EUROPEA ... MICS

EUROPEAN MACROECONOMICS

Robert Barro and Vittorio Grilli

MACMILLAN

First published 1994 by
THE MACMILLAN PRESS LTD
Houndmills, Basingstoke, Hampshire RG21 2XS
and London
Companies and representatives throughout the world

ISBN 0–333–57763–9 hardcover
ISBN 0–333–57764–7 paperback

A catalogue record for this book is available
from the British Library.

Copy-edited and typeset by Povey–Edmondson
Okehampton and Rochdale, England

Printed in Hong Kong

Contents

1

The Approach to Macroeconomics

In macroeconomics we study the overall or aggregate performance of an economy. We consider, for example, the total output of goods and services as measured by the **gross national product (GNP)** and the **gross domestic product (GDP)**. We look also at the aggregates of employment and unemployment, and at the breakdown of GNP into consumer expenditures, investment (which are purchases of new capital goods), government purchases of goods and services, and net exports.

The above terms refer to the quantities of goods or work effort. We shall also be interested in the prices that relate to these quantities, that is, the domestic currency prices of the goods and services that the economy produces (e.g. pound prices in the UK, franc prices in France and peseta prices in Spain). When we look at the price of the typical basket of goods, we refer to the **general price level**. But we are also interested in the **wage rate**, which is the price of labour services, the **interest rate**, which determines the cost of borrowing and the return to lending, and the **exchange rates** between the currencies of different countries.

We shall want to know how the economy determines the various quantities and prices and how government policies affect these variables. Specifically, we shall consider monetary policy, which involves the determination of the quantity of money and the design of monetary institutions, and fiscal policy, which pertains to the government's expenditures, taxes, and budget deficits.

The performance of the overall economy is of substantial concern for everyone because it influences job prospects, incomes, and prices. Thus, it is important for us – and even more important for our government policymakers – to understand how the macroeconomy works.

Unfortunately, as it is obvious from reading the newspapers, the theory of macroeconomics is not a settled scientific field. There is much controversy among economists about what is a useful basic approach, as well as about the detailed analyses of particular economic events and policy proposals. There has been, however, a great deal of progress in recent years in designing a more satisfactory macroeconomic theory. The main objective of this book is to convey that progress to students in an accessible form.

Macroeconomics and the World Economy

In this book we will be concerned with the general economic performance of market economies. One important aspect of our approach is that we do not want to constrain ourself to the analysis of the economy of a particular country. Familiarity with the working of one macroeconomic system is, nowadays, hardly satisfactory. This is especially true in Europe, where the geographic boundaries are becoming blurred as far as economic relations are concerned. Since the end of World War II, Europe has been proceeding toward economic integration at an accelerating speed. National economies have become more and more internationalized by their membership in organizations like the European Community and the European Free Trade Association. It would be impossible to have a clear picture of the evolution of, say, the French economy, without any knowledge of how the German economy works, and vice versa.

Our task, however, is less difficult than it may appear at first. We will show that there are basic economic relationships and empirical regularities

Box 1.1   The European Community

The importance of the European Community for the economic development of Western Europe after World War II (and in perspective for that of Eastern Europe) cannot be over-emphasized. It is useful, therefore, to provide some basic notions about its history and its operations. Formal economic cooperation in Europe began in 1951, with the founding of the **European Coal and Steel Community (ECSC)** between Belgium, France, Germany, Italy, Luxembourg and the Netherlands. In 1957, the same six countries signed the Treaty of Rome, establishing the **European Economic Community (EEC)**, and the treaty establishing the **European Atomic Energy Community (EURATOM)**. EEC, EURATOM and ECSC were amalgamated in 1967 and they are now known as the **European Community (EC)**. During the following twenty years, in three enlargement waves, the EC membership doubled. In 1973, the United Kingdom, Ireland and Denmark joined. They were followed, in 1981, by Greece, and in 1986 by Portugal and Spain.

Formal cooperation agreements in Europe were not limited to the EC. In 1960, Austria, Denmark, Norway, Portugal, Sweden, Switzerland and the United Kingdom signed the Stockholm Convention, establishing the **European Free Trade Association (EFTA)**. Later, Finland and Iceland became EFTA members but, as we have seen above, Denmark, Portugal and the United Kingdom left subsequently to join the EC. EFTA has close ties with the EC. Custom duties and other restrictions between the two areas have been removed and, *de facto*, EC and EFTA form an integrated common market. Given that Austria, Finland and Sweden have already filed for EC membership, the existence of EFTA as a separate entity from the EC will probably be short-lived.

In Figure 1.1, we illustrate the relationship between the three EC institutions that are most important from the point of view of economic policy: the European Parliament, the European Commission and the Council of Ministers.[1]

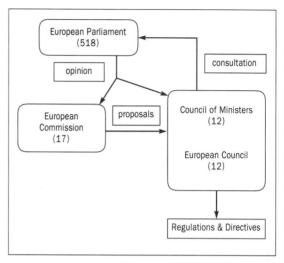

Figure 1.1   The European Community

The institutional engine of the EC is the **European Commission**. It is the executive organ of the EC, having the role of initiating, supervising and implementing the actions of the Community. Its main function is to draft and present proposals to the Council of Ministers and to carry out the decisions taken by the Council. The Commission is based in Brussels and has 17 members, two from each of the larger members (France, Germany, Spain, Italy, and the United Kingdom) and one from each of the other seven. They are appointed for a renewable four-year term by the Council of Ministers, following the indication of national governments. Heading the commission is its president, who is the most prominent member of the permanent staff of the EC.

Although the Commission and its president have the ability to set the Community's agenda, the actual decisions are taken by the **Council of Ministers**, which is, therefore, the most powerful institution of the EC. The ministers of the governments of the member states sit in the Council. Its composition depends on the subject under discussion. If fiscal issues are debated, then the Council consists of the finance ministers; if agricultural policies are discussed, then the agricultural ministers will meet, and so on. Of particular importance is the Council of Ministers at the foreign ministers level, also known as the General Affairs Council. Member states have rotating six-month terms at the presidency of the Council. Twice a year the Council meets at the head of government level, also known as the **European Council**. Although not a formal institution of the EC, the European Council has now a central role in the decision making of the Community. It is at these semi-annual summits that the most difficult issues are discussed and the most important decisions are taken.

The third major EC institution is the **European Parliament**. The plenary sessions of the European Parliament are usually held in Strasbourg, although its other activities take place in Brussels and Luxembourg. The European Parliament has 518 members, directly elected by the people of the member states. The number of members of parliament that each country sends to Strasbourg depends on its size. Unlike national parliaments, the powers of the European Parliament are very limited. Its main role is to supervise the work of the Commission and the Council and to approve the Community budget. It has no direct legislative power but only an advisory role to the Council and the Commission.

In addition to its political institutions, the EC has developed its own monetary system, the **European Monetary System (EMS)**. We postpone a detailed description of the EMS to Chapter 11. Part of the EMS accord was the introduction of the **European Currency Unit (ECU)** as the unit of account of the Community and possibly the future common European currency. In the examples in the book, we shall use ECUs to denominate nominal quantities.

that hold true for all of the industrialized countries. Therefore, we will need just one basic macroeconomic framework to understand the behaviour of the main economic aggregates in the United Kingdom, Germany, or most of the industrialized countries. This is not to say that all countries are identical. To the contrary, there are substantial differences among them, in particular in their institutional and political structures which, undoubtedly, have an impact on economic activity. When they play a crucial role, we will describe these differences and discuss their likely effects. However, to understand many crucial macroeconomic issues, these cross-country differences can be left aside.

To properly account for the international dimension that modern economies have acquired, the traditionally closed-economy[2] approach to macroeconomics has to be amended. Therefore, we shall devote considerable time to modelling the international economic links that arise from a country's trade in goods, services, real and financial assets, and the labour force. We will show how changes in the outside world economy impact the performance of a country and how economic events in a country spill over to the rest of the world.

Output, Unemployment, and the Price Level in the Major Industrialized Economies

To get an overview of the subject matter, we now consider the historical record on the main macroeconomic variables for some of the major industrialized economies. Figure 1.2 shows the total output of goods and services for the six world largest economies (i.e. France, Germany, Italy, Japan, the United Kingdom and the United States), which we will refer to as the **G-6**,[3] from 1950 to 1990. There are two commonly used measures of aggregate output: the gross national product (which is used in Figure 1.2 for Germany, Italy, Japan and the United States), and the gross domestic product (used in Figure 1.2 for France and the United Kingdom), both expressed in

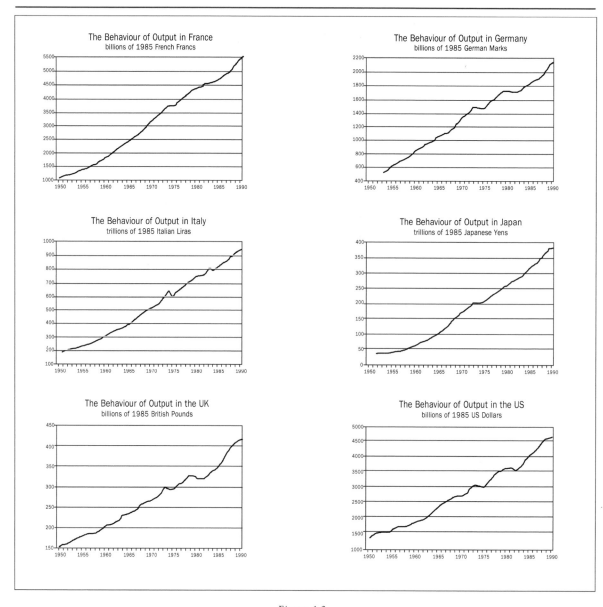

Figure 1.2

terms of values for a base year, which happens to be 1985. These measures are called **real GNP** and **real GDP**, respectively. As we shall see in a later section on national-income accounting, these two measures are closely related and, for most countries, they are very similar.

The general upward trend of real GNP (GDP) in Figure 1.2 reflects the long-term growth or economic development of these economies. Figure 1.3(a) shows the average growth rate of real GNP from 1955 to 1990 for the major industrialized countries. It ranged from 2.5% per year in the United Kingdom to 6.7% in Japan. Consequently, between 1955 and 1990, the total output increased almost threefold in the United Kingdom and more than ninefold in Japan. If we divide through by population to determine real **per capita GNP**, we find that the average growth rate ranged from

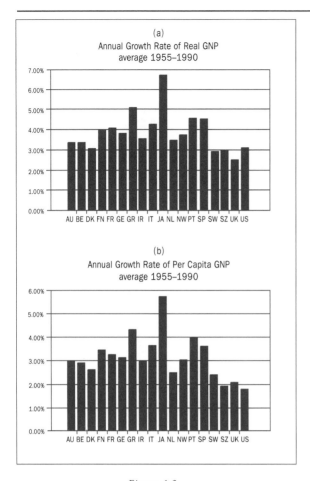

(a)
Annual Growth Rate of Real GNP
average 1955–1990

(b)
Annual Growth Rate of Per Capita GNP
average 1955–1990

Figure 1.3

1.9% per year in the United States to 5.8% in Japan – i.e. the average growth rate of real GNP (3.1% in the United States and 6.7% in Japan) less the average growth rate of population (1.2% in the United States and 0.9% in Japan). Hence, between 1955 and 1990, output per person increased by a factor of almost two in the United States and a factor of almost seven in Japan.

Figure 1.4 shows the annual growth rate of real GNP for the G-6 countries. Notice in this figure the recurring ups and downs of output. These movements are called **aggregate business fluctuations** or the **business cycle**.[4] When real GNP falls toward a low point or trough, the economy is in a **recession** or an economic contraction. These are periods characterized by negative rates of growth.

Conversely, when real GNP expands toward a high point or peak, the economy is in a **boom** or an economic expansion. These are periods characterized by high rates of growth. Notice that all the G-6 countries experienced a recession in 1974–75. This is also the only time, in the period between 1950 and 1990, in which France and Japan experienced negative rates of growth. The other four countries, instead, experienced more than one recession in this period. The United States, for example, experienced recessions in 1954, 1958, 1970, 1974–75 and 1980–82, and 1990–91. On the up side, notice the high rates of growth in output that all these countries experienced in the 1960s.

Figure 1.5 reports the unemployment rate for the G-6 countries. The unemployment rate is the fraction of the labour force that has no job. (We discuss the precise meaning of this variable in Chapter 10.) Although the growth rate of output displayed a similar behaviour across countries, there are visible differences in the pattern of the unemployment rate. In the United States, the unemployment rate follows business fluctuations closely. That is, the unemployment rate tends to be high during recessions and low during booms. In contrast, the unemployment rate in the European countries displays more persistent swings than output growth. Finally, the rate of unemployment in Japan has been very stable at levels considerably lower than in the other G-6 countries.

Figure 1.6 shows an index of the general level of prices in the G-6 countries. (We discuss the details of the particular measure – the deflators for the gross national product and the gross domestic product – toward the end of this chapter.) The first observation is the persistent rise in prices in all countries in this period. This pattern did not apply before World War II when prices displayed movements both up and down. In fact, there are long periods in the earlier history – eg 1869–92 and 1920–33 for the United States – during which prices fell persistently. The second observation is the different speed with which prices increased across countries and across periods. To gain more insight on this issue, Figure 1.7 looks at the year-to-year growth

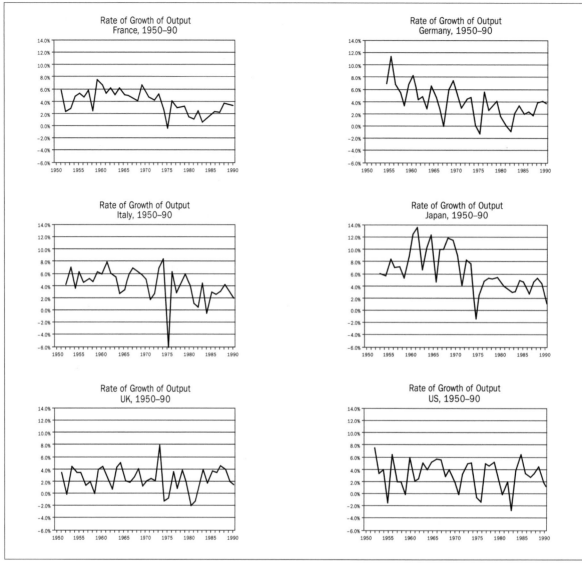

Figure 1.4

rate of the general price level, that is, the **inflation rate**. Notice how, on average, inflation has been higher in France, Italy and the United Kingdom than in Germany, Japan, and the United States. Note, also, that all countries experienced the highest rates of inflation in the period between the mid-1970s and the early 1980s.

In subsequent chapters we shall relate the behaviour of the general price level to monetary developments, especially to changes in the quantity of money. This monetary behaviour depends, in turn, on the nature of monetary institutions, such as the characteristics of the national central bank and of the banking sector, and the type of exchange rate regime that a country adopts.

Some Key Facts about Business Fluctuations

One of the main objectives of macroeconomics is to understand business fluctuations. To get a

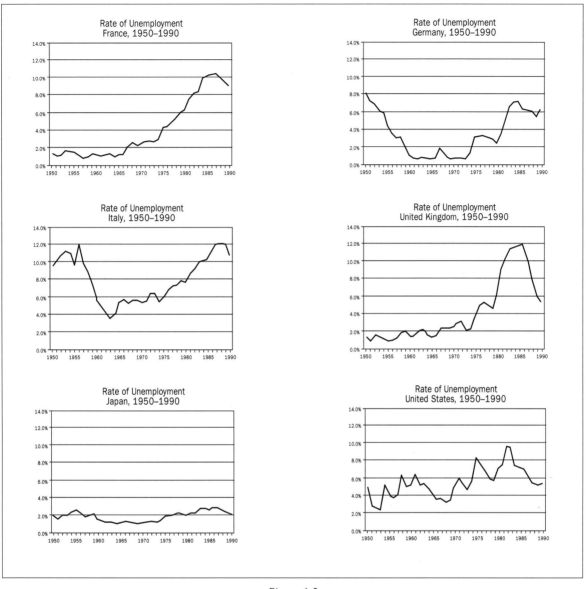

Figure 1.5

clear picture of the main issues, we now examine some detailed characteristics of business fluctuations in the main industrialized countries in the period 1950–90[5]. These facts are interesting in themselves and help to focus the theoretical discussion in later chapters. We shall want to see how well the economic model that we develop fits the observed features of business fluctuations.

The solid lines in Figure 1.8 show the path of real GNP (GDP) on a proportionate scale, essentially the same pictures that appeared in Figure 1.2. A good way to assess business fluctuations is to look at the departure of real GNP (GDP) from a trend line that captures the longer-run evolution of output. The dotted lines in the figure, obtained from a statistical smoothing procedure,[6] represent such trends. The gap

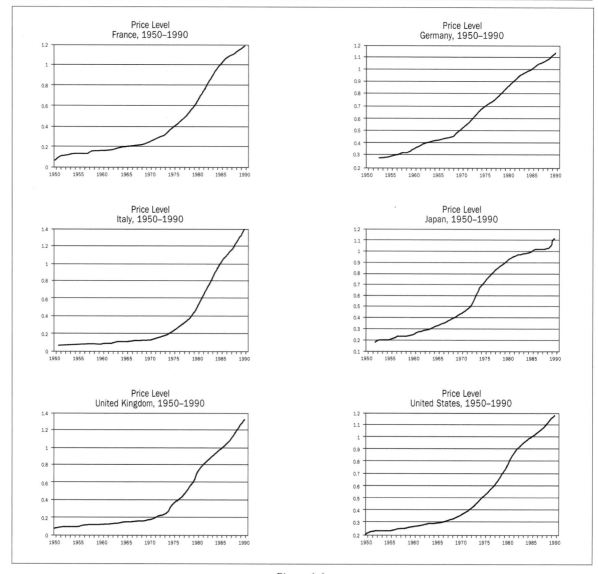

Figure 1.6

between real GNP (GDP) and the trend line, which we refer to as *detrended GNP (GDP)* or the *cyclical component of GNP (GDP)*, is shown by the dashed lines. The average of detrended GNP is zero by construction, and the value at any date – read off the left scale – shows the percentage deviation from the trend. In 1982, for example, real GNP (GDP) was below trend by 0.1% in France, by 3.0% in Germany, by 0.9% in Italy, by 2.0% in Japan, by 5.2% in the United Kingdom

and by 5.6% in the United States. Conversely, in 1989 GNP (GDP) was above trend by 0.5% in France, by 1.1% in Germany, by 0.2% in Italy, by 1.1% in Japan, by 2.5% in the United Kingdom, and by 1.7% in the United States.

A useful way to summarize the volatility of real GNP is to compute the standard deviation of the cyclical component.[7] These numbers are displayed in Figure 1.9. For example, the standard deviation of the cyclical component of French

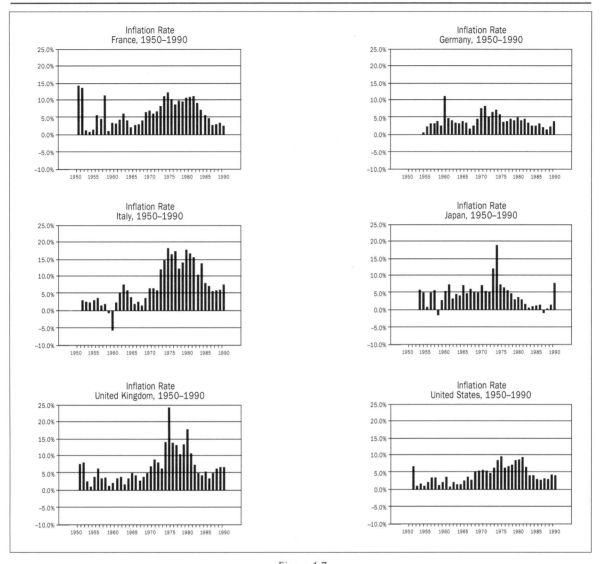

Figure 1.7

output is 1.9%, whereas that of Japanese output is 3.7%. The cyclical fluctuations are, in other words, large enough so that French real GNP is often 1.7% (3.7% for Japan) or more above or below its trend line.

We saw that output in 1982 was below trend in all G-6 countries. Similarly, in 1989, output was above trend in all G-6 countries. This observation raises the obvious and important question of whether business cycles are related across countries. Do recessions and booms occur at similar times in different countries or, instead, does the timing of output fluctuations vary across countries? In Figure 1.10 we present the correlation coefficients between the cyclical component of GNP (GDP) for each of the G-6 countries with those of several industrialized countries. The correlation coefficient is a statistical measure of how two variables move together. It can take values between one and minus one. A value of the correlation coefficient close to zero indicates the absence of a statistical relationship between the

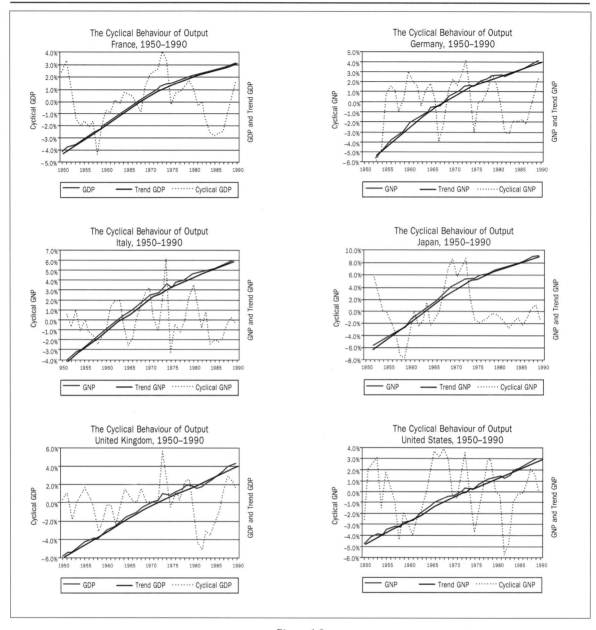

Figure 1.8

two variables. Positive values of the correlation coefficient indicate that the two variables tend to move in the same direction. The closer is the correlation coefficient to one, the stronger is this *positive correlation*. Conversely, negative values of the correlation coefficient indicate that the two variables tend to move in opposite directions. The closer the correlation coefficient to minus one, the stronger is this *negative correlation*. Figure 1.10 shows that business cycles are positively correlated across the major economies (the only exception being Norway). Also, the positive correlation is stronger for the European countries and Japan than for the United States.

The Components of GNP

We can get more information about business fluctuations by comparing detrended real GNP with the detrended data for its various components. We look here only at the domestic parts of spending and defer until Chapter 7 a discussion of the foreign sector.

The largest component of output is private consumption. Figure 1.11 shows that the average share of this component in real GNP for the main industrialized countries from 1950 to 1990 ranged from 54% to 76%. We can apply the methodology that we used for GNP (GDP) to decompose private consumption and the other components of output between trend and cyclical components. One important observation is that consumer spending typically moves in the same direction as GNP. Figure 1.12(a) shows that the correlation between the cyclical components is positive and large, ranging from 0.62 to 0.96. If this correlation is positive – that is, if a variable usually moves cyclically in the same direction as real GNP – then economists say that the variable is *procyclical*. A variable that moves in the opposite direction is *countercyclical*, and one that has little relation to real GNP is *acyclical*. Private consumer spending is therefore a procyclical variable.

Figure 1.9 shows that the volatility of the cyclical component of consumer expenditure is similar to that of real GNP (GDP): in France, Japan, and the United States consumer spending is slightly less volatile than GNP (GDP), whereas in Germany, Italy, and the United Kingdom it is slightly more volatile. Private consumption can, however, usefully be divided into two components: (i) spending on non-durable goods and services and (ii) purchases of consumer durables. Durable goods are the equipment used by

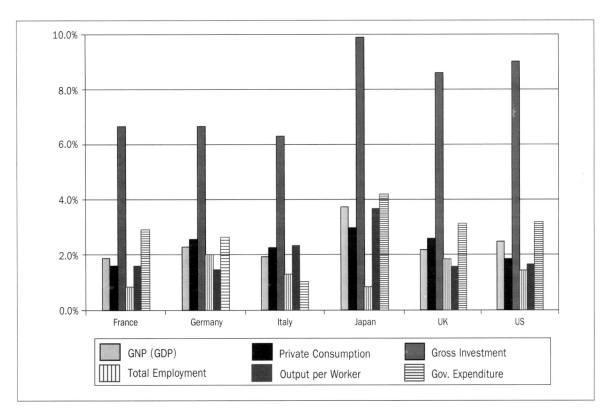

Figure 1.9 Volatility of cyclical aggregates (standard deviation, 1950–90)

Figure 1.10

households; for example automobiles, appliances, and furniture are a form of investment. Purchases of durable goods by households, in fact, behave similarly to the spending on equipment by businesses, one of the components of gross investment that we discuss later. Consumer spending on non-durables and services is quite

stable. In the United States, for which data are available for the period under consideration, the standard deviation of this type of consumer spending is about one-half that for GNP. Because spending on non-durables and services is relatively stable, this component contributes much less to business fluctuations than would be

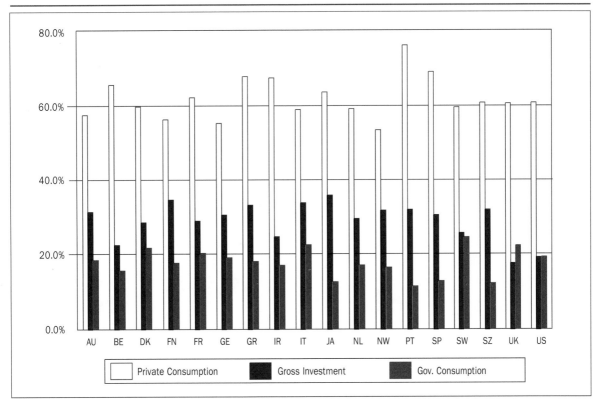

Figure 1.11 The components of output (% of GNP (GDP), average 1950–90)

expected from the average size of this component (54% of GNP in the United States compared to 7% for consumer spending in durables).

The second component of GNP (GDP) is gross investment – spending on structures, equipment, and inventories by businesses, and purchases of residential housing by households. As shown in Figure 1.11, the average rate of gross investment to GNP (GDP) ranged between 18% and 36% in the main industrialized countries. Figure 1.12(b) shows that gross investment is procyclical: the correlations of the cyclical components with detrended real GNP are between 0.47 and 0.90. The contrast with private consumption, and especially with consumer spending on non-durables and services, is that gross investment is substantially more volatile than real GNP. Figure 1.9 shows that the standard deviation for gross investment was 2.5 to 4 times larger than that for GNP. Thus, this variable contributes far more to business fluctuations than would be expected

from its average shares of real GNP. Although gross investment averages less than a third of GNP, the volatility of this component and its high correlation with detrended GNP mean that it accounts for the bulk of overall business fluctuations. It will therefore be important later on (especially in Chapter 9) to see whether our economic model can explain the key role of investment in business fluctuations.

The third component of GNP (GDP) is government purchases of goods and services. Figure 1.11 shows that its average rate to GNP (GDP) ranged between 12% and 25%. Figure 1.9(c) shows that this component is about as volatile as GNP – the standard deviation for government purchases ranges between 1.0% and 4.1%. The new finding, however, is that the relationship between detrended government purchases and output is not very strong: the correlation is as low as −0.04 and never exceeds −0.58. Government purchases are, in most

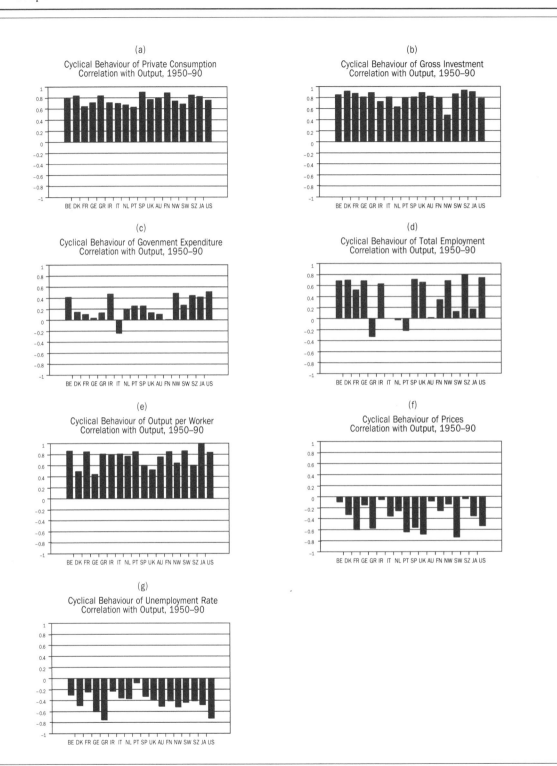

Figure 1.12

countries, acyclical, that is, their movements are not related to the movements of real GDP. Although government purchases are large and moderately variable, the low correlation with GNP indicates that this component of spending has little to do with the typical pattern of business fluctuations.

Labour Input and Productivity

Underlying the cyclical fluctuations in real GNP are substantial movements of labour input. As a measure of labour input we consider here total employment, that is, the number of persons with jobs. Figure 1.9(d) shows that this variable is markedly procyclical for the majority of countries – the correlations exceeding 0.60. In some countries – Austria, Finland, Italy, the Netherlands, Portugal and Sweden – this labour variable is acyclical. We shall discuss the possible reasons for these cross-country differences in Chapter 13. The volatility of employment (Figure 1.9) is less than that of GNP.

The cyclical behaviour of *labour productivity* – the output generated per unit of labour – depends on the relative movements of output and labour. We consider here as measures of productivity *output per worker*, that is, real GNP divided by the number employed. In contrast to total employment, productivity is highly procyclical in all countries: the correlations with detrended GNP range between 0.41 and 0.98 (Figure 1.12(e)). These results mean that output expands proportionately more than labour in a boom and falls proportionately more than labour in a recession.

Because employment is typically procyclical, it is not surprising that the unemployment rate is countercyclical. The correlation of the detrended unemployment rate with detrended GNP ranges between -0.25 and -0.92 (see Figure 1.12(g)).

The Price Level

Later we shall find it useful to see how the general level of prices relates to business fluctuations. We use the measure of the price level shown in Figure 1.6, the deflator for the GNP (GDP). Figure 1.12(f) shows that the overall price level was countercyclical in most countries from 1950 to 1990.

The Approach to Macroeconomics

This section describes the basic theoretical approach that this book uses to design a useful macroeconomic model. In setting up this model, we shall spend a good deal of time on economic theory. In this context we worry about whether the theory seems sensible, whether it is internally consistent, and so on. But we should always remember that the main test of the model will be its ability to explain the behaviour of macroeconomic variables in the real world. We therefore devote considerable space to comparisons of the theory with the real world, that is, with empirical evidence.

Microeconomic Foundations of Macroeconomics

We begin by developing the basic price theory – or **microeconomic foundations** – that underlies the macroeconomic analysis of the aggregate variables in an economy. Much of this microeconomics will be familiar to students from previous courses in economics. In that sense, the macroeconomic approach in this book is a continuation of the economic reasoning used to explain the behaviour of individual households and businesses. Here we apply this same economic science to understand the workings of the overall economy – that is, to study real GNP, employment and unemployment, the general price level and inflation, the wage rate, the interest rate, the exchange rate, and so on. Many basic textbooks in economics unfortunately do not follow this general approach when dealing with macroeconomics. Students could, in fact, easily reach the conclusion that macroeconomics and microeconomics were two entirely distinct fields. A central theme of this book is that a more satisfactory macroeconomics emerges when it is linked to the underlying microeconomics. The term 'more satisfactory' means, first, that the macroeconomic theory avoids internal inconsistencies, and second, that it provides a better understanding of the real world.

In Chapter 2 we examine the choice problems of an isolated individual, similar to the Robinson Crusoe of Daniel Defoe's novel. We assume that Crusoe's choices are guided by enlightened self-interest – that is, we exploit the central economic postulate of optimizing behaviour. In the initial framework, the only choice problem concerns the level of work effort, which then determines the quantities of production and consumption. But by studying Crusoe's behaviour, we can understand the trade-off between leisure and consumption that applies in complicated market economies. Also, by looking at an isolated individual, we bring out the role of a resource or **budget constraint** in its simplest form. When goods cannot be stored over time, Crusoe's budget constraint dictates that his consumption equals his production. As we shall see, extensions of this simple constraint are central to correct macro-economic analyses in economies that include many consumers and producers, as well as a government.

We can use the model of Robinson Crusoe to predict his responses to changes in production opportunities – for example, to harvest failures or to discoveries of new goods or methods of production. Many of these results carry over to the predictions for aggregate output and employment in more realistic settings. In particular, when we consider the economy's responses to changes in production opportunities – such as the oil crises of 1973–74 and 1979 – we usually get the right answer by thinking of the parallel situation for Robinson Crusoe.

Chapters 3 and 4 develop the microeconomic foundations needed to go from an analysis of Robinson Crusoe to a study of many persons who interact on various marketplaces. Once again we exploit the postulate of optimizing behaviour, subject to budget constraints, to assess the responses of individuals to different circum-stances. To simplify matters, we start with only two markets. On the first market, households buy and sell goods in exchange for money. The monetary cost on this market is the theoretical counterpart of the general price level. On the second market, households buy and sell bonds in exchange for money. This credit or loan market establishes an interest rate, which borrowers must pay to lenders.

The introduction of the goods market allows people to specialize in production activities, a setup that adds to the economy's productivity. (Robinson Crusoe did not have this option.) Chapter 3 explores the incentives to hold non-interest-bearing paper money rather than finan-cial assets that bear interest. The **demand for money** arises out of the process of carrying out transactions, which use money as a **medium of exchange**. Because households use money when they buy or sell goods or financial assets, it would require a great deal of planning and effort to hold little or no money. We then discuss how the quantity of money demanded depends on the price level, the interest rate, the level of income, and other variables.

Chapter 4 explores the credit market, i.e. the market where households can borrow and lend. The existence of the credit market means that a household's expenditure during any period can diverge from its income during that period. Thus, unlike Robinson Crusoe, a household with a given income has choices about consuming now versus later. Similarly, households can choose between working now versus later. We discuss these choices by considering incentives to save, that is, to accumulate assets that pay interest income. We stress the idea that a higher interest rate motivates people to save more; thereby, they consume less today and plan to consume more later. Similarly, we show that various forces can induce people to rearrange their work and production from one period to another.

In a later chapter (Chapter 6), we introduce a labour market on which labour services are bought and sold at an established wage rate. But to simplify the basic model, we do not include this market at the outset. Rather, we pretend that households work only on their own production processes – that is, each household owns its own business and provides the labour input for this business. For many purposes – such as studying the main determinants of aggregate output and work effort, the general price level, and the interest rate – this simplification will be satisfactory. But to explore some other topics – such as unemployment and wage rates – we have to deal explicitly with the labour market.

The analysis stresses the role of budget constraints, which ensure a balance between each household's sources and uses of funds. Although these budget conditions may seem tedious at times, it is important to keep these matters straight. Many serious errors in macroeconomic reasoning occur when economic theorists forget to impose the appropriate budget constraints in their models. We shall see that these conditions are especially important in evaluating temporary versus permanent changes in income, in studying the effects of interest rates on lenders and borrowers, and in evaluating the effects of money holdings. Also, when we introduce government policies in later chapters, we shall find it crucial to impose the government's budget constraint. Many errors in analyses of the government's expenditures and budget deficits result from a failure to impose this budget constraint.

Market-Clearing Conditions

We note in Chapter 5 that certain conditions must hold when we add up the actions of all households. For example, the total of goods sold by suppliers must equal the total bought by demanders. Similarly, the total amount loaned on the credit market must equal the total borrowed. We refer to conditions such as these as **aggregate-consistency conditions**. These conditions tell us something about how aggregate quantities must behave for the analysis to be internally consistent. Any reasonable macromodel must satisfy these conditions.

One way to ensure that the aggregate-consistency conditions hold is to assume that the various markets – say, for goods and credit – always clear. Clearing means that the price level and the interest rate adjust simultaneously so that the aggregate demand for goods equals the aggregate supply, and the aggregate of desired lending equals the

aggregate of desired borrowing. We use this **market-clearing approach** to satisfy the aggregate-consistency conditions in the basic model.

The idea that markets clear is closely related to the notion that private markets function efficiently. With cleared markets, it is impossible to improve on any outcomes by matching potential borrowers and lenders or by bringing together potential buyers and sellers of goods. Cleared markets already accomplish all of these mutually advantageous trades. We can see that market clearing is reminiscent of the optimizing behaviour of individuals. On the one hand, people determine their individual choices of work, consumption, and so on to make themselves as well off as possible. On the other hand, market clearing means that the people who participate in and organize markets – and are guided by the pursuit of their own interests – do not waste resources, and thereby end up achieving efficient outcomes. Market clearing is therefore the natural complement at the macro level to the microfoundations that underlie the model.

It is possible to satisfy the aggregate-consistency conditions without imposing market clearing in the sense described above. One important idea is that imperfect information makes it impossible to make the best decisions about production and work at all times. We shall consider later some macroeconomic models that incorporate incomplete information (particularly in Chapter 20). But it is best to explore the workings of the economy under full information before going on to this advanced topic. Thus, we do not introduce incomplete information into the model at the outset.

Another alternative to market clearing is the **Keynesian model**, originally developed by the British economist John Maynard Keynes. This model assumes that some prices (usually of labour services or commodities) are sticky and that some rationing of quantities bought or sold comes into play. It turns out that outcomes are generally inefficient in the Keynesian model: some mutually advantageous trades do not take place. As a reflection of this 'market failure', there tends to be chronic unemployment and underproduction. These conclusions from the Keynesian model have led many economists to advocate 'corrective' policy actions by the government.

The Keynesian model depends crucially on the assumption that prices are sticky. Thus, not surprisingly, the rationale for price stickiness has been the subject of substantial and still unresolved debate. The Keynesian theory is, in any case, another advanced topic that cannot be appreciated without first working through the logic of a market-clearing model. We therefore take up the Keynesian model (in Chapter 21) after the market-clearing analysis has been completed.

To summarize, the basic model relies on two key elements for making predictions about the behaviour of quantities and prices in the real world. First, we use the model's microfoundations, which derive from the optimizing behaviour of individuals subject to budget constraints. Second, we exploit the notion of market clearing, a process that reflects the efficient matching of potential buyers and sellers of goods, credit, labour services, and so on.

Using the Market-Clearing Model

Chapter 5 lays out the central theoretical apparatus used throughout the remainder of the book. After this point, the discussion amounts to extensions of the basic model to apply the reasoning to various topics in macroeconomics. The list of applications eventually includes supply shocks, inflation, business fluctuations, long-term economic growth, government purchases and public services, monetary and fiscal policies, international borrowing and lending, exchange rates, financial intermediation, incomplete information and rational expectations, and the Keynesian model.

We first use the model in Chapter 5 to study various disturbances that affect opportunities for production. Specifically, we assess the effects of supply shocks on output, employment, the price level, and the interest rate. We then relate the findings to some of the characteristics of business fluctuations that we explored in this chapter.

Chapter 6 brings in a labour market and allows for business firms as distinct economic units. In this extended model, we can show how the clearing of the labour market determines the wage rate and the quantity of employment. For most purposes, however, the extended model yields results that coincide with those in Chapter 5. We therefore return in most of the subsequent analysis to the simpler setting that neglects the labour market and considers only one type of economic unit. We can think of this unit as a combination of a household and a firm: this unit merges the consumption and working activities of households with the production and hiring activities of businesses. The main reason we use this device is that it simplifies the analysis without causing any mistakes.

Chapter 7 extends the theory from the economy of one country to that of many countries, which interact on international markets for goods and credit. We simplify the analysis by assuming that all countries use the same currency and quote prices in units of this currency. We can then readily apply the previous framework to analyze a country's **balance of international payments**. We explore, for example, how shocks to technology and fiscal policies influence a country's incentive to borrow or lend internationally.

Chapters 8 and 9 introduce the possibility of chronic rises in the general price level, that is, inflation. We look at inflation as primarily a monetary phenomenon. One of the major themes is that inflation and monetary growth can be largely independent of the variations in output and employment, the 'real' variables in the model. The interaction of monetary phenomena with output, employment, and other real variables is a major issue in macroeconomics but one that is not fully resolved. In this book we deal first with simple models in which the interaction between monetary forces and the real variables is unimportant. Then we extend the analysis (in Chapters 18–20) to bring in more interesting possibilities for this interaction.

Chapter 10 introduces financial intermediaries and studies the creation of deposits and the lending operations of banks and other institutions. The analysis stresses the role of intermediaries in promoting economic efficiency. Thus, a contraction in the amount of financial intermediation – such as that during periods of financial crisis – tends to reduce the levels of production and employment. In addition, there are important effects of changes in financial intermediation on the general price level.

Chapter 11 allows for different currencies and considers the determination of exchange rates. We consider the distinction between fixed and flexible exchange rates and we study the European Monetary System. We discuss how exchange rates interact with interest rates and the balance of international payments.

Chapters 12–14 apply the theory to business fluctuations and economic growth. Chapter 12 introduces investment, which is the accumulation of capital goods. We already noted that business fluctuations feature most greater variations in investment rather than consumption. The theory can explain this pattern and other characteristics of business fluctuations as responses to shocks that affect technology or preferences. These types of disturbances have been the focus of a recent area of research called **real business cycle theory**. (The approach contrasts with monetary theories, which stress the effects of monetary disturbances on the economy.)

Chapter 14 studies how investment shows up over the longer term as an increase in the stock of capital and thereby in economic growth. By allowing also for growth in population and for improvements in technology, we can apply the theory to an economy's long-term development. Accordingly, we can use the model to study the behaviour of the major macroeconomic variables in the regions of western Europe and the United States. In addition, we apply the theory to the growth experiences of the individual US and European states and to a large number of developing countries.

Chapter 13 expands the model to allow for unemployment. We view unemployment as arising from the problem of matching workers to jobs. Specifically, we relate the average level and dynamics of unemployment to the rates at which people find and lose jobs. Then we show how various economic forces influence the rates of job finding and job separation. We show, in particular, why unemployment rises during a recession.

Chapters 15–18 bring in government expenditures, taxes, and public debt and thereby allow us to consider fiscal policies. First, we introduce government purchases of goods and services, expenditures that we assume are used to provide public services to consumers and producers. Then we consider how households react to income taxes and to transfer programmes, such as social security. Finally, by introducing the public debt, we can evaluate the economic consequences, both domestically and internationally, of the government's financing its spending by budget deficits rather than taxes.

Chapters 19–22 deal with interactions between monetary forces and real economic activity. Chapter 19 explores the main pieces of empirical evidence that concern the interaction between monetary variables and the real economy. The theory can explain much of the evidence but not all of it. Specifically, using the model that we have developed up to this point, we cannot rationalize significant effects of purely monetary shocks on real economic activity.

Chapter 20 extends the market-clearing model to account for real effects of monetary disturbances. The new feature is that individuals have incomplete information about prices in various markets and about the overall monetary picture. When people do not observe something directly – such as the general price level – they are motivated to use their available information to forecast the unobserved variables as accurately as possible. This type of expectation is called *rational*, and hence the approach is often called *rational-expectations macroeconomics*. In this setting monetary disturbances can affect real economic activity more or less as appears in the data on business fluctuations.

The theory in Chapter 20 has intriguing implications for monetary policy: the effects on real variables derive only from the erratic part of monetary policy, and the effects tend to be adverse. Thus, the main message is that monetary policy should be predictable rather than erratic.

Chapter 21 develops the model of business fluctuations that was stimulated by the research during the 1930s of the British economist, John

Maynard Keynes. This theory departs from the previous analysis by assuming that some prices do not adjust instantaneously to clear all markets. That is, the prices of goods or wages of labour are assumed to be sticky rather than perfectly flexible. We begin with a simple version of the Keynesian model, a version that brings out the idea that shocks to the economy can have multiplicative effects on output. Then we work out the **IS/LM model**, which is a popular extended version of this theory.

A basic conclusion from the Keynesian model is that recessions can result when monetary contractions or other disturbances lead to decreases in the aggregate demand for goods. There is more scope for active monetary and fiscal policies in this model than there was in the market-clearing framework.

For many years, the Keynesian model was the most popular tool of macroeconomic analysis. The popularity of this model has diminished since the late 1960s, however, especially at the frontiers of macroeconomic research. There are two main reasons for this decreased popularity. First, the Keynesian model does not deal very well with inflation or supply shocks, two problems that have been important since the late 1960s. Second, despite many attempts, economists have not found satisfactory ways to provide the Keynesian macromodel with internally consistent and plausible microfoundations. There is, in any event, another reason to postpone the consideration of the Keynesian model until late in the book: the model cannot be fully understood – and the distinctive features of it cannot be appreciated – until the market-clearing analysis has been worked out. Thus, whatever one's ultimate judgment about the usefulness of the Keynesian model, it would not be very useful to begin a study of macroeconomics with this model.

Chapter 22 discusses a new line of macroeconomic theory developed to explain the formation of monetary policies. This approach retains the framework of market clearing and rational behaviour and builds on Keynesian models (Chapter 21) and on models of incomplete information about prices (Chapter 20) to justify the existence of real effects from monetary disturbances. Although people form expectations rationally, the incomplete information means that surprise increases in money and the general price level can induce expansions in the quantities of production and work.

Although it would be better for the policymaker to avoid using monetary policy to systematically increase output, a commitment to do so may lack credibility. In this situation, the outcome is a high level of inflation with no gains in output. We discuss, next, ways to make anti-inflation monetary policy credible. We present evidence that delegating monetary policy to an independent central bank can solve in part the credibility problem.

We extend the model in two directions: first, by introducing shocks to output and by assuming that the monetary authority had, in addition to an output targeting objective, an output stabilization objective. Once again, because of the policymaker systematic attempt to increase output, the economy suffers an inflationary bias, and the scope for stabilization is reduced. Second, we look for open-economy implications of this framework and we study the problem of international policy coordination and of the possible introduction of a monetary union in the EC.

A Note on Mathematics and Economic Reasoning

This book does not use any advanced mathematics. Rather, it relies on graphical methods and occasional algebraic derivations. Although calculus would speed up the presentation in some places, this technique is unnecessary for the main economic arguments Students should therefore not find the book difficult on technical grounds.

What will be demanding from time to time is the economic reasoning. It is this aspect of economics that is the most difficult – as well as the most rewarding. Unfortunately, not all of this difficulty can be avoided if we wish to understand the economic events that take place in the real world. The feature that should help students to master the material is the use of a single, consistent model, which is then successively refined and applied to a variety of macroeconomic problems. Anyone who invests enough effort to understand the basic model will eventually see the simplicity of the approach, as well as the applicability to a wide variety of real-world issues. Conversely, anyone who fails to master the basic model will be in serious trouble later.

Elements of National-Income Accounting

Up to this point, we have used terms such as *gross national product* (GNP), *gross domestic product* (GDP), *consumer expenditure*, *investment*, the *general price level*, and so on without defining them precisely. Now, by looking at the **national-income accounts**, we develop the meanings of these terms. There are many difficult issues that arise in the construction of these accounts. We consider here only the basic concepts, which will be adequate for the subsequent analysis.

Nominal and Real GNP and GDP

We begin with the GNP. Nominal GNP measures the value of all the goods and services that an economy produces during a specified time period in current prices. In 1992, for example, the nominal GNP in the United Kingdom was £598.4 billion, and in the United States, the largest world economy, it was $5950.7 billion.

Consider the definition of nominal GNP one step at a time. The word 'nominal' means that the GNP is measured in units of some currency, such as pounds, dollars, marks, yen, ECUs and so on. For most goods and services – pencils, automobiles, haircuts, and so on – the currency value is the price for which these items sell in the marketplace. However, governmental services – which include national defence, the justice system, and police services – are not exchanged on markets. These items enter into nominal GNP at their cost of production.

It is important to understand that the GNP includes only the goods and services that an economy produces during a given time period: current GNP measures only current production. The construction and sale of a new house therefore count in GNP, but the sale of a secondhand house (which was produced earlier) does not count.[8]

The nominal GNP can be misleading because it depends on the overall level of prices, as well as on the physical amounts of output. The top part of Table 1.1 illustrates this problem. Think about a simple economy that produces only butter and golf balls. We show the hypothetical quantities and prices of these goods for 1992 in the first columns of the table. Notice that the nominal GNP for 1992 is 500 ECUs. The columns labelled 1993A and 1993B show two possibilities for prices and outputs in 1993. Nominal GNP rises in both cases by 10% to 550 ECUs. In case A, however, the production of both goods has declined, whereas in case B the production of both has increased. Thus, identical figures on nominal GNP can conceal very different underlying movements in production.

Economists construct a measure of real GNP to solve the problem of changing price levels. Real GNP uses prices from a single year, called the base year. If the base year is 1985, for example, then we refer to real GNP as 'GNP in 1985 ECUs' or as 'GNP in constant ECUs,' because we use a set of constant (1985) prices. Similarly, we refer to nominal GNP as 'GNP in current ECUs', because it uses the prices of the current period.

We compute real GNP by multiplying the current quantity of output of each good by the price of that good in the base year. Then we sum up over all these multiples to get the economy's aggregate real GNP. Because the prices used in this calculation do not vary from year to year, we end up with a reasonable measure for the changes over time in the overall level of production.

The bottom portion of Table 1.1 illustrates this calculation, using 1992 as the base year. Consider the values of real GNP for the cases labelled 1993A and 1993B. These values differ substantially, although the values of nominal GNP are the same. In the 1993A example, real GNP falls below the 1992 level by 7.6%. This figure is a weighted average of the fall in butter production

	1992			1993A			1993B	
P_{1992}	Q_{1992}	Market value at 1992 prices	P_{1993A}	Q_{1993A}	Market value at 1993A prices	P_{1993B}	Q_{1993B}	Market value at 1993B prices
Butter								
ECU 2.00/lb	50	ECU 100	ECU 2.30/lb	44	ECU 101.20	ECU 1.80/lb	70	ECU 126.00
Golf Balls								
ECU 1.00/ball	400	ECU 400	ECU 1.20/ball	374	ECU 448.80	ECU 0.80/ball	530	ECU 424.00
Nominal GNP		ECU 500			ECU 550.00			ECU 550.00

P_{1992}	Q_{1992}	Market value at 1992 prices	P_{1993A}	Q_{1993A}	Market value at 1992 prices	P_{1993B}	Q_{1993B}	Market value at 1992 prices
Butter								
ECU 2.00/lb	50	ECU 100	ECU 2.00/lb	44	ECU 88.00	ECU 2.00/lb	70	ECU 140.00
Golf Balls								
ECU 1.00/ball	400	ECU 400	ECU 1.00/ball	374	ECU 374.00	ECU 1.00/ball	530	ECU 530.00
Real GNP (1992 base)		ECU 500			ECU 462.00			ECU 670.00

Note: P and Q refer to price and quantity, respectively, for the year indicated by the subscript.

Table 1.1   The calculation of nominal and real GNP

by 12% and that in golf ball production by 6.5%. Thus, real GNP gives a more accurate picture of the change in output than does the 10% increase in nominal GNP. Similarly, for the 1993B case, real GNP rises by 34% (a remarkable achievement for one year!). This figure is a weighted average of the rise in butter production by 40% and that in golf ball production by 32%.

Notice that the proportional change in real GNP is a weighted average of the proportional changes in production for the various goods, which are butter and golf balls in the example. Generally, there would be many ways to define the weights in this calculation. It turns out that the standard method for computing real GNP – which we employed in Table 1.1 – uses as weights the shares of each good (butter or golf balls) in

GNP for the base year. That is, as seems reasonable, this calculation gives more weight to the goods that account for a larger share of the economy's output (in the base year). But as we move away from the base year, these shares can change significantly. For that reason, the designation of the base year is changed from time to time.

Although it reveals a lot about the economy's overall performance, the real GNP is not a perfect measure of welfare. Some of the problems with using real GNP as a measure of well-being are the following:

- Aggregate GNP does not consider changes in the distribution of income across households.
- The calculated GNP excludes a variety of nonmarket goods, among them legal and

illegal transactions in the 'underground economy', as well as services that people perform in their homes. For example, if someone mows his or her own lawn, then GNP does not increase – but if the person hires someone to mow the lawn (and the transaction is reported to the government), then GNP increases.

- The GNP assigns no value to leisure time.

Despite these shortcomings, we typically learn a great deal about an economy – in terms of short-run fluctuations and long-term development – by studying the changes in aggregate real GNP.

We have seen that several countries use as the main measure of their output not GNP, but **gross domestic product (GDP)**. The difference between these two concepts is that GDP does not include the *net factor income from abroad*, which is instead part of GNP. This item measures the contribution to production by domestic labour and capital that is used in other countries, net of the contribution of foreign labour and capital to domestic production. As shown in Table 1.2, this difference is small for the G-6 countries.

The Gross National Product and the Gross Domestic Product: Expenditure, Production, and Income

We can think about GNP and GDP in three different ways. First, we can consider the expenditures on goods and services by different groups – households, businesses, all levels of government, and foreigners. Second, we can measure the production of goods by various industries – agriculture, manufacturing, wholesale and retail trade, and so on. Finally, we can calculate the incomes earned in the production of goods – compensation of employees, rental income, corporate profits, and so on. The important point is that all three approaches will end up with the same total for GNP. To see this, we take up each approach in turn, beginning with a breakdown by type of expenditure.

Measuring GNP and GDP by Expenditures

The national accounts divide GNP and GDP into four parts, depending upon who or what buys the goods or services. The four sectors are households, businesses, all levels of government, and foreigners. Table 1.2 shows the details of this breakdown for 1989 for the G-6 countries. The first column lists values in current price and the second refers to real price – that is, values for the base year, 1980 for Germany, France, Italy and the United States, and 1985 for the United Kingdom and Japan.

The purchase of goods and services by households for their own use is called **private final consumption expenditure**. This spending accounts for the bulk of GNP (GDP) – for example, between 55% and 65% of real GDP in the G-6 countries in 1989 (see Table 1.2).

The national accounts distinguish between purchases of consumer goods that will be used fairly quickly, such as toothpaste and various services, and those that will last for a substantial time, such as automobiles and appliances. The first group is called **consumer nondurables and services**, and the second is called **consumer durables**. The important point is that consumer durables yield a flow of services in future periods, as well as currently. Table 1.2 shows the division of consumer expenditures among durable goods, nondurable goods, and services.

The second major category of GNP (GDP) is **gross private domestic investment**, which is the purchase of goods and services by businesses. The 'fixed' part of these investments comprises firms' purchases of new capital goods, such as factories and machines. Note that business's capital goods are durables, which serve as inputs to production over many years. Thus, investment goods are similar to the consumer durables that we mentioned before. In fact, in the national accounts, an individual's purchase of a new home – which might be considered the ultimate consumer durable – is counted as a part of fixed business investment rather than personal consumer expenditure. For many purposes, we should add the other purchases of consumer durables to the national accounts' measure of gross investment to get a broader concept of investment.

	United States Billions of current $	United States Billions of 1980 $	United Kingdom Billions of current £	United Kingdom Billions of 1985 £	Germany(1) Billions of current DM	Germany(1) Billions of 1980 DM	France(1) Billions of current FF	France(1) Billions of 1980 FF	Italy(1) Trillions of current lire	Italy(1) Trillions of 1980 lire	Japan Billions of current Yen	Japan Billions of 1985 Yen
Private final consumption expenditure	3425.1	2304.6	326.7	270	1211.3	963.9	3665.3	2071.9	732.1	306.4	228.6	223.3
Durable goods	379.6	309.7	34.8	29.3			314.9	203.8			16.3	18.9
Nondurable goods	1190.4	877.7	144.1	123.8			1803.5	1048.4			88.6	87.9
Services	1854.8	1112.3	133.8	105			1569.6	832			118	109.6
Others	0.3	4.8	14	11.9			−22.7	−12.3			5.7	6.9
Gross private domestic investment	771.2	650	88.6	71.8	487.5	396.7	1311.4	783.1	256.4	117.5	99.8	101.8
Change in stocks	28.3	21.7	3	2.7	29.1	22.4	39.9	24.2	16.2	8.2	3.2	3.7
Gross fixed capital formation	742.9	628.3	86.6	458.4	374.3	1271.5	758.9	240.2	109.3	96.6	98.1	
Residential	226.1	161.6	15.8	15.8	119.1	93.9	310.4	188.2	57	23.7	23.1	21.7
Nonresidential	516.8	466.7	70.8	53.3	339.3	280.4	961.1	570.7	183.2	85.6	73.5	76.4
Government expenditure	1026.1	702.1	113.4	89.1	419	332.9	1119.2	629.8	199.6	72.6	62	58.5
Final consumption expenditure	919.3	619.9	99.5	77.2	419	332.9	1119.2	629.8	199.6	72.6	36.2	33.6
Change in stocks	−4.2	−4.2	0	−0.1						−0.2	−0.1	
Gross fixed capital formation	111	86.4	13.9	12							26	25
Net exports of goods and services	−90.5	−107.7	−18.8	117.7	52.3	17	−64.2	−1	−19.8	5.6	−3.3	
Exports	484.2	455.8	124.1	119.3	699.2	579.1	1425.1	848.8	244.2	123.1	42.4	51.5
Imports	574.7	563.5	142.9	138.2	581.5	526.8	1408.1	913	245.2	142.9	36.8	54.8
Statistical discrepancy			0.9	0.7								
Gross Domestic Product (GDP)	5131.9	3549	511.8	412.7	2235.5	1745.8	6112.9	3420.6	1187.1	476.7	396	380.3
Net factor income from the rest of the world	44.4		−1.2		25.7		−12		−12		2.9	
Factor income from the rest of the world	135.2		65.4		87.9		237.5		237.5		14.8	
Factor income paid to the rest of the world	90.8		66.6		62.2		249.5		249.5		11.9	
Gross National Product (GNP)	5176.3		510.6		2261.2		6100.9		1175.1		398.9	

Source: OECD, National Accounts.

Table 1.2   Expenditure composition of Gross National Product and Gross Domestic Product, 1989

Total investment is the sum of fixed investment and the net change in business's inventories of goods. In 1989 this total investment equalled between 18% and 27% of real GDP, or 27% and 32% if we include the purchases of consumer durables, in the G-6 countries (see Table 1.2).

The third component of GNP (GDP) is **government purchases** of goods and services. This category combines governmental consumption purchases with public investment. It is possible, however, to get a rough breakdown into the two components. There are two points about the government sector that sometimes cause confusion. First, it includes all levels of government, whether central or local. Second, it includes purchases of goods and services but excludes the government's **transfer payments**. (Examples of transfers are social security benefits and welfare payments.) The idea is that transfers do not represent payments to individuals in exchange for currently produced goods or services. These expenditures therefore do not appear in GNP. In 1989, government purchases accounted for between 15% and 22% of real GNP(GDP) (see Table 1.2).

Some of the goods and services produced in an economy are exported to foreign users. **Exports** must be added to domestic purchases to compute the economy's total production (GNP). Foreigners also produce goods and services that are imported into the domestic country. **Imports** must be subtracted from domestic purchases to calculate GNP. The foreign component therefore appears in GNP as **net exports**: the spending by foreigners on domestic production (exports) less the spending by domestic residents on foreign production (imports). Notice that net exports may be either positive or negative. In 1989 this component was between −4.6% and 3.0% of real GNP(GDP) in the G-6 countries.

Economists often omit net exports when they construct a macroeconomic model for a single economy. Then the model applies to a **closed economy** rather than an **open economy**, which includes the foreign sector. The rationale for assuming a closed economy is to simplify the theory. We follow the closed-economy tradition of macroeconomics until Chapter 7, where we allow for foreign trade. When we omit the foreign sector, we get the familiar division of GNP into three parts:

GNP = consumer expenditure +

gross investment + government purchases

One common error about national accounting arises because the spending on new physical capital is called 'investment'. This terminology differs from the concept of investment in ordinary conversation, a concept that refers to the allocation of saving among different financial assets, such as stocks, bonds, real estate, and so on. When we speak of a firm's investment, we refer to the purchase of physical goods, such as a factory. Do not be confused by these two different meanings of investment.

Another point about investment concerns **depreciation**. During any period, some of the existing stock of capital tends to wear out or depreciate. Thus, a part of gross investment merely replaces the old capital that has depreciated. The difference between gross investment and depreciation – called **net investment** – is the net change in the stock of capital goods. We shall discuss the difference between gross and net investment in Chapter 12. For now, note that the sum of consumption expenditures, *net* investment, government purchases of goods and services, and net exports is called **net national product (NNP)**. The difference between GNP and NNP reflects the difference between gross and net investment, which is the amount of depreciation. Hence, we have the condition

NNP = GNP − depreciation.

The NNP concept is useful because it measures output net of the amount needed to replace worn-out capital goods.

Measuring GNP and GDP by Production

Instead of breaking down GNP (GDP) into the sectors that do the spending, we can look at a breakdown by the sectors that do the producing (and selling). Table 1.3 shows such a breakdown for 1989 for GDP. The relative importance of different sectors is quite similar across the G-6 countries. In the United States, for example, in terms of shares of real GDP, the breakdown was 22.5% in manufacturing, 18% in wholesale and retail trade, 21% in finance, insurance and real estate, 11% in production by government and government enterprises, 6% in transportation and public utilities, 5% in construction, 3% in mining, and 3% in agriculture.

Often a firm produces **intermediate goods**, which another business uses as an input. In order not to double count intermediate goods in GNP, the national accounts give each business credit only for its **value added** to production. The value added by a firm is the difference between its revenues and the cost of goods that it buys from other firms. An example of an intermediate good is the flour that a baker uses to make bread. The baker's value added is the market value of the bread less the value of the flour used to produce the bread. The amounts shown in Table 1.3 are the value added to production by each industry.

	United States Billions of current $	United States Billions of 1980 $	United Kingdom Billions of current $	United Kingdom Billions of 1985 $	Germany Billions of current DM	Germany Billions of 1980 DM	France Billions of current FF	France Billions of 1980 FF	Italy Trillions of current lire	Italy Trillions of 1980 lire	Japan Billions of current Yen	Japan Billions of 1985 Yen
Agriculture	89.2	91.1	6.6		36.1	35.9	214.4	145.2	41.9	23.9	10.2	10.4
Mining	86.4	94.5			72.22	55.6	30.2	19.1	(a)	(a)	1.1	0.9
Manufacturing	862.2	742.7			695	521.6	1304.4	712.6	275.7	134.1	114.4	115
Electricity, gas and water	137.3	85.3				124.2	81.4	58.5	15.7	11.4	12.1	
Construction	220.7	151.3	30.3		116	94.4	321.6	205.2	63.4	27.1	37.6	33.3
Wholesale and retail trade, restaurant and hotels	767.7	592	62.1				943.9	482	219.7	84.6	50.4	51.4
Transport, storage and communication	274.2	204.2	30.1		129.6	113.5	346.5	245.3	74	27.8	25.9	24.4
Finance, insurance, real estate	1123.9	695.4			260	203.4	1315.5	657.2	275	105.3	66.9	64.2
Community, social and personal services	431.6	294.9			370.2	278.6	331	182.4	(b)	(b)	60.7	52.8
Statistical discrepancy	62.6	37.4										
Total Industries	4056	2988.8	389.9		1878.9	1470.1	4931.7	2730.6	1008.2	418.5	378.6	364.5
Government	536.4	362.9	63.6		239.1	190.9	966.5	531.1	144.8	48.1	30.8	27.2
Other producers			9.9		46.1	36			10.1	3.7	7.9	7.1
Imputed bank charges	−127.1	−77.4	−25.2		−89.2	−76.5	−298.5	−158.8	−49.1	−20.7	−20.2	−21.7
Import duties	15.4	13.1	40.7		23.1	21.1	11.2	11.1	74	26.9	1.9	2.9
Value added tax			31.9		137.5	104	502.5	306.5			−1.4	
Statistical discrepancy	-8.1	13.9	1								−1.7	0.3
Total adjustments	−119.8	−50.4	48.4		71.4	48.6	215.2	158.8	24.9	6.2	−21.4	−18.5
Gross Domestic Product (GDP)	4472.6	3301.3	511.6		2235.5	1745.6	6113.4	3420.5	1188	476.5	395.9	380.3

(a) Mining is included in item Manufacturing.
(b) Community, social and personal services are included in item Finance, Insurance, real estate.
(c) US data are for the year 1987.

Source: OECD National Accounts, table 12.

Table 1.3(a)   Production components of the Gross Domestic Product, 1989

	United States 1987 Billions of current $	United States 1987 Billions of 1980 $	United Kingdom Billions of current $	United Kingdom Billions of 1985 $	Germany Billions of current DM	Germany Billions of 1980 DM	France Billions of current FF	France Billions of 1980 FF	Italy Trillions of current lire	Italy Trillions of 1980 lire	Japan Billions of current Yen	Japan Billions of 1985 Yen
Agriculture	1.99	2.76	1.29		1.61	2.06	3.51	4.24	3.53	5.02	2.58	2.73
Mining	1.93	2.86			3.23	3.19	0.49	0.56			0.28	0.24
Manufacturing	19.28	22.50			31.09	29.88	21.34	20.84	23.21	28.14	28.90	30.24
Electricity, gas and water	3.07	2.58					2.03	2.38	4.92	3.29	2.88	3.18
Construction	4.93	4.58	5.92		5.19	5.41	5.26	6.00	5.34	5.69	9.50	8.76
Wholesale and retail trade, restaurant and hotels	17.16	17.93	12.13				15.44	14.09	18.49	17.75	12.73	13.52
Transport, storage and communication	6.13	6.19	5.88		5.80	6.50	5.67	7.17	6.23	5.83	6.54	6.42
Finance, insurance, real estate	25.13	21.06			11.63	11.65	21.52	19.21	23.15	22.10	16.90	16.88
Community, social and personal services	9.65	8.93			16.56	15.96	5.41	5.33			15.33	13.88
Statistical discrepancy	1.40	1.13										
Total Industries	90.69	90.53	76.18		84.05	84.22	80.67	79.83	84.87	87.83	95.63	95.85
Government	11.99	10.99	12.43		10.70	10.94	15.81	15.53	12.19	10.09	7.78	7.15
Other producers			1.93		2.06	2.06			0.85	0.78	2.00	1.87
Imputed bank charges	−2.84	−2.34	−4.92		−3.99	−4.38	−4.88	−4.64	−4.13	−4.34	−5.10	−5.71
Import duties	0.34	0.40	7.95		1.03	1.21	0.18	0.32	6.23	5.65	0.48	0.76
Value added tax			6.23		6.15	5.96	8.22	8.96			−0.35	0.00
Statistical discrepancy	−0.18	0.42	0.20								−0.43	0.08
Total adjustments	−2.68	−1.53	9.46		3.19	2.78	3.52	4.64	2.10	1.30	−5.41	−4.86
Gross Domestic Product (GDP)	100.00	100.00	100.00		100.00	100.00	100.00	100.00	100.00	100.00	100.00	100.00

(a) Mining is included in item Manufacturing.
(b) Community, social and personal services are included in item Finance, insurance, real estate.

Source: OECD National Accounts, table 12.

Table 1.3(b)   Production components of the Gross Domestic Product, 1989 (percent of GDP)

	Baker		Miller	
Revenue	*Costs and profits*		*Revenue*	*Costs and profits*
Total revenue from sale of bread ECU 600	Labour Flour Profit	ECU 200 ECU 350 ECU 50	Total revenue from sale of flour ECU 350	Labour ECU 250 Profit ECU 100

Table 1.4   Data for calculation of Gross National Product and National Income

	United Kingdom 1990 % of NI (billion £)		United States 1988 % of NI (billion $)	
Compensation of employees	316.4	75.22	2905	73.21
Proprietors' income	57.7	13.71	325	8.19
Rental income and net interest	38.4	9.14	411	10.36
Corporate profits	67.2	15.98	328	8.27
Imputed charges	4.3	1.02		
Total Domestic Income	484.0	115.06	3969.0	100.03
less				
Stock appreciation	6.4	1.52		
Gross domestic product, income estimate	477.6	113.54	3969.0	100.03
plus				
Statistical discrepancy	0.2	0.04		
Gross Domestic Product at factor cost	477.6	113.58	3969.0	100.03
plus				
Net property income from abroad	4.0	0.96		
Gross National Product at factor cost	481.8	114.54	3969.0	100.03
less				
Capital consumption	61.2	14.54		
National Income (Net National Product at factor cost)	420.6	100.00	3968.0	100.00

Source: UK National Accounts; OECD National Accounts.

Table 1.5   Composition of National Income

Income

The third way to look at GNP is in terms of the income earned in production. This income is called **national income**. To make clear the relation between production and income, think of a simple economy that has one firm producing bread as the only final product and another firm producing flour as the only intermediate good. Suppose that the miller uses only labour to produce flour, and the baker uses labour and flour to produce bread. Sample income statements for these firms appear in Table 1.4. In this table the only sources of income are labour income and profits. Total nominal GNP, which is the market value of the bread, is 600 ECUs. This amount also equals the total revenue of the baker. The income statement shows that this revenue divides up into 350 ECUs for the cost of flour, 200 ECUs for payments to labour (or, from the workers' standpoint, 200 ECUs of labour income), and 50 ECUs of profits (or the return on capital, that is the income assigned to the providers of capital). For the miller, the revenue of 350 ECUs goes for 250 ECUs of labour costs (or labour income) and 100 ECUs of profits. Thus, in this simple case, national income equals the total labour income of 450 ECUs plus total profits (return on capital) of 150 ECUs, which equals the 600 ECUs of GNP.

Table 1.5 shows the breakdown of national income in the United States and United Kingdom for 1990. For the United Kingdom, for example, 73% of the total is compensation of employees, 14% is income of proprietors (owners of farms and small businesses), less than 9% is personal rental income and net interest income and 15% is corporate profits.

Two complications disturb the equality between GNP and national income in the real world. First, suppose that the baker uses some capital goods in the production process. As the capital wears out, the baker subtracts depreciation charges from profits. Hence, the total income for labour and profit equals the baker's total revenue, which equals GNP, less the depreciation charges. That is, national income equals NNP, which is GNP less depreciation.

A second adjustment arises because of sales and excise taxes, which are called 'indirect taxes'. These levies create a gap between the market price of a good – which includes the tax – and the revenue received by the producer. (The gap shows up as revenue for the government.) In the example from Table 1.4, if there had been a 5% sales tax on bread, then the consumer would have paid ECU 630 for the bread, but the baker's total revenue would have remained at ECU 600. National income would still be ECU 600, but GNP (calculated at market prices) would be ECU 630. Generally, national income equals GNP less depreciation and less these indirect taxes. Table 1.6 demonstrates this calculation using US and UK data for 1990.

Recall that the definition of national income includes only the amounts earned in the production of output. Economists also calculate the amount of income that people actually receive, a concept called **personal income**. This measure differs from national income for several reasons. First, only a portion of firms' profits are paid out as dividends to individuals. Second, personal income excludes the contributions paid for social insurance, because households do not receive these amounts directly as income. Next there are

	United Kingdom 1990 (billion £)	United States 1988 (billion $)
Gross Domestic Product (GDP)	550.6	
plus		
Net factor income from abroad	4.0	
equals		
Gross National Product (GNP)	554.6	4864
less		
Depreciation	61.2	506.0
equals		
Net National Product (NNP)	493.5	4358
less		
Indirect business taxes (and related items)	72.9	390.0
equals		
National Income	420.6	3968.0
less		
Corporate profits	62.9	328.0
Contributions for social insurance	34.8	445.0
plus		
Government transfer payments	64.6	555.0
Dividends	70.5	96.0
Other		215
equals		
Personal income	458.1	4061.0
less		
Personal tax and nontax payments	73.5	590.0
equals		
Disposable personal income	384.6	3471.0

Table 1.6 Relations among national accounting aggregates

a series of adjustments to ensure that the amount of interest income in personal income corresponds to the amount that individuals receive. Finally, various transfer payments appear in personal income but not in national income. All these adjustments are detailed in Table 1.6.

Economists also calculate the amount of income that households have left after paying personal taxes, a variable called **disposable personal income**. Table 1.6 shows the calculation of disposable personal income from personal income.

Prices

One objective of macroeconomic theory is to explain the general level of prices and the changes in the price level over time. To use the theory, we need an empirical measure (or measures) of the general price level. The analysis of real and nominal GNP (GDP) provides one such measure. The **implicit GNP (GDP) price deflator** (or, more compactly, the GNP deflator) can be calculated as

implicit GNP price deflator

$$= [(\text{nominal GNP})/(\text{real GNP})] \times 100$$

It is conventional to multiply by 100 to obtain an index number that takes on the value 100 for the base year (for which nominal GNP equals real GNP).

For a concrete example, consider again the data from Table 1.2. For the 1993A case, the GNP deflator is (nominal GNP × real GNP) 100 = (550/462)100 = 119. In other words, the price of the 'average item' increased by 19% from 1992 to 1993. This number is a weighted average of the percentage increase in the price of butter (15%) and golf balls (20%). It turns out that the weights used to compute the average percentage change are the shares of the two goods in the real GNP for 1993. Thus, by using the GNP deflator to measure the general level of prices, we give more weight to the items that are currently more important in the economy's market basket of produced goods.[9]

The formula for the implicit price deflator can be rearranged to see why we call it a price deflator. The rearranged equation is

real GNP $= [(\text{nominal GNP})/(\text{implicit GNP}$

price deflator$)] \times 100.$

Thus, we effectively divide or deflate the nominal GNP by the price deflator to compute the real GNP.

This implicit GNP price deflator is called 'implicit' because it is not directly or explicitly calculated. Real GNP and nominal GNP are computed directly, and the GNP deflator is calculated by dividing the two as we have done. There are also explicit indexes of the general price level. Two important examples are the **consumer price index** (**CPI**) and the **producer price index** (**PPI**), which is also called **wholesale price index**. These are explicit indexes because they are calculated directly.

The CPI is based on a fixed market basket of consumer goods. Every few years the government takes a statistical survey to compile the base-year prices and expenditures on a large sample of goods that are consumed by typical individuals. The expenditure shares serve as fixed weights until the next survey is taken. To calculate the CPI we first compute the ratio of the current market price of each good to its base-year price. Then we sum up over the ratios, weighting each by the share of the good in base-year expenditures. Typically, we also multiply the result by 100 so that the CPI for the base year is 100.

The PPI is computed in a similar manner. This index measures prices at an early stage of production: the 'basket' in the PPI consists of a large number of items sold at wholesale. These goods are primarily raw materials and semi-finished goods.[10] It is possible to calculate inflation rates based on the CPI or the PPI, as well as on the GNP deflator (as shown in Figure 1.6). The inflation rates reported in the newspapers usually refer to the changes in the CPI or PPI. In our discussion of the general price level and inflation, we shall refer primarily to the GNP deflator. There are several reasons for this choice. First, the PPI is too narrow a concept to reflect the general level of prices. Second, the GNP deflator reflects the importance of the various items in current market baskets of produced goods, whereas the CPI refers to base-year market baskets, which can become less relevant over time. Third, the GNP deflator contains only the prices of goods that are produced domestically, whereas the CPI includes prices of imported goods. Our attempt to understand the domestic forces that contribute to changes in the domestic price level can be confused if we use the CPI.

Important Terms and Concepts

gross national product (GNP)

general price level

wage rate

interest rate

exchange rate

real GNP

recession

boom

Great Depression

gold standard

consumer nondurables and services

consumer durables

gross private domestic investment

government purchases of goods and services

transfer payments

exports

imports

net exports

closed economy

inflation rate

microeconomic foundations

budget constraint

demand for money

medium of exchange

aggregate-consistency conditions

market-clearing approach

Keynesian model

real business cycle theory

IS/LM model

balance of international payments

national-income accounts

personal consumption expenditure

consumer nondurables and services

open economy

depreciation

net investment

net national product (NNP)

intermediate goods

value added

gross domestic product (GDP)

national income

personal income

disposable personal income

implicit GNP price deflator

consumer price index (CPI)

producer price index (PPI)

Notes

1. The other main institutions of the EC are the Economic and Social Committee, the Court of Justice, the Court of Auditors and the European Investment Bank.

2. A 'closed-economy' is a country that does not have any economic exchange with the rest of the world.

3. The term G-6 is modelled on the well known term G-7, used to indicate the seven most industrialized countries, i.e. Canada, France, Germany, Italy, Japan, the United Kingdom and the United States.

4. The term *business cycle* is somewhat misleading because it suggests a more regular pattern of ups and down in economic activity than actually appears in the data. But the term is too entrenched in the economics literature to avoid entirely.

5. Not all data are available for all countries for the whole period 1950–90. We use, for each country, the longest possible sample.

6. Explain the statistical smoothing procedure; reference Kydland and Prescott from Minneapolis Fed Review.

7. The standard deviation is the square root of the variance. The variance is the average squared value of the cyclical component.

8. Activities related to the selling of a secondhand house, like the services by a notary, an evaluator and a solicitor, are all included in the calculation of GNP.

9. The GNP deflator, which weights by the importance of goods in current market baskets, is an example of a Paasche index of prices. For a discussion, see Edwin Mansfield (1985, pp. 105ff).

10. The CPI and PPI, which weight by the importance of goods in the base year, are examples of Laspeyres indexes of prices. See ibid. for a discussion.

2

The Economics of Robinson Crusoe

In any economic analysis, the determination of work effort, production, and consumption depends on opportunities for production and on preferences about working and consuming. This basic interaction between opportunities and preferences shows up even in the simplest possible economy, which consists of isolated individuals, each of whom resembles Robinson Crusoe. In this setting, which we develop in this chapter, we can readily analyze the economy's responses to changed opportunities in terms of **wealth effects** and **substitution effects**. The primitive environment of Robinson Crusoe contains the essence of choice problems that arise in complicated market economies. Therefore, the principal findings from this chapter remain valid when we extend the analysis in later chapters to settings that look more like modern industrialized economies.

We begin with a simple **production function**, which relates the quantity of output to the amount of work effort. This function determines the productivity of labour, which is the amount of extra output generated from more work. Next, we discuss preferences for consumption and leisure. Basically, people increase their work effort and accept less leisure only if they receive a sufficient addition to consumption.

Production Technology

The basic theoretical model contains one type of economic unit, which we can think of as a combination of a household and a firm. This single unit combines the consuming and working activities of households with the producing and hiring activities of businesses. For most purposes, this abstraction will be satisfactory because some households ultimately own the private businesses. Further, by merging the functions of households and businesses, we achieve some major simplifications of the analysis. From now on we refer to this composite unit simply as a household.

Each household uses its labour effort as an input to production. Note that, to simplify matters, we do not yet consider stocks of capital as inputs to the production process. This chapter concentrates on the economic incentives that make people work more or less in order to produce and consume more or fewer goods.

Formally, the quantity of a household's commodity output per period, denoted by y, is a function of the quantity of labour input, ℓ. We write this relation as

$$Y_t = f(\ell_t) \tag{2.1}$$

where f is the household's production function, which specifies the relation between the amount of work and the quantity of goods produced. The subscript t, which denotes the time period, is omitted when no ambiguity results.

Because the model contains a single physical type of commodity, there is no problem in measuring each household's output. The real-world counterpart of this output, when added up over all producers, is the gross national product (GNP). Many practical problems arise in using price indexes to add up goods that are physically different, but these difficulties do not arise in our simplified theoretical framework.

We assume in the basic model that people cannot store commodities from one period to the next, and thus we neglect inventories of goods. We can think of the commodities as perishable consumer goods. Examples include personal services, restaurant meals, and so on.

Work is productive in the sense that more work effort, ℓ, yields more output, y. The extra output produced by one more unit of work is called the **marginal (physical) product of labour**, henceforth designated **MPL**. We assume **diminishing marginal productivity**, which means that each successive unit of work effort generates progressively smaller, but still positive, responses of output.

Figure 2.1, which is the graphical representation of equation (2.1), shows the relation of output to the quantity of labour input. Note that the curve goes through the origin, which means that output is zero when labour effort is nil. The positive slope of the curve (that is, of a straight line that is tangent to the curve) at any point indicates the additional output that results from extra labour input, which is the marginal product of labour. For example, at the employment level ℓ_1, the MPL equals the slope of the straight line that is tangent to the production function at point A.

The shape of the production function in Figure 2.1 implies that the slope becomes less steep as work effort increases. This property reflects the diminishing marginal productivity of labour. For example, at the employment level ℓ_2, which exceeds ℓ_1, the slope of the tangent straight line at point B is smaller than that at point A. The full relation of the marginal product of labour, MPL, to the amount of work, ℓ, appears in Figure 2.2. Note that the marginal product declines as work effort increases. We refer to the graph of MPL versus ℓ as the *schedule* for the marginal product of labour. By a schedule, we mean the entire functional relation between MPL and ℓ.

The curves in Figures 2.1 and 2.2 apply at some initial level of technology, that is, for a given production function $f(\ell)$. We show this production function again as the solid curve in Figure 2.3. The dashed curve in the figure shows the level of output for an improved technology, denoted by $f(\ell)'$. The level of output is now higher at any given level of labour input.

What is the effect of an improvement in technology on the marginal product of labour? In general, a technological improvement may

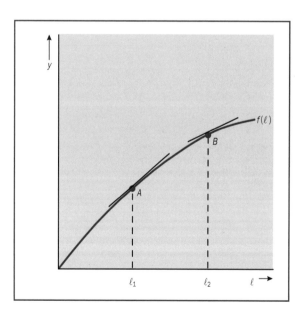

The curve shows the level of output as a function of the quantity of labour input. At point A the slope of the tangent straight line equals the marginal product of labour when $\ell = \ell_1$. The same is true for point B where $\ell = \ell_2$.

Figure 2.1   Graph of production function

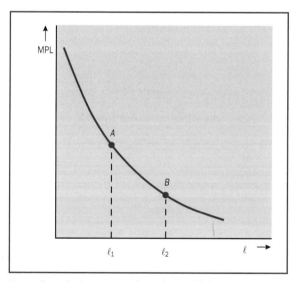

Since $\ell_1 < \ell_2$ the marginal product of labour at point A exceeds that at point B. That is the marginal product of labour falls as work effort rises.

Figure 2.2   Relation of marginal product of labour to level of work

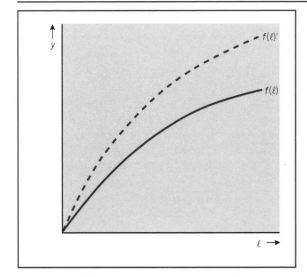

The curve $f(\ell)'$ corresponds to an improved technology, relative to the one labelled $f(\ell)$. This improvement raises the level of output for a given amount of labour input.

Figure 2.3 Effect of an improvement in technology on the level of production

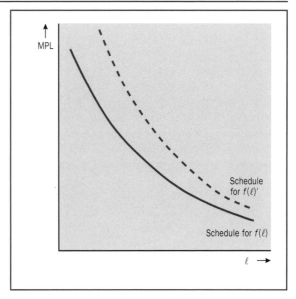

The dashed curve corresponds to an improved technology $f(\ell)'$ relative to the initial one $f(\ell)$. The technological advance shifts upward the schedule for the marginal product of labour.

Figure 2.4 Effect of an improvement in technology on the marginal product of labour

either raise or lower labour marginal product. For our purposes, we would like to capture the typical or average response. Studies of production functions at an economy-wide level suggest that, in the usual situation, an improvement in technology raises the marginal product of labour at any given level of work effort.

The construction of the curves in Figure 2.3 reflects the assumption that an improvement in technology raises the marginal product of labour. Namely, the curve labelled $f(\ell)'$ – which corresponds to the improved technology – is steeper than the initial curve at any level of work effort. Recall that the slopes of the curves measure the marginal product of labour, MPL, at each point. In Figure 2.4 we show explicitly that the technological advance leads to an upward shift in the schedule for the MPL.

Tastes for Consumption and Leisure

Suppose, as is true for Robinson Crusoe, that each person has no opportunity to exchange com-

modities or anything else with other households. In this case, each household's only option is to consume all the goods that it produces in each period. (Remember, there are no possibilities for storing commodities.) Then in the world of Robinson Crusoe we have

$$c_t = y_t = f(\ell_t) \tag{2.2}$$

where c_t is the amount of consumption in physical units. The equation says that each household's consumption equals its production, which depends on its quantity of work effort.

Consumption in each period is a source of happiness or **utility** for households. (Henceforth, we use the economist's standard jargon, *utility*.) Equation (2.2) implies that someone can consume more only if he or she raises production. Further, for a given technology, the quantity of goods produced, y_t, depends on the level of work effort, ℓ_t. So the amount of work is the key decision that households make in this model.

In the real world, households have a lot of flexibility in their choices of work effort. For example, someone might work four hours per day or eight hours. A person can pick a job that requires lots of hard work or one that does not. Someone might work for only part of the year, as is often the case for construction workers and professional sports figures. From the perspective of a family, there is a decision on how many members participate in the labour force. During this century, for example, there has been a strong increase in the number of families with two full-time workers. One evidence of this trend is the growing rate of participation of women in the civilian labour force, as reported in Table 2.1. The big increase in the labour force in the EC took place in the last thirty years. The percentage of women in the labour force rose in the EC, from 30.4% in 1960 (almost the same level as in 1910)

to 40.2% in 1990. In a longer time perspective, the amount of time spent at work depends also on the typical lengths of schooling and retirement.

We model this real-world flexibility of work effort by allowing people freely to choose their hours of work in each period. Thus, we neglect any constraints that, for example, permit people to work on some jobs for eight hours per day or four hours but not seven or two. This abstraction will be satisfactory when we think about the overall behaviour of work effort for a large number of households. In this context the constraints tend to average out.

Households have a fixed amount of time in each period, which they can divide between work and leisure. By the term *leisure* we mean to capture the full array of activities – other than work to produce goods – on which people spend their time. We assume that leisure time is

	1910	1950	1970	1989	% change 1910–1989	% change 1970–1989
Belgium	30.9	27.9	30.5	33.7	9.1	10.5
Denmark	31.3	33.7	36.0	44.5	42.2	23.6
France	35.6	36.0	36.2	39.8	11.8	9.9
Germany	30.7	35.1	36.0	37.3	21.5	3.6
Greece			25.7	26.6		3.5
Ireland			26.3	29.3		11.4
Italy	31.3	25.5	28.7	31.9	1.9	11.1
Netherlands	23.9	23.4	26.4	30.9	29.3	17.0
Portugal			24.8	36.6		47.6
Spain			19.4	24.4		25.8
United Kingdom	29.0	30.8	35.6	38.6	33.1	8.4
Austria	35.9	38.5	38.7	40.1	11.7	3.6
Finland	36.5	40.7	43.7	46.9	28.5	7.3
Norway	30.1	27.1	29.3	41.0	36.2	39.9
Sweden	27.8	26.4	35.7	44.5	60.1	24.6
Switzerland	33.9	29.7	32.7	36.6	8.0	11.9
Japan	38.9	38.5	39.0	37.9	−2.6	−2.8
United States	21.2	28.8	36.5	41.4	95.3	13.4
average 18	31.2	31.6	32.3	36.8	17.8	13.9
average EC			29.6	34.0		14.7
average EFTA			36.0	41.8		16.1
average G-6	31.1	32.5	35.3	37.8	21.5	7.0

Sources: First three columns from A. Maddison, *Dynamic Forces in Capital Development*, 1991; other column from World Bank, *World Tables*.

Table 2.1   Percent of women in total labour force

intrinsically more enjoyable than time at work. In other words, leisure is a source of utility for households.

Suppose that we can define a function to measure the amount of utility that derives each period from consumption and leisure. The form of this **utility function** is

$$u_t = u(c_t, \ell_t) \qquad (2.3)$$
$$(+) \, (-)$$

where u_t is the amount of utility (in units of happiness, which are sometimes called *utils*) that someone obtains for period t. We assume that the form of the utility function, u, is the same for all periods. The positive sign under the quantity of consumption, c_t, indicates that utility rises with consumption. The negative sign under work effort, ℓ_t, signifies the negative effect on utility of more work (that is, of less leisure). For convenience, we now drop the time subscripts and refer to period t's consumption and work as c and ℓ, respectively.

We analyze a household's decisions on working and consuming by exploiting the central economic postulate of optimizing behaviour. Each household opts for the levels of work and consumption that maximize utility in equation (2.3). Note, however, that this maximization is subject to the constraint from equation (2.2), which says that each household's consumption in any period equals its production for the same period. We want to use these facts to understand the household's selection of work and consumption.

To make progress in analysing the household's choices, we must characterize further the utility function, which expresses people's tastes for consumption and leisure. A basic assumption is that the utility gained from an extra unit of leisure, relative to that from an extra unit of consumption, diminishes as the ratio of leisure to consumption rises. In other words, if someone has a lot of leisure but relatively little consumption, he or she is more concerned with adding to consumption rather than leisure. Consider the amount of extra consumption needed to compensate for the loss of a unit of leisure time. If a

person starts with little consumption and a lot of leisure, it is important to add to consumption. Therefore, he or she is willing to work a lot more to get additional consumption. If the person is already working quite a bit and has a high level of consumption, leisure becomes more significant. Therefore, he or she is less willing to work more and give up leisure to obtain extra consumption.

The curve in Figure 2.5 summarizes this discussion. At zero work effort, $\ell = 0$, the curve specifies a level of consumption, c^0, on the vertical axis. This amount of consumption, together with full-time leisure ($\ell = 0$), determines some level of utility from equation (2.3). Denote this level of utility by u^1. The curve shown in the figure connects this initial point to all other possible combinations of work and consumption that provide the same level of utility, u^1.

Suppose that the person works a positive amount, so that leisure becomes less than a full-time activity. For concreteness, assume that work is one hour per day, represented by $\ell = 1$ in Figure 2.5. By itself, this reduction in leisure lowers utility. But we want to know how much additional consumption would restore the original level of utility. Denote by Δc^1 the required amount of extra consumption. Then the new combination of work and consumption, where $\ell = 1$ and $c = c^0 + c^1$, yields the same utility as the initial pair, where $\ell = 0$ and $c = c^0$. Hence, the person is indifferent between these two pairs of work and consumption. We show that these two points yield the same level of utility by connecting them with the curve shown in the figure.

If the person works another hour – that is, $\ell = 2$ – some additional consumption is again needed to maintain the level of utility. Figure 2.5 assumes that the required extra consumption is the amount Δc^2. Therefore, the point where $\ell = 2$ and $c = c^0 + \Delta c^1 + \Delta c^2$ again provides the same utility as the initial pair, where $\ell = 0$ and $c = c^0$.

We can continue this exercise as the amount of work rises. The result is the curve in Figure 2.5, which shows all pairs, (ℓ, c), that yield the same level of utility. Since people are indifferent among these pairs of work and consumption, the curve is called an **indifference curve**.

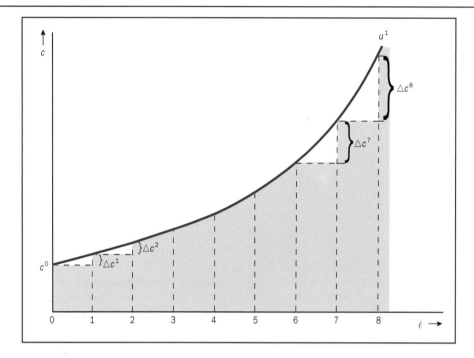

All points on the curve yield the same level of utility. Hence the household is indifferent among these pairs of work effort and consumption

Figure 2.5   An indifference curve for work and consumption

The previous discussion tells us something about the shape of an indifference curve. As someone works more, each additional unit of work requires a greater amount of extra consumption to maintain utility. Therefore, the size of each addition to consumption, Δc, is larger the higher is the associated number of work hours. Note, in particular, that $\Delta c^1 < \Delta c^2 < \ldots < \Delta c^7 < \Delta c^8$ in Figure 2.5.

At any point along the indifference curve, the slope of a tangent straight line indicates the increment in consumption that a person requires to make up for the loss of a unit of leisure. Each of the additions to consumption, Δc, that appear in Figure 2.5 approximates this slope in the vicinity of the corresponding level of work. For example, the amount Δc^2 is a good measure of the slope when the level of work lies between one and two hours per day. The previous results imply that the slope of the indifference curve rises as the amount of work, ℓ, increases.

The slope of the indifference curve in Figure 2.5 indicates the amount of consumption that someone needs to make up for the loss of a unit of leisure. Put alternatively, if a worker receives more than this amount of consumption, he or she would be better off. For example, when someone is already working seven hours per day, he or she is willing to work an additional hour if consumption thereby rises by at least the amount Δc^8 in the figure. If it turns out that the extra hour of work increases consumption by an amount greater than Δc^8, economic reasoning predicts that the worker will work that extra hour. This viewpoint allows us to determine the number of hours that people actually work.

All points on the curve in Figure 2.5 yield the same level of utility u^1. But suppose that we look along the vertical axis and raise the consumption level above c^0; then utility increases. Corresponding to this higher level of utility, say u^2, we can construct another indifference curve.

The new curve is similar to the one shown in the figure, but it lies wholly above this curve. That is, for any level of work, ℓ, the amount of consumption, c, is higher. That is why the new indifference curve corresponds to a higher level of utility. (We can also say that for any level of consumption, c, the amount of work effort, l, is smaller along the new curve.)

Similarly, we could lower the level of consumption below c^0 along the vertical axis. In this case, we can start the construction of an indifference curve for a lower level of utility. As a general matter, we can define a whole 'family' or 'map' of indifference curves, each of which corresponds to a different level of utility. Figure 2.6 shows five of these curves, labelled by their levels of utility, where $u^1 < u^2 \ldots < u^5$. Along any curve the level of utility is constant. But as a person moves vertically from one curve to others – thereby, raising consumption while keeping work fixed – the level of utility increases. We have already mentioned the central idea that the household wants to achieve the highest possible level of utility. Therefore, we can also say that the household's objective is to reach the highest possible indifference curve among the family of curves in Figure 2.6.

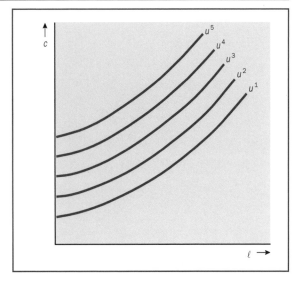

The level of utility rises as the household moves from the curve labelled u^1 to that labeled u^2 and so on.

Figure 2.6   A family of indifference curves for work and consumption

Deciding How Much to Work

Suppose that a household begins from a particular combination of work and consumption, (ℓ, c). Then we can consult Figure 2.6 to find the indifference curve to which this point corresponds. The slope of the indifference curve at this point indicates how much extra consumption, Δc, someone insists on to work an additional unit of time. To determine how much someone actually works, we combine the indifference curves with a description of people's opportunities for raising consumption when work effort rises. In the model, these opportunities come from the production function, which appears in Figure 2.1. The marginal product of labour, MPL, is the amount of extra output generated by an extra unit of work. Further, we know from equation (2.2) that each addition to

output corresponds to an equal addition to consumption.

The MPL is the addition to production – and therefore to consumption – that results from an extra unit of work. The slope of the indifference curve is the amount of extra consumption that a person needs to make up for less leisure time. Therefore, if the MPL exceeds the slope of the indifference curve, the person will be better off if he or she works more and uses the added output to expand consumption. However, as work rises, the MPL declines, and the slope of the indifference curve rises. Therefore, the increase in work lessens the initial excess of the MPL over the slope of the indifference curve. When the gap vanishes – that is, when the marginal product equals the slope of the indifference curve – it no longer pays to work more.

The results are in Figure 2.7. Consider the intersection of the production function, $y = f(\ell)$, with indifference curve u^1 at point D. At this position, the slope of the production function – which is the MPL – exceeds the slope of the indifference curve. An increase in work expands output and, hence, consumption by more than

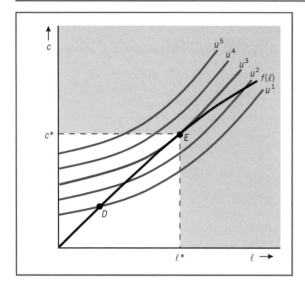

The household moves along the production function $f(\ell)$ to reach the highest possible indifference curve. This occurs at point E where the production function is tangent to indifference curve u^3

Figure 2.7 Combining the indifference curves with the production function

enough to maintain the level of utility. Graphically, by raising work and moving along the production function beyond point D, a household intersects higher indifference curves and thereby raises utility.

Assume that work rises enough to reach point E in Figure 2.7. At this point the slope of the production function equals the slope of the indifference curve. We show this graphically by drawing the production function, $f(\ell)$, as tangent to indifference curve u^3 at point E. Then we designate the associated levels of work and consumption as ℓ^* and c^*. Notice that, at this point, a movement along the production function beyond point E intersects lower indifference curves. In other words, the extra output and consumption are now insufficient to make up for the loss of utility from extra work. Therefore, utility declines if work rises above the amount ℓ^*.

To summarize, each household chooses the combination of work and consumption that maximizes utility. Therefore, the household selects the pair, (ℓ^*, c^*), at which the production function is tangent to an indifference curve.

The figures that we used to illustrate our analysis are theoretical analogues of situations and decisions that occur every day to almost everybody. While it is impossible to actually use in our figures 'real' production functions or 'actual' indifference curves, we should not conclude that these concepts are mere abstractions with no real content. On the contrary, it will soon be evident that these theoretical principles can be immediately applied to a number of practical cases and are very helpful in explaining and predicting real economic decisions and events.

Shifts in the Production Function

We want to understand how people alter their work effort and consumption when there are changes in the opportunities for production. Here, we represent these changes by shifts of the production function, $f(\ell)$. Remember that we are examining the choices of work and consumption for a single period. So think here of changes in the production function that apply for that same period.

There are many examples of economic disturbances that alter production opportunities. For instance, particularly severe weather conditions reduce agricultural output and thereby amount to a downward shift in the production function. The oil crises of 1973–74 and 1979 led to increases in the price of oil, which meant that users of energy had to give up more resources to carry out their production. From the standpoint of these users, the disturbance again looks like a downward shift in the production function, $f(\ell)$. On the other hand, discoveries of new technology – such as practical uses of electricity, nuclear energy, computer chips, and fibre optics – amount to upward shifts of the production function.

In analysing the reaction of households to economic changes, we shall find it useful to place the responses into two categories:

- wealth effects
- substitution effects

A wealth effect (which economists also call an **income effect**) concerns the overall scale of opportunities. If a change allows people to obtain more of the things that provide utility, then wealth increases. A substitution effect refers to the relative ease or cost with which people can obtain the various items that provide utility. We might, for example, have a change in the possibilities for transforming more work (and, hence, less leisure) into more consumption. More generally, we could have a change in the relative costs of obtaining any two goods, such as bread and television sets.

We shall use the concepts of wealth and substitution effects extensively throughout this book. To begin we consider the wealth effects for the model that we have been analysing. We assume throughout this discussion that people have a given pattern of tastes for consumption and leisure. Specifically, people's indifference curves, which appear in Figures 2.6 and 2.7, do not move around when the production function shifts.

Wealth Effects

As a general definition, a change raises wealth if it enables people to reach a higher level of utility. In contrast, wealth declines if the change forces people to a lower level of utility.[1] Unfortunately, this definition may be difficult to apply in some circumstances. We want to use the notions of wealth and substitution effects to assist in analyses of various economic changes, such as a harvest failure. In some cases, we do not know at the start whether a particular change will end up raising or lowering utility, so if we have to solve the whole problem to determine what happens to wealth, there may not be much point in using the concept.

We can usually test for the sign of the change in wealth by the following method. Start with a household's initial choices of work and consumption at the position (ℓ^*, c^*) in Figure 2.7. Then see how the economic change alters opportunities in the vicinity of this initial point.[2] For example, the initial quantity of work effort, ℓ^*, may allow the

household to consume at a higher level than before. Then wealth surely increases (because the household can attain a higher level of utility). Alternatively, the initial level of work effort, ℓ^*, may allow only a smaller quantity of consumption than before. In this case wealth probably declines.

Let's be more concrete about this method for the case of a shift to the production function. An increase in wealth arises if households can produce and consume more goods for the same amount of work effort. In the simplest case of a pure wealth effect, the production function shifts upward in a parallel manner. This shift means more output for a given amount of input but no change in the slope of the production function at each level of work. That is, the marginal product of labour does not change at a given level of work. We show this case in Figure 2.8. In this case, the new production function, $f(\ell)'$, parallels the old one, $f(\ell)$.

Recall that our previous case of a shift to the production function, as shown in Figure 2.3,

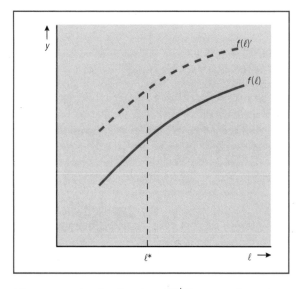

The new production function $f(\ell)'$ lies everywhere above the old one $f(\ell)$. With this type of parallel shift the two functions have the same slope at any given level of work effort.

Figure 2.8 A parallel upward shift of the production function

involved changes in the slope of the function. For the moment we neglect this type of change because it brings in substitution effects. The parallel shift shown in Figure 2.8 is easier because it involves only a wealth effect.

How do people respond to an increase in wealth? We find the answer in Figure 2.9 by combining the change to the production function with two of the indifference curves. The production function was initially tangent to an indifference curve at the point (ℓ^*, c^*). Then, as mentioned before, the upward shift of the production function enables a household to reach a higher indifference curve. The new production function, $f(l)'$, is tangent to a higher indifference curve at the point $[(\ell^*)', (c^*)']$. The figure indicates that consumption increases – $(c^*)' > c^*$ – and work effort decreases – $(\ell^*)' < \ell^*$. In other words, households respond to the increase in wealth by raising the quantities of both things that provide utility – consumption and leisure. We say that consumption and leisure are **superior goods** because the quantities of both rise in response to an increase in wealth. (Sometimes economists use the term **normal goods** instead of superior goods.) Alternatively, we can say that the wealth effect is positive for consumption and negative for work.

Generally, when there are many types of goods, we cannot be sure that the wealth effect is positive for all of them. Some goods may be 'inferior', which means that people desire less of them when wealth rises. But when thinking about only two broad categories of things that provide utility – consumption and leisure – we can be pretty sure that both goods are superior. That is, some reasonable assumptions about the nature of preferences guarantee this result. Hence, from now on, we assume that consumption and leisure are superior goods.

It is not surprising that the wealth effect on consumption is positive. Casual observation across families or countries immediately supports this proposition. Similarly, at the aggregate level, it is no surprise that consumption per person has grown along with the rise in output per capita.

The negative effect of wealth on work effort is somewhat harder to verify. But it does show up in

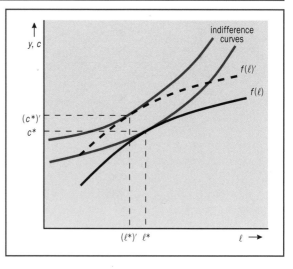

The parallel upward shift of the production function motivates the household to consume more and work less.

Figure 2.9 The response of work and consumption to an increase in wealth

the long-run negative influence of economic development on average hours of work. Table 2.2 shows the evolution of average annual hours of work over more than a century in several industrialized economies. In all the countries considered, hours of work almost halved since 1870. For example, if we were to assume a work day of eight hours for the whole period, we find that in 1870 the average G-6 worker spent 368 days a year on the job (a very long year!). By 1987, the number of days at work decreased to 206. The reduction in work effort has taken place both in terms of hours of work a day (or a week) and in the number of working days a year. Thus, in 1870, a typical worker in one of the G-6 countries might have worked 60 hours a week for 50 weeks a year, while in 1989 it decreased to 42 hours a week for 40 weeks.

If we look across countries at a point in time, we get some further indication of a negative wealth effect on work effort. For example, over the period 1953–60, the mean over ten industrialized countries for the average weekly hours in manufacturing was 43.9. (The ten are France, Germany, the Netherlands, the United Kingdom, Norway, Switzerland, Sweden, New Zealand, the

United States and Canada.) But the mean over ten less-developed countries was 47.4. (These ten are Yugoslavia, Colombia, the Philippines, El Salvador, Ecuador, Guatemala, Peru, Taiwan, Egypt, and Ceylon.)[3]

The negative effect of economic development on average hours of work seems to weaken at high levels of development. In Table 2.2 we observe that in many countries the reduction in the number of hours is greater in the period 1870–1938 than between 1950 and 1987. While the long-term downward trend in average hours worked per week has slowed down after World War II, it has still been substantial in some countries, even in recent years. For example, in France's manufacturing sector, average weekly hours worked fell from 46.3 in 1964 to 38.7 in 1990.

We have to go further with our economic analysis to explain the observations for the recent period. As mentioned before, we want to bring in substitution effects as influences on the choices of work and consumption.

Substitution Effects for Work versus Consumption

We started with a pure wealth effect where the production function shifted upward in a parallel manner, as shown in Figure 2.8. This change in technology allowed people to produce more goods for a given amount of work. There was no change, however, in the schedule for the marginal product of labour, MPL. This last condition is unrealistic, because technological advances tend to raise the MPL at each level of work.

Suppose that we want to understand the effects on households' choices from the type of upward shift to the production function that appears in Figure 2.10. The new function, $f(\ell)'$, is proportionately higher than the initial one, $f(\ell)$, at each level of work. Therefore, the slope of the new curve exceeds that of the initial one at each level of work. This change in slope brings in a

	1870	1913	1938	1950	1987	1989	% change 1870–1987	% change 1870–1938	% change 1950–1987
Belgium	2964	2605	2267	2283	1620		−45.3	−23.5	−29.0
Denmark	2945	2588	2267	2283	1669	1654	−43.3	−23.0	−26.9
France	2945	2588	1848	1926	1543		−47.6	−37.2	−19.9
Germany	2941	2584	2316	2316	1620	1607	−44.9	−21.3	−30.1
Italy	2886	2536	1927	1997	1528		−47.1	−33.2	−23.5
Netherlands	2964	2605	2244	2208	1387		−53.2	−24.3	−37.2
United Kingdom	2984	2624	2267	1958	1557	1552	−47.8	−24.0	−20.5
Austria	2935	2580	2312	1976	1595	1591	−45.7	−21.2	−19.3
Finland	2945	2588	2183	2035	1663	1655	−43.5	−25.9	−18.3
Norway	2945	2588	2128	2101	1486		−49.5	−27.7	−29.3
Sweden	2945	2588	2204	1951	1466		−50.2	−25.2	−24.9
Switzerland	2984	2624	2257	2144	1794		−39.9	−24.4	−16.3
Japan	2945	2588	2391	2166	2020	1998	−31.4	−18.8	−6.7
United States	2964	2605	2062	1867	1608	1604	−45.7	−30.4	−13.9
average 14	2949	2592	2191	2087	1611	1666	−45.4	−25.7	−22.8
average EC7	2947	2590	2162	2139	1561	1604	−47.0	−26.6	−27.0
average EFTA	2951	2594	2217	2041	1601	1623	−45.8	−24.9	−21.6
average G6	2944	2588	2135	2038	1646	1690	−44.1	−27.5	−19.2

Source: A. Maddison, *Dynamic Forces in Capital Development*, 1991.

Table 2.2   Annual hours worked per person

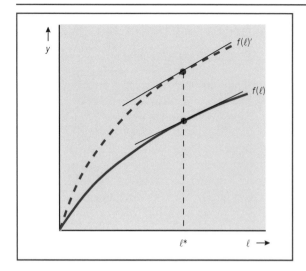

The new production function level is higher and more steeply sloped than the old one *f(ℓ)* at each of work

Figure 2.10   A proportional upward shift of the production function

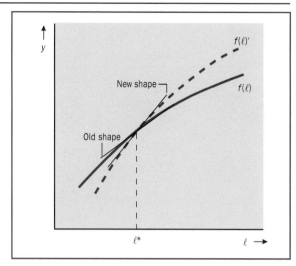

At ℓ* the level of output is the same for the two production functions. However, the new function $f(\ell)'$ is more steeply sloped than the old one *f(ℓ)* at any level of work

Figure 2.11   A twist of the production function

substitution effect, which we now have to consider.

The proportional shift in Figure 2.10 combines the parallel shift in Figure 2.8 with a counter-clockwise twist of the new function, $f(\ell)'$. Recall that we already understand the pure wealth effects from the parallel shift; therefore, we need only to study the consequences of this counter-clockwise twist of the production function to assess the type of proportional shift that appears in Figure 2.10. Figure 2.11 isolates this twist. Note that the new production function, $f(\ell)'$, is more steeply sloped than the old one, $f(\ell)$, at each level of work. Hence, the twist raises the marginal product of labour at any level of work.

Figure 2.12 shows the household's response to a twist of the production function. The initial function, $f(\ell)$, is tangent to an indifference curve at the point (ℓ^*, c^*). Since the new function, $f(\ell)'$, passes through this point, it would still be possible to work the amount ℓ* and consume the amount c*. Households were happy initially to stay at this point because the MPL equalled the slope of the indifference curve, but the MPL is now higher. Therefore, more work now generates enough additional output (and consumption) to

raise utility. That is, a movement along the new production function, $f(\ell)'$, in Figure 2.12, reaches higher indifference curves. Eventually, the household gets to one that is tangent to the new production function at the point $(\ell^*, c^*)'$. Then any more work would lower utility.

We have shown that a rise in the schedule for the marginal product of labour induces more work, $(\ell^*)' > \ell^*$, and more consumption, $(c^*)' > c^*$. Recall that a household always has the opportunity to work one more unit of time and use the additional MPL units of output to raise consumption. In terms of the two things that provide utility – leisure and consumption – households have the option to give up one unit of leisure in exchange for MPL extra units of consumption. When the schedule for labour marginal product shifts upward, this deal becomes more favourable. That is, households now get more consumption, MPL, when they give up a unit of leisure. Or, to put this another way, consumption has become less costly relative to leisure. A rational person who wants to maximize utility finds it desirable to substitute toward the items that have become cheaper. In our example,

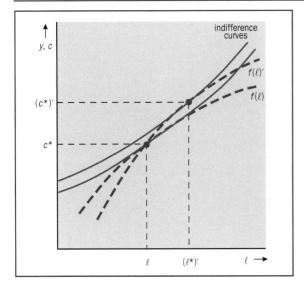

The schedule for the marginal product of labour shifts upward when the production function shifts from $f(\ell)$ to $f(\ell)'$. The response is an increase in work – from n^* to $(\ell^*)'$ – and a rise in consumption – from c^* to $(c^*)'$

Figure 2.12 Response of work and consumption effect

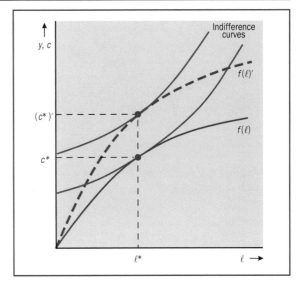

When the production function shifts upward proportionately there is an increase in consumption but an ambiguous change in work effort.

Figure 2.13 Response of work and consumption to combined wealth and substitution effects

this substitution effect motivates more consumption and less leisure (which means more work).[4]

Combining the Wealth and Substitution Effects

We can now work out the full effects from a proportional upward shift of the production function, as shown in Figure 2.10. This change combines an increase in wealth with a substitution effect from the rise in the schedule for the marginal product of labour.

Figure 2.13 shows the effects on the household's choices. Notice that consumption increases, $(c^*)' > c^*$. The effect on work effort is, however, ambiguous. Let's consider the nature of this ambiguity. The positive wealth effect leads to more consumption and more leisure and therefore to *less* work. The substitution effect from the higher schedule for the MPL implies more consumption and less leisure, which means *more* work. Notice that the wealth and substitu-

tion effects reinforce themselves with respect to consumption but oppose each other with respect to work and leisure. The proportional shift of the production function leads to less work and more leisure only if the wealth effect dominates the substitution effect. We cannot say in general which force will be more important.

Let's use the perspective of wealth and substitution effects to reconsider the facts on work hours that we looked at before. Recall that the major decline in average hours worked occurred during the first part of the century, i.e. at earlier stages of economic development.

Suppose that we think of economic development as represented by a series of proportional upward shifts to production functions. Figure 2.14 picks out three stages of economic development: a low level where the production function (for the typical producer) is $f(\ell)^{\mathrm{I}}$, a middle level at $f(\ell)^{\mathrm{II}}$, and a high level at $f(\ell)^{\mathrm{III}}$. We can think of the first curve as applying to any industrialized country before World War I, the second curve as applying at the end of World War II, and the third as applying in 1993.

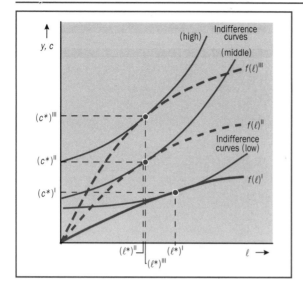

The figure shows three levels of the production function as the economy develops from $f(\ell)^{I}$ to $f(\ell)^{II}$ to $f(\ell)^{III}$. The indifference curves in the corresponding regions are labelled 'low', 'middle' and 'high'. Notice that work effort falls at early stages of economic development but changes little at more advanced stages.

Figure 2.14   Effect of long-term economic development on average work hours

Consider the patterns for households' tastes that would be consistent with the data on average work hours. Imagine first an economy at a low level of development; that is, a situation in which the production function allows the typical person to reach only a low indifference curve. In this circumstance, people are likely to be willing to work long hours to maintain their consumption levels, even if their marginal products are low and although they are already working a lot. Diagrammatically, the indifference curve marked *low* in Figure 2.14 is extremely flat up to a high level of work effort. The flat slope means that people are willing to work a lot to gain a small amount of extra consumption. Notice that the first production function is tangent to the low indifference curve at the point $[(\ell^*)^{I}, (c^*)^{I}]$. Here, people work many hours but produce and consume relatively little because of the low level of the production function.

When production opportunities improve to the second level, $f(\ell)^{II}$, the production function is tangent to the indifference curve labelled *middle* at the point, $[(\ell^*)^{II}, (c^*)^{I}]$, in Figure 2.14. The figure shows this middle indifference curve with a slope that is higher and more steeply rising than that for the low indifference curve. This shape means that extra leisure has become more important relative to additional consumption. For this reason a reduction in hours worked, $(\ell^*)^{II} < (\ell^*)^{I}$, accompanies the rise in consumption, $(c^*)^{II} > (c^*)^{I}$. In this range of economic development, the negative wealth effect on work effort dominates the substitution effect.

Finally, the move from the second production function, $f(\ell)^{II}$, to the third, $f(\ell)^{III}$, corresponds to the case that we explored before in Figure 2.13. Here, the wealth and substitution effects roughly cancel to yield little change in work hours. But consumption again increases, $(c^*)^{III} > (c^*)^{II}$.

Summary

In this chapter, households are isolated from each other and therefore behave like Robinson Crusoes. There are no markets on which people can trade, and each household uses its own labour to produce goods via a production function. Because we treat goods as non-storable, each household consumes what it produces.

We can express people's preferences in terms of their utility for consumption and leisure. Then we can translate these preferences into indifference curves for work and consumption. Basically, people work more only if they receive a sufficient addition to their consumption.

The combination of households' preferences with their opportunities for production determines the choices of work, production, and consumption. For convenience we analyze these choices in terms of wealth and substitution effects. An improvement in the production function increases wealth, which motivates less work and more consumption. That is, the wealth effect is positive for consumption and leisure.

The only substitution effect in the model involves the productivity of labour. If the schedule for labour marginal product shifts upward, then households can obtain more consumption for an extra hour of work. Because consumption becomes cheaper relative to leisure, households work more to raise their consumption. In other words, they substitute away from leisure and toward consumption.

Toward the end, we use the apparatus to analyze the long-term behaviour of work hours. Initially, as an economy develops, the increase in wealth motivates people to consume more and to work fewer hours per week. As the economy develops further, the substitution effect from labour higher productivity tends roughly to offset the wealth effect. Hence, there is little change in work hours, but consumption continues to rise.

Important Terms and Concepts

production function
wealth effect
substitution effect
marginal product of labour (MPL)
diminishing marginal productivity
utility
utility function
indifference curve
superior goods (or normal goods)
Inferior goods

Questions and Problems

Mainly for Review

2.1 What is a production function? How does it represent a trade-off that the individual *has* to make between work (and consumption) and leisure?

2.2 Distinguish between total product and marginal product. What are the implications for total product if marginal product is (a) positive and increasing, (b) positive and diminishing, and (c) negative?

2.3 What is a utility function? Show how to represent different levels of utility by a family of indifference curves. Can these curves shift in the way that the production function can?

2.4 Show how the slope of each indifference curve indicates the trade-off that the individual is willing to make between work (and consumption) and leisure. Explain why it may not be equal to the trade-off represented by the slope of the production function.

2.5 Suppose that to remain at the same level of utility an individual would have to receive one additional unit of consumption as compensation for one less unit of leisure. Would it be utility maximizing for the individual to work more if at that point the additional output obtained is more than one? if it is less than one? Restate your answer using the concepts of indifference curves and the production function.

2.6 Suppose there is an improvement in the production function. Assume that the improvement includes an upward shift in the schedule for the marginal product of labour. Will the individual work more to obtain more output; or work less, obtain the same or a greater amount of output, and enjoy more leisure than before? Explain your answer in terms of wealth and substitution effects. How does your answer change if either consumption or leisure is an inferior good?

Problems for Discussion

2.7 Properties of a Specific Production Function
Suppose that the production function has the form,

$$y = A.\sqrt{\ell} + B$$

where y is output, ℓ is labour input, A is a positive constant, and B is another constant, which may be positive, negative, or zero.
a. Graph the level of output, y, versus the quantity of labour input, ℓ.
b. Is the marginal product of labour positive? Is it diminishing in ℓ?
c. Describe the wealth and substitution effects from an increase in the coefficient A.
d. Describe the wealth and substitution effects from an increase in the coefficient B.

2.8 Effects of Shifts in the Production Function on the Choice of Work Effort
Assume again that the production function is $y = A.\sqrt{\ell} + B$. What are the effects on a household's work effort, ℓ, output, y, and consumption, c, from:
a. an increase in the coefficient A?
b. an increase in the coefficient B?

2.9   Temporary versus Permanent Changes in the Production Function

Suppose that the production function shifts upward. Assume, as in Figure 2.8, that the shift is parallel, so that no change occurs in the schedule for labour marginal product. Recall that we showed in Figure 2.9 that people respond by raising consumption and reducing work.

The improvement in the production function could be permanent – as in the case of a discovery of some new technology – or it might be temporary – as in the case of good weather for this period. What difference does it make for the results whether the change is permanent or temporary? That is, do we predict different responses of consumption and work effort in the two cases?

2.10   Changes in Labour-Force Participation

In the text we mentioned some variations over time in average hours worked per week. But we also see important changes in aggregate work effort that reflect shifts in labour-force participation. For example, people may alter their time spent at school or in retirement. Also, especially for married women in recent years, people may choose to work in the market rather than at home. Overall we can assess the changes in labour-force participation from the following table, which shows the ratio of the total labour force to the adult population aged less than 65.

Notice that labour-force participation behaved differently in the EC and in the US. Most of this change reflected the different dynamics in the labour activity of men and women.

What does our analysis of wealth and substitution effects say about this behaviour of labour-force participation? (Think here of effects on a family that

includes more than one potential worker.) Can we reconcile these patterns of labour-force participation with the tendency of average hours worked per worker to stay constant or fall slowly? (Note: This question does not have a clear-cut answer!)

2.11   Productivity

A popular measure of productivity is the ratio of output (say, real GNP) to employment (say, worker hours). In the graph of the production function below, this concept of productivity at the employment level ℓ^1 is given by the ratio, y^1/ℓ^1. Productivity at this point equals the slope of the dashed line that is drawn from the origin to intersect the production function at the employment level ℓ^1.

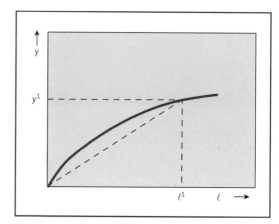

a. For the production function shown and for any employment level ℓ, show graphically that productivity, y/ℓ, always exceeds the marginal product of labour, MPL.

		Labour Force				
		EC			*US*	
	Total	*Male*	*Female*	*Total*	*Male*	*Female*
1990	66.6	79.7	53.6	76.6	85.2	68.1
1980	65.9	84.1	47.9	72.0	84.7	59.7
1960	67.9	96.2	41.3	66.2	90.5	42.6

Notes:
– Total labour force, % of total population aged 15 to 64.
– Male labour force, % of male population aged 15 to 64.
– Female labour force, % of female population aged 15 to 64.

Source: OECD Historical Statistics.

b. Consider a technological change that shifts the production function upward proportionately at all levels of ℓ (as shown in Figure 2.10). What happens to the choices of work effort, ℓ, and output, y? What happens to productivity, y/ℓ? (Empirically, long-run economic development is associated with a sustained rise in output per worker hour.)

c. Assume now that the form of the production function does not change. But suppose that people shift their tastes and become more willing to work. That is, at the initial levels of work and consumption, each person requires a smaller addition in consumption to give up a unit of leisure. What happens here to the choices of work effort, ℓ, and output, y? What happens to productivity, y/ℓ?

Notes

1. This viewpoint comes from John Hicks (1946, Ch. 2).
2. This general approach derives from the work of the Russian economist, Eugen Slutsky. For a discussion (in the context of markets for goods), see Hal Varian (1987, pp. 147–50).
3. The data are in Gordon Winston (1966, table 1). His study deals also with cross-county differences in labour-force participation.
4. Figure 2.12 shows that the household reaches a higher indifference curve. Therefore, the disturbance involves an increase in wealth as well as a substitution effect. Because the wealth effect is relatively unimportant, the example provides a close approximation to a pure substitution effect. To isolate the substitution effect exactly, we would have to include a small, parallel downward shift of the production function along with the twist shown in the figure. If this small shift were of the right size, then the household would remain on the initial indifference curve. But this minor modification would still leave people with higher levels of work effort and consumption. Thus, the elimination of the small wealth effect would not change any qualitative results.

3

The Basic Budget Constraint and the Demand for Money

In the previous chapter, each household was like Robinson Crusoe: there were no possibilities for trade between one household and another. This chapter and the next introduce two types of opportunities for exchange. First, there is a commodity market on which people can sell their outputs and buy those of others. On this market, the price level is the amount of money that exchanges for one unit of commodities. One important aspect of this market is that it allows people to specialize in their type of production. This specialization is a major element in efficient economic organization.

Second, there is a credit market on which households can borrow and lend. The interest rate determines the cost of borrowing and the return to lending.

The Commodity Market

In the real world, people consume very little of the goods that they help to produce in the marketplace. For example, an auto worker's contribution to the output of cars is much greater than that worker's expenditure on cars. Typically, a person works on one or a few products and receives income from the sale of these products or from the sale of labour services, which help to create the products. Then this income is spent on a wide range of consumer goods. As Adam Smith observed over two centuries ago, people tend to specialize with respect to occupations and production activities. This specialization aids efficiency. In fact, the national output would be many times smaller if

everyone participated in the production of all goods. In that case, people would learn each job badly and would spend most of their time shifting from task to task.

In the theoretical model, we want to capture the feature that individuals consume little of what they produce. To keep things workable, it is convenient to go to the extreme and assume that producers sell their entire output on a market on which people buy and sell commodities. Then sellers use their proceeds to buy other goods for consumption purposes.

The model would become unmanageable if we tried to keep track of the physical differences among many kinds of goods. Therefore, we continue to pretend that there is a single physical type of good, which households produce by one type of production process. As before, the production function is

$$y_t = f(\ell_t) \tag{3.1}$$

Money

Consider the sales and purchases of goods on the commodity market. We assume that it is inconvenient to trade one type of good directly for another. As economists have noted for hundreds of years, this form of **barter** exchange would require a person to find someone who wants exactly the goods that he or she has and has exactly the goods that he or she wants. We therefore assume that society has settled on a **medium of exchange**, called money. People sell their outputs for money and use money to buy other goods for consumption purposes. The use of money facilitates the exchange of one good for another.

The money in our model is analogous to paper **currency** issued by a government. At the present time, almost all governments issue currency. (Two exceptions are Panama and Liberia, which use US currency. Some others that lack their own paper money are Andorra, Greenland, Guadalupe, and Liechtenstein.) Money takes a paper form in the model, with no backing by gold or other commodities. The monetary roles of gold and silver were important historically but are much less significant under present-day arrangements.

Money is denominated in an arbitrary unit, such as a dollar, a pound or an 'ECU'. We shall often refer to ECU amounts as **nominal** magnitudes.[1] One important property is that, unlike some assets that we introduce later, money does not bear interest.[2]

Denote the ECU quantity of money that someone holds during period t by m_t. The aggregate quantity of money, denoted by M_t, equals the sum of the holdings by all individuals. (We adopt the convention of using a capital letter to represent an aggregate quantity.) For now, we assume that the aggregate quantity of money does not change over time.

The Price Level

Because goods are physically the same, we expect that all can be sold for the same number of ECUs on the commodity market. The number of ECUs that people receive for each unit of goods sold is the ECU *price* of the good. We denote the price by P and measure it in units of ECUs per good. Often, we refer to P as the **general price level**.

For a seller of commodities, the price P is the number of ECUs obtained for each unit of goods sold. For a buyer, the price is the number of ECUs paid per unit of goods. Since P ECUs buy 1 unit of goods, €∅ would buy $1/P$ units of goods. The expression $1/P$ is therefore the value of €1 in units of the commodities that it buys. Similarly, €m exchanges for $(m) \times 1/P$ units of commodities. Whereas the quantity m is the value of money in

terms of ECUs, the quantity m/P measures the value of this money in terms of the quantity of commodities that it buys. Expressions like m/P are in units of commodities or in **real terms**. By contrast, a quantity like m is in ECU or nominal terms.

In the present chapter, we assume that people perceive the price level to be constant over time. (We drop this unrealistic assumption in Chapter 8, which begins the study of inflation.) Throughout the analysis, we assume that each household views itself as sufficiently small that it can buy or sell any amount of goods in the commodity market without influencing the established price. Economists call this **perfect competition**.

The Credit Market

In the Robinson Crusoe model of Chapter 2, people had no way to shift resources over time. Goods could not be stored, and individuals could not borrow from others and repay these loans later. For now, we retain the assumption that goods cannot be stored, but we introduce possibilities for borrowing and lending on a credit market.

A person who makes a loan receives a piece of paper that indicates the terms of the contract. In our model we call this piece of paper a **bond**. The holder of a bond – the lender – has a claim to the amount owed by the borrower. Bonds in the model come in units of ECUs. When someone buys 1 unit of bonds with €1 of money, he or she lends €1 on the credit market. If a person issues 1 unit of bonds in exchange for €1 of money, he or she borrows €1.

To simplify matters, pretend that all bonds have a maturity of one period. Each ECU unit of these bonds commits the borrower to pay the lender the **principal**, €1, plus interest, €R, in the next period. The variable R is the **interest rate** – that is, the ratio of the interest payment, €R, to the amount borrowed, which is €1. For the buyer of a bond, the interest rate is the return per period to lending; for the issuer of the bond, the interest rate is the cost per period of borrowing.

We assume that the credit market treats all bonds alike, regardless of the issuer. That is, to keep things manageable, we do not differentiate among persons with respect to their credit-worthiness, the type of collateral that they put up for a loan, and so on. Accordingly, the interest rate, R, must be the same for all bonds. Further, any household is small enough to be able to buy or sell any amount of bonds without affecting the interest rate. Again, this is an assumption of perfect competition. We can modify this frame-work later to bring in various real-world complications, such as limitations on individuals' access to borrowing and the existence of bonds with various maturities.

Let b_t represent the number of bonds in ECU units that a household holds during period t. The amount of bonds may be positive or negative for an individual household. Notice, however, that for any ECU borrowed by one person, there must be a corresponding ECU lent by someone else. Hence, the *total* of positive bond holdings for lenders must exactly match the *aggregate* of negative bond holdings for borrowers. In the model we allow only one type of economic unit, households, to borrow and lend. In particular, we do not yet deal with governments, foreigners, financial institutions, or corporations as participants in the credit market. (We shall see later that the essential ideas do not change when we make these additions.) Therefore, in the model the *total* of bonds held by all households, denoted by B_t, must always be zero.

As noted before, b_{t-1} is the ECU amount of bonds that someone holds during period $t - 1$. In period t these bonds pay the interest, Rb_{t-1}, and principal, b_{t-1}. (Notice that the bonds bought or sold in period $t - 1$ do not bear interest until period t.) Thus, the receipts from bonds are positive for lenders – for whom b_{t-1} is positive – and negative for borrowers. Recall that the aggregate stock of bonds for period $t - 1$, B_{t-1}, is zero. Therefore, the aggregates of interest and principal payments for period t must also be zero. The total of interest receipts always balances the total of interest expenses.

We measure **saving** in the form of bonds as the net change in someone's asset position, $b_t - b_{t-1}$.

Note that this saving is a *flow*, which determines the *change* over one period in someone's *stock* of bonds. This saving is positive for some persons and negative for others. However, when we sum up across households, we know that $B_t = B_{t-1} = 0$. Therefore, the aggregate of saving in bonds, $B_t - B_{t-1}$, must also be zero in each period. In the aggregate, the additions to loans balances the additions to debts.

An individual's total of financial assets equals the sum of money and bonds, $m_t + b_t$. Recall that money holdings are non-negative for all persons – that is, $m_t \geq 0$. (Only the government can issue money!) In the aggregate, since $B_t = 0$, the stock of financial assets equals the total money stock, M_t.

The change in an individual's financial assets, $(m_t + b_t) - (m_{t-1} + b_{t-1})$, is the total amount that an individual saves during period t. When summing up across all households, we know that $M_t - M_{t-1} = 0$ (because we are assuming that the total stock of money is constant), and $B_t - B_{t-1} = 0$. Therefore, the aggregate of total saving is zero at all points in time in the present model. (When we introduce investment in Chapter 13, this result will change.)

The Budget Constraint

Each household receives income from sales of output, y_t, on the commodity market. The quantity of output depends on the amount of labour input, ℓ_t, through the production function, $y_t = f(\ell_t)$. Because the price of goods is P, the ECU income from selling output is Py_t. Recall that interest income from the bond market, Rb_{t-1}, is positive for lenders and negative for borrowers. Also, remember that people receive no interest income from their holdings of money.

Each household purchases the quantity of consumable goods, c_t, from the commodity market. Because the price of goods is P, the amount of consumption expenditure in ECUs is Pc_t.

For a given total of financial assets, a household can use the credit market to exchange money for bonds, or vice versa, and thereby achieve the desired composition of assets between bonds and money. The amount held as bonds, b_{t-1}, determines the interest income or expense for period t. The motivation for holding money, which does not bear interest, derives from its convenience in carrying out exchanges.

We can express the equality between a household's total sources and uses of funds in the form of a budget constraint. The condition for period t is

$$Py_t + b_{t-1}(1 + R) + m_{t-1} = Pc_t + b_t + m_t$$
$$(3.2)$$

The left side of equation (3.2) contains sources of funds, which include income from the commodity market, Py_t, the principal received on last period's bonds, b_{t-1}, the interest receipts from these bonds, Rb_{t-1}, and the amount of money held over from the previous period, m_{t-1}. The right side of the equation comprises uses of funds, which are consumption expenditures, Pc_t, holdings of bonds, b_t, and holdings of money, m_t. Because we treat the price level and interest rate as constants, these variables appear without time subscripts in the equation.

Rearrangement of equation (3.2) yields an expression for a household's nominal saving, which is the change over time in the ECU value of financial assets:

$$\text{nominal saving} = (b_t + m_t) - (b_{t-1} + m_{t-1})$$
$$= Py_t + Rb_{t-1} - Pc_t \quad (3.3)$$

Nominal saving equals the income from producing and selling output plus interest receipts less consumption expenditures.

Households can leave saving intact by making simultaneous changes in income and consumption. For example, suppose that someone works more in period t and raises income, Py_t, by ε1000. Then, if he or she also raises consumption spending, Pc_t, by ε1000, saving does not change. Therefore, the budget constraint allows people to work more and raise consumption during any period, without altering the amounts of assets that they carry over to the future. This trade-off between consumption and leisure in a single period was the only choice available to Robinson Crusoe in the model from Chapter 2. The expanded model retains this option but also introduces possibilities that exploit the credit market. Specifically, individuals can vary current saving, which is the difference between income and expenditure. Thereby, people alter the amount of assets that they carry over to the future.

Recall that equation (3.3) specifies the saving for one household. As mentioned before, the total of this saving across households is zero. When we add up the right side of equation (3.3) over all households, we find that aggregate income equals aggregate spending, $PY_t = PC_t$. (Remember that the aggregate stock of bonds, B_{t-1}, is zero.) For Robinson Crusoe, the equality between production and consumption holds individually at every point in time. Now, because of the credit market, *some* people can consume more than their income (dissave), while others consume less (save). But it is still true for *the economy as a whole* that total output cannot depart from total consumption. Consumption is the only use for commodities in the present model.

The budget constraint (3.2) points out that in our economy agents can choose between two forms of financial assets, money and bonds. But so far, we have not analyzed how much of these assets people hold or how these holdings change over time. In the rest of this chapter we provide the first building block in the model by explaining people's willingness to place part of their assets into money; that is, we explain the demand for money. We do this by setting up a simple model in which money is the medium of exchange and in which people economize on their costs of transacting by holding more money. For the most part, the results that we get from this simple model generalize to more complicated settings in which people hold money. We shall see, in any event, that the demand for money is a crucial determinant of the price level. In Chapter 4 we will consider the bond holding decisions.

The Nature of a Monetary Economy

We assume that money is the sole medium of exchange in the economy. Trades occur between money and commodities and between money and bonds but not directly between bonds and commodities or between the commodities that different households produce. As we noted above, the direct exchange of goods for goods, which is called barter, is inefficient for many types of transactions.[3] Barter requires a **double coincidence of wants**, that is, is a situation in which one person has the goods that someone else desires and vice versa. A general means of payments, such as money, avoids this problem. Buyers use money to purchase goods or bonds and sellers receive money in exchange for goods or bonds. The sellers accept money in payment because they know they can use it later to buy goods or bonds from someone else. Thus, the problem of double coincidence of wants does not arise.

Historically, commodities such as gold and silver served as money. These precious metals possess attractive physical characteristics, which classical economists enumerated as portability, indestructibility, homogeneity, divisibility, and cognizability.[4] But when paper money – such as pound notes – replaces commodity money, these physical characteristics no longer enter into the analysis. In our model we think of money as this kind of paper currency rather than gold, silver, or other commodities.

We assume that the interest-bearing bonds in the model are not money: these paper claims do not function as media of exchange. There are several reasons for this. First, the government may impose legal restrictions that prevent private parties, such as Ford or Volkswagen, from issuing small-size, interest-bearing notes that could serve conveniently as hand-to-hand currency. Further, the government may enact statutes that reinforce the use of its money, the so-called **legal tender** provision, which requires that all debts, public and private, be repaid with government money.[5] Second, there are costs of establishing one's money as reliable and convenient. These costs include the prevention of counterfeiting, the replacement of worn-out notes, the willingness to convert notes into different denominations and possibly into other assets, and so on. Because of these costs, money would tend to bear interest at a rate lower than bonds. In fact, because of the inconvenience

of paying interest on hand-to-hand currency, the interest rate on currency is typically zero.

We can relate our abstract concept of money to conventional measures of the money stock. The theoretical construct corresponds closely to currency held outside commercial banks. For example, at the end of 1992, the amount of this currency in the United Kingdom was £17.9 billion, which amounted to 3.0% of the nominal gross national product (GNP). In other words, British residents held a little more than 1.5 weeks' worth of GNP as currency in 1992. From Table 3.1, which shows data for 1990, we learn that ratio of currency to annual GNP ranged from a low of 2% for Finland to highs of 10% for Switzerland and 9% for Japan.

The term 'money' typically refers to a monetary aggregate that is broader than currency. One definition, called **M1**, attempts to classify as money the assets that serve regularly as media of exchange. This concept includes the checkable (or demand) deposits that people hold

Country	Currency	Checkable deposits	M1
Belgium	.067	.096	.199
Denmark	.050	.344	.396
France	.041	.151	.267
Germany	.065	.160	.226
Italy	.054	.299	.362
Netherlands	.071	.174	.247
Spain	.091	.201	.296
United Kingdom	.030	.362	.391
Austria	.060	.079	.140
Finland	.018	.066	.085
Norway	.046	.296	.365
Switzerland	.099	.122	.266
Australia	.036	.082	.119
Canada	.031	.117	.148
Japan	.087	.192	.279
United States	.046	.094	.156

Note: The ratio is the value of the monetary aggregate at the end of 1990 divided by the GNP or GDP for 1990.

Source: International Monetary Fund, *International Financial Statistics, Yearbook*, 1991.

Table 3.1 Ratios of money to GNP for some developed countries in 1990

at banks and some other financial institutions. The amount of these checkable deposits in the United Kingdom at the end of 1992 was £220.9 billion, or 37% of annual GNP. Therefore, M1 – the sum of currency and checkable deposits – equalled £238.8 billion at the end of 1992, or 40% of GNP. Put alternatively, M1 amounted to almost five months' worth of GNP in 1992 in the UK. From Table 3.1 we see that the ratio of M1 to annual GNP in 1991 ranged from a low of 7% for Finland to highs of 40% for Denmark. It should be kept in mind that the definition of M1 is less homogeneous across countries than that of currency. This is because the decision on which deposits to include and which to exclude is somewhat arbitrary.

Still broader definitions of money add other kinds of deposits. For example, **M2** includes money-market deposit accounts, savings and small-denomination time deposits, some Eurodollar accounts issued abroad, and repurchase agreements. Other broader aggregates, like **M3** and **M4**, encompass a larger set of financial accounts.

As mentioned, we can readily identify the money in the theoretical model with currency, but the concept does not correspond precisely to broader monetary aggregates, such as M1 or M2. When we expand the theoretical framework (in Chapter 10) to incorporate financial institutions such as banks, we can deal with checkable deposits or other types of deposits. For now, however, we should think of money as currency. We also assume that the government has a monopoly in the issue of money (that is, currency) and that the interest rate on money is zero.

Given that people use money to transact, how much money should they hold? Suppose that everyone synchronized each sale of goods or bonds with an equal-sized purchase of some other good or bond. Then although people used money for all exchanges, they would end up holding virtually zero cash. But to hold this low average money balance, each person would have to spend a lot of effort on financial planning. He or she would have to synchronize the timing of sales and purchases and would have to carry out a large number of transactions. It is typically more convenient to allow receipts to accumulate for a while as cash before spending these funds or converting them into bonds. As Milton Friedman put it, money serves as a *temporary abode of purchasing power*. As a general statement, people can reduce their average holdings of cash only by incurring more costs. These costs are often called **transaction costs**, which refer to the expenses of carrying out trades, as well as the costs of making financial decisions.

Given the total of financial assets, a lower average cash balance means a higher average stock of bonds. Hence, by economizing on money, people earn more interest (or pay less interest if they are borrowing). The demand for money reflects this trade-off between transaction costs and interest earnings. In the next section we use a simple model to illustrate this trade-off and show how it determines the demand for money. Although the model is only an illustration, it nevertheless brings out the general trade-offs that determine the demand for money.

A Model of Optimal Cash Management

Consider a retired person, who is living off previously accumulated assets. This person keeps financial assets primarily in bonds, since they pay interest, but holds some money to facilitate the purchases of consumer goods. For simplicity, assume that consumption expenditure is constant at the amount Pc ECUs per year. (We still pretend that the price level, P, does not change over time.) The retiree makes occasional withdrawals of funds from the stock of interest-bearing assets. Suppose that these withdrawals occur at the interval T. For example, if withdrawal occurs every month, then $T =$ one-twelfth of a year. Equivalently, the frequency of exchange is 12 per year. Note that this frequency is the reciprocal of the period between withdrawals, $1/T$.

Each exchange of interest-bearing assets for money involves a transaction cost. There may be explicit brokerage changes, but, more likely, the main expense is the time and trouble for carrying out the transfer. If a person spends more time transacting, then he or she has less time available for work or leisure. Suppose that each exchange costs $-\gamma$ (the Greek letter *gamma*) ECUs, which includes the ECU value attached to the time needed for the exchange. We assume a lump-sum transaction cost, which means that the charge is independent of the number of ECUs withdrawn. If the retiree transacts at the frequency $1/T$ per year, then the total of transaction costs per year is the ECU amount $-\gamma\cdot(1/T)$. Dividing by the price level, P, we find that the real transaction cost per year is

$$\text{real transaction cost} = (\gamma/P)\cdot(1/T) \qquad (3.4)$$

The term, γ/P, is the real cost per transaction.

When the retiree makes a withdrawal, he or she obtains the amount of money needed to meet expenses until the next withdrawal. In the present case, the money must cover the expenditures over an interval of length T. Since the person spends at the rate Pc ECUs per year, the amount needed is $Pc\cdot T$. The retiree spends these funds gradually to buy goods, running out of money when the time T has elapsed. At that point, he or she replenishes cash by making the next withdrawal from the stock of interest-bearing assets.

Figure 3.1 shows the time pattern of money holdings. Notice that a withdrawal of $Pc\cdot T$ ECUs occurs at date 0. The retiree spends gradually at the rate Pc ECUs per year and thereby just exhausts the stock of money at time T. Between dates 0 and T, the level of money is shown by the downward-sloping line in the figure. At date T there is another withdrawal of size $Pc\cdot T$ ECUs. Hence, money jumps upward – along the dashed line in the figure – to the level $Pc\cdot T$. Then the money balance declines steadily again until the time for a new withdrawal at $2T$. This sawtooth pattern for money holdings keeps repeating with the peaks spaced at interval T.

Given the form of cash management from Figure 3.1, the average money balance is half the vertical distance to the peak:

$$\bar{m} = \frac{1}{2}Pc\cdot T$$

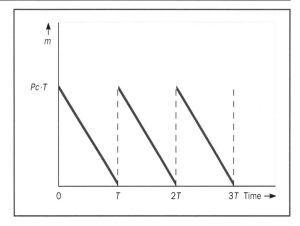

Money holdings reach a peak $Pc\cdot T$ just after each withdrawal. Then money declines gradually reaching zero when it is time to make the next withdrawal. Notice that the withdrawals occur at the interval T.

Figure 3.1   Time pattern of money holdings

where $\bar{m}$ denotes the average holding of money. If we divide by the price level, P, we can express the average holding of money in real terms as

$$\bar{m}/P = \frac{1}{2}cT \qquad (3.5)$$

Suppose that the retiree has already determined the amount of his or her total financial assets for each period. Then an increase in the average money balance must imply a reduction in the average holdings of bonds, and hence a decline in interest income. If the interest rate is R (per year), then the ECU magnitude of interest earnings foregone per year is the quantity $R\cdot\bar{m} = R\cdot(\frac{1}{2})PcT$. If all financial assets had been held as bonds, then the interest income per year would have increased by this amount. As usual, we can divide through by the price level to express this ECU magnitude in real terms. Therefore, the real amount of interest income foregone per year is given by

$$\text{interest foregone in real terms} = R\cdot\bar{m}/P$$
$$= R\cdot\frac{1}{2}cT \quad (3.6)$$

There are two types of costs in our cash-management problem.[6] First, we can think of the interest foregone in real terms, $R \cdot \frac{1}{2} cT$, as a cost of holding money. We graph this cost versus the transaction interval, T, in Figure 3.2. Note that this cost is a straight line from the origin with slope equal to $R \cdot \frac{1}{2} c$. Second, there is the real transaction cost, which is given in equation (3.4) by $(\gamma/P) \cdot (1/T)$. This cost appears as the rectangular hyperbola in Figure 3.2. Transaction costs approach zero as the interval between transactions tends toward infinity and approach infinity as the interval tends toward zero.

We show also the total of interest and transaction costs in Figure 3.2. This curve is U-shaped. Costs decline initially as the transaction interval rises above zero because transaction costs decline by more than interest costs increase. Eventually transaction costs do not fall as fast as interest costs rise. Therefore, total costs start to increase with increases in the interval, T. There is some amount of time between trips, denoted by T^* in the figure, which minimizes total costs.[7] Hence, a rational person chooses the interval T^*.[8]

For later purposes, the important point is that the choice of transaction interval, T, determines the average holding of real money from equation (3.5) as the amount, $\bar{m}/P = (\frac{1}{2})cT$. Therefore, a person's choice of transaction interval translates into that person's choice of an average holding of real money. Our main concern now is how various changes in the economy affect the transaction interval and thereby a person's average holding of real money.

There are three variables that determine the transaction interval, T^*, in the model: (1) the interest rate, R, (2) the real flow of expenditures, c, and (3) the real cost per transaction, γ/P. We can use graphical methods to study the effects of changes in any of these variables.

Figure 3.3 assumes an increase in the interest rate from R to R'. This change steepens the slope of the line that describes interest-foregone costs. In calculating total costs we find that the interest component has become more important relative to the transaction-cost component. Hence, we reach sooner the position at which increasing interest costs dominate over falling transaction costs. It follows that the minimum of total costs occurs at a shorter interval between withdrawals – that is, $(T^*)' < T^*$ in the figure.

We can interpret the result as follows. An increase in the interest rate makes it more important to economize on cash in order to avoid large amounts of foregone interest income. In our simple model, people can reduce average

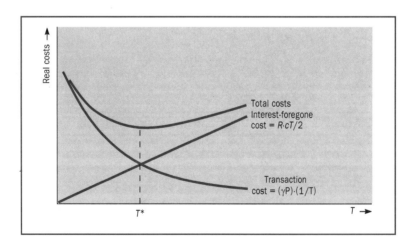

The interest foregone by holding money $R \cdot cT/2$ increases with the period between withdrawals T. Transaction costs $(\gamma P) \cdot (1/T)$ decline as the period rises. Total costs reach a minimum at the point T^*.

Figure 3.2 Costs of cash management

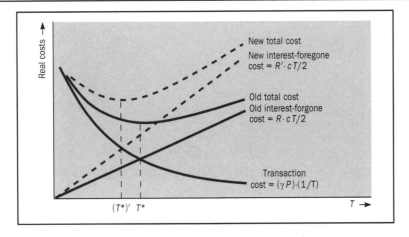

An increase in the interest rate from R to R' steepens the line that describes interest-foregone costs. People respond by lowering the period between withdrawals from T^* to $(T^*)'$.

Figure 3.3   Effect on the transaction interval of an increase in the interest rate

holdings of money only by transacting more frequently – that is, by shortening the period between financial exchanges, T. Although this process entails a higher transaction cost, people are motivated by the rise in the interest rate to incur these costs. Hence, the rise in the interest rate, R, leads to a decline in the interval between transactions.

Recall from equation (3.5) that the average real money balance equals $\frac{1}{2}cT$. Since the increase in the interest rate lowers the period, T, it must also lower the average holding of real money. In other words, a higher cost of holding money – a rise in the interest rate – reduces the real demand for money. We shall use this important result many times in the subsequent analysis.

We can use a similar method to assess changes in the real flow of spending, c. A rise in the spending flow shifts the interest-foregone cost exactly as shown in Figure 3.3. Hence, someone with a greater annual flow of real expenditure chooses a shorter interval between withdrawals, T. This result follows because an increase in the real volume of spending, c, makes the interest-foregone cost more important relative to the transaction cost. Households with more real spending – typically, households with higher income – find it worthwhile to devote more

effort to financial planning in order to economize on their cash.

Average real money balances equal the quantity, $\frac{1}{2}cT$. For a given choice of transaction interval, T, a rise in real spending, c, increases average real money balances proportionately. But we have just shown that the period, T, declines as the volume of spending increases. This response means that a rise in real spending leads to a less-than-proportionate increase in the average holding of real money.[9] Sometimes economists refer to this result as **economies of scale** in cash holding. This property means that households with a larger scale of spending hold less money when expressed as a ratio to their expenditures.

Finally, we can consider an increase in the real cost of transacting, γ/P. We can show graphically that this change leads to a lengthening of the period between exchanges, T. People transact less frequently when the cost of each exchange rises. Because the period, T, lengthens, average real money balances, $\frac{1}{2}cT$, increase.

Properties of the Demand for Money

The results tell us the effects on average real money balances from changes in the interest rate, R, the real volume of spending, c, and the real cost of transacting, γ/P. We can summarize these findings in the form of a function, ϕ (the Greek letter *phi*), for average real money demanded:

$$\bar{m}/P = \phi(R, c, \underset{(-)}{\gamma} / P) \tag{3.7}$$

Again the signs indicate the effect of each independent variable on the dependent variable, $\bar{m}/P$.

To find the average money balance in nominal terms, we can multiply through equation (3.7) by the price level. Then we get

$$\bar{m} = P \cdot \phi(R, c, \underset{(-)}{\gamma} / P) \tag{3.8}$$

Consider what happens if we double the price level, P, but hold fixed R, c, and γ/P. (Note that nominal spending, Pc, and the ECU cost of transacting, γ, double along with the doubling of the general price level.) These changes leave unaltered the curves in Figure 3.2, which describe the real cost of transacting and the real value of interest income foregone. Therefore, people do not change their choice of transaction interval, T. It follows that average *real* balances, $\bar{m}/P = \frac{1}{2}cT$, do not change in equation (3.7). But average *nominal* balances, $\bar{m} = \frac{1}{2}PcT$, double along with the doubling of the price level, as shown in equation (3.8).

The Aggregate Demand for Money

For an individual household in our model, the level of real money follows a sawtooth pattern and varies between zero and the amount cT. Equation (3.7) determines the average level of real money, $\bar{m}/P = \frac{1}{2}cT$. Suppose that we sum up over many households, each of which has the same average real balance. Then, unless the timing of transactions is synchronized across households, this aggregation smooths out the sawtooth pattern. In particular, aggregate real money balances at any date look like an individual's average amount, $\bar{m}/P$, multiplied by the number of households.

We can write out a function, Φ (Greek capital *phi*), for aggregate real money demanded as

$$M/P = \Phi(R, c, \underset{(-)}{\gamma} / P) \tag{3.9}$$

The function Φ looks like the individual's function ϕ in equation (3.7), but magnified to incorporate the adding up across many households. Similarly, the aggregate version of equation (3.8) for nominal money demand is

$$M = P \cdot \phi(R, c, \underset{(-)}{\gamma} / P) \tag{3.10}$$

Generalizations and Implications for Money Demand

Although we can complicate the theory of money demand in many ways, the properties that we derived from the simple model still tend to hold. That is because the simple model captures the basic trade-off that determines the demand for money: if people put more effort into transacting and financial planning, then they can lower their average holding of money. A lower money balance means, in turn, a greater amount of interest earnings. A person engages in various aspects of cash management up to the point at which the gain in interest income just compensates for the added transaction costs. Therefore, a basic result is that a higher interest rate motivates people to incur more costs in order to economize on money; hence, a higher interest rate reduces the demand for money.

An increase in the volume of real expenditures raises the benefits from financial planning. Therefore, although a higher level of spending means more money held, real money balances tend to rise less than proportionately with real spending. In the simple model, real spending corresponds to real consumption, C. Other components of spending, such as purchases of goods by businesses, also have a positive effect on the aggregate demand for money in a more general model.

The real demand for money rises less than proportionately with an increase in real spending if we hold fixed the real cost of transacting, γ/P. If we think about different households, then those with higher real income and, hence, real spending tend also to have a higher value of time. Since a major component of the transaction cost is the time wasted, the households with higher income likely have larger transaction costs. Since an increase in transaction costs means more real money held (recall equation [3.7]), the higher-income households hold more money on this count. Therefore, when we include this effect, the tendency to see economies of scale in cash holdings becomes weak. The more basic finding, which we rely on later, is that an increase in real spending raises the real demand for money.

The theory relates the demand for money in real terms to a set of real variables, which include the real flow of spending, the real costs of transacting, and the interest rate. A change in the general price level – with all the real variables held fixed – does not change the demand for money in real terms. Therefore, the nominal demand for money rises by the same proportion as the price level if all real variables do not change. For example, an increase in the price level by 10% raises the demand for nominal money, M, by 10%, so as to leave the real amount, M/P, unchanged.

In our simple model, the real transaction costs incurred per year, $(\gamma/P)\cdot(1/T)$, pertain to transfers from interest-bearing assets to money. More generally, transaction costs apply also to other forms of exchanges, such as the costs of buying commodities with money and the costs of making wage payments to workers.

We would want also to bring in the costs of financial planning and decision making. Typically, people who do more calculating manage to maintain a smaller average money balance and thereby achieve a greater amount of interest earnings. But this broader view of transaction costs does not alter the main conclusions with respect to the form of the functions for aggregate money demand in equations (3.9) and (3.10).

The costs of transacting change when there are technological innovations in the financial sector. For example, the use of computers by financial institutions makes it easier for customers to shift between money (defined as currency or demand deposits) and alternative assets. These improvements tend to lower the demand for money. Similarly, the development of convenient checkable deposits in the late nineteenth and early twentieth centuries had a negative effect on the demand for currency (and a positive effect on the holdings of demand deposits).

The possibilities for economizing on money holdings are influenced also by the use of credit. It is easier to synchronize receipts and payments –

The Payments Period and the Demand for Money

Irving Fisher (1971, pp. 83–85) stressed the dependence of the demand for money on the period between payments of wages. The effects of this period are analogous to those for the interval between withdrawals from a financial asset. In particular, a shorter payments period reduces the average holding of real money balances. This effect is important during extreme inflations – for example, during the German hyperinflation after World War I. In such situations the cost of holding money becomes very high. Therefore, people incur more transaction costs – such as the costs of making more frequent wage payments – to reduce their average holdings of real money. For 1923, the final year of the German hyperinflation, an observer reported, 'it became the custom to make an advance of wages on Tuesday, the balance being paid on Friday. Later, some firms used to pay wages three times a week or even daily' (Costantino Bresciani-Turroni, 1937, p. 303). Similarly, during the Austrian hyperinflation after World War I, 'The salaries of the state officials, which used to be issued at the end of the month, were paid to them during 1922 in instalments three times per month' (J. van Walre de Bordes, 1927, p. 163).

and thereby easier to achieve a lower average money balance – when people buy with credit rather than cash. Credit also favours the use of checks rather than currency.

A broader model would bring in uncertainties associated with the timing and size of receipts and expenditures. An increase in these uncertainties tends to raise the average holding of money because people hold cash partly to guard against unexpected delays in receipts or unanticipated opportunities for purchases. Therefore, we anticipate that an increase in uncertainties about receipts and expenditures tends to raise the real demand for money. Although the introduction of uncertainty adds some important new effects, this generalization does not eliminate the types of influences on aggregate money demand that we summarized in equations (3.9) and (3.10).

The Velocity of Money

When trying to predict future inflation or the future amount of real transactions, economists often focus on the relation between the average amount of money that someone holds, $\bar{m}$, and the amount of transactions carried out by that money. In our simple model, the ECU volume of transactions equals consumption expenditure, Pc. (In a broader context, the ECU volume of transactions might relate to GNP or even to broader totals that include various kinds of intermediate expenditures.) The ratio of transactions to the average money balance – measured as $Pc/\bar{m}$ if transactions are given by consumption expenditure – is called the **velocity of money**. The velocity is the number of times per unit of time, such as a year, that the typical piece of money turns over.

In our model, a person's average real money balance is given from equation (3.5) by $\bar{m}/P = \frac{1}{2}cT$. Therefore, velocity is $c/[\bar{m}/P] = 2 \cdot (1/T)$. Notice that the velocity of money depends directly on the frequency of exchange, $1/T$, between alternative financial assets and money. One variable that has an important effect on velocity is the interest rate, R.

An increase in R motivates a higher frequency of financial exchanges, $1/T$, and therefore a higher velocity.

The Velocity of Money in the G-6

Figure 3.4 shows the velocity of money in the G-6 countries from 1950 to 1990. Velocity is defined here as the ratio of aggregate personal consumption expenditures for the year, PC, to the annual average of the money stock. We define money as the broader monetary aggregate, M1, which includes both currency and checkable deposits. Since these checkable deposits are an alternative to currency as a medium of exchange, we can readily apply our theory of the demand for money to this broader concept.

The figure shows that the behaviour of velocity was different across countries. In the US and the UK, for example, velocity tended to rise, while in Germany to fall. In France, Italy and Japan, velocity fell in the first part of the period while in the second part it has been rising.

Two main factors account for the post-World War II behaviour of velocity. First, the movements of interest rates, which are also plotted in Figure 3.4.[10] For example, the interest rate paid on 3-month maturity US Treasury bills rose from 1.2% in 1950 to 2.9% in 1960, 6.5% in 1970, and a peak of 14.0% in 1981, but then declined to 7.5% in 1985 and 5.8% in 1987. Since then, the rate rose to 8.1% in 1989, but then fell to 5.4% in 1991. The rise in interest rates until the early 1980s motivated a reduction in real money balances relative to the volume of real spending – hence, velocity increased. But the decline in interest rates after the early 1980s tended to reverse this pattern. As it can be observed from Figure 3.4, changes in interest rates go a long way in explaining the variation in velocity in the G-6 countries.

The second factor is technological advances in financial management, changes that enable people to economize more easily on their money.[11] In our simple model, these developments appear as reductions in the real cost of financial exchanges, γ/P. These changes raise velocity because they induce people to switch

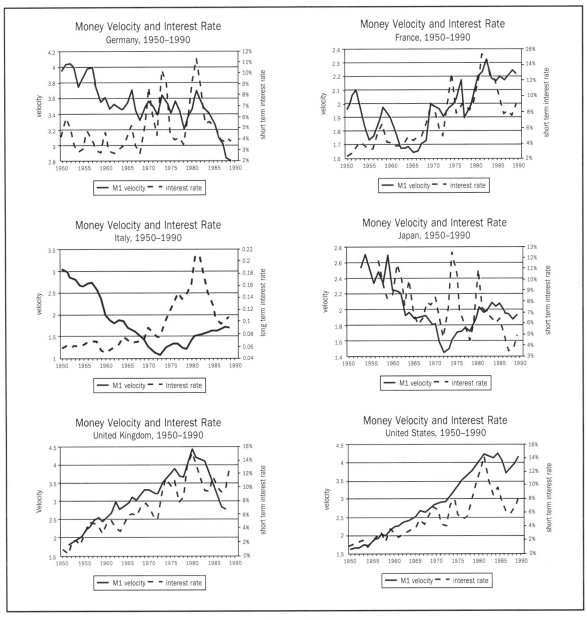

Figure 3.4

from holdings of money to holdings of alternative financial instruments. One common example of innovation in transaction technology is the use of credit cards. Figure 3.5 displays the relationship between money velocity and the use of credit cards. It shows that where the use of credit card is more widespread, the velocity of M1 is higher, as we would expect since people will feel less the need to keep monetary balance for their transactions. One notable exception is Japan which, while being the country with the largest diffusion of credit cards has a relatively low money velocity. One should be careful in comparing different financial systems since they are highly regulated and these regulations often differ considerably across countries.

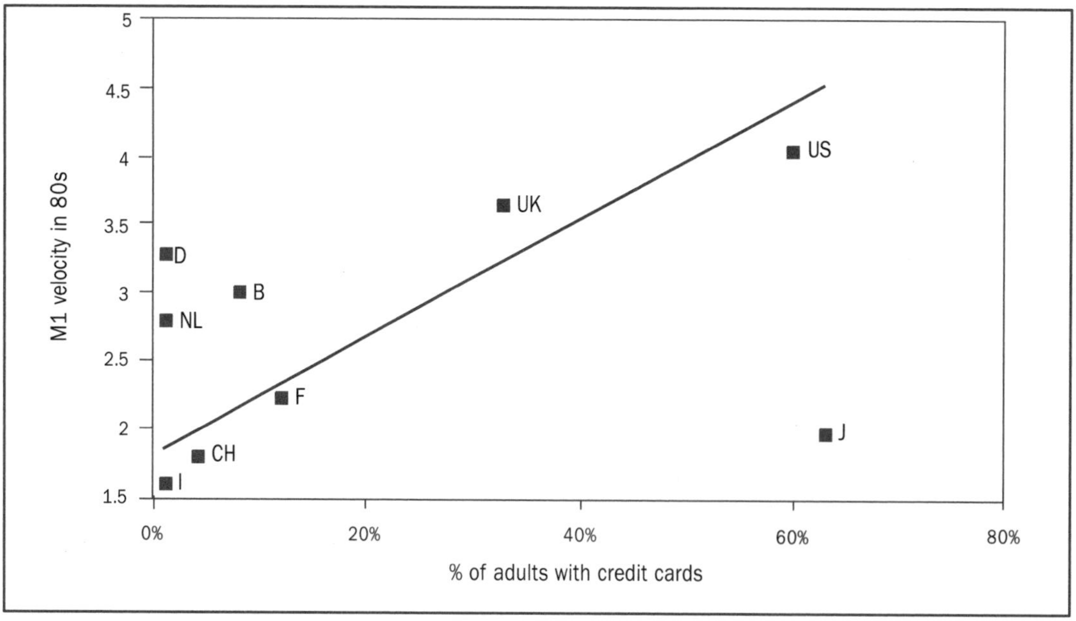

Figure 3.5 Money velocity and credit cards, 1990

Empirical Evidence on the Demand for Money

Our simple model provides a number of conclusions about the factors that influence the demand for money. We can summarize the main results as follows:

- An increase in the interest rate, R, reduces the real demand for money.
- An increase in real spending, measured by real consumption or a broader construct, raises the real demand for money. In some cases, the increase in real money demanded is smaller in proportion than the increase in real spending – that is, there are economies of scale in the holding of money.
- An increase in the price level, P, say by 10%, raises the nominal demand for money by 10% – hence, the real demand for money does not change.
- An increase in real transaction costs, γ/P, raises the real demand for money.

We want to know how these propositions accord with the facts. During the post-World War II period there have been many statistical studies of the demand for money, so that a good deal of empirical evidence is available.[12] Classic studies in this field are by Steven Goldfeld (1973, 1976) and refer to the United States. Similar investigations on the property of money demand have been conducted for most of the other industrialized countries. Notable examples are by Frowen and Arestis (1976) for Germany, by Spinelli (1980) for Italy and by den Butter and Fase (1981) for eight EC members (Belgium, Denmark, France, Germany, Ireland, Italy, the Netherlands, the United Kingdom).

The negative effect of interest rates on the demand for money is confirmed by investigators for several monetary aggregates. For example, den Butten and Fase found, in a period between 1961 and 1976, that a 10% increase in interest rates (say, a rise from 10 to 11%) reduced the real demand for M2 in the long run by about 1.2% (in Italy) to 3.1% (in Belgium).

There is strong evidence for a positive effect of real spending on the real demand for money but, in the EC, evidence of economies of scale in this relation is not present. For example, den Butten and Fase found that an increase by 10% in real GNP led in the long run to an increase by more than 10% in the real demand for M2 in all eight EC countries. The stronger response was measured for the UK, where the increase in real demand for M2 is roughly 19%. The appearance of economies of scale – that is, a less than 10% response of real money demand – was found, instead, by Goldfeld for the US. He measured that an increase by 10% in real GNP in the US implies a long-run expansion of real M1 by 6 to 7%.

Our model predicts that an increase in the price level raises the nominal demand for money by the same proportion. Also this proposition receives empirical support. For example, den Butten and Fase found that an increase of the price level by 10% led to an increase in the nominal demand for M2 ranging between 8.4% in the UK to 13% in Belgium and Germany.

Finally, our theory predicts that a decrease in transaction costs lowers the demand for money. This effect has been important since the early 1970s because a variety of financial innovations have made it easier for people to hold less currency and checkable deposits. As we mentioned above, innovations include automatic teller machines, the spread of credit cards, and various accounts that allow inexpensive computerized transfers between checkable and noncheckable deposits. In Table 3.2 we report, for several countries, the importance of credit cards and automatic teller machines.

Most economists, when trying to estimate the demand for money, ignored these financial innovations. Until about the mid-1970s, the estimated equations seemed to work well in that their predictions about the demand for money were fairly accurate. However, most of the developments that substantially reduced transaction costs have occurred only since the mid-1970s. It is in this period that the estimates that ignored financial innovations started to fail. In particular, the actual amount of money that people held was substantially less than the amount predicted by

	Percent of adults with credit cards 1991	Cash machines per 10 000 people 1991	M1 velocity (average 80s)
Belgium	8	0.9	3.00
France	12	2.5	2.22
Germany	1	1.4	3.27
Italy	1	1.7	1.58
Netherlands	1	1.8	2.79
United Kingdom	33	3	3.66
Japan	63	6.5	1.98
Switzerland	4	3.4	1.79
United States	60	3.3	4.06

Source: Datamonitor as reported by *The Economist* (27 June 1992).

Table 3.2 Technological changes in transaction technology

earlier evidence. (This result has sometimes been referred to as 'missing money'.)

A study on the United States by Michael Dotsey (1985) found that the volume of electronic funds transfers was a good proxy for the state of financial innovation. He showed thereby that recent financial innovations had a strong downward effect on holdings of checkable deposits.[13] Further, by including his measure of financial innovation, he derived a money-demand equation that looked stable before the early 1970s and since. His fitted equation showed effects from interest rates and real spending that were similar to those that included data only up to the early 1970s.

Summary

We introduced a commodity market on which people buy and sell goods at the price *P*. The existence of this market promotes economic efficiency because it allows producers to specialize. We also introduced a credit market on which people borrow and lend at the interest rate *R*. By using this market, individuals can choose a time pattern for consumption that differs from that for income.

We explained in this chapter why people hold part of their financial assets as money rather than interest-bearing bonds. The explanation involves, first, the role of money (but not bonds) as a medium of exchange and, second, the extra transaction costs that arise when people economize more on their holdings of money. We showed that the average amount of real money held involves a trade-off between transaction costs and interest-income foregone. A higher interest rate motivates people to incur more transaction costs in order to achieve a lower average real money balance.

Our theoretical model has the following major implications for the aggregate demand for money:

- An increase in the interest rate reduces the real demand for money.
- An increase in real spending raises the real demand for money, but possibly by a smaller proportion than the increase in spending.
- An increase in the price level raises the nominal demand for money by the same proportion.
- An increase in real transaction costs raises the real demand for money.

The empirical evidence generally supports these propositions.

Important Terms and Concepts

barter
medium of exchange
nominal
general price level
real terms·
economies of scale in the demand for money
transaction costs
M1, M2, M4
perfect competition
bond
currency
interest rate
double coincidence of wants
legal tender
velocity of money

Questions and Problems

Mainly for Review

3.1 What are the costs of transacting between money and financial assets? (You may want to make a list and include such items as the cost of a trip to the bank and the time spent waiting in line.) How would the development of electronic teller services affect this cost?

3.2 Suppose that an individual's consumption expenditure is ε6000 per year and that it is financed by monthly withdrawals of money from a saving account.

   a. Depict on a graph the pattern of the person's money holdings over a period of one year. What is the average money balance?
   b. Graph the pattern of money holdings when withdrawals of money are made only once in two months. Show that the average money balance is higher.

3.3 Refer to question 3.2. If consumption expenditure rises to ε9000 per year and withdrawals continue to be made monthly, then what is the average money holding? Is it optimal for the frequency of withdrawals to remain the same when consumption increases? Explain.

3.4 What is the definition of the aggregate velocity of money? Use the concept of velocity to explain how a given aggregate quantity of money balances can be used to pay for a relatively large volume of consumption expenditure over a year.

3.5 Consider the following changes and state whether their effect on the real demand for money is an increase, a decrease, or uncertain:
   a. A decrease in the interest rate.
   b. An increase in real transaction costs.
   c. An increase in real consumption.
   d. An increase in the price level.

3.6 Consider again the changes listed in question 3.5, and describe their effect on velocity.

Problems for Discussion

3.7 Transaction Costs and Households' Budget Constraints
   Assume that the real cost of transacting between bonds and money, γ/P, rises.
   a. How does this change show up in households' budget constraints? What is the effect on wealth?

b. We neglected transaction costs when considering households' choices of work effort, consumption, and saving. Suppose now that we bring in the wealth effect from part (a). What then is the effect of an increase in the real cost of transacting, γ/P, on households' work effort, consumption, and saving?

c. Have we left out a new substitution effect in part (b)? Think about the choice between consumption and leisure. Consumption involves market exchange, which requires the use of money. But people can 'buy' leisure without using money! So what substitution effect arises for consumption versus leisure when the real cost of transacting, γ/P, rises? How does this affect the answer to part (b)?

3.8 Further Aspects of Transaction Costs
In problem 3.7 we considered the effects of transaction costs on households' budget constraints. These costs might show up as purchases of financial services – for example, as brokerage fees or service charges by banks. Alternatively, transaction costs might just represent the time that it takes to go to the bank or to make a decision.

a. How do these two different views of transaction costs affect the way that the costs appear in households' budget constraints?

b. Do these differences affect our other answers to problem 3.7?

c. How should we think about the production of financial services? That is, how can we incorporate this 'good' into the model?

3.9 Effects of the Payment Interval on the Demand for Money
Think of a worker with an annual income of ε12000. Suppose that he or she receives wage payments once per month. Consumption spending is constant at ε12000 per year. Assume that the worker holds no bonds – that is, he or she holds all financial assets in the form of money.

a. What is the worker's average money balance?

b. What would the average money balance be if the worker were paid twice per month instead of once per month?

c. What is the general relation between the average money balance and the interval between wage payments?

3.10 Effects of Shopping Trips on the Demand for Money
Assume again the conditions of problem 3.9 with workers paid once per month. But instead of carrying out consumption expenditures in a uniform flow, the worker now makes periodic shopping trips. At each trip he or she buys enough goods (for example, groceries) to last until the next trip.

a. If the worker shops four times each month, then what is the average money balance? Why is the answer different from that in part (a) of problem 3.9?

b. What happens if he or she shops only twice each month?

c. What is the general effect on the average money balance of the interval between shopping trips? Compare the answer with that for part (c) of problem 3.9.

d. Suppose that the cost of making shopping trips rises – for example, because of an increase in the cost of gasoline. How would this change affect the frequency of shopping trips? What does the result imply about the effect of an increase in the cost of shopping trips on the average real holding of money? How does this effect compare with the impact of financial transaction costs, γ/P, which we explored in the text?

3.11 Expenditures and the Demand for Money
a. Consider an increase in the aggregate of real spending, C. What is the effect on the aggregate demand for real cash balances, M/P? Notice that aggregate real spending can rise for two reasons. First, there could be an increase in everyone's real spending, with no change in the number of people. Second, there could be an increase in the number of people, with no change in each person's level of real spending. How does the response of aggregate real money, M/P, depend on which case applies?

b. What should happen to the velocity of money as an economy develops? (Take a look at Figure 3.4 to see the history of velocity in the G-6.) In answering, be sure to specify what happens to the interest rate, R, and the real cost of transacting between money and interest-bearing assets, γ/P.

3.12 Effects of Other Variables on the Demand for Money
For given values of real income and spending, the interest rate, and real transaction costs, would you say that the following statements are true, false, or uncertain.

a. An agricultural society has lower real money demand than an industrial society.

b. Real money demand is higher in dictatorships than in democracies.

c. A country with a large fraction of elderly people has higher real money demand than a country with a small fraction of elderly.

d. A country with a higher literacy rate has lower real money demand.
(For evidence on these kinds of effects on money demand, see Lawrence Kenny, 1988.)

3.13 The Denominations of Currency (optional)
Consider how people divide their holdings of currency between large bills (say, of ε100 and over) versus small ones. How would the fraction of the

value of currency that someone holds as large bills change with

a. an increase in the price level?

b. an increase in a person's real income?

c. an increase in the interest rate?

d. a greater incentive to avoid records of payments (for example, to evade taxes or to engage in criminal transactions)?

Notes

1. We introduce the convention of using ε as the symbol for ECU.

2. Historically, it is rare for currency to pay interest. Some early forms of US Treasury notes, such as those issued from 1812 to 1815, paid interest and also had some limited use as media of exchange. However, because no denominations below \$100 were issued, these notes were used mostly as bank reserves. For a discussion, see Richard Timberlake (1978, pp. 13—17). ECUs, at present, exist mostly as bank deposits, and thus do carry interest. There are no ECU notes, only some ECU coins, but even these do not circulate since they are special issues with a gold or silver content that exceeds their face value.

3. The classic discussion of the difficulties with barter exchange is W. Stanley Jevons (1896, Chaps. 1-3). An interesting model of the evolution of specialized media of exchange appears in Robert Jones (1976).

4. See Jevons (1896, Ch. 5) and for an earlier discussion, John Law (1966, Chapter 1).

5. Notice that this type of provision does not determine the price at which currency exchanges for goods. If the price level were infinite, what would the legal-tender property mean?

6. The model is an example of the *inventory approach to money demand*, which was pioneered by William Baumol (1952) and James Tobin (1956). (The approach is often called the Baumol–Tobin model.) The two costs for holding money are analogous to those that arise when a firm holds an inventory of its product. The interest-foregone cost for money parallels the costs of foregone interest, storage, and depreciation, which apply to inventories of goods. The transaction cost for financial exchanges corresponds to the costs of restocking – that is, the transaction cost for ordering, shipping, and processing new goods from a supplier. More complicated models of inventories – whether of goods or money – stress the uncertainties in receipts and expenditures.

7. The answer can readily be found from calculus. We want the value of T that minimizes total costs, $R \cdot \frac{1}{2}cT + (\gamma/P) \cdot (1/T)$. The result from setting the derivative with respect to T to zero is $T^* = [2(\gamma/P)/Rc]$. Since $\bar{m}/P = \frac{1}{2}cT$, the solution for T^* implies $m/P = \sqrt{[c(\gamma/P)/2R]}$. The last result is sometimes called the *square-root formula*, because it relates $\bar{m}/P$ positively to $\sqrt{c}$.

8. In our example, the period T^* turns out to equalize the two components of the total costs. That is, in Figure 3.2, the interest-foregone line intersects the curve for transaction costs at the point T^*. This property depends on the details of our example; it does not hold more generally.

9. We can show that the decline in the transaction interval, T, is by a smaller proportion than the increase in real spending, c. Therefore, the average real money balance does rise on net. See note 7 above for an exact result using calculus.

10. In Figure 3.4 we use interest rates on short maturity Treasury bonds, usually 3–month bonds.

11. Some of these advances – particularly the ready availability of money-market funds – were triggered by the rise in interest rates. Therefore, the second factor for explaining the rise in velocity is partly related to the first one.

12. For surveys of the evidence, see David Laidler (1985, Ch. 4) and John Judd and John Scadding (1982).

13. Differences in financial sophistication are also important when considering the demand for money across countries. For some empirical estimates over the long term, see Michael Bordo and Lars Jonung (1981).

4

The Intertemporal Budget Constraint and the Demand for Credit

In the previous chapter we introduced two assets in the economy: money and bonds. We then analyzed the elements determining individuals' holding of money balances and we explained the determinants of aggregate money demand. In this chapter we examine the other financial decision of our typical economic agent: how much to borrow or lend. By using the credit market, people can avoid substantial fluctuations in their consumption even if their incomes vary a great deal from period to period. The effect of interest rate changes on the time pattern of consumption and work is one of the key relations in this chapter.

In order to understand the reasons for using the credit market it is necessary to expand the time horizon of our model. Borrowing and lending operations inevitably involve transactions in more than one period. The main logical innovation in this chapter is to extend the analysis of economic agents decisions to an intertemporal setting.

Budget Constraints for Two Periods

The discussion in the previous chapters brought out the effects of current consumption and work on the assets that a household carried over to the future. We can clarify this process by studying choices over two periods.

Recall the budget constraint we analyzed in Chapter 3. Equation (3.2) holds for any period.

For example, for period 1, the condition is

$$Py_1 + b_0(1 + R) + m_0 = Pc_1 + b_1 + m_1 \quad (4.1)$$

In order to focus on the bond holding decisions, it is convenient to assume that each household's money holdings are constant over time – that is, $m_1 = m_0$. Anyone who maintains a constant quantity of money carries out any saving or dissaving in the form of bonds. By making this assumption, we avoid a clutter of minor terms in the household's budget constraint over more than one period. But we shall return in the last section of this chapter to reconsider the case in which money holdings change over time.

Using the condition, $m_1 = m_0$, the budget constraint from equation (4.1) simplifies to

$$Py_1 + b_0(1 + R) = Pc_1 + b_1 \quad (4.2)$$

There is a similar one-period budget constraint for period 2:

$$Py_2 + b_1(1 + R) = Pc_2 + b_2 \quad (4.3)$$

The two budget constraints are not independent because b_1 appears as a use of funds in period 1 and as a source of funds in period 2.

We can combine the two one-period budget constraints into a single two-period budget constraint. First, solve equation (4.3) for b_1 to get

$$b_1 = Pc_2/(1 + R) + b_2/(1 + R) - Py_2/(1 + R)$$

Next, substitute for b_1 in equation (4.2) and collect terms into sources and uses of funds to get

$$Py_1 + Py_2/(1 + R) + b_0(1 + R)$$
$$= Pc_1 + Pc_2/(1 + R) + b_2/(1 + R) \qquad (4.4)$$

The sources of funds on the left side of equation (4.4) include the income from the commodity market for periods 1 and 2, Py_1 and Py_2, and the initial stock of bonds, b_0. The uses of funds on the right side involve the consumption expenditures over the two periods, Pc_1 and Pc_2, and the stock of bonds held at the end of the second period, b_2.

Observe how the incomes, Py_1 and Py_2, appear in equation (4.4). We divide next period's amount, Py_2, by the term $(1 + R)$ before adding it to this period's, Py_1. It is important to understand why incomes from the two periods, Py_1 and Py_2, are not just added together in the two-period budget constraint. Similarly, on the right side of equation (4.4), we divide next period's expenditure, Pc_2, by the term $(1 + R)$ before adding it to this period's, Pc_1. Again, we want to understand why we combine expenditures from different dates in this manner.

Present Values

If the interest rate is positive – that is, $R > 0$ – a given ECU amount of today's bonds translates into a larger number of ECUs next period. Accordingly, individuals who can buy or sell bonds on the economy-wide credit market (that is, people who can lend or borrow) regard a ECU's worth of income or expenses differently depending on when it arises. Specifically, ε1 received or spent earlier is equivalent to more than ε1 later. Or, viewed in reverse, ECUs received or spent in the future must be discounted to express them in terms that are comparable to ECUs in the present.

Suppose, for example, that $R = 10\%$ per year. Assume that someone has ε100 of income today but plans to spend these funds in the future. Then he or she can buy ε100 of bonds now and have ε110 available next year. Hence, ε100 today is worth just as much as ε110 next year. Equivalently, the ε110 is discounted to correspond to the amount of today's income needed to generate ε110 next year. We find this amount by solving the following equation:

$$(\text{Income needed today}) \times (1 + 10\%) = ε110$$

The required amount of current income is $ε110/(1.1) = ε100$.

More generally, if we substitute any value of the interest rate, R, for 10%, the income for next period, Py_2, is divided by the term $(1 + R)$ to find the equivalent amount for this period. The result, $Py_2/(1 + R)$, is the **present value** of the future income. Economists call the term $(1 + R)$ the **discount factor**. When we discount by this factor – that is, when we divide by the term $1 + R$ – we determine the present value of next period's income.[1]

Equation (4.4) shows that we express the second period's income as a present value, $Py_2/(1 + R)$, before combining it with the first period's income, Py_1. Thus, the sum, $Py_1 + Py_2/(1 + R)$, is the total present value of income from the production (and sale) of goods over periods 1 and 2. Similarly, we express next period's expenditure as the present value, $Pc_2/(1 + R)$, before adding it to this period's spending, Pc_1. The sum, $Pc_1 + Pc_2/(1 + R)$, is the total present value of consumption expenditures over periods 1 and 2.

The Household's Budget Line

The two-period budget constraint in equation (4.4) brings out the choices that a credit market allows to a household. Assume, for example, that a household raises today's spending, Pc_1, by ε1000, and thereby cuts today's saving by ε1000. This change reduces assets at the end of the first period, b_1, by ε1000 (see equation (4.2)). For the second period, the household loses ε1000 in receipts of principal from bonds and ε100 in receipts of interest (assuming that $R = 10\%$). With ε1100 less during the second period, the household can decrease next period's spending, Pc_2, by this amount to keep the final asset position, b_2, intact. Therefore, the increase in today's spending by ε1000 balances against a decrease in next period's spending by ε1100. More generally, the required decrease in spending for the next period, Pc_2, equals the increase in this period's spending, Pc_1, multiplied by the discount factor, $(1+R)$.

To study the choices of c_1 and c_2 it is convenient to express everything in real terms by dividing through equation (4.4) by the price level, P. If we rearrange terms to place those involving consumption on the left side, we get

$$c_1 + c_2/(1+R) = y_1 + y_2/(1+R)$$
$$+ b_0(1+R)/P$$
$$- b_2/P(1+R) \quad (4.5)$$

Note that each term in equation (4.5) is in real terms. For example, y_1 is period 1's real income from the commodity market, in the sense of indicating the number of commodity units that someone can buy during period 1 with the ECU income of Py_1.

Suppose that we fix the total of the items on the right side of equation (4.5) at some amount, which we can call x. So we can think of fixing the starting real value of bonds, $b_0(1+R)/P$, the real present value of bonds carried over to period 3, $b_2/P(1+R)$, and the total present value of real income from the commodity market, $y_1 + y_2/(1+R)$. Then we can rewrite equation (4.5) as

$$c_1 + c_2/(1+R) = x \quad (4.6)$$

where

$$x = b_0(1+R)/P - b_2/P(1+R) + y_1$$
$$+ y_2/(1+R).$$

Equation (4.6) makes clear that for a given quantity x, a household can change today's consumption, c_1, by making the appropriate adjustment in next period's consumption, c_2.

The straight line in Figure 4.1 shows the possibilities. If the household consumes nothing in the second period, so that $c_2 = 0$ (which would

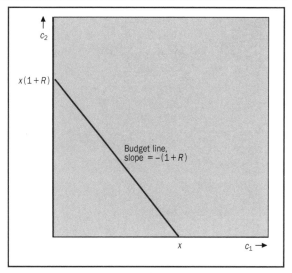

The budget line with slope $-(1+R)$ shows the attainable combinations of consumption levels c_1 and c_2. Along this line, the total real present value of expenditures over the two periods equals the fixed amount x.

Figure 4.1 The possibilities for consuming now versus later

probably cause starvation and therefore be undesirable), then equation (4.6) says that today's consumption, c_1, equals x. Hence, the line in the figure intersects the horizontal axis at this point. Alternatively, if the household consumes nothing today, so that $c_1 = 0$, then the real present value of next period's consumption, $c_2/(1+R)$, equals x. In this case, next period's consumption is given by $c_2 = x(1+R)$. Therefore, the line in the figure intersects the vertical axis at this point.

The straight line in Figure 4.1 connects the value x on the horizontal axis to the value $x(1+R)$ on the vertical. This **budget line** shows all the combinations of consumptions, c_1 and c_2, that satisfy the household's budget condition from equation (4.6). The important point is that the budget line shows the attainable pairs of consumption, c_1 and c_2, for a given real present value of spending over the two periods.

The slope of the budget line in Figure 4.1 is $-(1+R)$. (The magnitude of the slope is the ratio of the vertical intercept, $x[1+R]$, to the horizontal, x.) Along this line, a decrease by 1 unit in today's real spending, c_1, is matched by an increase of $(1+R)$ units in next period's real spending, c_2. To put it another way, the interest rate R is the premium in future consumption for saving today rather than consuming.

So far, the analysis describes a household's opportunities for consuming in one period versus another. But we have not yet studied people's preferences for consumption at different dates. When we combine the opportunities with the preferences, we shall determine the actual choices of consumption over time. Thus, we now turn our attention to these preferences.

Preferences for Consuming Now versus Later

In Chapter 2 we derived indifference curves for consumption and work in each period. Now we want to think about choices over time; specifically, about consumption in period 1 versus

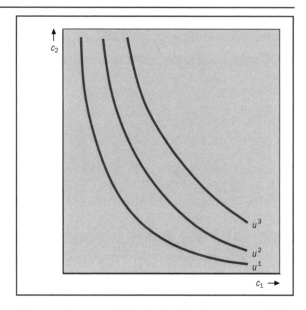

Along each curve the level of utility is constant. Utility increases as the household moves from the curve labelled u^1 to that labelled u^2 and so on.

Figure 4.3   A family of indifference curves for consumption now versus consumption next period

consumption in period 2 and about work in period 1 versus work in period 2. To begin, suppose that the two work efforts, ℓ_1 and ℓ_2, are given. Then we want to construct indifference curves to show the household's attitude toward different combinations of the two consumption levels, c_1 and c_2. Figure 4.2 shows such a curve. For high levels of c_1 relative to c_2, such as at point A in the figure, a household is more interested in next period's consumption than this period's. Hence, a small increase in c_2 makes up for the loss of a unit of c_1. Thus, the curve in the figure has a relatively flat slope at point A. Similarly, the curve has a steep slope when c_1 is relatively low, as at point B in the figure. At any point, the slope of the indifference curve reveals the amount of next period's consumption needed to make up for the loss of a unit of current consumption.

As in Chapter 2, we can define a family of indifference curves, each applying to a different level of utility. Figure 4.3 shows three of these curves, labelled by their levels of total utility, where $u^1 < u^2 < u^3$.

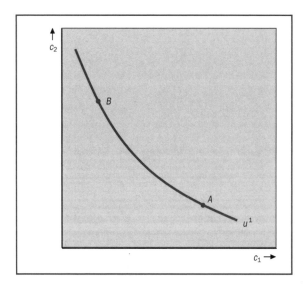

The household is equally happy with any combination of consumptions c_1 and c_2 that lie along the curve. Today's consumption is high relative to next period's at point A and low relative to next period's at point B. Hence, the curve is steeper at point B than at point A.

Figure 4.2   An indifference curve for consumption now versus consumption next period

Choosing Consumption over Two Periods

The budget line in Figure 4.1 describes how households can use the credit market to shift between consumption now and consumption in the next period. The family of indifference curves shown in Figure 4.3 describes people's willingness to exchange consumption now for consumption in the next period. If we combine the market opportunities from Figure 4.1 with the indifference map from Figure 4.3, we can determine the choices of consumption over the two periods.[2]

Figure 4.4 combines the budget line from Figure 4.1 with the indifference curves shown in Figure 4.3. Notice that the household moves along the budget line to reach the highest possible indifference curve. This occurs at the point of tangency, shown in the figure, at which the slope of the budget line equals the slope of an indifference curve. We label the corresponding levels of consumption for the two periods as c_1^* and c_2^*.

Recall that the slope of an indifference curve measures the bonus in next period's consumption

needed to compensate for the loss of a unit of this period's consumption. In contrast, the slope of the budget line is $-(1 + R)$, which determines the premium, R, for saving more. At the point of tangency shown in Figure 4.4 the premium from saving more just balances the willingness to defer consumption. For this reason, any choice along the budget line other than the point (c_1^*, c_2^*) leads to lower utility. This result is clear geometrically from Figure 4.4.

To sum up, we combined people's opportunities (the budget line) with their preferences (the indifference curves) to determine the choices of consumption over two periods. At the same time, we determined how much people save today. We can use this analysis to see how the time pattern of consumption and saving changes when there are shifts in the interest rate or other variables. The effects of changes in the interest rate turn out to be especially important for our subsequent macroeconomic analysis.

Wealth and Substitution Effects

As in Chapter 2, we can use the notions of wealth and substitution effects to analyze people's choices. In the present setting, wealth effects relate to the quantity previously denoted as x, which is the total present value of real consumption expenditures for periods 1 and 2. The important substitution variable for consuming now versus later, or for how much to save, is the interest rate, R.

Wealth Effects on Consumption

Before, we found that parallel shifts of the production function implied pure wealth effects. These wealth effects show up here as shifts in the total real present value of expenditures, x, which is given by

$$x = c_1 + c_2/(1 + R)$$
$$= y_1 + y_2/(1 + R) + b_0(1 + R)/P$$
$$- b_2/P(1 + R) \qquad (4.7)$$

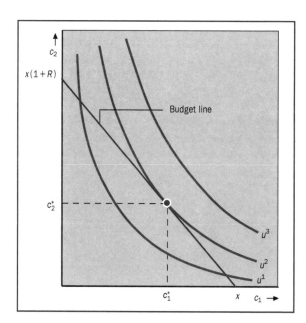

The choice of consumption levels c_1^* and c_2^* occurs where the budget line is tangent to an indifference curve.

Figure 4.4 Choosing consumption today and next period

Also, recall that the amounts of real income from the commodity market come from the production function as $y_1 = f(\ell_1)$ and $y_2 = f(\ell_2)$.

Assume that the production function shifts upward for periods 1 and 2. Think of parallel shifts that do not change the schedule for labour's marginal product. Assuming for the moment that work efforts, ℓ_1 and ℓ_2, do not change, there are increases in the amounts of real income, y_1 and y_2. Now suppose that we hold constant the initial and final stocks of bonds, b_0 and b_2. Then the increases in y_1 and y_2 raise the total real present value of spending, x, from equation (4.7).

Figure 4.5 shows that the increase in the total real present value of spending generates a parallel outward shift of the budget line. (The slope stays the same because the interest rate does not change.) The new budget line allows the household to reach a higher indifference curve than before. Note that the new point of tangency between the budget line and an indifference curve occurs at higher levels of consumption for each period. Hence, the wealth effect is positive for c_1 and c_2 – or equivalently, c_1 and c_2 are both superior goods.

The Interest Rate and Intertemporal Substitution

If the interest rate is R, each household faces the budget line that we label as 'old' in Figure 4.6. Given the total real present value of spending for periods 1 and 2, the household selects the consumption pair, (c_1^*, c_2^*) If the interest rate rises to R', then the new budget line is steeper than the old one. There are, however, many places that we could draw this new line in Figure 4.6. For present purposes, we want to isolate the substitution effect from a higher interest rate. If we held fixed the overall real present value of spending, x, then the new budget line would start from the value x on the horizontal axis but otherwise would lie to the right of the old budget line. But then the new budget line would allow the household to consume the same amount today, c_1^*, and more next period. Because wealth increases in this case, the shift would not be a pure substitution effect.

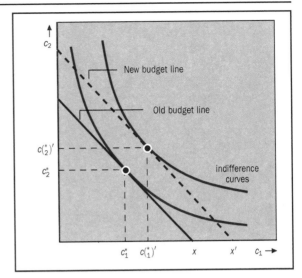

The total real present value of consumption expenditures for periods 1 and 2 rises from x to x'. Consumption increases from c_1^* to $(c_1^*)'$ in period 1 and from c_2^* to $(c_2^*)'$ in period 2.

Figure 4.5   Wealth effects on consumption

We can approximate a pure substitution effect by rotating the budget line around the point at which the household initially chose the levels of consumption. When drawn this way, the new budget line shown in Figure 4.6 intersects the old one at the point (c_1^*, c_2^*): the household therefore retains the option to buy this initial pair of consumptions. But the household cannot increase either quantity without giving up some of the other.

Although the new budget line passes through the point (c_1^*, c_2^*) in Figure 4.6, the line is not tangent to an indifference curve at this point. Because the new budget line is steeper than the indifference curve, the premium to saving more, R', exceeds the amount needed to motivate more saving. It follows that the household would raise saving – that is, c_1 falls and c_2 rises. The new choices, labelled $[(c_1^*)', (c_2^*)']$ in the figure, correspond to the tangency between the new budget line and an indifference curve.[3] The important point is that the increase in the interest rate motivates people to raise future consumption, c_2, relative to current consumption, c_1. Equivalently, the rise in the interest rate

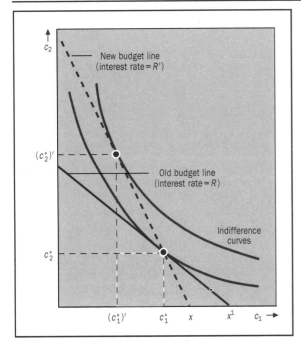

When the interest rate is R on the old budget line, the household chooses the consumption pair (c_1^*, c_2^*). If the interest rate rises to R' on the new budget line the household opts for the pair $[(c_1^*)', (c_2^*)']$. Notice that the increase in the interest rate motivates people to choose a higher ratio of consumption next period to consumption this period.

Figure 4.6 Effect on consumption from an increase in the interest rate

induces households to save a larger fraction of current income.

Recall that the total real present value of spending over periods 1 and 2 is $c_1 + c_2/(1 + R)$. Note again that we divide c_2 by the discount factor, $(1 + R)$, before adding it to c_1. A rise in R lowers the cost of next period's consumption relative to that of current consumption because a person can obtain more units of consumption next period for each unit of current consumption foregone. It is this change in relative costs that motivates people to substitute future goods, c_2, for current ones, c_1. Economists call this mechanism an **intertemporal-substitution effect**.

Choosing Work Effort at Different Dates

In Chapter 2 we studied the choice of work and consumption for a single period. There we stressed substitution effects from changes in the schedule for labour's marginal product. Also, we explored wealth effects from shifts in the position of the production function.

In this chapter, we have examined an individual's choices of consumption over time. But so far we have not considered the choices of work effort. If we combine the previous analysis

Box 4.1 Empirical Evidence on Intertemporal Substitution of Consumption

Our theoretical analysis predicts that a higher interest rate motivates people to defer consumption from the present to the future. An empirical study by David Runkle (1988) isolated this effect by examining the behaviour of food consumption over time (1973–82) for a sample of 1100 US households. (The data come from the Panel Study on Income Dynamics, which is constructed at the University of Michigan.) Runkle found that an increase in the annual interest rate by one percentage point raised the typical family's growth rate of consumption by about one-half percentage

point per year. (Runkle's estimates adjust the interest rate for inflation and taxes in ways that we shall explore in Chapters 8 and 16, respectively.) The response of consumption growth to the interest rate turned out to be larger for households that had substantial liquid assets (such as stocks, bonds, and bank deposits) than for those without such assets. Economists have been less successful at finding these types of effects in aggregate consumption data. For a discussion of this evidence, see Robert Hall (1989).

of work and consumption with the present analysis of consumption over time, we shall understand how households choose work effort over time.

Wealth Effects on Work Effort

We can write the household's budget constraint for two periods as

$$f(\ell_1) + f(\ell_2)/(1+R) + b_0(1+R)/P$$
$$= c_1 + c_2/(1+R) + b_2/P(1+R) \qquad (4.8)$$

Note the substitutions, $y_1 = f(\ell_1)$ and $y_2 = f(\ell_2)$, in the expression for the real sources of funds on the left side. Suppose that the production function shifts up in a parallel fashion for periods 1 and 2. For given amounts of work, ℓ_1 and ℓ_2, the real sources of funds increase on the left side of equation (4.8). As we saw before, households respond by raising c_1 and c_2.

Recall from Chapter 2 that people also react to more wealth by taking more leisure. Hence, the levels of work, ℓ_1 and ℓ_2, tend to decline rather than stay fixed. Macroeconomists usually stress the positive wealth effect on consumption but neglect the effect on leisure. However, the evidence on hours of work, which we reviewed in Chapter 2, indicates that this effect on leisure is important. For example, at early stages of economic development, the wealth effect is strong enough that average hours worked tend to diminish as an economy develops.

The Interest Rate and Choices of Work Effort

Figure 4.6 shows that an increase in the interest rate motivates households to reduce current consumption, c_1, and raise next period's consumption, c_2. Notice from the right side of equation (4.8) that an increase in R makes next period's consumption, c_2, cheaper relative to this period's, c_1. That is why people substitute toward c_2 and away from c_1 when R rises. But the same argument holds for leisure in the two periods. If someone takes leisure in period 2, he or she

discounts the loss in output, $f(\ell_2)$, by the factor $(1+R)$. Therefore, when R rises, the leisure from period 2 becomes cheaper relative to that in period 1. The conclusion is that an increase in the interest rate motivates people to substitute toward next period's leisure and away from this period's. Or, equivalently, this period's work, ℓ_1, rises relative to next period's, ℓ_2. Note also that the increase in ℓ_1 reinforces the effect of the decrease in c_1 in raising current saving.

Overall, an increase in the interest rate has two types of intertemporal-substitution effects. First, today's consumption, c_1, declines relative to next period's, c_2. Second, today's work, ℓ_1, rises relative to next period's, ℓ_2. Both effects – the reduction in current spending and the increase in current income – show up as an increase in current saving. Thus, both responses reflect the positive response of an individual's desired saving to the return from saving, which is the interest rate.

Empirical Evidence on Intertemporal Substitution of Work Effort

Macroeconomists typically stress the effect on saving that results from intertemporal substitution of consumption but neglect the effect from changes in work effort. There is, however, some evidence that intertemporal substitution of work effort is also important. George Alogoskoufis (1987b) found for US data from 1948 to 1982 that an increase in the annual interest rate by one percentage point lowered the growth rate of work by about 0.6 percentage point per year. For British data from 1950 to 1982, the corresponding estimate (Alogoskoufis, 1987a) was about 0.2. These results applied if aggregate work effort was measured by the total number of employees. If work effort was measured instead as hours worked per person, then the results were not statistically significant. Thus, these findings suggest that intertemporal substitution of work effort is more important for the number of workers than for hours worked per person. Thomas MaCurdy (1981) reports additional evidence that supports the importance of intertemporal substitution of work effort.

Budget Constraints over Many Periods

Thus far, we have examined the behaviour of households over two periods. To carry out this analysis, we had to hold fixed the amount of bonds that someone carries over to later periods. This amount is, in fact, not a given, because it depends on people's plans for consuming and earning income in the future. We now make this connection explicit by dealing with households' plans over many periods. Another important reason for extending the model to more than two periods is to be able to distinguish between future temporary and permanent shocks. In fact, with only two periods, second period (i.e. future) events have always a permanent nature since they cannot be reversed.

Budget Constraints for Any Number of Periods

Start with the two-period budget constraint from equation (4.4):

$$Py_1 + Py_2/(1 + R) + b_0(1 + R)$$
$$= Pc_1 + Pc_2/(1 + R) + b_2/(1 + R)$$

The final stock of bonds from the second period, b_2, determines the initial stock for period 3. Specifically, for period 3 the budget constraint is

$$Py_3 + b_2(1 + R) = Pc_3 + b_3$$

We can use this equation to solve out for the stock of bonds, b_2, and substitute the result into the two-period budget constraint to get the three-period budget constraint:

$$Py_1 + Py_2/(1 + R) + Py_3/(1 + R)^2 + b_0(1 + R)$$
$$= Pc_1 + Pc_2/(1 + R) + Pc_3/(1 + R)^2$$
$$+ b_3/(1 + R)^2 \qquad (4.9)$$

By now we see how to construct a budget constraint for any number of periods. The budget constraint for j periods is

$$Py_1 + Py_2/(1 + R) + Py_3/(1 + R)^2 + \ldots$$
$$+ Py_j/(1 + R)^{j-1} + b_0(1 + R)$$
$$= Pc_1 + Pc_2/(1 + R) + Pc_3/(1 + R)^2 + \ldots$$
$$+ Pc_j/(1 + R)^{j-1} + b_j/(1 + R)^{j-1} \qquad (4.10)$$

Notice that the previous examples of budget constraints are special cases of equation (4.10). For $j = 2$ we get the two-period budget constraint in equation (4.4) and for $j = 3$ we get the three-period constraint in equation (4.9).

Notice two things about the budget constraint for j periods in equation (4.10). First, the right side involves the stock of bonds, b_j, held at the end of period j. Second, we calculate the present value of income or expense for any period t by dividing by the factor $(1 + R)^{t-1}$. This factor represents the accumulation of interest between period 1 and period t – that is, over $t - 1$ periods.

The Household's Planning Horizon

Suppose that a household is choosing today's consumption and work effort, c_1 and ℓ_1. Typically, households make these choices in the context of a long-term plan that considers future levels of consumption and income. These future values relate to the current choices through the j-period budget constraint shown in equation (4.10). We can refer to the number, j, as the household's **planning horizon**.

How long is the horizon that people consider in making current decisions? Because we are dealing with households that have access to a credit market, a long planning horizon is appropriate. That is, by borrowing or lending, people can effectively use future income to finance current spending, or current income to pay for future spending. When expressed as a present value, prospective incomes and expenses from the distant future are as pertinent for current decisions as are today's incomes and expenses.

Economists often assume that the planning horizon is long but finite. For example, in a class of theories called **life-cycle models**,[4] the horizon, j, represents an individual's expected remaining lifetime. If people do not care about things that occur after their death, then they have no reason to carry assets beyond period j. Accordingly, they set to zero the final asset stock, b_j, which appears on the right side of the budget constraint in equation (4.10). (We also have to rule out the possibility of dying in debt, which would correspond to $b_j < 0$.)

Researchers who use life-cycle models usually assume that the working span, which is the interval for which $\ell_t > 0$, is shorter than the length of life. In this case, people have retirement periods during which consumption must be financed either from savings accumulated during working years or from transfer payments. These transfers could come from the government (**social security**) or from children.

It is straightforward to define the anticipated lifetime – and thereby the finite planning horizon – for an isolated individual who has no concern for descendants. The appropriate horizon is, however, not obvious for a family in which the parents care about their children. (The children may also care about their parents!) In this context, the applicable horizon extends beyond someone's expected lifetime, and people would give some weight to the expected future incomes and expenses of their children. Further, since children care about the welfare of their children – should they have any – and so on for each subsequent generation, there is no clear point at which to terminate the planning period. Of course, this argument does not imply that anticipated incomes and expenses for the distant future count as much as those for a few years off. But by using present values, we already place a large discount on incomes and expenses from the distant future.

Instead of imposing a finite horizon, we can think of the household's plan as having an **infinite horizon**. There are two good reasons for proceeding in this way:

- First, if we think of the typical person as part of a family that has concerns about the members of future generations – children, grandchildren, and so on – into the indefinite future, then this setup is the correct one: it would be inappropriate to identify the horizon with the typical person's expected lifetime.

- Second, although it is not obvious at this point, an infinite horizon is the easiest framework to use.

Budget Constraints for an Infinite Horizon

When the planning horizon is infinite, the budget constraint includes the present values of incomes and expenses for the indefinite future. Then, using equation (4.10), we have

$$
\begin{aligned}
&Py_1 + Py_2/(1+R) + Py_3/(1+R)^2 + \ldots \\
&\quad + b_0(1+R) \\
&= Pc_1 + Pc_2/(1+R) + Pc_3/(1+R)^2 + \ldots
\end{aligned}
$$
(4.11)

We no longer terminate the sums for incomes and expenses at some finite date, j, as we did in equation (4.10). Notice also that the final stock of bonds, b_j, does not appear in the budget constraint. In effect, there is no 'final' period to consider here.

For most purposes, we prefer to deal with the budget constraint in real terms. If we divide through equation (4.11) by the price level, P, then we get

$$
\begin{aligned}
&y_1 + y_2/(1+R) + y_3/(1+R)^2 + \ldots \\
&\quad + b_0(1+R)/P \\
&= c_1 + c_2/(1+R) + c_3/(1+R)^2 + \ldots
\end{aligned}
$$
(4.12)

Equation (4.12) says that the present value of real income from sales to the commodity market over an infinite horizon, plus the real value of the receipts from the initial stock of bonds, equals the present value of real consumption expenditure over an infinite horizon. We shall use this form of the budget constraint when studying households' choices over many periods.

Choices over Many Periods

Before, we discussed the choices of consumption over two periods, c_1 and c_2. Now we consider the entire path of consumption, $c_1, c_2, c_3, \ldots$. In some of our previous discussion, we thought about a given total present value of real spending over two periods, $x = c_1 + c_2/(1 + R)$. Here we proceed analogously by looking at the total present value of real spending over an infinite horizon. Using the budget constraint in equation (4.12), we have

$$x = c_1 + c_2/(1 + R) + c_3/(1 + R)^2 + \ldots$$
$$= y_1 + y_2/(1 + R) + y_3/(1 + R)^2 + \ldots$$
$$+ b_0(1 + R)/P \qquad (4.13)$$

The Interest Rate and Intertemporal Substitution

Given the total present value of real spending over an infinite horizon, a household can still substitute between c_1 and c_2. Just as before, for each unit of c_1 foregone, a household can obtain $(1 + R)$ additional units of c_2. But there is nothing special about periods 1 and 2. People can substitute in a similar manner between c_2 and c_3, c_3 and c_4, and so on. In general, if someone gives up one unit of c_t, the credit market allows him or her to raise c_{t+1} by $(1 + R)$ units.

Consider an increase in the interest rate, R. As before, we want to abstract from wealth effects to isolate the substitution effect from this change. In the two-period case, we know that an increase in R motivates people to reduce c_1 relative to c_2. That is because the higher interest rate makes today's consumption more expensive relative to the next period's. But the same reasoning applies to any pair of consumptions, c_t and c_{t+1}. An increase in R lowers c_t relative to c_{t+1}.

When we allow for variable work effort, we find that changes in the interest rate also have intertemporal-substitution effects on work and leisure. The generalization from the two-period model is that an increase in R motivates people to take less leisure in one period relative to that in the next period. That is, ℓ_t rises relative to ℓ_{t+1}.[5]

Finally, note that the decrease in c_1 and increase in ℓ_1 both imply an increase in current saving. Thus, as in the two-period case, a higher interest rate motivates people to save more.

Wealth Effects

As before, wealth effects involve changes in the total present value of real spending, x, which is given in equation (4.13). Remember that the aggregate value of the initial stock of bonds, B_0, is zero. Therefore, if we think about the typical or average household, for which $b_0 = 0$, then wealth effects will arise only from changes in the present value of real income from the commodity market, $y_1 + y_2/(1 + R) + \ldots$. For a given amount of work effort in each period, these changes must involve shifts in the production function.

Permanent Shifts of the Production Function

Consider first the case in which the production function, $f(\ell_t)$, shifts upward in a parallel fashion for all periods. As examples, we can think of discoveries of new technology or natural resources – that is, changes that create permanent improvements in productive capacity. Given each period's amount of work, ℓ_t, each period's level of output, y_t, rises. Hence, the total real present value of spending, x, increases in equation (4.13).

As a generalization of the results for two periods, we find that the increase in the present value of real spending, x, leads to increases in consumption, c_t, for each period. Consumption in any period is a superior good and the wealth effect is positive. Similarly, we find that more wealth leads to more leisure in each period. Therefore, an increase in wealth implies less work effort, ℓ_t, at each date.

The Marginal Propensities to Consume and Save

Suppose that real income, y_t, rises by one unit in each period. One possibility is that consumption, c_t, also increases by one unit in each period. (This response would satisfy the budget constraint in equation (4.13).) If someone responds in this way, economists say that his or her **marginal propensity to consume** – defined as the change in consumption during a period relative to the change in that period's income – is one. Since consumption and income change by equal amounts in all periods, there is no change in saving for any period. In other words, the **marginal propensity to save** – defined as the change in saving for a period relative to the change in income for that period – is zero.

If income, y_t, changes by one unit in each period, as before, but a household increases current consumption, c_1, by less than one unit, then the current marginal propensity to consume is less than one. Correspondingly, the current marginal propensity to save is positive. Households must, however, use this extra saving to expand some future level of consumption. Hence there must be at least one subsequent period during which consumption, c_t, rises by more than one unit.

Suppose that a household planned initially for a constant amount of consumption. Then the increase in period t's consumption, c_t, by more than one unit means that this consumption

increases relative to today's, c_1. That is, consumption shifts away from the present and toward the future. We know that this type of shift is appropriate if the interest rate increases. But since the interest rate does not change here, the household would tend to maintain the relative amounts of consumption at different dates. For the case at hand, this balance results only if the household increases consumption in every period by one unit. Hence, if the improvement in the production function is permanent, then we predict that the marginal propensity to consume would be close to one. Correspondingly, the marginal propensity to save would be near zero.

Temporary Shifts of the Production Function
Suppose now that the parallel upward shift of the production function lasts only for the current period. So instead of discoveries of new technol-

---

Box 4.2   Empirical Evidence on the Marginal Propensity to Consume

Empirical research provides strong evidence that the marginal propensity to consume out of permanent changes in income is much greater than that for temporary changes. Some of the clearest evidence comes from special circumstances in which there are windfalls of income, which people surely regard as temporary. One example is the receipt by Israeli citizens of lump-sum, non-recurring restitution payments from Germany in 1957–58 (see Mordechai Kreinin, 1961, and Michael Landsberger, 1970). The payments were large, with a value that roughly equalled the average family's annual income. For this case, the data indicate that the typical family's consumption expenditure during the year of the windfall rose by no more than 20% of the amount received. Further, the measure of consumer spending includes purchases of consumer durables. Because these goods last for many years, we should view these purchases as partly saving rather than consumption. Therefore, the true marginal propensity to consume out of the windfall was much less than 20%.

Another example is the payment in 1950 to US World War II veterans of an unanticipated, one-time life insurance dividend of about $175. At the time, this amount represented about 4% of the average family's annual income. In this case, the statistical estimates indicate that consumption rose by 30 to 40% of the windfall (see Roger Bird and Ronald Bodkin, 1965). But since the data again include purchases of consumer durables, the true marginal propensity to consume would be much lower than 30%.

More generally, statistical studies of consumer behaviour indicate that the marginal propensity to consume out of permanent changes in income is large and not much different from one. In contrast, the marginal propensity to consume out of temporary income is only about 20 to 30% (see Robert Hall, 1989). Although this response to temporary changes is somewhat greater than that predicted by our theory, the important point for our analysis is that the response of consumer demand to permanent changes in income is much greater than that to temporary changes.

ogies or resources, we can think of the effects of weather, temporary changes in the supply of raw materials, strikes, and so on.

If work efforts do not change, then the increase in real income occurs only in the current period. Households would like to spread this extra income over consumption in all periods. But to raise future consumption, households now have to raise current saving. Hence, current consumption, c_1, rises by much less than the increase in current real income, y_1. In other words, if the improvement of the production function is temporary, then the marginal propensity to consume is small, and the marginal propensity to save is positive and nearly equal to one.[6]

Wealth Effects from Changes in the Interest Rate

Thus far, we have looked only at intertemporal-substitution effects from changes in the interest rate. Now let's see whether a change in the interest rate leads to a wealth effect.

We can test for the effect on wealth by using the budget constraint, which is again

$$y_1 + y_2/(1+R) + \ldots + b_0(1+R)/P$$
$$= c_1 + c_2/(1+R) + \ldots$$

Abstract from the term that involves the initial stock of bonds, $b_0(1+R)/P$, because this term will equal zero when we sum up over all households.

Suppose that we hypothetically hold fixed the paths of real incomes, y_1, y_2, ..., and expenditures, c_1, c_2, ... Then consider the separate effects of an increase in R on the left and right sides of the budget constraint. The rise in R reduces the present values of real income, $y_1 + y_2/(1+R) + \ldots$, and real spending, $c_1 + c_2/(1+R) \ldots$. But the important question is which sum falls by the greater amount. If the present value of real spending falls by more, then the given path of real income would be sufficient to continue purchasing these goods and still have something left over. Then the household could increase consumption for some periods without necessarily decreasing it for others. Hence, wealth increases. The opposite conclusion applies if the

present value of real spending falls by less than that of real income.

The budget constraint indicates that the terms that decline most with the rise in R are those that are most distant into the future. That is, the discount factor for period t is $1/(1+R)^{t-1}$, which is more sensitive to changes in R the higher the value of t. When R rises, the present value of real spending declines by more than that of real income if the path of spending is more heavily concentrated in the future than is the path of income. For the case in which the initial bonds, b_0, equal zero, this property applies for someone who has positive saving in most of the earlier years and negative saving in most of the later years. In other words, people who plan usually to be lenders experience an increase in wealth when the interest rate rises. Conversely, those who plan usually to be borrowers have a decline in wealth.

Although either situation may hold for an individual, neither case can apply for the average person. Because the aggregate stock of bonds is always zero in our model, we know that the average household is neither typically a lender nor typically a borrower. Therefore, in the aggregate, the wealth effect from a change in the interest rate is nil.[7] This result is important. It says that for aggregate purposes we can neglect wealth effects from changes in the interest rate, and we should focus on the intertemporal-substitution effects from these changes.

Shifts in the Schedule for Labour's Marginal Product

A rise in the schedule for labour's marginal product typically accompanies an improvement in the production function. As we know, a higher schedule for labour's marginal product motivates people to work more. If the change is the same for each period, then work and hence real income rise by roughly equal amounts in each period. In this case the marginal propensity to consume would be close to one and each period's consumption would increase by roughly the same amount as income. In other words, saving would not change.

A permanent improvement in labour's productivity means that consumption becomes cheaper relative to leisure at each date. Therefore, people work and consume more in every period. Because there are no changes in the relative costs of consumption or leisure for different periods, the responses in work and consumption tend to be the same in each period; hence, there are no effects on saving.

We should be careful to distinguish the substitution between consumption and leisure from the intertemporal-substitution effect. The intertemporal effect involves the cost of taking consumption or leisure in one period rather than another. For example, an increase in the interest rate motivates people to reduce today's consumption and leisure relative to future consumption and leisure. In contrast, the schedule for labour's marginal product determines the relative cost of consumption and leisure at a point in time. Therefore, a shift in this schedule induces changes in the relative amounts of consumption and leisure. But if the change in labour's productivity is permanent, then there are no intertemporal-substitution effects.

The results are different if the change in productivity is temporary. As an example, think of a gold rush or other temporary profit opportunity, which makes the reward for today's work effort unusually high. We can represent this case by shifting the schedule for labour's marginal product only for the current period. Then the new element is that today's leisure becomes more expensive relative to future leisure or consumption. Therefore, people have an incentive to expand today's work to increase future consumption and leisure. Thus, a temporary improvement of productivity stimulates saving: today's output rises by more than today's consumption.

Money and Households' Budget Constraints

We want now to incorporate the discussion of money demand of Chapter 3 into our treatment of households' budget constraints. Recall the form of the budget condition for period t:

$$Py_t + (1 + R)b_{t-1} + m_{t-1} = Pc_t + b_t + m_t \tag{4.14}$$

We simplified the analysis before by pretending that each household's money balance was constant over time: $m_t = m_{t-1}$. Then the money-balance terms on each side of equation (4.14) cancelled, and terms involving money did not appear in the budget constraint over an infinite horizon. Now we want to reconsider this analysis when households can alter their holdings of money.

In our model of the demand for money, the cash position moved up and down during a period in accordance with the sawtooth pattern shown in Figure 3.1. For the purpose of constructing a budget constraint over an infinite horizon, it is satisfactory to neglect these ups and downs of money within a period. Hence we now pretend that a household's money holding equals m_t during period t. This amount is constant during the period, but can change from one period to the next.

Consider a household that starts with the money balance m_0 and that plans to hold the amount m_1 in period 1. We allow m_1 to differ from m_0, but it is convenient to pretend for the moment that all future balances also equal m_1 : $m_1 = m_2 = m_3 \ldots$. We can use the one-period budget constraint from equation (4.14) as we did in Chapter 3 to derive a budget condition that applies for any number of periods. For an infinite horizon, the result is

$$y_1 + y_2/(1 + R) + \ldots + b_0(1 + R)/P + m_0/P$$
$$= c_1 + c_2/(1 + R) + \ldots + m_1/P \tag{4.15}$$

Equation (4.15) differs from equation (4.12) only by the addition of a monetary term on each side of the equation. The sources of funds on the left side now include the initial real money balance, m_0/P. This term makes sense because households can use their initial money to buy goods.

The uses of funds on the right side now include m_1/P, which represents the real money balance that the household plans to hold forever (because $m_1 = m_2 = \ldots$). The funds held (forever) as money cannot also be spent on consumption:

therefore, m_1/P shows up on the right side of equation (4.15) as a use of funds.

Suppose that a household's initial real money balance, m_0/P, rises, while the planned future real balance, m_1/P, does not change. The increase in real money is then equivalent to an increase in household wealth. We expect, therefore, that the household would increase consumption and leisure in all periods.

Alternatively, assume that m_1/P rises by the same amount as m_0/P. Equation (4.15) then shows that no resources are available for the household to raise consumption and leisure. The increase in m_0/P is just sufficient to maintain the expansion of m_1/P (forever). Nothing is left over for other purposes.

The important result is that consumer demand and desired leisure depend positively on the term, $m_0/P - m_1/P$. For a household that plans to maintain a constant real money balance – that is, $m_0/P = m_1/P$ – the net effect is nil. Because the typical person will end up in this situation (in the market-clearing analysis of Chapter 5), this last result turns out to be important.

The same type of result holds if we allow m_t; to vary after period 1. Instead of m_1/P, the right side of equation (4.15) contains a complicated average of the real money balances that the household plans to hold in all future periods. It remains true that an increase by one unit in all future values of m_t/P (for $1, 2, \ldots$) raises the uses of funds on the right side of equation (4.15) by one unit. Therefore, if m_0/P and all future values, m_t/P, rise by the same amount, then the household would not change its choices of consumption and leisure.

The Real-Balance Effect

Consider the wealth effect from a change in the price level, P. Look at the household's budget condition in real terms from equation (4.15). Suppose that we hold fixed the levels of output, y_1, y_2, $\ldots$, and consumption, c_1, c_2, $\ldots$. Also, hold constant the interest rate, R, the planned level of *real* money balances, m_1/P, and the initial *nominal* money holding, m_0. Finally, think about the average person, for whom the initial bonds, b_0, equal zero.

Consider the effects on the left and right sides of equation (4.15) from a decline in the price level. Given our assumptions, nothing changes on the right side, which measures the uses of funds in real terms. The only effect on the left side (since $b_0 = 0$) is an increase in the real value of the initial money balance, m_0/P. Wealth therefore increases because people can use these higher initial real balances to raise consumption and leisure. The increase in wealth from a decline in the price level is called the **real-balance effect**.[8] As with other wealth effects, we predict that this one leads to increased consumption and leisure at all dates.

The real-balance effect operates only when there is a change in initial real money, m_0/P, relative to the planned future holdings, represented here by m_1/P. In most of our subsequent analysis, we shall look at situations in which the aggregates of actual and planned real money balances move by equal amounts. Then, as discussed before, there are equal changes to the left and right sides of the budget constraint in equation (4.15). In these cases, the change in real money balances will not involve net wealth effects on the aggregates of consumption and leisure.

The aggregate real value of bonds, B_0/P, is always zero and therefore cannot be affected by a change in the price level. A change in the price level nevertheless can have important distributional effects if some households are lenders and others are borrowers. Lenders, for whom $b_0 > 0$, benefit from a decline in the price level. They have more wealth and therefore tend to increase consumption and leisure. Borrowers, with $b_0 < 0$, lose from a decline in the price level and tend to reduce consumption and leisure.

We know that the aggregate effect from a decline in the price level on real bond holdings is nil because $B_0 = 0$. Our analysis also assumes that the increases in consumption and leisure for creditors balance the decreases for debtors. That is, we assume that the responses of creditors and debtors to changes in wealth are quantitatively about the same. In this case, we can neglect the distributional effects from price-level changes when we study the determinants of aggregate consumption and leisure. The distributional effects would, however, be central if we wanted to analyze the political pressures for changes in the price level: creditors would like lower price levels and debtors would like higher price levels.

Summary

We introduced a credit market on which people borrow and lend at the interest rate R. By using this market, individuals can choose a time pattern for consumption that differs from that for income.

We began with a budget constraint over two periods but then extended the analysis to any number of periods. For most purposes, we can think of the behaviour of households over an infinite horizon. We motivated the infinite planning period by thinking about a family in which parents care about their children, who care about their children, and so on.

An increase in the interest rate motivates households to shift away from consumption over the near term and toward that in the future. The opposite responses apply to work effort. These intertemporal-substitution effects mean that a higher interest rate motivates people to save more.

Improvements in the production function have wealth effects that are positive on consumption and negative on work for each period. If the shift is permanent, then the marginal propensity to consume is near one, and the marginal propensity to save is near zero. If the shift is temporary, then the marginal propensity to consume is small, and the marginal propensity to save is almost one. We also showed that a change in the interest rate has no aggregate wealth effect.

A permanent upward shift in the schedule for labour's marginal product raises work and consumption in each period but does not affect saving. In contrast, a temporary upward shift in the schedule raises current output by more than current consumption and thereby raises saving.

We incorporated the holdings of money into households' budget constraints over an infinite horizon. If the planned future holdings of real money equal the initial holding, then there is no impact on the sources of funds net of the uses. In these cases, we therefore do not have to worry about wealth effects from real money balances on the aggregates of consumer demand and leisure.

Important Terms and Concepts

barter
medium of exchange
nominal
currency
general price level
interest rate
principal of bond
saving
present value
real terms
marginal propensity to save
real-balance effect
perfect competition
bond
discount factor
budget line

intertemporal-substitution effect
planning horizon
life-cycle model
social security
infinite horizon
marginal propensity to consume
permanent income
real balance effect

Questions and Problems

Mainly for Review

4.1   Why would individuals be interested only in the real value of consumption expenditures, income, and assets such as money and bonds? Would a fall in the ECU amount of consumption spending leave the individual worse off when it is accompanied by an equiproportionate fall in the price level?

4.2   Distinguish clearly between an individual's initial asset position and the change in that position. Which is affected by current consumption and saving decisions? Is an individual who is undertaking negative saving necessarily a borrower in the sense of having a negative position in bonds?

4.3   Derive the two-period budget constraint, and draw a graph of it. Why are there no terms involving money holdings on the side of sources of funds?

4.4   Show how taking a present value involves giving different weights to ECU values in different periods. Why is income in the present more 'valuable' than income in the future? Why is consumption in the future 'cheaper' than consumption in the present?

4.5   Review the factors that determine an individual's choice of consumption over two periods, c_1 and c_2, and show this choice graphically. Why is the individual best off when the budget line is tangent to an indifference curve?

4.6   What factors determine whether the marginal propensity to consume is less than one or equal to one? Can the marginal propensity to consume be greater than one?

4.7   Review the effects of the following changes on current consumption and work, distinguishing clearly between wealth effects and substitution effects.
   a.   A permanent parallel shift of the production function.
   b.   A change in the interest rate.
   c.   A temporary change in the marginal product of labour.

Problems for Discussion

4.8   Discount Bonds
   The one-period bonds in our model pay a single interest payment or 'coupon' of εR and a principal of $\varepsilon 1$. Alternatively, we could consider a one-period discount bond. This type of asset has no coupons but pays a principal of $\varepsilon 1$ (or, more realistically, $\varepsilon 10\,000$) next period. Let P^B be the ECU price for each unit of discount bonds, where each unit is a claim to $\varepsilon 1$ next period.
   a.   Is P^B greater or less than $\varepsilon 1$?
   b.   What is the one-period rate of interest on discount bonds?
   c.   How does the price, P^B, relate to this one-period rate of interest?
   d.   Suppose that instead of coming due next period, the discount bond comes due (matures) two periods from now. What is the interest rate *per period* on this bond? How do the results generalize if the bond matures j periods from now?

4.9   Financial Intermediaries
   Consider a financial intermediary, such as a bank or savings and loan association, that enters the credit market. This intermediary borrows from some people and lends the proceeds to others. (The loan to a bank from its customers often takes the form of a *deposit*.)
   a.   How does the existence of intermediaries affect the result that the aggregate amount of loans is zero?
   b.   What interest rate would the intermediary charge to its borrowers and pay to its lenders? Why must there be some spread between these two rates?
   c.   Can you give some reasons to explain why intermediaries might be useful?

4.10   Wealth Effects
   Consider the household's budget constraint in real terms over an infinite horizon,

$$y_1 + y_2/(1+R) + \ldots + b_0(1+R)/P$$
$$= c_1 + c_2/(1+R) + \ldots .$$

   Using this condition, evaluate the wealth effect of the following:
   a.   An increase in the price level, P, for a household that has a positive value of initial bonds, b_0. (The result has implications for the effects of unexpected price changes on the wealth of nominal creditors and nominal debtors.)
   b.   An increase in the interest rate, R, for a household that has $b_0 = 0$ and $c_t = y_t$ in each period.
   c.   An increase in the interest rate, R, for a household that has $b_0 = 0$, $c_t > y_t$ for $t > T$, and $c_t < y_t$ for $t < T$, where T is some date in the future.

4.11   Short-Term and Long-Term Interest Rates
   Assume that $\varepsilon 1$ worth of one-period bonds issued at the end of period 0 pays out $\varepsilon(1 + R_1)$ during period 1 – that is, the principal of $\varepsilon 1$ plus the interest payment of εR_1. Assume that $\varepsilon 1$ worth of one-period bonds issued at the end of period 1 will pay out $\varepsilon(1 + R_2)$ during period 2. Suppose that people also market a two-period bond at the end of period 0. $\varepsilon 1$ worth of this asset pays out $\varepsilon(1 + 2R)$ during period 2. Lenders from date 0 to date 2 have the option of holding a two-period bond or a succession of one-period bonds. Borrowers have a similar choice between negotiating a two-period loan or two successive one-period loans.
   a.   What must be the relation of R to R_1 and R_2? Explain the answer from the standpoint of borrowers and lenders.
   b.   If $R_2 > R_1$, what is the relation between R (the current *long-term interest rate*) and R_1 (the current *short-term interest rate*)? The answer is an important result about the *term structure of interest rates*.

4.12 The Household's Budget Constraint with a Finite Horizon

Consider the household's budget constraint for j periods from equation (4.10):

$$Py_1 + Py_2/(1+R) + \ldots + Py_j/(1+R)^{j-1}$$
$$+ b_0(1+R)$$
$$= Pc_1 + Pc_2/(1+R) + \ldots + Pc_j/(1+R)^{j-1}$$
$$+ b_j/(1+R)^{j-1}$$

Assume that $y_t = 0$ for $t > T_1$, and $c_t = 0$ for $t > T_2$. Here, T_2 might represent the expected lifetime and T_1 the anticipated working span for an individual.

a. Assume that the household uses the planning horizon, $j = T_2$. Why might the household do this? What value would the household select for b_j? What does the j-period budget constraint look like in this case?

b. Discuss the pattern of saving, $b_t - b_{t-1}$, for the 'retirement period', where $T_1 < t < T_2$. What can be said about saving for the typical working year where $0 < t < T_1$? (This result concerns the *life-cycle* motivation for household saving.)

c. Suppose that the government forces people to retire earlier than they would otherwise choose. How would this action affect the choices of work effort, consumption, and desired saving for people who are still working but anticipating an earlier retirement?

d. Given that individuals care about their children (and parents), what difficulties arise in specifying a value for the finite planning horizon, $j = T_2$?

4.13 Permanent Income (optional)

The idea of permanent income is that consumption depends on a long-run measure of income rather than just on current income. Operationally, we can define permanent income to be the hypothetical, constant flow of income that has the same present value as a household's actual sources of funds.

a. Use the budget constraint in equation (4.12) to obtain a formula for permanent income. Explain the various terms in the formula.

b. What is the marginal propensity to consume out of permanent income?

c. If consumption is constant over time, what is the value of permanent income?

Notes

1. If we were to allow for uncertainty, the discount factor would not be equal to the interest rate. However, at this stage of the analysis, this is not an important issue, although it will play an important role later on.

2. This method comes from Irving Fisher (1930, especially Ch. 10).

3. Note that the household reaches a higher indifference curve. Hence, wealth increases, even though we rotated the budget line through the point at which the household initially chose consumption, (c_1^*, c_2^*). But it turns out that this wealth effect becomes negligible, relative to the substitution effect, when we look at smaller and smaller changes in the interest rate. So at least for small changes, we can neglect the wealth effect as a satisfactory approximation.

4. See Franco Modigliani and Richard Brumberg (1954) and Albert Ando and Franco Modigliani (1963).

5. We should not interpret the decision of increasing leisure following a decrease in the interest rate as a decision to quit working. The issue of quits, layoffs and other aspects of the labour market remain to be discussed later, in Chapter 13. A better real-life example has to do with the decision of working overtime, or of taking extra time off in the form of holidays.

6. Our findings about permanent and temporary changes of the production function correspond to Milton Friedman's (1957, Ch. 2, 3) concept of permanent income. The general idea is that consumption depends on a long-term average of incomes – called permanent income – rather than just current income. If the change in income is temporary, then permanent income and hence consumption rise relatively little. Hence, as in our earlier discussion, the marginal propensity to consume out of temporary income is small.

7. For further discussion of this result, see Martin J. Bailey (1971, pp. 106–8).

8. The effect has been stressed by many economists. See, for example, Gottfried Haberler (1939, especially Chs 8, 11), A. C. Pigou (1947), Don Patinkin (1948), and Robert Mundell (1971). Even if it may induce a positive wealth effect, a reduction in price level is not so welcome and it has been often seen as one of the major problems in the great depression.

5

The Basic Market-Clearing Model

In Chapter 2, we considered how isolated households chose their work effort and thereby their production of commodities. With no possibilities for trades with other households or for storing goods, production was equal to consumption for each household. In Chapters 3 and 4, we allowed people to buy and sell goods at the price P and to borrow and lend at the interest rate R. With these market opportunities, a household could save or dissave, so that consumption and production need not be equal in every period. The accumulation of saving over time determined a household's stock of financial assets, which could be held as money or bonds, and we studied how savings are allocated between these two assets.

In the discussion of a market economy in Chapter 3, we mentioned three conditions that must hold when we sum up over all households. First, since consumption is the only use for output in the model, total production, Y_t, equals total consumption, C_t. Second, because each ECU lent by someone on the credit market corresponds to a ECU borrowed by someone else, the aggregate stock of bonds, B_t, equals zero in every period. Finally, since the stock of money does not change over time, the total that people hold in each period, M_t, equals the given quantity, M_0. We shall refer to these three conditions as aggregate-consistency conditions.

Aggregate-Consistency Conditions and the Clearing of Markets

How do we know that the totals of individuals' choices satisfy the three aggregate-consistency conditions? For example, on the commodity market, individuals think that they can sell, or *supply*, a desired quantity of goods, and also buy, or *demand*, a desired quantity. We need something to guarantee that the total of commodities supplied equals the total demanded.

Similarly, on the credit market, each person thinks that he or she can borrow or lend any amount at the going interest rate, R. For a particular interest rate, there is no reason to think that the total of desired holding of bonds, B_t, would be zero. But then we have an inconsistency because the total that people want to borrow does not equal the total that others want to lend. One way or another, the credit market has to balance the overall amounts of borrowing and lending.

Finally, with respect to money, each person believes that he or she can hold the quantity that he or she demands. Yet somehow the total of these demands must equal the given aggregate quantity of money.

The classical solution is that the interest rate, R, and the price of commodities, P, adjust to ensure that

- the total of commodities supplied equals the total demanded,
- the total of desired holdings of bonds is zero, and
- the total of money demanded equals the aggregate quantity of money.

This viewpoint is called the market-clearing approach. In this approach the various prices, which are R and P in our model, adjust so that each market clears. By clearing we mean that the quantity supplied of each good – bonds, money, or commodities – equals the quantity demanded. When this condition holds simultaneously for every good, **general market clearing** applies.

When all markets clear, no one is unable to buy or sell commodities at the going price or unable to extend or receive credit at the going interest rate. Everyone can buy and sell as much as they want of each good at the market-clearing prices.

Recall that each household regards the interest rate, R, and the price level, P, as given. However, the aggregates of households' choices determine R and P to satisfy the market-clearing conditions. Hence, R and P cannot be independent of the aggregate of people's choices about bonds, money and commodities. But any individual's transactions are assumed to be a small fraction of the totals on any market. Therefore, as a good approximation, each person can disregard the effects of his or her behaviour on the market-clearing values of R and P. So we can continue to use the analyses of individual choices that we worked out in Chapters 3 and 4.

As mentioned before, we need to ensure that the three aggregate-consistency conditions hold. But why do we use market clearing to ensure these conditions? This device amounts to assuming that private markets function to allocate resources efficiently. When the markets clear, it is impossible to improve on any outcomes by matching potential borrowers and lenders or by bringing together potential buyers and sellers of commodities. Cleared markets already accomplish all of these *mutually advantageous trades*. Thus, the assumption that markets clear is tied closely to the view that the individuals who participate in and organize markets – and who are guided by the pursuit of their own interests – end up generating efficient outcomes.

We could use some concept other than market clearing to ensure that the aggregate-consistency conditions hold. One alternative is the Keynesian model, in which some markets do not clear in the sense of our concept of cleared markets. Rather, some prices are sticky, and some rationing of quantities comes into play. For example, households may be unable to sell all of the goods or labour services that they desire at the going price. We shall explore this viewpoint in Chapter 22. But the subtleties of Keynesian arguments cannot be appreciated without first understanding the workings of a market-clearing model. Therefore,

it is best to begin by studying a framework in which markets clear.

Economists often use the term *equilibrium* to signify market clearing. But because the concept of an equilibrium has been used in so many different ways in the economics literature, its meaning has become unclear. For example, some economists think of the Keynesian model as a *disequilibrium* framework, and others view it as a different concept of equilibrium. We shall avoid the terms equilibrium and disequilibrium in our discussion. But we should emphasize two ideas that are central to our thinking about markets. First, we have some aggregate-consistency conditions, which must be satisfied by any reasonable model. Second, we assume in most of the analysis that the interest rate and price level adjust to clear the markets. That is how we satisfy the aggregate-consistency conditions in the market-clearing model. We shall see later how the Keynesian model modifies the second idea but not the first one.

Walras' Law of Markets

Consider again a household that faces a given price level, P, and interest rate, R. Denote by y_1^s the quantity of goods that the household decides to produce and *supply* to the commodity market during period 1. By the amount supplied, we mean the quantity offered for sale at the going price. Similarly, let c_1^d represent the quantity of goods that a household offers to buy – or *demands* – from the commodity market. Finally, let b_1^d and m_1^d denote the household's planned stocks of financial assets for period 1 – that is, b_1^d is the demand for bonds and m_1^d is the demand for money.

Suppose that a household carries over from period 0 the stocks of financial assets, b_0 and m_0. Then the household's budget constraint in real terms for period 1 is

$$y_1^s + b_0(1 + R)/P + m_0/P = c_1^d + b_1^d/P + m_1^d/P$$

$$(5.1)$$

Summing up equation (5.1) over all households gives the aggregate form of the budget constraint for period 1:

$$Y_1^s + B_0(1 + R)/P + M_0/P$$
$$= C_1^d + B_1^d/P + M_1^d/P \qquad (5.2)$$

Since every ECU lent during period 0 must correspond to a ECU borrowed, we must have $B_0 = 0$. Using this condition and rearranging terms, equation (5.2) simplifies to

$$(C_1^d - Y_1^s) + (B_1^d/P) + (M_1^d/P - M_0/P) = 0 \qquad (5.3)$$

Equation (5.3) shows how the market-clearing model deals with the three aggregate-consistency conditions that we mentioned before. For period 1, these conditions are:

- $C_1^d = Y_1^s$ – the total demand for commodities equals the total supply,
- $B_1^d = 0$ – any ECU that someone wants to lend corresponds to a ECU that someone else wants to borrow,
- $M_1^d = M_0$ – people willingly hold the outstanding stock of money, M_0.

But look at equation (5.3). Suppose that the first two aggregate-consistency conditions hold – that is, $C_1^d = Y_1^s$ and $B_1^d = 0$. Then equation (5.3) guarantees that the third condition, $M_1^d = M_0$, holds also. In fact, if any two of the three conditions hold, then the third one must hold. Thus, we have to worry about satisfying only two of the three conditions for aggregate consistency. The third follows automatically from the aggregate form of households' budget constraints in equation (5.3). This result is called **Walras' Law of Markets**, in honour of the nineteenth-century French economist, Leon Walras, who pioneered the study of models under conditions of general market clearing. (Economists refer to his analysis as *general equilibrium theory*.)

We shall obtain the same results regardless of which pair of aggregate-consistency conditions that we examine. Macroeconomists typically look at the condition for clearing the commodity market, $C_1^d = Y_1^s$, and at the one for money to be willingly held, $M_1^d = M_0$. We shall find it

convenient to follow this practice. Remember, however, that the results would not change if we substituted for one of these conditions the condition that the credit market clear, $B_1^d = 0$.

Clearing the Commodity Market

We want to ensure that the aggregate quantity of commodities supplied, Y_1^s, equals the aggregate quantity demanded, C_1^d. We refer here to quantities for the current period, which is period 1, but it is convenient now to drop the time subscripts.

The previous analysis isolated several variables that influence the aggregate supply and demand for commodities, including the following:

- The interest rate, R: A higher rate implies intertemporal-substitution effects, which reduce current demand, C^d, and raise current supply, Y^s (by raising current work).
- Wealth effects from changes in the position of the production function: An increase in wealth raises demand, C^d, but lowers work effort. (This decline in work partially offsets the direct effect from an improvement in the production function on the supply of goods, Y^s.)
- Substitution effects from changes in the schedule for the marginal product of labour: An upward shift leads to an increase in supply, Y^s (because people work more), and an increase in demand, C^d.

We can write out the condition for clearing the commodity market during the current period as

$$Y^s(R, \ldots) = C^d(R, \ldots) \qquad (5.4)$$
$$(+) \qquad\quad (-)$$

The function Y^s refers to the aggregate supply of commodities and the function C^d refers to the aggregate demand. Later in the book aggregate demand will have other components, i.e. investment demand, government demand and net demand from abroad (or net export). We indicate explicitly only the effects of the interest rate in these functions. The omitted variables in the functions, denoted by . . ., include the wealth and substitution effects that arise from changes in the production function.

Equation (5.4) deals with the summation over a large number of households. We would like to use this analysis even when households are not identical – for example, when they differ by productivity, age, tastes, initial assets, and so on. In some cases, the aggregation over different types of people will not cause major problems. For example, a change in the interest rate implies the same type of intertemporal-substitution effect for everyone. We can also handle shifts in production functions when these shifts are similar for all producers. However, some changes benefit some people and harm others. For instance, we discussed before how move-

ments in the price level or the interest rate have positive or negative effects on wealth, depending on someone's status in the credit market. These types of changes shift the distribution of resources across households without changing the aggregate value of these resources. Economists call these kinds of changes **distributional effects**. However, we have no presumption about how distributional effects influence the aggregates of commodities supplied or demanded. So, as is customary in macroeconomics, we assume (hope) that we can neglect distributional effects for the purpose of aggregate analysis.

Recall some variables that do not influence aggregate supply and demand in equation (5.4). The aggregate quantity of bonds, B_0, is zero and therefore does not appear. We discussed in Chapter 4 the role of initial real money balances, M_0/P. We showed there that, as long

---

Box 5.1   Why Does the Price Level Not Affect Commodities Supplied and Demanded?

It seems odd that the price level, P, would not appear in the condition for clearing the commodity market, equation (5.4). Intuitively, we would expect a higher price of commodities to discourage demand and encourage supply. Let's think about what happens when P rises. The production function, $f(\ell)$, does not change. Therefore, given ℓ, a household's nominal income from sales of commodities, $P \cdot f(\ell)$, goes up along with P. But real income, $f(\ell)$ (obtained by dividing the nominal income by P), does not change. Since real income from production is the same, it is reasonable on this count that consumption demand and labour supply would not change.

We are also holding fixed the interest rate, R. Therefore, a once-and-for-all increase in the price level, P, does not affect the relative costs of consumption or leisure in different periods. That is, the change in P has no intertemporal-substitution effects.

For a given amount of nominal bonds, b_0, an increase in P would reduce the real amount,

b_0/P. This effect is bad for someone with positive bond holdings but correspondingly good for someone with negative bond holdings. The effect is nil in the aggregate because the total of bond holdings, B_0, is zero and because we neglect distributional effects.

Finally, the increase in P lowers M_0/P. Real wealth falls on this count, and households would respond by lowering consumer demand and raising labour supply. In Chapter 4 we called this mechanism the real-balance effect. We know, however, that in a position of general market clearing, households will be motivated to hold the existing money – that is, M_1^d/P will end up being the same as M_0/P. In this situation, we know from Chapter 4 that there will be no net wealth effect on consumption demand and labour supply. That is why we can ignore the real-balance effect when we think about positions of general market clearing. That is also why the price level, P, does not appear in equation (5.4).

as we consider only positions where $M_0/P = M_1^d/P$ – which will hold when we have general market clearing – the level of real money balances has no net wealth effect on consumption demand and labour supply. It follows that M_0/P – and the price level P itself – do not appear in equation (5.4).

Finally, we demonstrated in Chapter 4 that a change in the interest rate, R, has no aggregate wealth effect. (A rise in R is good for people who are usually lenders but correspondingly bad for those who are usually borrowers.) Therefore, the effects of R shown in equation (5.4) refer only to intertemporal-substitution effects. For this reason, we know that a rise in R lowers current consumer demand, C^d, and raises current commodity supply, Y^s.

Because the interest rate has important influences on commodities supplied and demanded, we shall find it convenient to depict equation (5.4) graphically with R on the vertical axis. Figure 5.1 shows that the interest rate has a positive effect on aggregate supply, Y^s, and a negative effect on aggregate demand, C^d. When R changes, the responses of supply and demand show up as *movements along the curves* in the figure. (We show the curves as straight lines only for convenience.)

The positions of the supply and demand curves in Figure 5.1 depend on the omitted elements, denoted by . . ., in equation (5.4). When any of these elements change – for example, because of a shift in the production function – the effects on commodity supply and demand show up as *shifts of the curves* in the figure. For given values of these elements, we can read off from the figure the value of the interest rate, R^*, that corresponds to the clearing of the commodity market, $Y^s = C^d$. Generally, we use an asterisk to signal that the value of a variable, such as $R = R^*$, derives from a market-clearing condition. Notice from the figure that the market-clearing level of output is the quantity $Y^* = C^*$.

Remember that each household's quantity of output, y, depends on the level of work, ℓ, through the production function, $y = f(\ell)$. We assume that we can use an aggregate form of this relation

$$Y = F(L) \qquad (5.5)$$

The aggregate production function connects the aggregate amount of work, L, to the aggregate quantity of output, Y. Once we know the market-clearing level of output Y^* from Figure 5.1, we can use equation (5.5) to compute the corresponding level of aggregate work effort, L^*.

The market-clearing diagram in Figure 5.1 is the central graphical tool for the subsequent study of macroeconomic disturbances. Even when we complicate the model, we shall be able to use a version of this diagram to derive the main results. It is therefore worth reviewing the basic ideas behind this diagram. First, a higher interest rate stimulates the desire to produce and sell goods today but deters the desire to buy goods. These forces underlie the upward slope of the supply curve and the downward slope of the demand curve. Second, we determine the market-clearing values of the interest rate and the quantity of output by equating aggregate supply to aggregate demand.

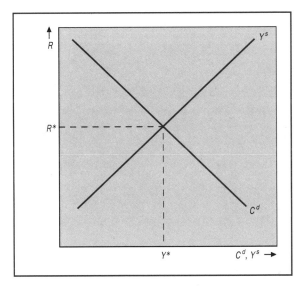

Clearing of the commodity market $C^d = Y^s$ occurs at the interest rate R^*. At this point the level of aggregate output is $Y^* = C^*$.

Figure 5.1 Clearing the commodity market

The Quantity of Money Equals the Quantity Demanded

The second aggregate-consistency condition requires the stock of money, M_0, to equal the aggregate quantity demanded during period 1, M_1^d. For convenience, we again drop the time subscripts.

In Chapter 3 we derived a function for the aggregate demand for money. When expressed in real terms – that is, as M^d/P – this demand depends negatively on the interest rate, R, and positively on the real amounts of spending, C, and income, Y. Therefore, we can write the condition for money to be willingly held as

$$M = P \cdot \Phi(R,\ Y, \ldots) \qquad (5.6)$$
$$(-)\ (+)$$

Note that the function, Φ, on the right side of equation (5.6) determines the demand for money in real terms, M^d/P. Therefore, $P \cdot \Phi(R, Y, \ldots)$ is

the nominal demand for money, M^d. For convenience, we include aggregate output, Y, as the measure of real transactions in the money-demand function. (Recall that $C = Y$ will apply in this model.) The omitted terms, denoted by . . ., include any effects on real money demanded other than the interest rate and the level of output. For example, transaction costs would enter here.

Figure 5.2 shows graphically the equality between the quantity of money and the quantity demanded. We shall find it convenient to put the price level, P, on the vertical axis. Then the quantity of money is the constant M, which appears as a vertical line in the figure. The nominal demand for money is $M^d = P \cdot \Phi(R, Y, \ldots)$. For given values of R and Y, this demand is directly proportional to P. Hence, we show it in the figure as a positively sloped straight line, starting from the origin. Notice that the quantity of money equals the quantity demanded when the price level is the value P^*.

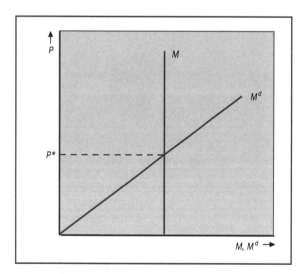

The nominal demand for money is $M^d = P \cdot \Phi(R, Y, \ldots)$. For given values of Y and R this demand is a straight line starting from the origin. The nominal quantity of money is the constant M. The amount of money demanded equals the quantity of money when the price level is the value P^*.

Figure 5.2   The demand for money equals the quantity of money

General Market Clearing

We want to determine the values of the interest rate, R^*, and the price level, P^*, that are consistent with the two aggregate-consistency conditions:

- the commodity market clears, as in Figure 5.1, and
- the quantity of money equals the quantity demanded, as in Figure 5.2.

Remember from Walras' Law that these two conditions ensure that the credit market clears, $B^d = 0$. Thus, it is appropriate to refer to R^* and P^* as the general-market-clearing values of the interest rate and the price level.

We can readily see the basic workings of the model. The market-clearing diagram from Figure 5.1 determines the interest rate, R^*, and the level of aggregate output, Y^*. We can substitute the values for R^* and Y^* into the money-demand function on the right side of equation (5.6). Then for a given quantity of money, M, Figure 5.2

determines the general-market-clearing value of the price level, P^*.

The procedure for solving the model is this simple because the price level does not appear in equation (5.4), which is the condition for clearing the commodity market. To put it another way, changes in P do not shift the curves in Figure 5.1. For this reason, we do not have to know the general-market-clearing value of the price level, P^*, when we determine the interest rate, R^*. We can just look at Figure 5.1 to determine R^*. Then, conditional on this result, we can use equation (5.6) and Figure 5.2 to solve out for P^*. The best way to clarify the workings of the model is to work through some examples, which are of substantial interest for their own sake.

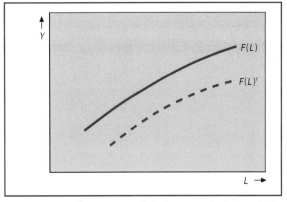

We examine here a parallel downward shift of the production function from $F(L)$ to $F(L)'$.

Figure 5.3 A parallel downward shift of the production function

Supply Shocks

Economists use the term **supply shocks** to refer to sudden changes in the conditions of production. Adverse effects include harvest failures, strikes, natural disasters, epidemics, and political disruptions. The most important recent examples of supply shocks are the oil crises of 1973–74 and 1979, and to a lesser extent 1990. In fact, most economists became interested in supply shocks only after these dramatic changes in the market for oil.

For some reason, the term 'supply shock' always refers to a negative effect on the supply of goods. But there can also be positive developments, such as technical innovations, bountiful harvests, or the sharp reduction in the price of oil in 1986. Our analysis applies to either favourable or unfavourable changes in productive conditions. As in some previous discussion, however, we shall find it important to distinguish temporary from permanent changes.

A Temporary Shift of the Production Function

Start with a temporary adverse change to the production function, say a shift that lasts for only the current period. As examples, we can think of the drought of 1988 that limited US agricultural

output and coal strikes that lowered production in Great Britain.

Consider first a purely parallel downward shift of the production function, as shown in Figure 5.3. This case is the simplest example of a supply shock because it does not alter the schedule for the marginal product of labour. Hence, there are no substitution effects from changes in the relative costs of consumption and leisure.

Effects on the Interest Rate and Output

One effect of the supply shock is that output decreases for a given level of work effort. On this count, the supply of goods, Y^s, falls.

Second, the disturbance reduces wealth. Because the change is short-lived, the wealth effects are small: we predict a small decrease of aggregate consumer demand, C^d, and a small increase of aggregate work effort. The increase in work implies a rise in goods supplied, Y^s. But since the wealth effect is weak, this increase offsets only a small part of the initial cutback in supply. Thus, the net effect is a decrease in aggregate supply, Y^s, which exceeds the small decline in aggregate demand, C^d.

Figure 5.4 shows the changes to the commodity market. Before the shift, the market cleared at the interest rate R^*. Then the disturbance causes the aggregate supply curve to shift leftward from the one labelled Y^s to that labelled $(Y^s)'$. At the same time, the aggregate demand curve shifts leftward from the one marked C^d to that marked $(C^d)'$. As discussed before, the shift of the supply curve is larger than that of the demand curve. Hence, there is **excess demand** for commodities – $(C^d)' > (Y^s)'$ – at the initial interest rate R^*. (In the opposite situation – a temporary favourable shift of the production function – there would be excess supply of commodities.)

The excess of goods demanded over those supplied means that – at the going interest rate – everybody would like to reduce their saving or borrow more. That is because the worsening of the production function is temporary. Instead of cutting their consumption, individuals would like to absorb most of their temporarily depressed income by reducing current saving or by increasing current borrowing. People plan to repay their debts or build up their assets later when income is higher. But we know that everybody cannot reduce their saving or increase borrowing because aggregate saving must end up being zero. The interest rate has to adjust to make the aggregate of desired saving conform to the economy's

possibilities: zero total saving. To put this point another way, the interest rate must change to clear the commodity market.

Figure 5.4 shows that the new interest rate, $(R^*)'$, exceeds the initial one, R^*. This rise in the interest rate eliminates people's desires to carry out negative aggregate saving. Equivalently, the increase in the interest rate lowers the quantity of goods demanded along the curve $(C^d)'$ and raises the quantity supplied along the curve $(Y^s)'$. At the new interest rate, $(R^*)'$, the commodity market again clears – that is, $(Y^s)' = (C^d)'$.

The new level of output, $(Y^*)'$, can be read off the intersection of the new supply and demand curves in Figure 5.4. Notice that the disturbance – the temporary worsening of the production function – leads to a fall in output. From the perspective of commodity demand, $(C^d)'$, it is clear that output must be lower: the decrease in wealth shifts the demand curve leftward and the increase in the interest rate reduces the quantity demanded along the new curve, $(C^d)'$. It follows that aggregate demand – and hence output, which equals the quantity demanded – must decline overall.

From the standpoint of commodity supply, $(Y^s)'$, there is the initial leftward shift of the curve. Then the rise in the interest rate raises the amount supplied along the curve $(Y^s)'$. This increase in quantity supplied only partially offsets the initial decrease because supply and demand are again equal at the new interest rate, $(R^*)'$, and we have just shown that the quantity demanded is lower.

Effects on Work Effort

The forces that operate on work effort are closely related to those that affect consumer demand. The decline in wealth raises work and lowers leisure and the rise in the interest rate reinforces these effects. Consequently, aggregate work effort rises and aggregate leisure declines. This result makes sense because the disturbance does not change the terms on which people can transform leisure into consumption – that is, the schedule for labour marginal product does not shift. If the quantities of consumption and leisure change, then we would expect them to change in the same

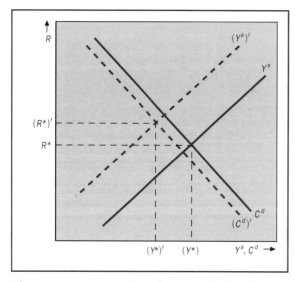

The temporary worsening of the production function lowers aggregate supply by more than demand. Therefore clearing of the commodity market requires the interest rate to rise.

Figure 5.4   Effect of a supply shock on the commodity market

direction. In the present example, the aggregates of consumption and leisure both decrease.

The supply shock leads overall to less output and consumption, but to more work. Recall from the analysis in Chapter 2 that we reached similar conclusions when we confronted Robinson Crusoe with a downward shift of the production function. We might have expected some differences because people can use the credit market to borrow and lend in the present model, whereas Robinson Crusoe could not borrow and lend. But the interest rate adjusts in the market economy to ensure that the aggregate of desired saving is zero. The typical person therefore ends up saving zero, just like Robinson Crusoe. For this reason, we end up with similar predictions about the effects of a worsening of the production function on work effort, production, and consumption.

Remember from Chapter 1 that the reductions in output during recessions are regularly accompanied by declines in labour input, measured by employment or worker-hours. That is, labour input is a strongly procyclical variable. The present example does not fit this pattern because work effort moves in the direction opposite to output. We shall find below that we can get the 'right' pattern for work effort by allowing for a shift to the schedule for labour marginal product.

Effects on the Price Level
To determine the price level, we use the condition that all money be willingly held. Recall that this condition is

$$M = P \cdot \Phi\,(R, \quad Y, \ldots)$$
$$\quad\quad\quad (-)\ \ (+)$$

We know that the disturbance lowers aggregate output and raises the interest rate. Both changes reduce the real demand for money, which appears on the right side of the equation. Therefore, Figure 5.5 shows that the demand for money shifts leftward from the line labelled M^d to that labelled $(M^d)'$. Notice that the price level rises from the initial value P^* to the higher value $(P^*)'$. This change is necessary to restore equality between the amount of money demanded and the fixed quantity of money, M.

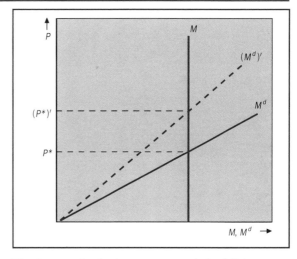

The increase in the interest rate and the fall in output imply a leftward shift to money demand. The price level rises from P^* to $(P^*)'$ to restore equality between the amount of money demanded and the fixed quantity of money M.

Figure 5.5   Effect of a supply shock on the price level

Note that shifts to the production function lead to movements in opposite directions for output and the price level – for example, an adverse shock lowers output and raises the price level. Recall from Chapter 1 that the general price level was, in fact, a countercyclical variable, at least from 1954 to 1991. The theoretical results therefore accord in this respect with the empirical pattern.

We can use the analysis to understand the effects on the price level from the oil crises of the last twenty years. Sharp increases in the price of oil, relative to that of other goods, occurred in 1973–74, 1979–81, and in August 1990 with the start of the Persian Gulf crisis. Although oil crises do not directly affect production opportunities, the effects on most industrialized countries' businesses resemble those from downward shifts to production functions. Because oil is an important input to production, a cutback in the supply of oil – as reflected in an increase in its relative price – tends to deter the production of other goods. In addition, an increase in oil's relative price means that oil-importing countries, such as most of the industrialized countries, pay out more of their income to foreigners per unit of oil purchased. Therefore, for a given amount of work effort and production, an oil-importing country ends up with less income to spend on consumption.

Overall, the oil crises created adverse shifts of the type shown in Figure 5.4. (These changes apply if people perceived the increase in oil's relative price to be temporary.) Then we find that output falls, the interest rate rises, and the real demand for money declines. Hence, for a given quantity of money, the general price level increases. By similar reasoning, we find that the reductions in the relative price of oil in 1983–84, in 1986, and in 1991 after the end of the Persian Gulf War helped to hold down the overall level of prices in most countries.

We should not conclude that an increase in the relative price of any commodity leads to a rise in the general price level. By the general price level, we mean the number of ECUs that it takes to buy a typical market basket of goods. This general level of prices can move up or down while some relative prices increase and some decrease. As an example, consider a poor year for wine grapes that affects all countries but not France. The price of wine rises relative to the price of other goods. From the standpoint of France as an exporter of wine, the disturbance amounts to a temporary upward shift of the production function. Hence, there is an increase in real money demanded, which leads to a decline of the overall price level in France.

The Dynamics of Changes in the Interest Rate and the Price Level

We have figured out how a particular disturbance, such as a temporary worsening of the production function, changes the general-market-clearing values of the interest rate and the price level. We know that the aggregate-consistency conditions will not be satisfied unless we get to the new position of general market clearing. But we have not really explained how R and P move from one position of market clearing to another.

We mentioned before that a temporary worsening of the production function makes everyone want to save less at the initial interest rate. This decline in offers to lend funds relative to the offers to borrow tends to bid up the interest rate on loans. This reaction is consistent with the increase in the market-clearing value of the interest rate.

We noted also that the disturbance creates excess demand for commodities. It seems reasonable that suppliers would react to this excess demand by raising the price, P, at which they are willing to sell. This response accords with the increase in the market-clearing value of the price level.

The above sketch suggests that some plausible stories about market pressures would lead the economy toward the new position of general market clearing. Economists have, in fact, constructed some elaborate models of these dynamics. But it remains true that economists do not understand these processes very well. For one thing, it is difficult to explain how people behave while the aggregate-consistency conditions do not hold.[1] But if we look only at positions in which these conditions hold, then we limit our attention to situations of general market clearing.

In the subsequent analysis, we focus on the characteristics of market-clearing positions. Along the way, we sometimes provide dynamic stories to motivate the changes in the price level and the interest rate. But these stories should be treated with caution since they do not correspond to fully worked-out models. Our main propositions about the real world come from seeing how particular disturbances influence the conditions for general market clearing. This method usually provides answers that accord well with real-world observations. From an empirical standpoint, therefore, the lack of a formal dynamic theory of price changes may not be that much of a shortcoming.

Summarizing the Results

Let's review our findings for a temporary worsening of the production function. We found that this disturbance leads to cutbacks in output and consumption but to a rise in work effort. The interest rate and the price level rise.

Consider why the interest rate rises. Because everyone regards the fall in output as temporary, they would like to borrow funds to maintain their levels of consumption. Since not everyone can borrow at once, the interest rate increases to restore the balance between desired borrowing and lending. Anyone who lends funds in this depressed situation receives a premium in terms of a high rate of interest.

Consider why the price level rises. The decline in current consumption and output, combined with the rise in the interest rate, reduce the real demand for money. Because the quantity of money is fixed, the price level must rise for the amount of money demanded to equal this fixed quantity.

Including a Shift to the Schedule for the Marginal Product of Labour

We have just studied an example in which the production function shifted downward in a parallel fashion. In the typical case, however, the cutback in the production function would be accompanied by a worsening in the schedule for labour marginal product. There may, for example, be a proportional downward shift of the production function, as shown in Figure 5.6: in this case, the marginal product of labour falls at a given level of work effort. We assume again that the change to the production function applies only for the current period – that is, people still perceive the disturbance to be temporary.

We again have the changes to the commodity market shown in Figure 5.4, but we have to add some new effects that concern the decrease in labour marginal product. We discuss here *only* these new effects. The fall in productivity induces people to work less today and to increase current leisure and consumption. Because the worsening in production opportunities is temporary, people also want to shift toward current leisure and away from future leisure and consumption. That is, an intertemporal-substitution effect reinforces the reduction in today's work effort. The overall reduction in current work implies a reduction in the current supply of goods, Y^s, and a corresponding decline in current income. Households spread this fall in today's income over reductions in current and future consumption and future leisure. Current consumer demand, C^d, therefore

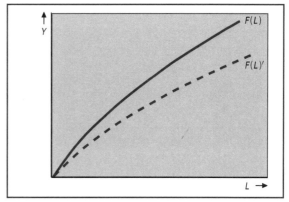

We examine here a proportional downward shift of the production function from $F(L)$ to $F(L)'$.

Figure 5.6 Proportional downward shift of the production function

decreases, but by only a small amount relative to the cut in current income.

To incorporate the new effects, we have to make modifications to Figure 5.4. First, we add a leftward shift to the supply curve, $(Y^s)'$. Second, we add a smaller leftward shift to the demand curve, $(C^d)'$. Notice that these changes do not alter the general configuration of the curves shown in Figure 5.4. Hence, we still conclude that output and consumption decrease and the interest rate rises. Because of the fall in the schedule for labour marginal product, these effects are all larger than before.

The only qualitative difference in the results concerns the behaviour of work effort. We found before that work effort increased. Recall that this response reflected the decrease in wealth and the increase in the interest rate. But now people want to work less because of the fall in the marginal product of labour (MPL). Hence, it is now uncertain whether work effort rises or falls on net.

Think of this last result again in terms of a harvest failure. People want to work a lot today because output is low (the wealth effect) and because the interest rate is high (the intertemporal-substitution effect). But if the harvest failure makes additional labour today relatively unproductive, then people prefer to take leisure instead of work. People work less on net if the

---

Box 5.2   Supply Shocks and the Interest Rate in Nineteenth-Century France

David Denslow and Mark Rush (1989) studied the effects of agricultural harvests on French interest rates over the period 1828 to 1869. This sample was attractive for several reasons: agriculture was a major part of output (roughly 50%), short-term fluctuations in agricultural output reflect mainly the influence of weather (which is a force from outside the economy and is therefore easy to interpret), the French economy had some aspects of an economy without international trade (as in our theoretical model), and good data are available. Denslow and Rush found that a temporary shortfall of wheat production had a statistically significant, inverse effect on the long-term interest rate in France: a 10% decline in the output of wheat raised the interest rate by 0.1 percentage point above the comparable interest rate in England. Thus, these results are consistent with our theoretical analysis.

---

dominant effect is this substitution between work and leisure – the main concern then is to work relatively little when productivity is low, but to work hard and long when productivity is high. Labour input is then low along with output in response to an adverse shock and high along with output in response to a favourable shock. Recall from Chapter 1 that economies exhibit this procyclical pattern for labour input.

When we look at the condition that money be willingly held, as shown in equation (5.6) and Figure 5.5, we again find that the disturbance raises the price level. Because output and the interest rate move by more than before, we conclude that the increase in the price level is greater than previously.

A Permanent Shift of the Production Function

Return to the case of a parallel downward shift of the production function, for which labour marginal product does not change. But suppose now that this change is permanent rather than lasting for just one period.

The difference from the previous case concerns the size of the wealth effects. There is now a strong negative effect on consumer demand. Also, there is a strong positive effect on work effort, so that the supply of goods falls by less than before. Recall that our analysis in Chapter 4 showed that a permanent shift in the production function had

little effect on desired saving: people do not want to borrow more today because future income will be just as low as current income. It follows, for a given interest rate, that the decreases in commodities supplied and demanded would be roughly equal. We use the market-clearing diagram in Figure 5.7 to illustrate this case. Notice that the

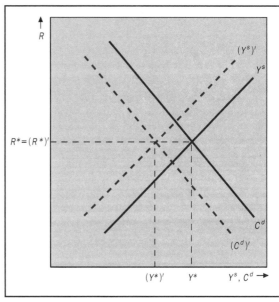

The permanent worsening of the production function reduces aggregate supply and demand by comparable amounts. Therefore the interest rate does not change.

Figure 5.7   Effect of a permanent downward shift of the production function on the commodity market

leftward shifts to the supply and demand curves are the same. Commodity supply still equals commodity demand at the initial interest rate, R^*, and the new market-clearing interest rate, $(R^*)'$, equals R^*.

Output and consumption again decline. Since the interest rate does not change, the reduction in consumer demand now reflects only the decrease in wealth. Similarly, the fall in wealth implies an increase in work effort.

Since output declines and the interest rate does not change, we know that real money demanded declines. We can therefore still use Figure 5.5 to see that the price level rises. Overall, the results for output and the price level resemble those that we found before when the change in the production function was temporary.

The major difference in results is the rise in the interest rate when the worsening of the production function is temporary but no change when the worsening is permanent. The interest rate is a signal that tells people the cost of using resources now rather than later. Specifically, a high interest rate attaches a high cost to current consumption and leisure, relative to future consumption and leisure. When the production function declines temporarily, there is a scarcity of goods today relative to the future. A high interest rate makes sense in this situation because it makes people take today's relative scarcity into account when they decide how much to consume and work. Conversely, a permanent worsening of the production function means that fewer goods are available at all times; there is no shift in today's position relative to tomorrow's. The interest rate stays the same because there is no change in the cost of using resources today rather than tomorrow.

The results tell us something important about movements in interest rates. Interest rates change when there are economic disturbances that alter present conditions relative to prospective ones. Harvest failures, natural disasters, and major strikes fall into this category. As we stress in a later chapter, war may be empirically the most important example of a disturbance that has a temporary effect on the overall economy. In contrast, we do not predict that permanent shocks will generate large changes in interest rates. (*Warning*: The analysis has so far left out two important influences on interest rates: inflation and shifts to investment demand. We study inflation in Chapters 8 and 10 and investment in Chapter 13.)

As before, we can also include a downward shift to the schedule for the marginal product of labour. This extension does not change most of the results. We still predict that a permanent decline of the production function has no effect on the interest rate. As in the analysis of a temporary shift, the response of work effort is ambiguous. That is because the reduction in wealth motivates more work, and the fall in labour marginal product motivates less work. Work effort again falls along with output if the dominant effect is the shift in labour productivity.

Changes in the Stock of Money

In the previous examples, we deduced the change in the price level by examining the condition that money be willingly held. We found that changes in output and the interest rate altered the demand for real money balances. Then the price level changed to equate the nominal quantity of money demanded to the given nominal quantity of money. Essentially, we have dealt with changes in the demand for money while holding fixed the aggregate supply of nominal money, M.

Many economists have argued that changes in the quantity of money, M, are empirically the major source of variations in the price level. To study this linkage, we have to allow for changes in the stock of money. Therefore, we now construct a simple device that enables us to study these changes.

Think of a case in which the initial stock of money, M_0, and all subsequent stocks, M_t for $t > 0$, rise by the same amount. We consider, in other words, a permanent increase in the quantity of money. This change would arise if the government, on a one-time-only basis, printed up some extra money and gave it to people. In Chapters 8 and 9 we shall examine more realistic ways in which new money gets into the economy.

The condition for clearing the commodity market, $Y^s(R, \ldots) = C^d(R, \ldots))$, does not involve the level of the money stock, M. Therefore, we know right away that the change in the number of ECU bills outstanding does not alter the market-clearing value of the interest rate, R^*, or the levels of output and consumption, $Y^* = C^*$.

Consider again the condition that the money stock be willingly held:

$$M = P \cdot \Phi (R, \; Y, \ldots)$$
$$(-) \; (+)$$

Since the interest rate and the level of output do not change, there is no change in the real demand for money, $\Phi(R, Y, \ldots)$, which appears on the right side of the equation. Therefore, the line labelled M^d in Figure 5.8 does not shift. The figure shows, however, that the nominal quantity of money increases from M to M'. It follows that the price level rises from P^* to $(P^*)'$. In order for the change in the nominal amount of money demanded, M^d, to equal the change in the quantity of money, the price level must rise by the same proportion as the money stock. In other words, the real quantity of money, M/P, does not change. This result makes sense because the real amount of money demanded, $\Phi(R, Y, \ldots)$, also does not change.

We can, as before, outline a dynamic story that makes plausible the increase in the price level. At the initial level of prices, households have more money than they wish to hold and they therefore try to spend the excess money on goods, leisure, and bonds. (The increased demand for bonds corresponds to the heightened demand for future goods and leisure.) These responses represent the real-balance effect. Remember that this effect operates when − as at present − households have more money than they plan to hold in the future. Since the real-balance effect raises the aggregate demand for goods above the supply, there is upward pressure on the price level.[2] Further, this increase in prices continues until the outstanding amount of money is willingly held. At this point, households no longer have excess money that they wish to spend, and there is no further pressure for the price level to rise.

The Neutrality of Money

The results exhibit an important property that is called the **neutrality of money**. Once-and-for-all changes in the aggregate quantity of money affect nominal variables but leave real variables unchanged. For example, if the money stock doubles, then the price level doubles, as does the nominal value of production and consumption, $PY = PC$. But no changes occur in the real variables, which include output and consumption, $Y = C$, real money balances, M/P, and the quantity of work, L. The interest rate, R, also does not change. We should think of the interest rate as a real variable: it signals the cost of buying consumption or leisure today rather than tomorrow. In later chapters, we explore further aspects of monetary neutrality.

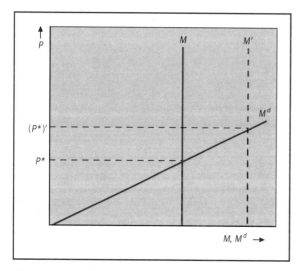

The quantity of money rises from M to M'. In order for this money to be willingly held the price level rises from P^* to $(P^*)'$.

Figure 5.8 Effect of a change in the stock of money

The Quantity Theory of Money and Monetarism

The **quantity theory of money** refers to a body of thinking about the relation between money and prices. This viewpoint goes back hundreds of years, with some of the most interesting statements coming from David Hume, Henry Thornton, and Irving Fisher.[3] There are two common elements in these analyses. First, changes in the quantity of money have a positive effect on the general price level. Second, as an empirical matter, movements in the money stock account for the major longer-run movements in the price level.

Some writers refined the quantity theory to apply to changes in the stock of money relative to changes in the quantity of goods on which people could spend their money. The last element corresponds in our model to the total output of goods, Y. But output is only one variable that affects the demand for real money balances. To go further, some quantity theorists stress that the price level increases when the quantity of money rises in relation to the real balances that people want to hold. Hence, most movements in prices would reflect movements in money if the variations in the nominal quantity of money are much greater than the fluctuations in the demand for real money balances.[4]

Sometimes economists identify the quantity theory of money with the statement that monetary changes are neutral. Then we have our previous proposition that shifts in the stock of money have proportional effects on the price level but no effects on real variables. Many quantity theorists regard this hypothesis as accurate in the long run but not for short-run variations in money. The quantity theory allows for the possibility that fluctuations in money have temporary effects on real economic activity. At this point, our model does not admit these short-run real effects of money, but we shall reexamine this matter in later chapters.

More recently, economists and journalists have used the term **monetarism** to describe a school of thought that is similar to modern versions of the quantity theory of money. As with most other terms that are common in the popular press, this one has been used in contradictory ways. But it is clear that monetarists regard the quantity of money as the major determinant of the price level, especially over the long run. Thus, monetarists stress control of the money supply as the central requirement for price stability. Also, monetarism allows for important short-term effects of monetary fluctuations on real economic activity. But monetarists typically regard these effects as unpredictable. Therefore, they argue that stable money is the best policy for avoiding erratic movements of the real variables.[5]

Changes in the Demand for Money

As mentioned, we can determine the price level by looking at the condition that money be willingly held:

$$M = P \cdot \Phi(R, \ Y, \ldots)$$
$$(-) \ (+)$$

We have just studied changes in the money stock: shifts in the quantity of money change the price level in the same direction. Earlier, we examined disturbances to the production function, which ended up changing output, Y, and the interest rate, R. With the money stock held constant, these changes affect the price level by shifting the real demand for money. Notice that the price level moves in the direction opposite to changes in the real demand for money.

An economy may experience changes in the demand for money that do not reflect movements in output or the interest rate. For example, in our model of the demand for money from Chapter 3, there may be changes in the cost of transacting between interest-bearing assets and money. These costs have declined significantly in recent years with the development of money-market funds, automated bank tellers, and other financial innovations. We predict that these types of changes reduce the demand for real money balances.

To represent this type of change, suppose that the real demand function for money, $\Phi(R, Y, \ldots)$, shifts leftward, as shown in Figure 5.9. The result is that the price level must rise for the nominal amount of money demanded to remain equal to the given nominal quantity, M. Hence, we predict

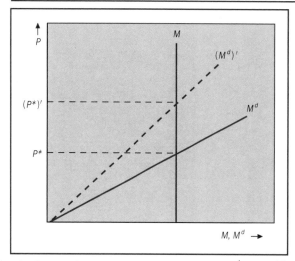

The demand for money shifts leftward from M^d to $(M^d)'$. The price level rises from P^* to $(P^*)'$ to restore equality between the amount of money demanded and the fixed quantity of money M.

Figure 5.9   Effect of a decrease in the demand for money on the price level

that the financial innovations of recent years – which reduced the demand for real money balances – raise the price level for a given behaviour of the nominal quantity of money. Notice also that these innovations lead to a lower level of real money balances, M/P.

In our model the change in the real demand for money – and the resulting change in real money balances – do not influence the condition for clearing the commodity market, $Y^s(R, \ldots) = C^d(R, \ldots)$. Therefore, these changes do not affect the market-clearing values of output or the interest rate.

Summary

Any macroeconomic model must satisfy some conditions for aggregate consistency. In our context these are, first, total output equals total consumption; second, any ECU that someone lends corresponds to a ECU that someone else borrows; and third, people hold the outstanding stock of money. We use the idea of market clearing to satisfy these conditions – the supply of commodities equals the demand, the aggregate demand for bonds is zero, and the amount of money demanded equals the quantity outstanding.

The households' budget constraints imply that the three aggregate-consistency conditions are not independent. Walras' Law says that we can use any two of the three conditions. We focus on the condition for clearing the commodity market – that the supply of commodities equals the demand – and on the condition that the stock of money be willingly held.

We constructed a market-clearing diagram to show how the condition for clearing the commodity market determines the interest rate and the level of output. The condition that money be willingly held determines the price level for a given nominal quantity of money.

We use the market-clearing apparatus to analyze supply shocks, which we represent as shifts to the production function. A temporary adverse shock lowers output, raises the interest rate and price level, and has an ambiguous effect on work effort. When the unfavourable shift to the production function is permanent rather than temporary, the main difference is that the interest rate does not increase. That is because a higher interest rate signals the scarcity of goods today relative to later. When things get permanently worse, there is no reason for the interest rate to change.

Shifts in the nominal quantity of money are neutral in the model: the price level changes in the same proportion as money, but no real variables change. Shifts to the demand for money change the price level in the opposite direction. The only real variable that changes in this case is the quantity of real money balances.

Important Terms and Concepts

general market clearing
Walras' Law of Markets
distributional effects
supply shock
excess demand
excess supply
neutrality of money
quantity theory of money
monetarism

Questions and Problems

Mainly for Review

5.1 How are transactions in different markets, such as consumption and borrowing, linked in individual budget constraints? How does Walras' Law show that this linkage carries over to the markets as a whole?

5.2 How does a change in (a) the interest rate, (b) wealth, and (c) the production function affect the aggregate demand and supply of commodities? Describe the effects graphically, making sure to distinguish between *shifts in* and *movements along* the demand and supply curves.

5.3 Why is a change in the price level not effective in reducing excess demand or supply in the commodity market? Explain how a change in the price level can ensure that the outstanding quantity of money is held willingly.

5.4 Consider a parallel upward shift of the production function, which raises the aggregate supply of commodities. Use a graph to convince yourself that:
  a. If consumption demand shifts by an equivalent amount, then the interest rate does not change.
  b. If consumption demand shifts by a smaller amount, then the interest rate declines.

5.5 Describe your results in question 5.4 in terms of the marginal propensity to consume. Which of the two possibilities is likely to hold when the shift in the production function is temporary?

5.6 What is meant by the neutrality of money? Explain its implications for the popular notion that an increase in the quantity of money reduces the interest rate.

5.7 Consider a decline in the transaction cost of converting financial assets into money. Describe its effect on (a) the price level, (b) the real quantity of money, and (c) velocity. Do these effects contradict the neutrality of monetary changes?

Problems for Discussion

5.8 Walras' Law of Markets
  a. Show how to derive Walras' Law of Markets (equation [5.3]) by using the households' budget constraints.
  b. We seem to have three independent conditions for aggregate consistency: zero aggregate demand for bonds, $B_1^d = 0$; the money stock is willingly held, $M_0 = M_1^d$; and equality between commodities supplied and demanded, $Y_1^s = C_1^d$. Walras' Law says that only two of these conditions are independent. Explain this result.
  c. How do the number of independent conditions for aggregate consistency compare with the number of market prices that we have to determine in the model? By the term *market prices*, we mean to include both the price level, P, and the interest rate, R. (The interest rate is the price of credit.)
  d. Write out Walras' Law in the form of a sum of aggregate excess demands, $C^d - Y^s$, $M_1^d/P - M_0/P$, and B_1^d/P. What does the law say in this form?

5.9 Effects of a Change in Population
  Assume a one-time decrease in population, possibly caused by an onset of plague or a sudden out-migration. The people who left are the same as those who remain in terms of productivity and tastes. The aggregate quantity of money does not change.
  What happens to aggregate output, Y, work effort, L, the interest rate, R, and the price level, P?

5.10 Effects of a Change in the Willingness to Work
  Suppose (in a magical, unexplained fashion) that all households change their preferences to favour consumption over leisure. That is, people raise their willingness to work. Assume that no change occurs in preferences for expenditures now versus later, so that aggregate desired saving does not change at the initial interest rate.
  What happens to aggregate output, Y, work effort, L, the interest rate, R, and the price level, P? Can you think of some real-world events that might raise everybody's willingness to work?
  (*Note*: We will be in trouble if we permit unrestricted fluctuations in preferences. A basic strength of the economic approach – and the basis for forming hypotheses that we can conceivably reject from observed data – is the assumption of stable tastes. Then we can analyze changes to production possibilities and other disturbances in terms of wealth and substitution effects, as we did in the text. In this manner, we end up with predictable influences on observable variables, such as output and the price level. But if tastes are unstable, then we

can reconcile any observed behaviour by invoking the appropriate shift in unobservable preferences. This capacity for explaining all data means that the model has no predictive value. Also, unaccountable shifts in preferences are more plausible for an individual than for the aggregate of households. Usually there is no good reason for everyone to become more eager to work at precisely the same time.)

5.11 Effects of a Shift in Desired Saving
Suppose that all households increase their preference for current expenditures over future expenditures. In particular, desired saving declines at a given value of the interest rate.

What happens to aggregate output, Y, work effort, L, the interest rate, R, and the price level, P? (The note attached to problem 5.10 applies also to the change in tastes assumed in this problem.)

5.12 Temporary Changes in the Price Level
Consider again the analysis of a temporary worsening of the production function (Figures 5.4 and 5.5). We showed that the price level rises from its initial value, P^*, to a higher value, $(P^*)'$. But since the disturbance is temporary, the price level would return in later periods to the initial value, P^*. At least, this would happen if nothing else changes, including the quantity of money.

So far, the analysis assumes that people expect the price level to remain constant over time. But we just showed that the current price level is above its expected future values when there is a temporary worsening of the production function. Think about how to modify the analysis to take account of expected future changes in the price level. (Do not spend too much time on this problem, since we shall study this topic in detail in Chapters 8 and 10.)

5.13 Consumption, Saving, and the Interest Rate (optional)
According to the theory, an increase in the interest rate motivates people to reduce current consumption relative to current income. Correspondingly, people increase current saving. Yet although a temporary downward shift of the production function leads to an increase in the interest rate, it does not lead to any change in the ratio of aggregate consumption to aggregate income (which equals one in this model). Also, there is no change in aggregate saving, which equals zero.
a. Explain these results.
b. Researchers often attempt to estimate the effects of a change in the interest rate on an individual's choices of consumption and saving. Many studies look at the relation between the interest rate and either the ratio of aggregate consumption to aggregate income or the amount of aggregate saving. What does the theory predict for this

relation? Why does it not reveal the effect of a change in the interest rate on an individual's desire to consume and save?
c. The theory says that an increase in the interest rate motivates people to raise next period's consumption, c_2, relative to this period's, c_1. Suppose that we look at the relation of the interest rate, R_1, to the ratio of aggregate consumptions, C_2/C_1. Does this relation reveal something about the behaviour of individuals?
d. Suppose that we want to use aggregate data to figure out the effects of the interest rate on an individual's choices of consumption and saving. What do the answers to this question suggest that we should look at?

5.14 The Dynamics of Changes in the Price Level
In the text, we examined a case in which the real demand for money declined. Then the price level increased, but the interest rate did not change.
a. Outline a dynamic story that describes the pressures for the price level to rise.
b. Does the interest rate stay fixed or move around while the price level adjusts in part (a)?
c. Can you tell a story in which the price level jumps immediately to its new market-clearing position rather than adjusting gradually in accordance with the sketch in part (a)?

5.15 A Currency Reform
Suppose that the government replaces the existing monetary unit with a new one. For example, Germany might shift from the Deutsche Mark to the ECU, which equals 2 Deutsche Marks. People can exchange their old currency for the new one at a ratio of 2 to 1. Also, any contracts that were written in terms of Deutsche Marks are converted at the ratio of 2 to 1 into ECUs.
a. What happens to the price level and the interest rate?
b. What happens to the quantities of output, consumption, and work effort?
c. Do the results exhibit the neutrality of money?

5.16 Temporary versus Permanent Changes of the Production Function (optional)
Consider the parallel downward shift of the production function in Figure 5.3. This type of change does not affect the schedule for labour marginal product. Suppose first that this change is permanent.
a. We dealt with this type of disturbance for an isolated individual, Robinson Crusoe, in Chapter 2. We found that Crusoe reduced output and consumption but raised work effort. How do these results compare with those that we obtained in the present chapter, which includes markets for commodities and credit? Think of the typical or representative household: does that

household's responses of output, consumption, and work effort differ from those of Robinson Crusoe?

b. Suppose now that the change to the production function is temporary. Compare again Robinson Crusoe's responses of output, consumption, and work effort with those of the typical household in the model from the present chapter.

c. For Robinson Crusoe, how do the responses of output, consumption, and work effort depend on whether the improvement to the production function is temporary or permanent? (Problem 2.9 in Chapter 2 deals with this matter.)

d. Put together the results from parts (a), (b), and (c). They tell us how to compare temporary and permanent changes in the production function for the model in the present chapter, which includes markets for commodities and credit. How do the responses of output, consumption, and work effort for the typical household depend on whether the change in the production function is permanent or temporary?

Notes

1. Walras thought of an auctioneer who adjusted various prices along the lines of our dynamic sketch, but no trades were concluded until all markets cleared. In this case, we would not have to worry much about how people behaved when markets did not clear. Of course, the device of an auctioneer who adjusts prices should not be taken literally for most markets. The idea is that buyers and sellers will manage quickly to establish prices that accord with the market-clearing conditions.

2. We noted that households attempt to spend some of their excess money on bonds. This increase in the demand for bonds tends to drive down the interest rate. A lower interest rate causes excess demand for commodities and thereby reinforces the pressure toward higher prices. As the price level rises, the increase in the nominal demand for money reverses the pressure on the bond market and causes the interest rate to rise. At the new position of general market clearing – in which the quantity of money, the price level, and the nominal demand for money have all risen in the same proportion – the net change in the interest rate is nil.

3. See Eugene Rotwein (1970) and Henry Thornton (1978).

4. Milton Friedman stresses the stability of the demand for money as the hallmark of a modern quantity theorist. See Friedman (1956, p. 16).

5. The term 'monetarism' originates with Karl Brunner (1968). Brunner (p. 9) stresses three major features of the monetarist position: 'First, monetary impulses are a major factor accounting for variations in output, employment, and prices. Second, movements in the money stock are the most reliable measure of the thrust of monetary impulses. Third, the behaviour of the monetary authorities dominates movements in the money stock over business cycles.'

6

The Labour Market

To simplify matters, we pretended that households used only their own labour to produce goods. Now we make things more realistic by introducing a market in which people exchange labour services. The people who buy labour services are the firms or employers in the economy. Those who sell services are the employees.

Think of the labour market as a place in which people supply and demand labour services. The clearing of this market – along with those for commodities and credit – determines the aggregates of work and output. One objective of this chapter is to see how the presence of the labour market and the existence of firms change the way that work and output are determined. For most macroeconomic questions, it turns out that the answer is, 'not much'. Our previous simplified setting in which people work only on their own production processes is satisfactory for most purposes. The extensions in this chapter do, however, allow us to explore the determination of wage rates and the manner in which a labour market promotes economic efficiency. The extended framework will also be essential later when we study unemployment (in Chapter 13).

Setup of the Labour Market

Suppose, for simplicity, that everyone's labour services are physically the same. But instead of working on one's own production process, people now sell their labour services on the labour market. This market establishes a single wage rate, which we denote by w and measure in units of ECUs per person-hour. (For convenience, we omit time subscripts here.) By the wage rate we mean that buyers of labour services pay w ECUs for each hour that someone works for them. Correspondingly, sellers of labour services receive w ECUs for each hour of work. As in our treatment of the commodity market, we assume that each individual buyer and seller regards the wage rate, w, as a given.

Denote by ℓ^s the number of person-hours of labour services that a household supplies to the labour market during a period. Correspondingly, this household receives the ECU quantity, $w \cdot \ell^s$, of labour income.

Suppose that some of the households – who are inclined to be entrepreneurs – set themselves up as **firms**. These firms hire other people as workers. Let ℓ^d denote the number of person hours of labour services that a firm demands from the labour market. Correspondingly, the firm pays the ECU amount, $w \cdot \ell^d$, as wage payments to its workers.

Each firm uses its input of labour services, ℓ^d, to produce commodities. The quantity produced and supplied to the commodity market is

$$y^s = f(\ell^d) \tag{6.1}$$

where f is again the production function. Since the goods sell at the price P, the firm's gross revenue from sales is $P \cdot y^s$. The firm's **profit** (or earnings) equals gross revenue less wage payments – that is,

$$\text{profit} = P \cdot y^s - w \cdot \ell^d = P \cdot f(\ell^d) - w \cdot \ell^d \tag{6.2}$$

Note that firms do not issue or hold bonds at this stage of our analysis. The potential to borrow becomes important in Chapter 13 when we allow for investment.

A firm's earnings go to the household or households that own the firm. We could introduce a **stock market**, on which people bought and sold the ownership rights in businesses. Then the profits would go to the current shareholders in the form of dividend payments. To keep things simple, we do not introduce a stock market and assume that the ownership rights in firms are distributed in some manner among the households.[1] In any event, it is important to note that all firms must be owned 100% by some households. Each household's total income now includes its share of profits from firms, as well as wage income, $w \cdot \ell^s$, and interest income.

The Demand for Labour

Think about a household that owns all or part of a firm. The household's utility depends on its consumption, c^d, and work, ℓ^s. Hence, the firm's demand for labour, ℓ^d, matters to the household-owner only through its effect on the firm's profit, which appears in equation (6.2). If the firm acts to benefit its owners – which we assume – then it sets its demand for labour, ℓ^d, to maximize profit in each period.

An increase in labour input, ℓ^d, has two effects on profit. First, an extra hour of work means that output, $f(\ell^d)$, increases by the marginal product of labour, MPL. Gross sales revenue therefore rises by the ECU amount, $P \cdot \text{MPL}$. Second, the wage bill increases by the ECU wage rate, w. Profit rises with an increase in labour input if the value of labour's marginal product, $P \cdot \text{MPL}$, exceeds w. To maximize profit a firm expands employment, ℓ^d, up to the point at which the value of the marginal product just equals the wage rate – that is, until $P \cdot \text{MPL} = w$. If we divide through by the price level, then the condition that each firm satisfies in every period is

$$\text{MPL} = w/P \qquad (6.3)$$

Notice that the right side of equation (6.3) is the **real wage rate**, w/P. This variable is the quantity of commodities that someone can buy with the ECU amount w. Equation (6.3) says that a producer chooses the quantity of labour input,

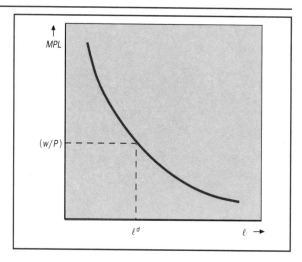

Labour's marginal product, MPL declines as the quantity of labour increases. Producers set the demand for labour, ℓ^d, at the point where the marginal product equals the real wage rate, w/p.

Figure 6.1 Demand for labour

ℓ^d, so that the marginal product, MPL, equals the real wage rate. At that point, the last unit of labour contributes just enough to output, MPL, so as to cover the extra cost of this labour in units of commodities, which is the real wage rate.

Figure 6.1 illustrates the results. The curve shows the negative effect of more labour input on the marginal product, MPL. Notice that firms set their demand for labour, ℓ^d, at the point where the marginal product equals the real wage rate, w/P.

The Gains from Equalizing Labour's Marginal Product Across Firms

At a point in time, each worker receives the same real wage rate because we assumed that all labour services are identical. Labour's marginal product therefore ends up being the same on all production processes. This result holds even if there are differences across firms in production functions or across households in their willingness to work. It is efficient to equalize these marginal products: otherwise the economy's total output could rise, without changing total work effort, by shifting workers from one place to another. The increase in output results if a worker moves from an activity where his or her marginal product is low to one where it is high.

There is no reason for workers' marginal products to be equal if a labour market does not exist. In our earlier model, in which people worked only on their own production processes, workers might end up with large differences in marginal products. Because one person could not work on another's production activity, there was no mechanism to equalize the marginal products.

Consider two isolated regions, *A* and *B*. The technology in *A* is primitive and workers end up with the low marginal product and real wage rate, $\text{MPL}^A = (w/P)^A$. Region *B* is more advanced and ends up with a higher marginal product and real wage rate, $\text{MPL}^B = (w/P)^B$. Now suppose that an economy-wide labour market develops, and this market allows people from region *A* to work in region *B* and vice versa. As we set things up, the workers from the low-wage region *A* would migrate to region *B*. Then, by working with the better technology, these workers can produce more goods without working any harder. The movement of workers out of *A* and into *B* continues until the marginal products and real wage rates are equalized in the two regions. This equalization results partly through a higher marginal product in *A* (in which work declines) and partly through a lower marginal product in *B* (in which work increases). But for our purposes, the important point is that the opening up of the economy-wide labour market allows for an expansion of aggregate output without requiring an increase in total work effort. In that sense the economy operates more efficiently when the labour market exists.

As with the commodity and credit markets, we find that the existence of the labour market aids economic efficiency: this market exhausts all the potential gains from movements of workers from one place to another. Because everyone's marginal product and real wage rate end up being the same, there are no gains of this type that remain unexploited.

Properties of the Demand for Labour

We can use Figure 6.1 to see how various changes affect the demand for labour. It follows at once that a decrease in the real wage rate, w/P, means a higher quantity of labour demanded. When the real cost of hiring workers decreases, firms expand employment until labour's marginal product falls by as much as the decrease in w/P.

An upward shift in the schedule for labour's marginal product – that is, an upward shift of the curve in Figure 6.1 – leads to a greater quantity of labour demanded at any given real wage rate. Employment expands until the marginal product again equals w/P.

We can summarize the results by writing down a function for the aggregate demand for labour. This function takes the form

$$L^d = L^d(w/P, \dots) \qquad (6.4)$$
$$(-)$$

where the expression $\dots$ again refers to characteristics of the production function.

Recall that each firm's choice of labour input determines its supply of goods through the production function, $y^s = f(\ell^d)$. Since labour demanded decreases with the real wage rate, we can write the function for the aggregate supply of goods as

$$Y^s = Y^s(w/P, \dots) \qquad (6.5)$$
$$(-)$$

Labour Supply and Consumption Demand

The introduction of the labour market does not greatly alter our earlier analysis of work effort and consumption demand. The main modification concerns the household's choice between consumption and leisure at a point in time. In our previous model the schedule for labour's marginal product, MPL, tells people the terms on which they can substitute consumption for leisure. When someone works an extra hour on his or

---

Box 6.1   Empirical Evidence on the Response of Labour Supply to Time Variations in Real Wage Rates

We discussed in Chapter 4 the estimates of George Alogoskoufis (1987a, 1987b) for inter-temporal-substitution effects on labour supply. Aside from the influence of interest rates, which we mentioned before, these studies also consider the response of labour supply to anticipated variations in real wage rates. For the United States, an increase by one percentage point per year in the expected growth rate of real wages raised the growth rate of the number of workers by about one percentage point per year. For the United Kingdom the results showed less sensitivity of work effort to variations in real wages; an increase by one percentage point per year in the expected

growth rate of real wages raised the growth rate of the number of workers by only about 0.4 percentage point per year. For both countries, the results were weaker if work effort was measured by hours worked per person rather than the number of workers: the relation between the expected growth rate of real wages and the growth rate of hours worked per capita was not statistically significant. The evidence therefore suggests that intertemporal substitution of labour supply in response to time variations of wages is more important for the number of people working than for hours worked per person.

---

her own production process, he or she can use the additional output (of MPL units) to raise consumption. Now households sell their labour services at the real wage rate, w/P, rather than working on their own production. The real wage rate therefore indicates the terms on which people can substitute consumption for leisure. Someone who works an extra hour can use the additional w/P units of real income to expand consumption.

For a household, the real wage rate now appears where previously the schedule for labour's marginal product appeared. Specifically, an increase in the real wage rate motivates households to increase labour supply and consumption demand. But recall that the choice of labour demand by firms guarantees that the real wage rate equals the economy-wide marginal product of labour. Therefore, the effects from the real wage amount, ultimately, to corresponding effects from the schedule for labor's marginal product.

As before, wealth effects can arise from shifts in production functions. These effects show up first on firms' profits (and on stock prices if we had introduced a stock market). But it is important to remember that the profits go to

the households that own the firms. Therefore, the shifts in production functions ultimately have wealth effects on households, as in our earlier model that ignored firms.

One new consideration is the wealth effect from a change in the real wage rate, given the position of the production function. An increase in w/P benefits the households that sell labour services. But this benefit is matched by an extra cost for the firms, which buy labour services. Since the firms are owned by households, the overall wealth effect on households from a change in w/P is nil. (There would be distributional effects if households differ by their relative amounts of wage and profit income. But we follow our usual practice of neglecting distributional effects on the aggregates of labour supply and consumption demand.)

The interest rate, R, has the same intertemporal-substitution effects as before. An increase in R motivates households to save more by reducing current consumption demand and raising current labour supply. An additional intertemporal-substitution effect arises if people anticipate variations over time in the real wage rate. Suppose, for example, that workers regard the current real wage rate as high relative to future values. Then they increase current labour supply and plan to reduce labour supply in the future. Before, we found similar effects if people anticipated changes in the schedule for labour's marginal product.

We can summarize the results in this section by writing down functions for the aggregates of labour supply and consumption demand. These functions take the forms

$$L^s = L^s(w/P, R, \ldots) \qquad (6.6)$$
$$(+) \ (+)$$

and

$$C^d = C^d(w/P, R, \ldots) \qquad (6.7)$$
$$(+) \ (-)$$

The omitted terms, denoted by . . ., include characteristics of the production function, as well as any elements that generate departures of expected future real wage rates from the current value.

Clearing of the Labour Market

The labour market clears when the aggregate supply of labour, L^s, equals the aggregate demand, L^d. Therefore, using equations (6.4) and (6.6), the condition for clearing the labour market is

$$L^d(w/P, \ldots) = L^s(w/P, R, \ldots) \qquad (6.8)$$
$$(-) (+) \ (+)$$

Recall that the terms denoted by . . . include characteristics of the production function.

As before, there are also conditions for clearing the commodity market and for ensuring that all money is willingly held. These conditions must hold along with equation (6.8) to ensure the clearing of all markets. When we take these conditions together, we shall be able to determine the nominal wage rate, w, as well as the interest rate, R, and the price level, P. In other words, we add one new market-clearing condition, equation

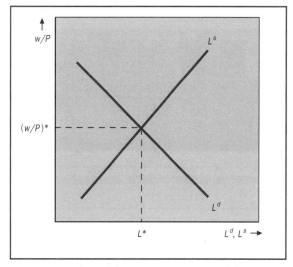

For a given value of the interest rate, R, and for a given form of the production function, the labour market clears when the real wage rate is $(w/P)^*$ and the quantity of work is L^*.

Figure 6.2   Clearing of the labour market

(6.8), and thereby determine one more 'price' – the price of labour services, w. For now, we focus on the new condition for clearing the labour market.

Figure 6.2 shows the clearing of the labour market. For convenience, we place the real wage rate, w/P, on the vertical axis and labour demand and supply on the horizontal. The quantity of labour demanded by firms falls with w/P and the quantity of labour supplied by households rises with w/P.

Notice from Figure 6.2 that the aggregates of labour demand and supply are equal when the real wage rate is $(w/P)^*$ and the level of work is L^*. We can think of this overall level of work effort as corresponding to aggregate **employment** (number of persons working) or to total hours worked by all persons. Figure 6.2 allows us to relate the market-clearing values of the real wage rate and employment (or total hours worked) to variables that shift either the labour-demand curve or the labour-supply curve. These variables include the interest rate, R, the forms of production functions, and prospective changes in the real wage rate. For example, an increase in the interest rate shifts the labour-supply curve rightward in Figure 6.2. Employment, L^*, therefore rises and the real wage rate, $(w/P)^*$, declines.

Clearing of the Commodity Market

Using equations (6.5) and (6.7), we can write the condition for clearing the commodity market as

$$C^d(w/P,\ R,\ldots) = Y^s(w/P,\ldots) \qquad (6.9)$$
$$\ \ (+)\ \ (-) \qquad\qquad (-)$$

We want to show that this condition is essentially the same as the one for clearing the commodity market in Chapter 5. That is, we want to demonstrate that the introduction of the labour market and firms leaves intact our previous analysis of the commodity market. This finding is important because it means that all of our results from Chapter 5 carry through to the extended model that includes a labour market.

Recall that the condition for clearing the labour market in equation (6.8) (and Figure 6.2) determines w/P. This condition implies that an increase in the interest rate, R, shifts the labour-supply curve rightward in Figure 6.2. Hence, w/P falls when R rises. We can use this result to substitute out for the real wage rate, w/P, in the condition for clearing the commodity market, equation (6.9). After substituting for w/P in terms of R, we get the simplified condition for clearing the commodity market:

$$C^d(R,\ldots) = Y^s(R,\ldots) \qquad (6.10)$$
$$(-) \qquad\quad (+)$$

As usual, the expression . . . includes characteristics of the production function.

Notice that w/P does not appear in equation (6.10) because we have replaced it by the various elements, including R, that determine the real wage rate. In particular, since Y^s depends on w/P in equation (6.9), and since w/P depends on R, Y^s depends indirectly on R. Therefore, when we

solve out for w/P, Y^s depends directly on R in equation (6.10).

Let's examine in detail how the interest rate enters into the condition for clearing the commodity market in equation (6.10). Recall that an increase in R shifts the labour-supply curve rightward in Figure 6.2 and thereby causes a decline in w/P. This decline in w/P leads, as shown in equation (6.9), to an expansion of goods supply, Y^s. Therefore, the positive effect of R on Y^s in equation (6.10) picks up this channel of effects.

On the demand side, the change in the interest rate has two effects. First, from equation (6.9), an increase in R lowers consumer demand, C^d, for a given value of w/P. Second, because an increase in R leads to a lower value of w/P, there is a further decline in consumer demand. The negative effect of R on C^d in equation (6.10) picks up both channels of effect.

The important point is that equation (6.10) looks just like the condition for clearing the commodity market that we used in Chapter 5.[2] Because the condition for clearing the commodity market is essentially the same as before, we can still use our previous analysis to determine the interest rate and the quantities of output and work effort for each period. To see how this works, let's reconsider the example of a shift in the production function.

An Improvement in the Production Function

Assume a permanent proportional upward shift of the production function. This change means that the level of aggregate output and the marginal product of labour increase for a given amount of aggregate work effort.

Figure 6.3 shows the effects on the labour market. Because the disturbance raises wealth, the supply of labour declines for a given value of w/P. Because of the upward shift to the schedule for labour's marginal product, the demand for labour rises for a given value of w/P. Hence, Figure 6.3 shows that the real wage rate increases, but the change in the quantity of labour is uncertain. As in some previous cases, the wealth

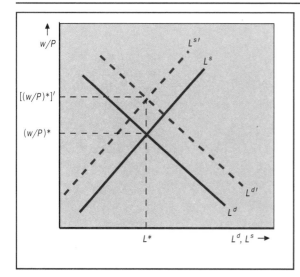

The permanent upward shift of the production function raises the demand for labour but lowers the supply. Therefore the real wage rate increases, but the change in work is uncertain.

Figure 6.3 Effect of an improvement in the production function on the labour market

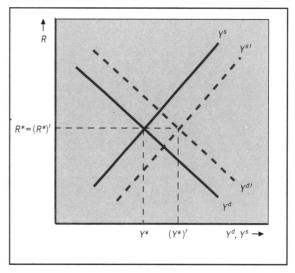

The permanent upward shift of the production function raises the demand and supply of commodities by roughly equal amounts. Hence output increases but the interest rate does not change.

Figure 6.4 Effect of an improvement in the production function on the commodity market

effect suggests less work, but the improvement in productivity suggests more work. If the dominant element is the effect on productivity, then work effort rises in response to a favorable shock.

Figure 6.4 shows the effect on the commodity market. We use the market-clearing condition from equation (6.10), which takes account of the determination of the real wage rate from the labour market. Notice first the rightward shift in consumer demand. This shift reflects partly the wealth effect from the improvement in the production function and partly the substitution effect (toward consumption and away from leisure) from the rise in the real wage rate.

The supply of goods rises with the improvement in the production function but falls because of the increase in the real wage rate. Recall, however, that the shift in the production function and the resulting change in w/P are permanent in this example. The aggregate of desired saving would therefore change little, if at all, at the initial interest rate. This result means that goods supply, Y^s, shifts rightward on net by roughly the same amount as C^d. We conclude from Figure 6.4

that output increases, but the interest rate does not change.[3]

An important observation is that the results coincide with those that we reached earlier, when people worked on only their own production processes. A permanent improvement in production opportunities raises aggregate output but has an ambiguous effect on work effort. Labour input is procyclical, as in the data, if the positive response of labour demand to the improvement in productivity dominates over the negative response of labour supply to the increase in wealth. Further, because the shift in the production function is permanent, there is no change in the interest rate.

The Behaviour of the Real Wage Rate

The model predicts that the real wage rate would be procyclical: favourable shocks to the production function raise output and the real wage rate, whereas unfavourable shocks lower output and the real wage rate. Moreover, if the response of labour demand to the change in productivity dominates over the reduction in labour supply due to more wealth, then labour input is also procyclical. The quantity of labour rises in booms along with the expansions of output and real wage rates, and vice versa in recessions.

This last result relies on the shifts in labour demand due to changing productivity in Figure

6.3. If the labour demand curve did not shift – because the production function did not change or because we allowed only for parallel shifts in the production function – then shifts in the labour-supply curve would trace out the fixed labour-demand curve. Since the labour-demand curve slopes downward, the quantity of labour and the real wage rate would have to move in

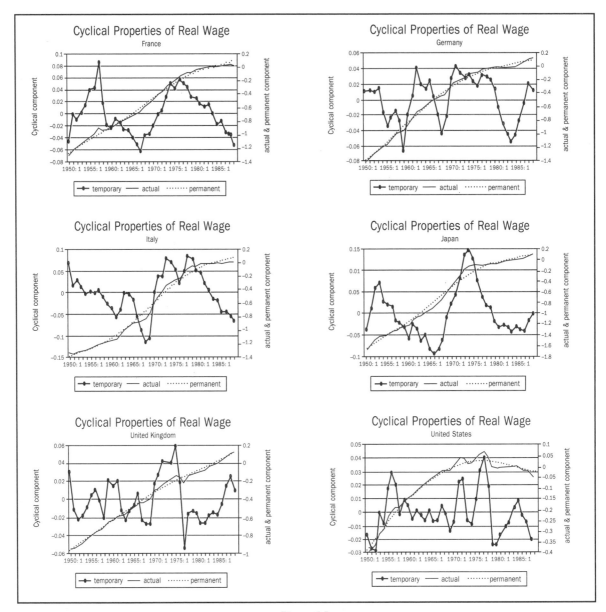

Figure 6.5

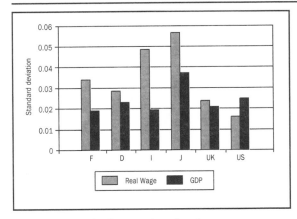

Figure 6.6   Cyclical properties of real wage

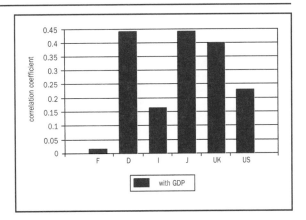

Figure 6.7   Cyclical properties of real wage

opposite directions and therefore could not *both* be procyclical. This result is important because the data indicate that both variables are procyclical. To fit the theory to these facts we have to allow for shifts to labour demand that reflect changes in the productivity of labour.

We discussed in Chapter 1 the procyclical behaviour of labour input, measured by employment or worker-hours. The dotted lines in Figure 6.5 show the real wage rates on a proportionate scale from 1950 to 1990 for the G-6 countries. We measure the real wage rate by the ratio of average hourly earnings of production workers in manufacturing to the consumer price index (CPI). The dashed lines in the figure are smooth trend lines that filter out the longer-run movements of the real wage rate. (See the discussion of trend lines in Chapter 1.) The solid lines are the detrended real wage rates – the difference between the actual and trend values. Recall that each of these detrended values represents a proportionate deviation from the long-run path. From Figure 6.6 we see that the real wage rate moves substantially around its trend. While in the US detrended real wage is less volatile than detrended real GNP – the respective standard deviations are 0.016 and 0.025, in all the other G-6 it is more volatile. In Italy, for example, the standard deviation of detrended real wage was 0.048, while that of output was 0.019. In Figure 6.7 we also notice that the real wage rate is clearly procyclical: the correlation of the detrended real wage rate with detrended real GNP is always

positive, and as high as 0.44 for Germany and Japan.[4] This pattern fits with the model's predictions and therefore provides some support for the theory.

In a long-run context, the development of an economy involves a series of permanent improvements to the production function of the sort considered in Figures 6.3 and 6.4. Our analysis therefore predicts that economic development leads to continuing increases in the real wage rate. From Figure 6.5 we see that this proposition accords with data for all the G-6 countries, except for the US. The United States, therefore, displays a unique pattern for the real wage rate, as shown in Figure 6.5. While the real wage rate in the US grew strongly from 1954 to 1973, at an average rate of 1.7% per year, it has not grown since. (The growth rate from 1973 to 1991 was −0.5% per year.) It is possible to look at a broader measure of real labour compensation, one that applies to the entire economy and that includes some parts of fringe benefits.[5] This measure shows a small increase from 1973 to 1991 – the average growth rate was 0.3% per year – but the dramatic decline in real wage growth after 1973 is still present. The behaviour of real wage growth before and after 1973 in the US mirrors the patterns in labour productivity. Output per worker-hour grew at 2.1% per year from 1954 to 1973 and by 0.4% per year from 1973 to 1991. Although the diminished growth rate of labour productivity is well known, the sources of this reduced growth are not well understood.

Nominal Wage Rates

To determine nominal wage rates and other nominal variables, we again consider the condition for money to be willingly held. This condition looks as it did in Chapter 5:

$$M = P \cdot \Phi(R, \ Y, \ldots) \tag{6.11}$$
$$\underset{(-)}{} \underset{(+)}{}$$

The aggregate real demand for money, $\Phi(\cdot)$, would now include money held by firms as well as households. The form of this function would not, however, differ greatly from that in our earlier analysis: the amount of real money demanded still falls with an increase in the interest rate, R, and rises with an increase in real spending as measured by real output, Y.

The full market-clearing model now consists of equation (6.11) plus the conditions derived earlier for clearing the labour and commodity markets:

$$L^d(w/P, \ldots) = L^s(w/P, \ R, \ldots) \tag{6.12}$$
$$\underset{(-)}{} \underset{(+)\ (+)}{}$$

and

$$C^d(w/P, R, \ldots) = Y^s(w/P, \ldots) \tag{6.13}$$
$$\underset{(+)\ (-)}{} \underset{(-)}{}$$

We have already seen that equations (6.12) and (6.13) determine the real wage rate, w/P, the interest rate, R, and the levels of output, Y, and employment, L.

We showed in Chapter 5 that an increase in the quantity of money, M, was neutral. The price level, P, rose in the same proportion, but all real variables – including Y, L, R, and M/P – were unchanged. This property of monetary neutrality still holds in the model that includes a labour market. We should, however, add the real wage rate, w/P, to the list of real variables that do not change and we should add the nominal wage rate, w, to the list of nominal variables that rise in the same proportion as the quantity of money.

To verify these results, remember that equations (6.12) and (6.13) determine R and Y. These variables then determine the real demand for money, $\Phi(\cdot)$. Given this real demand, equation (6.11) implies that an increase in M raises P in the same proportion. Real money balances, M/P, therefore do not change when there is a once-and-for-all shift in the nominal quantity of money.

Recall that equations (6.12) and (6.13) determine w/P and L. In fact, the real wage rate equals the marginal product of labour at this value of L. We can find the nominal wage rate, w, by multiplying the real wage rate, w/P, by the price level, P, which we have already determined. Notice that an increase in M raises P in the same proportion but does not change w/P. An increase in M therefore raises w (as well as P) in the same proportion.

The Labour Market in the Macroeconomic Model

Consider how the introduction of the labour market and firms affects our analysis. We have shown that these new features do not change the way that shifts to the production function affect the interest rate and the aggregate quantities of output and work effort. We also found that the extensions did not change the interaction between money and prices. In other words, our earlier simplification – which neglected the labour market and the existence of firms – allows us to get reasonable answers to many important questions. For most of the subsequent analysis, we shall therefore find it satisfactory to return to the simpler framework, which does not deal explicitly with the labour market or firms. The main place in which we reintroduce firms and the labour market is Chapter 13, which deals with unemployment.

Summary

We introduced a labour market in which firms demand labour and households supply labour at a going wage rate. This market clears when the aggregate demand for labour equals the aggregate supply. One important aspect of a cleared labour market is that it equates each worker's marginal product to the real wage rate. This market therefore exhausts all the gains in output that can result by shifting workers from one production activity to another.

The requirements for general market clearing are that the labour market clears along with the markets for commodities and credit. In comparison with our previous analysis, we have added one new condition – that the labour market clear – and one new 'price', the wage rate for labour services.

The inclusion of the labour market allows us to study the effects of various disturbances on the real wage rate. Shifts to the production function generate procyclical movements of the real wage rate, a pattern that appears in the G-6 data. In a long-run context, the real wage rate will increase as an economy develops, a proposition that also accords with empirical evidence.

The conditions for determining the aggregate quantities of output and work, as well as the interest rate and the price level, turn out to be similar to those from before. For many purposes, we can therefore carry out the analysis by pretending, as before, that households work on only their own production processes. (We have to consider firms and a labour market later when we study unemployment.)

Important Terms and Concepts

firm
profit
stock market
real wage rate
employment

Questions and Problems

Mainly for Review

6.1 How does an increase in the real wage rate affect the demand for labour? Where does the assumption of diminishing marginal productivity of labour come in?

6.2 Consider two individuals, *A* and *B*; they have the same production function, but *A* has a greater willingness to work. If each individual is isolated on an island, who will work more? Who will have the higher marginal product? Show how total output can increase, with no increase in total labour, by exchanging labour services for goods between the two islands – that is, by opening up a labour market.

6.3 Suppose that the interest rate increases. How does this change affect the supply of labour and hence the real wage rate?

6.4 Explain why economic development tends to raise the real wage rate.

6.5 Suppose that the quantity of money, *M*, increases.
   a. The increase in the nominal wage rate suggests that workers will be better off. Why is this not so?
   b. The increase in the price level suggests that workers will be worse off. Is this correct?

Problems for Discussion

6.6 The Labour Market and Efficiency
   In the text we considered two isolated regions, *A* and *B*. The technology in *A* was inferior to that in *B*. Therefore, we found that the opening up of an economy-wide labour market led to higher aggregate output without requiring an increase in aggregate work effort. In this sense the new market improved the economy's efficiency.
   a. Does the result mean that everyone is better off? In answering, consider the position of workers and firms (and the owners of firms) in both regions.
   b. Does your answer suggest that some groups might oppose moves to free up markets, even when there would be gains in the aggregate? Can you think of any real-world examples of this phenomenon?

6.7 Walras' Law
   a. When we introduce the labour market, what new aggregate-consistency condition arises?
   b. Use the aggregate form of households' budget constraints to derive Walras' Law of Markets. How does the law differ from that in Chapter 5?

6.8 Wealth Effects from Changes in the Real Wage Rate
   Suppose that the real wage rate, w/P, increases.
   a. Why are there offsetting effects on wealth? What would you predict for the wealth effect on aggregate consumption demand and labour supply?

b. Suppose that most suppliers of labour own relatively little of the ownership rights in firms. What would you predict for the wealth effect on aggregate labour supply?

6.9 Temporary Shifts of the Production Function
Consider a temporary, parallel downward shift of the production function.
a. What are the effects on the interest rate, the real wage rate, and the quantities of output and employment?
b. Do the results differ from those in Chapter 5, where people worked only on their own production processes?
c. How do the answers change if the shift of the production function is proportional rather than parallel?

6.10 Short-Run Movements of the Real Wage Rate (optional)
Consider again a temporary, parallel downward shift of the production function.
a. Using the results from problem 6.9, what is the pattern of association between changes in the real wage rate and changes in the quantities of employment and output?
b. Assume, more realistically, that the schedule for labour's marginal product shifts downward. Assume, in particular, that this shift is large enough so that work effort declines. What then is the pattern of association between changes in the real wage rate and changes in the quantities of employment and output?

c. Suppose that business fluctuations result from temporary shifts of the production function. What do you predict for the 'cyclical' behaviour of real wage rates: do real wage rates move together with or inversely to output and employment? (There is some debate about the cyclical behaviour of real wage rates. Most researchers find a procyclical pattern in the US data since the 1950s: real wage rates tend to be high when output and employment are high.)

6.11 The Short-Run Behaviour of Productivity (optional)
Suppose that we use the popular definition of labour productivity as the ratio of output to employment, Y/L.
a. How does this measure of productivity relate to the marginal product of labour?
b. Assume, as in problem 6.10, that business fluctuations result from shifts of the production function. How would productivity behave? In particular, is productivity high or low when output is high?

6.12 Determination of Stock Prices (optional)
Suppose that there are a fixed number of firms in the economy, each with access to the same production function, $f(\ell)$. Assume that the owner of a firm prints up and sells 100 ownership certificates (shares), each of which entitles the holder to 1% of the firm's profits. What would be the price of each share?

Notes

1. The ability to buy and sell stocks in various businesses becomes more interesting if we allow for uncertainties about each firm's earnings. Then households have an incentive to diversify their holdings of stock across many types of businesses. Because we have not introduced these uncertainties, a stock market would not add much to the analysis.

2. The only difference is that the labour market ensures that everyone's marginal product of labour, which equals the real wage rate, is the same. The equality of real wage rates arises only because we assumed, first, that everyone's labour services were physically identical and, second, that all jobs had similar working conditions. We could expand the analysis to deal with different levels of skills and different characteristics of jobs. Then we would find that real wage rates were higher for people who were more productive and on jobs that were less pleasant. But these considerations would not change the major macroeconomic results.

3. Because the interest rate does not change, we do not have to modify the analysis of the labour market in Figure 6.3. Recall that this diagram applies for a given value of the interest rate.

4. The procyclical nature of the real wage rate would be even stronger if we were able to adjust for cyclical changes in the quality of the labour force. This average quality (measured by education, experience, or lifetime real wages) tends to rise during recessions because the lesser skilled workers typically lose jobs quicker than the more skilled. Similarly, firms reduce their standards for hiring during booms. Because the average quality of the labour force is countercyclical, the real wage rate per unit of labour quality is more procyclical than the rate per worker-hour.

5. The data on real compensation per hour for the overall business sector are from *Economic Report of the President*, 1992, table B-44. See also the discussion of real wage growth in *ibid*, pp. 95–6.

7

World Markets in Goods and Credit

Thus far, we have dealt with the macroeconomic performance of a single, closed economy. In particular, we have neglected the interactions among countries on international markets. Until recently, macroeconomic theory was developed in a closed economy framework, mostly because the analysis is simpler under that assumption and because the impact of the rest of the world on the domestic economy was deemed to be small. However, after the opening up of international markets over the last two decades, the practice of ignoring the rest of the world has become increasingly unsatisfactory. This is especially true for Europe in which international trade is an essential component of economic activity.

One reason for the importance of international trade in Europe is the geographical proximity and relatively small size of each country. Proximity alone, however, does not explain the extraordinary growth in trade among European countries. A crucial element in this process has been the creation of the European Community (EC), which permitted the removal of tariffs and quotas among its members. In 1990, for example, EC exports of goods and services were 29.4% of GDP, whereas US exports were only 9.4% of GDP. However, almost 60% of EC trade was directed to other countries within the Community. If we consider only the EC external trade, that is, trade with countries outside the Community, then the ratio of export to GDP is 9.1%, a number comparable to that for the United States.

In many respects, the interaction among western European countries is similar to that among the various regions of the United States. But there are important differences as well. In the United States monetary policy and a large part of

fiscal policy are centralized at the federal level. This centralisation does not apply to the European Community (EC), in which member countries retain individual monetary and fiscal policies. This diversity of policy adds complexity to the analysis, because we have to allow for differences in national price levels, interest rates, and for the existence of exchange rates between different currencies. Within the EC, these complications will be considerably reduced if the European Monetary Union (EMU) comes into existence. We shall analyze this possibility and its implications later in the book. It is important to keep in mind, however, that the creation of EMU, or even of a European Political Union (EPU), does not mean that international factors will become unimportant. International considerations will continue to be crucial for the analysis of the interactions between the EC and the rest of the world.

This chapter extends the model presented in the previous chapters to allow for trade in goods and credit across national borders. With these extensions we will be able to analyze international economic issues that have become important in recent years. In particular, we will be able to discuss the macroeconomic causes of current-account surpluses and deficits, a hot topic in economic and political discussions because of the persistent trade imbalances of Japan with the rest of the world.

We shall find that our previous analysis of a closed economy applies to the macroeconomics of the world economy, whereas our earlier treatment of individuals carries over to the behaviour of a small economy that operates on world markets. We can use this perspective to think about international borrowing and lending, changes in the prices of commodities such as oil, and the factors that determine a country's balance of international payments.

One Currency World

Consider a world economy, composed of several countries, for example the EC member states. From the perspective of each individual country, we want to add the possibilities of buying goods from abroad or of selling goods to foreigners. That is, we will extend the analysis of the commodity market to include imports and exports. To carry out this extension, we begin with a number of unrealistic assumptions, which we will later relax. Assume first that the goods produced in each country are physically identical. In addition, suppose that transport costs and barriers to trade across national borders are small enough to neglect. (In this sense, the analysis applies when international markets are relatively open, as is true in the main countries in recent years, especially within the EC.) Finally, pretend at this stage that instead of using their own currency all countries use a **common currency**, such as the ECU (the European Currency Unit). The residents of each country hold ECUs and quote prices in units of ECUs.

Given our assumptions, goods in all countries must sell at the same ECU price P. Otherwise, households and firms would want to buy all goods at the lowest price and sell all goods at the highest price. This result is the simplest version of the **law of one price**. Therefore the ECU price level in all countries is the same, equal to P.

Suppose that each country has a central bank and that this bank holds a quantity of **international currency**. This currency could be pieces of paper denominated in US dollars, Japanese yen or other national units or could be a commodity such as gold. The precise form of the international currency is unimportant for our purposes, except that we assume that the nominal interest rate on this currency is zero.

Let $\bar{H}_t$ denote period t's world quantity of international currency, denominated in units of ECUs. (An overbar means that the variable

pertains to the entire world.) For simplicity, we assume that $\bar{H}_t$ does not change over time; that is, $\bar{H}_t$ equals the constant $\bar{H}$. The domestic central bank demands the real quantity, H_t/P, of this international currency to facilitate transactions between domestic residents and foreigners. (Later in the book, we shall discuss further this demand for international currency.)

Assume that a single credit market exists in the world. If we abstract from differences in creditworthiness among borrowers, the interest rate, R, on this world credit market must be the same for lenders and borrowers from every country.

International Borrowing and Lending

Consider the situation from the standpoint of the residents of a particular country, which might be the United Kingdom. We refer to this country as the domestic or home country, and we refer to other countries as the rest of the world. Let Y_t represent the total of goods and services produced domestically, which is the real gross domestic product (GDP). Correspondingly, the ECU income from this source is the amount PY_t.

For the residents of a single country, the total of funds lent need no longer equal the total borrowed. Rather, the total amount lent on net by domestic residents corresponds to the total borrowed on net from this country by foreigners. Let B_t^f represent the net holding of foreign bonds by domestic residents at the end of period t, that is $B_t^f = B_t^X - B_t^M$, where B_t^X are the holdings of foreign securities by domestic agents and B_t^M are the holdings of domestic securities by foreign agents. If $B_t^f > 0$, then the home country is a net creditor to the rest of the world, whereas if $B_t^f < 0$, then the country is a net debtor. Correspondingly, the amount RB_{t-1}^f is the net interest income (positive or negative) for period t to domestic residents from abroad.[1]

If we add up for the entire world, then we must have that the total amount borrowed equals the total lent. Hence, the world aggregate for the net holding of foreign bonds, $\bar{B}_t^f$, is zero. This result for the world parallels the condition that we had before for a single country when we neglected foreigners. In our previous setting, an isolated country had no place to borrow from. Although this constraint no longer applies to an individual country, it still holds for the entire world (if we neglect the possibility of borrowing from Mars). Correspondingly, the world aggregate of net interest income from abroad, RB^f_{t-1}, is also zero.

Suppose that the net interest income from abroad is the only source of income from the rest of the world.[2] Then the total ECU income of domestic residents during period t is the gross national product, which equals gross domestic product, PY_t, plus the net interest income from abroad, RB^f_{t-1}. This total income can be spent in the following ways:

- Personal consumption expenditures, PC_t, whether on goods and services produced domestically, PD^g_t, or abroad, PM^g_t.
- **Net foreign investment**, which is the name given to the net acquisition of interest-bearing claims from abroad, $B^f_t - B^f_{t-1}$, plus any accumulation of international currency, $H_t - H_{t-1}$. Typically the change in international currency is a small fraction of GNP.

Putting the results together yields the budget constraint for the home country:

$$PY_t + RB^f_{t-1} = PC_t + (B^f_t - B^f_{t-1}) + (H_t - H_{t-1}) \tag{7.1}$$

Equation (7.1) is the simplest form of a **budget constraint for an open economy**. For a single economy in isolation (a closed economy), the gross domestic product, PY_t, must equal the total expenditure by domestic residents for goods and services, PC_t. When we open the economy to the rest of the world, we introduce some new items, which can create a divergence between the gross domestic product and the total of domestic expenditures on goods and services. The left side of equation (7.1) includes the net factor income from abroad, RB^f_{t-1}. The right side includes net foreign investment, which equals the net acquisition of interest-bearing claims,

$B^f_t - B^f_{t-1}$, plus the accumulation of international currency, $H_t - H_{t-1}$.

The term $B^f_t - B^f_{t-1}$ is called the **balance on capital account** for the home country. If $B^f_t - B^f_{t-1}$ is positive, then there is an **outflow of capital**. (If it is negative, then there is an **inflow of capital**.) An outflow of capital means that the home country acquires interest-bearing claims on foreigners and thereby provides funds for the foreigners to purchase goods and services.

Domestic residents have a total income of $PY_t + RB^f_{t-1}$ (which equals GNP) and a total expenditure on goods and services of PC_t. The difference between income and expenditure corresponds to saving by domestic residents in the form of additional assets acquired from the rest of the world and is called the **current-account balance**. Notice from equation (7.1) that

Current-account balance

$$= PY_t + RB^f_{t-1} - PC_t$$
$$= \text{net foreign investment}$$
$$= B^f_t - B^f_{t-1} + H_t - H_{t-1} \tag{7.2}$$

This expression is the basic identity for the balance of international payments. The equation says that the current-account balance equals net foreign investment, which is the sum of the net capital flow, $B^f_t - B^f_{t-1}$, and the change in international currency, $H_t - H_{t-1}$. If the current-account balance is positive (or negative), then a country is said to have a **surplus** (or **deficit**) **on current account**. Notice that as an accounting identity, a surplus on current account must have an offsetting financial transaction in the form of an increase in interest-bearing claims, B^f, or international currency, H.

Now consider an alternative view of a country's position with respect to the rest of the world. In an open economy, the home country can exchange goods and services with the rest of the world. Exports, PX^g_t, are the goods and services produced by domestic residents that are sold to foreigners. Imports, PM^g_t, are the goods and services produced by foreigners that are bought by domestic residents. The difference between exports and imports of goods and services is referred to as the **trade balance**. In an open economy, moreover, $PY_t = PD_t^g + PX_t^g$, because the domestic production of goods and services, PY_t, must be sold to domestic residents, PD_t^g, or foreigners, PX_t^g. Similarly, recall that $PC_t = PD_t^g + PM_t^g$, because total expenditure by domestic agents, PC_t, falls on domestic products, PD_t^g, or foreign products, PM_t^g. If we substitute these relationships (and $B_t^f = B_t^X - B_t^M$), into Equation 7.2, then we get:

Current-account balance
$$
\begin{aligned}
&= PY_t + RB_{t-1}^f - PC_t \\
&= PD_t^g + PX_t^g + R(B_{t-1}^X - B_{t-1}^M) - PD_t^g - PM_t^g \\
&= PX_t^g + RB_{t-1}^X - (PM_t^g + RB_{t-1}^M) \quad (7.3)
\end{aligned}
$$

The export of goods and services plus the net income received from abroad is called **total exports**, PX_t. The sum of imports of goods and services and the interest income paid to foreigners is called **total imports**, PM_t. A country's **net exports** is the difference between its total exports and its total import, $P(X_t - M_t)$. Rearranging equation 7.3 leads to the customary definition of the gross national product:

$$
\text{GNP} = PY_t + RB_{t-1}^f = PC_t + P(X_t - M_t) \quad (7.4)
$$

Figure 7.1 shows the ratio of the current-account balance to GNP from 1960 to 1990 for the EC, the US and Japan. The EC current account displayed several cycles. It was in deficit only for the periods 1963–65, 1974–76, 1979–82, and 1990. However, these aggregate figures conceal the differences in the pattern of the current accounts of the individual EC member states. For example, the current accounts of Germany and the Netherlands have been mostly in surplus during this period. In contrast, the current accounts of Denmark and Greece have typically been in deficit. As a whole, however, the behaviour of the current account of the EC is similar to that for Japan. In particular, both current accounts moved into deficit during the oil-price shocks of 1973–74 and 1979–80. Also, the EC and Japan showed large current account surpluses during the 1980s.

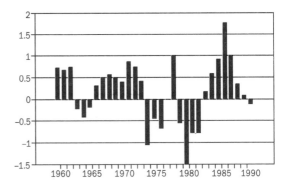

Note: From 1960 to 1967 the current-account figure does not include Portugal and France; from 1968 to 1972 it does not include Portugal.

Figure 7.1 (a)　EC current-account balance (percent of GNP (or GDP))

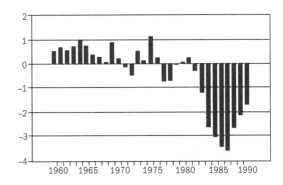

Figure 7.1 (b)　United States current-account balance (percent of GNP (or GDP))

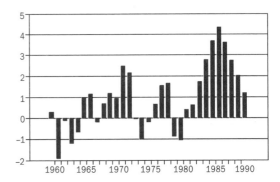

Figure 7.1 (c)　Japan current-account balance (percent of GNP (or GDP))

The behaviour of the EC current account contrasts with that for the United States. First, the United States was less affected by the two oil-price shocks. This outcome is not too surprising as the United States is far less dependent than the EC on foreign oil. Second, the US current account exhibited large deficits in the 1980s, the largest recorded this century. To find US current-account deficits of comparable size as a percent of GNP, we have to go back to the early 1870s and late 1890s.

The Role of the International Credit Market

For an individual in a closed economy, the credit market allows for divergences between income and spending. For example, if a disturbance temporarily lowers a person's income, then he or she can borrow – or spend out of accumulated assets – to avoid a temporary decline in consumption or investment. Similarly, an individual can save most of a windfall of income to spread it over extra consumption in future periods.

On the other hand, when a closed economy experiences an economy-wide disturbance – such as a temporary decline in everyone's production opportunities – it is impossible for *everyone* to borrow more. In this case, the real interest rate adjusts so that the aggregate of desired borrowing equals the aggregate of desired lending. Hence, in a closed economy, the credit market cannot cushion spending against an economy-wide disturbance, even if it is temporary.

A single country functions in a world credit market much like an individual functions in the credit market of a closed economy. Assume that the home country initially has a zero balance on current account. Then suppose that a temporary supply shock, such as a harvest failure or a natural disaster, makes everyone in the home country desire to borrow more at the initial real interest rate. If the home country's economy is **small**, then the world credit market can accommodate the increase in borrowing without significant changes in the world's real interest rate.

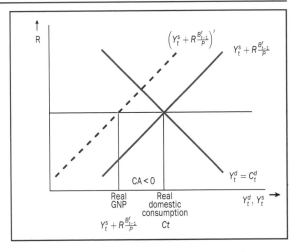

Figure 7.2   Temporary supply shocks in a small country

Figure 7.2 illustrates this case of a temporary supply shock when the home country is small. The vertical axis plots the interest rate, R, which prevails on the international credit market. For a small economy, which has access to the world credit market and exerts little effect on this market, it is appropriate to treat the interest rate as a given, represented by the solid horizontal line. The downward-sloping solid curve in the figure shows the domestic residents' aggregate demand for goods, $Y_t^d = C_t^d$. As in our previous analysis of a closed economy, a lower real interest rate stimulates this demand.

The upward-sloping solid curve in the figure shows the domestic residents' aggregate supply of goods, $Y_t^s + RB_{t-1}/P$. Note that this concept corresponds to real GNP, which is the total of goods produced by domestic residents, including the real interest income from abroad. (We define supply in this way so that an equality between supply and demand for goods corresponds to a balance on the current account.) As in previous analyses, a higher real interest rate raises the quantity of goods supplied.

We draw the solid lines in the figure so that, at the given world real interest rate, the domestic residents' aggregate quantity of goods demanded, Y_t^d, is initially equal to the aggregate quantity supplied, $Y_t^s + RB_{t-1}/P$. Hence, real domestic expenditure on goods and services initially equals real GNP. It follows from equation 7.2 that the current account is in balance. Hence, if the home country's holding of international currency is constant $(H_t = H_{t-1})$, then the capital account is initially in balance $(B_t^f = B_{t-1}^f)$. Notice that a balance on the current account does not imply a balance of trade. Assume, for example, $B_{t-1}^f/P > 0$, so that the home country is a net creditor abroad. The home country can use the income received as interest payments to import goods and services. In other words, a lender country can have, at the same time, a balanced current account and a trade deficit. Conversely, a debtor country requires a trade surplus to maintain a zero current account.

Now suppose that a temporary supply shock reduces the home country's supply of goods but has a negligible effect on demand. Then the new supply curve is the one shown by the dashed line in Figure 7.2. At the going world real interest rate, R, the quantity of goods demanded by domestic residents now exceeds the quantity supplied. In the world economy this imbalance can be accommodated by the home country's borrowing from abroad. The difference between the quantity of goods supplied, $Y_t^s + RB_{t-1}^f/P$, and the quantity of goods demanded, C_t, is the real deficit on current account (see equation (7.2)). If there is no change in the home country's holding of international currency, then equation (7.2) says that the current-account deficit corresponds to a capital inflow from abroad, that is, to a negative value for the change in earning assets, $B_t^f - B_{t-1}^f$. Hence, a temporary supply shock induces the home country to borrow from abroad to avoid a cutback in current spending.

Consider now the case in which the country is not small with respect to the world credit market. The main difference is that the world interest rate is now affected by changes in domestic demand and supply. For simplicity, consider the case in which the world is composed of only two countries of equal size, say the EC and the US. Figure 7.3 describes the initial world equilibrium. The left quadrant refers to the US economy and the right quadrant to the EC. We have constructed the example so that the EC (and thus the US) current account is zero. Also, we have

assumed, without affecting the results, that $B_{t-1}^f = 0$. Suppose now that the EC experiences a negative supply shock similar to the one analyzed above, as shown in Figure 7.4. At the initial interest rate there is a world excess demand. To restore equilibrium the interest rate must rise. The increase in the interest rate reduces demand and stimulates supply in both countries. Equilibrium is achieved at R', where the excess supply of goods in the US is equal to the excess demand for goods in the EC. The EC borrows from the US and thus runs a current-account deficit. In comparison with the previous case of a small economy, the world interest rate is higher, the EC current-account deficit and consumption are smaller. As a general proposition, the larger the country that experiences a temporary shock, the greater is the impact on the world interest rate and the smaller is the ability of the country to absorb the reduction in consumption by borrowing or lending in the international credit market.

Suppose now that the supply shock applies to the whole world, and not just to the EC. The universal desire to borrow cannot be satisfied in this case. Figure 7.5 illustrates this situation. Consumption smoothing is not possible, and the only effect is on the interest rate that must increase worldwide. The current account has still a zero balance. Notice that this treatment of a worldwide disturbance, including the determinants of the world interest rate, corresponds to

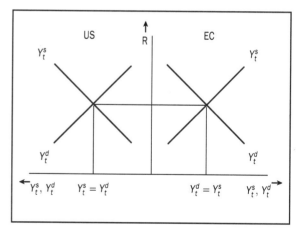

Figure 7.3   Two-country world equilibrium

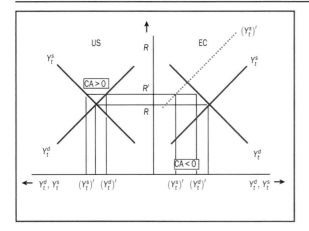

Figure 7.4   Temporary supply shock in the EC

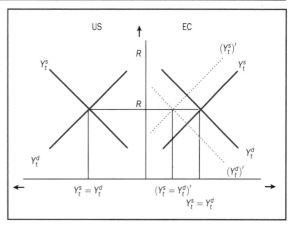

Figure 7.6   Permanent supply shock in the EC

the analysis of a closed economy that we carried out in the previous chapter.

Finally, consider the case of a shock that persists over time. Figure 7.6 shows the extreme case of a permanent negative supply shock in the EC. As we discussed in the previous chapter, the wealth effect on consumption in this case is large, and the demand schedule shifts by roughly the same amount as the supply schedule. These shifts leave the interest rate unchanged and the current account in balance. If the shock is not permanent, but persists only for a few periods, then the wealth effect on consumption is reduced. The shift in the demand schedule would be smaller

than the shift in supply and, thus, the interest rate increases and the EC runs a current-account deficit. Compared to the case of temporary shock, the effects on the current account and interest rate are now smaller. As a general proposition, therefore, the higher the degree of persistence of a shock, the smaller the effects on the interest rate and the current account.

Examples of International Borrowing and Lending

We can identify various situations in which a country borrows heavily on the world credit market. Consider Poland from 1978 to 1981, when harvest failures and labour-force problems meant that output fell well below the anticipated average level of future output. An estimate of real product for Poland shows a decline of 14% from 1978 to 1981 (see Robert Summers and Alan Heston, 1988). Thus, the situation resembles that shown in Figure 7.2, where external borrowing avoids a sharp decline in current real spending. The gross foreign debt of Poland reached $25 billion in 1981, about half the country's annual output of goods and services. (The centrally planned economies of Eastern Europe used to report a concept called 'net material product', which is analogous to net national product.)

For a second situation in which a country borrows heavily, consider Mexico. In this case,

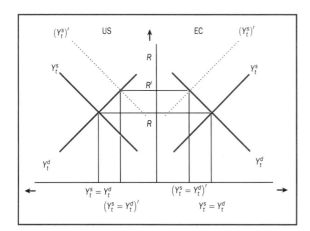

Figure 7.5   Temporary worldwide supply shock

there was a major discovery of a natural resource, oil, which promised large amounts of income in future periods. By 1974, Mexico's oil prospects were great, but a significant volume of production had not yet appeared. In this situation, the increase in prospective income motivates an increase in consumption (and an expansion of government projects) before most of the oil revenue materializes. In addition, the oil discoveries motivated an increase in investment in oil-related industries. Thus, the case corresponds to an increase in the aggregate demand for goods. The conclusion is that Mexico would borrow from abroad to finance its increase in current expenditures. In fact, Mexico's gross external debt rose from $3.5 billion or 9% of GDP in 1971 to $61 billion or 26% of GDP in 1981.[3] Of course, this type of foreign borrowing runs into trouble when, as in 1982–86, the relative price of oil falls unexpectedly, so that Mexico's income turns out to be lower than predicted. (Whether the trouble applies mainly to Mexico or to Mexico's international creditors is another question.)

Borrowing from abroad reflects a shortfall of national saving. For Poland and Mexico, the borrowing reflected a drop in saving, which resulted from a decline in current income (Poland) or an increase in prospective income (Mexico). By contrast, the countries that lend internationally are those with high desired saving, where current income is high relative to long-run income. Included in the category of international lenders are the mature industrialized countries, such as the United States through 1983 and Switzerland. Another example of an important international creditor is Saudi Arabia, whose flow of oil income through 1981 was high relative to the long-term prospective flow. The estimate net international investment position of Saudi Arabia (including international reserves) was about $145 billion in 1982 but declined to about $99 billion in 1986 because of the drop in oil revenues (see Economist Intelligence Unit, 1987).

One important point is that – just as in the case of a credit market in a closed economy – the existence of an international credit market tends to be advantageous for both borrowers and lenders. Obviously this market enables borrow-ing countries to spend more than their current income, an action that is warranted in the cases mentioned above. But the potential to lend abroad also allows countries that have a relatively large amount of desired saving to achieve higher rates of return than would be available domestically. Therefore, although there have been significant recent troubles with foreign loans, we should not conclude that the existence of the international credit market is a bad idea overall.

Notice that throughout this analysis we assumed a 'perfect' world credit market, where the interest rate was the same for each country. However, as the residents of a country increase their borrowing – with the government of the country often doing the borrowing or guaranteeing the loans – there may be an increasing risk of default. When a government borrows abroad, we particularly have to consider that 'sovereignty' makes it difficult for foreign creditors to enforce loans. (Governments are sovereign in that they are above any meaningful international law; in particular, it is difficult for a creditor to foreclose on government property.) The increasing default risk implies that the real interest rate paid by a country tends to rise as the amount borrowed increases.[4] Consequently, a country (or an individual) has difficulty in using the credit market to smooth out spending when there are major fluctuations in income.

When we take account of this effect, we find that the results are a composite of those that we found before for a closed economy with those discussed in this chapter for a perfect world credit market. For example, a temporary disturbance to a small country's income shows up partly as a change in that country's real interest rate and level of real expenditure and partly in the amount of borrowing from abroad. International borrowing then buffers only a portion of the variations in a small country's income.

The Terms of Trade

Up to now we have assumed that there existed only one good in the world and that all countries were producing and consuming it. This assumption is satisfactory for the analysis of most closed economy macroeconomic issues. As we have seen above, in an open economy context this assumption is useful to capture the crucial relationship between a country's saving behaviour and its current account. There are, however, other influences on the pattern of international trade that can be understood only by increasing the complexity of the model. One of the main insights of the theory of international trade is that countries will not produce exactly the same goods. Countries tend to specialize in the production of goods and services in which they have a comparative advantage, either because of their technology or because of their particular mix of factors of production. In an extreme case, a country may not produce any of the goods it desires to consume domestically. Instead, it will export the goods it produces and use the receipts to import foreign goods for consumption. The first implication of this result is that, even if the balance of trade is equal to zero, imports and exports can be positive (and, in reality, they are always so). Therefore, an important source of economic disturbance for an open economy is a variation in the price of the goods it exports relative to the price of the goods that it imports. In Table 7.1, we report the main category of imports and exports for several countries. For example, a change in the price of copper or in the price of tea would have a major impact on the economies of Chile or Kenya. We now model the effects of this type of shock.

To keep things simple, consider again the case of a small economy. Pretend that this country produces and exports a single good (or market basket of goods) that sells at the ECU price P, and imports another good (or market basket of goods) from the rest of the world at price $\bar{P}$. The ratio between the prices of the domestic and foreign goods, $P/\bar{P}$, is called the **terms of trade**.[5] If the ratio increases, then the home country's terms of trade improve. That is, for each unit of goods that a home country produces and sells abroad (exports), it can now purchase more units of foreign goods (imports).

We have to modify the condition for the current-account balance to allow for differences

Country	Export	% of Total export	Import	% of Total import
Australia	Wool	(13.7)	Capital goods	(27.6)
Chile	Copper	(48.5)	Industrial supplies	(53.4)
China	Textile & clothing	(27.5)	Machinery & transp. equip.	(36.0)
Denmark	Agricul.& foodstuff	(21.0)	Machinery & electrical prod.	(18.6)
Germany	Motor vehicles	(18.1)	Agricul.& foodstuff	(13.1)
India	Gems & jewellery	(21.7)	Capital Goods	(19.0)
Japan	Motor vehicles	(18.4)	Energy Prod.	(20.5)
Kenya	Coffee & tea	(45.0)	Machinery	(22.5)
New Zealand	Meat, wool & dairy prod.	(41.0)	Machinery & mechanical Appl.	(30.0)
Norway	Oil & gas	(36.3)	Machinery	(22.5)

Source: The Economist, *World in Figures*.

Table 7.1 Principal import and export of selected countries, 1988

between domestic and foreign prices of goods. To simplify the analysis, without affecting the main results, pretend that the entire gross domestic product, Y_t^s, is sold at price P and exported, whereas all of domestic consumption is on goods produced abroad (imports) and bought at price $\bar{P}$. Then the current-account balance is

$$\text{current account balance} = PY_t^s + RB_{t-1}^f - \bar{P}C_t^d \tag{7.5}$$

The current-account balance is still equal to national saving. But national saving depends now on the two prices, P and $\bar{P}$. For the purposes of discussion, assume that the current account has a zero balance at the initial values of P and $\bar{P}$, and that B_{t-1}^f is equal to zero. It is also convenient to express the current account in real terms, that is, in terms of one of the two goods, say the foreign good. If we divide equation 7.6 by $\bar{P}$, then we get

$$\text{real current account balance} = (P/\bar{P})Y_t^s - C_t^d \tag{7.6}$$

126 European Macroeconomics

Equation 7.6 shows that what matters is the **relative** price of imports and exports, not the two nominal prices. Consider an improvement in the terms of trade – say an increase in P for a given value of $\bar{P}$ – that reflects a disturbance in the rest of the world. For example, Chile may face an increase in the relative price of copper, or Australia may experience a rise in the relative price of wool. Since the disturbance originates from the rest of the world, Chile's capacity to produce copper or Australia's to produce wool does not change. We also assume, as is likely for the case of changes in wool and copper prices, that people view the shift in P as temporary.

Suppose that the home country did not change its supply of goods, Y_t^s, or its demand for goods, C_t^d. Then equation (7.6) implies that the improvement in the terms of trade leads to a surplus on the current account. With an increase in $P/\bar{P}$, the unchanged volume of real exports – corresponding here to total domestic production

Y_t^s – leads to a rise of real export revenues, $(P/\bar{P})Y_t^s$. Since real import expenditure, C_t^d, is unchanged, the current account moves into surplus. (This result still holds if not all production is exported and if some of the expenditures are on domestic goods at price P rather than on imports at price $\bar{P}$.)

The improvement in the terms of trade, however, motivates some changes in goods supplied and demanded. Since the disturbance is temporary, wealth effects are minor. The main responses that we have to consider involve substitution effects. We discuss these effects with the help of Figure 7.7(a). This graph is a little more complicated than usual, so it needs some extra words of explanation. In the north-east quadrant is plotted the supply of domestic goods as a function of the relative price between domestic and foreign goods, that is, the terms of trade. The supply schedule is positively sloped. In deciding on work effort and production, house-

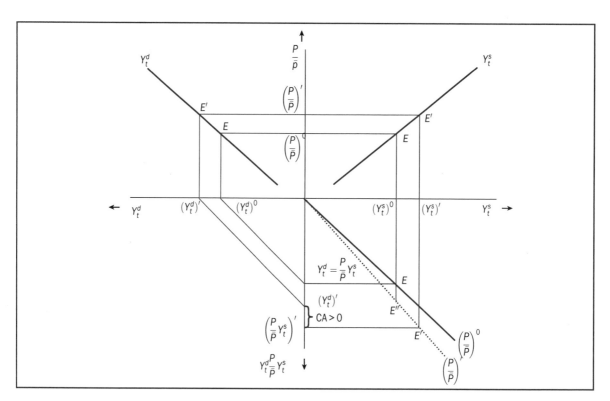

Figure 7.7a Temporary improvement of the terms of trade

holds (in their role as workers and producers) looked before at the marginal product of labour, MPL. The difference now is that producers sell all of their output at the domestic price, P, but buy goods for consumption at the foreign price, $\bar{P}$. (The nature of the results would not change if, as is more realistic, households buy some goods at price P and others at price $\bar{P}$.) An increase in $P/\bar{P}$ means that households obtain more in consumption (of foreign goods) for each unit of work and production. Therefore, just as in the case of an improvement in the schedule for labour's marginal product, the substitution effect from an increase in $P/\bar{P}$ motivates an expansion of work effort and a corresponding rise in the supply of domestic goods, Y_t^s. In the north-west quadrant we represent the domestic demand for foreign goods as also a positive function of the terms of trade. As the foreign good becomes cheaper relative to the good produced domestically, its demand from domestic residents increases. Notice that, in addition to the terms of trade, aggregate demand and supply depend, as usual, on the world interest rate and domestic wealth. Changes in these variables would induce shifts in the location of the schedules in the graph.

The assumption that the domestic country is small implies that prices – the terms of trade and the interest rate – are determined at the world level and are not affected by the domestic economy. In other words, from the point of view of the home country, foreign demand for domestic goods is perfectly elastic (horizontal) at price $P/\bar{P}$, and so is the supply of foreign goods. Notice that in the north-east quadrant quantities are in terms of domestic goods, whereas in the north-west quadrant they are in terms of foreign goods. To compute the current-account balance, in the south-east quadrant, we use the terms of trade to evaluate domestic goods in terms of foreign goods. The slope of the line stemming from the origin is $P/\bar{P}$. Therefore, it translates quantities of domestic goods on the horizontal axis into corresponding quantities of foreign goods on the vertical axis. Nothing really happens in the south-west quadrant. The values of domestic consumption of foreign goods from the horizontal axis of the north-west quadrant are simply copied to the vertical axis of the south-east quadrant.

We are now ready to use Figure 7.7(a). Under our assumption of a zero current-account balance, the initial equilibrium is given by points E in the three quadrants. At $(P/\bar{P})^0$, domestic consumption of foreign goods, $(Y_t^d)^0$, equals the domestic production and export of domestic goods, expressed in terms of foreign goods, $(P/\bar{P})^0 (Y_t^d)^0$. Consider now the effects of a temporary improvement in the terms of trade, that is, an increase in $P/\bar{P}$. This change implies a vertical shift in the terms of trade line in the north quadrants and a clockwise turn in the terms of trade line in the south-east quadrant. Imports and exports increase. But the impact on exports is stronger because of the combination of two effects. First, there is an increase in the value of domestic exports in terms of foreign goods due to the increase of the terms of trade to $(P/\bar{P})'$. This effect is represented by the movement from E to E'' in the south-east quadrant. Second, there is an increase in the physical number of units of the domestic good produced and exported –represented by the movement from E'' to E' in the south-east quadrant. The net effect is a current account surplus.[6]

Figure 7.7(b) describes the above experiment in the usual graph plotting aggregate demand and

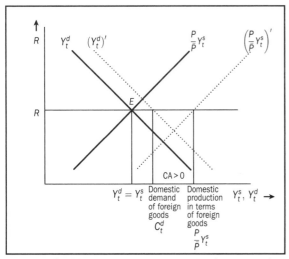

Figure 7.7b Temporary improvement in the terms of trade

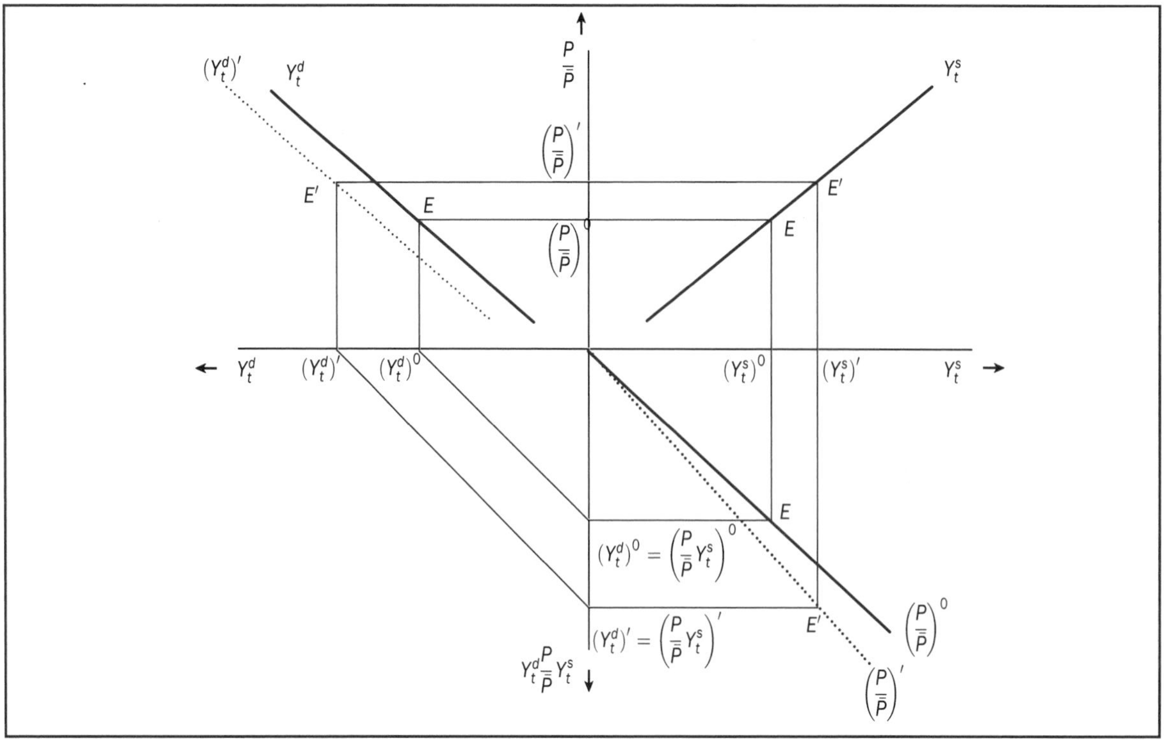

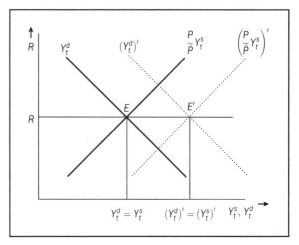

Figure 7.8a   Permanent improvement of the terms of trade

supply as functions of the interest rate. All quantities are expressed in terms of foreign goods. The initial equilibrium is at point E, where the current-account balance is zero. The increase in $P/\bar{P}$ produces a rightward shift in $(P/\bar{P})Y_t^s$ and C_t^d. However, for the reasons discussed above, the shift in supply dominates the shift in demand. Hence, the country runs a current-account surplus and thus accumulates foreign assets. Households, therefore, spread their temporarily high current income over more consumption in many periods.

Consider now the case in which the improvement in the terms of trade is permanent. This case is described in Figures 7.8(a) and 7.8(b). The crucial difference is that the permanent nature of the increase in $P/\bar{P}$ produces a strong wealth effect. The schedule for the demand for imports therefore shifts left. The new equilibrium is such that demand and supply (expressed in the same unit) increase by the same amount. At the new

equilibrium point, E', the current-account balance is zero.

Figure 7.8b   Permanent improvement in the terms of trade

In Figure 7.9 we present, as an example, the behaviour of the current account and the terms of trade for Belgium, Germany and the United States. Notice the sharp deterioration in the terms of trade for all three countries, after the oil-price shocks of 1973–74 and 1979–80. Recall from the above analysis that a temporary improvement in the terms of trade should lead to an increase in the current-account surplus (a reduction of its deficit), whereas a temporary deterioration of the terms of trade should lead to an increase in the current-account deficit (a reduction of its surplus). Judging from Figure 7.9, this interpretation seems to fit reasonably well the case of Belgium, less well the case of Germany, and poorly the case of the US. There are several reasons for these cross-country differences in the relationship between terms of trade and current account. First, as we have learned above, in order to evaluate the impact of a change in the terms of trade we have to establish how persistent the shock was expected to be. This is often a difficult task. Second, the current account can be affected by supply and demand shocks that do not show up, at least in the short run, in movements in the terms of trade.

Finally, other factors, which we have not yet discussed, can change the current account. In the case of the United States, for example, several economists have claimed that the current account has been strongly affected by the behaviour of the US government debt. We will discuss this hypothesis later on in the book when we examine the macroeconomic effects of fiscal policies.

A classic example of the impact of changes in the terms of trade is the current-account balance for the Organization of Petroleum-Exporting Countries (OPEC). Table 7.2 shows that OPEC's current account was nearly balanced in 1972. Then the sharp increases in oil prices during 1973–74 led to a current-account surplus of $60 billion in 1974. From 1974 to 1978, the relative price of oil fell somewhat. But more important, the growing perception that the relative price of oil would remain high motivated the OPEC countries to adjust their expenditures to their higher long-run incomes. By 1978 the current account of OPEC was again nearly balanced but at much higher ECU levels of exports and imports. Then the surprise increases in oil prices in 1979–80 led again to a large surplus on the

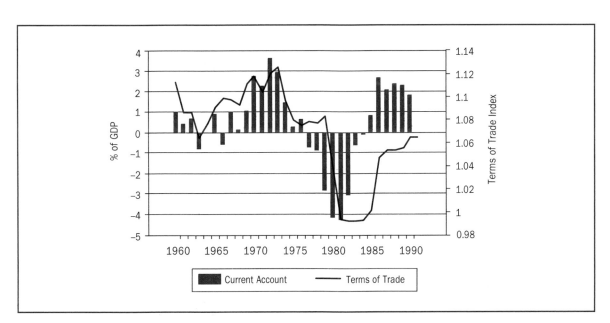

Figure 7.9a   Terms of trade and current account, Belgium

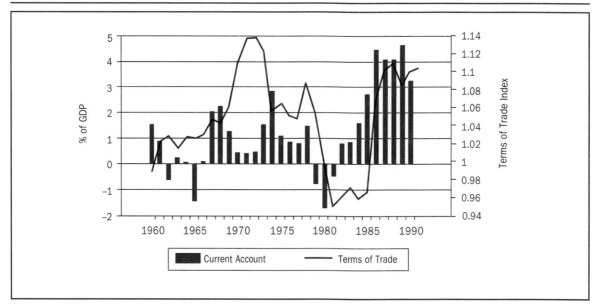

Figure 7.9b   Terms of trade and current acccount, Germany

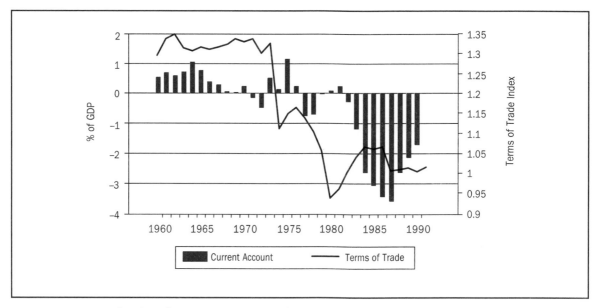

Figure 7.9c   Terms of trade and current account, United States

current account ($104 billion in 1980). In this case the upward adjustment of expenditures moved the current account to a small deficit by 1982. Then the sharp decline in the price of oil in 1986 led to a current-account deficit of $28 billion.

Terms-of-trade movements, in particular those related to the change in the price of raw materials, have attracted much attention after the oil shocks of the 1970s. However, they are not unique to this recent period. The large size and

Year	Current-account balance ($ billion)
1972	1
1974	60
1976	37
1978	−3
1980	104
1982	−10
1984	−7
1986	−28

Source: OECD, *OECD Economic Outlook* (June 1988, July 1983, July 1979).

Table 7.2 Current-account balance of oil-exporting countries (OPEC)

effects of changes in the price of commodities in the 1930s were the reason behind John Maynard Keynes's proposal to create an international organization whose main goal was to stabilize the price of raw materials. In the Appendix to the memorandum to the UK Treasury in which he outlines the plan for such organization, Keynes analyzed the behaviour of the price of four benchmark commodities (rubber, cotton, wheat and lead) in the decade ending in 1938. He reports that the average annual price change for these commodities was 67%, certainly a big number! Keynes stressed the importance of these price changes because of their impact on the terms of trade: 'the tendency of international trade is to make many countries increasingly dependent on individual crops, for which they are specially suited, so that the social consequences of large movements in the prices of these specialized products are severe'.[7]

Box 7.1   Free Trade and Europe 1992

The analysis thus far has posited world free trade in goods and services. In particular, we have assumed that countries did not impose any tariff or quota restrictions on foreign import. In reality, tariffs and quotas are used, to different extent, by most countries. Historically, revenues from import duties have been a non-trivial proportion of government revenues. Since the early 1950s, however, we have observed a worldwide reduction of tariffs and quotas. At a global level, these reductions have been the result of several rounds of negotiations within the framework of the General Agreement on Tariffs and Trade (**GATT**). Thus far, seven rounds of negotiations have been completed, the last being the Tokyo Round in 1979. The eighth one, the Uruguay Round, is currently under way. These negotiations have led to sweeping reductions in the level of tariffs. Today tariff barriers are only a small fraction of what they were just forty years ago. For example, the average tariff level in the United States was around 25% right after the end of World War II, and it is now just above 3%.

Not all tariff reductions, however, have taken place within GATT. In Europe, the European Community had the leading role in promoting free trade. In 1958, tariffs were still significant in the founding members in the Community, as reported in Table 7.3. The Treaty of Rome called for the removal of all tariff barriers inside the Community within twelve years, that is by the end of 1969. This goal was attained, almost two years earlier, by 1968. Denmark, Ireland and the UK, which entered later in the EC, eliminated their tariffs by 1977.

At the beginning of the 1980s, however, it became apparent that, despite the elimination of official tariffs and quota, real free trade in the Community was not yet achieved. Attention shifted to **non-tariff barriers**, national practices and regulations that, even if not explicitly designed to discriminate against foreign products, discourage international

	%
Transport equipment	22
Clothing	21
Footwear	19
Rubber manufactures	18
Building parts and fitting	17
Furniture	17
Manufactures of metal	16
Textiles, except clothing	16
Instruments	16
Wood manufactures, except furniture	16
Electric machinery	15
Paper, paperboard, etc.	15
Non-metallic mineral manufactures	13
Machinery other than electric	13
Chemicals	12
Leather, etc.	12
Ordnance	11
Iron and steel	10
Silver, platinum, gems, jewellery	6
Average	**15**

Source: El-Agraa, *The Economics of the European Community*, 1990.

Table 7.3   Average tariffs in the EC founding members, 1958

trade. In 1985 the EC summit endorsed the European Commission's *White Paper on Completing the Internal Market*, which detailed the steps to be taken in order to create a single European market. Three main types of non-tariff barriers were identified:[8]

- **physical barriers**, mainly associated with frontier formalities like intra-EC border stoppages, customs controls, and related paperwork;
- **technical barriers**, associated with difficulties in meeting divergent national product standards and technical regulations, and in accessing nationally protected public procurement markets;
- **fiscal barriers**, deriving from divergent rates of value added tax and excise duties.

The main obstacle to the elimination of these barriers was political. Community decisions regarding the internal market required unanimity, and few measures had the unconditional support of all member states. The turning point was reached in 1986, with the approval of the *Single European Act*, which formally established 31 December 1992 as the deadline for the completion of the internal market. The Act amended the voting procedure of the Community by introducing the concept of a **qualified majority** for decisions aimed at the establishment and functioning of the internal market. According to this principle, countries are given a different number of votes, depending on their size. France, Germany, Italy and the UK each have 10 votes; Spain 8; Belgium, Greece, the Netherlands and Portugal 5; Denmark and Ireland 3; Luxembourg 2. A decision by qualified majority requires at least 54 votes. This change in voting procedure speeded up the legislative process at the Community level. The goal of drafting and approving in time the over 300 different regulations and directives that were needed to complete the single market project, was made possible.

But how important are non-tariff barriers in practice? What costs did they impose on the Community and what gains should we expect from their removal? Was the 1992 project worth the trouble? The European Commission has tried hard to answer these questions. They estimated that the gain from a single European market would amount, over a five-year period, to between 70 and 190 billion ECUs. This figure is between 2.5% and 6.5% of 1988 Community GDP. These estimates have been criticized for a variety of reasons, mainly for being over-optimistic. Some authors, however, suggested that the gains from 1992 could be much larger than those predicted by the Commission. Richard Baldwin, for example, argued that, by ignoring the dynamic effects of the integration, the Commission might have underestimated the true impact of 1992 by as much as 450%.[9]

Estimating the gains of 1992 is very difficult. Quantifying the total effect of such a complex process is, as the Commission itself admitted, hazardous.[10] It is fair to say, however, that the general opinion of the business community is

I. *Ranking of Market Barriers* (1 = most important, 8 = least important)

	B	DK	D	GR	E	F	IRL	I	L	NL	P	UK	EUR12
Administrative barrier	1	2	2	1	1	2	1	1	1	1	1	2	1
National standards	2	1	1	7	6	1	2	4	2	3	4	1	2
Physical frontier delays and costs	3	3	4	3	2	4	3	3	3	2	2	3	3
Community laws	7	4/5	3	6	4	6	8	6	6	5	7	6	4
Restrictions in capital market	4	6	7	2	5	7/8	5	5	4	6	6	7	5
Regulation in freight and transport	5	4/5	5/6	4/5	3	5	4	8	5	4	5	5	6/7
Differences in VAT	8	7	5/6	4/5	7	3	6	7	7	8	8	8	6/7
Government procurement	6	8	8	8	8	7/8	7	2	8	7	3	4	8

II. *Opinion on the Effects on Costs of Removing Barriers* (replies in %)

	B	DK	D	GR	E	F	IRL	I	L	NL	P	UK	EUR12
Very significant cost reduction	27	1	0	10	8	8	6	26	20	11	32	8	25
Slightly significant cost reduction	58	52	52	61	41	45	61	57	60	44	36	50	37
No effect/no answer	15	46	47	23	34	40	30	17	10	45	30	37	36
Slightly significant cost increase	0	0	0	1	0	0	0	0	0	0	1	0	2
Very significant cost increase	0	1	1	5	2	7	3	0	10	0	1	0	0

III. *Source of Cost Reduction* (1 = most important, 6 = least important)

	B	DK	D	GR	E	F	IRL	I	L	NL	P	UK	EUR12
Distribution costs	1	1	1	3/4	2/3	1	1	1	1	1	3	1	1
Costs of imported materials	3	4	3	2	1	2	3/4	2/3	4/5	2	1	3	2
Production process	2	2/3	2	5	4	3	5	4	3	3	2	2	3
Banking costs	4	5/6	4/5	1	2/3	4	3/4	2/3	2	4	4	5	4
Marketing costs	5	2/3	4/5	6	5	6	6	6	6	5/6	6	4	5
Insurance costs	6	5/6	6	3/4	6	5	2	5	4/5	5/6	5	6	6

B = Belgium; DK = Denmark; D = Germany; GR = Greece; E = Spain; F = France; IRL = Ireland; L = Luxembourg; NL = Netherlands; P = Portugal; UK = United Kingdom

Source: Michael Emerson et al., *The Economics of 1992. The EC Commission's Assessment of the Economic Effects of Completing the Internal Market* (1992), Paolo Cecchini, *The European Challenge, 1992 – The Benefits of a Single Market* (1988).

Table 7.4   Business perceptions of 1992

that gains exist and are significant. As part of their effort to establish the benefit of a single market, the Commission organized wide-ranging surveys of about 11 000 businesses around the Community. As can be seen from Table 7.4, the large majority believes that non-tariff barriers are important and that the costs of conducting business in the EC will be reduced after 1992. The main source of gains is thought to be the abolition of administrative barriers and the harmonization of national standards. These changes should ease the process of product distribution across the Community.

Nontraded Goods

Thus far we assumed that all goods were tradable across countries. But some items, such as services and real estate, are difficult to transport across national borders. Economists account for this phenomenon by including **nontraded goods** in the analysis.[11] Recall that the terms of trade refers to the price of tradables produced in the home country relative to the price of tradables produced in the rest of the world. Given the terms of trade, it is possible for the price of the home country's nontradables to change relative to the price of its tradables. In particular, since the nontradables do not enter into international commerce (by definition), the home country's relative price of nontradables and tradables tends to be more sensitive than the terms of trade to disturbances that originate at home. (In the extreme case of a closed economy, none of its goods enters into international trade and only the domestic disturbances matter.)

Consider how the presence of nontraded goods affects the analysis of a change in the terms of trade. The main consideration is that an improvement in the terms of trade raises the price of the home country's tradables relative to its nontradables. This change motivates the home country to shift production and employment away from the nontradables sector and toward the tradables sector. Hence, the existence of nontradables reinforces the positive effect of the terms of trade on the production of tradables. However, the expansion in the tradables sector may go along with a contraction of production and employment in the nontradables sector. Despite these new effects, it is important to note that the existence of nontradables does not affect our main predictions about the relation between the terms of trade and the current-account balance.

Summary

We began by introducing international trade in goods and credit. These possibilities allow for the efficient specialization of production across countries and for an individual country's spending to diverge temporarily from its income.

In this simple economy, the current-account balance equals national saving. A temporary supply shock in one country reduces desired saving and thereby leads to a deficit on the current account. If the shocks apply to the entire world, there is no one abroad to borrow from. In this situation the typical country does not (and cannot) run a deficit on the current account. We showed that this type of analysis could account for some observed behaviour of international borrowers and lenders.

A temporary improvement in the terms of trade raises desired national saving. Therefore, the current account moves toward surplus. In contrast, a permanent improvement in the terms of trade has little effect on desired national saving. Therefore, the current account does not change. Some evidence of the predicted linkages between the terms of trade and the current-account balance comes from the recent experience of the OPEC countries.

Important Terms and Concepts

common currency
law of one price
international currency
net factor income from abroad
direct investment abroad
net foreign investment
balance on capital account

outflow (inflow) of capital
current-account balance
surplus (deficit) on current account
tradable goods
terms of trade
nontraded goods

Questions and Problems

Mainly for Review

7.1 Equation (7.2) states that the current account balance is identically equal to net foreign investment. If GNP or domestic expenditure changes, why is there a change in net foreign investment rather than a change in the real interest rate? What is the accompanying change in net exports?

7.2 Explain why an improvement in the terms of trade need not be associated with an increase in net exports.

7.3 Why is it infeasible for all countries to run a current-account deficit at the same time?

7.4 If a country runs a trade balance deficit must it also run a current-account deficit?

Problems for Discussion

7.5 Wealth Effects from Changes in the Real Interest Rate

Consider the wealth effects from a change in the world real interest rate.
a. What is the effect for a single country?
b. What is the aggregate effect for the world?
c. How do these results compare with our earlier findings for a closed economy?

7.6 Supply Shocks for a Single Country

Consider a supply shock that adversely affects the home country's production of tradable goods. Assume that the shock is temporary and that no significant change occurs in the terms of trade.
a. If the country can borrow from abroad at the world real interest rate, what happens to the home country's consumption and current-account balance?
b. How do the results differ if the home country cannot borrow from abroad?
c. Assume now that the domestic industries are owned primarily by foreigners. (In other words, domestic residents had diversified their ownership of assets internationally so as not to be too susceptible to local supply shocks.) How does this change affect the answers?

7.7 A Change in the Terms of Trade

In the text we considered a change in the terms of trade that reflected a disturbance from the rest of the world. Suppose instead that a supply shock at home leads to an increase in the relative price of the home country's tradable goods. For example, a harvest failure in Brazil would raise the relative price of coffee. What are the effects from this type of disturbance on the home country's:
a. wealth and consumption of various goods, and
b. current-account balance?
   (*Hint*: Did you assume that the disturbance was temporary or permanent?)

7.8 Tariffs (optional)

Suppose that a small country levies a tariff on imports of a tradable good from abroad. If the good sells at price $\bar{P}$ abroad and if the rate of tariff is 10%, domestic residents pay $1.1 \cdot \bar{P}$ for each unit of the good. Assuming that the tariff is permanent, what are its effects on the home country's:
a. consumption of the various tradable and non-tradable goods,
b. production of tradables and nontradables, and
c. balance on current account?
   Re-do the analysis for the case where the tariff is temporary.

Notes

1. More generally, the variable B_t^f includes not only interest-bearing securities but also any other net claims of domestic residents on the rest of the world. Specifically, it includes ownership of capital abroad, which arises from direct investment in foreign countries. The term RB_t^f encompasses the income from this ownership of capital.

2. Our formulation neglects transfer payments from one country to another and also ignores any net labour income from abroad. This net labour income equals the earnings of domestic residents working in foreign countries, less that of foreigners working in the home country. This category of income is unimportant for most countries. It is, however, a significant negative item for Germany, which imports many foreign workers as *gastarbeiter*, and a significant positive item for countries like Pakistan and Turkey, which export workers to other places. If we included this net labour income, we would add it to the net interest income to measure the overall net factor income from abroad. The term 'factor income' means that the income flows to the factor labour or to the factor 'capital', which corresponds here to the net claims, B^f, on assets abroad.

3. The data on gross domestic product for Mexico and Brazil (mentioned below) are from *International Financial Statistics* (1982 Yearbook, April 1983). The data on external debt for Mexico and Brazil are from Organization of American States, *Statistical Bulletin of the OAS*, vol. 4, nos

1–2 (January-June 1982), table SA-5, p. 30; and Morgan Guaranty Trust, *World Financial Markets* (February 1983), table 2, p. 5.

4. For a discussion of these issues, see Jonathan Eaton, Mark Gersovitz and Joseph Stiglitz (1986), and Jeremy Bulow and Ken Rogoff (1988).

5. The terms of trade should not be confused with the real exchange rate, a concept analyzed in Chapter 11.

6. The effect of a temporary improvement in the terms of trade on the current account is not as unambiguous as described above. As the reader might have guessed, it depends crucially on the assumption about the elasticity of demand and supply of import and export. The international trade literature has studied at length the conditions under which a deterioration of the terms of trade might lead to an increase in the current-account surplus. These are known as the Marshall–Lerner condition and the Bikerdicke–Robinson–Metzler condition.

7. J.M. Keynes (1936) p. 314.

8. See Cecchini, *The European Challenge*, 1992.

9. Richard Baldwin, 'The Economic Effects of 1992', *Economic Policy*, vol. 9.

10. Michael Emerson *et al.*, *The Economics of 1992. The E.C. Commission's Assessment of the Economic Effect of Completing the Internal Market*, Oxford University Press.

11. There are problems in implementing this idea since considerations such as transport costs mean that tradability is a relative matter. Although some goods enter more easily than others into international trade, with enough incentive, almost anything – including the services of workers – becomes a tradable good.

8

An Introduction to Inflation and Interest Rates

This chapter begins the study of **inflation**. By inflation, we mean a continuing upward movement in the general price level. The theoretical analysis suggests some possible sources of inflation. To sort out the possibilities, we shall find it convenient to think about the condition that all money be willingly held:

$$M = P \cdot \Phi(R, \ Y, ...) \qquad (8.1)$$
$$(-) \ (+)$$

One way for the price level to increase is through a downward movement in the real demand for money. For example, a permanent downward shift in the production function would lower aggregate output, Y, and thereby decrease the real quantity of money demanded. But notice that a single disturbance of this type creates a single increase in the price level rather than a continuing series of increases in prices. To generate inflation along this line, we would need a succession of downward shifts to the production function. There is no doubt that adverse shocks to the production function – such as oil crises, harvest failures, and strikes – can influence the general level of prices over short periods. But there is no evidence that these forces can account for inflation in the sense of persistent rises in prices. In fact, the typical pattern for most countries is one of growing output. Since this growth raises the real demand for money, we predict that prices would fall over time if the nominal stock of money, M, did not change.

There can also be reductions in the real demand for money that reflect increasing finan-cial sophistication. As we have seen in Chapter 3, for example, many countries have developed financial instruments and procedures that make it easier for people to economize on money. These financial innovations have led to a downward trend in the real demand for money. This element can account, however, for only a small amount of inflation: something like 1 to 2% per year is a reasonable estimate. Therefore, we cannot use this idea to explain the persistently high rates of inflation that have prevailed in many countries since the late 1960s.

The remaining suggestion from the previous analysis is a link between inflation and increases in the quantity of paper money, M. At an empirical level it is clear, first, that the quantity of money often grows at a high rate over long periods of time and, second, that **rates of monetary growth** differ substantially across countries and over time for a single country. Monetary growth is therefore a good candidate as a source of inflation.

Cross-Country Data on Inflation and Monetary Growth

To assess the role of money as a determinant of inflation, let's examine some data. Table 8.1 shows the experiences of 83 countries during the post-World War II period. The table reports the average growth rates of an index of consumer prices and of money, defined as hand-to-hand currency. (The results are similar for the broader monetary aggregate, M1, which includes check-

Country	$\Delta P/P$	$\Delta M/M$	$\Delta M/M-$ $\Delta P/P$	$\Delta Y/Y$	Time span	Country	$\Delta P/P$	$\Delta M/M$	$\Delta M/M-$ $\Delta P/P$	$\Delta Y/Y$	Time span
Brazil	77.8	77.4	−0.4	5.6	1963–90	New Zealand	7.6	6.4	−1.2	2.6	1954–89
Argentina	76.0	72.8	−3.2	2.1	1952–90	El Salvador	7.6	8.1	0.5	3.3	1951–90
Bolivia	48.0	49.0	1.0	3.3	1950–89	South Africa	7.5	10.1	2.6	3.7	1950–90
Peru	47.6	49.7	2.1	3.0	1960–89	Cameroon	7.5	10.7	3.2	5.5[a]	1963–88
Uruguay	43.1	42.4	−0.7	1.5	1960–89	Ivory Coast	7.3	12.0	4.7	5.0[a]	1962–86
Chile	42.2	47.3	−5.1	3.1	1960–90	Italy	7.3	10.3	3.0	4.6	1950–90
Yugoslavia	31.7	38.7	7.0	8.7[a]	1961–89	Ireland	7.2	7.9	0.7	3.3	1950–89
Zaire	30.0	29.8	−0.2	2.4	1963–86	India	7.2	10.7	3.5	4.2	1960–89
Israel	29.4	31.0	1.6	6.7	1950–90	Pakistan	6.8	10.7	3.9	4.7	1955–90
Sierra Leone	21.5	20.7	−0.8	3.1	1963–88	Syria	6.7	15.0	8.3	5.3	1957–87
Turkey	20.1	22.9	2.8	5.9[a]	1955–88	Finland	6.7	8.6	1.9	4.2	1950–90
Ghana	19.3	18.6	−0.7	2.5	1950–88	Togo	6.6	13.8	7.2	4.4[a]	1963–85
Iceland	18.8	18.4	−0.4	4.3[b]	1950–90	United Kingdom	6.5	6.4	−0.1	2.4	1951–90
Mexico	18.7	23.2	4.5	5.4[a]	1950–89	Congo	6.4	9.6	3.2	–	1960–89
Somalia	18.2	21.7	4.5	–	1960–88	Australia	6.4	8.5	2.1	3.9	1950–90
Colombia	13.9	18.5	4.6	4.7	1950–88	France	6.2	7.0	0.8	4.1	1950–90
Korea (South)	12.8	22.1	9.3	8.6	1953–90	Sweden	6.2	7.4	1.2	2.9	1950–90
Paraguay	12.5	16.9	4.4	4.8	1952–88	Denmark	6.1	7.7	1.6	3.0	1950–89
Sudan	12.0	16.3	4.3	2.3[a]	1956–86	Norway	6.1	6.4	0.3	3.8	1950–90
Costa Rica	11.8	16.5	4.7	4.6	1960–90	Burkina Faso	5.9	10.1	4.2	3.6[a]	1962–85
Ecuador	11.6	15.7	4.1	4.7	1951–89	Sri Lanka	5.9	10.6	4.7	5.0[a]	1950–90
Jamaica	11.2	15.6	4.4	1.8	1960–89	Chad	5.8	7.2	1.4	–	1960–77
Nigeria	10.8	14.2	3.4	4.1	1955–89	Niger	5.8	9.9	4.1	3.2[a]	1963–89
Portugal	9.9	11.5	1.6	4.7	1953–86	Saudi Arabia	5.5	15.0	9.5	6.1	1968–89
Iran	9.9	18.5	8.6	4.7[a]	1959–88	Morocco	5.5	11.1	5.6	3.9	1958–89
Gambia	9.8	11.5	1.7	3.2[a]	1964–86	Tunisia	5.5	11.0	5.5	6.1[a]	1960–90
Guyana	9.8	13.8	4.0	−0.4[a]	1960–88	Libya	5.4	25.0	19.6	5.7[a]	1964–79
Greece	9.5	14.9	5.4	4.7	1953–87	Guatemala	5.4	9.1	3.7	3.9	1950–89
Madagascar	9.5	8.8	−0.7	1.5[a]	1964–86	Thailand	4.9	9.4	4.5	6.8	1955–90
Spain	9.2	13.1	3.9	4.5	1954–90	Honduras	4.9	9.5	4.6	3.6	1950–90
Senegal	8.7	12.2	3.5	1.1	1967–86	Haiti	4.8	9.8	5.0	1.8	1953–89
Mauritius	8.6	12.7	4.1	3.9	1963–90	Japan	4.7	11.2	6.5	6.9[b]	1953–90
Dominican Republic	8.6	13.2	4.6	4.7	1950–90	Iraq	4.7	14.1	9.4	6.6[a]	1965–75
Trinidad and Tobago	8.5	10.5	2.0	1.9	1960–89	Canada	4.6	8.1	3.5	4.2	1950–90
Central African Republic	8.3	11.4	3.1	–	1963–89	Austria	4.5	7.1	2.6	3.9	1950–90
Egypt	8.0	12.0	4.7	4.1[a]	1955–89	Cyprus	4.5	10.5	6.0	5.2	1960–90
Nepal	8.0	14.4	6.4	3.1	1964–89	Netherlands	4.2	6.4	2.2	3.7[b]	1950–89
Venezuela	8.0	10.7	2.7	4.4	1950–90	United States	4.2	5.7	1.5	3.1[b]	1950–90
Philippines	7.8	11.3	3.5	4.8[b]	1950–90	Belgium	4.1	4.0	−0.1	3.3[b]	1950–89
Gabon	7.6	10.0	2.4	5.3[a]	1962–87	Malta	3.6	9.6	6.0	6.2	1960–88
						Singapore	3.6	10.8	7.2	8.1	1963–89

Table 8.1 continues on p. 139

Switzerland	3.2	4.6	1.4	3.1	1950–90
Germany (West)	3.0	7.0	4.0	4.1[b]	1953–90

Note: All growth rates are annual averages for the sample periods shown in the right column. $\Delta P/P$ is the growth rate of consumer prices. $\Delta M/M$ is the growth rate of the stock of currency. $\Delta Y/Y$ is the growth rate of real gross domestic product.

[a]Data on real domestic product were unavailable for these countries. ΔY was calculated by subtracting the average growth rate of consumer prices, ΔP, from the average growth rate of nominal gross domestic product.

[b]Real gross national product was used instead of real gross domestic product.

Source: All data are from issues of *International Financial Statistics*.

Table 8.1 Annual growth rates of prices, money, and output for 83 countries in the post-World War II period (arranged by decreasing order of the inflation rate)

able deposits. However, because of differences in the nature of financial institutions, the meaning of M1 varies more across countries than does that of currency.) The table arranges the countries in descending order with respect to their average rates of inflation. Note the following:

- The average growth rates of prices and money are positive for all countries since World War II.
- The average growth rates are typically high. For example, the median inflation rate for the 83 countries is 7.6% per year, with 23 of them exceeding 10%. For the average growth rate of currency, the median is 11.3% per year, with 57 of the countries above 10%.
- There is a broad cross-sectional range for the average growth rates of prices and money. The average inflation rates vary from 78% for Brazil and 76% for Argentina to 3% for Germany and Switzerland. The growth rates of currency have a comparable range, varying from 77% for Brazil and 73% for Argentina to 4% for Belgium and 5% for Switzerland.
- The average growth rate of currency exceeds that of prices in almost all cases. That is, growing real money balances are typical in the post-World War II period. The median growth rate of real currency across the countries is 3.5% per year.

- Most significant, there is a strong positive correlation (0.97) across countries between the average rates of price change and the average rates of monetary growth.

Figure 8.1 shows the positive correlation between inflation and the growth rate of currency. Each increase by one percentage point per year in the rate of monetary growth is associated with an increase by roughly one percentage point per year in the rate of inflation. The relation between inflation and monetary growth is, however, closer for the more extreme cases than for the moderate ones. For example, the association is less dramatic for countries in which the average rate of monetary growth is between 5 and 15% per year.

If the growth rate of money exceeds the growth rate of prices, then real money balances, M/P, increase over time. Because money is willingly held at each date, the growth rate of real balances must equal the growth rate of real money demanded. Recall that our previous analysis of the demand for money suggested several factors that could lead to increases over time in the quantity of real money demanded. The most important is the growth rate of output. Table 8.1

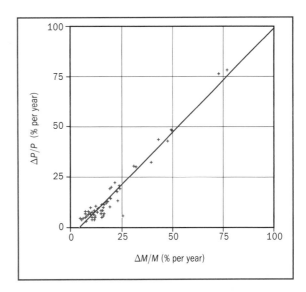

Figure 8.1 Graph of the inflation rate versus the growth rate of currency for 83 countries

shows the average growth rate of output for 79 countries (those for which data are available). Figure 8.2 graphs the growth rate of real money balances against the growth rate of output: the two are positively related (correlation = 0.51). In addition, the median growth rate of output, 4.2% per year, is close to the median growth rate of real money balances, 3.5% per year. The positive effect of growing output on the growth of real money balances means that a country with a higher growth rate of output tends to have a lower rate of inflation for a given rate of monetary growth. Therefore, differences in the growth rates of output explain some of the imperfect association between monetary growth and inflation, as shown in Figure 8.1.

Another variable that influences the demand for money is the interest rate, R, which determines the cost of holding money. Other things equal, we predict that the average growth rate of real money balances will be lower for countries in which the interest rate has increased, and vice versa. Notice that the change in the interest rate, rather than the average level of the interest rate, matters here. Although researchers have verified this proposition for industrialized countries, we cannot demonstrate it for the

substantial number of countries that lack organized securities markets on which interest rates are quoted. We shall see, however, in this and the next chapter that interest and inflation rates are closely related. In particular, increases in the inflation rate mean that money depreciates in real terms at a faster rate and, hence, that the cost of holding money is greater. It follows that an increase in the rate of inflation tends to reduce the real demand for money. We therefore predict that the average growth rate of real money balances will be lower for countries in which the inflation rate has increased. (Notice again that what matters here is the change in the inflation rate rather than the average level of the rate.) As examples, the sharp rises in inflation rates explain the negative growth rates of real money balances that show up in Table 8.1 for Argentina, Zaire, and Sierra Leone.

Overall, the cross-country data suggest a significant, positive association between monetary growth and inflation. This relation is closer than it first appears if we consider additional variables, such as the growth rate of output and changes in interest rates and inflation rates, which affect the real demand for money.

Time Series Data on Inflation and Monetary Growth

Additional evidence on the association between monetary growth and inflation can be found in the analysis of historical data. Table 8.2 reports data for Italy, the United Kingdom and the United States on average rates of inflation and monetary growth over long time periods between 1870 and 1989. Over the entire 130–year span, the average inflation rate was 8.9% per year in Italy, 3.3% in the UK and 2.0% in the US. The average growth rate of money was 11.9% per year in Italy, 4.6% in the UK and 5.3% in the US. Correspondingly, the average growth rate of real money balances was 3.1% per year in Italy, 1.3% in the UK and 3.3% in the US. Notice that this figure accords with the average growth rate of output, which was 2.6% per year in Italy, 1.9% in the UK and 3.4% in the US.

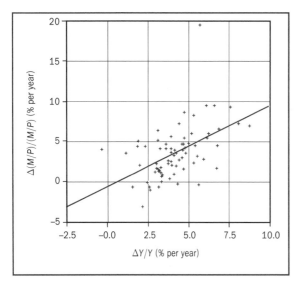

Figure 8.2 Graph of the growth rate of real money balances versus the growth rate of output for 79 countries

	Italy				United Kingdom				United States			
	(1) Money growth	*(2)* Inflation rate	*(3)* GDP growth	*(4)* (1) – (2)	*(1)* Money growth	*(2)* Inflation rate	*(3)* GDP growth	*(4)* (1) – (2)	*(1)* Money growth	*(2)* Inflation rate	*(3)* GDP growth	*(4)* (1) – (2)
1870–1913	3.9	0.7	1.9	3.2	1.4	–0.1	1.9	1.5	3.6	–0.5	3.9	4.2
1913–50	18.2	19.1	1.5	–0.8	5.9	3.2	1.3	2.7	7.4	2.6	2.8	4.8
1950–73	14.3	3.9	5.6	10.4	6.1	4.6	3.0	1.5	3.4	2.6	3.6	0.7
1973–89	15.2	13.0	2.9	2.2	9.0	10.4	2.0	–1.4	7.3	6.5	2.7	0.8
1870–1989	11.9	8.9	2.6	3.1	4.6	3.3	1.9	1.3	5.3	2.0	3.4	3.3

Sources: – Italy: Money before 1960 is a broad money measure (comparable to M2) from Spinelli (1980).
 – Italy: Money after 1960 is M2 from the IMF International Financial Statistics.
 – Italy: Consumer Prices and GDP are from Maddison (1991).
 – UK: Money before 1982 is Monetary Base from Capie and Webber (1985).
 – UK: Money after 1982 is Monetary Base from the IMF International Financial Statistics
 – UK: Consumer Prices and GDP are from Maddison (1991).
 – US: Money before 1960 is Monetary Base from Friedman and Schwartz (1963).
 – US: Money after 1960 Monetary Base from the IMF International Financial Statistics.
 – US: Consumer Prices and GDP are from Maddison (1991).

Table 8.2   Growth rates of money, inflation, and output

Notice that there are substantial differences in the various periods. For example, inflation was very low, in fact negative in the UK and the US, before 1913. Conversely, inflation was high between 1973 and 1989. Also, real money balances grew at very different rates across time and across countries. As in our previous analysis, we can explain some of the divergences between monetary growth and inflation by considering variables that alter the demand for money. These include the growth rate of output, changes in interest rates, and the development of financial institutions. Moreover, international monetary arrangements regarding the type of exchange rate regime can play an important role in the determination of inflation. For example, in the period between 1950 and 1973, which was characterized by fixed exchange rates, inflation was on average lower than between 1973 and 1989, a period characterized by floating exchange rates.[1] We shall come back to the relationship between exchange rate regime and monetary discipline in Chapter 11.

Inflation as a Monetary Phenomenon

Casual observation of two types of data – across countries and over time – suggests that we should consider seriously Milton Friedman's (1968b, p. 29) famous statement, 'Inflation is always and everywhere a monetary phenomenon.' We should, however, remember some important points. First, the analysis will not rule out effects of real disturbances, such as supply shocks, on the price level. We expect, however, that these effects will be more important for isolated episodes of price changes than for chronic inflation. Second, we should view the expression *monetary phenomenon* as incorporating variables that influence the real demand for money, as well as the nominal supply of money. Third, we would eventually like to know why monetary growth behaves differently in different countries and at different times. This question would require us to explore a number of new subjects, including governmental incentives to print more or less money. We sidestep the theory of money supply in this and the next chapter and look only at the consequences for inflation and other variables of a given – unexplained – time path of money. This type of analysis is crucial for an understanding of inflation, although it does not constitute a full study of the topic.

Actual and Expected Inflation

We now begin the process of incorporating inflation into the theoretical model. The inflation rate between periods t and $t + 1$ is defined as

$$\pi_t \equiv (P_{t+1} - P_t)/P_t \qquad (8.2)$$

where π is the Greek letter *pi*. Notice that the inflation rate equals the rate of change of the price level between periods t and $t + 1$. By rearranging equation (8.2), we can solve out for the next period's price level as

$$P_{t+1} = (1 + \pi_t)P_t \qquad (8.3)$$

Hence, prices rise over one period by the factor, $1 + \pi_t$. Although we focus on rising prices – that is, positive rates of inflation – we can also consider declining prices. These cases are called **deflations**.

In making various decisions, such as the choice between consuming now or later, people want to know how prices will change over time. People therefore form forecasts or **expectations of inflation**. We use the symbol π_t^e to denote an expectation of the inflation rate π_t. Usually we think of someone as forming this expectation during period t. Because people already know the current price level, P_t, the expectation of inflation, π_t^e, corresponds to a forecast of the next period's price level, P_{t+1}.

In general, forecasts of inflation are imperfect: the actual rate of inflation is typically higher or lower than the average person's expectation. The forecast error – or **unexpected inflation** – is therefore usually non-zero. People do, however, have incentives to form their expectations *rationally* – making efficient use of the available information on past inflation and other variables

– to avoid systematic mistakes. This rationality implies that unexpected inflation would not exhibit a systematic pattern of errors over time. For example, if unexpected inflation is positive this period, then it may be either positive or negative in the next period.

Real and Nominal Interest Rates

As before, let R_t be the interest rate on bonds. If a person buys ε1 of a bond (with a maturity of one period) during period t, then he or she gets $\varepsilon(1 + R_t)$ as receipts of principal plus interest during period $t + 1$. The ECU value of assets held as bonds therefore rises over one period by the factor $1 + R_t$. We can think of the rate R_t as the ECU or **nominal interest rate**.

What happens over time to the real value of assets that people hold as bonds? If the price level is constant, as in previous chapters, then the real value of these assets also grows at the rate R_t. Thus, in a world of constant prices, the nominal interest rate, R_t, would also be the **real interest rate** – that is, the rate that determines the growth over time in the real value of assets.

If the inflation rate is positive, then equation (8.3) indicates that the price level rises over one period by the factor, $1 + \pi_t$. Therefore, if the ECU value of assets rises over one period by the factor, $1 + R_t$, then the real value of assets rises by the proportion, $(1 + R_t)/(1 + \pi_t)$. Note that the numerator indicates that the ECUs available next period grow by the factor $1 + R_t$, whereas the denominator recognizes that the price level is higher by the factor $1 + \pi_t$.

If households hold assets in the form of bonds, then the real value of these assets rises over one period by the factor $(1 + R_t)/(1 + \pi_t)$. We can define the real interest rate, r_t, to be the rate at which assets held as bonds grow in real terms. Then the real interest rate satisfies the condition

$$(1 + r_t) = (1 + R_t)/(1 + \pi_t) \qquad (8.4)$$

It is the real interest rate, rather than the nominal rate, that determines the amount of extra consumption that someone can get in period

$t + 1$ if he or she foregoes a unit of consumption in period t. If, for example, someone lowers c_t by one unit, then he or she saves P_t extra ECUs (in the form of bonds) and thereby has an additional $P_t \cdot (1 + R_t)$ ECUs to spend in period $t + 1$. This amount buys $P_t \cdot (1 + R_t)/P_{t+1}$ units of additional consumption in period $t + 1$. This term equals $(1 + R_t)/(1 + \pi_t)$, which is the same as $1 + r_t$ from equation (8.4).

The results imply that households will look at the real interest rate, not the nominal rate, when they decide how much to consume, work, and save in various periods. For this reason we want to explore further the meaning and measurement of the real interest rate.

We can obtain a more useful expression for the real interest rate, r_t, if we manipulate equation (8.4). Multiply through on both sides by the term $1 + \pi_t$, and simplify the result to get the condition

$$r_t + \pi_t + r_t \pi_t = R_t \tag{8.5}$$

Recall that we measure each variable – R_t, π_t and r_t – as a growth rate per period, say per month. If we think of interest and inflation rates that are no larger than, say, 20% per year, then the rates per month – R_t, π_t, and r_t – will be no greater than 2%. It follows that the interaction term, $r_t \pi_t$, will be very small in equation (8.5): less than $0.02 \times 0.02 = 0.0004$. We can therefore neglect this term and satisfactorily approximate the real interest rate as

$$r_t \approx R_t - \pi_t \tag{8.6}$$

where the symbol, $\approx$, means approximately equal to.[2]

Recall that the nominal interest rate, R_t, determines how the ECU value of assets held as bonds grows over time. By contrast, the real interest rate, r_t, determines how fast these assets grow in real terms. Equation (8.6) says that the real interest rate, r_t, equals the nominal rate, R_t, less the rate of inflation, π_t. Thus, the real rate is lower than the nominal rate if the inflation rate is positive. Further, the real rate is positive only if the nominal rate exceeds the inflation rate. If the nominal rate is less than the inflation rate, then

the real interest rate is negative. In this case the rise in ECU value at the rate R_t does not cover the rise in prices at the rate π_t.

Actual and Expected Real Interest Rates

We usually think of situations in which people observe the nominal interest rate on bonds, R_t. To calculate the **expected real interest rate** between periods t and $t + 1$, people have to subtract from R_t their expectation of inflation, π_t^e. The expected real interest rate, denoted by r_t^e, is then given by

$$r_t^e \approx R_t - \pi_t^e \tag{8.7}$$

Recall that the actual inflation rate, π_t, can be above or below its expectation, π_t^e. If inflation turns out to be surprisingly high – that is, $\pi_t > \pi_t^e$ – then the real interest rate r_t is less than its expectation, r_t^e. In other words, if we combine equations (8.6) and (8.7), then the unexpected part of the real interest rate, $r_t - r_t^e$, is

$$r_t - r_t^e \approx -(\pi_t - \pi_t^e) \tag{8.8}$$

Errors in forecasts of inflation, $\pi_t - \pi_t^e$, generate errors of the opposite sign in forecasts of the real interest rate.

It is possible to have different institutional arrangements in which borrowers and lenders specify in advance the real interest rate, r_t, rather than the nominal rate, R_t. In this case the nominal payments for principal and interest adjust to compensate for inflation. These adjustments ensure that the actual real interest rate equals the prespecified value. People would then know the real interest rate in advance but would be uncertain about the nominal interest rate.

The financial arrangements in which people contract in advance for real interest rates are called **indexation** or **inflation correction**. These systems tend to exist in countries in which extreme inflation is chronic, such as Brazil and Israel. Recently, as we discuss below, the British government issued a long-term indexed bond of this type. Economists do not know why private parties and governments typically prefer to borrow and lend at prespecified nominal interest rates rather than real rates.[3]

Nominal and Real Interest Rates in the Post-World War II Period

Figure 8.3 shows the relation between the inflation rate, and nominal and real interest rates for the G-6 countries over the post-World War II period. The nominal rate is the average for each year on long-term government securities. The inflation rate for each year, π_t, is the rate of change of the general price level, measured by the consumer price index (CPI). The real interest rate for each year comes from the formula, $r_t = R_t - \pi_t$.

One point to notice in Figure 8.3 is that the nominal interest rate rose dramatically from the end of World War II until the early 1980s in all countries except Germany and Japan. For example, in the UK the rate increased from 3% per year in 1950 to about 6% in the early 1960s, 8 to 9% in the late 1960s, 13% in 1979, and 14.7% in 1981. Even more dramatic was the increase in the nominal interest rate in Italy, which reached a peak of about 21% in 1982. The experiences in France and the US were similar. Further, despite the appearance of a generally upward drift in interest rates, it would not have been easy to forecast this 'trend'. In any event, someone who foresaw this pattern could have made a fortune by speculating on bond prices. After 1981, the interest rate fell in all these four countries. The nominal interest rate in Germany and Japan, on the other hand, did not display the same upward trends before 1981, nor the dramatic reduction afterwards. The movements in the interest rate have been smaller in these two countries. The nominal rate fluctuated between 5% and 10%.

Figure 8.3 also plots the inflation rate and the real interest rate. If the real interest rate were constant, then the nominal interest and the inflation rate would move together on a one-to-one basis. Although r_t varied over time, the striking feature of the graph is the tendency for R_t and π_t to move in the same way. In the subsequent analysis (in Chapter 10), we shall want to understand why nominal interest rates move roughly on a one-to-one basis with inflation rates.

The behaviour of real interest rates differs markedly from that of nominal rates. The real rate, r_t, showed no trend from 1950 to 1972. It fluctuated around a mean as low as 1% in Italy and as high as 4% in Germany. Then the rate fell from 1973 to 1980 and, with the exception of Germany, it was negative on average. In the 80s the real rate rose to an average between 3% (in Italy) and 4.8% (in the US).

The actual rate of inflation, π_t, may diverge substantially from the rate that people expected, π_t^e. In that case the real interest rate, r_t, differs from the expected rate, r_t^e. Because the expected real interest rate will be important for the subsequent analysis, we should make some effort to measure expected inflation.

Measures of Expected Inflation
Economists have employed at least three methods to measure expectations of a variable like inflation or the real interest rate.

1. Ask a sample of people about their beliefs.
2. Use the hypothesis of **rational expectations**, the idea that people's beliefs correspond to optimal predictions, given the available information. Then use statistical techniques to figure out these optimal predictions.
3. Use market data, such as interest rates or prices of financial contracts, to infer what people believe.

The main shortcoming of the first approach is that the sample may not be representative of the whole economy. Also, economists have a better theory of how people take actions than of how they answer questions on surveys. Unlike in a market in which the participants back up their statements with money, it is less clear what it means when someone just expresses opinions about inflation or other variables.

The second approach, based on rational expectations, has produced some successes and some difficulties.[4] One problem arises in figuring out what information people have when they

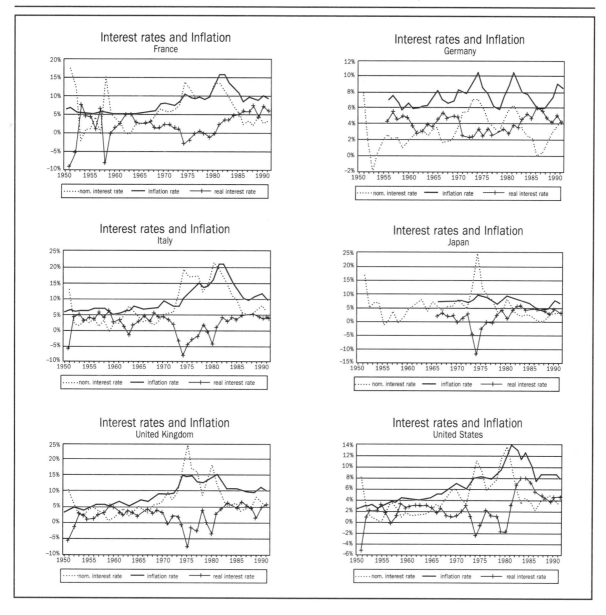

Figure 8.3

form expectations. Another concerns the choice among statistical models. In any event, the results about expected inflation from some of these studies do not differ in many respects from the survey findings that we consider below.

The third approach, which relies on market data, has had limited success thus far for measuring expected inflation.[5] One interesting

source of data is the futures contract based on the US CPI that was traded for a while on the Coffee, Sugar & Cocoa Exchange in New York. Traders in this market essentially bet on the value of the US CPI in future periods. Then these traders won or lost money depending on the value that the US CPI actually took later on. By looking at these bets, we can infer traders' expectations of future changes in the price level in the US. For example, in February 1986, people anticipated an inflation rate of 4.5% for the remainder of 1986, 7.3% for 1987, and 8.1% for 1988. By June 1986, however, the expected inflation rates had fallen to 4.4% for 1987 and 6.6% for 1988. The actual inflation rates – far below expectations as revealed by the CPI futures market – turned out to be 0.6% for 1986, 3.7% for 1987, and 4.6% for 1988. It is, unfortunately, impossible to bring these data up to date because insufficient trader interest has prevented this futures market from operating.

Return now to the first approach, which uses survey data to measure expected inflation. Joseph Livingston, a Philadelphia journalist, began in 1946 to survey about 50 economists (fewer in the early years of the sample) for their forecasts of the US CPI 6 to 12 months in the future. The variable denoted π_t^e in Table 8.3 is the average of the two 6-month-ahead forecasts for each year, when expressed as the implied prediction for the annual rate of inflation.[6] The last column in Table 8.3 shows the corresponding value of the expected real interest rate, $r_t^e = R_t - \pi_t^e$.

Only recently, similar surveys of inflationary expectations have become available for other countries. In Table 8.4 we use one of these surveys to construct the expected real interest rate for the G-6 countries from 1989 to 1992. In contrast with Figure 8.3, the nominal interest rate refers here to short-term government securities (between two and three months). The inflation expectations that we report have been computed by a London-based firm that surveys, every month, about 180 market forecasters world-wide. One important observation from Table 8.4 is the cross-country differences in the expected real rate. In 1991, for example, the expected real rate was about 3% in Germany but over 6% in France. Because there are participants in the financial markets who can move readily between various government bonds, we would anticipate that the expected real interest rates on these assets would be similar. Otherwise, some people would switch to the bond that promised the higher real yield. This process of switching, or **international arbitrage**, would continue until the prices of the bonds adjusted to keep the expected real interest

Year	R_t	π_t	r_t	π_t^e	r_t^e
1948	1.0	0.4	0.6	1.2	-0.2
1949	1.1	-2.8	3.9	-4.0	5.1
1950	1.2	8.0	-6.8	-0.2	1.4
1951	1.6	4.3	-2.7	3.1	-1.5
1952	1.8	0.4	1.4	1.1	0.7
1953	1.9	0.7	1.2	-0.6	2.5
1954	1.0	-1.4	2.4	-0.9	1.9
1955	1.8	0.0	1.8	0.3	1.5
1956	2.7	3.5	-0.8	0.5	2.2
1957	3.3	3.4	-0.1	1.3	2.0
1958	1.8	1.3	0.5	0.1	1.7
1959	3.4	1.3	2.1	0.6	2.8
1960	2.9	1.6	1.3	0.7	2.2
1961	2.4	0.6	1.8	0.6	1.8
1962	2.8	1.3	1.5	1.0	1.8
1963	3.2	1.5	1.7	1.0	2.2
1964	3.6	0.9	2.7	1.0	2.6
1965	4.0	2.1	1.9	1.1	2.9
1966	4.9	3.2	1.7	1.7	3.2
1967	4.3	3.4	0.9	2.1	2.2
1968	5.3	3.8	1.5	2.8	2.5
1969	6.7	5.5	1.2	2.9	3.8
1970	6.5	4.5	2.0	3.6	2.9
1971	4.4	3.3	1.1	3.8	0.6
1972	4.1	3.7	0.4	3.3	0.8
1973	7.0	9.5	-2.5	3.6	3.4
1974	7.9	11.3	-3.4	6.2	2.7
1975	5.8	6.4	-0.6	6.7	-0.9
1976	5.0	5.2	-0.2	5.6	-0.6
1977	5.3	5.9	-0.6	5.6	-0.3
1978	7.2	8.1	-0.9	6.2	1.0
1979	10.1	11.4	-1.3	7.6	2.5
1980	11.4	10.2	1.2	10.4	1.0
1981	14.0	7.6	6.4	9.7	4.3
1982	10.7	4.1	6.6	6.1	4.6
1983	8.6	4.0	4.6	4.5	4.1
1984	9.6	3.1	6.5	5.3	4.3
1985	7.5	3.2	4.3	4.2	3.3
1986	6.0	0.6	5.4	3.5	2.5
1987	5.8	3.7	2.1	3.5	2.3
1988	6.7	4.7	2.0	4.2	2.5
1989	8.1	5.1	3.0	5.0	3.1
1990	7.5	5.4	2.1	3.9	3.6
1991	5.4	2.2	3.2	3.7	1.7

Notes to Table 8.3 continued on p. 147

Note: The inflation rate, π_t, refers to the change in the CPI from January of each year to January of the next year. We use the figures that exclude the shelter component to avoid some problems of measuring mortgage interest costs. The nominal interest rate, R_t, is the average annual rate on secondary markets for US Treasury bills with a three-month maturity. The real interest rate, r_t, equals $R_t - \pi_t$.

Source: The data are from the *Citibase* data bank. The variable π_t^e, from the Livingston survey, comes from the Federal Reserve Bank of Philadelphia. The figures are an average for each year of the 6-month forecasts (from December of the previous year and June of the current year).

Table 8.3   Inflation rates, nominal interest rates, and real interest rates for recent US experience (% per year)

rates close to each other. There are elements, however, that would allow the expected real interest rate to differ across countries. First, bonds of different countries may have different amounts of risk. For example, the return on a French bond could be perceived as riskier because there may be more uncertainty about inflation in France than in Germany. To compensate the investor for this greater risk, the interest rate would be higher on French bonds than on German bonds. Second, different countries have different tax treatment of the interest income deriving from bond holdings. Therefore, the net (of taxes) expected real interest rate, which is what drives international arbitrage, can be very different from the gross expected return reported in Table 8.4. Finally, international investors are not necessarily concerned with rates of return in terms of the currency of denomination of the bonds (as reported in Table 8.4), but in terms of the currency of their country of residence. Therefore, in order to calculate the relevant expected real interest rate we have to compute the expected rate of appreciation or depreciation of the currency of denomination of the bond. Again, this could produce different figures from those calculated in the table. Moreover, since exchange rate movements are uncertain, investors have to bear different amounts of risk which is related to the variability of the value of the currency of denomination of the bonds. We shall expand on the reasons for the existence of interest-rate differentials in Chapter 11.

	nominal interest rate	expected inflation	actual inflation	expected real interest rate	ex-post real interest rate
France					
1989	9.4	3.4	3.4	5.9	5.9
1990	10.2	3.1	3.5	7.2	6.7
1991	9.7	3.3	2.9	6.4	6.8
1992	10.3	3.1	2.3	7.2	8.0
Germany					
1989	4.6	3.0	2.7	1.6	1.9
1990	5.7	3.0	2.8	2.8	2.9
1991	6.7	3.4	4.0	3.2	2.7
1992	7.8	3.9	3.7	3.9	4.1
Italy					
1989	10.2	6.5	6.6	3.6	3.6
1990	9.6	5.9	6.3	3.7	3.4
1991	10.9	6.5	6.1	4.4	4.8
1992	12.1	5.4		6.7	
Japan					
1989	3.0	2.5	3.5	0.5	-0.5
1990	5.0	2.1	3.9	2.9	1.2
1991	5.4	3.2	2.1	2.2	3.3
1992	4.0	2.2	2.5	1.9	1.5
UK					
1989	13.4	7.7	7.7	5.8	5.8
1990	14.1	7.4	9.0	6.7	5.2
1991	10.8	6.1	4.1	4.7	6.7
1992	9.7	4.1	5.5	5.7	4.3
US					
1989	8.4	4.8	5.1	3.6	3.3
1990	7.5	4.4	5.4	3.1	2.1
1991	5.4	4.6	2.2	0.8	3.2
1992	3.9	3.2	3.0	0.7	0.9

Note: The inflation rate refers to the change in the CPI from January of each year to January of the next year. The nominal interest rate is the average annual rate on secondary market for Treasury bills with a three-month maturity. The ex-post real interest rate is the difference between the nominal interest rate and the rate of inflation. The expected real interest rate is the difference between the nominal interest rate and the expected rate of inflation.

Source: Nominal interest rates and consumer prices are from DATASTREAM.

   The expected rates of inflation are from Consensus Economics Inc., London.

   The figures are an average for each year of the 6-month forecasts (from December of the previous year and June of the current year).

Table 8.4   Inflation rates, nominal interest rates and real interest rates for recent G-6 countries' experience (% per year)

The comparison of Tables 8.3 and 8.4 provides further evidence of the problems of using survey data on expectations. The expected rates of inflation for the US in the years available in both surveys are close, but do not coincide. The reason is that opinions differs across individuals. Therefore, it is difficult to calculate expected real interest rates objectively and accurately. Nonetheless, the expected real interest rate is a crucial concept; it is important to learn about this concept, even if we can measure it only imprecisely.

Expected Inflation and Expected Real Interest Rate in the Post-World War II Period

Given the limited amount of survey data for most countries, we now construct expected inflation by using the second type of methodology we described above, i.e. that of using statistical techniques to compute people's best predictions of future inflation.[7] As we said before, the results from this type of analysis do not differ substantially from the survey findings, mainly because many of the individuals that respond to the surveys use this type of statistical technique to firm up their belief about inflation. In Figure 8.4 we plot quarterly data for the actual inflation rate, the expected inflation rate and the difference between the two – the inflationary surprise – for the G-6 countries. The figure shows that expected inflation tracks closely actual inflation most of the time and, thus, inflationary surprises fluctuate around zero. Nonetheless, there are periods in which inflationary surprises are large. For example, in the mid-1970s, expected inflation was well below actual inflation in most countries.

In Table 8.5 we report average nominal interest rates, inflation rates, expected inflation, actual and expected real interest rates for selected periods over the sample 1960 to 1990. The behaviour of expected real interest rates differs markedly from that of nominal interest rates. In the period from 1960 to 1973, the expected real rate, r_t^e, averaged between 0.3% in Italy and 3.2% in Germany, while the average nominal interest rate ranged between 4.0% in Italy and 7.6% in Japan. Between 1974 and 1979, while the nominal interest rate increased in all six countries, the

expected real interest rate fell to an average of zero across the G-6, ranging between −3.5% in the UK to 2.2% in Germany. In the period from 1980 to 1984, nominal interest rates increase further, but this time expected real interest rates also rose to an average of 3.6%. Finally, between 1985 and 1990, nominal interest rates decreased substantially in all six countries, but expected real interest rates decreased only in Germany, Japan and the US, while they increased in France, Italy and the UK.

Another fact to note from Table 8.3 is that deviations of actual from expected inflation, $\pi_t - \pi_t^e$, explain some of the behaviour of actual real interest rates, r_t. Remember that, for a given value of r_t^e, the inflation surprise, $\pi_t - \pi_t^e$, reduces r_t one-to-one. In particular, surprise inflation – $\pi_t > \pi_t^e$ – accounts for some of the smallest real interest rates. In the period 1974–79, expected inflation was below realized inflation in all six countries. In the G-6, actual inflation in this period was, on average, 11% while expected inflation was 9%. This explains why actual interest rates were negative in this period – −2.0 on average.

In a longer-run context, the average of the expected inflation for the G-6 countries from 1960 to 1990 was 5.6%, compared to an average for actual inflation of 6.6%. Correspondingly, the average expected real interest rate, r_t^e, of 2.1% was above the average of the actual rate, r_t, of 1.2%. In fact, expected real interest rates were above actual interest rates in all the G-6 countries. In other words, the persisting tendency to underpredict inflation is a partial explanation for why r_t averaged only slightly above zero.

To use inflation surprises to explain high real interest rates, we have to search for unexpectedly low inflation. Mainly we find this pattern in the second part of the 1980s. Consequently, the average of r_t in the G-6 from 1985 to 1990 was 4.3%, compared to an average for r_t^e of 3.7%.

Interest Rates on Money

We have discussed the nominal and real interest rates on bonds. But the same analysis applies to

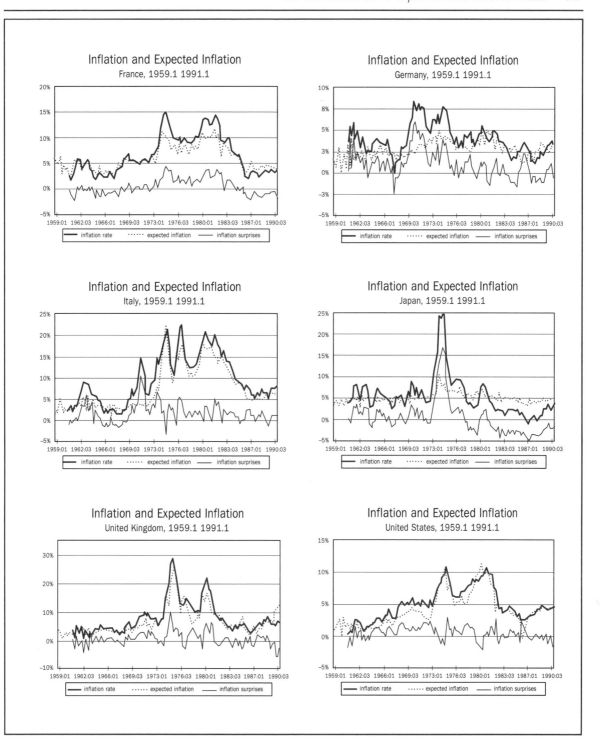

Figure 8.4

	France	Germany	Italy	Japan	UK	US	Average G-6
			Nominal interest rates				
1960–1973	5.5	5.7	4.0	7.6	5.9	4.4	5.5
1974–1979	9.2	5.7	13.9	7.7	10.2	6.8	8.9
1980–1984	13.2	8.5	17.6	7.6	11.9	10.9	11.6
1985–1990	8.8	5.4	12.1	5.1	11.3	6.9	8.3
1960–1990	8.1	6.1	9.7	7.1	8.7	6.4	7.7
			Inflation rates				
1960–1973	4.5	4.4	5.8	6.1	5.2	3.6	5.0
1974–1979	10.7	4.7	16.0	10.2	16.2	8.0	11.0
1980–1984	11.2	3.8	16.6	3.9	9.7	6.8	8.7
1985–1990	3.6	2.5	7.2	1.5	5.7	3.7	4.0
1960–1990	6.7	4.0	9.9	5.6	8.2	5.1	6.6
			Expected inflation				
1960–1973	4.7	2.4	3.8	4.8	4.4	2.6	3.8
1974–1979	8.7	3.6	13.8	6.7	13.6	7.3	9.0
1980–1984	9.2	3.7	14.4	5.4	8.6	6.6	8.0
1985–1990	4.5	2.4	6.3	4.4	6.2	3.6	4.6
1960–1990	6.1	2.9	7.9	5.2	7.2	4.4	5.6
			Expected real interest rates				
1960–1973	0.8	3.2	0.3	2.8	1.5	1.8	1.7
1974–1979	0.5	2.2	0.1	1.0	−3.4	−0.5	−0.0
1980–1984	4.1	4.8	3.2	2.2	3.3	4.3	3.6
1985–1990	4.3	3.0	5.8	0.6	5.2	3.3	3.7
1960–1990	1.9	3.2	1.7	1.9	1.5	2.0	2.1
			Actual real interest rates				
1960–1973	1.0	1.3	−1.8	1.4	0.8	0.9	0.6
1974–1979	−1.5	1.0	−2.1	−2.5	−6.0	−1.2	−2.0
1980–1984	2.0	4.6	1.0	3.7	2.2	4.1	2.9
1985–1990	5.2	2.9	5.0	3.6	5.7	3.2	4.3
1960–1990	1.5	2.1	−0.1	1.4	0.6	1.4	1.2

Table 8.5   Interest rates and inflation rates (average over period)

money once we specify that the nominal interest rate on money is zero rather than R_t. Recall that the real interest rate on any asset equals the nominal rate less the rate of inflation, π_t. The real rate for bonds is therefore $r_t = R_t - \pi_t$. Since money (currency) has a nominal interest rate of zero, the real interest rate is $-\pi_t$. Positive inflation means that the purchasing power of money erodes over time.

As with bonds, we can distinguish the expected real interest rate on money from the actual rate. The expected real interest rate on money is the negative of the expected inflation rate, $-\pi_t^e$.

Remember that the money in our model is like currency, which pays a zero nominal interest rate. Most forms of checkable deposits pay interest. For these types of 'moneys', we would calculate the real interest rate just as we do for bonds: the real rate equals the nominal interest rate paid on deposits less the rate of inflation.

Summary

We began by examining data on monetary growth and inflation across countries and over

Box 8.1 Indexed Bonds in the United Kingdom

We mentioned before that indexed bonds adjust their nominal payments to provide a known real interest rate.[8] We therefore do not have to measure expected inflation to compute expected real interest rates (which equal the actual rates in this case).

The British government began in March 1981 to issue marketable bonds ('gilts') that linked the nominal interest payments and principal to a broad index of retail prices.[9] Table 8.6 shows that real interest rates on British indexed bonds rose from 2.4% in 1981 to 4.3% in 1991. From 1982 to 1990, the average value of 3.4% coincides with the average for expected real interest rates, r_t^e, in the United States (see Table 8.3). The UK yields were, however, lower in the earlier part of the period (3.1% for the United Kingdom versus 4.1% for the United States from 1982 to 1985) and higher in the later part (3.7% versus 2.8% from 1986 to 1990). In 1991, the UK yield of 4.3% was more than double the US value of 1.7%.

Notice that the real interest rates for the years 1989–91 in Table 8.6 are different from the corresponding ones in Table 8.4. The reason is that the debt studied in Table 8.6 has a maturity of about 25 years, whereas the Treasury bills considered in Table 8.4 have a maturity of 3 months. If we were to use in Table 8.4 the nominal interest rate on long-term government securities, the corresponding expected real interest rate would have been 3.1% in 1989, 4.6% in 1990 and 4.0% in 1991, which are much closer to the figures in Table 8.6.

Period	Real Interest Rate[a]
1981 (April–December)	2.4
1982	2.8
1983	2.9
1984	3.3
1985	3.3
1986	3.5
1987	3.7
1988	3.8
1989	3.6
1990	4.1
1991	4.3

[a]The rate applies to bonds with roughly a 25-year maturity.

From April 1981 to March 1982, the values are estimated from the yield on bonds due in 1996.

For 1981–83, Buckmaster & Moore, *Index-Linked Gilt Book*, May 1985; for 1984–88, Bank of England; for 1989–90, Central Statistical Office (U.K.), *Financial Statistics*; for 1991, Bank of England *Quarterly Bulletin*.

Table 8.6   Real interest rates on indexed bonds in the United Kingdom

time. These data suggest that variations in monetary growth account for a good deal of the variations in inflation rates.

The real interest rate on bonds, r_t, equals the nominal rate, R_t, less the inflation rate, π_t. If a bond specifies the nominal interest rate in advance, then the expected real interest rate, r_t^e, depends inversely on the expected inflation rate, π_t^e. We examined the data since World War II on government securities, the CPI inflation rate, and survey data of expected inflation. Over the long term, the nominal interest rate moved together with the actual and expected rates of inflation.

Important Terms and Concepts

inflation
rate of monetary growth
deflation
expectation of inflation
unexpected inflation
nominal interest rate
real interest rate
expected real interest rate
indexation
inflation correction
rational expectations
international arbitrage

Questions and Problems

Mainly for Review

8.1 Monetarists hold that changes in the price level are primarily the results of changes in the quantity of money. Can this conclusion be based solely on theoretical reasoning? Explain.

8.2 Define the real interest rate. Why does it differ from the nominal interest rate in the presence of inflation?

8.3 Why does the actual real interest rate generally differ from the expected rate? How does this relation depend on whether bonds prescribe the nominal interest rate or the real interest rate?

8.4 Consider the data from surveys of inflationary expectations. What are the pluses and minuses of using this type of information to measure expected rates of inflation?

Problems for Discussion

8.5 Monetary Growth and Inflation
Suppose that the money-demand function takes the form

$$(M/P)^d = \Phi(R, \ Y, ...) = Y \cdot \Psi(R)$$
$$\quad\quad\quad (-) \quad (+) \quad\quad\quad (-)$$

where Ψ is some function. This form says that an increase in real output by, say, 10% raises the real demand for money by 10%.
  a. Is it possible that this form of the demand for money accords with our theory of money demand from Chapter 3?
  b. Consider the relation across countries between the average growth rates of money and prices. If the functional form shown above for money demand applies, how does the average growth rate of real output affect the relation between the growth rates of money and prices?
  c. What is the relation between the average growth rates of money and prices for a country in which the nominal interest rate, R, has increased?
  d. If the expected real interest rate is constant, then what is the relation between the average growth rates of money and prices for a country in which the expected inflation rate, π^e, has increased? How does this result apply to countries for which we do not observe the nominal interest rate, R, on an organized credit market?

8.6 Statistical Relations between Monetary Growth and Inflation (optional)
Students who have studied econometrics and who have access to a statistical package on a computer should do the following exercise.
  a. Use the data in Table 8.1 to run a regression of the inflation rate, ΔP, on a constant and the growth rate of money, ΔM. What is the estimated coefficient on money growth and how should we interpret it? What is the meaning of the constant term?
  b. Run a regression of the growth rate of real money balances, $\Delta M - \Delta P$, on the growth rate of real output, ΔY, and a constant. Interpret the coefficient on ΔY.
  c. Suppose that we add the variable, ΔY, to the regression run in part (a). What is the estimated coefficient on ΔY and how should it be interpreted?

8.7 Prepayments of Mortgages and Callability of Bonds
Mortgages typically allow the borrower to make early payments of principal, which are called *prepayments*. Sometimes the mortgage contract specifies a penalty for prepayments and sometimes there is no penalty. In recent years some governments have prohibited prepayment penalties on mortgages. (Lenders do, however, usually charge some fees for setting up a new mortgage.) Similarly, long-term bonds typically allow the issuer to prepay the principal after a prescribed date and with a specified penalty. When the bond issuer exercises this option to prepay, he or she is said to 'call' the bond. Bonds that allow this option are said to be *callable* or to have a *call provision*.
  a. When would a borrower want to prepay (or call) his or her mortgage or bond? Would we see more prepayments when nominal interest rates had unexpectedly increased or decreased?
  b. From the late 1970s until 1982 banks and savings and loan associations were eager for their customers to prepay their mortgages. Why was this the case? More recently, the customers wanted to prepay: why is that?

c. Suppose that there is an increase in the year-to-year fluctuations of nominal interest rates. (These fluctuations were particularly great from the mid-1970s through the early 1980s.) From the standpoint of a borrower, how does this change affect the value of having a prepayment option – that is, callability – in his or her mortgage or bond?

8.8 Rational Expectations and Measures of Expected Inflation

How would the hypothesis of rational expectations help us to measure inflationary expectations? What seem to be the pluses and minuses of this approach?

8.9 Indexed Bonds

Consider a bond that costs ε1000. Suppose that the bond pays a year later the principal of ε1000 plus interest of ε100.

a. What is the nominal interest rate on the bond? What are the actual and expected real interest rates? Why is the nominal rate known, but the real rate uncertain? Suppose that someone issues an indexed bond, which adjusts the payments to compensate for inflation. For example, assume that the total amount paid a year later is the quantity $ε1100 \cdot (1 + \pi)$, where π is the inflation rate over the year.

b. What is the real interest rate on the indexed bond? Why is the real rate known but the nominal rate uncertain?

c. Can you think of other types of indexed bonds? Are the real and nominal interest rates both uncertain in some cases?

Notes

1. Between March 1979 and September 1992, the fluctuations of the lira were formally restricted within a band, as prescribed by the Exchange Rate Mechanism of the European Monetary System. Until the mid-1980s, however, the wideness of the band and the frequent realignments of the central parity around which the band was defined, implied that the lira was effectively in a flexible rate system.

2. The approximation becomes better the shorter the length of the period (and becomes perfect as the length approaches zero). The length of the period actually plays no economic role in the model and we use these periods – *discrete time* – solely for convenience. We can therefore assume that a period is extremely brief and, hence, that equation (8.6) is accurate.

3. There have been some suggestions: (1) People use and hold money – an asset that is denominated in nominal units – which makes it desirable to borrow and lend in the same units. (2) The government enforces contracts in nominal units more diligently than contracts in other units. (3) The tax treatment of indexed bonds is unclear. (4) It is hard to agree on a price index to use in making inflation corrections.

4. For uses of this approach to measure expected inflation, see, for example, James Hamilton (1985).

5. Eugene Fama (1975) suggested that nominal interest rates were good measures of expected inflation. But his estimated relationships broke down after the early 1970s. For some discussion of this topic, see Charles Nelson and William Schwert (1977).

6. For a discussion of the Livingston survey, see John Carlson (1977).

7. The statistical technique we used to compute expected inflation is that of linear least squares forecast based on an autoregressive representation of inflation. This is a common technique and the interested reader should consult, for example, Sargent (1979) Ch. 11, for a detailed discussion.

8. The famous economist, Irving Fisher, had his company, Cardex Rand, issue an indexed bond in the 1920s, but it was not very popular.

9. Because the index linking involves a lag of eight months, the real yield varies somewhat with actual inflation. But as a first approximation, we can treat the real interest rate as known in advance.

9

Money, Inflation, and Interest Rates in the Market-Clearing Model

This chapter uses the market-clearing model to study inflation and nominal interest rates. For the main analysis we return to the setting from Chapter 5 that does not deal explicitly with a labour market or firms. As we saw in Chapter 6, this simplification will be satisfactory for most purposes. The basic approach will be to specify a given time path of the money stock, M_t. Then we figure out what time path of the price level, P_t – hence, of the inflation rate, π_t – and of the nominal and real interest rates, R_t and r_t, satisfy the conditions for general market clearing.

We shall focus on the consequences of different rates of anticipated inflation and monetary growth. Even when the inflation rate, π_t, varies over time, we assume that people forecast these changes accurately. Put another way, people have **perfect foresight** about future price levels, so that there is always equality between the actual and expected inflation rates, $\pi_t = \pi_t^e$. Accordingly, if people know the nominal interest rate, R_t, then there is also equality between actual and expected real interest rates, $r_t = r_t^e$.

The analysis is limited because it does not address unanticipated inflation and monetary growth. (We shall explore these matters later.) But it is useful to study anticipated inflation as a separate topic. In particular, the changes in anticipated inflation explain the principal longer-term movements in nominal interest rates since World War II.

Incorporation of Inflation and Monetary Growth into the Model

We want to incorporate into the model the new elements that were discussed in Chapter 8. These new features include inflation and the distinction between real and nominal interest rates. To analyze the link between monetary growth and inflation, we also have to extend the model to allow for changes in the stock of money.

For simplicity, we begin with situations in which the nominal interest rate, R, and the inflation rate, π, are constant over time. Therefore, the real interest rate, $r = R - \pi$, is also constant. Because we assumed equality between actual and expected inflation, $\pi = \pi^e$, there is also equality between actual and expected real interest rates, $r = r^e$.

Monetary Growth and Transfer Payments

We choose the simplest possible way to introduce monetary growth into the model: new money shows up as transfers from the government to households. (Later we shall see that the main results still hold for other, more realistic methods of introducing new money into the economy.)

Denote by v_t the ECU amount of transfer that a household receives during period t. This amount need not be the same for everyone. The government finances the total of transfers, V_t, by printing and distributing new money. The change in the aggregate quantity of money, $M_t - M_{t-1}$, therefore equals the aggregate amount of transfers:

$$V_t = M_t - M_{t-1} \qquad (9.1)$$

Equation (9.1) is a simple version of a **governmental budget constraint**.

The left side is total government expenditures, all of which take the form of transfers at this point. The right side shows government revenues. At present, this revenue derives solely from the printing of new paper money.

We can think of transfer payments as arising via a 'helicopter drop' of cash.[1] Our public officials effectively stuff a helicopter full of paper currency and fly around dropping money randomly over the countryside. The transfer payments occur when people pick up the money. Despite the unrealistic flavour of this story, the only important aspect of it is that each person's transfer is independent of his or her level of income, previous amount of money holdings, and so on. Economists refer to these kinds of transfers as **lump-sum transfers**: the amount that someone receives is independent of his or her level of work effort, holdings of money, or other activities. Because the transfers are lump sum, an individual understands that changes in his or her holdings of money, m_t and m_{t-1}, have no impact on the size of his or her transfer, v_t.[2]

We have to modify households' budget constraints to include the transfer payments. Each household's budget constraint for period t is

$$P_t y_t + b_{t-1}(1+R) + m_{t-1} + v_t = P_t c_t + b_t + m_t \qquad (9.2)$$

As before, the sources of funds on the left side include the ECU receipts from the commodity market, $P_t y_t$, plus the values of the bonds and money that were held last period, $b_{t-1}(1+R) + m_{t-1}$. The new element is the ECU amount of transfer, v_t, which is an additional source of funds

for a household. The right side of equation (9.2) contains the same uses of funds as before: the nominal purchases of commodities, $P_t c_t$, plus this period's holdings of bonds and money, $b_t + m_t$. Notice that we date the price level, P_t, because it will no longer be constant over time. Since we assume that the nominal interest rate, R, is constant, we do not have to date it.

Budget Constraints over an Infinite Horizon

We have to make some adjustments to incorporate inflation into households' budget constraints over an infinite horizon. Let's put aside the various monetary terms, which include the initial stock of real money balances, the transfers received from the government, and the interest foregone by holding money. (The appendix to this chapter shows that this omission is satisfactory.) Then, when written in terms of nominal present values, the budget constraint over an infinite horizon looks basically like it did before. Since we assume that the nominal interest rate R is constant, the condition is

$$P_1 y_1 + P_2 y_2/(1+R) + P_3 y_3/(1+R)^2 + \ldots$$
$$+ b_0(1+R)$$
$$= P_1 c_1 + P_2 c_2/(1+R) + P_3 c_3/(1+R)^2 + \ldots \qquad (9.3)$$

The only new element in equation (9.3) is the dating of the price level.

Recall that we assume a constant rate of inflation, π. Therefore the price levels for any two adjacent periods satisfy the condition, $P_t = (1+\pi)P_{t-1}$. We can use this condition repeatedly to express each future level of prices in terms of the current price, P_1, and the inflation rate π. Then we get the sequence:

$$P_2 = (1+\pi)P_1,$$
$$P_3 = (1+\pi)^2 P_1,$$
.
.
.

If we substitute these results into the budget constraint from equation (9.3), then we get the revised condition

$$P_1[y_1 + y_2 \cdot (1+\pi)/(1+R) +$$
$$y_3 \cdot (1+\pi)^2/(1+R)^2 + \ldots] + b_0(1+R)$$
$$= P_1[c_1 + c_2 \cdot (1+\pi)/(1+R) +$$
$$c_3 \cdot (1+\pi)^2/(1+R)^2 + \ldots] \quad (9.4)$$

Notice that the next period's real income and spending, y_2 and c_2, enter multiplicatively with the factor $(1+\pi)/(1+R)$. But recall from Chapter 8 that the relation between real and nominal interest rates is $(1+r) = (1+R)/(1+\pi)$. The term in equation (9.4), $(1+\pi)/(1+R)$, is therefore equal to $1/(1+r)$. Hence, to express the next period's real income and spending, y_2 and c_2, as present values, we divide by the discount factor, $1+r$. This result makes sense because the real interest rate tells people how they can exchange goods of one period for those of another. In particular, it is the *real* interest rate, rather than the *nominal* rate, that matters here.

The same idea applies for any future period. For example, the real income and spending for period 3, y_3 and c_3, enter into equation (9.4) as a multiple of the factor, $(1+\pi)^2/(1+R)^2$, which equals $1/(1+r)^2$. If we make all these substitutions into equation (9.4) – and also divide through by the current price level, P_1 – then we end up with a simplified form of the budget constraint:

$$y_1 + y_2/(1+r) + y_3/(1+r)^2 + \ldots$$
$$+ b_0(1+R)/P_1 = c_1 + c_2/(1+r) +$$
$$c_3/(1+r)^2 + \ldots \quad (9.5)$$

(The nominal interest rate appears in the term $b_0(1+R)$ because this term is the nominal value of the bonds carried over to period 1.)

Equation (9.5) is the budget constraint in real terms over an infinite horizon. The new element is that the real interest rate, r, appears instead of the nominal rate, R, in the various discount factors.

Intertemporal-Substitution Effects

We discussed before how the interest rate has intertemporal-substitution effects on consumption, leisure, and saving. These effects involve the relative costs of taking consumption or leisure at one date rather than another. In making these comparisons an individual wants to know, for example, how much extra consumption he or she can get next period by reducing consumption this period. As we worked out before, an individual can save and thus transform each unit of consumption foregone this period into $1+r$ units of added consumption for the next period. An increase in the real interest rate, r, motivates people to reduce current consumption and leisure to raise future consumption and leisure. In other words, a higher r motivates people to save more today. The important point is that the real interest rate matters here rather than the nominal rate. Thus, our previous discussions of intertemporal-substitution effects remain valid if we replace the nominal interest rate by the real rate.

Recall that in this chapter we treat the real interest rate, r, as a known quantity. More generally, the expected real interest rate, $r^e = R - \pi^e$, is what matters for intertemporal-substitution effects. No one shifts their planned time paths of consumption and leisure, and hence their saving, unless they anticipate that the real interest rate will be either higher or lower. For intertemporal-substitution effects to arise, there must be a change in the nominal interest rate, R, relative to the expected rate of inflation, π^e.

Interest Rates and the Demand for Money

Recall that the demand for money involves a trade-off between transaction costs and interest foregone. Further, the interest foregone depends on the differential between the interest rate on bonds and that on money. Since the nominal interest rate on money is zero, this differential equals the *nominal* interest rate, R (and not the *real* interest rate, r). It follows that the demand-for-money function involves the nominal interest rate, R. Therefore, as in our previous analysis that neglected inflation, the function for the aggregate real demand for money takes the form

$$(M_t/P_t)^d = \Phi(Y_t, R, \ldots) \qquad (9.6)$$
$$\quad\;\; (+)\;(-)$$

Notice an important point. It is the (expected) real interest rate, r, that exerts intertemporal-substitution effects on consumption and work. But it is the nominal interest rate, R, that influences the real demand for money.

Market-Clearing Conditions

We know from Chapter 5 how to express the conditions for general market clearing. First, the aggregate supply of goods, Y_t^s, equals the demand, C_t^d:

$$Y^s(r_t, \ldots) = C^d(r_t, \ldots) \qquad (9.7)$$
$$\;\;(+) \qquad\qquad (-)$$

Equation (9.7) shows the intertemporal-substitution effects from the real interest rate, r_t. As usual, this effect is positive on the supply of goods and negative on the demand. The omitted terms, denoted by . . ., include various aspects of the production function.

Second, we have the condition that all money be willingly held. We can write this condition for period t as

$$M_t = P_t \cdot \Phi(Y_t, R_t, \ldots) \qquad (9.8)$$
$$\qquad\quad (+)\;(-)$$

On the left is the actual quantity of money. On the right is the nominal demand for money, which depends positively on the price level, P_t, and aggregate output, Y_t, and negatively on the nominal interest rate, R_t. Any other factors that influence money demand, such as transaction costs, are denoted by the expression . . . in equation (9.8). We assume that these factors do not change over time.

The Superneutrality of Money

Before we explore the details of the link between monetary behaviour and inflation, we can already

see an important property from the condition for clearing the commodity market. Consider the underlying real factors in the model, which include the forms of production functions, the level of population, and the preferences of households. These elements enter into the demand and supply of commodities through the omitted terms, which we denote by . . . in equation (9.7). For given values of these elements, equation (9.7) determines the real interest rate, r_t, and the level of aggregate output, $Y_t = C_t$, at each date. If the underlying real elements do not change over time, then the market-clearing values of the real interest rate and output are constants.

The important point is that the real interest rate and output are determined independently of the path of money. Although changes in money will end up affecting the paths of the price level and the nominal interest rate, these monetary changes will not affect at least some of the real variables in the model. If all real variables are invariant with the behaviour of money, then economists say that money is **superneutral**. The term 'superneutral' indicates an extension of another concept, the neutrality of money, which we discussed before. Neutrality of money means that once-and-for-all changes in the quantity of money affect nominal variables but not real variables. Superneutrality extends this idea from one-time changes in the stock of money to arbitrary variations in the entire path of money.

We know from before that money is neutral in the model. One point we want to consider in this chapter is whether money is superneutral. To the extent that money is not superneutral, we shall find some effects of money and inflation on real variables.

Monetary Growth, Inflation, and the Nominal Interest Rate

We want now to examine the details of the linkages among monetary growth, inflation, and the nominal interest rate. We carry out this analysis for given values of the real interest rate, r, and output, Y. By holding these variables fixed, we are making two types of assumptions. First, we use the property that anticipated variations in money and prices do not affect the real interest rate and output. Second, we assume that no other shifts occur over time to the functions for aggregate commodity demand and supply. Generally these types of changes would lead to movements in the real interest rate and output.

More specifically, the analysis neglects any systematic growth of output. Recall from Chapter 8 that countries with higher average growth rates of output tend to have less inflation for a given average growth rate of money. Although it is not hard to incorporate this feature into the analysis, we assume that output is constant to bring out the major points in the easiest possible way.

The main results can be illustrated by assuming a constant rate of monetary growth:

$$M_t = (1 + \mu)M_{t-1} \qquad (9.9)$$

where μ (the Greek letter *mu*) is the monetary growth rate. Assume that equation (9.9) governs the behaviour of money from the current date, $t = 1$, into the indefinite future.

We want to calculate the price level at each date, given that money grows at a constant rate. We already determined the real interest rate and output to equate aggregate commodity supply and demand in equation (9.7). Further, if these supply and demand functions do not shift over time, then the real interest rate, r, and output, Y, are constants. Given these results, the price level, P_t, must satisfy the condition that money be willingly held. Writing this condition in real terms, we have

$$M_t/P_t = \Phi(Y, R_t, \ldots) \qquad (9.10)$$
$$(+) \ (-)$$

In Chapter 5 we found that once-and-for-all increases in the quantity of money raised the price level in the same proportion. It is therefore reasonable to consider the possibility that the price level, P_t, grows at the same rate as the money stock, M_t. In this case the inflation rate, π, is constant and equal to the rate of monetary growth, μ. So let's make this guess and see whether it accords with the condition from equation (9.10) that all money be willingly held.

If money and prices grow at the same rate, then the ratio of these two, which is the level of real money balances, M_t/P_t, does not change over time. Therefore, the amount of real money, which appears on the left side of equation (9.10), is constant.

Recall that the nominal interest rate, R_t, equals the quantity $r_t + \pi_t$. But we already know that the real interest rate is constant. Therefore, if the inflation rate is constant, then the nominal interest rate is also constant. This result means that the real demand for money, $\Phi(\cdot)$, which appears on the right side of equation (9.10), is constant. (Remember that output, Y, does not change over time.)

Since real money balances and the real amount of money demanded are each constant, we have only to be sure that the two constants are the same. This condition holds if we determine the current price level, P_1, to equate the amount of real money balances, M_1/P_1, to the real quantity demanded, $\Phi(\cdot)$. Then, since actual and desired real money do not vary over time, we can be sure that all money will be willingly held at each date: equation (9.10) holds in every period.

We have now verified that our guess – prices growing at the same rate as money – satisfies the conditions for general market clearing. This path of prices is therefore the one that will prevail in our market-clearing framework. To summarize, the results are as follows:

- Prices grow at the same rate as the money stock: $\pi = \mu$.
- Aggregate real money balances, M_t/P_t, are constant.
- The nominal interest rate, R, is constant and equal to $r + \pi$.
- The aggregate demand for real balances, $\Phi(Y, R, \ldots)$, is constant.
- The current price level, P_1, equates the quantity of real money balances, M_1/P_1, to the real amount demanded, $\Phi(Y, R)$.

The results imply that the growth rate of money, μ, shows up one-for-one in the inflation rate, π, and in the nominal interest rate, $R = r + \pi$. But recall that a higher nominal interest rate means a lower level of real money demanded. Therefore, a higher growth rate of money corresponds to a lower level of aggregate real money balances, M_t/P_t.

A Shift in the Monetary Growth Rate

We can better understand the results by studying a change in the monetary growth rate. Suppose that the money stock has been growing for a long time at the constant rate, μ. Further, assume that everyone expects this behaviour to persist indefinitely. Hence, the inflation rate is the constant, $\pi = \mu$, and the nominal interest rate is given by

$$R = r + \pi = r + \mu$$

We show this initial situation on the left side of Figure 9.1. Consider how the quantity of money, M_t, behaves over time. We have the sequence

$$M_1 = (1 + \mu)M_0$$
$$M_2 = (1 + \mu)M_1 = (1 + \mu)^2 M_0$$
.
.
.

Therefore, for any period t, the quantity of money is given by

$$M_t = (1 + \mu)^t M_0 \qquad (9.11)$$

We shall find it convenient to graph the quantity of money, M_t, on a proportionate or logarithmic scale. Then each unit on the vertical axis corresponds to an equal proportionate change in a variable – say, a 1% change in the stock of money. Since money grows at the constant proportionate rate μ, the graph of money versus time is a straight line on a proportionate scale. Further, the slope of the line equals the growth rate, μ. The left side of Figure 9.2 therefore shows the quantity of money, M_t, as a straight line with slope μ.[3]

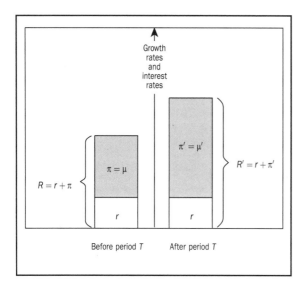

Before period T the growth rate of money is μ. Hence, the left side of the figure shows that the inflation rate is $\pi = \mu$ and the nominal interest rate is $R = r + \pi = r + \mu$ After period T the growth rate of money is the bigger value μ'. Consequently the new inflation is $\pi' = \mu'$ and the new nominal interest rate is $R' = r + \pi' = r + \mu'$.

Figure 9.1 Growth rates of money and prices and levels of interest rates: effects of an increase in the monetary growth rate

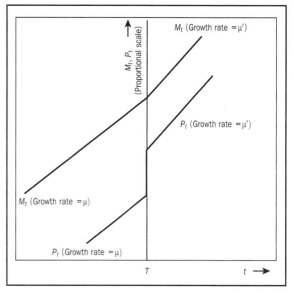

We show the behaviour of money and prices before and after an increase in the monetary growth rate at date T. Notice that a jump in the price level occurs at date T.

Figure 9.2 Effect of an increase in the monetary growth rate on the path of the price level

We found before that the price level grows also at the constant rate, $\pi = \mu$:

$$P_t = (1 + \pi)^t P_0 = (1 + \mu)^t P_0 \qquad (9.12)$$

The left side of Figure 9.2 therefore shows the graph of the price level, P_t, as a straight line with slope μ. This line parallels the one for the stock of money, M_t.

Assume now that the growth rate of money rises from μ to μ' at some date T. Here, we think of this change as a surprise – that is, before date T no one anticipated the acceleration of money. But once it happens, we assume that everyone expects the new monetary growth rate, μ', to persist indefinitely. Hence, we study here the consequences of a once-and-for-all increase in the rate of monetary expansion.

After the change in the monetary growth rate, the economy is in the same type of situation as before. The only difference is that the growth rate of money is μ' rather than μ. Therefore, we show on the right side of Figure 9.1 that the new inflation rate is $\pi' = \mu'$. We know, in addition, that the change in monetary behaviour does not affect the real interest rate, which remains at the value r. The new nominal interest rate is therefore $R' = r + \pi' = r + \mu'$. Hence, the inflation rate and the nominal interest rate rise by as much as the increase in the monetary growth rate.

We show the levels of money and prices after date T on the right side of Figure 9.2. Because the growth rate of money rises after date T, the line for the money stock, M_t, has the slope μ', which exceeds the original slope. Note, however, that there is no immediate jump in the stock of money at date T; money just starts to grow faster at this point.

Since prices grow at the rate $\pi' = \mu'$ after date T, the figure again shows the line for the price level, P_t, as parallel to that for the money stock. But notice an important complication in the graph of P_t in Figure 9.2: there is a jump in P_t at date T. Let's see why this jump takes place.

The acceleration of money at date T raises the nominal interest rate from $R = r + \mu$ to $R' = r + \mu'$. Recall that an increase in the nominal interest rate reduces the real demand

for money. Hence, the existing amount of money will be willingly held at date T only if the actual real balances, M_T/P_T, fall by as much as the real demand. But there is no sudden change in the nominal quantity of money at date T – only an increase in the rate of growth. Therefore, real balances can fall to equal the smaller amount demanded only if there is an upward jump in the price level at date T.

We can say something about the size of the jump in the price level. The proportionate rise in the price level equals the proportionate fall in real money balances, which equals the proportionate decline in the real demand for money. Further, the magnitude of the decline in money demand depends on two things: first, the change in the nominal interest rate, which is $\mu' - \mu$, and second, the sensitivity of real money demanded to changes in the nominal interest rate. The jump in the price level is therefore greater the larger is the acceleration of money, $\mu' - \mu$, and the greater is the sensitivity of money demand to changes in the nominal interest rate.

The Increase in the Nominal Interest Rate

Let's think about why the acceleration of money at date T leads to a rise in the nominal interest rate. At date T, people learn that henceforth the government will pursue a more expansionary monetary policy. They know also that this policy means a rate of inflation, $\pi' = \mu'$, which exceeds the initial rate, $\pi = \mu$. Consider what the higher expected rate of inflation does at date T in the credit market. Borrowers now regard the old nominal interest rate, R, as a better deal. That is because the real interest rate that they must pay has fallen from the value $R - \mu$ to the lower value, $R - \mu'$. Hence, if the nominal interest rate did not change, then borrowers would raise their demand for loans. On the other side, lenders see that their real rate of return has deteriorated. Therefore, if the nominal interest rate did not change, then lenders would decrease their supply of loans. A balance between loans demanded and supplied applies – that is, the credit market clears – only if the nominal interest rate rises.

The new nominal interest rate, R', exceeds the old one, R, by the increase in the inflation rate, μ' − μ. Lenders view this rise in the nominal rate as just sufficient to compensate them for the loss of purchasing power over time due to the higher inflation rate. Similarly, borrowers are willing to pay the higher nominal interest rate because they expect to repay their loans with more heavily deflated ECUs. In other words, the increase in the nominal interest rate incorporates fully the change in expected inflation. Thereby, the acceleration of money and prices does not change the real interest rate, r.

The Jump in the Price Level

Consider now the intuition for why the price level jumps upward at date T. The sudden prospect of higher inflation and the consequent rise in the nominal interest rate lead to a fall in the real demand for money at date T. If the price level did not adjust, then people's actual real money balances, M_T/P_T, would exceed the desired amount. Consequently, everyone would attempt to spend their excess money by buying either goods or bonds. The rise in the demand for goods puts upward pressure on the price level, and the economy returns to a position of general market clearing only when the price level rises enough to equate actual and desired real money. This condition is the one that we used to determine the size of the jump in the price level in Figure 9.2.

Wage Rates

If we added a labour market to the model, then we would find that the real wage rate, w/P, and the quantity of employment, L, were independent of money: money is also neutral with respect to these two real variables. The path of nominal wage rates must therefore parallel the path of prices, which appears in Figure 9.2. This result means that nominal wages grow at the rate μ up to date T and at the higher rate μ' after date T. Further, the nominal wage rate would jump upward at date T.

Summarizing the Results for an Acceleration of Money

Let's summarize the results for a once-and-for-all increase in the growth rate of money (a decrease in the growth rate of money just reverses the signs of all effects):

- There are no changes in the real interest rate, the real wage rate, or the levels of output and employment.
- The inflation rate and the nominal interest rate (and the growth rate of nominal wages) rise by as much as the increase in the growth rate of money.
- The real demand for money and the actual quantity of real money balances decrease.
- The price level jumps upward to equate actual real money balances to the smaller quantity demanded.

Let's use these results to see whether money is superneutral – that is, whether the path of money matters for real variables. Recall that the path of money does not affect the real interest rate, the real wage rate, and the quantities of output and employment. However, because the acceleration of money raises the inflation rate, it also raises the nominal interest rate and thereby lowers the amount of real money demanded. The resulting fall in real money balances is one real effect of the change in monetary behaviour. Anticipated monetary growth and inflation are therefore not quite superneutral in the model.

Underlying the decline in real money demanded is an increase in the transaction costs that people incur to economize on money. Since these costs absorb resources, the increase in these costs is an adverse real effect from the increase in monetary growth. Our analysis neglected any effects of transaction costs on households' choices of work effort, consumption, and saving. These kinds of effects are small in ordinary circumstances – that is, unless inflation is extreme – and we can safely ignore them for most of our analysis. But for very high inflation rates, such as those that we discuss later for the German **hyperinflation**, the resources spent on transaction costs can have significant effects on output, work effort, the real interest rate, and other real variables. The independence of real variables from anticipated monetary growth and inflation is therefore only an approximation, which is satisfactory when transaction costs are small.

Remember that the present analysis assumes perfect foresight about future price levels.[4] The model therefore features equality between actual and expected inflation and between actual and expected real interest rates. We saw in Chapter 8 that unexpected inflation has important effects on realized real interest rates. If inflation and real interest rates are uncertain, then there are a variety of real effects that would arise. We shall explore some of these effects in Chapter 20. For now, the important point is that the analysis deals only with anticipated inflation.

The Dynamics of Inflation

Consider again the case in which monetary growth rises at date T from the initial value, μ, to the higher value, μ'. Let's think further about the transition from the initial rate of inflation, $\pi = \mu$, to the subsequent rate, $\pi' = \mu'$. Because the nominal interest rate increases, the level of real money balances decreases. For real money to fall, there must be a transition period during which prices rise by proportionately more than money. So far our analysis says that this transition occurs in an instant at date T by an upward jump in the price level. But in the real world there are a number of considerations that stretch out the transition. Here, we introduce some of these features to study some aspects of the dynamics of inflation.

Gradual Adjustment of the Demand for Money

Return to the case in which people first learn at date T that money will be growing at a higher rate. Recall that the size of the jump in the price level at date T depends on the extent of the fall in real money demanded. Suppose now that people reduce their demand for money only gradually when the nominal interest rate increases. Then we may find only a small jump in the price level at date T. Most of the extra upward kick to the price level shows up only gradually as people reduce their real demand for money.

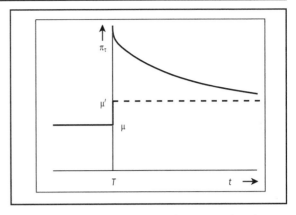

The growth rate of money rises from μ to μ' at date T. The solid line shows that the inflation rate π_t stays above μ' for a while but eventually approaches μ'.

Figure 9.3   Effect of higher monetary growth on inflation including gradual adjustment of the demand for money

Recall that a person's real demand for money reflects some underlying decisions about the frequency of transactions, financial planning, and so on. If the nominal interest rate rises, then it is reasonable that people would take some time to modify these aspects of their behaviour. Hence, in the aggregate, the real demand for money would decline gradually in response to an increase in the nominal interest rate.

Slow adjustment in the demand for money effectively spreads out the jump in the price level over a transition interval. When money accelerates at time T, the inflation rate reacts something like the solid line shown in Figure 9.3: the inflation rate, π_t, exceeds the new growth rate of money, μ', over an extended interval. The excess of π_t over μ' means that real money balances, M_t/P_t, fall over time to match the gradual decline in the real demand for money. Eventually, π_t approaches its new long-term value, μ': in the long run, the real quantity of money remains constant but at a lower level than initially.

Anticipated Changes in Monetary Growth

Our analysis can deal with situations in which the growth rate of money either rises or falls. But so far, we have assumed that the change in actual monetary growth coincides with the change in perceptions about future monetary growth. That is, two things happen at date T in the previous examples. First, money accelerates or decelerates permanently. Second, people first learn at date T that this acceleration or deceleration will occur.

People may receive advance information that allows them to forecast increases or decreases in monetary growth and inflation. This type of information could derive from news about the prospects for war and peace or from political changes that foreshadow changes in the monetary regime. In the 1890s, for example, William Jennings Bryan campaigned for the US presidency on a programme of easy money (free coinage of silver). His defeat probably lowered expectations of future monetary growth and inflation. Similarly, the election of Margaret Thatcher in 1979 probably lowered expectations of future monetary growth and inflation in the UK. Another example of advance information concerns the post-World War I hyperinflation in Germany. People apparently anticipated for several months before November 1921 that a **monetary reform** was coming.[5]

If people forecast an acceleration or deceleration of money, then the path of inflation differs from those already discussed. To avoid a good deal of complicated details, the subsequent discussion just sketches the types of effects that arise.

Suppose that people learn currently that an acceleration of money is coming at the future date T. Then they know also that inflation rates and nominal interest rates will be higher in the future. When people know that the cost of holding money will rise after date T, they tend to reduce their demand for money before date T. Otherwise they will get caught holding money at date T when the big increase in prices occurs. Thus, the expectation of future inflation has a negative effect on people's willingness to hold money today. This reduction in today's demand for money means that today's price level must rise. In other words, although the acceleration of money has not yet occurred, the expectation of a future monetary acceleration leads to a higher current

rate of inflation. Finally, since this higher rate of inflation becomes anticipated, the nominal interest rate also rises before the acceleration of money.

The precise path of inflation depends on when people learn about the acceleration of money. But, as mentioned, the key point is that changes in expectations about future money can generate variations in inflation and the nominal interest rate that precede the changes in monetary growth. Thus, although the analysis stresses monetary factors as the source of inflation, significant divergences can arise in the short run between the growth rates of money and prices. These divergences are likely to be important in an environment – such as those present today in many countries – in which a volatile monetary policy induces frequent revisions in forecasts of monetary behaviour. Such an environment would also be marked by volatility in inflation rates and nominal interest rates.

The Transition from One Inflation Rate to Another

Let's stress a basic feature of the results concerning changes from one long-term inflation rate to another. Although jumps in the price level need not occur, an acceleration of money must involve a transition during which prices rise by proportionately more than money. This conclusion follows inevitably from the eventual decline in real money balances.

We can turn the results around to deal with a case in which money decelerates. Although a downward jump in the price level need not occur, the transition must involve a period in which prices grow by proportionately less than money. This result holds because the lower nominal interest rate raises the real demand for money.

Suppose, as an example, that the government reduces monetary growth permanently from 10% per year to 5%. Presumably the objective of this policy is to reduce long-term inflation. Our analysis implies that there is a transition period during which the inflation rate is even less than 5% per year. There may, in fact, be deflation – falling prices – for a while. Thus, in designing a monetary policy to end inflation, economic advisers have to think about the potential for very low or negative rates of inflation as a temporary side effect.

Box 9.1   Money and Prices during the German Hyperinflation

We can assess some of the theoretical results by examining the data on the post-World War I German hyperinflation. Here, we have something close to a laboratory experiment for studying the consequences of high and variable rates of monetary growth and inflation.[6] Over the period from 1921 to 1923, the rates of inflation ranged from near zero to over 500% per month! Further, the available data suggest that relatively small changes occurred in aggregate real variables, such as total output and employment. Hence, aggregate real money demanded would not be affected very much by changes in real spending.

When inflation rates are volatile, it is impossible to predict accurately the real interest rate on loans that prescribe nominal interest rates. This type of lending therefore tends to disappear during hyperinflations, such as the one in Germany. For this reason, when analysing the demand for money during the German hyperinflation, we have no useful measures of the nominal interest rate. In this environment the best indicator of the cost of holding money comes directly from the expected rate of inflation, π^e. This rate tells people how much they lose by holding money rather than consuming or holding a durable good that maintains its value in real terms.

Table 9.1 summarizes the behaviour of the monetary growth rate, μ, the inflation rate, π, and real money balances, M/P, in Germany from 1920 until 1925. In most cases the table indicates the average growth rates of money and prices over six-month intervals. The level of real money balances pertains to the ends of each of these intervals.

At the beginning of 1920 the growth rates of money and prices were already at the very high

Table 9.1   Monetary growth, inflation, and real money balances during the German hyperinflation

Period	μ	π	M/P
	(% per month)		
Feb to June 1920	5.7	6.0	1.01
June to Dec 1920	3.0	1.1	1.13
Dec 1920 to June 1921	0.8	0.1	1.18
June to Dec 1921	5.5	8.4	0.99
Dec 1921 to June 1922	6.5	12.8	0.68
June to Dec 1922	29.4	46.7	0.24
Dec 1922 to June 1923	40.0	40.0	0.24
June to Oct 1923	233	286	0.03
Reform period			
Dec 1923 to June 1924	5.9	−0.6	0.44
June to Dec 1924	5.3	1.4	0.56
Dec 1924 to June 1925	2.0	1.6	0.57
June to Dec 1925	1.2	0.4	0.60

Note: M is an estimate of the total circulation of currency. Until late 1923 the figures refer to total legal tender, most of which consists of notes issued by the Reichsbank. Later, the data include issues of the Rentenbank, private bank notes, and various 'emergency moneys'. However, especially in late 1923, many unofficial emergency currencies, as well as circulating foreign currencies, are not counted. The numbers are standardized so that the quantity outstanding in 1913 is 1.0. P is an index of the cost of living, based on 1913 = 1.0.

Source: *Sonderhefte zur Wirtschaft und Statistik*, Berlin, 1925.

rate of about 6% per month. (When talking about hyperinflations, economists typically measure these rates per month rather than per year!) Then there was a deceleration of money to an average rate of less than 1% per month for the first half of 1921. Notice that, as the theory predicts, the growth rate of prices, π, fell by more than the growth rate of money, μ, when money decelerated. Correspondingly, real money balances increased by about 20% from early 1920 to early 1921. (The level of real money in early 1920 was roughly equal to that from before the war in 1913.)

In 1922 money accelerated dramatically to an average growth rate of nearly 30% per month toward the end of the year. During this period the growth rate of prices, π, exceeded that of money, μ. Hence, by late 1922 real money balances fell to about a quarter of the level prevailing in early 1920.

During the first half of 1923 there was some let-up in the acceleration of money, and money and prices grew together at the extraordinary average rate of 40% per month. Correspondingly, although the rate of inflation was enormous, the level of real money remained fairly stable. But late in 1923 the hyperinflation built to its climax with rates of monetary expansion of 300 to 600% per month for October–November. Again, the acceleration of money led to rates of inflation that exceeded the growth rates of money. Real money balances reached their low point in October 1923 at about 3% of the level for early 1920. If we neglect variations in aggregate real income from 1920 to 1923 – which is satisfactory as a first-order approximation – then the reduction in real money implies a rise in velocity by over 30-fold. In other words, if in 1920 people held the typical piece of currency for two weeks before spending it, then in October 1923 they held it for about half a day.

A major monetary reform occurred in Germany during November 1923. This reform included the introduction of a new type of currency, a promise not to print new money beyond a specified limit to finance government expenditures or for other purposes, some changes in government spending and taxes, and a commitment to back the new currency by gold.[7] In any event, there was a sharp curtailment in monetary growth and inflation after December 1923. For example, during 1924 monetary growth averaged 5 to 6% per month. But because of the deceleration of money after November 1923, the average inflation rate was even less – below 1% per month for 1924. Most dramatically, the quantity of real money balances rose from 3% of the early 1920 level in October 1923 to 56% of that level by December 1924.[8] (Much of the increase in real money arose as an infusion of new types of currency during the reform months of November and December 1923.)

In 1925 the growth rate of money fell to 1 to 2% per month, and the inflation rate remained at roughly 1% per month. Real money balances rose slowly to reach 60% of the early 1920 level by late 1925. Although the inflation rate remained low for the remainder of the 1920s, the level of real money did not reattain the early 1920 level. Perhaps this discrepancy reflects a long-lasting negative influence of the hyperinflation on people's willingness to hold money.

Real Effects of Inflation

Some Effects from Unanticipated Inflation

Our analysis in this chapter focuses on anticipated inflation. But let's note briefly some real effects that arise from unexpected inflation. During the German hyperinflation, one effect of this type was a substantial redistribution of wealth. Before the extreme inflation began, some households and businesses had nominal debts (including mortgages and other loans), and others held nominal assets. The hyperinflation – which was not anticipated at the time when people acquired these nominal debts and assets – wiped out most of the real value of claims that had a predetermined nominal value. Therefore, debtors gained while creditors lost. The general point is that unexpected inflation can have significant effects on the distribution of wealth.

The unpredictability of inflation reduces the willingness of people to enter into contracts that specify nominal values in advance. Thus, as we already noted, the usual types of bond and loan markets tended to disappear during the German hyperinflation and other extreme inflations. Although other kinds of markets may still function (such as a stock market and transactions denominated in foreign currencies in hyperinflation Germany or indexed bond markets in modern inflations), the loss of the traditional types of bonds and loans is an adverse real effect from unpredictable inflation.

Effects of Anticipated Inflation on Real Money Balances and Transaction Costs

In the discussion of superneutrality of money, we mentioned that some real variables, such as aggregate output, were at least approximately independent of anticipated variations in money and the general price level. But even if aggregate output changes little, one real effect from an increase in expected inflation is the reduction of real money balances. During the German hyperinflation, this response was dramatic, with aggregate real money falling to about 3% of its initial level.

Corresponding to the increase in expected inflation and the reduction in real money, people expend more resources on transaction costs. Although we regard these costs as small in normal times, we cannot neglect them during extreme circumstances, such as the German hyperinflation. For example, people spent a significant portion of their time on the process of receiving wage and other payments once or twice per day and in searching rapidly to find outlets for their cash. Given these magnitudes, we would also predict that extreme inflation would have significant effects on aggregate output. For the German case, there is some evidence that the process of dealing with the severe inflation in late 1923 had adverse effects on aggregate output and employment.

The Revenue from Money Creation

A different real effect from inflation involves the **government's revenue from printing money**. In our theory thus far, the government uses this income solely to finance transfers. More realistically, governments use the printing press to pay for a variety of expenditures.

Recall that the real amount of revenue for period t is the quantity $(M_t - M_{t-1})/P_t$. The condition, $M_t = (1 + \mu)M_{t-1}$, implies that we can rewrite the expression for real revenue as

$$\text{real revenue from printing money} =$$
$$(M_t - M_{t-1})/P_t = \mu \cdot M_{t-1}/P_t \qquad (9.13)$$

A higher value of μ implies a higher value of the inflation rate, π, which implies a higher value of the nominal interest rate, $R = r + \pi$. A higher growth rate of money therefore increases the cost of holding money: people forego interest at a higher rate by holding money. For this reason, economists often refer to the government's revenue from money creation as the **inflation tax**. These revenues are also referred to as **seigniorage**. The government raises the tax rate on real money holdings when it raises μ and thereby raises R. We can also say that the higher value of π, caused by the higher value of μ, means that the real value of money declines at a faster rate.

Note from equation (9.13) that the real revenue from money creation is the product of the growth rate of money, μ, and a term that approximates the level of aggregate real money held, M_{t-1}/Pt. Recall that an increase in μ leads to a reduction in real money balances. Hence, if μ rises from, say, 10% per month to 20% per month – or by a factor of 2 – then the government's real revenue increases if real money balances decline by less than 50%. This condition holds empirically except for the most extreme cases. During the German hyperinflation, for example, the condition was apparently not violated until the growth rate of money approached 100% per month between July and August 1923. Until then, the government successfully extracted more real revenue by printing money at higher rates.

In normal times for most countries, the government obtains only a small portion of its revenue from printing money. In Table 9.2 we report some estimates of the seigniorage revenues in eight EC countries in the period 1979–86. In Greece, Italy, Portugal and Spain seigniorage has been an appreciable source of revenue during this period. From the table we also see that the size of the inflation tax revenues is positively associated with the size of the monetary base in the system. Since seigniorage is a tax on money holding, the larger are money balances in the economy, the greater are the revenues from this source of taxation. From the table it is also clear that the large cross-country differences in the size of the monetary base are not due to differences in the demand for currency, but to differences in the demand for money by banks in the form of bank reserves. The inflation tax, in practice, is often a tax on commercial banks and, therefore, it can affect the international competitiveness of the banking sector. To fully appreciate this point we have to study in more detail how financial intermediaries are organized and how they operate. This is the subject of the next chapter.

In a few high-inflation countries, the revenue from money creation is quite important. As an extreme example, for Argentina over 1960–75, money creation accounted for nearly half of government revenues and for about 6% of GNP. Some other countries in which the revenue from printing money has been important are Chile (5% of GNP over 1960–77), Libya (3% of GNP over 1960–77), and Brazil (3% of GNP over 1960–78).

During the German hyperinflation and in some other hyperinflations (such as Austria, Hungary, Poland, and Russia after World War I), money creation became the primary source of government revenue. The amounts obtained eventually approached 10 to 15% of GNP, which appears to be about the maximum obtainable from printing money. There was a close month-to-month connection in Germany between the volume of real government spending and the growth rate of the money supply. The variations in monetary growth – and hence, inflation – were driven in this case by shifts in real government spending (see Zvi Hercowitz, 1981). Much of the government spending over this period went to reparations payments associated with World War I. The reduction in these payments after November 1923 was therefore a major factor in the success of the German monetary reform.

Summary

We introduced monetary growth into the model by allowing for governmental transfer payments. By considering the government's budget constraint, we found that the aggregate of these transfers equals the change in the stock of money.

We modified the households' budget constraints to include inflation. The main result is that these constraints involve the real interest rate rather than the nominal rate. Similarly, the intertemporal-substitution effects on consumption and leisure depend on the real interest rate. When there is uncertainty about inflation, it is the expected real interest rate that matters in the budget constraints and for intertemporal-substitution effects.

The nominal interest rate, R, still determines the cost of holding money rather than bonds. Therefore, although the real interest rate matters for choices of consumption and work, it is the nominal rate that appears in the demand-for-money function.

We used the market-clearing model to analyze the interactions among monetary growth, inflation, and nominal and real interest rates. An important result is that the real interest rate, the

Seigniorage (% of tax revenues) 1979–86 average	Monetary Base (% of GDP 1986)			Bank reserves to deposit ratio %
	Total	Currency	Bank reserves	
Greece	9.1	22.6	9.8	12.8	26.5
Italy	6.2	18.6	6.8	11.8	17.7
Portugal	11.9	20.5	9.5	11.0	28.6
Spain	5.9	19.3	7.5	11.8	19.6
Belgium	0.4	8.2	7.8	0.4	1.2
France	1.3	5.9	4.5	1.4	3.8
Germany	0.8	9.9	5.8	4.1	7.8
UK	0.5	4.6	3.6	1.0	2.1

Source: Drazen (1989), Giavazzi (1988).

Table 9.2   Revenue from money creation

real wage rate, and the aggregates of output and employment are invariant with anticipated variations in the quantity of money. Money is, however, not superneutral in the model. (By superneutral, we mean that variations in the path of money have no real effects.) The behaviour of money influences the level of real money balances, the nominal interest rate, and the

volume of transaction costs. Further, the invariance of the real interest rate and aggregate output holds only as an approximation.

An increase in the growth rate of money shows up in the long run as equal increases in the inflation rate, the nominal interest rate, and the growth rate of nominal wages. However, because the higher nominal interest rate reduces the real

---

Appendix: The Wealth Effects from the Monetary Terms

We argued in Chapter 3 that we could neglect wealth effects associated with money if we ignore transaction costs. We now want to show that these wealth effects can still be neglected in the model that adds monetary growth and inflation.

Consider the household's budget constraint in nominal terms in equation (9.3). The first amendment when we consider the monetary terms is to add the initial nominal balance, m_0, as a source of funds on the left side of the equation.

The second change is that each household receives the nominal transfer, v_t, from the government in each period. The present value of these transfers should be added as a source of funds on the left side of equation (9.3).

If the household always held the constant *nominal* balance, m_1, from period 1 onward, then we would modify the right side of equation (9.3) to include m_1 as a nominal use of funds. The constancy of nominal money balances is, however, unlikely in the presence of inflation. (Real money held would then decline steadily over time.) Suppose instead that the household adds the amount, $m_2 - m_1$, to its money balance during period 2. This change in money enters into the budget constraint like period 2's nominal consumption expenditure, Pc_2. The quantity, $m_2 - m_1$, would therefore be discounted by the factor, $1 + R$, on the right side of equation (9.3). We can treat similarly all future changes in money: $m_3 - m_2$ like P_3c_3, and so on.

The budget constraint that extends equation (9.3) to include all the monetary terms is therefore:

$$P_1 y_1 + P_2 y_2/(1 + R) + \ldots + b_0(1 + R) +$$
$$m_0 + v_1 + v_2/(1 + R) + \ldots$$
$$= P_1 c_1 + P_2 c_2/(1 + R) + \ldots + m_1 +$$
$$(m_2 - m_1)/(1 + R) + \ldots$$
$$(9.14)$$

The difference between the new sources and uses of funds in equation (9.14) is given by

$$v_1 + v_2/(1 + R) + \ldots - (m_1 - m_0) -$$
$$(m_2 - m_1)/(1 + R) - \ldots$$
$$(9.15)$$

Each term that is being subtracted in (9.15) involves the change in nominal money, $m_t - m_{t-1}$. But recall from equation (9.1) that, in the aggregate, the change in nominal money, $M_t - M_{t-1}$, equals the government's nominal revenue, which equals the total nominal transfer to households, V_t. The expression in (9.15) therefore equals zero for the aggregate of households. In the aggregate, the additional sources of funds exactly balance the additional uses. Therefore, if we follow our usual practice of neglecting distributional effects, then we can ignore any wealth effects from the monetary terms.

demand for money, there must be a transition interval during which the rate of inflation exceeds the growth rate of money. In a simple case the transition occurs in an instant by an upward jump in the price level. But if we bring in some realistic extensions of the model – such as gradual adjustment of money demand and foreknow-ledge of the acceleration of money – then we find a richer dynamics of prices during the transition. One general property is that the inflation rate exceeds the growth rate of money during the transition.

Similar results apply to a decrease in long-run inflation brought about by a decline in the growth rate of money. The process of reducing inflation involves a transition period with unusually low rates of inflation, which may even be negative.

We illustrated some of the results by observing the dynamics of monetary growth and inflation during the post-World War I German hyperinfla-tion. Higher rates of monetary growth led to lower levels of real money balances, whereas reductions in monetary growth had the opposite effect. We also discussed the effects of inflation on transaction costs and on the real revenue that the government obtains from printing money.

Important Terms and Concepts

governmental budget constraint
lump-sum transfer
perfect foresight
superneutrality of money
inflation tax
seigniorage
hyperinflation
monetary reform
government's revenue from printing money

Questions and Problems

Mainly for Review

9.1 Consider an individual who lives for two periods, earns a nominal income of ε1000 in each period, and has zero initial and terminal assets. The nominal interest rate, R, on ECU loans is 15%, and the expected rate of inflation, π^e, between the two periods is 10%. Assume that the price level in the first period is 1.
  a. What is the real value of period 1 income?
  b. What is the maximum amount of ECUs that could be borrowed in period 1? Find the real value of this amount, and add it to the real value of period 1 income to see the maximum amount of (real) consumption possible in period 1.
  c. What is the price level in period 2? What is the real value of period 2 income?
  d. What is the maximum amount of ECUs that can be obtained in period 2 by saving in period 1? Find the real value (in period 2) of this amount and add it to the real value of period 2 income to

see the maximum amount of (real) consumption possible in period 2.
  e. As in question 4.3 of Chapter 4, plot a graph to show the consumption possibilities in the two periods.
  f. What is the slope of the budget line that you drew in part (e)? Show that it is equal to $-(1+R)/(1+\pi^e)$.

9.2 Based on your answer to question 9.1, explain why $(1+R)/(1+\pi^e)$, rather than $1+R$, is the correct measure of the trade-off between real consumption in the two periods. In what situation would it be appropriate to use the nominal interest rate?

9.3 Distinguish between the measures of nominal saving implicit in equations (9.3) and (9.5). Explain why, when inflation is positive, the first measure is an overestimate of saving for a net lender (an individual for whom $b_{t-1} > 0$). Can we make a similar comparison for a net debtor (an individual for whom $b_{t-1} < 0$)?

9.4 Suppose that the commodity market clears at a real interest rate of 4%.
  a. If the inflation rate is zero, what is the nominal interest rate? If the inflation rate is 10%, what is the nominal interest rate?
  b. If the nominal interest rate did not go up by the same amount as the inflation rate, what would happen to the commodity market – that is, would there be excess supply or excess demand?

9.5 Which of the following statements is correct?
  a. A constant rate of increase in the price level will lead to a continuous rise in the nominal interest rate.
  b. A continuous increase in the inflation rate will lead to a continuous rise in the nominal interest rate.

9.6 What would be the effect on the nominal interest rate of each of the following events?

   a. The announcement of a one-time increase in the money stock.

   b. The announcement of a planned increase in the rate of monetary growth.

      Why does the price level jump in both instances? Does the velocity of money increase in both cases?

9.7 Critically review the following statement: 'The quantity theory of money predicts that the rate of inflation must equal the rate of monetary growth. In fact, the two are not equal; therefore the theory is wrong.' How do factors such as anticipated increases in inflation or gradual adjustments in the demand for money alter the prediction? What about factors considered in Chapter 8, such as growth in output?

9.8 Can the government always increase its revenue by raising the rate of monetary growth? How does the answer depend on the response of real money demanded to the nominal interest rate?

Problems for Discussion

9.9 Inflation and the Demand for Money

   Suppose that households hold stocks of goods – for example, groceries – as well as money and bonds. Assume that these goods depreciate in a physical sense at the rate δ per year (δ is the Greek letter *delta*).

   a. What is the 'nominal interest rate' on holdings of these goods? Does this interest rate affect the demands for stocks of goods and money?

   b. Assume that the nominal interest rate on bonds, R, does not change, but the expected inflation rate, π^e, rises. What happens to the demand for money?

   Note: This problem shows that the demand for money can involve substitution between money and goods, as well as between money and bonds. The demand for money may therefore change with a shift in the expected inflation rate, even if the nominal interest rate on bonds does not change.

9.10 Wealth and Substitution Effects from Inflation (optional)

   Suppose that the expected inflation rate, π^e, and the nominal interest rate, R, each increase by one percentage point. Thus, the expected real interest rate on bonds does not change.

   a. What happens to the real demand for money?

   b. Underlying this change in the demand for money, what happens to the real amount of transaction costs that people incur?

Assume now that we do not neglect the role of transaction costs in households' budget constraints.

   c. What is the effect of higher inflation on people's wealth? How do consumption and leisure respond?

   d. Does higher expected inflation also exert substitution effects on consumption and leisure? (Note that, unlike consumption, leisure does not require people to use money.) Therefore, what is the overall effect of higher expected inflation on consumption and leisure?

9.11 The Superneutrality of Money

   a. What is the meaning of the term *superneutrality of money*?

   b. Is money superneutral in the model? In particular, if the behaviour of money changes, which real variables change and which do not change? Explain the factors that underlie these results.

9.12 Inflation and Saving (optional)

   a. Suppose that we define a household's real saving to be the change in the real value of its assets, bonds and money. Use the household's budget constraint from equation (9.2) to derive an expression for real saving. Does real saving equal real income less real consumer expenditure? In the expression for real income, how do we measure the real interest income on bonds? In particular, does it involve the nominal interest rate, R, or the real interest rate, $R - \pi$? Is there also a term for real 'interest income' on money?

   b. Nominal saving equals real saving multiplied by the price level P_t. What is the formula for nominal saving?

   c. Suppose as an alternative that we define nominal saving to be the change in the nominal value of a household's assets held as bonds or money. (The standard national accounts follow this practice.) Compare the results with those from part b. What differences arise in the measurement of interest income on bonds and money?

   d. Suppose that we define real saving to be nominal saving divided by the price level, P_t, where nominal saving is defined as in part c. Does this concept of real saving measure the change in the real value of assets? Compare the result with that from part a, which does measure the change in the real value of assets.

9.13 A Case of Counterfeiting

   In 1925 a group of swindlers induced the Waterlow Company, a British manufacturer of bank notes, to print up and deliver to them 3 million pounds worth of Portuguese currency (escudos). Since the company also printed the legitimate notes for the Bank of Portugal, the counterfeit notes were indistinguishable from the real thing (except that the serial numbers turned out to be duplicates of those from a previous series of legitimate notes). Before the fraud was discovered, 1 million pounds' worth of the 'counterfeit' notes had been introduced into circulation in Portugal. After the scheme unravelled (because the duplication of serial numbers was discovered), the Bank of Portugal made good on the fraudulent notes by exchanging them for newly printed, valid notes. The bank subsequently sued the Waterlow Company for damages. The company was found liable, but the key question was the amount of the damage award. The bank argued that the damages were 1 million pounds (less funds collected from the swindlers).

The other side contended that the bank suffered only negligible real costs in having to issue an additional 1 million pounds' worth of new money to redeem the fraudulent notes. (Note that the currency was a purely paper issue, with no promise of convertibility into gold or anything else.) Thus, the argument was that the only true costs to the bank were the expenses for the paper and printing itself. Which side do you think was correct? (The House of Lords determined in 1932 that 1 million pounds was the right measure. For discussions of this fascinating episode in monetary economics, see R.G. Hawtrey, 1932, and Murray Bloom, 1966.)

Notes

1. We believe that the original source of this popular story is Milton Friedman (1969, pp. 4–5).
2. The discussion assumes positive transfers, although we could deal with negative ones. Negative transfers are taxes, which can also be lump sum – that is, independent of individuals' levels of income, amount of money holdings, and so on. Whereas we view transfers as financed by a helicopter drop of cash, we can view taxes as collected by a giant vacuum cleaner.
3. We ignore the discrete length of periods in this graph. In effect, we treat this length as being extremely brief.
4. The exception is the jump in the price level that accompanies the surprise acceleration of money at date T. The inflation rate (infinity) exceeds the expected inflation rate at this point.
5. Robert Flood and Peter Garber (1980) and Laura Lahaye (1985) provide quantitative estimates for these expectations of impending monetary reform.
6. Not surprisingly, the topic has fascinated many economists. Two of the more important studies are by Costantino Bresciani-Turroni (1937) and Phillip Cagan (1956).
7. For discussions of the reform, see Bresciani-Turroni (1937), Thomas Sargent (1982), and Peter Garber (1982). Sargent's analysis deals also with the ends of the hyperinflations in Austria, Hungary, and Poland in the early 1920s. He stresses the rapidity with which inflations can be ended once governments make a credible commitment to limit money creation in the long run.
8. The biggest hyperinflation on record occurred in Hungary after World War II: the price level rose by a factor of 3×10^{25} over the 13 months from July 1945 to August 1946. In the stabilization period from August 1946 to December 1947, the inflation rate declined to about 15% per year, and real money balances rose by a factor of 14. For a discussion, see William Bomberger and Gail Makinen (1983).

10

Financial Intermediation

Up to now the model treats money as currency, non-interest-bearing pieces of paper issued by the government. When we studied the demand for money in Chapter 3, we focused on the role of money as a medium of exchange. Households held money because they used it for purchases or sales of goods, bonds, and labour services. To reduce their average real money balance, households had to incur extra transaction costs, which might involve going more often to the bank or the store.

Checkable Deposits and M1

We mentioned in Chapter 3 that currency is not the only medium of exchange in the real world. The most important alternative is checkable deposits. These deposits are issued by various financial institutions, such as commercial banks and savings and loan associations. The holder of a deposit can purchase goods, bonds, and labour services by writing a cheque on his or her account. The cheque instructs the financial institution to transfer funds from the account of the cheque writer to that of another person. The important point is that 'checkable' deposits are often preferable to currency as a medium of exchange.

The most popular definition of money, M1, attempts to classify together the assets that serve commonly as media of exchange. Thus, M1 is the sum of currency held by the public and demand (checkable) deposits. In most industrialized countries, demand deposits account for the bulk of M1. For example, in 1991, demand deposits were about 70% of M1 in Germany, Japan and the United States and over 90% in the United Kingdom (see Table 3.1).

Some economists have argued that 'money' should also include deposits that are not checkable but can be converted readily into checkable form or into currency. The broader aggregate M2 includes consumer time deposits at various financial institutions, money-market deposit accounts, and some other items. Still broader monetary aggregates, such as M3, include additional types of financial assets. The problem is that once we go beyond the definition of money as common media of exchange, there is no clear place to draw the line. In the box below we consider some interesting attempts to solve this problem by constructing indices of monetary aggregates.

For our purposes, it is unimportant to settle on a precise definition of money. But we do want to extend the model to assess the economic consequences from the existence of various types of deposits and various kinds of financial institutions.

Let's begin by noting that bank deposits differ in the following ways:

- Whether they can be withdrawn on demand at face value. This privilege applies to **demand deposits** and usually to **savings deposits**. In contrast, **time deposits** have a stated maturity date, with some penalties typically attached to premature withdrawals.
- Whether people can write cheques that instruct the financial intermediary to make payments to a third party. Usually, all demand deposits are checkable.
- Whether they pay interest and at what rate.
- Whether they are insured.

Box 10.1   Indexes of Money

Some economists have used an index-number approach to measure the money supply. The general idea is to construct an aggregate that weights different assets according to their 'degree of moneyness.' One approach, used by William Barnett, Edward Offenbacher, and Paul Spindt (1984), begins with the observation that people hold currency although it bears zero interest. Other assets, such as various kinds of deposits, provide fewer monetary services and therefore must pay positive interest rates to induce people to hold them. Then the general idea is to weight the quantities of various assets inversely to their interest rates (which are observable) and hence in direct relation to their amounts of monetary services (which are unobservable). Currency counts one-to-one as money, checkable deposits (which bear low but positive interest rates) count somewhat less than one-to-one, time deposits (which bear higher interest rates) count still less, and so on. Using this technique, Barnett *et al.* have constructed a time series of a weighted monetary aggregate,

which behaves somewhat differently from M1 or other concepts.

One difficulty with the approach is that differences in interest rates among assets reflect characteristics other than monetary services. Also it is sometimes hard to measure the implicit interest rate from free services to holders of deposits. To get around these problems, Paul Spindt (1985) took a different approach. He made direct estimates of monetary services by observing how frequently the various kinds of assets were used in exchanges. Thus, currency and checkable deposits – which have high velocities – received a high weight for monetary services. In contrast, time deposits – which have low velocity – received a low weight as money. Using this procedure, Spindt calculated a time series for another weighted monetary aggregate, which showed somewhat different behaviour from the one described above. It is likely that economists will make increasing use of these weighted monetary aggregates in future research.

Households and firms decide how much to hold of the various deposits by considering the above characteristics as well as the interest rate paid. The main point is that these deposits are often more attractive than either currency or bonds. By bonds, we mean interest-bearing obligations of governments, businesses, or households. By holding a bond, a household or firm lends funds directly to governments or to other households or firms. In contrast, deposits are liabilities of financial institutions. By holding a deposit, a household or firm lends funds to a financial institution. As we shall see, the financial institution then acts as an intermediary by lending its funds to governments or to other households or firms.

We want to understand why households and firms typically use the services of financial intermediaries rather than making loans directly. Then we can also see how the existence of financial intermediaries and the amount of financial intermediation affect the performance of the economy.

Financial Intermediaries and the Credit Market

Thus far in our model, the people who hold bonds make direct loans to others. A lender may, for example, hold a mortgage on someone's house, a loan collateralized by someone's car, or a loan to a business for investment purposes. But this type of direct lending is often inefficient. First, it requires households and firms to evaluate the creditworthiness of borrowers, a process that is often difficult. Second, unless individual households and firms hold portions of many different types of loans, they risk the loss of a large part of their assets when a single loan goes bad. But it is hard for a single household or business to diversify by holding lots of different loans. Finally, the form of claim that someone holds – say, a home mortgage – must match the form of the loan in terms of its maturity. In the case of a 20-year loan to a home owner, the lender can cash in this claim only by selling it to someone else or by convincing the borrower to pay it off.

Financial intermediaries, such as commercial banks, can solve these problems. First, these institutions are in a good position to evaluate and collect on loans and to assemble a variety of loans by type and maturity. The credit market works better when loans are evaluated and administered by financial specialists rather than by households and non-financial firms. Second, as we already noted, financial institutions can attract funds by offering deposits, which are desirable forms of assets for households and businesses. In normal times, during which financial institutions hold a sound, well-diversified portfolio of assets, the deposits are safe and easy to understand.

Financial markets and financial intermediaries are heavily regulated. The government intervenes and directly participates in these markets even in countries that have a traditional free market attitude toward most of the other sectors in the economy.[1] The degree of public intervention goes beyond the usual legislative activity. The public authorities directly participate in the transactions that take place in these markets through the actions of the national **central bank**. The way in which financial markets are structured and regulated differ considerably across countries. It is therefore difficult to generate theoretical conclusions that apply to all times and places. Nonetheless, in all the developed countries, the basic principles and mechanisms that determine the relationship between the monetary sector and the real economy are the same, even if the details differ. Given our macroeconomic perspective, these details are not crucial. However, before we concentrate on the general principles of financial intermediation, it is useful to have a sense of the cross-country differences and complexity of this sector.

Financial intermediaries are not just commer-

cial banks. Financial intermediation is conducted by a variety of institutions, such as savings and loan associations, money-market funds, mutual savings banks, pension funds, investment companies, insurance companies, and the government's mortgage associations. The institutional structure and the importance of these different intermediaries vary greatly across countries.

We can identify three general forms of institutional organization of financial intermediaries, depending on the degree of separation between banking and security activities. The essential difference is in the type of assets that an intermediary holds. Banking activities are associated with loans, which can be direct loans or purchases of bonds. Security activities involve equity stakes in companies through the purchase of corporate stocks.

In the first system, typical of the US, Canada and Japan, banking and security activities are considered intrinsically different, especially in terms of risk. As a prudential measure, the same institution is prevented from carrying on both activities. The opposite point of view characterizes the universal banking systems. Here, the same institution is allowed to perform the full range of financial activities including banking, brokerage and portfolio management activities. Countries like Germany, the Netherlands and Switzerland, that adopt this system, believe that by differentiating across these different operations, the risk of financial failure arising from losses in a particular activity is reduced. The third system, in use for example in Belgium, France and Italy, is a compromise between the two extremes. Here, the financial institutions resemble universal banks with the exception that their participation in the secondary markets works only through the services of a licensed broker.[2]

Table 10.1 gives a more complete picture of the regulations determining the range of markets and activities in which various types of financial intermediaries can participate. These different regulations, together with innumerable country-specific historical developments, have resulted in very different national banking sectors. Table 10.2 provides some indication of this cross-country heterogeneity.

	Primary markets	Secondary markets	Collective investment	Portfolios and counselling
Belgium	I, VI	I, II	III	I, II, IV, VI
Denmark	I, II, VI	I, II, VI	III	I, II, VI
France	I	I, II	I, II, III, V	I, II, IV
Germany	I	I, II	III	I, VII
Greece	I, II	I, II	III	I
Ireland	I, II	I, II, VII	I, III, V	I, II, IV
Italy	I, IV	I, II	I, III, V	
Luxembourg	I, II	I, II	I, II, III	I, II
Netherlands	I, II	I, II	III	I, II
Portugal	I, III	I, II, III	I, III	I, III
Spain	I, II	I, II	I, III	I, II
UK	I, II, VII	I, II	VI	I, II, V
Australia	I, II, VII	I, II, VII	I, II, VII	
Canada	I, II	I, II	I, VII	I, II, V
Japan	II	II	III	II, V
Switzerland	I, IV	I, IV	III	I, IV
USA	I*, IV	I*, II	I*, III	I*, II, IV

Table 10.1 Notes

I: Commercial banks
II: Brokers (Stockbrokers, Security Firms, Dealers, Discount Brokers)
III: Mutual Funds, Pension Funds, Investment Funds, Investment Associations, Investment Societies
IV: Investment Banks, Financial Companies
V: Insurance Companies
VI: Other Credit Institutions
VII: Other Financial Institutions

* Limited to US government, state, local, municipal bonds and certain money market investments.

Table 10.1 Institutions allowed to perform security-related operations in different markets and different forms of investment

	No. commercial banks	No. savings & mutual banks	No. foreign banks	No. domestic banks	Market share five largest institutions
Belgium	86	31	61	56	70
Denmark		219	5	214	78
France	367	624	131	860	50
Germany	252	598[1]	148	702	44
Greece	33	2	19	16	83
Ireland	42	17		59	
Italy	200	85	38	247	55
Luxembourg	122		102	20	30
Netherlands	81	67	0	108	84
Portugal		27	9	18	78
Spain	136	213	36	300	46
UK	611	140	300	451	36
EEC	2176	17777		3064	13
Japan	141[2]	1088[3]	64	1165	20
Switzerland	233	215	109	339	65
US	14130	3563	459	17234	10

[1] Does not include 3604 cooperative credit institutions.
[2] Includes city and regional banks.
[3] Includes 929 credit associations and credit cooperatives.

Table 10.2　Summary statistics on selected banking systems, end of 1986

The Balance Sheet of a Financial Intermediary

A financial institution's deposits appear on the liabilities side of its balance sheet, and various loans appear on the assets side. Table 10.3 shows a typical balance sheet. To be concrete, the figures apply in 1991 to an actual commercial bank – Banca Commerciale Italiana – which had total assets of ε76 billion.

The main items on the asset side of the balance sheet are as follows:

- Cash of ε5147 million. This item includes currency (often called **vault cash**) and deposits held on the books of the national central bank (Banca d'Italia). The total of currency and deposits held at the central bank is called **reserves**.
- Securities of ε6519 million. This category includes government bonds and short-term money-market instruments, such as commercial paper and certificates of deposit issued by other financial institutions.
- Loans of ε34 952 million. The principal items are commercial loans, mortgages, and instalment loans.
- Interbank deposits and loans of ε20 758 million. These are deposits held at and loans made to other financial intermediaries. The short-term end of this market (often over-

night) is referred to as the **interbank market**. Banca Commerciale Italiana had ε4121 million of these loans outstanding at the end of 1991. The interest rate charged on these short-term loans is called the interbank rate or the **money market rate**.[3]

The principal items on the liability side are the following:

- Demand deposits of ε23 260 million.
- Time deposits of ε12 085 million.
- Borrowings from the central bank of ε898 million. The central bank lends to financial institutions at the *discount window*. The interest rate charged on these loans is the central bank **discount rate**.
- Deposits and loans from other financial institutions of ε26 763 million. Of these, the short-term borrowings from the interbank market were ε5989 million.
- Shareholders' equity of ε3564 million. This 'book value' is the sum of paid-in capital plus accumulated profits (as measured by accountants).

Reserves – Required and Excess

Financial intermediaries hold earning assets, by which we mean loans and securities, to obtain a flow of interest income. They hold physical capital and deposits at other financial institu-

Assets		Liabilities	
Cash and funds with the Central Bank	5147	Demand deposits	23 260
of which: required reserves	4575	Time deposits	12 085
Securities and other financial assets	6519	Borrowing from the Central Bank	898
Deposits and due from other banks	20 758	Deposits and due to other banks	26 763
of which: at sight or undefined maturity	4121	*of which: at sight or undefined maturity*	5989
Loans	34 952	Other liabilities	9527
Other assets	8721	Shareholders' equity	3564
Total	76 097	Total	76 097

Note: This is the consolidated balance sheet of the BCI group. This includes the accounts of Banca Commerciale Italiana, SpA (the Parent Company) and that of other banks and finance companies involved in banking activities in which the Parent Company holds a majority stake.

Source: Banca Commerciale Italiana Annual Report and Accounts 1991.

Table 10.3   Balance sheet of Banca Commerciale Italiana, 31 December 1991 (millions of ECU)

tions to carry out their business efficiently. What about cash? Because banks and some other depository institutions stand ready to convert their deposits into currency on demand, they keep some currency to meet the possible withdrawals of depositors. Another, and often more important, determinant of cash holdings by these institutions is the **reserve requirement** imposed by the central bank. Most countries' central bank specifies the quantity of reserves that must be held against various categories of deposits. Legally the reserves can be held either as currency (vault cash) or as deposits on the books of the central bank. Banca Commerciale Italiana held ε4575 million in required reserves in 1991.

As reported in Table 10.4, there are large cross-country differences in banks' reserve requirements. In 1991, Italian banks had to have a minimum of 22.5% of all categories of deposits in the form of reserves, whereas UK banks had to hold less than 0.5%. Nowadays, several central banks pay interest on the reserves that commercial banks hold with them. However, this interest rate is below the market rate. The difference between the interest rate on reserves and the market rate acts as a tax on deposit institutions and is a source of seigniorage, as mentioned in Chapter 9. This difference has sometimes been substantial.

Belgium	0
Denmark	reserve requirment abolished in March 1991
France	4.1
Germany	6.6–12.5 depending on the size of deposits
Greece	8
Ireland	8
Italy	22.5
Luxembourg	0
Netherlands	not applicable
Portugal	17
Spain	5
United Kingdom	0.45
United States	12
Japan	2.5

Source: Padoa-Schioppa and Saccomanni (1992); Banca Commerciale Italiana, *Tendenze Monetarie*, Nov. 1991; Batten *et al.* (1990).

Table 10.4 Required reserves on demand deposits (in percent, 1991)

Figure 10.1 shows how the ratio of required reserves to checkable deposits behaved from 1918 to 1991 for the US, the country for which a long time series exists. The main source of change in this ratio is shifts in legal requirements. But some requirements attach also to time and savings deposits, which do not enter into the total of checkable deposits. Also, the requirements depend on the total volume of deposits of the financial institution. Some changes in the ratio of required reserves to checkable deposits therefore reflect shifts in the composition of deposits (between checkable and time or savings and among the categories of financial institutions).

Instead of keeping non-interest-bearing cash, financial institutions prefer to hold assets that bear interest. Because these institutions can shift rapidly in and out of short-term securities or the interbank market, even a moderate interest rate induces them to keep very little reserves above the required amount. Economists use the term **excess reserves** for the difference between total and required reserves.

Figure 10.2 shows the ratio of total reserves to total bank deposits for the G-6 countries in the post-war period. Again, the long-run movements of the reserve ratios are driven by changes in reserve requirement. The same is true for the cross-country differences in average reserve holdings. For this reason, for example, in Germany and Italy total reserves are much higher than France or Japan. Notice that, over

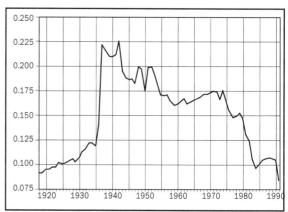

Figure 10.1   Ratio of required reserves to checkable deposits

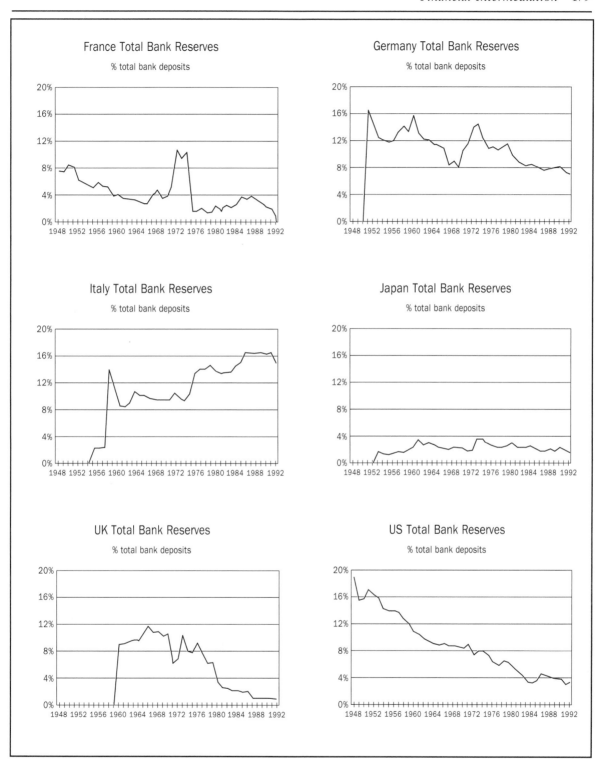

Figure 10.2

this period, the UK and the US have been characterized by a continuous decline in reserve holdings, while Italy experienced a continuous increase. Notice that in France, Germany and the UK reserves peaked between 1972 and 1974, a period of financial distress that followed the collapse of the Bretton Woods system of fixed exchange rates (we will discuss this episode in the next chapter). A similar situation was experienced in the 1930s in the US, reflecting the financial crises of the Great Depression, as well as the extremely low interest rates on safe assets (we shall discuss this episode in detail later.)

Excess reserves provide funds that a financial institution can dip into during emergencies. By contrast, required reserves do not serve this purpose. For a given amount of deposits, a depository institution is not permitted to let its reserves fall below the required amount.

Deposits and Earning Assets

Suppose that a depository institution attracts an additional ε100 of deposits. For concreteness, think about a checkable deposit for which the required-reserve ratio is 12%. Then the institution holds ε12 out of the extra ε100 as required reserves. The rest of the ε100 may be divided as the institution chooses between loans and securities (which bear interest) or excess reserves (which bear zero or below market interest).

The change in the institution's net earnings equals the interest on the additional earning assets, less the added costs of evaluating and collecting on loans or dealing in securities, less any extra costs of servicing the deposits (if no separate fees are charged), less the interest paid on the new deposits. For the institution to profit from this enterprise, it must be that the interest rate on deposits, call it R^d, is less than that on loans and securities, which we still call R. In particular, the spread, $R - R^d$, must cover the cost of the funds that the intermediary holds in non-interest-bearing form, the transaction costs associated with deposits and earnings assets, and some return on the capital invested in the business of being an intermediary. Call the total of these items the **costs of intermediation**. Competition among intermediaries would drive the interest

rate on deposits high enough so that the spread, $R - R^d$, just covered the costs of intermediation.[4] It follows that the interest rate paid on deposits, R^d, would rise with the interest rate on loans and securities, R, and would decline with an increase in the costs of intermediation, such as a rise in the required-reserve ratio.

Deposit Interest Rates and Financial Intermediation

The amount of deposits that households and firms want to hold – and hence the amount of funds that financial intermediaries have to loan out – depends on the interest rate on deposits, R^d. Deposits become more attractive relative to currency if R^d increases. (Note that the nominal interest rate on currency is fixed at zero.) Deposits become less attractive relative to bonds if the spread, $R - R^d$, rises.

Suppose, for example, that the required-reserve ratio declines. For a given value of R, our analysis of competition among financial intermediaries predicts that the deposit interest rate, R^d, would rise. Households and firms would therefore hold more deposits at the expense of currency and bonds. The increase in deposits means that financial intermediaries would expand their holdings of assets. Thus overall, we find that a lower reserve requirement leads, first, to more of M1 held as deposits rather than currency and, second, to more financial intermediation.

Notice also that changes in reserves requirements can have important repercussions on the international competitiveness of banks. Compare, for example, the situation of Italian and British banks. Because of the higher reserve requirement, Italian banks will have, other things equal, a larger interest rate spread, $R - R^d$, to cover their costs. Hence, depositors will receive a lower return on deposits held at an Italian bank than on deposits held at a British bank and will, therefore, prefer to use British banks to Italian banks. This observation suggests that Italian banks would disappear, since they cannot compete with British banks. Why are they still around? There are two, interconnected, reasons. First, until recently, the residents of many countries (including Italy) could not choose to use foreign financial intermediaries. The set of measures preventing domestic residents from accessing foreign financial institutions and markets are referred to as **capital controls**. In the EC, most capital controls have now disappeared, as part of the 1992 liberalization programme. The second reason is that the large majority of individuals are small depositors for whom the costs involved in using a foreign bank are too large compared to the benefit of a small increase in R^d. Also, foreign banks tend to offer deposits denominated in their own currencies. Depositors then have to bear transaction costs and foreign exchange risk. To avoid these costs, most depositors would still use domestic banks.[5]

Borrowing from the Central Bank

Borrowing from the central bank can be advantageous if the central bank's discount rate is below the rates at which financial institutions can otherwise borrow. Such borrowing may not always be desirable, however, even if the discount rate is relatively low. That is because, first, the central bank tends to examine banks more carefully when they borrow frequently at the discount window and, second, the central bank can refuse to lend to banks that ask 'too often'. In any case the lower the discount rate is, relative to market interest rates, the greater is the incentive for banks to borrow from the central bank.

Figure 10.3 shows the credits (as a percentage of total deposits) received by banking institutions from the central bank in France, Germany, Italy and Japan between 1960 and 1992. Notice that these borrowings were important in France at the beginning of the period, when they where above 40% of total deposits. For the other countries, however, their relevance has been much smaller.

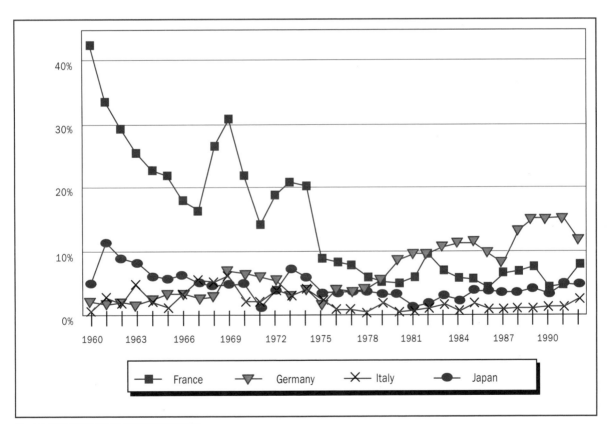

Source: IMF *International Financial Statistics*.

Figure 10.3 Credit from the central bank (as percentage of total deposits)

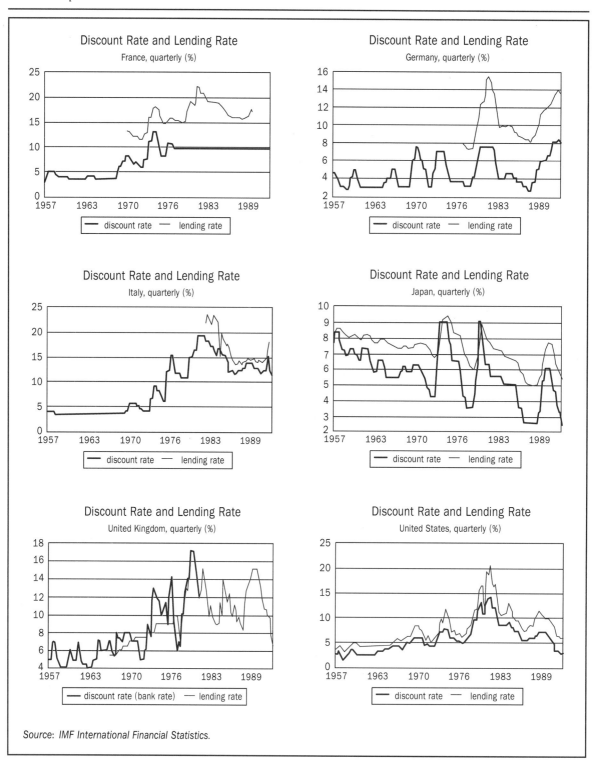

Figure 10.4 Discount rates and lending rates in the G-6

The average borrowings in Germany were 7.2% of total deposits, in Italy 1.8% and in Japan 5.2%.

Figure 10.4 shows how the annual average discount rate at the central bank of the G-6 countries compares to the interest rate on medium-term maturity (i.e. less than a year) commercial paper.[6] Although the two interest rates tended to move together, the discount rate typically has been lower than the commercial paper rate. The loans from the central bank therefore usually involved a subsidy to the borrower.

The Central Bank

We have already seen that national central banks have important roles in domestic financial markets.[7] Central banks have evolved over the years along with monetary and financial developments. **The Bank of England**, the central bank of the United Kingdom, was funded in 1694 as a joint stock company, i.e. a private company.[8] Even if not a public institution, the Bank of England was granted from the beginning a privileged position with respect to other banks, in particular with respect to the power to issue banknotes. Common to other countries' experience, the Bank of England's initial main role was to serve as an agent to the Treasury. During the nineteenth century it gradually assumed the functions that we commonly associate with a central bank, such as the control of the overall money supply and of interest rates and the supervision of other banking institutions. Despite its clear public role, the Bank of England did not become a public institution until its nationalization in 1946.

The **Deutsche Bundesbank**, the German central bank, is a relatively recent institution. Its precursor was the Reichsbank, which began its operations in Berlin in 1876 but in fact had existed since 1847 as the Prussian Bank. After World War II and the division of Germany, the Reichsbank ceased to exist. It was replaced, in 1948, by the Bank Deutscher Länder (Bank of German States) organized by the Allies to resemble the US Federal Reserve System. In 1957, after the creation of the Federal Republic of Germany, the Bank Deutscher Länder was transformed into the current Bundesbank.

Since 1914 the **Federal Reserve System** has functioned as the central bank in the United States. There are 12 regional Federal Reserve banks, each of which was set up as a separate, quasi-private corporation. In the early days of the system, the 12 presidents of the regional banks served on the Governors' Conference, which had substantial influence over the Fed's policies. However, following the Great Depression and the Banking Act of 1935, the Governors' Conference was abolished and the Fed's power was centralized in Washington, D.C. Since 1935 the main authority has resided with the Board of Governors of the Federal Reserve System.

We have already mentioned that the central bank's activities include issuing notes, acting as an agent for the government, and supervising the banking system. Another important role is the management of the payment system, that is, the process through which payments (like cheques or wire transfers) are cleared. Not all central banks perform all of these activities. As shown in Table 10.5, which refers to the EC countries, issuing notes, acting as an agent for the government, and supervising the payment system are functions common to all the central banks. In the EC, however, national central banks differ in the degree of their involvement in the management of the payment system and in the supervision of the banking sector. Unlike the other EC countries, the central banks of Belgium, Denmark, Germany, and France, are not the only supervisors of their banking system. This role is shared with other public agencies.

The other major role of a central bank is the conduct of monetary policies. Once again, central banks differ in the way they manage monetary policies. Table 10.6 summarizes these differences for the EC countries. Notice that we distinguish between two means of conducting monetary policies: dealing in the domestic financial market, for example by buying and selling bonds on the secondary market for short-term government paper bills; and dealing with individual banks, for

		B	DK	D	GR	E	F	IRL	I	L	NL	P	UK
1.	Note Issue	yes	yes	yes	yes	yes	yes	yes	yes	yes	yes	yes	yes
2.	Treasury service for the government	yes	yes	yes	yes	yes	yes	yes	yes	yes	yes	yes	yes
3.	Payment System												
3.1	Oversight	yes	yes	yes	yes	yes	yes	yes	yes	yes	yes	yes	yes
3.2	Management of clearing system	no	yes	partial	yes	no	yes	no	yes	no	no	yes	no
3.3	Liquidity facilities	yes	yes	yes	yes	yes	yes	yes	yes	yes	yes	yes	yes
4.	Involvment in banking supervision												
4.1	Regulation	I	0	II	III	III	II	III	III	III	III	III	III
4.2	Authorization	0	0	0	III	III	II	III	III	III	III	III	III
4.3	Prudential	0	0	II	III	III	III	III	III	III	III	III	III

0 = nil
I = limited
II = intermediate
III = extensive

Source: Padoa-Schioppa and Saccomanni (1992).

Table 10.5   Role of the central bank in the EC countries

		B	DK	D	GR	E	F	IRL	I	L	NL	P	UK
1.	Operation with the domestic market												
1.1	Extent of use	III	I	III	I	III	III	III	III		II	III	III
1.2	Use of repurchase agreements	III	I	III	I	III	III	III	III		III	I	I
1.3	Degree of discretion in determining quantity of liquidity supplied	II	III	III	III	III	III	III	III		I	0	0
1.4	Degree of discretion in determining the cost of liquidity supplied	III	III	III	III	III	III	III	I		III	III	III
1.5	Ability to influence market rates	III	I	III	III	III	III	II	III		III	III	III
2.	Operations with individual intermediaries												
2.1	Extent of use	I	III	III	I	I	0	I	I		II	I	I
2.2	Degree of discretion in determining quantity of liquidity supplied	I	II	II	0	II	0	I	II		II	III	III
2.3	Degree of discretion in determining the cost of liquidity supplied	III	III	III	0	III	0	III	II		II	III	III
2.4	Ability to influence market rates	II	III	II	0	I	0	II	III		I	0	0

0 = nil
I = limited
II = intermediate
III = extensive

Source: Padoa-Schioppa and Saccomanni (1992).

Table 10.6   The central bank monetary policy operations

example by lending to an intermediary at the discount window. A third option involves dealing on the market for foreign exchange. We postpone the discussion of this topic to the next chapter. Now we want to focus on the domestic instruments for controlling the quantity of money. We begin by looking at the balance sheet of, arguably, the most influential central bank in Europe: the Deutsche Bundesbank.

Table 10.7 shows the balance sheet at the end of 1991. The main items on the asset side are the following:

- Gold account of DM 13.7 billion. In past years, when most countries were on the gold standard, variations in the quantity of gold resulted mainly from dealings with other central banks. Now changes are mainly due to adjustments in the official price of gold.
- Claims on international organizations: on the International Monetary Fund of DM8.3 billion and on the European Monetary Cooperation Fund (in connection with the European Monetary System) for DM17.3 billion
- Foreign assets of DM58 billion. These are balances with foreign banks, holdings of foreign assets, notes and coins.
- Loans to depository institutions of DM225.3 billion. These are the borrowings of depository intermediaries through repurchase agreement operations and at the discount window.

- Securities and coins of DM6.4 billion. These are mainly bonds issued by the Federal Republic of Germany.

Notice that the bulk of the Bundesbank assets are loans to domestic banks. This is not true for all central banks. For example, the great bulk of Federal Reserve assets takes the form of US government securities: unlike the central banks of many other countries, the Fed engages in little direct lending to the private sector.

The liability side of the Bundesbank's ledger includes the following main items:

- Banknotes (currency) of DM181.3 billion. At present, these notes are the only significant form of currency outstanding.
- Deposits of banks of DM72.4 billion. These mainly comprise the minimum required reserves of depository intermediaries. In Germany, like France, Spain and the US, these deposits do not bear any interest. In other countries, however, like Greece, Ireland, Italy and Portugal, required reserves pay interest.
- Public authorities' deposits of DM12.7 billion. These deposits constitute the federal and state governments' checking accounts, which are held at the Bundesbank. This is part of the treasury services for the government that we mentioned above.

The total of banknotes and deposits of depository institutions (DM253.7 billion in Germany) is

Assets		Liabilities	
Gold	13 687.5	Banknotes in circulation	181 300.2
Reserve position in the IMF	8 313.6	Deposits of banks	72 438.9
Claims on the EMCF	17 328.7	Deposits of public authorities	12 722.4
Foreign assets and claims on foreign institutions	58 015.6	Deposits of other domestic depositors	9 757.1
Loans to domestic banks	225 318.1	Deposits of foreign depositors	39 449.2
Securities and coins	6 353.2	Other liabilities	28 978.7
Other assets	30 843.2	Profit	15 213.4
Total	359 859.9	Total	359 859.9

Source: Annual Report of the Deutsche Bundesbank, 1991.

Table 10.7 Balance sheet of the Deutsche Bundesbank (31 December 1991) (DM million)

called the **monetary base** or **high-powered money** (or sometimes M0). This sum represents the total of the central bank's monetary liabilities (aside from those held by the public authorities or as foreign deposits). At the end of 1991, 71% of the monetary base took the form of currency in Germany. In the same year, currency was 91% of the monetary base in the US and only 36% in Italy (remember the high required reserve requirement in Italy).

Control of the Monetary Base

Open-Market Operations

In most industrialized countries, open-market operations have become the principal instrument for controlling the monetary base. Monetary authorities often express their monetary policy in terms of monetary aggregates. The aggregate targeted varies from the narrow M0 (in the UK) to the broad M3 (in Germany). During the 1980s, most central banks have de-emphasized the targeting of monetary aggregates and have expressed their policy in terms of a variety of economic indicators, for example the inflation rate or the exchange rate. Regardless of the aggregates used in the formulation of their policy, these objectives are achieved by controlling the behaviour of monetary aggregates directly and/or through changes in the short-term interest rates.[9]

As we shall see later, we can relate the behaviour of broader monetary aggregates to changes in the monetary base and, hence, to open-market operations. There are two main types of open market operations: **outright** or by **repurchase agreement**. An outright purchase (sale) is a once and for all purchase (sale) of a security on the market. With a repurchase agreement, at the time of the purchase (sale) of the security, the central bank agrees with the seller (buyer) to reverse the transaction after a prespecified period of time (usually very short, sometimes as short as one day). We can think of a repurchase agreement as a sequence of two, opposite, outright operations. Therefore, in the following discussion, we concentrate on outright open-market operations.

Consider now the effect of open-market operations on the monetary base. In the case of an open-market purchase, the central bank writes a cheque to buy, say, ε1 million of government securities. Suppose that the seller of the bonds is a commercial bank, which we call People's Bank. (We would end up with the same results if the seller were a household or, more likely, a large corporation.) The central bank credits this bank with ε1 million more of reserves in the form of book-entry deposits at the central bank. At this point, the balance sheets of the central bank and People's Bank change as shown in Table 10.8. Notice that the central bank has 1 million more of assets in the form of government bonds. This amount balances the extra ε1 million of liabilities, which show up as more deposits of depository institutions (in this case of People's Bank). Correspondingly, People's Bank has ε1 million more of assets in the form of deposits held at the central bank but 1 million less of government bonds, a form of interest-bearing assets that are included in the bank's portfolio of loans and securities.

The balance sheets shown in Table 10.8 are not the end of the story because People's Bank probably does not want to keep ε1 million more of non-interest-bearing reserves at the central bank. But let's hold off on this matter for now to focus on the behaviour of the monetary base. The open-market purchase of securities shown in Table 10.8 raises the monetary base by ε1 million, an increase that shows up initially as an extra ε1 million in reserves held by depository institutions at the central bank. Note also that an

Assets	Liabilities
Central Bank	
Government securities:	Deposits of depository institutions:
+ε1 million	+ε1 million
People's Bank	
Loans and securities: −ε1 million	
Deposits at Fed: +ε1 million	

Table 10.8 Effects on the balance sheets of the central bank and depository institutions from an open-market purchase of government bonds

open-market sale of securities would just reverse the process. If the central bank sells ε1 million of government bonds, then the monetary base declines by ε1 million.

In Germany and the US, open-market operations involve only government bonds, whereas in other countries, such as France, Japan and the UK, these operations also involve private bills, certificates of deposits and commercial paper. It makes little difference, however, if the central bank holds private bonds instead of the public debt. In this case, the private sector ends up holding more of the public debt but owes correspondingly more to the central bank. The central bank has more claims on the private sector but less on the national Treasury. Overall, the net positions of the private sector, the central bank, and the Treasury are the same.

Loans to Depository Institutions

The central bank can also control the monetary base by varying the quantity of loans to depository institutions. The central bank can engineer these changes by shifting either the discount rate or other aspects of its lending policies to induce depository institutions to borrow more or less at the discount window. During the 1980s the importance of the discount window has declined and open-market operations have become the major instrument of monetary policy. Only Japan, among the major countries, still emphasizes discount-window operations.

Suppose, for example, that People's Bank decides to borrow an additional ε1 million from the central bank. Then the central bank records a loan of ε1 million to People's Bank and also credits this bank with an extra ε1 million of deposits. If People's Bank just holds these deposits at the central bank (perhaps because if would otherwise have fallen short of its reserve requirement), then the balance sheets of the central bank and People's Bank change as shown in Table 10.9.

Notice that the borrowings show up as ε1 million more in loans to depository institutions on the asset side of the central bank's books. Simultaneously, on the liability side, there is an increase by ε1 million in the deposits of

	Assets	Liabilities
Central Bank	Loans to depository institutions:	Deposits of depository institutions:
	+ε1 million	+ε1 million
People's Bank	Deposits at the central bank:	Borrowing from the central bank:
	+ε1 million	+ε1 million

Table 10.9 Effects on the balance sheets of the central bank and depository institutions from central bank lending at the discount window

depository institutions. There are corresponding changes on the books of People's Bank. The main point is that, as before, the monetary base rises by ε1 million.

An increase in borrowings by depository institutions at the discount window is essentially the same as an open-market purchase of securities by the central bank. In both cases the monetary base increases. The only difference is that in one case (the open-market purchase) the central bank ends up holding more securities, whereas in the other (lending at the discount window), the central bank ends up with more loans to depository institutions. Correspondingly, People's Bank ends up holding fewer securities in the first case, and more debt to the central bank in the second. Overall, the difference amounts to a shift from the central bank's holding of securities to the central bank's holding obligations on a private bank. But as mentioned before, these types of changes have no major consequences. The only significant difference concerns the subsidy that the central bank provides to depository institutions because the discount rate is typically set below market interest rates.

Economists often say that a shift in the discount rate is significant not for its direct impact on borrowings but rather as an announcement of the central bank's intentions. Over the longer term, the central bank moves the discount rate to match changes in market interest rates. Hence, most of the movements in the discount rate are reactions to changes in the economy, rather than vice versa. But the timing and sometimes the amount of a shift in the discount rate are at the central bank's discretion. It is possible that some of these changes are a useful signal about the future behaviour of the monetary base. No one has yet shown, however, that changes in the discount rate can actually help to predict the future quantity of the monetary base or other economic variables. The suggestion that shifts in the discount rate have an 'announcement effect' is therefore an interesting, but unproven, idea.

Many economists think that the central bank should stop subsidizing borrowers – that is, it should set the discount rate at a penalty level above market interest rates. Of course, if the discount rate were actually a penalty rate, it would have to be above the rate at which an individual institution could otherwise borrow. But then, no institution would ever borrow from the central bank. Hence, the suggestion for a penalty discount rate amounts to a proposal for closing the discount window.

From the standpoint of controlling the monetary base, the existence of the discount window adds nothing to open-market operations. Thus,

the argument for the central bank's lending to depository institutions comes down to the desirability of subsidizing selected financial institutions – presumably, mainly institutions that are in trouble.

The Monetary Base and Monetary Aggregates

Thus far, our discussion shows how the central bank can control the monetary base. But we already mentioned that the central bank might adjust the base to achieve a target value for a broader monetary aggregate, such as M1 or M2. Recall that these aggregates add various categories of deposits to the amount of currency held by the public. To study the relation between the monetary base and these monetary aggregates, we have to understand the behaviour of deposits.

Return to the case shown in Table 10.8 in which the open-market purchase of securities raised the monetary base by ε1 million. Instead of a single bank, consider now the effects on financial intermediaries as a whole. Table 10.10 shows that in step 1 these intermediaries have 1 million more of deposits at the central bank and ε1 million less of loans and securities.

| | Financial intermediaries (FIs) | | Households | | The central bank | |
	Assets	Liabilities	Assets	Liabilities	Assets	Liabilities
Step 1:	Loans and securities: −ε1 million				Securities: +ε1 million	Deposits of FIs: +ε1 million
	Deposits at central bank +ε1 million					
Step 2:	Loans and securities: +ε1 million	Customer deposits: +ε1 million	Deposits at FIs: +ε1 million	Loans from FIs: +ε1 million		
Step 3:	Loans and securities: +ε880 000	Customer deposits: +ε880 000	Deposits at FIs: +ε880 000	Loans from FIs: +ε880 000		

Table 10.10   Effect of open-market purchases of bonds on the financial system

Suppose that the extra ε1 million of deposits at the central bank are excess reserves, which the financial intermediaries do not wish to hold. Rather, these institutions place these funds into earning assets. To be concrete, assume that they make an additional ε1 million of loans to households. The results would be the same, however, if the intermediaries bought more securities. In any event, the recipients of the loans have an extra ε1 million, which we suppose that they keep initially as deposits at a financial intermediary. Thus, the balance sheet of these intermediaries changes as shown in step 2 of Table 10.10. On the asset side there is an additional ε1 million of loans and securities, a change that offsets the initial decline by this amount. On the liability side, there is an added ε1 million of customer deposits.

The recipients of the loan probably do not want to hold an extra ε1 million of deposits. But as they spend these funds they are transferred to the accounts of others. Ultimately people are either induced[10] to hold an extra ε1 million of deposits at financial intermediaries, or they are motivated to redeem all or part of this ε1 million for currency (which the intermediaries stand ready to provide to depositors). For the moment, we shall ignore this important possibility of moving into currency. Then we eventually reach the situation shown as step 2 in Table 10.10.

The extra ε1 million in customer deposits raises the required reserves of the financial intermediaries. For illustrative purposes, assume a reserve ratio of 12%. Thus, required reserves rise by ε120 000. But then the financial institutions still have ε880 000 (ε1 million less the ε120 000) of excess reserves. They therefore again place these funds into earning assets, which we assume take the form of loans. When people are motivated to hold these additional funds as deposits we arrive at step 3 in Table 10.10. Here, the intermediaries' loans and securities rise along with its deposits by another ε880 000.

If we continue to work through this process, then we find that the deposits held at financial institutions rise by a large multiple of the expansion in the monetary base. Specifically, the deposits increase eventually by the amount

ε1 million $\cdot (1/0.12) = $ ε8.33 million. In other words, the increase by ε1 million in base money leads to an increase by ε8.33 million in deposits. At this point, the intermediaries' required reserves are up by 0.12· ε 8.33 million = ε1 million, that is, the additional base money is all held as required reserves.

An important amendment to this **multiple expansion of deposits** concerns the households' demand for currency. In the G-6 countries, the ratio of currency to checkable deposits was between 0.08 (in the UK) and 0.49 (in the US) in 1991. Using the value 0.4 for this ratio and assuming no changes in the relative attractiveness of currency and deposits, we predict that people will hold an additional 40 cents of currency for each extra dollar of deposits.

Table 10.11 modifies the analysis to take account of currency. Now, with an extra ε1 million of funds in step 2a, the public is eventually motivated to hold (approximately) ε700 000 more in deposits and ε300 000 more in currency. As the public redeems deposits to obtain this extra currency, the financial intermediaries must get this currency by running down their deposits at the central bank. Thus, in step 2a, the liabilities of financial institutions show ε700 000 more in customer deposits, and their assets show ε300 000 less in deposits at the central bank. Notice that required reserves are now up by ε84 000 (0.12 · ε700 000 of deposits) rather than the ε120 000 in the previous step 2. But actual reserves are higher by only ε700 000 rather than the previous ε1 million. Thus, excess reserves are higher by ε616 000 (ε700 000 less ε84 000) instead of the previous ε880 000 (ε1 million less ε120 000). The 'leakage' of funds into currency means that the financial intermediaries end up with less excess reserves than otherwise.

For the central bank, the additional currency outstanding of ε300 000 corresponds to an equivalent reduction in the book-entry deposits of financial institutions. As shown in step 2a of Table 10.11, there is no change in the monetary base, which consists of currency plus the deposits of the financial institutions at the central bank. Thus, the monetary base remains higher by ε1 million.

	Financial intermediaries (FIs)		Households		The central bank	
	Assets	Liabilities	Assets	Liabilities	Assets	Liabilities
Step 1a:	Loans and securities: −ε1 million Deposits at central bank +ε1 million				Securities: +ε1 million	Deposits of FIs: +ε1 million
Step 2a:	Loans and securities: +ε1 million Deposits at central bank: −ε300 000	Customer deposits: +ε700 000	Deposits at FIs: +ε700 000 Currency: +ε300 000	Loans from FIs: +ε1 million		Deposits of FIs: −ε300 000 Currency: +ε300 000
Step 3a:	Loans and securities +ε616 000 Deposits at central bank: −ε176 000	Customer deposits: +ε440 000	Deposits at FIs: +ε440 000 Currency: +ε176 000	Loans from FIs: +ε616 000		Deposits of FIs: −ε176 000 Currency: +ε176 000

Table 10.11   Effect of open-market purchases of bonds on the financial system, including the responses of currency

The rest of the analysis proceeds as before, except that some funds leak out to currency at each stage. We can find the ultimate position from the following set of equations, where the symbol Δ represents the change in the associated variable:

Δ (monetary base) = Δ (required reserves) + Δ (currency) = ε1 million
Δ (required reserves) = $0.12 \cdot \Delta$(deposits)
Δ (currency) = $0.4 \cdot \Delta$(deposits)

Substituting the second and third conditions into the first leads to

$0.12 \cdot \Delta$(deposits) + $0.4 \cdot \Delta$(deposits) = ε1 million

Solving for the change in deposits, we get the results:

Δ(deposits) = ε1 million/0.52 = ε1 920 000
Δ(currency) = $0.4 \cdot \Delta$(deposits) = ε770 000

Δ(required reserves) = $0.12 \cdot \Delta$(deposits) = ε230 000

Thus, the incorporation of currency has a dramatic effect on the results. Instead of rising by ε8.33 million, the deposits held at financial intermediaries end up increasing by only ε1.92 million. Generally the ultimate expansion of deposits is larger the smaller is the ratio of reserves to deposits (fixed at 0.12 above) and the smaller is the ratio of currency to deposits (0.4 above).

Given the changes in deposits and currency, we can calculate how an open-market operation affects various monetary aggregates. If we limit attention to checkable deposits (with a required-reserve ratio of 0.12), then the change in M1 is the sum of the changes in deposits and currency, or ε2 690 000 above. Since an increase by ε1 000 000 in high-powered money leads to an expansion by ε2 690 000 in M1, we can say that the **money multiplier** (the ratio of M1 to the base) is 2.69.

	F	D	I	J	UK	US
Money multiplier	4.73	2.06	2.46	2.78	10.30	2.74
Required reserves on demand deposits (%)	4.1	10*	22.5	2.5	0.45	12
Currency demand deposits	0.27	0.45	0.18	0.41	0.08	0.49

* Average

Source: IMF *International Financial Statistics* and Table 10.4.

Table 10.12 Money multiplier, 1991

Generally the money multiplier is higher the lower are the ratios of reserves and currency to deposits. Table 10.12 shows the money multiplier in 1991 for the G-6 countries. The table also shows the ratios of required reserve to deposits and of currency to deposits. The largest money multipliers are the ones for the UK and France. These countries have low reserve requirements and low ratios of currency to deposits.

Effects of Central Bank Actions

The Neutrality of Open-Market Operations

In Chapter 5 we found that once-and-for-all changes in the quantity of money were neutral. A one-time shift in the monetary base led only to proportional responses in the price level and other nominal variables. These results do not change when we introduce financial intermediation. But we have to include as nominal variables the quantities of the various deposits and reserves. Then we find that these nominal magnitudes rise along with the other nominal variables in proportion to the change in the monetary base. An open-market operation leaves unchanged the real quantities of deposits and reserves, the ratio of deposits to currency, the ratio of reserves to deposits, and so on.

Among the variables that do not change when there is a one-time open-market operation are the nominal interest rate on earning assets, R, and the nominal interest rate, R^d, paid on deposits. Because these interest rates are unchanged, households and firms would not alter their desired holdings of currency and deposits in real terms. Thus, the results are consistent with the unchanged real quantities of currency and deposits.

The financial intermediaries also end up in the same real position as before the open-market operation: there are no changes in the intermediaries' real quantities of deposits, reserves, and loans and securities. If these institutions held reserves initially only because of requirements – say, 12% of deposits – then the final holdings of reserves again equal the required amount.

The Amount of Financial Intermediation

Financial intermediation is important because it facilitates the matching of borrowers and lenders, as well as the carrying out of transactions. The reflection of this process is the real quantity of deposits and the real quantity of loans and securities held by financial intermediaries. We can think of these real quantities as a measure of the amount of financial intermediation in an economy.

The amount of financial intermediation that occurs depends on the benefits and costs. As mentioned before, the benefits relate to the efficient evaluation of loans, the diversification of assets by risk and maturity, and the convenience of deposits. The costs include the expenses of servicing deposits and loans, the return to capital in the intermediary business, reserve requirements, and the costs of evading restrictions for paying interest on deposits. If these costs of intermediation rise, then we predict that less intermediation will occur.

Suppose, as an example, that the central bank increases reserve requirements. Since financial intermediaries must hold more non-interest-bearing reserves for each dollar of deposits, these institutions end up paying a lower interest rate, R^d, on deposits. Households switch accordingly from deposits to currency or earning assets, and financial institutions end up with smaller real quantities of deposits and assets. That is, there is less financial intermediation in the economy. Note that we would reach the same conclusion if, instead of assuming an increase in reserve requirements, we postulated a higher cost for financial intermediaries to service deposits or police loans. The economy ends up again with less financial intermediation.

When there is less financial intermediation, it becomes harder for resources to flow toward investors whose projects have the greatest marginal products or toward consumers who have the greatest desires to consume now rather than later. On both counts, the economy operates less efficiently. Typically this loss of efficiency shows up as smaller aggregates of the capital stock and output. But the principal conclusion is that less financial intermediation means a poorer match of resources to their ultimate uses.

To some extent, the costs of intermediation reflect the underlying expenses of policing borrowers and servicing deposits. We can think of these elements as part of the technology or production function that generates intermediating services. Then the amount of intermediation that results tends to be optimal, given this technology. But, as already noted, reserve requirements, government regulation of interest rates on deposits, and so on artificially raise the cost of intermediation. More restrictive policies – such as higher reserve requirements – tend to discourage intermediation, a response that leads to a less efficient allocation of resources.[11]

Financial Intermediation and the Price Level

The degree of financial intermediation also interacts with the determination of the price level. To see how this works, recall how the price level is determined in a closed economy. (The results would be the same for an open economy under flexible exchange rates.) The key condition is the equation of the demand for money to the supply.

We now identify money with the monetary base, that is, as the sum of currency in circulation and the reserves held by financial institutions at the central bank. Suppose that the central bank controls the dollar quantity of base money, M, through open-market operations, as discussed above. Then the process of financial intermediation influences the price level because it affects the real demand for base money, M^d/P. For a given dollar quantity of base money, anything that raises the real demand leads to a fall in the price level. This effect works just like the various increases in the real demand for money that we considered in previous chapters.

Suppose, as an example, that the central bank raises the required-reserve ratio on deposits. For a given quantity of deposits, this change increases the demand for reserves by depository institutions. Hence, the real demand for the monetary base goes up.

Some additional effects arise because the higher reserve ratio tends to reduce the interest rate paid on deposits. If households shift out of deposits and into currency, then the real demand for the monetary base increases further. (That is because the demand for base money varies one-to-one with the demand for currency but varies only fractionally with the amount of deposits.) If households move away from deposits and into earning assets, then the real demand for base money tends to decline. (That is because the reduction in deposits reduces the real demand for reserves by financial institutions.) Thus, the shifting of households' assets among deposits, currency, and earning assets has an ambiguous overall effect on the real demand for the monetary base.[12]

Because of the direct positive effect on the demand for reserves, we can be pretty sure that the overall effect of an increase in the required-reserve ratio is to raise the real demand for base money. For a given nominal quantity of base money, the rise in the real demand for base money means that the price level falls.

Historically, the main examples of large short-term variations in the real demand for base money involve financial crises. It is therefore worthwhile to consider some of these episodes.

Banking Panics

Banks and other financial intermediaries promise to convert their demand deposits into currency immediately at face value. These institutions typically also extend this instantaneous conversion privilege to savings deposits, for which some notice of withdrawal can legally be required. Intermediaries do not, however, hold nearly enough cash or liquid securities to allow for the simultaneous conversion of all deposits into currency at face value.[13] Even if the underlying loans and securities are sound, financial institutions can get into trouble if too many customers want their cash at the same time. If people become concerned about a bank's ability to convert its deposits into currency at face value, then each individual has an incentive to get into line first to cash in. This incentive is especially great when the deposits are not insured. When many people attempt to cash in their deposits simultaneously, there is a 'run on the bank'. Sometimes a bank responds by temporarily *suspending* the privilege of converting demand deposits into currency. When this happens simultaneously at many banks or other financial institutions, economists say that a **banking panic** occurs.

The hallmark of a banking panic is a sudden increase in the demand for currency rather than deposits. As a response, banks and other intermediaries tend to increase their demands for excess reserves and other liquid assets to meet their customers' possible demands for cash. Overall, the banking panic leads to increases in the real demand for base money – partly in the form of the public's currency and partly as reserves of financial institutions. Hence, the previous analysis implies that a banking panic has two types of effects. First, it makes financial intermediation more difficult, a result that has adverse consequences for the efficient allocation of resources. Production and investment are, in particular, likely to decline. Then, second, unless

there is substantial increase in the nominal quantity of base money, the sharp increase in the real demand for base money puts downward pressure on the price level.

Banking panics occurred fairly often in Europe and in the United States until the 1930s. The panics typically exhibited increases in the ratios of the public's currency and banks' excess reserves to deposits. They also tended to show decreases in prices and in real economic activity. It is, however, hard to sort out the independent influence of the banking panics on output and other real variables. That is because, under the monetary system that was in place at that time, poor economic conditions tended automatically to generate financial crises.[14] Economists think that these crises also made real economic conditions worse, but it is not easy to prove this proposition through statistical analysis.

Bank panics were especially frequent and devastating in the US. Panics tended to spread quickly in a domino-like effect and embroil sometimes hundreds of banks. Banking crises in Europe tended to be more contained partly because of the role played by the national central bank that acted as a **lender of last resort** through the operation of its discount window.[15] When a financial crisis threatened, the lender of last resort would lend liberally to financial institutions at the discount rate, which would be set below market interest rates.

Several European banking crises are worth mentioning. In England, those connected with the collapse of Overend, Gurney & Co. Ltd in 1866 and with the failure of Baring Bros in 1890. In Italy, the one related to the financial troubles of the Società Bancaria Italiana in 1907. Finally, involving several countries, the one following the collapse of the Austrian bank Credit-Anstalt in 1931.[16] The first three episodes are ones in which the lender-of-last-resort actions of the central bank – the Bank of England in the Gurney and Baring crises and the Banca d'Italia in the Societa' Bancaria Italiana crisis – were crucial in containing the panic and avoiding the spreading of the crisis to the rest of the financial system. The episode of 1931, instead, is an example of how financial crises can quickly propagate, even internationally, in the absence of appropriate actions by the monetary authorities. The crisis originated in Vienna, due to the collapse of Credit-Anstalt, the largest Austrian bank at the time. Even if the Austrian government was eventually able to arrange an international loan from the Bank of International Settlements (in Basel) to try to rescue Credit-Anstalt, the loan was too little and too late to allow the Austrian National Bank to play effectively the role of lender of last resort. The crisis spread across the country, investing the foreign currency market and quickly moved across national boundaries reaching Czechoslovakia, Germany, Hungary, Poland and Romania.

A major reason for the founding, in 1914, of the Federal Reserve in the US was the desire to moderate financial crises, by creating an institutional lender of last resort. Despite the existence of a central bank, however, the worst banking panics in US history occurred from 1930 to 1933 during the Great Depression.[17] Between 1930 and 1933 there was an unprecedented number of bank suspensions – roughly 9000 out of about 25 000 banks that existed at the end of 1929. In March 1933, President Roosevelt proclaimed a 'banking holiday', which temporarily closed all of the banks. About one-third of those that had existed in 1929 never reopened.

In addition to a lender of last resort, another safeguard measure introduced to prevent the spreading of banking panics is the creation of institutions that insure deposits at banks. When the government guarantees the redemption of deposits, people lose most of their incentive to withdraw their funds when they are unsure about an institution's financial position. It therefore becomes harder for a bank run to start, or for one bank's problems to spread to others. Accordingly, we no longer have this major source of instability in the real demand for base money and, hence, in the price level.

Not all countries have a formal deposit insurance scheme. In the EC, for example, Greece and Portugal do not yet have a deposit protection programme. Moreover, as reported in Table 10.13, deposit protection schemes vary across countries in terms of the amount guaranteed and the circumstances under which the insurance is activated.

On the negative side, the presence of deposit insurance reduces the incentives of financial institutions to use caution in accepting risky loans. (This effect arises because an institution's insurance premium does not depend on the riskiness of that institution's portfolio of loans.) Some economists argue that this incautious attitude accounts for the high incidence of

		B	DK	D	GR	E	F	IRL	I	L	NL	P	UK
1.	Source of financing	Private	Private	Private		Public & private	Private	Private	Private	Private	Private		Private
2.	Amount guaranteed (thousand ECUs)	11.8	31.9	30% of bank capital	(deposit protection not yet introduced)	11.7	57.3	19.5	651.7	11.8	17.3	(deposit protection not yet introduced)	28.5
3.	Total or partial compensation	Total	Total	Total		Total	Total	Max	Full up	Total to 130.3	Total		75% intro-duced
									75% of remaining				
4.	Scope of intervention												
	4.1 In case of bankruptcy	Yes	Yes	Yes		Yes	Yes	Yes	Yes	Yes	Yes		Yes
	4.2 Independently of bankruptcy	Yes	No	Yes		Yes	Yes	No	Yes	No	No		No

Source: Padoa-Schioppa and Saccomanni (1992).

problems in lending to real estate developers, oil explorers, and foreign governments. Thus, deposit insurance has likely caused the problem of banking panics to be replaced by the problem of greater incidence of insolvency for financial institutions.

Summary

Financial institutions use the funds generated from deposits to make loans to households, businesses, and the government. This intermediation between deposit holders and borrowers is useful because it allows financial specialists to evaluate and collect loans. In addition, the process creates various types of deposits, which are convenient as stores of value and as media of exchange. The conventional definition of money, M1, adds those deposits that are checkable to the public's holding of currency. Thus, M1 attempts to measure the assets that serve as common media of exchange.

The amount of financial intermediation depends on the costs of intermediating; these costs include expenses for servicing deposits and loans, returns to capital in the intermediary business, and requirements to hold non-interest-bearing reserves. An increase in these costs – such as a rise in reserve requirements on deposits – leads to less financial intermediation. The adverse effects from the reduced intermediation include a greater difficulty of matching borrowers and lenders. These effects tend to show up as reductions in the quantities of investment and output.

National central banks control the size of the monetary base (the sum of the public's currency and the reserves of financial institutions) mainly through open-market operations. These operations involve exchanges between base money and securities, mostly government bonds. Central banks' loans to financial institutions at the discount window affect the monetary base in a similar manner.

An increase in the monetary base leads to a multiplicative expansion of deposits and of monetary aggregates, such as M1. The money multiplier, which is the ratio of M1 to the base, is greater the smaller are the ratios of reserves and currency to deposits. The money multiplier is highest in the UK where the reserve requirement and the currency to deposit ratios are lowest.

Open-market operations are still neutral in the model: they affect the price level and other nominal variables but do not change any real variables (aside from the private sector's holdings of real government bonds). Among the real variables that do not change are the ratios of deposits to currency and of deposits to reserves.

Given the quantity of base money, the price level depends inversely on the real demand for the monetary base. Historically, the major short-term movements in this demand stemmed from banking panics. These panics featured sharp increases in the public's demand for currency and in banks' demands for excess reserves. The existence of deposit insurance reduces the risk of banking panics but also increases the tendency for financial institutions to make risky loans and become insolvent.

Important Terms and Concepts

financial intermediaries
demand deposits
savings deposits
time deposits
discount rate
reserve requirement
excess reserves
costs of intermediation

open market operation: outright
  or repurchase agreement
central bank
capital controls
lender of last resort
vault cash
reserves (of depository institutions)
Federal Funds market

Federal Funds rate
interbank market
money market rate
monetary base
high-powered money
multiple expansion of deposits
money multiplier
banking panic

Questions and Problems

Mainly for Review

10.1   What considerations limit the amount of excess reserves held by financial institutions? Explain how the volume of reserves can be less than the volume of deposits.

10.2   What factors account for the spread between the interest rate on earning assets and the interest rate on checkable deposits? Is an increase in the spread associated with a lower volume of deposits?

10.3   Show that for an increase in the monetary base to be matched by an equivalent increase in reserves and currency held by the public, there must be a multiplicative expansion of deposits. How much would deposits expand if the reverse requirement were 100%?

10.4   Why does the expectation of a bank failure give individuals an incentive to cash in their deposits? Show that this expectation can be a self-fulfilling prophecy. How does the provision of deposit insurance reduce the likelihood of this event?

10.5   Explain why a shift by households away from currency and toward demand deposits would raise the price level.

Problems for Discussion

10.6   The Central Bank's Discount Rate and Borrowing at the Central Bank
    How does the volume of borrowing at the central bank depend on the discount rate and the interest rate on earning assets?
    Suppose that the central bank lowers the discount rate and that borrowings by banks increase. Are the effects on the economy the same as those from an open-market purchase of bonds?

10.7   Reserve Requirements
    Suppose that the central bank increases the required-reserve ratio on checkable deposits.
    a. How does this change affect the real demand for base money?
    b. How does it affect the price level?

c. How does it affect the nominal quantity of M1?
d. What real effects occur from the increase in reserve requirements?
    Pretend now that the government imposes reserve requirements on something that has nothing to do with 'money'. The requirement could, for example, be on refrigerators – anyone who owns a refrigerator must hold ε10 of non-interest-bearing reserves at the central bank.
    How does this new policy affect the real demand for base money and the price level? What other effects arise (for example, on the number of refrigerators)? In what ways do the answers differ from those for the usual case in which the requirements apply to checkable deposits?

10.8   Reserve Requirements in Italy
    From 1947 until December 1962, cash and government securities could be held in any combination to satisfy reserve requirements in Italy. Between 1963 and 1965, however, the Banca d'Italia required that at least 44% of obligatory reserves be held in cash.
    If the monetary base did not change for 1963–65, then how would the new treatment of required reserves affect the price level?

10.9   Interest on Reserves Held at the Bundesbank
    At present, reserves held at the Bundesbank bear no interest. Suppose that, following the example of Italy, reserves were paid interest in Germany, at a rate that was some fraction of the interest rate on commercial paper. If the quantity of base money stayed the same, then how would this change affect the following:
    a. the interest rate paid on checkable deposits?
    b. the dollar amount of checkable deposits?
    c. the price level?
    d. the amount of intermediation in the economy?
    e. the profits of the Bundesbank?

10.10   Gold and the Monetary Base in the UK
    Suppose that the British Treasury receives £1 billion of gold from abroad. Then the British Treasury deposits the gold at the Bank of England, so that the Bank of England's gold account and the Treasury's deposits at the Bank of England each rise by £1 billion.
    a. What happens to the monetary base if the Treasury holds the extra £1 billion in deposits?
    b. What happens if the Treasury spends the extra £1 billion and thereby restores its deposits to their initial level?
    c. How can the Bank of England offset the effect of the gold inflow on the monetary base? (If it takes this action, then the Bank of England is said to 'sterilize' the inflow of gold.)

10.11 Membership in the Federal Reserve System

Until 1980 only commercial banks that were members of the Federal Reserve System were subject to the Fed's reserve requirements. (There were also some services, such as cheque clearing and access to the discount window, that were provided free to members.) Membership was optional for banks with state charters but required for those with federal charters. (In 1980 only 30% of all commercial banks had national charters. But these institutions accounted for 55% of the deposits at commercial banks.)

The fraction of state banks that were members of the Federal Reserve System declined from 21% in 1948 to 10% in 1980. Why do you think this happened?

10.12 Runs on Financial Institutions

In the text we discussed runs on banks. How does the analysis differ if the run applies to other financial intermediaries, which do not offer checkable deposits?

10.13 Deposit Insurance (optional)

We discussed the role of deposit insurance, which reduces the risk of banking panics. A number of unresolved questions about this insurance are worth considering:

a. Could private companies satisfactorily provide insurance on deposits? Would the private sector end up providing the 'right' amount of insurance? Would private companies also charge for this insurance in accordance with the riskiness of an institution's earnings? What problems can arise if the government provides the insurance but does not take proper account of risk? More generally, why is deposit insurance an area in which the government should be involved?

b. Is there a reason for the government to be in the insurance business for deposits but not for other things, such as corporate obligations? (In the US, the federal government has, in fact, entered into the business of insuring the debt of doubtful borrowers – such as New York City and the Chrysler Corporation – as well as pension obligations and accounts at stockbrokers.)

Notes

1. See Goodhart (1989), chapter 9, for a discussion of the arguments in favour and against financial regulation.
2. Primary markets are financial markets in which new issues of securities, bond and shares, are sold. Secondary markets are financial markets in which previously issued securities can be resold.
3. In the United States the interbank market is called the Federal Funds market, and the corresponding interest rate, the Federal Funds rate.
4. For further discussion, see Benjamin Klein (1974).
5. The problem of lack of competitiveness due to large obligatory reserve can be solved if the central bank were to pay the market interest rate on required reserves. The Banca d'Italia pays interest on required reserves, but below the market rate.
6. British data should be interpreted with caution since the Bank of England no longer engages in discount window operations. In fact, data on the Bank of England Rate are not available after 1981.
7. Economists have debated whether a central bank is a necessary element of a financial system. For a discussion, see Goodhart (1989), chapter 8.
8. In several countries the central bank was originally a private institution.
9. For a discussion of monetary policy procedures in the major industrialized countries, see Batten *et al.* (1990).

10. As we show in the following section, the inducement derives in the present case from a higher price level.
11. For the argument that the financial industry should be fully deregulated, see Fischer Black (1970) and Eugene Fama (1983).
12. For further discussion of these types of effects, see James Tobin (1971a, 1971b).
13. By *liquid*, we mean that little cost attaches to the quick sale of an asset. Thus, government bonds are liquid, but real estate is relatively illiquid. Loans that are costly to evaluate– such as those to local businesses and consumers–may also be illiquid.
14. Phillip Cagan (1965, pp. 265 ff.) argues that the banking panics have major elements that are independent of changes in business conditions. But Gary Gorton (1986) finds a close relationship between business failures and banking panics.
15. For an early discussion of the lender-of-last-resort role played by the Bank of England, see Walter Bagehot (1873).
16. A classic reference for financial crises is Charles Kindleberger (1978).
17. Milton Friedman and Anna Schwartz (1963, ch. 7) argue convincingly that this financial crisis would have been much less severe if the Fed had not existed. That is because, under the earlier environment, the banks would not have relied on corrective measures from the Fed, actions that turned out not to materialize. The Fed failed, specifically, to act as a lender of last resort.

11

International Monetary Linkages

In Chapter 7 we discussed the interactions of an economy with the rest of the world by analyzing the international markets for goods and credit. Now that we are familiar with the domestic monetary sector we are ready to explore the other major international linkages, those deriving from foreign exchange markets. In Chapter 7, we could not discuss exchange rates because we assumed that all countries used a common currency, the ECU, and that all prices were quoted in units of this currency. To analyze exchange rates, we have to introduce different types of currency (pounds, dollars, yen, marks, etc.) and allow for prices to be quoted in these different currency units. This chapter makes the necessary extensions to consider these matters.

It is important to note that, even without discussing exchange rates, Chapter 7 brought out various factors that influenced the current-account balance, including variations in the terms of trade. The extensions to include exchange rates do not invalidate any of these results. We shall find that some of the forces that affect the current-account balance lead also to movements in exchange rates. But the underlying shocks that cause countries to borrow or lend internationally will be the same as those that we studied before.

Different Monies and Exchange Rates

Suppose, as in Chapter 7, that the world's supply of international currency is fixed at the amount $\bar{H}$. We still assume that this currency is denominated in some nominal unit, such as the

US dollar, and that the nominal interest rate on international currency is zero.

In the real world, each country issues and uses currency in its own unit – whether dollars, pounds, yen, or whatever – instead of using a common currency. To allow for this fact, let M^i be the quantity of domestic currency for country i. We measure this money in domestic currency units, such as British pounds.

A typical setup is that the central bank of country i holds international currency, H^i, and then issues the domestic currency, M^i. Thus we would have the simplified balance sheet for a central bank as shown in Table 11.1. The central bank's assets include international currency, H^i, foreign interest-bearing assets, and domestic interest-bearing assets, which include bonds issued by the home government. The holdings of domestic earning assets are called the central bank's **domestic credit**. The central bank's liabilities consist of domestic currency, M^i. (As we have seen in the previous chapter, the liabilities also include deposits of financial institutions held at the central bank.)

The domestic price level in country i, P^i, now expresses the number of local currency units, say pounds, that exchange for a unit of goods. To start, think again of a case in which the goods

Assets	Liabilities
International currency, H^i	Domestic currency, M^i
Foreign interest-bearing assets	
Domestic interest-bearing assets	
(domestic credit)	

Table 11.1 Simplified balance sheet of a central bank

produced in all countries are physically identical. Then the same product sells for P^i units of one currency (pounds) in country i and for P^j units of another currency (say, German marks) in country j.

We now must introduce a new market, called a *foreign exchange market*, on which people trade the currency of one country for that of another. For example, traders might exchange Japanese yen for US dollars or for German marks. The foreign exchange market establishes exchange rates among the various currencies. Currencies can be exchanged in organized markets, like futures and options markets. However, most of the foreign exchange transactions are executed directly, through phone or computer lines, by financial intermediaries such as commercial banks, investment banks, and pension and mutual funds. For these reasons, foreign exchange transactions tend to be concentrated in large financial centres, where financial intermediaries are numerous. The largest foreign exchange market is London, followed by New York and Tokyo. The volume of transactions that takes place in these market is enormous. In 1989, the average *daily* turnover in London was $187 billion, in New York $129 billion, and in Tokyo $115 billion.[1] To put this in perspective, consider that it took less than a working week at the London foreign exchange market to exchange currencies in an amount equivalent to the annual UK GDP (it was $838 billion in 1989).

There are two major foreign exchange markets: a **spot market** and a **forward market**. On the spot market, the exchange of currencies takes place on the same day as the price (i.e. the exchange rate) and the amount of funds involved in the transaction are agreed upon.[2] In the forward market, the exchange rate and the amount of funds to be exchanged is determined some time before the transfer of funds. The actual delivery of funds takes place after a prespecified period of time: 30 days, 90 days, six months or even years later. For example, on 31 July 1992, 1.47 German marks exchanged for $1.00 on the spot market, so that each mark was worth about 0.68 dollars. Similarly, 0.52 British pounds exchanged for $1.00, so that a British pound was worth about 1.93 dollars on the spot market.[3] On the same

day, 1.50 German marks exchanged for $1.00 on the forward market for delivery in 90 days, so that each mark was worth about 0.67 dollars on the 90 days forward market. Similarly, 0.53 British pounds exchanged for $1.00 at 90 days, so that a British pound was worth about 1.89 dollars on the 90 days forward market. Notice that the dollar was worth more in the forward market than in the spot market. In other words, on 31 July 1992, there was a *forward premium* on the dollar with respect to both the German mark and the British pound. Equivalently, there was a *forward discount* on the mark and the pound with respect to the dollar.

The exchange rates for German marks and British pounds in terms of US dollars determine the exchange rate between marks and pounds. That is, on the spot market, 1.47 German marks could buy $1.00, which could then be converted into 0.52 British pounds. Hence, 1.47/0.52 = 2.83 German marks could buy one British pound on the spot market. Thus, the spot exchange rate between marks and pounds was 2.83 marks per pound. (In practice, traders can make these exchanges directly rather than going through US dollars.) We could derive the 90 days forward exchange rate between marks and pounds in an analogous manner.

Let ϵ_t^i (the Greek letter *epsilon*) be the dollar spot exchange rate for country i at time t: ϵ_t^i units of country i's currency (say, mark) exchange for $1.00 at time t. Alternatively, we see that the dollar value of one unit of country i's currency (1 mark) is $1/\epsilon_t^i$. Notice that a *higher* value of the exchange rate, ϵ_t^i, means that country i's currency is *less* valuable in terms of dollars because it takes more of country i's currency to buy $1.00.

For any two countries, i and j, we observe the dollar exchange rates, ϵ_t^i and ϵ_t^j. These rates prescribe the number of units of each currency that trade for $1.00 at time t. Hence, ϵ_t^i units of currency i (say, 1.47 German marks) can buy ϵ_t^j units of currency j (say, 0.52 British pounds). We can now define the exchange rate between any two currencies i and j, ϵ_t^{ij}, as the number of units of currency i needed to buy one unit of currency j. This exchange rate equals $\epsilon_t^i/\epsilon_t^j$ (1.47/0.52 = 2.83 marks per pound). Alternatively, for one unit of currency *i*, people can get $\epsilon_t^{ji} = \epsilon_t^j / \epsilon_t^i$ units of currency *j*.

Figures 11.1 and 11.2 show the spot exchange rates between eight major currencies (those for France, Italy, Japan, the Netherlands, Spain, Sweden, the United Kingdom, and the United States) and the German mark from 1950 to 1992. The figures show the proportionate deviation of the exchange rate for each year from the value that prevailed for the particular country in 1950. With the exception of the Japanese yen, all currency depreciated considerably with respect to the German mark during this period. For example, in 1950, 0.83 French francs exchanged for one German mark, whereas in 1992, it took 3.4 French francs to buy one German mark. Figure 11.1 shows accordingly that the exchange rate for the French franc in terms of German marks rose by about 300% from 1950 to 1992. (Remember that the rise in the exchange rate means that the French franc became less valuable relative to the German mark.)

We can define the forward exchange rate in a similar way. Let $f_{t,t+\Delta}^i$ be the Δ-period dollar forward rate for country *i*: at time *t* it is established that $f_{t,t+\Delta}^i$ units of country *i*'s currency (say, mark) will exchange for $1.00 Δ-periods later (say, 90 days). If we work with monthly data, 90 days forward exchange rate can be expressed as $f_{t,t+3}^i$, the three-month forward exchange rate. Analogously, we can define the forward exchange rate between any two curren-

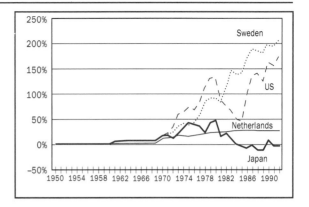

Figure 11.2 Exchange rates in terms of DM, 1950–92

cies *i* and *j*, $f_{t,t+\Delta}^{ij}$, by taking the ratio of their respective forward exchange rates with respect to the dollar.

In Figure 11.3 we show monthly observations, starting in 1976, of the 90 days forward discount (expressed in percent of the corresponding spot exchange rate) on the German mark and the Italian lira with respect to the dollar. Formally, the **forward discount** with respect to the dollar is given by: $fd_{t,t+3}^i = (f_{t,t+3}^i - \epsilon_t^i)$. Recall that a positive value of the forward discount means that currency is valued less if sold forward than if sold spot. In Figure 11.3 we see that in almost every period, the lira was sold at a discount with respect to the dollar in the forward market. Conversely, the mark was almost always sold at a premium, i.e. at a negative discount, in the forward market. Later in the chapter, we will be able to explain this different behaviour of the mark and the lira.

In the next two sections we study the determination of exchange rates. The fundamental force linking the value of two currencies, and therefore determining exchange rates, is **international arbitrage**. With international arbitrage we mean the buying and selling activities through which economic agents ensure that analogous commodities and assets are priced equally, independently of the currency in which they are quoted. We already discussed an implication of international arbitrage for commodity markets in Chapter 7, the law of one price. In the next section we extend that concept to a multicurrency

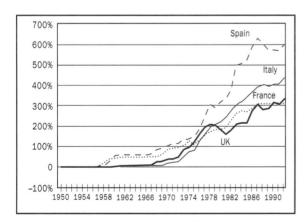

Figure 11.1 Exchange rates in terms of DM, 1950–92

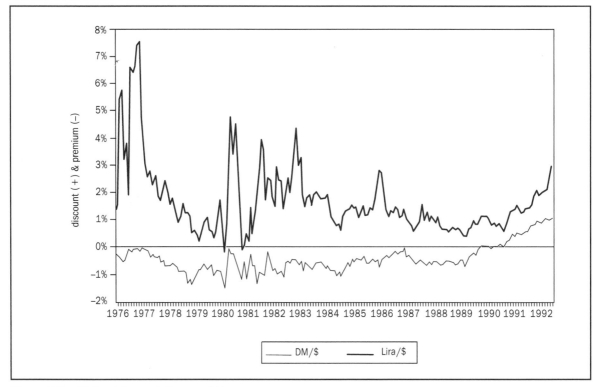

Figure 11.3   90 days' forward discount (%)

environment, and derive the basic law of one price for international commodity markets: the **purchasing-power parity**. International arbitrage, however, does not only apply to commodities but also to assets. Next, therefore, we derive the version of the law of one price that must hold for securities: the **interest parity condition**.

Arbitrage in Goods and Services: Purchasing-Power Parity

Suppose that we can think of all goods as tradable and physically identical. A resident of country i can use local currency to buy goods domestically at the price P_t^i or can exchange money into the currency of country j to buy goods at the price P_t^j. For each unit of currency i, a person gets $1/P_t^i$ units of goods domestically. Alternatively, by using the exchange market, he or she gets $\epsilon_t^{ji} = \epsilon_t^j/\epsilon_t^i$ units of currency j for each unit of

currency i. Then, buying at the price P^j, the person gets $\epsilon_t^{ji} \cdot (1/P_t^j) = 1/(\epsilon_t^{ij} \cdot P_t^j)$ units of goods. For things to make sense, the two options *must* result in the same amount of goods: otherwise everyone would want to buy goods in the cheap country and sell goods in the expensive country. Once again, this idea is a version of the law of one price, a concept that we used in Chapter 7. Thus, we must have that $1/P_t^i = 1/(\epsilon_t^{ij} \cdot P_t^j)$, or, after rearranging terms,

$$\epsilon_t^{ij} = P_t^i/P_t^j \qquad (11.1)$$

Equation (11.1) says that the exchange rate between any two currencies, ϵ_t^{ij}, equals the ratio of the prices of goods in the two countries, P_t^i/P_t^j. This condition is called **purchasing-power parity (PPP)**. It ensures that the purchasing power in terms of goods for each currency is the same regardless of where someone uses the currency to buy goods. In Figure 11.4 we describe this

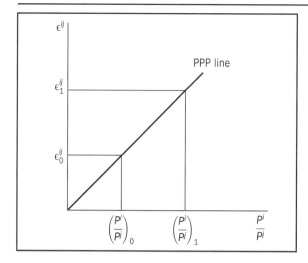

Figure 11.4　Exchange rate and PPP

relationship. The vertical axis measures the exchange rate between currencies i and j. The horizontal axis measures the ratio of the price of goods in country i to that in country j. The 45° degree line is the PPP line, i.e. the locus on which the ratio of the two prices is equal to the exchange rate. If the price ratio increases from $(P^i/P^j)_0$ to $(P^i/P^j)_1$, i.e. prices in country i increase with respect to prices in country j, then the exchange rate ϵ^{ij} will increase, that is, the currency of country i will decrease in value.

Define the change of country i's dollar exchange rate, $\epsilon^i_{t+1} - \epsilon^i_t$, to be $\Delta\epsilon^i$. Note that a positive value for $\Delta\epsilon^i$ means that country i's currency becomes *less* valuable over time in terms of dollars: it takes more of country i's currency to buy one dollar. We can say equivalently that country i's currency *depreciates* over time relative to the dollar. Conversely, if $\Delta\epsilon^i$ is negative, then country i's currency *appreciates* over time relative to the dollar.

The PPP condition implies that the rate of change of any exchange rate is related to the inflation rates in the two countries. If we update equation (11.1) to time $t+1$ and divide by the corresponding relationship at time t, then we obtain:

$$\epsilon^{ij}_{t+1}/\epsilon^{ij}_t = (P^i_{t+1}/P^i_t)\cdot(P^j_t/P^j_{t+1})$$

or, by defining the respective inflation rates $\pi^i = \Delta P^i/P^i$ and $\pi^j = \Delta P^j/P^j$,

$$1 + (\Delta\epsilon^{ij}/\epsilon^{ij}) = (1 + \pi^i)/(1 + \pi^j) \qquad (11.2)$$

A frequently used approximation of (11.2) is:

$$\Delta\epsilon^{ij}/\epsilon^{ij} \approx \pi^i - \pi^j \qquad (11.2')$$

The approximation arises because we have neglected the term $(\Delta\epsilon^{ij}/\epsilon^{ij})\cdot\pi^j$, which involves products of rates of change. This term approaches zero if we consider very small intervals of time. Equations (11.2) and (11.2') say that the higher a country's inflation rate, π^i, the higher the rate of depreciation of that country's currency, $\Delta\epsilon^{ij}/\epsilon^{ij}$. This equation is called the **relative form of PPP**, whereas equation (11.1) is called the **absolute form of PPP** (in the sense of involving levels of prices and exchange rates rather than changes).

In deriving equations (11.1) and (11.2) we assumed that all countries produced the same tradable good. The prices, P^i and P^j, therefore, referred to the same tradable good. But in macroeconomics we are mostly interested in the general price levels of countries, and not so much in the price of any specific good. For this purpose, we can generalize the PPP condition by thinking of P^i and P^j in equations (11.1) and (11.2) as the prices of market baskets of goods produced or consumed in countries i and j, respectively. We can, in practice, measure these prices by the deflators for the GDP or by consumer or wholesale price indexes. In this case, the PPP condition tells us that the rate of change of the exchange rate between two currencies depends on the inflation differential, measured say by the growth of the GDP deflator, between the two countries. For example, if the general price level in the United States grows faster than in Germany, then the dollar will depreciate with respect to the German mark. Conversely, if the rate of inflation is larger in the UK than in the US, then the dollar will appreciate with respect to the British pound.

Figure 11.5 shows the relationship between the rate of inflation and the rate of depreciation of

Box 11.1   Purchasing-Power Parity in Terms of the Big Mac

The *Economist* magazine has explored purchasing-power parity by looking at the cost of a simple product, McDonald's Big Mac hamburger, in various countries. The good is not perfectly tradable – because its provision requires local labour and land and because of differences in tax policies – but we would nevertheless predict that the ratio of prices across countries should relate to the exchange rates.

The *Economist* of 18 April 1992 reported that the prices of Big Macs and market exchange rates in April 1992 were as reported in the table.

If the PPP condition in equation (11.1) held exactly for Big Macs, then the ratio of the local price to the US$ price would coincide with the market exchange rate (local currency per US$). It is clear from the table that the price ratios and exchange rates are positively related, but not perfectly.

If the price ratio in a country exceeds the exchange rate, then Big Macs are relatively more costly to obtain in that country. Or, to put it another way, the market exchange rate undervalues the US dollar by the percentage shown in the last column. The table shows that in April 1992 the US dollar was undervalued in the majority of countries and in all of the

western European countries. This result emerges also if one constructs prices of a market basket of goods, not just Big Macs.

The Hamburger Standard

Country	Local price of Big Mac	Local price US Price	Market exch. rate (local currency per US$)	Over (+) or under (-) valuation of US$ (%)
Argentina	Peso 3.30	1.51	0.99	−34
Australia	A$ 2.54	1.16	1.31	+13
Belgium	BFr 108	49.32	33.55	−32
Brazil	Cr 3800	1735	2153	+24
Britain	£ 1.74	0.79	0.57	−28
Canada	C$ 2.76	1.26	1.19	−6
China	Yuan 6.30	2.88	5.44	+89
Denmark	DKr 27.25	12.44	6.32	−49
France	FFr 18.10	8.26	5.55	−33
Germany	DM 4.50	2.05	1.64	−20
Holland	Fl 5.35	2.44	1.84	−24
Hong Kong	HK$ 8.90	4.06	7.73	+91
Hungary	Forint 133	60.73	79.70	+31
Ireland	I£ 1.45	0.66	0.61	−8
Italy	Lire 4100	1872	1233	−34
Japan	Yen 380	174	133	−24
Russia	Rouble 58	26.48	98.95	+273
Singapore	S$ 4.75	2.17	1.65	−24
S. Korea	Won 2300	1050	778	−26
Spain	Ptas 315	144	102	−29
Sweden	SKr 25.50	11.64	5.93	−49
United States	US$ 2.19	1.00	1.00	0
Venezuela	Bs 170	77.63	60.63	−22

the exchange rate for 128 countries for the period 1969–88.[4] The vertical axis measures the left-hand side of equation (11.2), that is, (one plus) the rate of depreciation of each currency with respect to the US dollar. The horizontal axis measures the right-hand side of equation (11.2), that is, the ratios between (one plus) the rate of inflation of a country and that of the US. Figure 11.5 shows the positive relationship between the rate of depreciation of a country's exchange rate with respect to the dollar and its inflation differential with respect to the US. For example, prices in Chile grew 17 000 times more than in the US during these 20 years. Correspondingly, in 1988, a Chilean peso was worth, in dollars, 25 000

times less than it was in 1969. In contrast, in Switzerland prices increases by only one-third as much as they did in the US in this period. Correspondingly, in 1988, a Swiss franc was worth, in dollars, three times as much as it was in 1969.

Figure 11.5 also makes clear that the relationship between changes in the exchange rate and in the price level is not as precise as equation (11.2) suggests. If relative PPP held exactly, then all the observation in the figure would lie on the 45° line. In practice, we regularly observe deviations from relative PPP. These deviations are particularly severe if, instead of looking at 20-year periods, we were to analyze shorter time spans, say a year or

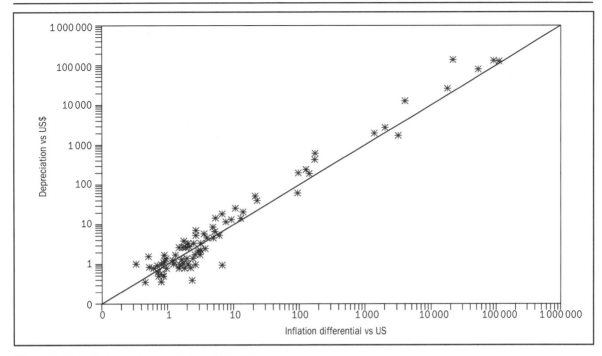

Figure 11.5 Inflation and depreciation, 1969–88

less. But there are good reasons why the PPP conditions need not hold exactly.

One reason for the failure of PPP conditions is that countries specialize in the production of different tradable goods, whose relative prices can change. As we have seen in Chapter 7, movements in a country's terms of trade can be substantial, and these can explain some of the violation of PPP. Suppose, as an example, that country i's terms of trade improve. That is, the prices of tradables produced in country i rise relative to the prices of tradables produced elsewhere. If P^i and P^j refer to market baskets of produced goods, then P^i/P^j must rise for a given exchange rate, ϵ^{ij}, because the goods produced in country i have become more expensive relative to those produced in country j. The general point is that various real disturbances can shift the PPP condition in equation (11.1).

But there are other elements that work against PPP. Recall that the force underlying PPP is the international arbitrage of goods. In order for PPP to hold, it is necessary for market agents to identify price differences for similar products

across countries. Collecting information on international prices is relatively simple for a wide range of products, especially for goods that are traded on organized markets whose prices are regularly reported by the financial press. These include, for example, coffee, sugar, wheat, several other agricultural products, and metals. For other commodities, however, prices may not be readily available, and thus some field research might be necessary.

Moreover, information gathering is just a small part of the costs associated with international arbitrage. Suppliers must be located in the country in which the goods are less expensive, and transport to the countries in which the goods are more expensive must be arranged. Finally, buyers must be found and a sales network organized. In other words, international arbitrage of goods is a costly activity. When all the costs are added up, it is possible that the cross-country differences in prices will not provide a sufficient return for the operation. For several products prices may have to move apart substantially before arbitrage could become profitable. Moreover, for some products, arbitrage may be infeasible for any conceivable price differential. We refer to these products as **nontradable** goods and services. They include, for example, house rental, theatre shows and government services. Because nontradables cannot move from one country to another, the purchasing power of a currency in terms of nontradables may depend on where one buys them.

To summarize, several factors prevent equation (11.1) from holding exactly. As we mentioned above, international arbitrage is not limited to goods and services, but includes also assets. In fact, arbitrage in securities is easier than arbitrage in commodities. Information about asset prices is readily available, transportation and other transaction costs are very small. We analyze the implications of arbitrage in assets next.

Arbitrage in Assets: Interest-Rate Parity

Suppose that there is a market-determined nominal interest rate in each country. The nominal rate in country i, R^i, will be expressed in units of its own currency – for example, as pound paid per year per pound lent out today.

Consider, for example, an investor who is evaluating whether to lend in country i, say the UK, at interest rate R^i, or in country j, say Japan, at interest rate R^j. At date t the person can invest £1.00 in London and receive $(1 + R^i)$ pounds at period $t+1$. Alternatively, at date t, the person can exchange £1.00 for $1/\epsilon_t^{ij}$ units of Japanese currency. By lending in Tokyo at the interest rate R^j, the person receives $(1 + R^j)/\epsilon_t^{ij}$ units of yen at date $t+1$. If he or she converts back to pounds using period $t+1$'s exchange rate, ϵ_{t+1}^{ij}, then the amount of pounds received is $\epsilon_{t+1}^{ij} \cdot (1 + R^j)/\epsilon_t^{ij}$. Notice that, if the exchange rate rises at a higher rate, that is if the pound depreciates with respect to the yen, then the pound value of next period's yen holdings rises for a given value of Japan's nominal interest rate R^j.

If there are no restrictions on the flows of assets across national borders (that is, no *capital controls*), then people can hold assets in any country. If the return on assets is not the same for all countries, then everyone would want to lend where the amount was greatest and borrow where it was smallest.[5] In our example, if the value of lending in yen is greater than the value of lending in pounds, everyone would want to lend in Tokyo and finance the operation by borrowing funds in London. Thus, as another implication of the law of one price – applied here to the returns on assets – the amounts must be the same for any country i and j. This condition is called **interest-rate parity**:

$$(1 + R^i) = (1 + R^j) \cdot (\epsilon_{t+1}^{ij}/\epsilon_t^{ij})$$

or, rearranging:

$$\epsilon_{t+1}^{ij}/\epsilon_t^{ij} = (1 + R^i)/(1 + R^j) \qquad (11.3)$$

If we use the definition of the change in the exchange rate, $\Delta \epsilon^{ij} = \epsilon_{t+1}^{ij} - \epsilon_t^{ij}$, then the quantity of pounds received becomes $(1 + R^j) \cdot [1 + (\Delta \epsilon^{ij}/\epsilon^{ij})]$, where $\Delta \epsilon^{ij}/\epsilon^{ij}$ is the rate of change of the exchange rate for British pound with the Japanese yen. We can then approximate (11.3) by:

$$\Delta \epsilon^{ij}/\epsilon^{ij} = R^i - R^j \qquad (11.3')$$

The approximation arises because we have neglected the term $(\Delta \epsilon^{ij}/\epsilon^{ij}) \cdot R^j$. This term approaches zero if we consider very small intervals of time.

Equations (11.3) and (11.3') tell us that the higher the rate of change of a country's exchange rate, $\Delta \epsilon^{ij}/\epsilon^{ij}$ – that is, the more rapid the depreciation of a currency – the higher must be that country's nominal interest rate, R^i. Notice the similarity between this condition and the purchasing power parity. The purchasing power parity states that the rate of change of the exchange rate between two countries equals the inflation differential between the two countries. The interest parity condition states that the rate of change of the exchange rate between two countries equals the nominal interest rate differential between the two countries.

Since ϵ_{t+1}^{ij} is not known at time t, the changes in the exchange rates cannot, in practice, be known in advance. Then, as a first-order approximation, we would replace the variable, ϵ^{ij}, by its expectation, $(\epsilon_{t+1}^{ij})^e$, to get:

$$(\epsilon_{t+1}^{ij})^e / \epsilon_t^{ij} = (1 + R^i)/(1 + R^j) \qquad (11.4)$$

or

$$(\Delta \epsilon^{ij})^e / \epsilon^{ij} \approx R^i - R^j \qquad (11.4')$$

where $(\Delta \epsilon^{ij})^e = (\epsilon_{t+1}^{ij})^e - \epsilon_t^{ij}$. Equation $(11.4')$ says that a higher expected rate of change of the exchange rate, $(\Delta \epsilon^{ij})^e / \epsilon^{ij}$, implies a correspondingly higher nominal interest rate, R^i.

Notice that the interest parity condition (11.4) can be expressed in terms of the current exchange rate, that is

$$\epsilon_t^{ij} = (\epsilon_{t+1}^{ij})^e \cdot (1 + R^j)/(1 + R^i). \qquad (11.4'')$$

Figure 11.6 describes this relationship. The vertical axis measures the exchange rate between currency i and j, ϵ^{ij}, and the horizontal axis the ratio of the nominal interest rate in country j and country i, $(1 + R^j)/(1 + R^i)$. The solid line from the origin is the interest rate parity line. Its slope equals the expected future exchange rate, $(\epsilon_{t+1}^{ij})^e$.

For concreteness, suppose that in Figure 11.6 country i is Britain and country j is Germany, and that initially $R^j = R^i$. Equilibrium is at point A, where the interest rate ratio equals one, and the current exchange rate between pounds and marks equals ϵ_0^{ij}.[6] Suppose now that the interest rate in Germany increases so that the interest rate ratio goes up to $[(1 + R^j)/(1 + R^i)]_1 > 1$. Suppose, also, that people's expectations about the future level of the exchange rate are unchanged, that is, $(\epsilon^{ij})^e$ is still the same as before. Individuals will now sell bonds denominated in pounds and buy bonds denominated in marks since their return has increased. This response tends to reduce the value of the pound with respect to the mark. The new equilibrium is at point B where the exchange rate has increased to ϵ_1^{ij}, that is, the pound has depreciated with respect to the mark.

Notice that a depreciation of the pound could occur without any interest rate changes. Suppose,

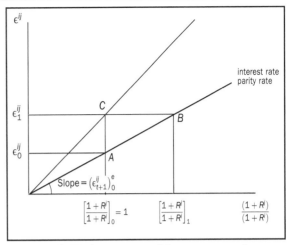

Figure 11.6 Exchange rate and interest rate parity

in fact, that individuals revise their exchange rate expectations, and now believe that the pound will depreciate in the future, that is $(\epsilon_{t+1}^{ij})^e$ increases to $(\epsilon_{t+1}^{ij})_1^e$. This change implies an increase in the slope of the interest rate parity line, which rotates to its new position given by the dotted line. The new equilibrium is at point C where the exchange rate has depreciated to ϵ_1^{ij}. Therefore, even if all the relevant current variables are unchanged, the exchange rate has moved because of the change in expectations.

This result illustrates an important property of exchange rates: exchange rates are **forward looking** variables. Changes in agents' expectations are often considered the main source of exchange rate variations. Although it is possible to attribute virtually all changes in exchange rates to expectational changes, this approach is not a satisfying explanation for macroeconomists. Since it is hard to measure agents' expectations, this type of explanation typically cannot be tested and thus cannot be verified empirically.

Purchasing Power Parity, Interest Rate Parity and Real Interest Rates

If purchasing-power parity holds in relative form, then equation (11.2) implies that the growth rate of the exchange rate, $\Delta \epsilon^{ij} / \epsilon^{ij}$, equals the difference in the inflation rates, $\pi^i - \pi^j$. In terms of expectations, the relative PPP condition is

$$(\Delta \epsilon^{ij})^e / \epsilon^{ij} = (\pi^i)^e - (\pi^j)^e \qquad (11.5)$$

If we combine equation (11.5) with the interest-rate parity condition from equation (11.4'), then we find that the expected real interest rates must be the same:

$$R^i - (\pi^i)^e \approx R^j - (\pi^j)^e \qquad (11.6)$$

For the main developed countries, expected real interest rates tend on the whole to move together,[7] a finding that supports equation (11.6) as a first-order proposition. The more detailed empirical evidence does, however, reveal significant divergences in expected real interest rates among these countries.[8] To explain these divergences we have to allow for departures from the relative PPP condition in equation (11.5). Recall that the PPP conditions need not hold if the price levels, P^i and P^j, refer to market baskets of goods produced or consumed in the two countries.

Suppose, for example, that the expected rate of inflation for country i is low relative to the expected rate of change of its exchange rate, all expressed in relation to country j:

$$(\pi^i)^e - (\pi^j)^e < (\Delta \epsilon^{ij})^e / \epsilon^{ij} \qquad (11.7)$$

Thus, in contrast with relative PPP from equation (11.5), the cost of obtaining goods in country i is expected to fall relative to that in country j.

If we use condition (11.7) together with the interest-rate parity condition from equation (11.4'), then we get

$$R^i - (\pi^i)^e > R^j - (\pi^j)^e \qquad (11.8)$$

Thus, the expected real interest rate is relatively high for the country in which people expect relatively low inflation, in the sense of condition (11.7).

It is plausible that goods in country i will become relatively cheaper over time if the relative cost of goods in country i is currently high, that is, if

$$P^i / P^j > \epsilon^{ij} \qquad (11.9)$$

This condition represents a departure from absolute PPP in equation (11.1). Condition (11.9) tends to lead to condition (11.7) because of the long-run tendency for absolute PPP to hold: if countries are relatively expensive today, then they tend to become relatively less expensive over time.

We can also look at condition (11.9) as a statement that country j's currency is highly valued, that is, ϵ^j is low in relation to the PPP value, P^j / P^i. We therefore conclude that *an overvalued currency is associated with relatively high expected real interest rates* (condition [11.8]).

Covered and Uncovered Interest Rate Parity

A number of real-world considerations prevent interest-rate parity (11.4) from holding exactly. These considerations include the tax treatment of interest income in different countries and governmental restrictions on international borrowing and lending. Conceptually, however, the most important reason is the uncertainty about asset returns and exchange-rate movements. Equation (11.4) makes clear that, in the presence of uncertainty, there is risk involved in the type of arbitrage operation that we described at the beginning of the section. For example, although we may expect the pound to appreciate with respect to the yen, it may not do so, in which case having invested £1.00 in London would turn out to have been less profitable than investing it in Tokyo.

Condition (11.4) is referred to as **uncovered interest-rate parity**, because it does not take into consideration the elements of risk in the exchange rate. Agents could, however, eliminate this risk from their arbitrage operations. The action is risky because at time t (when the investment decision is made), people do not know the *spot* exchange rate that will prevail at time $t + 1$ (when the proceeds of the investment are converted from one currency to another). Recall, however, that the forward exchange market allows a person to fix at time t the exchange rate that will be used at time $t+1$.

Consider the example of an investor evaluating whether to lend in the UK or in Japan, but this time allowing him or her to use the forward exchange market. At date t the person can invest £1.00 in London and receive $(1+R^i)$ pounds at period $t+1$. Alternatively, at date t, the person can exchange £1.00 for $1/\epsilon_t^{ij}$ units of Japanese currency. By lending in Tokyo at the interest rate R^j, the person will receive $(1+R^j)/\epsilon_t^{ij}$ units of yen at date $t+1$. At time t the agent can sell forward the $(1+R^j)/\epsilon_t^{ij}$ yen at the rate $f_{t,t+1}^{ij}$. Therefore, at time $t+1$, the amount of pounds received will be $f_{t,t+1}^{ij} \cdot (1+R^j)/\epsilon_t^{ij}$. If we use the condition for the forward discount, $fd_{t,t+1}^{ij} = f_{t,t+1}^{ij} - \epsilon_t^{ij}$, then the quantity of pounds received becomes $(1+R^j)\cdot[1+(fd_{t,t+1}^{ij}/\epsilon^{ij})]$, where $fd_{t,t+1}^{ij}/\epsilon^{ij}$ is the forward discount expressed as a percentage of the current spot exchange rate.

This time there is no uncertainty about the amount of pounds to be received at time $t+1$. The exchange rate risk has been eliminated from this transaction. The law of one price then requires that the return on the two assets must be the same, that is

$$(1+R^i) = (1+R^j)\cdot[1+(fd_{t,t+1}^{ij}/\epsilon_t^{ij})] \quad (11.10)$$

which can be approximated by

$$fd_{t,t+1}^{ij}/\epsilon_t^{ij} \approx R^i - R^j \quad (11.10')$$

This relationship is called **covered interest-rate parity**, because it assumes that the exchange rate risk has been 'covered' by using the forward exchange market.

Comparing equations (11.4) and (11.10) we see that the expected exchange rate and the forward exchange rate are closely related. In a world without uncertainty, the two rates would be exactly the same. In the presence of uncertainty, however, they may differ. The difference between the two is referred to as a risk premium, ρ_t:

$$f_{t,t+1}^{ij} = (\epsilon_{t+1}^{ij})^e + \rho_t^{ij} \quad (11.11)$$

Notice, first, that the risk premium can be either positive or negative. For example, if currency i has a positive risk premium with respect to currency j, i.e. $\rho_t^{ij} > 0$, then currency j has a negative risk premium with respect to currency i, $\rho_t^{ji} < 0$.

A positive risk premium compensates investors for holding a relatively risky currency. There are two main factors that determine the relative riskiness of a currency, factors that should be well known to students familiar with portfolio theory. The first is the variability of a currency. The more volatile is currency i, the more likely it is that expectations about the future value of this currency will turn out to be incorrect, that is, $(\epsilon_{t+1}^{ij})^e \neq \epsilon_{t+1}^{ij}$ with respect to any other currency j. The second factor is the correlation of the value of a currency with respect to that of the other assets held by investors. A large and positive correlation implies that, when all other assets are doing poorly on average, the value of this currency will also be low. The presence of the currency in a portfolio, therefore, adds to the total riskiness of the investment. Investors, in this case, will want to be compensated for the risk by a positive premium. On the other hand, a negative correlation implies that when all other assets are doing poorly on average, the value of the currency will be high. The presence of this currency in a portfolio, therefore, reduces the total riskiness of the investment. Investors, in this case, will be willing to pay more for this currency, and thus the risk premium will be negative.

Reconsider now Figure 11.3. We saw there that the German mark typically displayed a forward premium with respect to the US dollar, while the lira displayed a forward discount. From the definition of the forward discount and equation (11.11) we obtain

$$fd_{t,t+1}^{ij} = [(\epsilon_{t+1}^{ij})^e - \epsilon_t^{ij}] + \rho_t^{ij} \quad (11.12)$$

The German mark displayed a forward premium $(fd_{t,t+1}^{ij} < 0)$ because investors expected the mark to appreciate with respect to the dollar, $(\epsilon_{t+1}^{ij})^e < \epsilon_t^{ij}$, or they perceived the mark to be less risky than the dollar, $\rho_t^{ij} < 0$. The opposite was true for the Italian lira.

Flexible Exchange Rates

Figures 11.1 and 11.2 show that exchange rates behaved very differently before and after 1971. From 1950 to the early 1970s, the exchange rates between the eight major currencies and the German mark moved infrequently and by small amounts compared with what came later. Until the early 1970s and except during major wars, most countries typically maintained **fixed exchange rates** among their currencies. Since the early 1970s, many countries have allowed their exchange rates to vary or float more or less freely to clear the markets for foreign exchange. As is clear from a glance at Figures 11.1 and 11.2, the exchange rates of the eight major currencies with the German mark have fluctuated substantially over this period. It is easier to study first the determination of exchange rates in a flexible-rate environment, since in the previous sections we were implicitly thinking in terms of flexible exchange rates. We postpone the study of fixed exchange rates to the next section.

We learned that there are two main relationships driving the exchange rate: purchasing power parity and interest rate parity. In Figure 11.7 we describe these two conditions by combining Figure 11.4 (in the left panel) and Figure 11.6 (in the right panel). Suppose that arbitrage in both goods and assets can take place at no cost and instantaneously. The initial equilibrium is at points A and A', where the exchange rate is ϵ_0^{ij} and both interest parity and PPP are satisfied. For simplicity, assume that expectations are given at $(\epsilon_{t+1}^{ij})^e$. Consider an increase in R^j resulting from, say, an increase in the real interest rate in country j associated with a temporary negative productivity shock in that country. This implies that the interest rate ratio increases to $[(1+R^j)/(1+R^i)]_1$. For given expected exchange rate, interest rate parity requires a depreciation of currency i: the exchange rate increases to ϵ_1^{ij}. At an unchanged level of prices, at point C', goods of country i are cheaper than goods of country j. Individuals will purchase goods in country i and sell them in country j, increasing the price level in country i

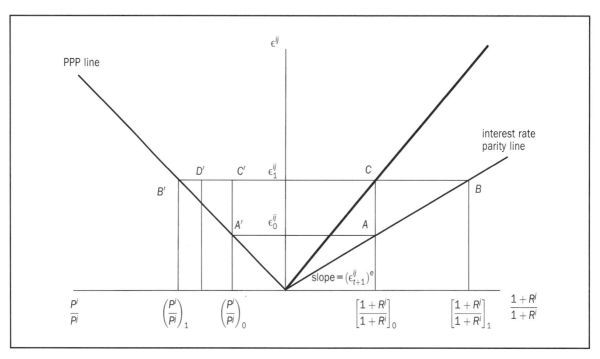

Figure 11.7 Equilibrium under flexible exchange rates

and decreasing it in country j, until PPP is restored. The new equilibrium is at points B and B'.[9]

If arbitrage in the goods market is imperfect because of informational and transaction costs, then it is possible to observe deviations from PPP. Because of the imperfect arbitrage in goods and services, the price ratio may fail to increase sufficiently. In this case, the equilibrium would be at point B and a point between B' and C', say D'. The distance between points D' and B' provides a measure of the deviation from PPP. Economists measure this distance by taking the ratio between points like B' and D', i.e. between ϵ^{ij} and P^i/P^j. This ratio – that is, $\epsilon^{ij} \cdot P^j/P^i$ – is called the **real exchange rate**. It indicates the quantity of goods produced in country i that exchanges for one unit of goods produced in country j. (A person can sell one unit of goods of country j for P^j units of country j currency, which can then be exchanged for $\epsilon^{ij}P^j$ units of country i's currency. This much currency buys $(1/P^i) \cdot \epsilon^{ij}P^j = \epsilon^{ij} \cdot P^j/P^i$ units of country i's goods. This last term equals the real exchange rate.) A rise – that is, a depreciation – in the real exchange rate means that goods produced in country i have become cheaper relative to those produced in country j. Or, to put it the other way, country j goods have become relatively more expensive. In order to distinguish it from the real exchange rate, economists sometimes refer to the ordinary exchange rate, ϵ^{ij}, as the **nominal exchange rate**. We shall discuss the empirical properties of the real exchange rate later in this chapter, after we discuss fixed exchange rates.

We now consider the link between the exchange rate and equilibrium in the market for money, as analyzed in Chapter 3. For simplicity, we now abstract from any deviations from PPP, but the main points would still be valid if we allowed for the type of deviation from PPP that we described above.

The monetary authority of country i determines its domestic money supply, M^i, through open-market operations or other means. Given the quantity of domestic money, the domestic price level, P^i, is determined to ensure that this money is willingly held. Recall from Chapter 3 that the money market equilibrium condition is given by:

$$M^i = P^i \cdot \Phi\left(Y^i, R^i, \ldots\right)$$

or, by rearranging the terms:

$$P^i = M^i / \Phi(Y^i, R^i, \ldots) \tag{11.13}$$

A similar relationship holds for country j. The PPP condition, $P^i = \epsilon^{ij} \cdot P^j$, implies that the exchange rate between country i and country j is given by

$$\epsilon^{ij} = P^i/P^j = [M^i/\Phi(Y^i, R^i,)] \cdot [\Phi(Y^j, R^j,)/M^j],$$

or, after rearranging terms,

$$\epsilon^{ij} = P^i/P^j$$
$$= [M^i/M^j] \cdot [\Phi(Y^j, R^j, \ldots)/\Phi(Y^i, R^i, \ldots)] \tag{11.14}$$

The exchange rate, ϵ^{ij}, is determined by the monetary authorities' choice of M^i and M^j and the values of Y^i, Y^j, R^i and R^j. (Note that R^i equals $r + \pi^i$, and π^i is the growth rate of P^i, which is determined from equation (11.13). A similar relationship holds for R^j.) Consider a once-and-for-all monetary expansion in country i. The price level in country i will increase and, according to equation (11.14), the country's currency will depreciate. In the left panel of Figure 11.7, we move along the PPP line, from point A' to point B'.

How is equilibrium established in the asset market? There is no reason for interest rates to move. Since we assumed a once-and-for-all increase in M^i, expected inflation is unchanged and thus R^i will not change. However, since the price level in country i is permanently higher, agents know that, according to PPP, the future exchange rate will also be higher and will revise their expectation accordingly. The increase in $(\epsilon^{ij}_{t+1})^e$ implies an increase in the slope of the interest rate parity line. The new equilibrium is achieved at points C and B'.

Summarizing, in a flexible exchange rate system, countries can make independent choices about their monetary policies. Each central bank can decide autonomously about the quantity of money or the level of the discount rate in their own country. The purchasing power parity condition and the interest rate parity condition force the exchange rate to move to equilibrate the differences in price levels and interest rates generated by national monetary policies. As we shall see next, the independence of national monetary policy is lost in a fixed exchange rate system.

Fixed Exchange Rates

Until the early 1970s and except during major wars, most countries typically maintained **fixed exchange rates** among their currencies. For the countries considered, the main exceptions to fixed exchange rates in this period were the fluctuations in the Canadian dollar rate until the early 1960s and some realignments in the rates for the French franc, German mark, and British pound. We explored a simple but unrealistic system of fixed exchange rates in Chapter 7. In that setting all countries used a common currency, so the fixity of exchange rates held trivially.

The fixed-rate regime that actually applied to the major developed countries from World War II until the early 1970s is called the **Bretton Woods System**.[10] Under this system, the participating countries established narrow bands within which they pegged the exchange rate, ϵ^i, between their currency and the US dollar. Country i's central bank stood ready to buy or sell its currency at the rate of ϵ^i units per dollar. The German Bundesbank, for example, provided dollars for marks when people wanted to reduce their holdings of marks, and vice versa when people wished to increase their holdings of marks. To manage these exchanges, each central bank maintained a stock of assets in the form of US currency or, more likely, in interest-bearing assets such as US Treasury bills that could be readily converted into US currency. Then the United States stood ready to exchange dollars for gold (on the request of foreign official institutions) at a fixed price, which happened to be $35 per ounce.

Thus, by maintaining a fixed exchange rate with the US dollar, each country indirectly pegged its currency to gold. (This setup is sometimes called a *gold-exchange standard*.)

Another example of a system of fixed exchange rates is the classical **gold standard**. Britain was effectively on the gold standard from the early eighteenth century until World War I, except for a period of suspension because of the Napoleonic wars from 1797 to 1821. Britain returned to the gold standard in 1926 but departed from the system during the Great Depression in 1931. The United States was on the gold standard from 1879 until the trough of the Great Depression in 1933, when the dollar price of gold was increased from $20.67 to $35.00 per ounce. Earlier periods in the United States involved a greater role for silver in the context of a *bimetallic standard*. From an international perspective, the gold standard reached its high point from 1890 to 1914, when most of the countries in Europe and the Americas pegged their currency to gold.

Under a gold standard, each country pegs its currency directly to gold instead of to a central currency, such as the US dollar. An ounce of gold might, for example, be set at $20 in New York and at £4 in London (roughly the values prevailing in 1914). Then the exchange rate between US dollars and British pounds would have to be close to $5 per pound. Otherwise (subject to the costs of shipping gold), it would be profitable for people to buy gold in one country and sell it in the other. As with the Bretton Woods System, the classical gold standard would – if adhered to by the participants – maintain fixed exchange rates among the various currencies.

To see the workings of a system with fixed exchange rates like Bretton Woods, start by letting P represent the dollar price of goods in the United States. Then, if the absolute PPP condition from equation (11.1) holds, country i's price level is

$$P^i = \epsilon^i \cdot P \tag{11.15}$$

(Note in equation (11.1) that the US dollar exchange rate with itself is unity.) If country i's exchange rate with the US dollar, ϵ^i, is fixed, then the price level in country i, P^i, must maintain a constant ratio to the US price level, P.

We can generalize the result by introducing deviations from absolute purchasing-power parity. As mentioned before, the reasons for these deviations include shifts in the terms of trade and a variety of other real disturbances. But we would retain the basic result – namely, a country cannot choose independently its exchange rate, ϵ^i, and its general price level, P^i. If absolute PPP tends to hold in the long run, then a fixed exchange rate means that a country's price level must maintain a given relation to the US price level.

If the US price level, P, changes, then equation (11.15) says that country i's price level, P^i, changes in the same proportion. In other words, any country that maintains a fixed exchange rate with the US dollar experiences roughly the same inflation rate, π^i, as the US rate, π.

Given fixed exchange rates, the interest-rate parity condition from equation (11.3) implies that country i's nominal interest rate, R^i, equals the US rate, R. Thus, under fixed exchange rates, a single nominal interest rate would prevail in the world. (Again, differences in taxes and in riskiness of returns mean that this result would not hold exactly.)

The Quantity of Money under Fixed Exchange Rates

When we considered, in Chapter 3, a closed economy and, in the previous section, when we analyzed an open economy under flexible exchange rates, we stressed the relation between a country's quantity of money, M^i, and its price level, P^i. Yet we have determined a country's price level in equation (11.15) without saying anything about that country's quantity of domestic currency. Let us now investigate the relation between domestic money and prices in an open economy under fixed exchange rates.

It is still the case that the residents of country i demand a quantity of real money, M^i/P^i, which depends on variables like domestic output, Y^i, and the world nominal interest rate, R. (We assume here that the residents of country i use

and hold their own currency rather than that of other countries.) The condition that all domestic money in country i be willingly held is

$$M^i = P^i \cdot \Phi(Y^i, R, \ldots) \tag{11.16}$$
$$(+)(-)$$

If absolute purchasing-power parity holds, then we can substitute in equation (11.16) for the domestic price level as $P^i = \epsilon^i \cdot P$ from equation (11.15). Then we get the condition for the domestic quantity of money:

$$M^i = \epsilon^i \cdot P \cdot \Phi(Y^i, R, \ldots) \tag{11.17}$$

Given the exchange rate, ϵ^i, the US price level, P, and the determinants of the real demand for money in country i, $\Phi(\cdot)$, equation (11.17) determines the nominal quantity of money, M^i, that must be present in country i. Hence, the quantity of domestic money *cannot* be regarded as a free element of choice by country i's central bank. If the central bank pegs the exchange rate at the value ϵ^i, then there is a specific quantity of money, M^i, that is consistent with this exchange rate.

To understand these findings, assume that the domestic price level, P^i, accords initially with absolute purchasing-power parity, as specified in equation (11.15) and that the quantity of domestic money, M^i, is the amount prescribed by equation (11.17). Then the quantity of money equals the amount demanded.

Now suppose that the monetary authority increases the quantity of domestic money, M^i, say, by an open-market purchase of government securities. In Table 11.2 we illustrate this case in step 1 by assuming that the domestic currency and the central bank's holdings of interest-bearing domestic assets each rise by ε1 million.

Our previous analysis of flexible exchange rates suggests that the increase in the quantity of domestic currency would raise the domestic price level, P^i. But then the price level in country i would exceed the value dictated by the PPP condition in equation (11.15). Hence, for a given exchange rate, goods bought in country i would become more expensive relative to goods bought

Assets	Liabilities
Step 1 Domestic interest-bearing assets:	Domestic currency, M^i
+ ε1 million	+ ε1 million

Assets	Liabilities
Step 2 International currency:	Domestic currency, M^i
− ε1 million	− ε1 million

Note: In step 1 the open-market purchase raises domestic currency by ε1 million. But in step 2, the loss of international currency means that domestic currency declines by ε1 million.

Table 11.2   Effects of open-market operations on the central bank's balance sheet

elsewhere. In response, households and firms would move away from buying goods in country *i* and toward buying goods in other countries (or toward goods imported from country i). This reaction tends to keep the domestic price level P^i from rising; that is, the domestic price level stays in line with the prices prevailing in the rest of the world. But at this price level, domestic residents would be unwilling to hold the additional ε1 million of domestic money, M^i. Accordingly, people would return their excess domestic currency to the central bank to obtain US dollars or other currencies. (Since the central bank pegs the exchange rate, ϵ^i, it stands willing to make these exchanges at a fixed conversion ratio.) Thus, in step 2 of Table 11.2, we show that the quantity of domestic currency and the central bank's holdings of international currency each decline by ε1 million.

Instead of reducing its holdings of international currency, the central bank could sell off other assets to get the international currency that people were demanding. The more general point therefore is that the return of domestic currency to the central bank causes the bank to lose some type of asset.

To complete the story, we must assess the central bank's reaction to its loss of international currency or other assets. As one possibility, the bank allows the domestic quantity of money, M^i, to decline. Then, as people return money to the bank, the domestic quantity of money falls back toward the level that is consistent with PPP in equation (11.17). This automatic response of domestic money is a central element of the gold standard or other systems of fixed exchange rates.

On the other hand, when the automatic mechanism tends to reduce the quantity of domestic money, M^i, the central bank might offset this tendency, for example, by further open-market purchases of securities. When the bank acts this way, economists say that it attempts to **sterilize** the flow of international currency. By sterilization, economists mean that the central bank tries to insulate the quantity of domestic money, M^i, from changes in the bank's holdings of international currency or other assets. Eventually this type of policy can lead to a sufficient drain on assets so that the central bank becomes unwilling or unable to maintain the exchange rate. That is, the central bank may no longer provide dollars at the fixed rate of ϵ^i units of domestic currency per dollar. Instead, there may be a **devaluation**, which means that the exchange rate rises above ϵ^i units of domestic currency per dollar. Thus, the tendency of central banks to sterilize the flows of international currency threatens the viability of fixed exchange rates.[11]

We should mention another possible reaction of government policy to the loss of central bank assets. Recall that this drain results in the present case from the central bank's excessive monetary creation, a policy that tends to make domestic goods more expensive relative to foreign goods. To counter this tendency, the home government might impose trade restrictions, which artificially raise the cost of foreign goods for domestic residents. Alternatively, the government might subsidize exports to make these goods cheaper for foreigners. The main point is that the government can interfere with free trade across national borders to prevent purchasing-power parity from holding. Thus, there are two types of potential ill-effects from excessive monetary expansion under fixed exchange rates. One is the loss of international currency, an outcome that leads eventually to devaluation. But to avoid either devaluation or domestic monetary contraction, governments may interfere with free trade. In fact, the frequency of these interferences during the post-World War II period was a major argument used by opponents of fixed exchange rates (see Milton Friedman, 1968a, ch. 9).

World Prices under Fixed Exchange Rates

A system of fixed exchange rates, centred on the US dollar, determines each country's price level, P^i, as a ratio to the US price level, P (see equation [11.15]). To complete the picture, we have to determine the US price level. The analysis is similar to the determination of the world price level in the common-currency system considered in Chapter 7. We have to equate the demand for international currency to the supply.

Suppose that all countries hold their international currency in the form of US dollars (as was reasonably accurate under the Bretton Woods System). Then the total real demand for US currency includes the holdings of US residents plus the holdings of foreigners in the form of international currency. Given the dollar quantity of US currency, M, we can determine the US price level, P, in the manner of our closed-economy analysis. Specifically, a greater amount, M, means a higher US price level, P, and a correspondingly higher price level, P^i, in each other country. Conversely, an increase in the real demand for US currency – whether by US residents or by foreigners – lowers the US price level, P, and correspondingly reduces the price level, P^i, in each other country.

Under the international regime that prevailed after World War II, there were a number of factors that constrained the US Federal Reserve's choice of the quantity of US money, M. First, if the Federal Reserve pursued a monetary policy that was inconsistent with stabilization of the US price level, P, then US currency would become less attractive as an international medium of exchange. That is, other countries would not like it if their price levels – which were constrained to follow the path of the US price level – grew too fast or fluctuated a great deal. Consequently, these countries might no longer find it desirable to peg their exchange rates to the US dollar or to

hold dollars as a form of international currency. This element constrained the expansion of US money to the extent that the US monetary authority wished to maintain the role of the US dollar as the centrepiece of the international monetary system.

More important, the United States had a commitment to exchange US dollars for gold at the rate of $35 per ounce. If the US price level rose substantially – as it did during the late 1960s – then it would become attractive for foreign central banks to trade their dollars for gold. As it lost more and more gold, the United States would become unable to maintain the dollar price of gold. Eventually the system would break down, as it did at the beginning of the 1970s. In 1971, President Richard Nixon decided that the United States would no longer provide gold to foreign central banks in exchange for US dollars.

Devaluation

Return now to the situation of a typical country in a regime of exchange rates tied to the US dollar. As suggested before, a country that typically pegs its exchange rate, ϵ^i, occasionally faces pressure to shift this rate. Consider, for example, a disturbance that tends to increase the domestic price level, P^i, relative to the US price, P. The disturbance could be a rapid expansion of the domestic currency, M^i, or a decrease in the demand for country i's real money, M^i/P^i. The central bank tends in these circumstances to lose international currency or other assets. In response, the bank may raise the exchange rate, ϵ^i, that is, devalue the domestic currency in terms of the US dollar.

A disturbance that tends to lower the domestic price level, P^i, relative to the US price, P, implies gains in the central bank's assets. The bank is likely to react in this case by lowering the exchange rate, ϵ^i, that is, by appreciating the domestic currency in terms of the dollar. Economists call this change a **revaluation**.

Devaluations and revaluations typically do not involve long periods during which the central bank gradually loses or gains international currency. That is because the expectation of a shift in the exchange rate leads to **speculation**, a response that tends to hasten the central bank's actions. If people anticipate a devaluation, then they have an incentive to act in advance to exchange their domestic money at the central bank for international currency, which might be US dollars. People react this way because they expect the domestic money to become less valuable relative to other moneys. But since the speculative decline in the demand for domestic money leads to further losses of international currency by the central bank, the devaluation tends to occur sooner.

Figures 11.1 and 11.2 provide some examples of sudden devaluation and revaluation during the mainly fixed-rate period before the early 1970s. France devalued the franc by a total of 40% in 1957–58, Germany revalued the mark by 4% in 1961 (but not with respect to the Dutch guilder), and Britain devalued the pound by 14% in 1967.

Consider now the effects of a devaluation – that is, an increase in the exchange rate, ϵ^i. As noted before, this change may be a symptom of inflationary pressure, possibly caused by excessive expansion of the domestic currency, M^i. But let's consider here the effects of an autonomous devaluation, that is, a devaluation that comes out of the blue rather than as a response to changes in domestic money supply or demand.

If the domestic price level P^i (measured, say, in terms of pounds per unit of goods) did not change, then an increase in the exchange rate ϵ^i (pounds per dollar) means that goods in country i would become cheaper in terms of dollars. For a given US price level, P, the demand for goods sold by country i would rise accordingly. This increase in demand suggests that the price level, P^i, would rise. This response would accord with the PPP condition, equation (11.15), which shows that a devaluation (a higher value of ϵ^i) leads to a higher domestic price level, $P^i = \epsilon^i \cdot P$.

If we treat the devaluation and the rise in the domestic price level as one-time events, then the higher domestic price level implies a greater demand for domestic money in nominal terms (see equation [11.16]). The rise in the nominal quantity of money, M^i, can come about in two ways. First, the central bank may create more

money through open-market operations or other means. Second, if the central bank does not act, then individuals would bring international currency to the central bank to get more domestic currency. As the bank exchanges domestic for international currency, the quantity of domestic money, M^i, rises. Thus, a one-time devaluation tends to increase the central bank's international currency along with the increase in the quantity of domestic money, M^i.

Notice that there is a two-way direction of association between devaluation and the behaviour of domestic prices and money. First, expansionary monetary policy creates pressure for devaluation. In this sense, domestic inflation causes devaluation. Second, a devaluation tends to raise domestic prices and money. In this sense, devaluation is itself inflationary.

Thus far, the analysis treats the changes in the exchange rate, ϵ^i, and the domestic price level, P^i, as one-time happenings. But, in practice, countries that devalue once tend to devalue again. This outcome makes sense if we think of devaluation as primarily a symptom of pressure for domestic inflation; in particular, as an indication that the domestic central bank is increasing the quantity of money at a rapid rate, for example to raise revenues through the inflation tax. Countries that act this way today are likely to continue this behaviour later. Hence, a devaluation can create expectations of future increases in the exchange rate, ϵ^i. Then the interest-rate parity condition from equation (11.4) implies that the domestic nominal interest rate, R^i, would rise above that in the United States. This change reduces the real demand for country i's money, M^i/P^i: consequently, a devaluation of country i's currency may no longer generate an increase in country i's holdings of international currency.

The European Monetary System

Exchange rates need not be fully fixed or perfectly flexible. After the collapse of the Bretton Woods system, most national central banks have not committed themselves to any specific exchange rate parity. Nonetheless, they still intervene in the exchange rate market to stabilize their currency. These interventions are, in most cases, not systematic but purely at the discretion of the monetary authorities.

A notable exception is the **Exchange Rate Mechanism (ERM)**. In March 1979 the **European Monetary System (EMS)** was inaugurated as a way to bring exchange rate stability to the EC area. According to the EMS, the EC countries agreed to limit the fluctuations of their bilateral exchange rates (the ERM) and to provide each other with credit facilities to help finance foreign exchange market interventions. Although all EC countries were, since the beginning, members of the EMS, only eight of them – Belgium, Luxembourg, Denmark, France, Germany, Ireland, Italy, and the Netherlands – initially participated in the ERM. In 1989, Spain also joined the ERM, followed, in 1990, by the UK and, in 1991, by Portugal, leaving only Greece outside the ERM. In September 1992, however, following a major exchange rate crises, Italy and the UK decided to suspend their participation to the ERM (see Box 11.2).

The ERM is an example of a fixed exchange rate regime that has no role for gold or some other commodity. Instead of using gold, the European Monetary System uses as an international currency unit the *European currency unit (ECU)*, which is a basket containing specified amounts of various European currencies. Each of the currencies participating in the ERM has an official central rate with respect to the ECU. These parities are displayed in Figure 11.8. For example, the central rate for the Dutch guilder is 2.20 guilders per one ECU, that of the German mark is 1.95 marks per one ECU. The central parities with respect to the ECU implicitly define a set of bilateral central parities between all the EC currencies. For example, dividing the central parity of the guilder with respect to the ECU by that of the German mark with respect to the ECU, we obtain the central parity of the guilder with respect to the mark, 1.13 guilders per one mark. According to the ERM agreement, each country in the system is committed to maintain the fluctuations of its exchange rate within ±2.25% around these central parities. The

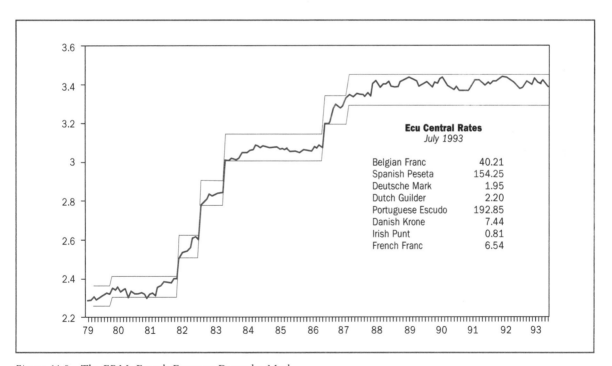

Figure 11.8 The ERM: French Franc vs Deutsche Mark

Box 11.2   The ERM Crisis of 1992

After a period of unprecedented stability, the ERM almost collapsed at the end of 1992. Five years had passed without any realignment in exchange rate parities (the last realignment occurred in January 1987).[12] In the meantime, three new countries had joined the system without creating major disruptions – Spain in June 1989, the UK in October 1990, and Portugal in April 1992. Encouraged by the apparent success of the ERM, European monetary policy goals became more ambitious. New impetus was given to the idea of moving from a system of semi-fixed exchange rates, like the ERM, to a European monetary union (EMU), requiring the creation of a single European currency that would replace the various national currencies. The appeal of the project was the elimination, once and for all, of the problem of exchange rate instability, at least within the EC. The EMU plan gathered considerable momentum with the approval, in December 1991, of the Maastricht Treaty, which defined the objective, the timing and the rules of the future monetary union.

The first sign of the storm to come was the Danish rejection of the Maastricht Treaty in a national referendum, in May 1992. This event started rising doubts about the political feasibility of EMU. The surprising defeat of the Maastricht Treaty in Denmark created a climate of uncertainty regarding a similar kind of referendum to be held in France the coming September. Unexpectedly, electoral polls revealed a strong opposition to EMU and its possible defeat. This triggered a massive speculation against the French franc, the Italian lira, the British pound, the Spanish peseta and the Portuguese escudo, considered to be the weak currency in the ERM. While the French franc survived the crisis, the other currencies did not. On 13 September 1992, the Italian lira was devalued by 7%. On 16 September the UK suspended its participation in the ERM followed, the next day, by Italy, once it was realized that the devaluation was unable to stop speculation against the lira. The same day, the Spanish peseta was devalued by 5%. As shown in Figure 11.9, the Spanish peseta did not leave the ERM, but was devalued again, together with the Portuguese escudo, in November 1992 and May 1993.

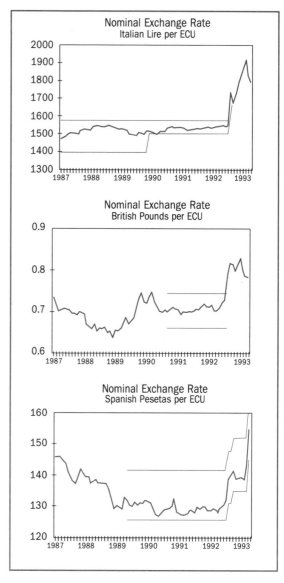

Figure 11.9   The ERM crisis of September 1992

recent entrants in the system – Spain and Portugal (and the UK up to September 1992) – are allowed, on a temporary basis, a wider band of fluctuation of ±6%.

The system, centred around the ECU, was created as a symmetric system, that is where no currency should have a privileged role like the dollar had during Bretton Woods. In practice, however, the ERM is not a symmetric system. The German mark is the central currency in the system, and the Bundesbank policies have a leading role.

The ERM is a combination of flexible and fixed exchange rates. The exchange rates can fluctuate on a day-to-day basis, but there exist fixed limits to these fluctuations. Even when the exchange rate is well within its band it does not behave like a pure flexible rate. In particular, we would expect the fluctuation of the exchange rate between two ERM currencies to be smaller than those of a purely flexible rate.

There are two reasons for the smoother behaviour of ERM exchange rates. First, in contrast to a pure float, the central banks that participate in the ERM intervene in the exchange market to stabilize their currencies even when they are not near the edge of their bands. The second reason is more subtle and involves the effect of the existence of the ERM on expectations. Equation (11.4″)

$$\epsilon_t^{ij} = (\epsilon_{t+1}^{ij})^e \cdot (1 + R^j)/(1 + R^i) \qquad (11.14'')$$

shows that the exchange rate is a forward looking variable, that is, it depends on the expectation of the future exchange rate, $(\epsilon_{t+1}^{ij})^e$. In a purely flexible exchange rate regime, the future exchange rate is, in principle, unconstrained. For example, the public may expect that the future value of the French franc will be lower by 20% with respect to the German mark, say because the French monetary authorities are expected to expand money supply substantially next period. If we assume for simplicity that French and German nominal interest rates are the same, then equation (11.4″) implies that the current FF/DM exchange rate will depreciate immediately by 20%. In other words, in a purely flexible exchange rate,

expectational changes can generate substantial fluctuations in the current exchange rate. One important effect of a system like the ERM is to limit these expectational changes and thus, to limit the fluctuations of exchange rates. Agents would not expect a future devaluation of the French franc by 20% because they realize that the Banque de France will intervene to confine the fluctuations of the franc with respect to the mark within the 2.25% limit. The strength of this effect on expectations depends on the credibility of the system. The ERM crisis of September 1992 is a clear indication of how, for some countries, the commitment to defend the exchange rate parity is not fully credible.

Giavazzi and Giovannini (1989), show that the reduction in volatility of the nominal exchange rate has been substantial since the start of the ERM. The stabilizing effect of the ERM was particularly strong between 1987 and 1992. Before 1987 and after September 1992, several central parity realignments took place and thus ERM currencies appreciated or depreciated far more than 2.25% of their initial central rates, or left the system altogether. Figure 11.8 shows, for example, that the central parity between the French franc and the German mark was devalued six times since 1979. Consequently, between March 1979 and January 1987 (the time of the last realignment), the French franc depreciated 45% with respect to the German mark.

The stabilizing effect of the ERM on expectations is limited for some currencies because the frequent use of realignments make agents doubt the commitment of some central banks to fixed central parities. Evidence of this initial lack of credibility of the ERM appears in Figure 11.10, where we plot the 90-days forward discount on the French Franc with respect to the German mark. Recall from the previous discussion that the forward discount is given by the expected depreciation plus the risk premium (see equation [11.12]). If the central parity were perfectly credible, then we should not expect to see a significant forward discount or premium. The forward discount should fluctuate narrowly around zero. Figure 11.10 shows, however, that a positive forward discount existed for most of the ERM period. At the beginning of 1981, the risk premium decreased toward zero, but then increased to almost 4%, preceding the realignment of October 1981, and remained positive for the next ten years. Although the French franc has not been devalued since January 1987, the risk premium remained positive until November 1991. This observation suggests that it takes several years for a central bank to restore the credibility of its exchange rate policies.

If proposals for European monetary integration go forward, then the system of fixed exchange rates with the ECU as its central unit may eventually be transformed into a regime with a common currency under a European Monetary Union. We postpone the discussion of this subject to Chapter 22, after we analyze business cycle fluctuations.

Purchasing-Power Parity under Flexible and Fixed Exchange Rates

Many economists have noted that purchasing-power parity seems to hold less well under the flexible exchange rates that have prevailed since the early 1970s than under the fixed rates that prevailed earlier for most countries. We have already mentioned that economists often measure deviations from PPP by the ratio of ϵ^{ij} to P^i/P^j, that is, the real exchange rate. We already looked in Figures 11.1 and 11.2 at the behaviour of nominal exchange rates for eight of the major developed countries with respect to Germany. To see the implications for PPP, we have to adjust these exchange rates to take account of the divergent movements in domestic price levels.

Figures 11.11 and 11.12 show the price levels (consumer price indexes) for the eight countries from 1950 to 1992. Each price level is expressed as a ratio to the German price level – that is, the values correspond to P^i/P^j from our previous discussion. The figures show for each year the proportionate deviation of the price ratio from the value that prevailed in 1950. For the UK in Figure 11.11, for example, the value for 1992 was 335% above that in 1950 because the average UK inflation rate from 1950 to 1992 was higher than that in Germany. For periods in which a country's inflation rate exceeded the German value, the lines shown in Figures 11.11 and 11.12 rise over time.

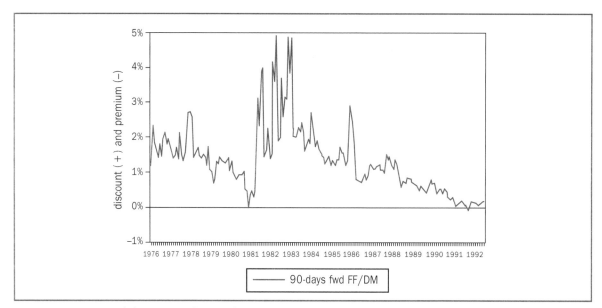

Figure 11.10   Forward discount on the French Franc

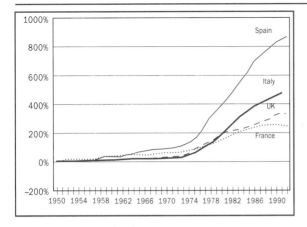

Figure 11.11 Price levels, 1950–92

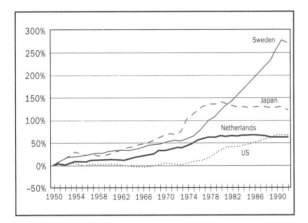

Figure 11.12 Price levels, 1950–92

Figures 11.13 and 11.14 show the ratio of the nominal exchange rate, ϵ^i, to the relative price, P^i/P^j. As in previous figures, the numbers plotted represent the proportionate deviation from the value that prevailed in each country in 1950. If relative PPP held, then the numbers would all equal zero. Deviations in relative PPP show up as movements above or below zero in Figures 11.13 and 11.14. As an example, for the Netherlands in Figure 11.14, the value of -17% for the real exchange rate in 1970 means that German goods could be exchanged for about 17% less goods in the Netherlands, compared to the situation that prevailed in 1950. Thus, Dutch goods became more expensive relative to German goods from 1950 to 1970. Recall that the nominal exchange

rate was essentially fixed at this time (see Figure 11.2). The fall in the real exchange rate therefore reflected a *higher* average inflation rate in the Netherlands (4.0% per year from 1950 to 1970) than in Germany (1.8% per year) – see Figure 11.12. The real exchange rate for the Netherlands continued to fall after 1970, so that Dutch goods exchanged for more and more German goods, until reaching the value -0.27% in 1978. Then the rate rose back to -0.23% in 1989, where it remained until 1992. A similar pattern was followed by the Swedish Kronar and the Japanese yen. Since 1980 to 1992 the Japanese inflation rate has been *lower* than that in Germany (the average inflation rate in this

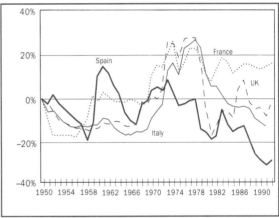

Figure 11.13 Real exchange rates in terms of DM 1950–92

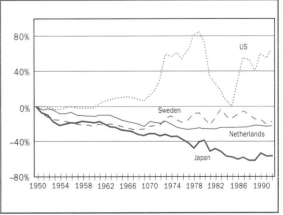

Figure 11.14 Real exchange rates in terms of DM 1950–92

period was 3% in Germany and 2.6% in Japan). The periods of decline in the real exchange rate for Japan therefore reflected decreases in the nominal exchange rate (Figure 11.2).

France, Italy, and the UK in Figure 11.13 and the US in Figure 11.14 experienced broadly similar patterns of real exchange rates. Each currency showed strong real depreciation from 1968 to 1978, followed by real appreciation until 1981. Afterwards, in Italy the real appreciation continued until 1992, whereas it reverted to a real depreciation in France, starting in 1981, and in the US, starting in 1985. In the UK, after a period of real depreciation between 1981 and 1987, the pound appreciated in real terms until 1991.

One interesting point, brought out by a comparison of Spain and Japan, is that the real exchange rates behaved similarly even when the domestic price levels and nominal exchange rates moved in very different ways. From 1970 to 1992, the Spanish inflation rate averaged 7.7% per year more than that in Germany (Figure 11.11), and the Spanish nominal exchange rate depreciated at an average rate of 6.1% per year (Figure 11.1). Thus, the real exchange rate for Spain *appreciated* by 1.6% per year (Figure 11.13). Over the same period, the average Japanese inflation rate was 1.6% per year below that in Germany (Figure 11.12), and the Japanese nominal exchange rate appreciated at an average rate of 0.1% per year (Figure 11.2). Thus, as with Spain, the real exchange rate for Japan appreciated by 1.65% per year (Figure 11.14).

The lesson from the comparison between Japan and Spain is that very different patterns for nominal variables – domestic price levels, nominal exchange rates, and, it turns out, underlying rates of monetary growth – can coexist with similar patterns for real exchange rates. That is because the nominal exchange rates, which were flexible in the 1970s, behaved sufficiently differently in Japan and Spain so as to offset the divergent trends in domestic price levels. Although the real exchange rates between each country and Germany have changed substantially since the early 1970s, the suggestion is that some real disturbances – rather than the nominal policies – were at work. Economists

have, unfortunately, not been so successful in isolating the important real disturbances.

We know for high-inflation countries, such as those on the right-hand side of Figure 11.5, that differences in inflation rates explain most of the divergent movements in nominal exchange rates. For the nine developed countries that we have been considering, the inflation rates are relatively moderate, and the fluctuations of inflation account for only a small part of the year-to-year variations in nominal exchange rates. Over the longer term, however, the differing behaviour of domestic price levels does explain a large fraction of the movements in nominal exchange rates. From 1973 to 1992 for the eight developed countries, the different movements in domestic price levels (shown in Figures 11.11 and 11.12) explain about 70% of the divergences in nominal exchange rates (Figures 11.1 and 11.2).

Let us try to summarize some of the major facts about real exchange rates in the post-World War II period.[13] Some of these observations follow directly from Figures 11.1–11.2 and 11.11–11.14, and others come from more detailed statistical analysis of these and other data.

(1) Real exchange rates have not been constant. The extent of year-to-year fluctuations during the flexible-exchange-rate period from 1973 to 1990 turns out to be roughly twice as great as that from 1951 to 1972, when most nominal exchange rates were fixed.[14] Departures from relative PPP have therefore been important, especially since the early 1970s. There were, however, some substantial movements in real exchange rates in the earlier period when nominal exchange rates were fixed. Thus, fixed nominal exchange rates do not guarantee stability in real exchange rates.

(2) The past experience of movements in real exchange rates provides little guide to future changes. For example, the real appreciation of the German mark against Italian, French, UK and US currencies from 1968 to 1974 (Figures 11.13 and 11.14) would not have allowed us to predict the continuation of real depreciations from 1975 to 1978. Similarly, the real depreciation of the German mark from 1978 to 1981 would not have allowed us to predict the following appreciations with respect to France, the UK

and the US or the following depreciation with respect to Italy. People who state confidently that any currency will rise or fall over some short-run horizon should not be taken seriously.

(3) There is no clear connection between the behaviour of real exchange rates and a country's experience with inflation or monetary growth. As an example, recall our comparison of Spain and Japan. Probably we can think of the movements in real exchange rates as reflecting primarily real changes, involving the terms of trade, the relative prices of traded and nontraded goods, trade restrictions and tax policies, and so on. But the details of the links between these real variables and the real exchange rates have not been worked out empirically.

(4) Supply shocks, such as the changes in oil prices, have been unusually large since the early 1970s. These shocks imply shifts in the terms of trade and thereby in real exchange rates. Hence, the change to flexible exchange rates is not responsible for all of the increased variability of real exchange rates since the early 1970s. (The increased importance of real shocks may make flexible exchange rates more attractive. In this sense, the volatility of real exchange rates helps to explain why we have flexible exchange rates, rather than vice versa.)

(5) Fluctuations in real exchange rates reflect market forces that no economist (or politician!) understands very well. With flexible exchange rates, these forces show up as variations in nominal exchange rates. Under fixed exchange rates, the forces exert pressure for change in domestic price levels and money stocks. Policymakers may resist these tendencies by carrying out offsetting monetary policies. Since these monetary actions cannot work in the long run, the ultimate reaction is likely to be restrictions on trade in goods and assets. Because of these restrictions, it may turn out that real exchange rates are less volatile under fixed exchange rates than under flexible rates. But because of the interferences with trade, the volume of international commerce would also be smaller. Although real exchange rates have been volatile since the early 1970s, it is important to remember that the volume of world trade increased substantially in comparison with the pre-1970 period.

Exchange Rates and the Current-Account Balance

Exchange rates are often discussed in conjunction with the current account. A common argument, for example, is that the British pound has to depreciate in real terms in order for the UK current account to move toward a surplus. That is, UK goods have to become cheaper relative to foreign goods to eliminate an excess of imports over exports.

It seems plausible that a real depreciation of the pound would deter imports and encourage exports. But suppose for the moment that the physical quantities of goods imported and exported did not change. Then a depreciation of the pound means that the pound revenues from exports would not change (if the pound price of export goods does not change), whereas the pound expenses on imports would rise. The current account would therefore show a larger deficit. The problem is that importers now pay more in terms of pounds (or in terms of goods produced in the United Kingdom) for each unit of foreign goods.

The offsetting force is that a fall in the relative price of UK products tends to lower the physical quantity of goods imported and raise the physical quantity of goods exported. The current-account balance moves toward surplus if these responses more than offset the adverse effect from having to pay more for each unit of goods imported.

To think about the net effect from a real depreciation of the pound, recall from Chapter 7 that the current-account balance equals national saving. The current-account balance moves toward surplus if national saving rises. To go further, we have to say something about where a shift in the real exchange rate came from.[15]

To take a case that we considered before, suppose that a real depreciation of the pound reflects an adverse shift in the UK terms of trade. That is, the tradable goods produced in the

United Kingdom become less valuable relative to the tradable goods produced elsewhere. We discussed in Chapter 7 the response of the current-account balance to this kind of disturbance. If the shift in the terms of trade is temporary, then national saving falls and the current account moves accordingly toward deficit. If the shift is permanent, then national saving changes little, and the current account is not affected. Although the real exchange rate depreciates in both cases, the current account moves toward a deficit in one situation and is not affected in the other.

We could think of other reasons for a real depreciation of the pound, such as a shift in the price of UK nontradables relative to UK tradables. Then we would find that the current-account balance could move toward surplus or deficit or remain unchanged. The general lesson is that a real depreciation of the pound may go along with a move in either direction in the current-account balance: the results depend on the details of the disturbances that led to the decline in the pound.

Empirically, it is difficult to find any clear pattern in the relation between current-account balances and real exchange rates. We can find episodes where the real exchange rate and the current-account balance moved together, others in which they moved in opposite directions, and others where there is no apparent relationship between them. From 1970 to 1980, for example, the US dollar depreciated dramatically in real terms relative to most other major currencies (see Figure 11.14). Over this period, the US current-account balance averaged roughly zero (0.02% of GNP) and showed no regular pattern over time. On the other hand, from 1980 to 1985, the US dollar appreciated in real terms, and the current-account balance moved toward a substantial deficit. Between 1981 and 1983 the French Franc depreciated in real terms and the French current account moved into deficit.

The overall indication is that movements in real exchange rates provide little or no information about what the current account is doing. This empirical observation is consistent with our theoretical reasoning because different underlying disturbances would lead to different patterns of association between the real exchange rate and the current-account balance.

Another point is that the real exchange rate is not a variable that is very amenable to government policy. The nominal exchange rate can readily be influenced by governments, for example, by changing the growth rate of money in a setting of flexible exchange rates. Governments also choose whether to have a system with fixed or flexible exchange rates. But we should think of the real exchange rate as a relative price, specifically, as the price of domestic goods relative to the price of foreign goods. Governments can influence the real exchange rate in the same way that they can affect other relative prices, for example, by restricting international trade in goods and assets or by tax policies (including tariffs and subsidies). If an economist urges a country's government to engineer a rise or fall of its currency in real terms, then he or she is really advocating this kind of interference with market forces. Such advice is, unfortunately, rarely accompanied by a rationale for the necessary form of government intervention.

Summary

Two main relationships drive exchange rates movements: purchasing-power parity (PPP) and interest-rate parity. Purchasing-power parity connects a country's exchange rate with, say, the German mark to the ratio of that country's price level to the German price level. In relative form, the PPP condition relates changes in exchange rates to differences in inflation rates. A variety of real factors, including changes in the terms of trade, shifts in the relative prices of traded and nontraded goods, and variations in trade restrictions and tax policies, can lead to deviations from PPP. Such deviations – corresponding to variations in real exchange rates – have been especially important since the early 1970s.

Interest-rate parity implies that differences in nominal interest rates across countries correspond to differences in expected rates of change of exchange rates. We discussed two versions of interest-rate parity: uncovered interest-rate parity, which involves the future expected spot exchange rate, and covered interest parity, which involves the forward exchange rate. Differences in taxes and in riskiness of returns can lead to deviations from interest-rate parity, but these deviations are minor for the main developed countries. If purchasing-power parity holds in relative form, then interest-rate parity implies that expected real interest rates are equal across countries. If relative PPP fails, then expected real interest rates will diverge. We showed that a country with a highly-valued currency – one that is expected to depreciate in real terms over time – tends to have a high expected real interest rate.

Examples of regimes with fixed exchange rates are the classical gold standard, the Bretton Woods System, and a world with a common currency. When the exchange rate is fixed to the US dollar, a country's price level is determined mainly by the US price level. Then, to satisfy the PPP condition, there is a specific quantity of money that is consistent with a country's chosen exchange rate. The flows of international currency tend to generate this quantity of money automatically. However, countries sometimes sterilize the flows of international currency to maintain a higher quantity of domestic money. These actions often lead to devaluation of the currency or to trade restrictions. Inflation and devaluation are related in two ways: domestic inflation tends to cause devaluation, and devaluation can itself be inflationary.

Flexible exchange rates have been prevalent since the early 1970s. The flexibility of exchange rates leaves intact the main results about international trade in goods and credit: the conditions for purchasing-power parity and interest-rate parity apply in the same manner as before. Under flexible exchange rates, however, each central bank can make an independent choice of monetary growth and, hence, inflation.

In the Exchange Rate Mechanism of the European Monetary System, exchange rates can fluctuate within fixed bands. The ERM has produced a considerable reduction in the volatility of the nominal exchange rate within the EC, between 1987 and 1992. Before 1987 and after September 1992, several central parity realignments took place and thus several ERM currencies appreciated or depreciated substantially. The frequent use of realignments made agents doubt the commitment of some central banks to fixed central parities. This scepticism was reflected in forward discounts of currencies with respect to the centre currency, the German mark.

It is difficult to find a regular pattern of association between the real exchange rate and the current-account balance. On theoretical grounds, the relationship depends on the underlying disturbance that caused the real exchange rate to change.

Important Terms and Concepts

international reserves
international arbitrage
domestic credit
purchasing-power parity (PPP)
absolute form of PPP
relative form of PPP
covered interest-rate parity
uncovered interest-rate parity
fixed exchange rate
Bretton Woods System
gold standard
forward looking

European Monetary System (EMS)
risk premium
sterilization
devaluation
monetary approach to the balance of payments
revaluation
speculation (on exchange rate)
spot and forward exchange rate
flexible exchange rate
real exchange rate
nominal exchange rate

Questions and Problems

Mainly for Review

11.1 Explain how the real exchange rate differs from the nominal exchange rate? Which rate is pegged in a system of fixed exchange rates? Can the government readily influence both rates?

11.2 Explain the conditions for absolute and relative purchasing-power parity in equations (11.1) and (11.2). How do these conditions relate to the behaviour of real exchange rates?

11.3 Under fixed exchange rates, does the central bank have discretion over the money supply? Show how an attempt to exercise an independent monetary policy may result in devaluation or revaluation. Why might the attempt lead to trade restrictions?

11.4 Under flexible exchange rates, a country that has a persistently high rate of inflation will experience a steady increase in its exchange rate. Explain why this happens. Why might the central bank like this system?

11.5 We mentioned that examples of regimes with fixed exchange rates were the classical gold standard, the Bretton Woods System, and a setup with a common currency. Explain how each of these regimes would ensure fixed exchange rates.

Problems for Discussion

11.6 Shifts in the Demand for Money
Consider an increase in the real demand for money in country i.
a. Under a fixed exchange rate, what happens to country i's price level, P^i, and quantity of money, M^i? What happens to the country's quantity of international currency, H^i?
b. Under a flexible exchange rate – with a fixed quantity of domestic money, M^i – what happens to the country's price level, P^i, and exchange rate, ϵ^i?

11.7 Monetary Growth under Flexible Exchange Rates
Equation (11.14) relates a country's exchange rate ϵ^{ij} to domestic money supply and demand. Suppose that a country raises its growth rate of money, μ^i, once and for all. Describe the effect of this change on the path of ϵ^{ij}. (Assume that the foreign price level, P^j, the world real interest rate, r, and the path of domestic output, Y^i, do not change.)

11.8 Flexible Exchange Rates and Inflation Rates
a. Show, by using the condition for relative purchasing-power parity in equation (11.2), that the growth rate of the exchange rate, $\Delta\epsilon^i/\epsilon^i$, is approximately equal to the difference between country i's inflation rate, π^i, and the US inflation rate, π.
b. Using the IMF's *International Financial Statistics* (yearbook issue), calculate the values of $\Delta\epsilon^i/\epsilon^i$ and $\pi^i - \pi$ for some countries in the post-World War II period. What conclusions emerge?

11.9 Nixon's Departure from Gold in 1971
Under the Bretton Woods System, the United States pegged the price of gold at $35 per ounce.
a. Why did trouble about the gold price arise in 1971?
b. Was President Nixon right in eliminating the US commitment to buy and sell gold (from and to foreign official institutions) at a fixed price? What other alternatives were there – in particular,
i. What was the classical prescription of the gold standard?
ii. The French suggested a doubling in the price of gold. Would that have helped?

11.10 Shipping Gold under the Gold Standard
Suppose that the price of gold is $5 per ounce in New York and 1 pound per ounce in London.
a. Assume that the exchange rate is $6 per pound. If a person starts with dollars in New York, then what can he or she do to make a profit? If the cost of transporting gold is 1% of the amount shipped, then how high does the exchange rate have to go above $5 per pound to make this action profitable?
b. Make the same calculations when the exchange rate is below $5 per pound, using the perspective of someone who starts with pounds in London.
(The results determine a range of exchange rates around $5 per pound for which it is unprofitable to ship gold in either direction. The upper and lower limits of this range are called *gold points*. If the exchange rate goes beyond these points, then it becomes profitable to ship an unlimited amount of gold. Can you show that the potential to ship gold guarantees that the actual exchange rate will remain within the gold points?)

11.11 Futures Contracts on Foreign Exchange
If a person buys a one-month futures contract on the German mark, then he or she agrees to purchase marks next month at a dollar exchange rate that is set today. The buyer of this contract goes 'long' on the mark and does well if the mark appreciates (more than the amount expected) over the month. Similarly, the seller of a one-month futures contract agrees to sell marks next month at a dollar exchange rate that is agreed on today. The seller goes 'short' on the mark and does well if the

mark depreciates (more than expected) over the month.

Consider a German bond with a maturity of one month. This bond sells for a specified number of marks today and will pay out a stated amount of marks in one month. How can a person use the futures market to guarantee the dollar rate of return from buying the German bond and holding it for one month?

11.12 Changes in the Quantity of International Currency (optional)

Our analysis treated the quantity of international currency as the constant, $\bar{H}$. What modifications have to be made to allow for changes over time in this quantity? In answering, consider the following regimes:

a. International currency consists of US dollar bills.

b. International currency is a pure bookkeeping entry, such as the European currency unit used by the European Monetary System.

c. International currency is gold.

11.13 Alternative Systems of Exchange Rates (optional)

In Chapter 7 we assumed a system with a common world currency. In this chapter we found that fixed exchange rates could be obtained by other means, such as a gold standard or an arrangement like the European Monetary System. We also found that exchange rates could be flexible rather than fixed. What seem to be the benefits and costs from the different setups? In particular,

a. Is it better to have fixed or flexible exchange rates?

b. Is it a good or bad idea for all countries to use a single form of currency?

(*Note*: This question is very difficult, and economists would not agree about the answer.

In thinking about the issues involved, you might consider the following: Are there transaction benefits from having just one type of currency and just one unit for quoting prices? Do governments want to have independent monetary policies and perhaps to get revenue from printing money? Is it costly for governments or individuals to hold stocks of gold? Can we be sure that central banks will stick to their announced policies of fixed exchange rates? Is it useful in some respects for different countries to use different units for quoting prices? Is it true that real exchange rates have become more volatile since the early 1970s because of the move toward flexible exchange rates?)

11.14 Nontraded Goods and Real Exchange Rates (optional)

Suppose that each country produces some goods and services (such as haircuts and rents on buildings) that are not traded internationally. Assume that the price of nontraded goods in country i rises relative to the price of traded goods, but no change occurs in the relative price of nontraded and traded goods in country j. What happens to country i's real exchange rate, $\epsilon^{ij}/(P^i/P^j)$? (Assume that P^i and P^j are the consumer price indexes for country i and country j, respectively.)

In answering, note that the general price levels, P^i and P^j, include the prices of traded and nontraded goods. The law of one price says that the purchasing power of any currency should be the same for traded goods, regardless of where they are produced, but the same may not hold for nontraded goods.

Can you use the result to suggest an explanation for the movement in Japan's real exchange rate from 1950 to 1970 (see Figure 11.14)?

Notes

1. These figures are based on a survey of foreign exchange markets conducted by the major central banks in 1989. For more details, see *Bank of England Quarterly Bulletin*, Nov. 1989.

2. In practice, it may take two days for the funds to clear.

3. For convenience, we start by expressing all exchange rates in terms of the number of units of domestic currency that trade for $1.00 (US). Most foreign exchange markets express exchange rates in terms of US dollars, and thus dollar exchange rates play a particularly important role in foreign exchange markets. We shall show in a moment, however, how to derive and work with exchange rates between any two currencies.

4. The countries in Figure 11.5 are the same as those included in Table 8.1 plus: Algeria, Antigua and Barbuda, Australia,

The Bahamas, Bahrain, Barbados, Belize, Benin, Botswana, Burundi, China, Dominica, Ethiopia, Fiji, Grenada, Indonesia, Jordan, Kenya, Lesotho, Liberia, Luxembourg, Malawi, Malaysia, Mali, Mauritania, Nicaragua, Oman, Panama, Papua New Guinea, Poland, Rwanda, Seychelles, Solomon Islands, St. Lucia, St. Vincent and the Grenadines, Suriname, Swaziland, Tanzania, Uganda, United Arab Emirates, Vanuatu, Western Samoa, Zambia, Zimbabwe.

5. If there is uncertainty about the future level of the exchange rate, this is not necessarily the case. We deal with this complication in the next section.

6. Notice that, in this case, the interest parity condition requires the expected future exchange rate to equal the current one, $\epsilon_t^{ij} = (\epsilon_{t+1}^{ij})^e$.

7. See Robert Barro and Xavier Sala-i-Martin (1990).

8. See Robert Cumby and Maurice Obstfeld (1984) and Frederic Mishkin (1984).

9. Notice that, in this process, country j will be running a trade deficit. This is what we would expect when a country is hit by a temporary negative shock.

10. The system is named in honour of the meeting site, Bretton Woods, New Hampshire, where the regime was set up. For the details of this system, see James Ingram (1983, ch. 9).

11. The discussion in this and the following sections follows a viewpoint that is often called the monetary approach to the balance of payments. This approach was developed by Robert Mundell (1968, part II; 1971, part III). The early origins of this theory are in the eighteenth-century writings of David Hume; see Eugene Rotwein (1970).

12. As shown in Figure 11.9, in January 1990 the lira switched from a $\pm 6\%$ band to the smaller $\pm 2.25\%$ band.

13. For a related discussion, see Michael Mussa (1979, pp. 10–27).

14. The standard deviation of year-to-year changes from 1973 to 1990 is about twice as large as that from 1951 to 1972.

15. In the next chapter, where we introduce investment, we will see that the current account is the difference between national saving and domestic investment. Our discussion, however, would still be valid in the presence of investment.

12

Investment and Real Business Cycles

So far we have simplified matters by pretending that labour services were the only variable input to the production process. Now we want to be more realistic by including capital services as well. We shall think primarily of **physical capital**, such as machines and buildings used by producers. In the national accounts this category is called **producer's durable equipment and structures**. But we can broaden this concept of capital to include the goods held as **inventories** by businesses. We might also add consumer durables, such as homes (called residential structures in the national accounts), automobiles, and appliances. We could go further to include **human capital**, which measures the effects of education and training on the skills of workers. Although the general economic reasoning applies also to human capital, we shall confine most of the analysis here to physical capital.

The Capital Stock and Investment in the G-6

Table 12.1 shows how a standard concept of physical capital evolved from 1950 until 1987 in four of the G-6 countries. This concept, called **fixed capital**, includes business's durable equipment and structures, plus residential structures both private and public. The data are expressed in terms of GDP. In all the major economies, fixed capital stock has increased considerably in the last four decades. Table 12.1 shows that in Germany, Japan and the UK, fixed capital stock has increased faster than GDP. In contrast, in the US the ratio of fixed capital stock to GDP in 1987

(a) Ratio of gross fixed capital stock to GDP

	1890	1913	1950	1973	1987
Germany			3.55	3.60	4.43
Japan			2.82	2.26	3.41
UK			1.90	2.51	2.89
US			3.69	3.39	3.62

(b) Ratio of gross residential capital stock to GDP
(% of total fixed capital in italics)

	1890	1913	1950	1973	1987
Germany			1.48	1.21	1.44
			42%	34%	33%
Japan			1.02	0.53	0.64
			36%	23%	19%
UK			0.80	0.78	0.87
			42%	31%	30%
US			1.43	1.32	1.32
			39%	39%	36%

(c) Ratio of gross non-residential capital stock to GDP
(% of total fixed capital in italics)

	1890	1913	1950	1973	1987
Germany	2.29	2.25	2.07	2.39	2.99
			58%	66%	67%
Japan	0.91	1.01	1.80	1.73	2.77
			64%	77%	81%
UK	0.95	1.03	1.10	1.73	2.02
			50%	69%	70%
US	2.09	2.91	2.26	2.07	2.30
			61%	61%	64%

Table 12.1

was more or less the same as in 1950. Given that, in 1950, fixed capital stock in the US was significantly larger than in the other economies, this suggests that less developed countries may accumulate capital faster than more advanced ones. The idea that less developed economies tend to catch up with more developed ones will be discussed in detail in Chapter 14. From Table 12.1 (on the previous page) we also learn that in all of the countries considered the relative importance of residential capital stock has been decreasing. In 1987, non-residential capital stock accounted for at least two-thirds of total fixed capital.

Note that fixed capital excludes business inventories (which are not part of 'fixed' capital), and consumer durables other than homes. The sum of these durables and the standard measure of fixed capital provides a broader measure of fixed capital.

Changes in the capital stock correspond to fixed investment expenditures by firms, households, and the government. Figure 12.1 shows, for the G-6 countries, the average values of the various categories of real fixed investment, expressed as ratios to real GNP, for the period between 1970 and 1992. The investment numbers refer to actual expenditures (called gross investment) and do not adjust for estimated depreciation of capital stocks. An allowance for the usual estimates of depreciation would not disturb the general nature of the time patterns shown in Figure 12.1.

The behaviour of investment will be a particular concern in our study of business fluctuations. To this end, it is important to distinguish between **private investment** and **public investment**. The decision process underlying these two types of investment is very different. In particular, changes in public investment are often driven by political considerations and thus elude simple macroeconomic principles. In our theoretical discussion of investment, we will concentrate on understanding the determination of private investment. Neglecting public investment, however, is not very important for our study of the macroeconomy. As we will show in the next section, in fact, during the business cycle the movements in private investment are, by far,

more important than those of public investment. Figure 12.1 distinguishes between private and public investment for three G-6 countries – Japan, the UK, and the US. We notice how public investment is much less important in the US than in Japan and the UK. The ratio to GDP of public investment averaged, from 1970 to 1992, 8.3% in Japan, 5.9% in the UK and only 2.3% in the US. Although we do not have exact figures, it is reasonable to assume that in the other three European G-6 the relative importance of public investment is close to that of Japan and the UK. The smaller scale of the involvement of government in the economy is an important difference between the US and the other advanced economies.

For the broader category of fixed investment, which includes purchases of consumer durables and public investment, the ratio to GDP averaged between 25.0% and 34.0% in the G-6. Notice that for Germany this ratio is lower (21.5%) because consumer durables are not included. In the other countries, consumer durables ranged between 3.5% and 7.8% of GDP. In the three countries for which we can calculate the private fixed investment the ratio to GDP averaged between 21% and 26%. Consistently with our discussion of capital stock in Table 12.1, we see from Figure 12.1 that the size of residential investment is between a third and one-half of non-residential investment. The average ratio of private non-residential fixed investment was 16.1% in Japan, 11.3% in the UK, and 10.9% in the US.

These ratios are, however, not constant over time. One crucial aspect of investment is that it displays large movements over the business cycle. Compare, for example, the level of investment in 1975, a year of economic recession, with that of 1989, a year of economic expansion. In 1975, private non-residential fixed investment was 14.4% of GDP in Japan, 9.1% in the UK and 9.8% in the US. In contrast, in 1989, these ratios were 20.1% in Japan, 16.2 in the UK and 11.1% in the US.

Business's investment spending also includes additions to stocks of goods held as inventories of finished product or of goods-in-process. This inventory accumulation can be either positive or

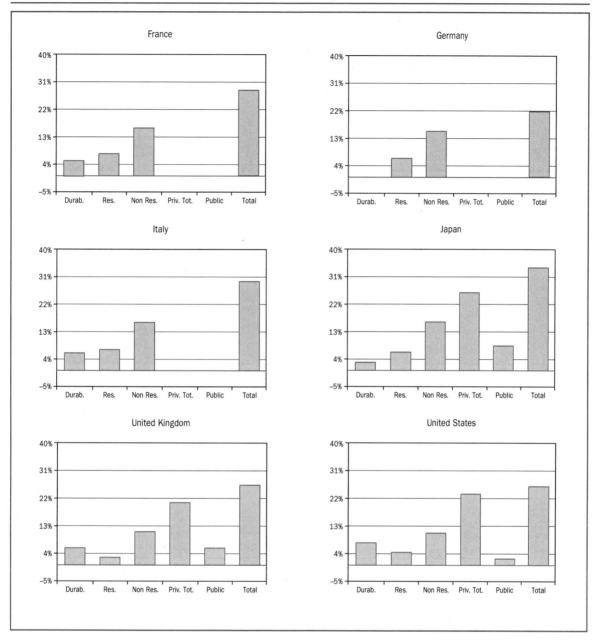

Figure 12.1   Ratios of fixed investment to GNP in the G-6 (%) (average 1970–92)

Note:
Total investment is the sum of durables, private and public investment.
For France, Germany and Italy, residential and non residential investment include both private and public investment.
For Japan, the UK and the US, instead, they refer only to private investment.
Notice that, due to lack of data, Germany's total investment does not include consumer durables.
Source: Datastream.

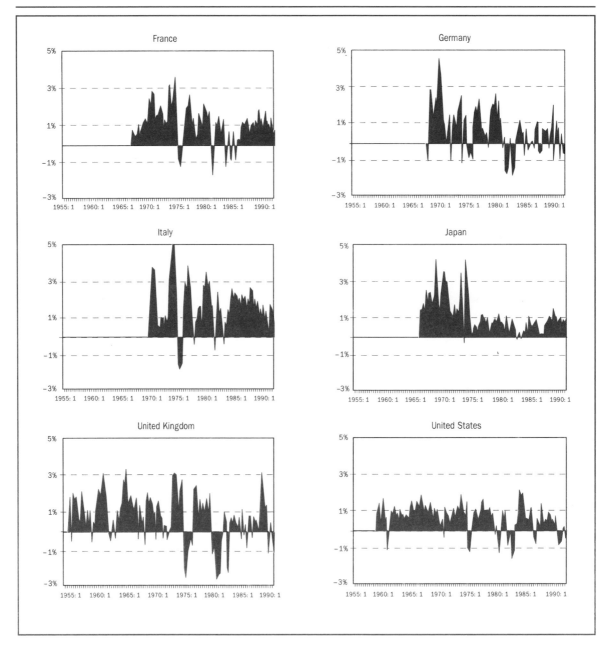

Figure 12.2 Inventory investment as a ratio to GNP in the G-6

Source: Datastream.

negative. Figure 12.2 shows the ratio of business's real inventory investment to real GNP for the G-6 countries. This ratio is extremely volatile, and, as with fixed investment, the low points tend to pick out the recessions. With the exception of Japan, for example, real inventory investment was negative in the recession of 1975, and they were large and positive in 1989.

Real GNP and its Components during Recessions

In this section we explore the behaviour of real GNP, and especially of its investment components, during economic downturns. If we examined times of economic upturn, then we would reach similar conclusions, except that all signs would be reversed.

We already stressed in Chapter 1 that the investment components of GNP are volatile and strongly procyclical. Table 12.2 highlights the role of investment during the recession of 1975 in the G-6 countries. We choose 1975 for convenience, since in that year all the G-6 countries experienced an economic downturn. The results would have been similar if we had analyzed other recessions. The data in the table use the analysis from Chapter 1 of the detrended values for the various components of real GNP.

Consider, for example, the behaviour of economic aggregates in Italy. Real GNP in the third quarter of 1975 was 3.7% below trend. The overall shortfall in real GNP can be allocated 20% to consumption of non-durables and services, 16% to consumer durables, 20% to total fixed investment, 69% to changes in business inventories, 0% to government purchases, and −25% to net exports. These allocations are based on the estimated cyclical components for the various parts of real GNP. If we aggregate the investment items – gross fixed investment plus changes in business inventories

	France	Germany	Italy	Japan	UK	US	G-6
Trough of recession	1975:3	1975:2	1975:3	1975:1	1975:3	1975:1	(average)
Shortfall of real GDP as % of Trend	−2.3%	−4.3%	−3.7%	−3.1%	−3.4%	−4.5%	−3.5%
% shortfall in real GDP accounted for by:							
1. Personal consumption	21%	17%	36%	5%	23%	47%	25%
1.a durables	13%		16%	11%	6%	20%	13%
1.b non-durables	8%		20%	−6%	17%	28%	13%
2. Private fixed investment				53%	13%	44%	37%
2.1a residential				41%	9%	30%	27%
2.1b non-residential				12%	4%	14%	10%
3. Public fixed investment				22%	−5%	−3%	5%
4. Total fixed investments (2 + 3)	49%	51%	20%	75%	8%	42%	41%
2.a residential	9%	35%	−4%	41%	9%		18%
2.b non-residential	39%	16%	25%	34%	−2%		23%
5. Change in inventories	88%	30%	69%	29%	40%	33%	48%
6. Government purchases of goods and services	2%	−4%	−0%	0%	−5%	0%	−1%
7. Net export	−58%	5%	−25%	−9%	34%	−22%	−12%
Summary							
Total investment (1.a + 4 + 5)	150%	81%	106%	115%	54%	97%	101%
Total private investment (1.a + 2 + 5)				93%	59%	97%	83
Total government (3 + 6)	2%	−4%	−0%	22%	−10%	−2%	1%
Ratio of trade balance to permanent GDP	−0.8%	−0.3%	−1.7%	−4.0%	0.0%	0.7%	−1.0%

Table 12.2 Behaviour of economic aggregates during the recession of 1975

plus purchases of consumer durables – then we account for 106% of the total shortfall in real GNP. Therefore, the movements in investment represent the bulk of the reduction in GDP.

The breakdown of the GNP shortfall among the various components in Italy conforms closely to the pattern for the other five countries.[1] The key findings, which apply to the average of the 1975 recession in the G-6 countries, are the following:

- Broadly defined investment accounts for the bulk of the fluctuations in real GNP, 101% on average. The large majority of these fluctuations are due to movements in private investment, 83% on average. Thus, as a first approximation, explaining recessions amounts to explaining the sharp contractions in the private investment components.
- Consumer spending on non-durables and services is relatively stable and accounts on average for only 13% of the shortfall of real GNP.
- Government purchases are not systematically related to recessions.
- Net exports are weakly countercyclical and account on average for –12% of the shortfall in real GNP (that is, the ratio of net exports to GNP is usually a little above trend during recessions).

We focus in this chapter on the behaviour of investment and consumption. We shall discuss government purchases in Chapter 15.

Capital in the Production Function

We now begin to incorporate capital into the theoretical model. To keep things manageable, imagine that there is a single type of capital, which we can measure in physical units – for example, as a number of standard machines. Denote by k_{t-1} the quantity of capital that a producer has at the end of period $t - 1$. Because it takes time to make new capital operational, we assume that the stock from period $t - 1$ is

available for use in production during period t. In other words, it takes one period for newly acquired capital to come on line.

The production function is now

$$y_t = f(k_{t-1}, \ \ell_t) \qquad (12.1)$$
$$(+) \ \ (+)$$

where the variable, k_{t-1}, is capital input and the variable, ℓ_t, is labour input. In the real world there are variations in the **utilization rate** of capital. By the utilization rate we mean the fraction of total time that a piece of capital is used. A factory may operate, for example, for one shift per day or two or could be open or closed on weekends. We neglect these changes in utilization for the production function shown in equation (12.1). Here, we can think of the quantity of capital, k_{t-1}, as always operating for one standard-length shift per day.

The plus signs under the two inputs in equation (12.1) signify that each is productive at the margin. That is, an increase in either input, with the other held fixed, leads to more output. Remember that the marginal product of labour for period t, MPL_t, is the effect on output, y_t, from an extra unit of work, ℓ_t. Note that we hold fixed the quantity of capital, k_{t-1}, when we measure the marginal product of labour. We define the **marginal product of capital** in a parallel manner. This marginal product, MPK_{t-1}, is the response of output, y_t, when capital, k_{t-1}, increases by one unit, while the amount of work, ℓ_t, does not change. The dating on this marginal product shows that it relates to the quantity of capital, k_{t-1}, from the end of period $t - 1$. Because of the lag in making new capital operational, this marginal product refers to the effect on output for period t.

We have discussed the diminishing marginal productivity of labour. Labour marginal product, MPL_t, falls as the amount of work increases, at least if the quantity of capital does not change. Now we make a parallel assumption about the marginal product of capital. This marginal product, MPK_{t-1}, declines as the quantity of capital, k_{t-1}, increases, at least if the amount of labour does not change.

Figure 12.3 shows how output responds as a producer uses more capital with a fixed quantity of labour. The curve goes through the origin, that is, a producer gets no output if the capital stock is zero. The slope of the curve is the marginal product of capital, MPK_{t-1}. The slope is positive

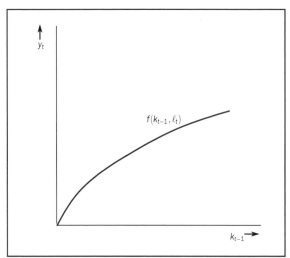

The graph shows the effect on output y_t from a change in capital input, k_{t-1}. Here, the quantity of labour input, ℓ_t, does not change.

Figure 12.3 Response of output to quantity of capital input

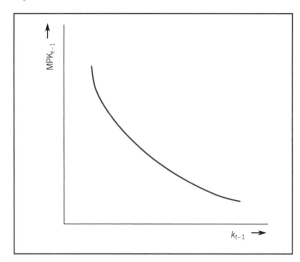

The graph shows that the marginal product of capital, MPK_{t-1} declines as the amount of capital, k_{t-1} increases.

Figure 12.4 Relation of the marginal product of capital to the quantity of capital

throughout but declines as the amount of capital increases. To stress this relationship, we show it explicitly in Figure 12.4.

Investment Goods and Consumer Goods

Investment is the purchase of capital goods – machines or buildings – from the commodity market. In the real world, most physical investment is carried out by businesses. But, as before, it is satisfactory not to distinguish firms from households. We can think of households in their role of producers as carrying out investment.

Capital goods generally differ physically from consumer goods. But to keep things simple, we assume that there is only one physical good that people produce and exchange on the commodity market. One household buys this good for consumption purposes, and another (perhaps a business) buys it to accumulate more capital – that is, for investment purposes.[2]

As before, producers sell all of their output, y_t, on the commodity market at the price P_t. Households or firms buy these goods either for consumption, c_t, or investment, which we denote by i_t. Therefore, if we think of households as doing the investment, a household's total demand for goods, y_t^d, equals the sum of consumption demand, c_t^d, and investment demand, i_t^d. Because all goods sell at the same price, suppliers do not care whether their goods are labelled as consumer goods or investment goods. We can therefore limit our attention to a producer's total supply of goods, y_t^s.

Depreciation

Capital goods do not last forever, but rather tend to depreciate – or wear out – over time. We model this process in a simple form, where the amount of depreciation during period t is a constant fraction of the stock of capital, k_{t-1}, that is carried over from period $t-1$ and used during period t. If d_t denotes the amount of depreciation in units of commodities, then

$$d_t = \delta k_{t-1} \qquad (12.2)$$

where δ (the Greek letter *delta*) is the constant rate of depreciation per period. To calculate the stock of capital, k_t, that is available for use in period $t+1$, we have to start with k_{t-1}, then add investment, i_t, and subtract depreciation, d_t:

$$k_t = k_{t-1} + i_t - \delta k_{t-1} \qquad (12.3)$$

Two concepts of investment are commonly used:

- Gross investment is the quantity of capital goods purchased, i_t.
- Net investment is the change in the capital stock, $k_t - k_{t-1}$, which equals gross investment, i_t, less the amount of depreciation, δk_{t-1}.

Correspondingly, there are two concepts of output:

- Gross product is the total amount produced, y_t.
- Net product equals gross product less depreciation, $y_t - \delta k_{t-1}$. That is, net product is the quantity of goods produced less the amount of capital goods worn out during the process of production.

Characteristics of Existing Capital

Remember that producers can call their output consumables or capital. But once a purchaser has put capital into place – for example, as a factory – it would be unrealistic to assume that these goods can be reclassified as consumables and then eaten up. Hence, we assume that the initial labelling choice as consumables or capital is irreversible: producers cannot consume their capital at a later date. They can, however, allow capital to depreciate and not replace it.

A second issue concerns the possibilities for moving capital goods from one production activity to another. Here we simplify the analysis by assuming that these movements are possible at negligible cost. This mobility of capital ensures that producers place all existing stocks in their most favourable use. Otherwise, someone could do better by shifting capital to another location. Recall also that we treat all units of capital as physically identical. Each unit must therefore end up with the same physical marginal product.

We shall sometimes find it convenient to think of resales of used capital. If a piece of capital has a low marginal product for one person, then he or she will find it advantageous to sell the capital to someone else. But since old and new capital are identical, the price of a unit of old capital during period t must equal that of new capital, which is P_t. We can therefore think of old capital goods as being sold along with new ones on the commodity market. Hence, we do not have to worry about a separate market for resales.

Investment Demand

Consider a producer's incentive to invest during period t. Recall that the stock of capital that will be available for production next period is the quantity

$$k_t = k_{t-1} + i_t - \delta k_{t-1}$$

At date t, the previous stock, k_{t-1}, and the amount of depreciation, δk_{t-1}, have already been determined by previous decisions. An increase by one unit in gross investment, i_t, therefore results in an increase by one unit in net investment, $i_t - \delta k_{t-1}$, and in the stock of capital, k_t. Hence, each producer decides how much to invest during period t by weighing the cost of this investment against the return from having more capital, k_t.

To raise investment by one unit, a producer must purchase an additional unit of goods from the commodity market at the price P_t. Hence, P_t is the nominal cost of an extra unit of investment.

There are two components of the return to investment. First, an additional unit of investment raises capital, k_t, by one unit. If we hold fixed the quantity of work for the next period, ℓ_{t+1}, then next period's output, y_{t+1}, rises by the marginal product of capital, MPK_t. Since producers sell this output at the price $P_t + 1$, the additional nominal sales revenue is $P_{t+1} \cdot \mathrm{MPK}_t$.

Remember that the fraction, δ, of each unit of capital disappears after one period because of depreciation. The remaining fraction, $1 - \delta$, is still around. We can simplify the analysis by pretending that producers sell their old capital on the commodity market at date $t + 1$. (If they like, they can 'buy back' this capital during period $t + 1$ to use for production at date $t + 2$.) Since goods sell at price P_{t+1} during period $t + 1$, the nominal revenue from the sale of used capital is $(1 - \delta)P_{t+1}$. Hence, this term is the second part of the return to investment.

Overall, an additional unit of investment costs P_t during period t and yields the amount $P_{t+1}(\text{MPK}_t + 1 - \delta)$ in period $t + 1$. The net nominal return on the investment is therefore $P_{t+1}(\text{MPK}_t + 1 - \delta) - P_t$. The ratio of this return to the nominal amount invested, P_t, determines the nominal rate of return to investment:

$$[P_{t+1}(\text{MPK}_t + 1 - \delta) - P_t]/P_t$$
$$= (1 + \pi_t)(\text{MPK}_t + 1 - \delta) - 1$$

where $P_{t+1} = (1 + \pi_t)P_t$ and π_t is the inflation rate for period t. The nominal rate of return from investment looks good or bad depending on how it relates to other returns. Specifically, households can earn the nominal interest rate, R_t, on bonds, or pay the rate R_t on debts to finance investment. If the nominal rate of return from investment exceeds R_t, then it pays to raise investment – that is, to buy more capital goods. But as the capital stock rises, diminishing marginal productivity implies that capital's marginal product, MPK_t, falls. This decline in the marginal product eventually reduces the nominal rate of return to investment enough to equal R_t. Producers then have no further incentive to expand investment.

Algebraically, investors act to satisfy the condition

$$(1 + \pi_t)(\text{MPK}_t + 1 - \delta) - 1 = R_t$$

where the left side is the nominal rate of return from investment. Recall, however, that the real rate of return on bonds, r_t, satisfies the relation $(1 + r_t) = (1 + R_t)/(1 + \pi_t)$. Using this condition, we can simplify the above result to the form

$$\text{MPK}_t - \delta = r_t \qquad (12.4)$$

The left side of equation (12.4) is the **real rate of return from investment** – the gross return, MPK_t, less the rate of depreciation, δ. Investors act to equate this return to the real rate of return on bonds, r_t. Any difference between these two rates makes it profitable to select either a higher or lower amount of investment. The amount of investment that households or firms choose therefore generates a marginal product, MPK_t, that equates the two real rates of return.

Figure 12.5 shows the results graphically. As the quantity of capital k_t rises, the marginal product MPK_t declines, as shown in the upper curve in the figure. The real rate of return from investment is the amount, $\text{MPK}_t - \delta$, shown by the lower curve in the figure. A producer chooses the quantity of capital, denoted by $\hat{k}_t$, at which the real rate of return from investment, $\text{MPK}_t - \delta$, equals the real interest rate, r_t.

Given the schedule for capital's marginal product, the **desired stock of capital**, $\hat{k}_t$, depends on the real interest rate, r_t, and the depreciation rate, δ. Hence, we can write the desired stock of capital as the function

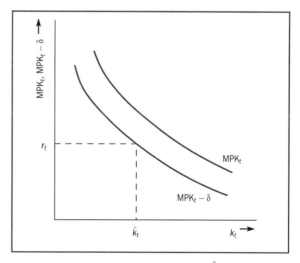

Producers aim for the quantity of capital $\hat{k}_t$ where the real rate of return from investment, $\text{MPK}_t - \delta$, equals the real interest rate on bonds, r_t.

Figure 12.5 Choice of capital stock

$$\hat{k}_t = \hat{k}(r_t, \quad \delta, \ldots) \qquad (12.5)$$
$$\quad\;\; (-)\,(-)$$

The expression ... represents the characteristics of the production function that affect the schedule for capital's marginal product. Note that an increase in r_t or δ means that the marginal product of capital, MPK_t, must be higher in equation (12.4). Therefore, for a given schedule of capital's marginal product, the desired stock of capital declines.

For given values of the real interest rate and the rate of depreciation, an upward shift in the schedule for capital's marginal product raises the desired stock of capital. We can show this result graphically by shifting the two curves upward in Figure 12.5.

Once we know the desired stock of capital, $\hat{k}_t$, we know also the choice of gross investment, i_t. Specifically, to attain the stock $\hat{k}_t$, a producer demands for investment purposes the quantity of goods i_t^d, where

$$i_t^d = \hat{k}_t - (1 - \delta)k_{t-1}$$

For given values of the starting capital stock, k_{t-1}, and depreciation, δk_{t-1}, gross **investment demand** varies one-to-one with changes in the desired stock of capital, $\hat{k}_t$. We can therefore use equation (12.5) to write out a function for gross investment demand as

$$i_t^d = \hat{k}(r_t, \quad \delta, \ldots) - (1 - \delta)k_{t-1}$$
$$\quad\;\; (-)\,(-)$$
$$= i^d(r_t, \quad \delta, k_{t-1} \ldots) \qquad (12.6)$$
$$\quad\;\; (-)\,(?)\,(-)$$

The implied amount of net investment demand is

$$i_t^d - \delta k_{t-1} = \hat{k}(r_t, \quad \delta, \ldots) - k_{t-1} \qquad (12.7)$$
$$\qquad\qquad\quad (-)\,(-)$$

Properties of Investment Demand

The main implications of the analysis for investment demand are the following:

- A reduction in the real interest rate, r_t, raises the desired stock of capital, $\hat{k}_t$, and investment demand.
- An upward shift in the schedule for capital's marginal product, MPK_t, raises the desired stock of capital, $\hat{k}_t$, and investment demand.
- Other things equal, investment demand declines if the previous stock of capital, k_{t-1}, rises. The phrase, 'other things equal', includes the various determinants of the desired stock of capital, $\hat{k}_t$.
- An increase in the rate of depreciation, δ, lowers the desired stock of capital, $\hat{k}_t$. Net investment demand, $\hat{k}_t - k_{t-1}$, therefore declines. Gross investment demand equals $\hat{k}_t - (1 - \delta)k_{t-1}$. Because δ rises and $\hat{k}_t$ falls, the overall effect on gross investment demand is ambiguous.
- Gross investment demand is positive if the desired stock, $\hat{k}_t$, exceeds the fraction, $1-\delta$, of the initial stock, k_{t-1}. For an individual, negative gross investment means that the sales of old capital goods exceed the purchases of new ones. We assumed before that capital goods cannot be converted back into consumables; that is, we assumed **irreversible investment.**[3] One person's negative gross investment (net sales of capital goods) must therefore correspond to someone else's positive gross investment: when we aggregate over all producers, gross investment, I_t, cannot be negative. To put this result another way, the aggregate stock of capital, K_t, cannot fall below the initial stock, K_{t-1}, by more than the amount of depreciation, δK_{t-1}. Correspondingly, aggregate net investment, $K_t - K_{t-1} = I_t - \delta K_{t-1}$, can be negative only up to the amount of depreciation, δK_{t-1}.

As shown in Table 12.1, there are periods in which, in some countries, the capital stock has declined. At these times, private net investment was negative. Our interpretation is that the aggregate desired stock of capital, $\hat{K}_t$, fell below the initial stock, K_{t-1}, during these years.

Quantitative Effects on Investment Demand
Data on net investment are not readily available due to the difficulty in computing capital

depreciation. For example, in the US fixed net investment (exclusive of purchases of consumer durables) has been estimated to be on average about 4% of the capital stock, K_{t-1}. Suppose that a change in the real interest rate, r_t, or in the schedule for capital's marginal product, MPK_t, lowers the desired stock of capital, $\hat{K}_t$, by 1%. The aggregate of net investment demand – over a period of, say, a year – would then decline by about 1% of the capital stock. If net investment demand were initially equal to 4% of the capital stock, then this change lowers it to 3% of the stock. Thus, a decline by 1% in the desired stock of capital translates into a fall by roughly 25% in net investment demand. Because one year's net investment is a small fraction – on the average about 4% – of the existing capital stock, small percentage changes in the desired stock generate large percentage changes in net investment

demand. We should therefore not be surprised by two features of the data that we noticed before. First, because net investment demand is volatile, the fluctuations of investment can account for a large share of the cyclical movements of real GNP. Second, the desired stock of capital is sometimes low enough – namely during deep recessions – for aggregate net investment to be negative.

Investment and Households' Budget Constraints

Remember that we can think of households, in their role as producers, as carrying out investment expenditures. To simplify the analysis, we consider first the case of a closed economy,

---

Box 12.1   Absence of a Resale Market

We determined the choice of investment by pretending that producers resold the undepreciated portion of their capital, $(1 - \delta)k_{t-1}$, on the commodity market during period t. Then, if they desired, producers bought back investment goods in period $t + 1$, resold them in period $t + 2$, and so on. By pretending that producers resold their old capital, we can easily calculate the rate of return to investment over one period. But this device is artificial. Typically, a firm or household keeps a piece of capital for many years. The sale of used capital goods is unusual for most types of producers' equipment and structures, although it is common for residences and automobiles.

In most cases our analysis of investment goes through even if resales are impossible. In the previous setup, a producer resold the quantity of capital, $(1 - \delta)k_{t-1}$, during period t, and then bought back the desired stock, $\hat{k}_t$. The difference between purchases and sales is $\hat{k}_t - (1 - \delta)k_{t-1}$, which equals gross investment demand, i_t^d. If we consider producers who always have positive gross investment

demand, then the potential for resale is irrelevant: someone with positive gross investment does not have to resell any capital. The producer just keeps the existing capital, and then buys new goods in the amount i_t^d. In this case, there are no changes if we eliminate the possibility for resale.[4] Remember that gross investment demand, i_t^d, equals net investment demand, $\hat{k}_t - k_{t-1}$, plus depreciation, δk_{t-1}. Therefore, for the previous results to hold, we do not need net investment demand to be positive for the typical producer. We need only to rule out net investment demand being so negative that it outweighs the positive amount of depreciation, δk_{t-1}.

For subsequent purposes, we assume that the previous analysis of investment demand is satisfactory. This analysis goes through if we allow resale of capital or if gross investment demand is always positive for every producer. But, of course, we shall also do okay as an approximation if – as seems plausible – gross investment demand is positive at most times for most producers.

Box 12.2 Gradual Adjustment of Investment Demand

The analysis assumes that producers purchase enough goods in a single period – which might be a year – to attain their desired stock of capital. That is, firms or households invest enough to close the gap between the capital carried over from the previous period, $(1 - \delta)k_{t-1}$, and the desired stock, $\hat{k}_t$.

We have ignored a variety of costs that arise when producers instal new capital goods. To place new plant and equipment into operation, a business normally goes through a phase of planning and decision-making, then a time of building and delivery, and finally an interval in which managers and workers familiarize themselves with the new facilities. Producers can speed up parts of this process but only by incurring extra costs. As examples, quicker decisions mean more mistakes, and faster service requires larger payments to workers and suppliers.

The costs for adjusting the levels of capital imply two types of lags in the investment process. First, a gap between the starting stock of capital, $(1 - \delta)k_{t-1}$, and the desired level, $\hat{k}_t$, stimulates higher investment over an extended interval. That is, since it takes time to build and instal new plant and equipment, investors stretch out their purchases of new capital goods over an interval of time. Second, the higher capacity for production becomes available only after the investment project is completed. (We capture some of this element by assuming that this period's capital stock affects production for the next period.)

Although adjustment costs for investment are quantitatively important, we continue to ignore these costs as a simplification.[5] The main features of the analysis would not change if we brought in these complications.

postponing the extension to an open economy to later in the chapter. When we include investment as another use of funds in a household's budget constraint, we get the condition

$$P_t y_t + b_{t-1}(1 + R) + m_{t-1} + v_t$$
$$= P_t c_t + P_t i_t + b_t + m_t \qquad (12.8)$$

As before, the left side shows the sources of funds, and the right side shows the uses. The new term is the expenditure for investment, $P_t i_t$, on the right side.

We have defined saving to be the change in the value of a household's assets, which could be held as bonds or money. In the presence of inflation, we have to distinguish the change in the real value of assets from the change in the nominal value: households would care about how the *real* value of their assets varies over time. We should define **real saving** accordingly to be the change in the real value of assets, the change in real bond holdings plus the change in real money balances.

(**Nominal saving** can then be calculated by multiplying real saving by the price level.)

Aside from bonds and money, households now have another store of value – physical capital goods. (Remember that the households own the capital goods.) A household's total real saving is therefore the change in the real value of bonds and money plus the change in the quantity of capital:

$$\text{Real saving} = (b_t + m_t)/P_t$$
$$- (b_{t-1} + m_{t-1})/P_{t-1}$$
$$+ k_t - k_{t-1} \qquad (12.9)$$

The last term in equation (12.9) is net investment. Hence, net investment is one component of real saving.

One way for a household to finance more net investment, $k_t - k_{t-1}$, is to raise real saving, which requires a cut in consumption or an increase in work effort (which would raise real income). But households can also finance investment by running down the real value of financial assets, bonds and money. A household (or business) can, for example, borrow to pay for additional capital goods. (A firm might borrow to finance a factory or a household might borrow to purchase a new home.) Hence, a household's or firm's decision to raise investment does not require a corresponding increase in that household's or firm's real saving.

From the standpoint of a single household or firm, the forces that influence net investment and real saving are different. Net investment demand expands, for example, with a fall in the real interest rate or an upward shift in the schedule for capital's marginal product. In contrast, a household's real saving increases when income is temporarily high or when the real interest rate rises.

If it were impossible to borrow and lend, then equation (12.9) would require each household's or firm's net investment to be financed only by that household's or firm's real saving. Producers could then exploit attractive investment opportunities only if they were willing to abstain from current consumption or leisure. The potential for running down financial assets or borrowing means that producers can undertake investments even if they are personally unwilling to save very much. In particular, the opportunities to borrow and lend ensure that all investment projects will be undertaken if the real rate of return to investment is at least as great as the real interest rate, r_t. Hence, the separation of individual decisions to invest from individual decisions to save promotes economic efficiency.[6]

What is the economy's aggregate of real saving? Since the total stock of bonds, B_t, in a closed economy is zero in each period, we find from equation (12.9) that

$$\text{Aggregate Real Saving} = M_t/P_t$$
$$- M_{t-1}/P_{t-1}$$
$$+ K_t - K_{t-1} \quad (12.10)$$

Let's ignore the part of aggregate real saving that consists of changes in aggregate real money balances, a part of real saving that is typically small in relation to aggregate net investment. Then equation (12.10) says that aggregate real saving equals aggregate net investment, $K_t - K_{t-1}$. Recall that individuals can invest by running down bonds or borrowing. But then others must be expanding their holdings of bonds – that is, lending. So, in a closed economy, greater net investment does require greater aggregate real saving.

We did not allow in previous chapters for investment. Then, if we neglected changes in aggregate real money balances, we found that aggregate real saving must be zero in a closed economy. Without investment, there is no way for a closed economy to save, that is, to change its real assets. But when the capital stock can vary, aggregate real saving can be non-zero: the economy can now adjust aggregate net investment to shift resources from one period to another. These possibilities for shifting resources over time were present before for an individual, who could borrow and lend on the credit market at the real interest rate, r_t. When we add a variable amount of capital stock to the analysis, the total economy has opportunities for real saving that resemble those available to individuals on the credit market. These opportunities have important consequences for the analysis of market-clearing conditions.

Clearing of the Commodity Market in a Closed Economy

There are still two aggregate-consistency conditions to satisfy: first, that the aggregate demand for commodities equal the supply and, second, that all money be willingly held. Because investment has major implications for the first condition but not the second, we focus on the condition for clearing the commodity market.

Clearing of the commodity market requires the aggregate supply of goods to equal the demand:

$$Y^s(r_t, \ldots) = C^d(r_t, \ldots) + I^d(r_t, \ldots) \quad (12.11)$$
$$(+) \qquad\quad (-) \qquad\quad (-)$$

The left side of the equation shows the positive intertemporal-substitution effect from the real interest rate, r_t, on the aggregate supply of goods, Y_t^s. This response reflects the positive effect on work effort, L_t. The omitted terms in the function, denoted by ..., include various characteristics of the production function, as well as the quantity of capital from the previous period, K_{t-1}.

The right side of equation (12.11) contains the two components of aggregate demand, consumption and gross investment. The real interest rate, r_t, has negative effects on consumer demand, C_t^d, and gross investment demand, I_t^d. The omitted terms include the characteristics of the production function, as well as the quantity of capital, K_{t-1}, and the depreciation rate, δ.

In Chapter 14, which considers long-term economic growth, it will be important to keep track of how the aggregate capital stock changes over time. Then we have to detail the role of the capital stock, K_{t-1}, in the market-clearing condition from equation (12.11). But for now we assume a given value of this stock. That is, we carry out a short-run analysis in which changes in the stock of capital are small enough to neglect.

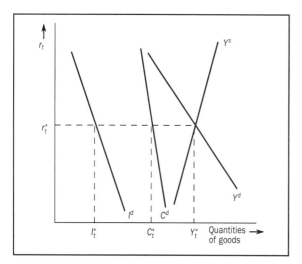

The commodity market clears at the real interest rate, r_t^*. Here, the total output, Y_t^*, breaks down into C_t^* of consumption and I_t^* of gross investment.

Figure 12.6　Clearing of the commodity market

This setting is adequate to study the main role of investment during business fluctuations.

Figure 12.6, which follows the approach developed in Chapter 5, graphs the aggregates of commodities supplied and demanded against the real interest rate, r_t. As before, the supply curve, Y^s, slopes upward, and the demand curve, Y^d, slopes downward. The figure breaks down aggregate demand into its two components, consumption demand, C^d, and gross investment demand, I^d. Each of these curves slopes downward versus r_t. We discussed before why investment demand would be especially sensitive to variations in the real interest rate. Therefore, the figure shows the I^d; curve with more of a negative slope than the C^d curve.

Figure 12.6 shows that the commodity market clears at the real interest rate r_t^*. Correspondingly, we label the level of output as Y_t^*. At this point, the uses of output break down between C_t^* of consumption and I_t^* of gross investment.

Real Business Cycles

We want to use the model that incorporates investment to see whether we can generate the key features of business fluctuations that we discussed in Chapter 1. We proceed by considering the types of supply shocks – shifts to the production function – that we examined in Chapter 5. The main question is whether these kinds of shocks will generate the cyclical patterns that appear in the data. If the answer is yes, then we will have to conclude that real business-cycle models – theories that rely on these types of disturbances – have considerable explanatory power.

We shall find it useful, as in Chapter 5, to distinguish temporary changes from permanent ones. Unlike in Chapter 5, however, we shall find it convenient to consider favourable shocks rather than unfavourable ones.

A Temporary Shift of the Production Function

Consider a temporary upward shift of the production function. To keep things simple, assume to begin with a parallel upward shift for period t. Then there are no changes in the schedules for the marginal products of labour, MPL_t, or capital, MPK_{t-1}. Also, we assume that there is no change in the schedule for the prospective marginal product of capital, MPK_t.

The improvement of the production function raises the aggregate supply of goods, Y_t^s, on the left side of equation (12.11). Wealth rises, but by only a small amount, because the increase in income is temporary. Consumer demand, C_t^d, therefore rises by a small amount, and work effort, L_t, falls by a small amount. This decrease in work offsets part of the increase in the supply of goods. Gross investment demand, I_t^d, does not shift because the schedule for capital's marginal product, MPK_t, has not changed.

Figure 12.7 shows the shifts to aggregate supply and demand. There is a rightward shift in supply and a smaller rightward shift in demand. In the figure the real interest rate labelled r_t^* is the one that cleared the market initially. At this real interest rate, the quantity of goods supplied now exceeds the quantity demanded: $Y_t^s > Y_t^d$. This excess supply arises because people react to the temporary abundance of production, and hence income, by raising their desired real saving. Thus, we can also say that the disturbance creates an excess of desired real saving over net investment demand.

The real interest rate must fall for the commodity market to clear: in Figure 12.7, the new market-clearing real interest rate, $(r_t^*)'$, is lower than the initial one, r_t^*. We can think of this decrease in the real interest rate as resulting from the excess of desired lending over desired borrowing.

Figure 12.7 shows that the new level of output, $(Y_t^*)'$, is above the initial amount, Y_t^*. This rise in output reflects partly an increase in consumption, $(C_t^*)' > C_t^*$, and partly a rise in gross investment, $(I_t^*)' > I_t^*$. (Since depreciation is fixed at the amount, δK_{t-1}, the change in net investment equals that in gross investment.) Note that the fall in the real interest rate raises consumption and investment demand. In addition, the increase in wealth reinforces the expansion of consumer demand. Finally, the lower real interest rate and

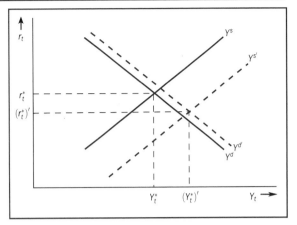

Figure 12.7 Effects of a temporary upward shift of the production function

the rise in wealth imply that the quantity of work effort, $(L_t^*)'$, falls short of the initial amount, L_t^*.

Consider the quantitative responses of consumption and work. Because the wealth effect is weak, the changes in consumption and work will be large only if there is a substantial decline in the real interest rate, r_t. Consider what happens, however, if investment demand is highly responsive to r_t. (We discussed before why this is likely.) In this case a small decrease in r_t is sufficient to equate desired real saving to net investment demand, that is, to clear the commodity market. Hence, most of the rise in output reflects an increase in investment, and there are only small changes in consumption and work.

An important conclusion is that fluctuations in investment partially insulate consumption from some types of temporary economic disturbances. When there is a temporary abundance of goods, everybody wants to save more or borrow less at the initial real interest rate. But if there are no possibilities for investment – the case that we considered in Chapter 5 – then it is infeasible for everyone to save more or borrow less. The real interest rate therefore falls enough to make the total of desired real saving equal zero. Households must then make substantial adjustments in their consumption and work. When we introduce investment, it becomes possible for aggregate real saving to change. By raising aggregate net investment, the economy does what each individual would like to do at a given real interest rate. In fact, if investment demand is highly sensitive to the real interest rate, as we anticipate, then the bulk of the rise in output shows up as increases in investment and real saving. In contrast, consumption changes relatively little.

Notice that the results imply that investment will absorb most of the short-term fluctuations in real GNP. This conclusion accords with the evidence from Table 12.2 that broadly-defined private investment accounts for 83% on average of the shortfall of real GNP during the 1975 recession in the G-6. The results also accord more generally with the observations from Chapter 1 that investment is highly volatile and strongly procyclical. Similarly, the theory is consistent with the finding that consumer spending on nondurables and services is procyclical, but is relatively stable and accounts on average for only a small fraction of the cyclical fluctuations in real GNP.

The Behaviour of Employment

One feature of the results that conflicts with the data is the behaviour of work effort. Labour input is procyclical and recessions are invariably accompanied by declines in employment and work-hours. But the analysis so far predicts that a temporary improvement to the production function leads to a small decrease in work.

Work effort falls in our example because we omitted a likely favourable effect of the disturbance on labour productivity. As mentioned in some earlier cases, an upward shift of the schedule for labour marginal product, MPL_t, usually accompanies a favourable shock to the production function. This change motivates people to raise work effort, L_t. In fact, because the improvement in productivity is temporary, there is an intertemporal-substitution effect, which reinforces the tendency for work to rise.

The increase in work effort implies additional rightward shifts to commodity supply and demand of the sort shown in Figure 12.7. Hence, there is a larger expansion of output. There is also a larger decrease in the real interest

rate and a correspondingly sharper increase in investment. The main new finding is the tendency for more work to accompany the rise in output. Labour input therefore tends to be procyclical as we found in Chapter 1.

The Cyclical Behaviour of the Real Interest Rate

We have found that a temporary improvement to the production function lowers the real interest rate. If we considered a temporary adverse shock, then we would find that the real interest rate would rise. Thus, the analysis predicts that the real interest rate would be countercyclical – low rates in good times and high rates in bad times. To see how this prediction matches up with empirical evidence, we now consider the G-6 countries' data on the cyclical behaviour of the real interest rate.

We argued, in Chapter 8, that the real interest rate that matters for decisions is the expected rate: the nominal interest rate observed directly less the inflation rate that people anticipate. We can measure this expected real interest rate by the interest rate on 3-month government bonds less an estimate of expected inflation for the corresponding three months. Our measure of expected inflation, available quarterly since 1960, is a statistical construct that represent the best forecast of inflation for each quarter that people could have generated, given the history of inflation observed up to the beginning of the quarter.[7] This measure does not differ greatly from the surveys of expected inflation that we discussed in Chapter 8.

In Table 12.3 we present the correlation coefficient between the cyclical component of GDP and the expected real interest rate.[8] The important observation for our purposes is that the expected real interest rate is countercyclical only in Italy and Japan. In France, Germany, the UK and the US the real interest rate is procyclical. However, in both cases, the correlation coefficients are small, between -0.30 and 0.28, indicating a weak cyclical pattern of real interest rates. The model, on the other hand, predicts that temporary shocks to the production function would generate a strongly countercyclical pattern of real interest rates. Therefore, we have to go further to fully reconcile the theory with the data.

France	0.14
Germany	0.30
Italy	−0.23
Japan	−0.03
UK	0.28
US	0.18

Correlation between detrended output and detrended real interest rate (quarterly data)

Table 12.3 Cyclicality of expected real interest rates, 1960–91

A Permanent Shift of the Production Function

One possible explanation for the lack of strong counter-cyclicality in the real interest rate is that we allowed for only temporary shifts to the production function, whereas several shifts that occur in practice tend to persist over time. For example, a discovery of a new product or an innovation to production techniques would have a persisting effect on the economy. To see how the duration of the shift affects the analysis, we now consider the polar case of a permanent upward shift of the production function. But start again with a parallel shift, which leaves unchanged the schedules for the various marginal products.

When the favourable shock is permanent, the wealth effects become important. There is a strong positive effect on consumer demand, C_t^d, and a strong negative effect on work effort, L_t. Recall from our discussion in Chapter 5 (Figure 5.7) that this type of permanent change to the production function exerts little net effect on desired real saving. Figure 12.8 shows accordingly that the rightward shift in demand equals that in supply. This result still holds if we include a permanent upward shift of the schedule for labour marginal product, although the curves shift by greater amounts.

The main point is that the supply of goods equals the demand at the initial real interest rate, r_t^*. (Equivalently, net investment demand still

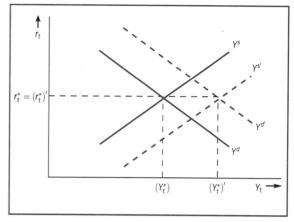

Figure 12.8 Effects of a permanent upward shift of the production function

equals desired real saving.) This analysis therefore predicts that the real interest rate will be acyclical. Therefore, combination of temporary and permanent shock can produce the weak cyclical behaviour revealed by Table 12.3.

Although the results for the real interest rate are better, the conclusions about investment and consumption are now unsatisfactory. Since the real interest rate does not change in Figure 12.8, investment stays at its initial value. All of the increase in output therefore reflects a rise in consumption. Thus, the model now predicts that investment would be acyclical, whereas consumption would be highly procyclical. As we know, this prediction conflicts dramatically with the data.

We cannot resolve the puzzle only by mixing the results from the temporary and permanent cases to allow for shocks to the production function that persist for awhile but not forever. As we move from the permanent to the temporary case, we enhance the procyclical response of investment and lessen the procyclical response of consumption – changes that achieve a better fit to the data. But we necessarily also introduce strongly countercyclical behaviour of the real interest rate, a pattern that conflicts with the facts. The key element in the gap between theory and data turns out not to be the permanence of the disturbance, but rather the invariance of the schedule for capital's marginal product. We therefore now consider the effects from changes in this marginal product.

Shifts to the Productivity of Capital

The previous examples dealt with disturbances that left unchanged the schedule for capital's marginal product, MPK_t. In these cases, there were no shifts to investment demand. Shocks to the production function tend, however, to shift the marginal products of the factor inputs and we have already shown how the changes in labour marginal product are crucial for generating the procyclical behaviour of labour input. We now allow also for the likely shifts to capital's marginal product and, hence, to investment demand.[9]

Assume now an upward shift to the schedule for capital's marginal product, MPK_t. Recall that this marginal product refers to the output for period $t+1$. To keep things simple, assume for the moment that no changes occur to the production function for period t. That is, we neglect the positive effects on the current supply of goods, Y_t^s, and the effects from increased wealth.

Recall that the condition for clearing the commodity market is (with time subscripts now omitted)

$$Y^s(r,\dots) = C^d(r,\dots) + I^d(r,\dots)$$
$$(+) \qquad\quad (-) \qquad (-)$$

Given our assumptions, the only effect from the disturbance is an increase in gross investment demand, I^d, on the right side of the equation. Figure 12.9 shows accordingly a rightward shift of the aggregate demand curve, Y^d, which reflects the rise in investment demand.

We see from the figure that the real interest rate and output increase. Note that the expansion of output reflects the positive effect of the higher real interest rate on work effort. The higher real interest rate leads also to a fall in consumption. Investment therefore rises by more than the increase in total output. Thus, this disturbance implies that the real interest rate, investment, and labour input would be procyclical, whereas

consumption would be countercyclical. Two problems with these predictions are, first, the real interest rate is not as strongly procyclical as this analysis would suggest, and second, consumption is procyclical. To match these facts we have to combine the analysis from Figure 12.9 with the previous discussion of effects from shifts in the production function.

Return now to the shocks to the production function that we considered in Figure 12.7 for a temporary change and in Figure 12.8 for a permanent change. These kinds of disturbances tend to be accompanied by the sort of upward shift to the schedule for capital's marginal product, MPK_t, that we considered in Figure 12.9. We can fit the various business-cycle facts that we have been discussing if we mix the results from Figures 12.7 and 12.8 – a case that applies if the disturbance persists for a while but not forever – and then also add the results from Figure 12.9. If we take the right mixture, then we get the following conclusions:

- The real interest rate can be either weakly procyclical or weakly countercyclical since positive shocks in the production function tend to shift the capital's marginal product so that the negative effect from the increase in desired real saving (Figure 12.7) is partially offset by the positive effect from the improvement in capital's productivity (Figure 12.9).

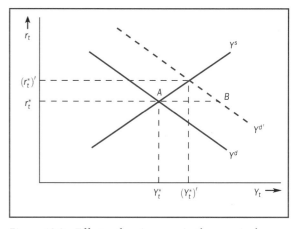

Figure 12.9   Effects of an increase in the marginal product of capital

- Investment is procyclical because of the direct effect from the shift to capital's productivity (Figure 12.9) and the reduction in the real interest rate. Because investment demand is highly sensitive to its determinants, including the marginal product of capital, the bulk of the fluctuations in output tend to show up in the investment component.
- Consumption is procyclical because of the positive effect from more wealth (Figure 12.8) and the lower real interest rate. Consumption can, however, account for only a small fraction of the overall movement in output: consumer demand responds little initially if the improvement to the production function is temporary (Figure 12.7), and the fall in the real interest rate is not large.
- Labour input is procyclical because the positive effects from labour enhanced productivity more than offset the small reduction in the real interest rate and the negative effect from more wealth.
- The real wage rate is procyclical, as discussed in Chapter 6, primarily because the improvement in labour productivity raises the demand for labour.

The main conclusion is that the model can account for all the features of business fluctuations that we have considered thus far. We now want to extend the analysis to account for international trade.

Saving and Investment in an Open Economy

In an open economy, domestic investment and changes in the aggregate amount of real money balances are not the only way in which the economy as a whole can save. As we have seen in Chapter 7, an economy can save by running current account surpluses. For an open economy, the budget constraint is

$$PY_t + R_{t-1}B^f_{t-1} = P(C_t + I_t) + (B^f_t - B^f_{t-1})$$
$$+ (H_t - H_{t-1}) \quad (12.12)$$

This relation extends equation (7.1) to allow for investment.

For a single economy in isolation (a closed economy), the gross domestic product, PY_t, must equal the total expenditure by domestic residents for goods and services, $P(C_t + I_t)$. As we have seen in Chapter 7, when we open the economy to the rest of the world, we introduce some new items, which can create a divergence between the gross domestic product and the total of domestic expenditures on goods and services. The left side of equation (12.12) includes the net factor income from abroad, $R_{t-1}B^f_{t-1}$ (which adds to GDP to get GNP). The right side includes net foreign investment, which equals the net acquisition of interest-bearing claims, $B^f_t - B^f_{t-1}$, plus the accumulation of international currency, $H_t - H_{t-1}$.

Domestic residents have a total income of $PY_t + R_{t-1}B_{-1}$ and a total expenditure on goods and services of $P(C_t + I_t)$. We have learned in Chapter 7 that the difference between income and expenditure corresponds to saving by domestic residents in the form of additional assets acquired from the rest of the world and is called the **current-account balance**. From equation (12.12) we get that the current-account balance is now given by

current-account balance
$$= PY_t + R_{t-1}B^f_{t-1} - P(C_t + I_t)$$
$$= S_t - PI_t \quad (12.13)$$

Thus, a country runs a surplus on current account – and thereby lends funds abroad – when its national saving exceeds its domestic investment. Equation (12.13) also says that national saving, S_t, ($PY_t + R_{t-1}B^f_{t-1} - PC_t$), can be used either for domestic investment, PI_t, or for net foreign investment, which equals the current-account balance.

Let us now reconsider the case of an increase in domestic investment demand, resulting from an upward shift to the marginal product of capital, MPK, as in Figure 12.9. If the disturbance applies only to the home country, and if the country is small with respect to the rest of the world, then it is appropriate to hold fixed the real interest rate at the world level, say r_t^*. At an unchanged real interest rate, there is no change in real GNP but an increase in real domestic expenditure. In this case, the home country borrows from abroad (runs a current-account deficit equal to the distance between points A and B) to finance its higher level of investment. The ability to borrow from foreigners means that a small country with a favourable investment opportunity can pay for the investment boom without having to raise current production (real GNP) and without having to curtail current consumption. Therefore, the effect on the domestic interest rate is reduced with respect to the closed economy case. This helps to explain the low cyclicality of real interest rates that we documented above.

The results differ if the disturbance applies globally rather than just to the home country. For example, suppose that some technical innovation leads to an increase in investment demand for all countries. Then the construction shown in Figure 12.9 applies to the world aggregates of supply and demand. In this case the real interest rate, r_t, rises to ensure balance between the world totals of real GNP and real expenditure on goods and services. For the world as a whole, it is not possible to finance an investment boom by borrowing from abroad. As in the case of a closed economy, the expansion of world investment must come from either an increase in production (the movement along the supply curve in Figure 12.9) or a decrease in consumption.

As another example, consider a developing country that has a high marginal product of capital. This type of country borrows abroad to finance large amounts of investment and thereby high growth rates of output. The potential to borrow abroad means that a developing country's level of consumption need not be depressed drastically during the period of high investment. A recent example of this behaviour is Brazil, which sustained an average growth rate of per capita real gross domestic product of about 5% per year from 1971 to 1980. Over this period, Brazil's gross external debt grew from $6 billion, or 11% of GDP, to $55 billion, or 22% of GDP.

For an earlier example of a rapidly developing country that borrowed heavily abroad, consider the United States. In 1890 the level of net foreign debt reached $2.9 billion, which amounted to 21% of GNP (see US Department of Commerce, 1975, p. 869). The United States was an international borrower for most years prior to 1890. Thus the situation of the United States in the late nineteenth century was roughly comparable to that of Brazil in the 1970s. Recall that borrowing from abroad reflects a shortfall of national saving, S, from domestic investment, I. For Brazil and the nineteenth-century United States, the borrowing reflected the high value of investment demand.

Summary

Investment fluctuates proportionately by much more than total output, which fluctuates by more than consumption. For a typical recession in the G-6 countries, the shortfall in total investment – gross fixed investment, changes in business inventories, and purchases of consumer durables – accounted on average for over 80% of the shortfall in real GNP. In contrast, consumer expenditures on nondurables and services declined relatively little during a recession.

We began the theoretical analysis of investment by introducing the stock of capital as an input into the production function. The marginal product of capital is positive but diminishes as the quantity of capital rises.

Gross investment is the quantity of capital goods that a producer buys from the commodity market. The total demand for goods is the sum of gross investment demand and consumption demand. The change in a producer's stock of capital – or net investment – equals gross investment less depreciation. In the aggregate, gross investment cannot be negative. Aggregate net investment, however, can be negative.

The real rate of return to investment is the marginal product of capital less the rate of depreciation. Producers determine their desired stocks of capital by equating this rate of return to the real interest rate. The desired stock of capital therefore rises if the real interest falls, if the schedule for capital's marginal product shifts

Box 12.3 The Relationship Between Saving and Investment in an Open Economy

Our discussion suggests that, in open economies, investment and saving can move independently from one another. An increase in domestic saving does not need to be matched by an increase in domestic investment, because domestic saving can be invested abroad. Similarly, a surge in domestic investment can be financed by foreign capital, and thus does not require an increase in domestic saving.

These theoretical results prompted several empirical investigations on the cross-country relationship between saving and investment. The first and most cited of these studies is by Martin Feldstein and Charles Horioka (1980). They argued that, if the mechanism described above were at work, then a country's level of investment should not be correlated with its level of saving. Contrary to this presumption, they found that saving and investment are highly positively correlated. They interpreted this result as evidence that international capital mobility is low and thus domestic saving is the most important determinant of domestic

investment. The essence of their result is described by Figure 12.10, which plots the ratio of domestic net investment to GDP against the ratio of domestic net saving to GDP for 18 developed countries. These ratios are averages for the period 1960 to 1986. The high correlation between saving and investment holds because most of the countries lie near to the 45° line, that is, the line that represents equality between saving and investment.

The inference that capital is not internationally mobile has, however, been criticized by several economists. The reason is that there are several scenarios in which saving and investment move together even under perfect international capital mobility. For example, if productivity shocks are positively correlated across countries, then it would be impossible for all countries to use international capital markets to finance their investment. In equilibrium, therefore, domestic investment will have to be close to domestic savings for each country. Moreover, if a country's net invest-

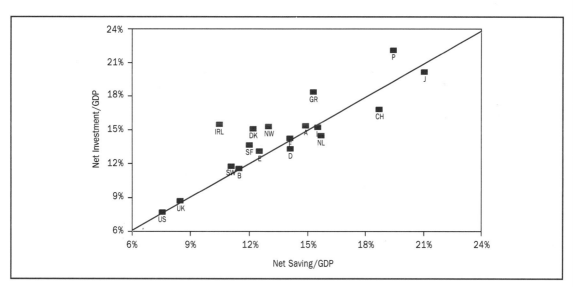

Source: Tesar (1991).

Figure 12.10   Net investment vs net saving (average 1960–86)

> ment is high because of a temporary favourable shock to its production function, then our theory predicts that the country's saving will be high at the same time (because of its temporary high income). In both cases the correlation between domestic saving and domestic investment would be high but this does not demonstrate that international capital markets are not working.

upward, or if the depreciation rate declines. Small percentage changes in the desired stock of capital translate into large percentage changes in net investment demand. This property explains why investment expenditure is volatile.

The existence of the credit market means that a household's or firm's decision to invest does not require that household or firm to save. The existence of investment therefore allows the whole economy to change its amount of real saving, even in the absence of international trade. In the presence of international capital mobility, there exist two ways in which the economy as a whole can save: by accumulating capital or by running a current account surplus. In an open economy, therefore, savings and investment do not need to be equal.

We modified the market-clearing analysis from Chapter 5 to include gross investment demand as a component of the aggregate demand for goods. We then used the modified framework to explore the effects from shocks to the production function. If we consider shocks that persist for a while but not forever and if we allow for shifts to the marginal products of labour and capital, then the model accords well with some observed features of business fluctuations. Specifically, the real interest rate is weakly countercyclical, investment is procyclical and accounts for the bulk of the fluctuations in output, consumption is procyclical but relatively stable, and labour input and the real wage rate are procyclical.

Important Terms and Concepts

physical capital
producers' durable equipment and structures
desired stock of capital
investment demand
irreversible investment
real saving
nominal saving
marginal product of capital (MPK)
real rate of return from investment
private fixed capital
inventories
human capital
utilization rate

Questions and Problems

Mainly for Review

12.1 What is meant by private domestic fixed investment? Does it include purchases of consumer durables? What about purchases of bonds?

12.2 Distinguish gross investment from net investment. When is net investment negative? Can gross investment be negative if capital goods cannot be resold?

12.3 Suppose producers expect inflation – that is, a higher price level in the next period. Will they want to increase their current purchases of capital goods? What if the nominal interest rate rises to reflect the higher expected inflation?

12.4 Does higher investment require higher saving on the part of an individual household or firm? For the economy as a whole, how do changes in the interest rate ensure that real saving rises to match an increase in investment?

12.5 Show graphically how the division of total output into consumption and investment is achieved through clearing of the commodity market. How does a temporary shift of the production function alter this division? Does your answer depend on the relative sensitivity of consumption demand and investment demand to changes in the interest rate?

12.6 Why does a decline in the productivity of capital reduce the interest rate? Could the interest rate fall so much as to leave the quantity of investment unchanged? Explain.

Problems for Discussion

12.7 The One-Sector Production Function
In our model, output can be labelled as either consumables or capital goods. Economists call this a one-sector production function.
  a. Why does the price of a unit of consumables always equal the price of a unit of capital in this model? What would happen if the price of consumables exceeded the price of capital goods, or vice versa?
  b. Suppose that everyone wants to undertake negative gross investment – that is, everyone wants to resell old capital on the commodity market. Can the price of capital goods fall below the price of consumables in this case?
  c. (optional) Consider a 'two-sector model', in which different production functions apply to consumables and capital goods. Would the price of a unit of consumables always equal the price of a unit of capital goods in this model?

12.8 Inventory Investment
Businesses hold inventories of goods, partly as finished products and partly as goods-in-process and raw materials. Suppose that we think of inventories as a type of capital, which enters into the production function. Then changes in these stocks represent investment in inventories. (Typically economists assume that the rate of depreciation on inventories is near zero.)
  a. How does an increase in the real interest rate affect the quantity of inventories that businesses want to hold? What happens therefore to inventory investment?
  b. Consider a temporary adverse shock to the production function. What happens to the amount of inventory investment? What do we predict therefore for the behaviour of inventory investment during recessions?

12.9 Investment Tax Subsidy
Suppose that some types of investments qualify for a government transfer. Assume that this governmental programme effectively refunds the fraction, *a*, of investment expenditures. How does the size of the refund percentage, *a*, influence producers' desired stocks of capital and, hence, their investment demand? (Assume that someone who resells capital has to return the investment credit on the amount sold.)

12.10 Capacity Utilization (optional)
One way for a producer to generate extra output is to use capital more intensively. That is, a producer can run more shifts per day or allow less down time for performing maintenance. Assume that more intensive utilization causes capital to depreciate faster.
  a. How does a producer determine the best intensity of use for capital?
  b. Show that an increase in the real interest rate, r_t, motivates producers to use their capital more intensively. What does this imply for the effect of the real interest rate on the supply of goods, y_t^s?

12.11 The Ownership of Capital (optional)
In our model, the people who use capital also own the capital. Suppose that these people print up certificates, each of which conveys ownership rights to one unit of capital. These certificates can be sold to others (on a stock market). But instead of using the capital themselves, the buyers of these certificates may allow other people ('businesses') to use the capital. Then the users pay a fee to holders of certificates. This fee may be either a fixed rental or a share of the profits.
  a. Why might it be a good idea to separate the ownership of capital from the use of that capital? (Remember that households or firms can already finance the purchase of capital by borrowing.) Why might it be a bad idea?
  b. What determines the nominal and real value of the ownership certificates if each is a claim to one unit of capital?
  c. In the real world why is the future real value of a certificate subject to great uncertainty? Specifically, why does the value depend on the fortunes of the company that issued it?

12.12 Investment Opportunities for Robinson Crusoe
In the market economy we found that investment takes the brunt of shocks to the production function. Suppose that we introduce opportunities for investment into the model of Robinson Crusoe, which we constructed in Chapter 2. How would Robinson Crusoe's investment and consumption respond to shocks to the production function? Are the results basically similar to those for the market economy?

Notes

1. Notice that the contribution of investment to the 1975 recession is smaller than usual in the UK. For example, in 1991, during the latest recession, the contribution of investment was above 100%.

2. This setup is called a *one-sector production technology*. This specification, which appears in most macroanalyses, has only one process that allows producers to use inputs to produce goods. Some economists use a *two-sector production model*. Then there is one process for producing consumer goods and another for capital goods. (There is, however, still only one physical type of capital and only one physical type of consumable.) For an example of a model with a two-sector production technology, see Duncan Foley and Miguel Sidrauski (1971, especially ch. 2).

3. If producers are uncertain about future conditions – such as the future state of technology – then the irreversiblility of investment becomes especially important. Basically, people are motivated to defer irreversible decisions, such as the initiation of investment projects, until the uncertainties are resolved. If the degree of uncertainty rises, then investment demand tends to fall. This element seems to underlie Keynes's (1935, ch. 22) belief that investment demand is volatile and therefore causes variability of aggregate economic activity. For a discussion of irreversible investment, see Ben Bernanke (1983a).

4. For a discussion of this issue and some related topics on investment, see Robert Hall (1977, especially pp. 71–4).

5. For discussions of adjustment costs in investment demand, see Robert Eisner and Robert Strotz (1963), Robert Lucas (1967) and S.J. Nickell (1978).

6. Irving Fisher (1930, especially chs, 7, 11) stresses this feature of a market economy.

7. The data are an updated version of the series reported in Robert Barro and Xavier Sala-i-Martin (1990).

8. The expected real interest rate was detrended following the same procedure used in Chapter 1.

9. John Maynard Keynes (1936, chs. 11, 12) stressed that shifts to investment demand, derived from changes in the perceived returns to investment, are a key element in business fluctuations.

13

Unemployment

We have shown that an adverse shock to the production function can lead to a decline in labour input that accompanies the fall in output. Thus, measures of labour input, such as employment and worker-hours, are procyclical.

We have not yet discussed **unemployment**, which is the number of people who are looking for work but have no job. The sum of unemployment and employment is the **labour force**. People who neither have a job nor are looking for one are classified as **outside of the labour force**, and the ratio of the number unemployed to the labour force is the **unemployment rate**. A key empirical regularity, already discussed in Chapter 1, is that the unemployment rate is countercyclical: the correlation between the detrended unemployment rate and detrended real GNP in the 18 developed countries considered is between -0.25 and -0.92 (see Figure 1.11). In this chapter, we want to explain why an adverse shock, which lowers output and employment, tends to raise the unemployment rate, and vice versa for favourable shocks.

In the labour market of Chapter 6, the wage rate adjusted to equate labour supply and demand. Hence, anyone who sought work at the going wage rate was able to get a job: unemployment was always zero, and employment equalled the labour force.

Whereas unemployment refers to unsuccessful job seekers, the term **vacancies** describes the number of jobs that firms have been unable to fill. In the model of Chapter 6, the wage rate adjusted so that firms were able to hire their desired number of workers. Hence, vacancies were always zero, and employment equalled the firms' demand for workers.

Although this model of the labour market can account for some of the fluctuations in employment (that is, the labour force) and worker-hours, it cannot explain why the quantities of unemployment and vacancies are non-zero. The model therefore cannot tell us why unemployment and vacancies change over time. Given these deficiencies, it is also likely that the model is not yet satisfactory for understanding all of the movements in production and labour input.

To explain unemployment and vacancies, we have to introduce some type of 'friction' into the workings of the labour market. Specifically, we have to explain why people without jobs take some time to find and accept employment. Similarly, we have to see why businesses with unoccupied positions take some time to fill them. Thus, the key to unemployment and vacancies is the process of workers searching for jobs and businesses searching for workers.

In our earlier discussion, we simplified matters by treating all workers and jobs as identical. In this context, the process of search among workers and firms would be trivial. Thus, to make the analysis meaningful, we have to allow for differences among workers and jobs. We can think, in fact, of the labour market as operating to find good matches between jobs and workers. Because jobs and workers differ, this matching process is difficult and time-consuming. Unemployment and vacancies arise as aspects of this process.

The next section develops a simple model of job matching. But before getting into the model, let's stress two important objectives. First, we want to explain why the levels of unemployment and vacancies are positive. Second, we want to see how these variables change over time and how they interact with the determination of production and labour input.

A Model of Job Finding

Consider a person who has just entered the labour force and is not yet employed – for example, a student who has just graduated from school and is seeking his or her first job or someone who is entering or reentering the labour force after raising a family. Suppose that this person searches for a position by visiting various firms. Each firm interviews job candidates to assess their likely qualifications for a position. As a result of each inspection, the firm estimates the value of the candidate's marginal product. To keep things simple, assume that the firm offers the person a job with a nominal wage, w, equal to this estimated value of marginal product. (We assume, only for simplicity, that the job entails a standard number of hours worked per week.)

The candidate must decide whether to accept an offer at the wage rate w. The alternative to taking a job is to remain unemployed and continue searching for another one.[1] More search pays off if a subsequent wage offer exceeds the initial one. The cost of turning down an offer is the wage income foregone while not working. This income foregone must, however, be measured net of any income that people receive because they are unemployed. This income includes **unemployment insurance**, which we shall discuss later, and any value attached to time spent unemployed (and searching for a job) rather than working.[2]

In evaluating an offer, the first thing to determine is how it compares with others that might be available. In making this comparison, a job seeker would have in mind a distribution of possible wages,[3] given the person's education, experience, locational preferences, and so on. Figure 13.1 shows a possible distribution of wage offers. For each value of wages on the horizontal axis, the height of the curve shows the relative chance or probability of receiving that wage offer. For the case shown, the offers usually fall in a middle range of values for w. There is, however, a small chance of getting either a very high wage offer (in the right tail of the distribution) or an offer near zero.

Figure 13.1 shows the value w^u, which is the effective wage received while unemployed. We know right away that a person would reject any offer that paid less than w^u. For the case shown in the figure, w^u lies toward the left end of the distribution of wage offers. This construction implies that most – but not all – wage offers would exceed w^u. Given the position of w^u, a job seeker's key decision is whether to accept a wage offer when $w > w^u$ applies.

As mentioned before, a person may refuse a wage that exceeds w^u to preserve the chance of getting a still better offer (see note 1). But there is a trade-off because the job seeker then foregoes the income, $w - w^u$, while not working. The balancing of these forces involves what economists call a **reservation wage** (or sometimes an acceptance wage), denoted by $\bar{w}$. Wage offers below $\bar{w}$ are refused, and those above $\bar{w}$ are accepted. If a person sets a high value of $\bar{w}$, then he or she will probably spend a long time (perhaps forever) unemployed and searching for an acceptable job. In contrast, a low value of $\bar{w}$ (but still greater than w^u) means that the expected time unemployed will be relatively brief. The expected wage received while employed is, however, lower the lower is $\bar{w}$.

The optimal value of $\bar{w}$ depends on the shape of the wage-offer distribution in Figure 13.1, as well as on the value of w^u and the expected duration of jobs.[4] For our purposes we do not have to go through the details of the calculation of the

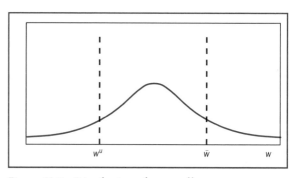

Figure 13.1   Distribution of wage offers

optimal $\bar{w}$. We can, however, note some properties that would come out of this calculation.

First, because some wage offers would generally be unacceptable – that is, $w < \bar{w}$ for some offers – it typically takes time for a job searcher to find an acceptable job. In the interim the person is 'unemployed' (although engaged in job search). Incomplete information about where to find the best job can therefore explain positive amounts of unemployment.

Second, an increase in the income while unemployed, w^u, motivates job seekers to raise their standards for job acceptance – that is, $\bar{w}$ increases. Given the distribution of wage offers in Figure 13.1, it becomes more likely that $w < \bar{w}$: hence, wage offers are more likely to be rejected. It follows that job searchers tend to take a longer time to find a job when w^u increases. For a group of workers, an increase in w^u therefore lowers the **job-finding rate** and raises the expected **duration of unemployment**.

Third, suppose that the whole distribution of job offers becomes better. A favourable shock to firms' production functions might mean, for example, that marginal products of labour were all 10% higher than before. This kind of shock therefore shifts the distribution of wage offers in Figure 13.1 to the right. (The height of the curve at the old wage w is now the height at the wage $1.1 \cdot w$.) For a given reservation wage, $\bar{w}$, wage offers are therefore more likely to be in the acceptable range, $w > \bar{w}$: hence, the job-finding rate rises, and the expected duration of unemployment falls.

A better distribution of wage offers also motivates people to raise their reservation wage $\bar{w}$. If the income obtained while unemployed, w^u, does not change, however, then the first effect tends to dominate.[5] A shift to a better distribution of wage offers – generated, for example, by a favourable shock to workers' productivity – raises the job-finding rate and lowers the expected duration of unemployment.

Search by Firms

Thus far, we have taken an unrealistic view of how firms would contribute to the job-search process. Firms received job applications, evaluated candidates in terms of likely marginal products, and then expressed wage offers.[6] This process does not allow firms to utilize the information that they have about the characteristics of their jobs, the traits of workers who are usually productive on these jobs, and the wages that typically have to be paid for such workers. Firms communicate this information by advertising job openings that specify ranges of requirements for education, experience, and so on, and also indicate a salary range. Such advertisements appropriately screen out most potential applicants and tend to generate more rapid and better matches of workers to jobs.

Although search by firms is important in a well-functioning labour market, the inclusion of this search leaves unaltered our major conclusions. In particular,

- It still takes time for workers to be matched with acceptable jobs, so that the expected durations of unemployment and vacancies are positive.
- An increase in workers' incomes while unemployed, w^u, lowers the job-finding rate and raises the anticipated duration of unemployment.
- A favourable shock to productivity raises the job-finding rate and reduces the expected duration of unemployment.

Job Separations

Workers search for jobs that offer high wages, relative to perceived opportunities elsewhere, and employers search for workers with high productivity, given the wages that must be paid. Although workers and firms evaluate their information as well as possible, they often find out later that they made mistakes. An employer may learn, for example, that a worker is less productive than anticipated, or a worker may discover that he or she dislikes the job (or boss). When a job match looks significantly poorer than it did initially, firms are motivated to discharge the worker, or the worker is motivated to quit.

Box 13.1   Vacancies and Unemployment: The Beveridge Curve

The likelihood that a job search will be successful depends on the number of jobs available: the more numerous the vacancies posted by firms, the more likely that a job seeker will find a 'good match'. Therefore, the flow of individuals who find a job and leave the unemployment pool depends positively on the number of vacancies. This observation suggests that the unemployment rate would be lower when the vacancy rate (i.e. the number of vacancies divided by the labour force) is high. This relationship, which is shown in Figure 13.2, is known as the **Beveridge curve**, after the British economist William Beveridge, or u–v curve, for unemployment–vacancy curve. The curve slopes down indicating that the unemployment rate increases as the vacancy rate decreases.

One puzzling aspect of the recent behaviour of unemployment, is that most countries' u–v curves have shifted considerably. Figure 13.3 shows the worldwide relationship between unemployment and vacancies during the period 1968–89. The most striking feature of this figure is that this relationship has been moving rightwards. In the early 1970s a 3% vacancy

rate corresponded approximately to a 3% rate of unemployment rate, whereas in the late 1980s, the same 3% vacancy rate corresponded roughly to a 6% unemployment rate. Richard Jackman, Christopher Pissarides and Savvas Savouri (1990) conducted a detailed examination of Beveridge curves for several OECD countries, and found substantial cross-countries differences. In particular, in the US during the second part of the 1980s the u–v curve returned to its late 1960s position, but in most European countries this return did not occur.

This shift in Beveridge curves is evidence that the effectiveness of job search has decreased over the last 20 years, at least in Europe. This finding implies that either workers have become less willing to accept job offers, perhaps for example because their reservation wage has risen, or firms have become less willing to fill their vacancies, possibly because employment-protection regulation has made it more difficult to fire workers in case of a bad match.

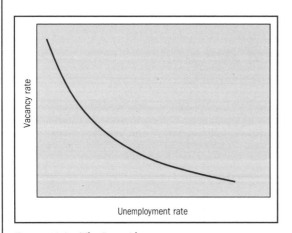

Figure 13.2   The Beveridge curve

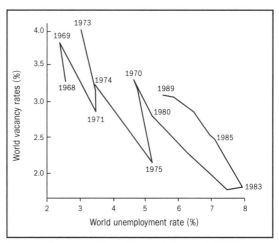

Source: Jackman, Pissarides and Savouri (1990).

Figure 13.3   World unemployment and vacancy rates, 1968–89

Either case results in a job separation, which typically reinstates a vacancy for the firm and unemployment for the worker. The main point is that a separation restarts the process of job search for firms and workers.

Separations also occur because of changed circumstances, even when firms and workers made accurate initial assessments of each other. An adverse shock to a firm's production function could, for example, lower its evaluation of a worker's marginal product and thereby lead to a discharge. (This type of job separation creates unemployment but not a vacancy.) If we distinguish the products of firms, then we would get a similar effect from a decline in the relative demand for a firm's product. Also, jobs are sometimes known to be temporary at the outset, as in the case of seasonal workers in agriculture or at sports facilities.

On the other side of the labour market, workers may experience changed circumstances with respect to family status, schooling, location, and retirement, as well as alternative job prospects. Shifts in these factors could induce a worker to quit a job. (This type of job separation tends to create a vacancy but not unemployment.)

For a group of employed workers, we can identify factors that influence the **job-separation rate**. The rate is higher, for example, among inexperienced workers who are harder to evaluate initially or for younger persons who are likely to experience changes in family size or job preferences. The separation rate would also be higher in industries that are subject to frequent shocks to technology or product demand.

If there were no separations (and no new persons entering the labour force), then the process of job search would tend eventually to eliminate unemployment and vacancies. But the existence of separations means that the finding of new jobs is continually offset by the loss of old ones – that is, by the creation of new unemployment and vacancies. The level and change in unemployment and vacancies involves the interplay between job finding and job separation. We now illustrate this process with a simple example, which focuses on the number of people employed and unemployed.

Job Separations, Job Finding, and the Natural Unemployment Rate

Let L be the number of people employed, and U the number unemployed. We assume here that the labour force, $L + U$, does not change over time. Hence, we do not allow for retirements or entry of new persons into the labour force. Because of the reevaluation of jobs and workers, some fraction of those employed experience a job separation in each period. In Figure 13.4 the box labelled L denotes the number employed, and the box labelled U shows those unemployed. The arrow from L to U represents the number of job separations. If the labour force is constant, and – unrealistically – if no job loser finds a new job immediately, then all those who lose jobs move from category L to category U. For the purpose of an example, assume that 1% of those employed lose their jobs each period, that is, the job separation rate is 1% per period.

As discussed before, the other thing that happens each period is that some fraction of those unemployed find jobs. In Figure 13.4 the arrow pointing from U to L represents the number of unemployed persons who find jobs during a period. Here (for the example to generate roughly the right numbers), assume that 15% of those unemployed find work each

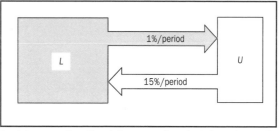

In this example, 1% of those employed (L) lose their jobs each period. Simultaneously 15% of those unemployed (U) find jobs each period. Therefore the net change in the number unemployed during a period is $15\% \cdot U - 1\% \cdot L$. Also the change in the number unemployed is the negative of the change in the number employed.

Figure 13.4 Movements between employment and unemployment

period. In other words, the job-finding rate is 15% per period.

We can work through the process of job separation and job finding to determine the numbers of people employed and unemployed. Table 13.1 assumes that the labour force is fixed at 100 million people (the actual size of the total EC labour force was 147 million in 1990), and the economy starts in period 1 with 90 million employed and 10 million unemployed. Thus, the unemployment rate is initially 10%. Of the 90 million workers, 1% – or 0.9 million people – lose their jobs in the first period. Simultaneously, 15% of those unemployed – or 1.5 million people – find jobs. Hence, the net change in employment during period 1 is 0.6 million. Correspondingly, unemployment falls by 0.6 million.

As the number of employed increases and the number of unemployed decreases, the quantity of job separations (1% of those employed) rises, and the quantity of job findings (15% of those unemployed) falls. The increase in employment therefore slows over time. The economy eventually approaches levels of employment and unemployment at which the number of job separations and findings is equal. Then, as long as the rates of job separation and job finding do not change, employment and unemployment are constant. In our example the balance between job separations and job findings occurs when employment equals 93.8 million and unemployment equals 6.2 million, that is, when the unemployment rate is 6.2%. Therefore, in this model, we can say that the **natural unemployment rate** is 6.2%. The economy tends toward this rate automatically, given the rates at which people lose and find jobs.

The model brings out some important points about the natural unemployment rate. First, although the unemployment rate eventually stays constant at this value, there is still a substantial amount of *job turnover*. Almost a million people lose and find jobs each period in the example when the unemployment rate is 6.2%. In this model – and in the real world – large flows from employment to unemployment, and vice versa, are a normal part of the operation of the labour market.

Second, the dynamics of employment and unemployment, as well as the value of the natural employment rate, depend on the rates of job separation and job finding. In the example these rates per period were set at 1% and 15%, respectively. More generally, our earlier analysis showed how the rates of job separation and job finding depended on various factors, such as a person's age and experience, the income available while unemployed, and the variability of an

Period	Number employed (L)	Number unemployed (U)	Number who lose jobs	Number who find jobs	Net change in employment	Net change in unemployment
1	90.0	10.0	0.9	1.5	0.6	−0.6
2	90.6	9.4	0.9	1.4	0.5	−0.5
3	91.1	8.9	0.9	1.3	0.4	−0.4
4	91.5	8.5	0.9	1.3	0.4	−0.4
5	91.9	8.1	0.9	1.2	0.3	−0.3
6	92.2	7.8	0.9	1.2	0.3	−0.3
.	.	.	.	.	.	.
.	.	.	.	.	.	.
∞	93.8	6.2	0.9	0.9	0	0

Note: We assume that the economy starts with 90 million people employed (L) and 10 million unemployed (U). Then, from Figure 13.4, 1% of those employed lose their job each period, but 15% of those unemployed find jobs. Therefore, the net change in employment is $15\% \cdot U - 1\% \cdot L$. Also, the change in unemployment is the negative of the change in employment. When the number employed reaches 93.8 million and the number unemployed reaches 6.2 million, the net changes in employment and unemployment are zero. Thus, the natural unemployment rate in this example is 6.2%.

Table 13.1   The dynamics of employment and unemployment and the natural rate of unemployment

industry's supply and demand conditions. To see how these factors influence employment and unemployment, we want to consider alternative values for the rates of job separation and job finding.

Let σ (the Greek letter *sigma*) be the job-separation rate and φ (the Greek letter *phi*) the job-finding rate. The change in the number employed during a period, ΔL, is given by

$$\Delta L = \phi U - \sigma L \qquad (13.1)$$

Note that the first term, ϕU, is the number of unemployed who find jobs during a period, and the second term, σL, is the number of employed who lose jobs. Equation (13.1) says that the change in employment equals job findings less job separations.

Equation (13.1) implies that employment increases if job findings, ϕU, exceed job separations, σL. In the reverse case, employment decreases. To determine the natural levels of employment and unemployment, we set the change in employment, ΔL, to zero in equation (13.1). Then, using the condition that the labour force, $L + U$, is fixed at 100 million, we find that

$$\phi U = \sigma L = \sigma(100 - U)$$

Solving this equation for the number unemployed, U, determines the natural values of unemployment and employment as

$$U = 100 \cdot \sigma/(\sigma + \phi)$$
$$L = 100 \cdot \phi/(\sigma + \phi) \qquad (13.2)$$

The natural unemployment rate is therefore

$$u = U/100 = \sigma/(\sigma + \phi) \qquad (13.3)$$

In our example, $\sigma = 0.01$ per period and $\phi = 0.15$ per period. Thus, $u = 0.01/0.16 = 6.2\%$, as we found before.

Equation (13.3) relates the natural unemployment rate to the rates of job separation, σ, and job finding, ϕ.[7] A higher rate of separation, σ, raises the natural unemployment rate, and a higher rate of finding, ϕ, lowers it. Thus, when we examine differences in natural unemployment

rates – either over groups of people or over time – we should look for differences in the rates of job separation and job finding. People who lose jobs more frequently or have more trouble in finding jobs will be unemployed a larger fraction of the time.

Movements in and out of the Labour Force

Before applying the theory to data on unemployment rates, we can usefully extend the analysis to include movements in and out of the labour force. Conceptually we classify people as outside of the labour force if they neither have a market job nor are currently looking for one. (Hence, the category includes full-time students and home-makers, who might reasonably think of themselves as 'employed'.) In practice, there are difficulties in distinguishing those outside the labour force from those unemployed: the distinction comes from people's answers to a survey question as to whether they are actively 'looking for work' during a particular period. To some extent, the number classified as unemployed underestimates the true number, because some of those labelled as outside of the labour force would also like market jobs (at some wage rate!). But on the other hand, many of those who call themselves unemployed are not actually interested in accepting employment on realistic terms.

For our purposes, the important new effects involve movements from inside the labour force to outside and vice versa. There are many good reasons for these movements – for example, when people retire, when they leave or re-enter school, when they have changes in marital status or in the number and ages of children, or when the nature of the available jobs changes.

Figure 13.5 shows the possible transitions among the three categories, employment, unemployment, and outside of the labour force. (Notice that the flows labelled 2 and 3 are those that we studied before.) The list of possibilities is as follows:

1. A change in job, without becoming unemployed or leaving the labour force. (This type

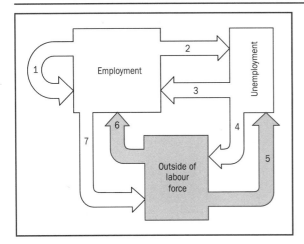

The diagram shows the possible movements from one category to another.

Figure 13.5 Flows of people among three categories: employment, unemployment and outside of the labour force

of shift is especially popular among sports figures and professors of economics – but, more generally, a large proportion of all job changes do not involve any unemployment; see Kim Clark and Lawrence Summers, 1979, p. 43.)

2. A loss of a job with a move to unemployment.
3. The finding of a job from the ranks of the unemployed.
4. A movement from unemployment to outside of the labour force, sometimes described as **discouraged workers**.
5. An entry or reentry to the labour force but initially unemployed.
6. An entry or reentry to the labour force with a job obtained at once (as in the case of most graduating majors in business and economics).
7. A loss of a job with a move outside of the labour force (a flow that includes permanent retirements, as well as withdrawals from the labour market to raise a family or return to school).

Total job separations are the sum of flows 1, 2 and 7, and total job findings are the sum of flows 1, 3, and 6. The difference between separations and findings is the change in employment. The change in unemployment is the sum of flows 2 and 5, less the sum of flows 3 and 4. Thus, because of the movements in and out of the labour force, the change in employment no longer coincides with the negative of the change in unemployment.

As before – but with greater complexity – people's tendencies to experience the various transitions shown in Figure 13.5 determine the levels of employment and unemployment over time. It is still true that employment tends to be lower the higher is the rate of job separation. Similarly, employment tends to be higher the greater is the rate of job finding. But the movements in and out of the labour force interact with these tendencies to lose and find jobs. For example, people who move frequently in and out of the labour force build up relatively little work experience. Hence, they tend to be the ones who are terminated first and hired last.

For unemployment, the new effects concern the possibilities for moving outside of the labour force. For example, the tendency for the unemployed to cease looking for work (flow 4 in Figure 13.5) reduces the number of persons counted as unemployed. But the tendency for people to shift from employment to outside of the labour force (flow 7) tends to raise unemployment. That is because, first, these people often become unemployed when they reenter the labour force (flow 5), and, second, they are more likely to lose a job later (flows 2 and 7).

The Behaviour of Unemployment Rates in the G-6

Unemployment rates vary considerably across countries and across categories of workers. In the period between 1950 and 1992 the average unemployment rate in the G-6 countries was 4.7%, being the lowest in Japan at 1.9% and the highest in Italy at 8.1%. As shown in Figure 13.6, unemployment rates differed not only in their mean but also in their dynamic behaviour. In particular, in France, Italy and the UK the unemployment rate displays a sharp and persis-

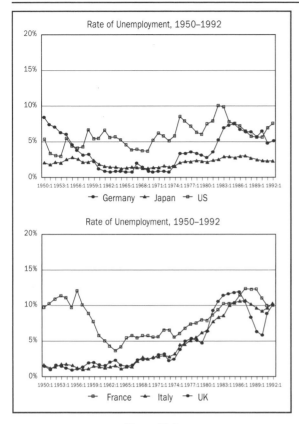

Figure 13.6

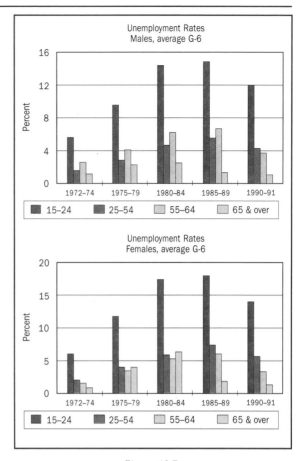

Figure 13.7

tent increase starting in the late 1970s. On the other hand, in Germany, Japan and the US, the unemployment rate displays some cyclical fluctuations and also a large increase in the late seventies but this increase was later reversed during the mid-1980s.

Figure 13.7 shows unemployment rates for various categories of workers by age and gender. The data are G-6 averages for five-year subperiods over the sample from 1972 to 1991. In this period, the average unemployment rate for all workers in the G-6 was 6%. The average unemployment rates varied substantially by demographic characteristics. For example, the average rate for females was 7.1%, whereas that for males was 5.4%. For both sexes, the average unemployment rate declines by age until people reach their 50s. But the sharpest distinction applies to people between 15 to 24, who had an average unemployment rate of 13%, compared to 4.5% for those at least 25 years of age.

Figure 13.7 does not indicate much change over time in the relative unemployment rates of the various demographic groups. The rate of unemployment for male workers aged 15 to 24, for example, averaged 1.9 times the overall rate, with no clear change in this relation over time. The rate of unemployment for male workers aged between 25 to 54 has been reasonably stable at around 0.7 times the overall rate. The rate of unemployment for females has been typically higher than that for males, but these rates have been similar since the early 1980s.

Table 13.2 shows considerable cross-country variations in the demographic composition of unemployment. In the period 1972 to 1992, the

	France	Germany	Italy	Japan	UK	US	Average G-6
Males							
15–24	12.0	5.7	22.0	4.2	15.1	12.6	11.9
25–54	4.0	3.8	2.7	1.6	7.1	4.8	4.0
55–64	5.0	6.7	1.4	3.9	10.2	3.9	5.2
65 & over	1.2	0.0	3.7	1.9	0.5	3.5	1.8
Total	5.2	4.4	5.6	2.2	9.0	6.3	5.5
Females							
15–24	20.1	7.0	30.3	3.7	11.2	12.8	14.2
25–54	7.2	5.5	7.5	2.0	3.3	5.8	5.2
55–64	6.0	7.3	3.1	1.5	4.6	3.7	4.4
65 & over	1.4	0.0	14.1	0.4	0.1	3.5	3.2
Total	9.2	5.9	13.0	2.1	5.2	7.2	7.1
Males & Females							
15–24	15.7	6.3	25.8	3.9	13.3	12.7	12.9
25 & over	5.3	4.7	4.3	1.9	5.8	4.9	4.5
Total	6.8	5.0	8.2	2.2	7.4	6.7	6.0

Source: Labour Force Statistics, OECD.

Table 13.2 Unemployment rates, averages 1972–91 (percent)

unemployment rate of males between 15 and 24 was highest in Italy at 22% and lowest in Japan at 4.2%. Similarly, that of females aged between 15 and 24 was as high as 30.3% in Italy and as low as 3.7% in Japan.

Cross-country differences are present also in the **participation rate**, i.e. the ratio of employment to population. Figure 13.8 shows the ratios of total employment (including the military) to total population. This ratio displays a long term increase in Japan and the US, a long-term decrease in France and Italy, while in Germany and the UK it does not have a particular trend. Despite the different behaviour of the total participation rate, all countries experienced a considerable increase in the labour-force participation rate of women and a slow decrease in that of men, as shown in Figure 13.9. This development means that there are now many more families with more than one income earner. A given overall rate of unemployment therefore does not have as much significance for the typical family's total earnings as it did in earlier years. (The existence of unemployment insurance and other welfare programmes also matters here.)

Nonetheless, deep differences in participation rates still remain across gender, age and country, as recorded in Table 13.3. Here the participation rate is calculated as the ratio of the total labour force for an age group divided by the total population for that age group.[8] For example, in the period 1972–91 the average participation rate for women aged 25–54 was 64.3% in the US but only 40.4% in Italy. On the other hand, the differences in the participation rate of males in the same age bracket is less pronounced, varying from 92.5% in Italy to 97.2% in Japan.

Causes for the Demographic Variations in Unemployment Rates

We can analyze the demographic disparities in unemployment rates by thinking about the determinants of the natural unemployment rates. Differences in the natural rates reflect variations in the rates of job separation and job finding. We can compare the rates of job separation across the demographic groups by looking at data on the **duration of jobs**: persons

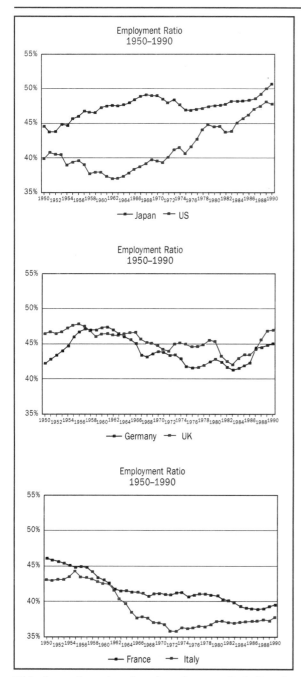

This shows the ratios of total employment (including the military) to total population.

Figure 13.8

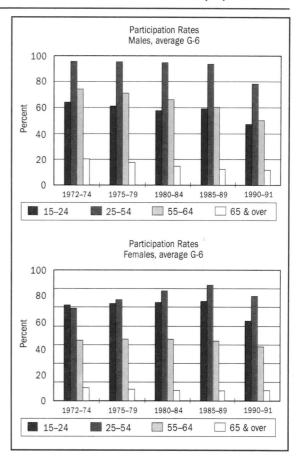

Figure 13.9

with high rates of job separation end up with short-term jobs, and vice versa. To get information about job-finding rates, we can examine data on the duration of unemployment. Persons who find jobs quickly end up with brief spells of unemployment, and vice versa.

The Duration of Jobs

The research by Robert Hall (1980a,b, 1982) on job separations allows us to understand some of the differences in unemployment rates by age, sex, and race. First, most new jobs that people get do not last very long. For example, using US data for 1973, Hall estimated that 61% of new jobs last less than one year, and the average duration of a new job is four years. But as people get older and try a variety of jobs, most workers eventually find a good job match, which lasts for a long time. Using data for 1978, Hall estimated that by age 50 over 70% of all workers have been on their

	France	Germany	Italy	Japan	UK	US	Average G-6
Males							
15–24	50.2	60.8	47.6	45.8	79.3	73.5	59.5
25–54	96.1	94.6	92.5	97.2	94.7	93.3	94.7
55–64	59.5	65.7	38.9	84.6	77.2	70.6	66.1
65 & over	8.4	7.7	6.8	40.2	11.1	18.0	15.4
Total	81.3	84.7	78.5	88.8	90.5	87.8	85.3
Females							
15–24	41.4	58.1	38.6	45.0	68.5	61.0	52.1
25–54	61.1	56.5	40.4	58.0	65.2	64.3	57.6
55–64	34.7	26.2	10.2	45.2	38.4	41.9	32.8
65 & over	3.5	3.4	1.7	15.7	3.8	7.6	6.0
Total	55.2	52.4	37.9	55.9	62.2	61.9	54.2
Males & Females							
15–24	45.8	61.1	43.1	45.4	74.0	67.3	56.1
25 & over	75.0	70.6	62.6	79.6	76.9	77.0	73.6
Total	68.2	68.4	57.8	72.2	76.3	74.6	69.6

Source: Labour Force Statistics, OECD.

Table 13.3 Participation rates, averages 1972–91 (percent)

present job for at least five years. By age 40, about 40% of all workers are currently in a very long-term job, which will eventually last at least 20 years. These results mean that job separations (flows 1, 2, and 7 in Figure 13.5) are much more common for younger workers, most of whom have not yet found a long-lasting job match. This element therefore explains a good deal of the higher unemployment rate for younger persons, especially teenagers.

A lower average duration of jobs can also explain some of the higher average unemployment rate for women than for men. Hall estimated for 1978 that about 50% of women who have jobs will eventually reach a tenure of at least 5 years on their job, and about 15% will reach at least 20 years. But the comparable figures for men are 64 and 37%, respectively. Historically, women moved in and out of the labour force (flows 4, 5, 6, and 7 in Figure 13.5) over their lifetime more often than men did. The narrowing in the gap between the unemployment rates of men and women (Figure 13.7) suggests that this distinction between the sexes may have become less important in recent years.

The Duration of Unemployment

The other main element that determines the average unemployment rate is the duration of a typical spell of unemployment. The longer it takes for an unemployed person to find a job or leave the labour force (flows 3 and 4 in Figure 13.5), the greater will be the measured number of unemployed at any point in time. Figure 13.10 shows this positive relationship between the duration of unemployment and the rate of unemployment. It shows that the countries with the highest percentage of long-term unemployed (i.e. over one year) have also the highest rates of unemployment. For example, in Spain 62% of unemployed were long-term unemployed in 1988 while in Norway they were only 6%. In the period between 1983 and 1988 Spain's unemployment rate was 20.1% while in Norway it was 2.7%.

Table 13.4 provides further evidence on the relationship between unemployment duration and unemployment rate. First, when we consider all workers, Britain had both an higher average duration of unemployment, 12.8 months, and an higher unemployment rate, 10.8%, than the US,

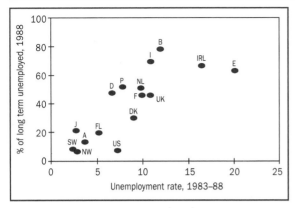

Figure 13.10 Long-term unemployed

2.6 months and 6.2% respectively. However, if we decompose the labour force in various categories according to labour skills, we notice that the relationship between unemployment duration and unemployment rate is not clear-cut. For example, in Britain and the US the unemployment rate of manual workers is about three times as large as that of professional and managerial workers. However, the difference in the unemployment duration of these two cate-

	Average duration of unemployment (months)	Unemployment rate (%)
Britain (1984)		
Professional & managerial	11.2	5.3
Clerical	10.1	8.0
Other non-manual	11.8	12.2
Skilled manual	14.2	12.6
Personal services & other manual	14.1	15.5
All	12.8	10.8
USA (1987)		
Professional & managerial	3.0	2.3
Clerical & other non-manual	2.6	4.3
Skilled manual	2.9	6.1
Personal services	2.4	7.7
Other manual	3.0	9.4
All	2.6	6.2

Source: Layard, Nickell and Jackman (1991).

Table 13.4 Unemployment duration by skill

gories of workers is small in both countries. Therefore, the higher unemployment rate for unskilled workers must reflect mostly the short duration of their jobs rather than a low rate of job finding.

Second, a considerable proportion of all spells of unemployment end in withdrawal from the labour force (flow 4 in Figure 13.5) rather than in employment (flow 3 in the figure). Then many of those who leave the labour force soon reappear as job searchers (flow 5 in the figure) and thereby count as a new spell of unemployment in the data. Clark and Summers argue that these spells of unemployment and the intervening periods outside of the labour force should be counted as long periods of unemployment. But many of these people (as well as some who never leave the labour force) may not be serious job seekers and should not be counted as unemployed in the first place. This ambiguity points out the fundamental problem of defining and measuring the concept of unemployment. It is easier to define and measure employment than unemployment.

Explaining the Differences in the Natural Unemployment Rate

There is a long list of factors – especially government policies – that economists think influence the natural unemployment rate for the whole economy. We consider briefly some of the more important possibilities: unemployment insurance, the minimum wage, and labour unions.

Unemployment Insurance

As we shall discuss in Chapter 15 (Table 15.3) most countries have an **unemployment insurance** scheme. This type of programme provides benefits to eligible persons who have lost their jobs and are currently 'looking for work'. Hence, those in the category labelled 'unemployment' in Figure 13.5 are candidates for these benefits.

A person's eligibility for benefits usually depends on a sufficient work history in a covered job.[9] An individual's benefits run out after a period which varies across countries and it ranges between three months to four years, as shown in

Figure 13.11. In some cases, in Finland for example, benefits last indefinitely; in others, like in the US during the recessions of 1982–83 and 1991, the government may extend the period of eligibility.

Unemployment benefits are one component of the income, w^u, that a person gets by not working. The ratio of the potential benefits to the wage from a prior job is called the **replacement ratio**. As shown in Figure 13.11, this ratio ranges from about 36% in the UK to 90% in Denmark.[10] Over time, the main changes in the unemployment-insurance programme have been extensions of coverage and increases in the allowable duration of benefits.

The existence of unemployment insurance makes the unemployed who are receiving benefits less eager to accept jobs or leave the labour force (flows 3 and 4 in Figure 13.5). The programme also makes the employed persons who will be eligible for benefits more willing to accept job separations (flow 2 in Figure 13.5).[11] In particular, unemployment insurance motivates **temporary layoffs**, short-term job separations during a period of slack production. Overall, a more generous programme of unemployment insurance leads to a higher natural rate of unemployment.

Many economists think that the generous unemployment-insurance programmes in some Western European countries – especially the long period of eligibility for benefits – are responsible for the large amount of long-term unemployment (see Gary Burtless, 1987, and Michael Burda, 1988). Figure 13.12 plots for 13 industrialized countries the amount of long-term unemployment (those unemployed at least 6 months, expressed as a percentage of total unemployment) against a measure of the generosity of the unemployment-insurance programme. This measure considers the programme's replacement ratio, as well as the allowable duration of benefits.[12] The figure shows that the countries with more generous unemployment-insurance programs have a greater incidence of long-term unemployment.

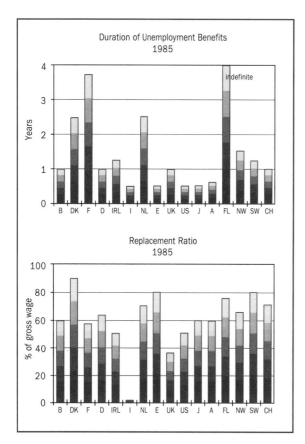

Figure 13.11

Source: Layard, Nickell and Jackman (1991).

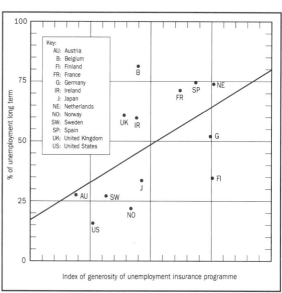

Figure 13.12 Unemployment insurance and long-term unemployment in industrialized countries

Similar results have been reported for non-European countries. Using data for the United States, some researchers report that unemployment insurance raises the natural unemployment rate by between 1/2 and 1 percentage point.[13] Lawrence Katz and Bruce Meyer (1988) focused on the duration of benefits. They estimated that an extension of allowable benefits by 1 week raises the mean duration of unemployment by between .16 and .20 week.

Although there is evidence that unemployment insurance raises the unemployment rate, there is not much indication that these programmes have become significantly more generous over the last two decades. It is therefore not easy to blame these programmes for the high unemployment rates experienced since the mid-1970s.

The Minimum Wage

When considering determinants of the natural unemployment rate, economists often mention the **minimum wage**. Unlike unemployment benefits, minimum wage regulations are not present in all countries. For example, Denmark, Germany, Italy and the UK do not have a minimum wage. On the other hand, Belgium, France, the Netherlands and the US do. The level of minimum wage differs substantially in these countries. In the US the minimum wage is about 40% of average manufacturing earning, while in the Netherlands this percentage is over 70%.

A higher minimum wage reduces the incentive of employers to hire low-productivity workers in sectors covered by the minimum wage. Empirically, researchers find that a higher minimum wage and greater coverage tend to reduce especially the employment of teenagers. Typical estimates suggest that an increase by 10% in the minimum wage lowers the quantity of teenagers employed by somewhat more than 1%.[14] There is also some indication of a negative effect on the employment of young adults aged 20–24 but no clear effect on older workers. In fact, because the minimum wage makes the labour of low-productivity workers artificially more expensive, it is likely that businesses would shift to more labour from high-productivity workers. Hence, labour unions tend to favour the minimum wage to protect their high-paid members from the competition of low-productivity, low-wage workers.

Although the adverse effect of the minimum wage on teenage *employment* is clear, the effect on teenage *unemployment* depends also on the response of labour-force participation. Because a higher minimum wage reduces the chance of finding a job, it also reduces the number of teenagers who declare themselves as looking for work. This response lessens the tendency for a higher minimum wage to raise the measured unemployment rate of teenagers.

In any event, the behaviour of the minimum wage cannot account for the high unemployment rates from the mid-1970s. That is because, first, the higher unemployment rates over this period applied as much to older workers as to teenagers and young adults and, second, high unemployment rates were present also in countries without minimum wage, like Italy and Britain.

Labour Unions

Economists sometimes suggest that labour unions cause unemployment. Mostly, unions can raise real wage rates and hold down the levels of employment in covered industries. Correspondingly, there is a higher supply of labour and lower real wage rates in uncovered sectors. Unions can therefore create inefficiencies, which include the inappropriate distribution of work and production between covered and uncovered areas. Conceivably, more union power would also lead to reductions in aggregate employment and output. But it is less clear that unions have anything to do with the amount of *unemployment*: the adverse effects on total work may correspond mostly to reductions in the labour force. Figure 13.13 shows the percentage of workers that were unionized in 1979 and the average unemployment rate during the 1970s. First, the importance of labour unions differs considerably across countries. In the US 25% of the workforce was unionized in 1979, while in Sweden almost 90%. Second, the figure shows that there is no clear relationship between unionization and unemployment rate. For example, although Sweden and Switzerland displayed the lowest unemployment rates in this period, the

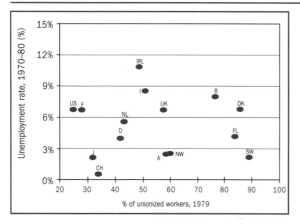

Figure 13.13   Unionization and unemployment

competitive forces to be able to work, but too small to internalize the negative impact of their requests on the aggregate economy. The crucial implication is that real wage demand and unemployment should be low in countries with either very low or very high degree of centralization, and high in countries with intermediate level of centralization. Figure 13.14 presents some evidence in favour of the theory. The horizontal axis ranks countries according to their degree of wage bargaining centralization. On the vertical axes we report the average unemployment level in the period 1983–88, and the percentage of long-term unemployed in 1988. As predicted by the theory, these relationships have a characteristic hump-shape.

Another way to look for effects of unions is by observing the changes in unionization over time.

Swedish workforce was very highly unionized, whereas the Swiss workforce was relatively little unionized.

On the basis of this evidence, researchers have suggested that the relationship between the wage bargaining process and the rate of unemployment may take less obvious forms. In recent work, Calmfors and Driffill (1988) suggest that more important than the density of unionization is the level of centralization of the wage bargaining process. Wage bargaining can be decentralized, taking place at the firm level, either because workers are not unionized or because unions are very localized, or can be fully centralized, with a national trade union covering all sectors of the economy. Between these two extremes, there is the intermediate case of large, but industry specific, unions. Their argument is that highly decentralized and highly centralized wage bargaining systems are conducive to real wage restraint, and thus do not impose excessive distortions on the economy. In the case of decentralized bargaining, competitive forces prevent excessive wage demands. In the case of a fully centralized system, the nation-wide unions realize the potential negative impact of excessive wage demands on the economy, and therefore they limit their demands at the negotiating table. According to this theory, the highest wage demands, and thus the highest unemployment, should be associated with the intermediate system of bargaining, i.e. when unions are too large for

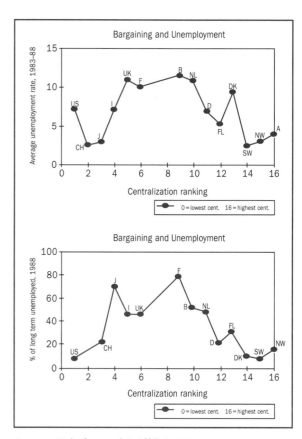

Source: Calmfors and Driffill (1988).

Figure 13.14

There is not much evidence that the degree of unionization is related to historical changes in unemployment. Figure 13.15 reports the percentage of unionized workers in 1970, 1979 and 1986/7 and the average unemployment rates for the three decades 1960s, 1970s and 1980s for the G-6 countries. Although unemployment rates increased in all countries, especially in the 1980s, union membership followed different patterns across countries. In Japan and in the US it decreased over the whole period, while in Germany it increased. In France, Italy and the UK it increased from 1970 to 1979, but then decreased. We cannot therefore attribute the increase in unemployment rates in these countries to an increase in unionization.

Employment and Unemployment during Recessions

We showed in Chapter 12 that shifts to the production function could account for some characteristics of real-world business fluctuations. In particular, an adverse shock to the production function could generate a recession that featured declines in real GNP and labour input. Now we can use the apparatus from this chapter to see how supply shocks affect unemployment. We consider the case of a fixed labour force, so that changes in unemployment reflect inverse movements in employment.

Suppose that an adverse shock reduces the marginal product of labour for the typical worker and job. One effect, which we noted earlier, is that the job-finding rate, ϕ, declines. That is because market opportunities – determined by labour marginal product – have become poorer relative to the income received while unemployed, w^u. For the same reason, existing job matches become less mutually advantageous for firms and workers. Job separations therefore tend to increase, especially in the form of layoffs and firings by firms: hence, the job-separation rate, σ, tends to rise.

To see the effects on unemployment and employment, return to the example in which the labour force was fixed at 100 million persons and the job-finding rates were initially 15% and 1%, respectively. Table 13.5 assumes that the economy begins in period 1 at the natural unemployment rate, 6.2% in this example. Then the adverse shock

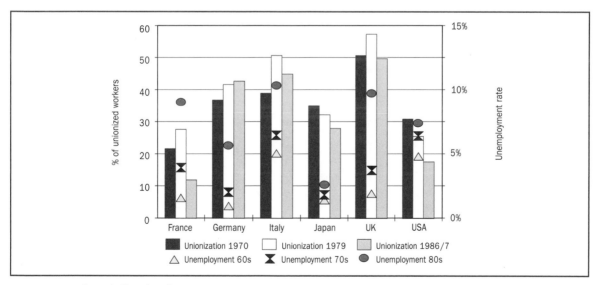

Source: Layard, Nickell and Jackman (1991).

Figure 13.15 Changes in unionization and unemployment

to production functions – the force that initiates a recession – means that the job-separation rate rises from 1% to, say, 1.5%, and the job-finding rate falls from 15% to, say, 10%.

Although some people still find jobs, they are outnumbered by those who lose jobs. Hence, Table 13.5 shows that the unemployment rate rises steadily from 6.2% in period 1 to 9.4% in period 6. The number employed falls correspondingly from 93.8 million to 90.6 million.

Suppose that the temporary adverse shock to the production function lasts through period 5. As of period 6, the job-separation rate is again 1%, and the job-finding rate is 15%. Although some people still lose their jobs, they are now outnumbered by those who find jobs. The unemployment rate therefore falls gradually toward the natural rate of 6.2%, and employment rises correspondingly back toward 93.8 million.

We should stress two realistic features of recessions that emerge from this example. First, the buildup of a recession involves a period of gradually rising unemployment and falling employment. Second, even after an economic recovery begins, it takes a substantial period for

the unemployment rate to return to its pre-recession level.

In this example, with a fixed labour force, the dynamics of employment is just the reverse of that of unemployment. Further, if we abstract from changes in the stock of capital, then the movements in production would parallel those in employment. Although these patterns capture the broad features of business fluctuations, some elements are missing. First, hours worked per worker, especially *overtime* hours, are more flexible than numbers employed. Hours and output per worker therefore tend to fall in a recession (or rise in a boom) before the corresponding changes in employment. Second, businesses can change their utilization of capital and hence the volume of production. With a given number of worker-hours, a decrease in utilization during a recession shows up as a reduction in output per hour worked.[15] Third, the labour force can vary. Except for young persons, however – who tend to drop out of the labour force in bad times – there turns out to be little association of the labour force with the level of real economic activity (see problem 13.7).

Period	Job separation rate (σ)	Job finding rate (ϕ)	Number employed (L)	Number unemployed (U)	Number who lose jobs	Number who find jobs	Net change in employment
1	0.015	0.10	93.8	6.2	1.4	0.6	−0.8
2	0.015	0.10	93.0	7.0	1.4	0.7	−0.7
3	0.015	0.10	92.3	7.7	1.4	0.8	−0.6
4	0.015	0.10	91.7	8.3	1.4	0.8	−0.6
5	0.015	0.10	91.1	8.9	1.4	0.9	−0.5
6	0.01	0.15	90.6	9.4	0.9	1.4	0.5
7	0.01	0.15	91.1	8.9	0.9	1.3	0.4
8	0.01	0.15	91.5	8.5	0.9	1.3	0.4
9	0.01	0.15	91.9	8.1	0.9	1.2	0.3
10	0.01	0.15	92.2	7.8	0.9	1.2	0.3
.	.	.	.	.	.	.	.
.	.	.	.	.	.	.	.
.	.	.	.	.	.	.	.
∞	0.01	0.15	93.8	6.2	0.9	0.9	0

Note: During the recession for periods 1 to 5, the job-separation rate is high – 1.5% rather than 1% – and the job-finding rate is low – 10% instead of 15%. Consequently, the unemployment rate rises from that natural rate 6.2% to 9.4% in period 6. When the job-separation and job-finding rates return to their normal values in period 6, the economy recovers gradually. In particular the unemployment rate again approaches the natual rate of 6.2%.

Table 13.5   The dynamics of employment and unemployment during a recession

Cyclical Behaviour of Employment and Unemployment Persistence

Figure 13.16 shows the behaviour of the cyclical component of output and of total employment in the period 1950–90 for the G-6 countries. The cyclical movement of a series around its trend are as those calculated in Chapter 1. First, Figure 13.16 shows that in France, Germany, the UK and the US total employment is strongly procyclical. The correlation coefficient between cyclical GDP and cyclical employment ranged from 0.51 in France to 0.75 in the US. On the other hand, in Japan and Italy the correlation between output and employment over the cycle is much weaker. The correlation coefficient was 0.15 in Japan and virtually zero in Italy. The second observation is that total employment is less volatile than GDP, that is, the average fluctuations in total employment have been smaller than those of GDP in all six countries. A measure of variability of the series, their standard deviations, are reported in Figure 13.17. The extreme case is that of Japan, where the variability of total employment was only 22% that of GDP. Notice that, since employment is procyclical and it fluctuates less than real GDP during the cycle, the ratio of real GDP to the number of workers – which is one measure of labour productivity – is procyclical, that is, it falls during recessions and increases during booms.

One of the most remarkable recent developments in the labour market in Europe has been the change in cyclicality of the rate of unemployment since the mid-1970s. As we have noted before, starting in the mid-1970s, unemployment rates have increased sharply worldwide. However, while in the US, Japan and Germany the rate of unemployment reverted in the mid-1980s to its 1960s' level, in most European countries it did not, as shown in Figure 13.18. In fact, in most of Europe, the recent increase in the unemployment rate does not seem to be cyclical but rather permanent.

Several explanations have been put forward for the worrying observation that negative shocks to employment tend to have a much higher persistence in Europe than in the US or Japan.

Several authors, e.g. Gottfries and Horn (1987), Blanchard and Summers (1986) and Lindbeck and Snower (1987, 1988), have suggested that an answer can be found by analyzing the wage bargaining process. In particular, they show different mechanisms through which wage bargaining can affect not only the steady state level of unemployment, but also its dynamics. For example, consider the case of a union in which the decision power is held by the members that are currently employed (often referred to as **insiders**), while the unemployed workers (referred to as **outsiders**), in general a minority, have little ability to affect wage negotiations. In this scenario, since the union gives privilege insiders' interests, wage demands will be too high to permit all the outsiders to be hired. Figure 13.19 illustrates this point. Start with the steady state equilibrium in which employment is at its natural rate level, L^*, and contract wages at their long-run level, $(w/p)^*$. Suppose that the economy suffers a negative productivity shock, so that the labour demand schedule shifts leftward to $L^{d'}$. Because the wage is fixed by contract, employment will drop to L_I, which represents the part of the union members that are still employed, i.e. the insiders. Consider now what happens after the shock disappears and the labour demand schedule returns to its long-run position L^d. If the union cares only about the insiders and if, at the renewal of the contract, it can dictate to the firm the new level of wages, it will demand $(w/p)'$ and the outsiders, $L^* - L_I$, will remain unemployed. Clearly this is an extreme that is unlikely to occur for two reasons. First, it may not be true that the union totally disregards the interests of the outsiders. After all, the current insiders could become outsiders in the future. Second, we have to consider that the firm, if the union demands are too high, can fire the insiders and hire some outsiders. If firing the insiders could be done at no costs, the only possible union demand would be $(w/p)^*$ and the whole of the outsiders will return to their jobs. However, firing the insiders is likely to be costly not just because the union can disrupt production in various ways, but because it is possible that the outsiders may have to be retrained before they

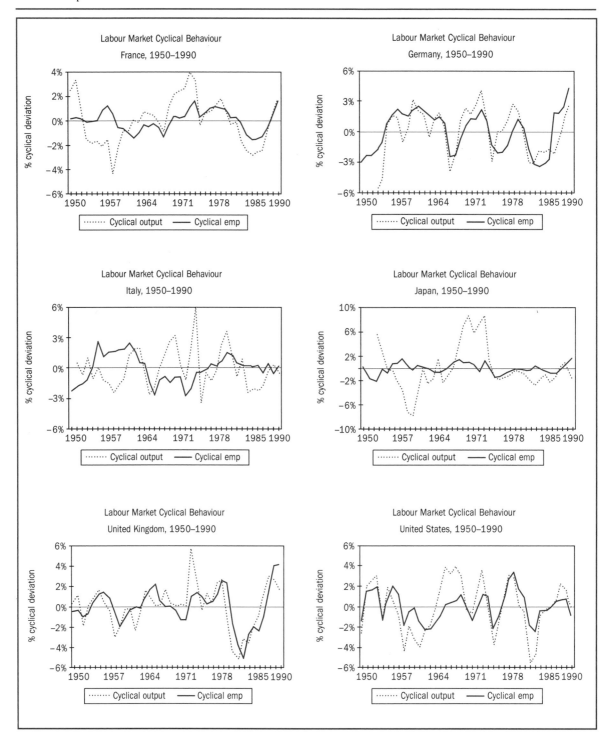

Figure 13.16

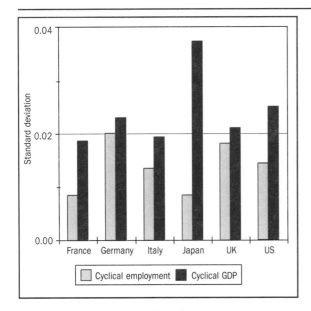

Figure 13.17 Variability of employment & output

can return to be as productive as the currently employed. The insiders, therefore, can exploit this difference in productivity to demand wages higher than $(w/p)^*$. Therefore, although it is unlikely that the union could or would want to demand $(w/p)'$, the new equilibrium wage could still be higher than $(w/p)^*$. As long as this is the case, employment will not return to L^*. Summarizing, in the presence of strong insider power, negative shocks can have a persistent effect on unemployment. The evidence on the relationship between the degree of unionization and this type of insider effects is not over-whelming. While Nickell and Kong (1992) find that insider effects are more important in industries with powerful unions, others have found that unions do not have this kind of impact.

Supply Shocks, Recessions, and Unemployment

The theory shows how shocks to the production function could cause the high unemployment characteristic of recessions. We would like to know how much these recessions actually were the result of identifiable supply shocks. Although

we cannot give a definitive answer to this question, there are some suggestive findings from recent empirical research.

Commodity Price Shocks

Most economists believe that the dramatic increases in oil prices in 1973–74 and 1979–80 were important factors in the recessions of 1974-75 and 1980–82, respectively. Layard *et al.* (1991, pp.408–412) estimated the impact of the increases in oil prices on the change in unemployment in the 1970s and 1980s in the OECD countries. They found that although oil shocks have been an important source of high unemployment in all these countries, their impact differed considerably across them. In particular, the impact was several times larger in countries with few primary commodities, like Belgium, Ireland and the Netherlands than in countries rich in raw materials like Australia, the UK, the US and Norway.

Sectoral Shifts

Aside from oil, economists have not been very successful in pinpointing identifiable supply shocks as regular elements in business fluctua-tions. It is possible nevertheless that an array of disturbances to productive conditions – which macroeconomists cannot identify directly – account for the recessions and booms. David Lilien (1982) pursued this idea by focusing on the changing composition of production. In industrial countries, the composition of production has moved away from traditional areas of manufac-turing, such as steel and automobiles, and toward high-tech industries and services. (The dominant movement earlier was from agriculture to manufacturing.) Lilien argues that the process of reallocating labour across sectors leads to high rates of job separation and therefore high rates of unemployment.[16] His empirical results (pp. 787–92) for the post-World War II United States show that periods of more rapidly changing industrial composition tend to be times of unusually high unemployment. Thus, the findings suggest that recessions derive in part from various shocks – such as technological innovations, changes in foreign competition, and variations in the relative

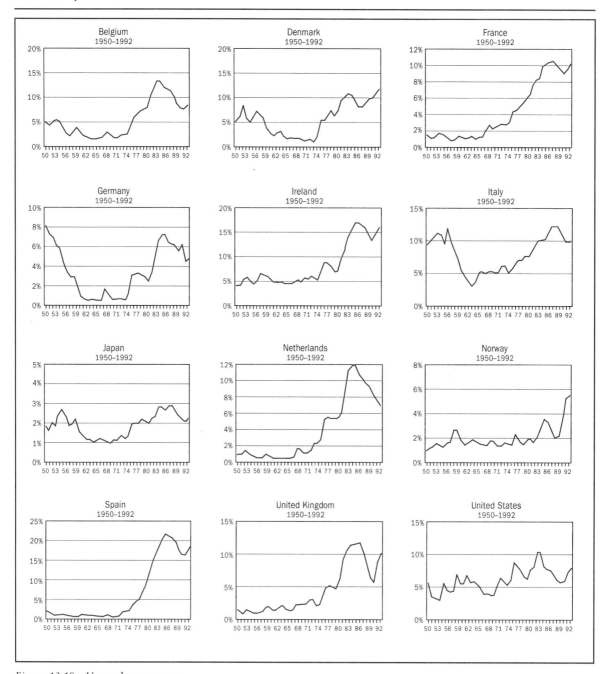

Figure 13.18   Unemployment rates

prices of raw materials – that induce shifts in the composition of industry.

A number of economists have extended or questioned Lilien's conclusions. Katharine Abraham and Lawrence Katz (1986) argue that Lilien's results would emerge if only aggregate shocks matter but sectors respond differentially to the aggregate shocks. Steve Davis and John

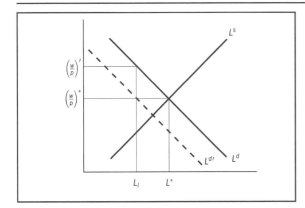

Figure 13.19 The effects of shocks in the presence of insiders

Haltiwanger (1992) show that recessions feature an unusually large volume of job reallocation, the sum of jobs created and jobs destroyed. Unemployment then emerges, as in Lilien, as a consequence of the frictions in the formation of new job matches. Davis and Haltiwanger demonstrate, however, that the process of reallocation is concentrated within sectors and therefore does not involve primarily the kinds of sectoral shifts that Lilien stressed. They also show that the jobs created and destroyed represent persistent changes in employment at the level of establishments. The changes in unemployment are therefore not concentrated in the temporary layoffs that are the focus of some theories, such as those that stress the role of unemployment insurance.

Summary

When workers and jobs differ, it takes time for people to match up well with jobs. Workers search for positions with high wages (and other desirable characteristics), and businesses search for productive workers. During the process of search, some job seekers remain unemployed, and some positions remain vacant. The rate of job finding depends on such things as the income available while unemployed and the level and shape of the distribution of wage offers.

Because workers or firms make mistakes in their initial assessments and because circumstances change, existing jobs sometimes end. The job-separation rate depends on workers' characteristics – such as age and experience – and the variability of an industry's supply and demand conditions.

The dynamics of employment and unemployment depend on the rates of job separation and job finding. If these rates are constant, then the economy tends automatically to a natural rate of unemployment. This natural rate rises with an increase in the job-separation rate but falls with an increase in the job-finding rate. Movements in and out of the labour force also influence the natural unemployment rate.

We use this framework to analyze differences in average unemployment rates by age, sex, and race: these differences reflect underlying variations in the duration of jobs and of unemployment. Younger workers, for example, have much higher job-separation rates and therefore exhibit a higher average unemployment rate.

We found before that an adverse shock to the production function can generate a recession in which output and labour input decline. Now we show that this kind of shock also lowers the job-finding rate and raises the job-separation rate. Unemployment thereby rises during a recession.

The main direct evidence for cyclical effects of supply shocks involves changes in oil prices. Some results about sectoral shifts and seasonal fluctuations suggest, however, that shifts in technology and preferences – the types of disturbances stressed in real business-cycle theories – can be quantitatively important in the short run.

Important Terms and Concepts

labour force
unemployment
unemployment rate
vacancies
reservation wage
job-separation rate
job-finding rate
natural unemployment rate
outside of the labour force
discouraged workers
insider and outsider workers
duration of jobs
duration of unemployment
unemployment insurance
replacement ratio (for unemployment insurance)
experience rating (for unemployment insurance)
participation rate
Beveridge curve, u–v curve
temporary layoffs
minimum wage

Questions and Problems

Mainly for Review

13.1 What is the definition of the unemployment rate? Since it does not include workers who moved from 'unemployment' to 'out of the labour force', is it an underestimate of the amount of unemployment in the economy? Can you think of any reason that the unemployment rate overstates unemployment?

13.2 Suppose that a job seeker receives a wage offer, w, that exceeds his or her income while unemployed, w^u. Why might the person reject the offer?

13.3 Once a worker and a firm find a job match, why would they ever choose to end this match? List some elements that influence the rate of job separation.

13.4 What is the natural rate of unemployment? When would unemployment differ from the natural rate? Can the natural rate itself change over time?

Problems for Discussion

13.5 The Job-Finding Rate
Discuss the effect on the job-finding rate and the expected duration of unemployment from the following:

a. an increase in unemployment-insurance benefits,
b. an increase in the minimum wage,
c. a technological shock that improves the available wage offers.
Consider a group of job seekers whose skills are hard to evaluate. For such people, the distribution of wage offers tends to have a wide dispersion. Would the job-finding rate be high or low for this group?

13.6 The Job-Separation Rate, the Job-Finding Rate, and the Natural Rate of Unemployment
Suppose that the labour force has 100 million people, of whom 92 million initially have jobs and 8 million are unemployed. Assume that the job-separation rate is 1% per period and the job-finding rate is 20% per period. Also, suppose that we can neglect movements in and out of the labour force. Trace out the path of employment and unemployment. What is the natural unemployment rate?

13.7 The Labour Force during Recessions
The data show little systematic response of the overall civilian labour force to recessions and booms. What response would you predict on theoretical grounds? (Hint: Think first about people's incentives to leave the labour force – that is, to stop looking for work – during a recession. But are there also incentives for some people to enter the labour force during bad times?)
The teenaged labour force declines during recessions. How can we explain this observation?

13.8 Women in the Labour Force
In the G-6 the unemployment rate for women averages about 1.5 percentage point higher than that for men (see Table 13.2). Further, in the G-6 the fraction of the civilian labour force that is female rose from 35.7% in 1970 to 41.4% in 1990. How would this increased role of women in the labour force affect the overall value of the natural unemployment rate?

13.9 The Minimum Wage Rate
How does an increase in the minimum wage rate affect the employment of:
a. high- and low-productivity workers in covered industries?
b. high- and low-productivity workers in uncovered industries?
What does a higher minimum wage rate mean for the unemployment rate of:
a. teenagers?
b. all workers?

13.10 Okun's Law

Okun's Law (named after the economist Arthur Okun) states that the ratio of the percentage shortfall in output during a recession to the percentage point increase in the unemployment rate is roughly equal to three.

How does Okun's Law relate to the behaviour of labour productivity during a recession?

13.11 Vacancies and Unemployment

We considered in the text how an adverse shock to production functions could lead to higher unemployment (as well as lower employment and production).

a. What would this type of disturbance do to the number of job vacancies? How would the number of vacancies therefore relate to the level of real economic activity?

b. Discuss this effect using the Beveridge curve.

Notes

1. We assume that it does not pay to accept a job and nevertheless keep searching. That is because the costs of getting set up in a job usually make it undesirable to take positions with short expected durations. It may also be easier to search while unemployed.

2. Presumably the unemployed have more leisure, even after considering the time required to search for a job. The basic results would not change, however, if people preferred time at work to time spent unemployed.

3. We assume for simplicity that the attractiveness of different jobs depends only on the wage paid. We could expand the model to consider an effective wage, which took account of working conditions, hours, job location, and so on.

4. For a discussion of models of job search that involve an optimal reservation wage, see Belton Fleisher and Thomas Kniesner (1984, pp. 477–507).

5. If w^u and all wage offers were higher by 10%, then the trade-off between the benefits and costs of accepting a job would not change. The job-finding rate and the expected duration of unemployment would therefore also not change. If we instead hold w^u constant – as we did in the text – then the net effect is equivalent to a fall in w^u. The net effect is accordingly an increase in the job-finding rate and a decrease in the expected duration of unemployment.

6. Since the marginal product of most people on most jobs would be negative (for example, of college professors as the chief executive officer of Volkswagen), we would have to allow wage offers to be negative. Usually, these negative offers would be unacceptable, so we can just as well think of no job being offered in such cases.

7. For more thorough analyses of this type of model, see Robert Hall (1979), Christopher Pissarides (1979,1990), Chitra Ramaswami (1983), and Michael Darby, John Haltiwanger and Mark Plant (1985).

8. The participation rate for the age group 25 and over is defined as the total labour force for this age group divided by the total population for ages 25–64. The participation rate for all ages (i.e. the item 'total'), is defined as the total labour force for all ages, divided by the total population for ages 15–64.

9. In some cases people who quit their jobs or are fired for cause are eligible for benefits, whereas in others they are ineligible. It is, of course, often hard to tell who quits or is fired for cause.

10. Italy is an unusual case. The basic unemployment benefits have been left at a very low level (the replacement ratio in 1985 was about 2%). In addition, there exists a special wage supplementation fund (Cassa Integrazione Guadagni), which pays about 80% of the salary of temporary layoffs. This, however, is not an automatic scheme, but is awarded by the government on a case by case basis.

11. This tendency diminishes if employers pay for the average benefits given to their ex-employees through a process called **experience rating**. With experience rating, a business that has a lot of job separations pays a larger amount into the fund that finances the unemployment benefits. This system therefore motivates employers to hold down their rates of job separation. There is some experience rating in the US system of unemployment insurance, but not in the systems of most other countries. For a discussion, see Robert Topel and Finis Welch (1980).

12. The data on the characteristics of the unemployment-insurance programmes are from Michael Emerson (1988, p. 90) and *The Employer*, Copenhagen, 10 August 1987, p. 6. The figures on long-term unemployment are from OECD (1987, p. 201).

13. See Daniel Hamermesh (1977, p. 52) and Kim Clark and Lawrence Summers (1982, table 10). Hamermesh focuses on changes in the duration of unemployment. He also distinguishes the effects in a year of high unemployment from those in a year of low unemployment, but the reported differences are small. Clark and Summers's estimates refer to 1978, for which the overall unemployment rate was 5.9%.

14. For a survey of the evidence, see Charles Brown, Curtis Gilroy and Andrew Koehn (1982).

15. A decrease in capacity utilization typically implies that fewer worker-hours would be required for current production. To the extent that worker-hours do not decline, firms are employing more labour than necessary for production. Economists have speculated whether this 'excess' labour is

underutilized (in that people work less intensively during recessions) or is instead used for activities that do not appear in measured output. Jon Fay and James Medoff (1985) found from a survey of 168 US manufacturing firms that the typical firm reacted to a recession by assigning an additional 5% of work hours to maintenance and overhaul of equipment, training, and other activities that would not show up in measures of current output. Thus, there seems to be a significant diversion of labour during recessions to these productive, but typically uncounted, activities.

16. Our simple theory, summarized in equation 13.3, says that the natural unemployment rate is $\sigma/(\sigma + \phi)$. Thus, we predict an increase in the unemployment rate if the job-separation rate, σ, rises proportionately more than the job-finding rate, ϕ.

14

Economic Growth

This chapter considers three key determinants of long-term economic growth: the accumulation of capital, population growth, and improvements in technology. Capital should be viewed in a broad sense to encompass physical capital (machines and buildings), as well as human capital (improvements in the quality of labour due to education, training, and experience). We shall see that the accumulation of capital is an important element of growth but that the workings of diminishing returns imply that growth cannot go on forever just by adding to the capital stock. We shall also find that population growth can sustain growth in the level of output but not in the levels of product and income per capita. Finally, we shall work out the role of technological advances as a crucial mechanism for sustaining growth in the long run.

Changes in the Stock of Capital

The previous chapter considered a production function that related a producer's output, y_t, to the previous period's stock of capital, k_{t-1}, and the quantity of labor input, ℓ_t. We shall find it convenient for exploring long-term growth to neglect the one-period lag that we assumed before between increments to the capital stock and the use of this capital to produce goods. We also want to focus now on the aggregate of outputs and inputs. Therefore, we write the production function in aggregate form as

$$Y = F(K, \ L) \qquad (14.1)$$
$$(+) \ (+)$$

where all variables refer to time t, but we omit the time subscripts on Y, K, and L for convenience.

We assume for now that overall population and aggregate labour input, L, are constant. We can therefore hold fixed L in equation (14.1) and focus on the relation between output, Y, and the capital stock, K. Figure 14.1 shows this relation (which we examined before in Figure 12.3). Recall that the positive slope of the curve at any point represents the marginal product of capital, MPK. As K rises (with L held fixed), the slope gets less steep because of the diminishing marginal productivity of capital.

The change in the economy's capital stock, ΔK, equals aggregate net investment, which equals gross investment less depreciation. As in Chapter 12, we assume that depreciation is the amount δK, where $\delta > 0$ is the depreciation rate.

We now focus our analysis on a closed economy, for which aggregate net investment

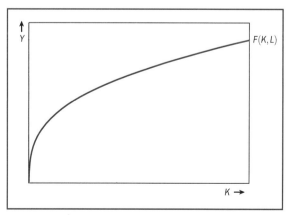

Figure 14.1 Relation between output and the capital stock

equals aggregate real saving. Therefore, in order to accumulate capital and to grow, an economy has to postpone consumption. The extension to an open economy would allow the economy to invest by borrowing from abroad by running current-account deficits, as we discussed in Chapter 12. This possibility does not alter the essence of argument. Moreover, the evidence by Feldstein and Horioka (1980) and others on the relationship between saving and investment, as discussed in Chapter 12, suggests that domestic investment and domestic saving move closely together. Therefore, as far as capital accumulation is concerned, not much is lost by ignoring movements in the current account.

We can define real **gross saving** to equal real saving plus depreciation. In the aggregate, real gross saving corresponds to gross investment or, equivalently, to the part of gross output, Y, that is not consumed. We now make the useful simplifying assumption that households set their real gross saving to equal the constant fraction, s, of gross output, Y. Then the change in the capital stock is given by

$$\Delta K = sY - \delta K = sF(K, L) - \delta K \qquad (14.2)$$

where s is the **saving rate**, which satisfies $0 < s < 1$.[1] Equation (14.2) says that net investment equals gross investment (and gross real saving), $sF(K, L)$, less depreciation, δK.

Figure 14.2 uses the graph of the production function from Figure 14.1 to illustrate the determination of net investment, ΔK. Gross investment, $sF(K, L)$, is the multiple s of the curve shown in Figure 14.1. Depreciation, δK, is the straight line from the origin with slope δ. Net investment is the difference between the two curves.

Figure 14.2 shows that net investment is positive for a range of capital stocks, $K > 0$. (If $K = 0$, then we assume that the economy cannot produce anything.[2]) But as K rises, diminishing returns set in and the slope of the gross investment curve, $sF(K, L)$, gets flatter. Eventually – at the capital stock K^* shown in the figure – the curve gets flat enough to cross the depreciation line, δK. At that point, gross

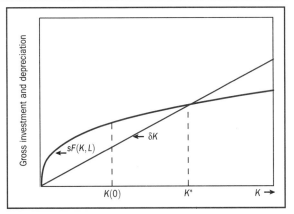

Figure 14.2   Determination of change in the capital stock

investment just covers depreciation, and net investment, ΔK, equals zero.

Suppose, as an example, that the economy starts with the capital stock $K(0)$ shown in Figure 14.2. Gross investment exceeds depreciation at this point, and net investment, ΔK, is positive. The stock of capital, K, therefore rises over time and the economy moves along the horizontal axis to the right of $K(0)$. This movement to higher values of K continues as long as ΔK is positive. That is, K increases over time as long as $K < K^*$, and K gradually approaches the value K^*. Once the capital stock gets to $K = K^*$, net investment becomes zero and K no longer changes over time. The stock then stays fixed forever at K^*. For that reason, K^* is called the **steady-state** capital stock.[3]

Note that the capital stock, K, determines aggregate output, Y, from the production function shown in Figure 14.1, $Y = F(K, L)$, where L is a given quantity. An increase in K therefore translates into an increase in Y. It follows that Y grows over time whenever K grows, that is, as long as $0 < K < K^*$ in Figure 14.2. If the economy begins at $K = K(0)$, then Y starts at $Y(0) = F[K(0), L]$ and then grows due to capital accumulation. Eventually, K approaches K^* and Y approaches its steady-state value, $Y^* = F(K^*, L)$. Thus, capital accumulation leads for a while to growth in output, but cannot sustain growth in output forever. The workings of diminishing returns imply that growth vanishes in the long run.

Figure 14.3 shows that a higher saving rate shifts upward the $sF(K, L)$ curve and thereby raises K^*. A proportional upward shift in the production function, $F(K, L)$, would shift the $sF(K, L)$ curve upward in the same way as an increase in s. Therefore, K^* would again increase. Figure 14.4 demonstrates that a lower depreciation rate, which shifts the δK line downward, also leads to a rise in K^*. Thus, an economy has more capital and output in the long run if it saves a higher fraction of its output or if it has a better technology (higher $F(K, L)$ or lower δ).

For some purposes, we want to use an algebraic determination of K^*, corresponding to the intersection between the $sF(K, L)$ and δK curves in Figure 14.2:

$$sF(K^*, L) = \delta K^* \tag{14.3}$$

We can, for example, use equation (14.3) to assess the effect on K^* from an increase in the level of population and, hence, the aggregate labour input, L.

To study the effects from a change in L, we need to know what happens to output, $Y = F(K, L)$, when the two inputs, K and L, expand together. If K and L double, does the economy produce twice as much output, or more or less than twice the output? If output exactly doubles, then the production function exhibits **constant returns to scale**. Alternatively, there are either **increasing or decreasing returns to scale** if

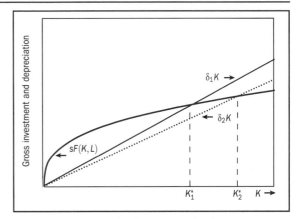

Figure 14.4 Effect of a decrease in the depreciation rate

output more or less than doubles, respectively. The main reason that constant returns to scale would not apply is that some inputs that we have not considered, such as land, do not double when capital and labour double. Output then probably less than doubles when K and L double because the land gets more crowded. To put it another way, constant returns to scale in K and L are likely to be a reasonable approximation if land does not represent an important constraint on production possibilities. We assume for our analysis that fixed factors like land are not so important and hence, that constant returns to scale in K and L are a reasonable approximation.

Go back now to equation (14.3) and assume that the aggregate labour input, L, doubles. If K^* doubles, then $Y^* = F(K^*, L)$ would double because of constant returns to scale. Therefore, the left-hand side of equation (14.3) would double. Because δK^* on the right-hand side also doubles, equation (14.3) must still hold. We have therefore verified that K^* doubles if L doubles. We can also get this result qualitatively from Figure 14.3 – an increase in L is another kind of change that leads to an upward shift in the $sF(K, L)$ curve.

We have found that a doubling of L leads to a doubling of K^*. Since both inputs double, Y^* must also double. More generally, K^* and Y^* change in the same proportion as L. Hence, a larger economy – with a greater population and, hence, a larger aggregate labour input, L – has

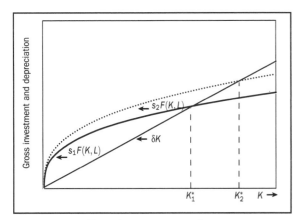

Figure 14.3 Effect of an increase in the saving rate

a proportionately higher capital stock and level of output in the long run. To put this result another way, the steady-state quantities *per worker*, K^*/L and Y^*/L, are independent of L.

We can use Figure 14.2 to think about economies with different levels of L if we measure K^* and $K(0)$ as quantities per worker. The model then describes how capital per worker, K/L, rises from its initial value, $K(0)/L$, to its steady-state value, K^*/L. Correspondingly, output per worker, Y/L, rises from $Y(0)/L$ to Y^*/L.

Although this simple model cannot explain growth in the very long run, it can illuminate the process of growth over the transition from an initial position, $K(0)$ and $Y(0)$, to the steady-state position, K^* and Y^*. For reasonable specifications of the model, this transition turns out to take a long time – several generations, rather than several years. The properties of this transition therefore provide important insights about the growth of capital and output over a long period.

Convergence

Consider a group of economies that has the same steady-state value, K^*, but different starting positions, $K(0)$. (Recall that we can allow for differences in L across economies by expressing K^* and $K(0)$ as quantities per worker.) In the model, K^* depends from Figure 14.2 and equation (14.3) on the position and slope of the production function, $F(K, L)$, and the saving and depreciation rates, s and δ. Thus, economies have similar K^* if they have access to about the same technologies – $F(K, L)$ and δ – and also have similar preferences about saving.

A key prediction of this model is that the initially poorer economies, with lower values of $K(0)$ and $Y(0)$, tend to catch up to the initially richer ones. The differences in capital stocks and outputs are gradually eliminated as each economy approaches the common steady-state values, K^* and Y^*. This tendency toward **convergence** means that the lower the starting values, $K(0)$ and $Y(0)$,

Box 14.1   How Long is the Transition Interval?

We found that the capital stock moves during a transition interval from its starting value, $K(0)$, to its steady-state value, K^*. A key determinant of the length of this transition interval is how rapidly the slope of $F(K, L)$ in Figure 14.1 flattens out as K rises, that is, how quickly diminishing returns to capital set in for given L. If the curve bends over rapidly, then it takes little time to reach K^* – a relatively small change in K causes the $sF(K, L)$ curve in Figure 14.2 to intersect with the δK line. Conversely, if $F(K, L)$ bends over slowly, then it takes a long time. If diminishing returns to capital do not set in at all, then the $sF(K, L)$ curve in Figure 14.2 becomes a straight line, which never intersects the δK line. The steady-state capital stock, K^*, is then infinite and the transition interval is also infinite. (Capital and output, K and Y, can grow forever in this case.)

We should take a broad view of capital to include human, as well as physical, components. Education and experience are capital just as much as business plant and equipment are capital. We should then interpret L as the quantity of raw labour, that is, labour input that is not yet augmented by investments in human capital. The broad array of potential investments in physical and human capital suggests that the economy would not experience diminishing returns to capital very quickly. The steady-state value, K^*, would be finite – because diminishing returns would set in eventually – but could be very far from the typical starting value, $K(0)$. The transition interval is then finite, but long. A reasonable estimate from a full specification of the model is that it takes about 35 years – roughly a generation – to eliminate half of the gap between $K(0)$ and K^*.

the higher the average growth rate during the transition: the faster growth rate is the mechanism whereby the economies with lower starting values catch up to those with higher starting values. The model predicts accordingly that poor economies grow faster on average than rich economies.

For the development of a single country over time, the model predicts that growth rates will be high when capital per worker is low and will decline as capital per worker rises. Thus, we expect to find higher growth rates at early stages of development – such as in the nineteenth century for the main industrial nations – than at later stages.

A low value of capital per worker also implies a high marginal product of capital and therefore a high real interest rate, r. (Recall from Chapter 12 that investors equate capital's marginal product, MPK, to $r + \delta$.) It follows that the real interest rate would decline along with capital's marginal product as an economy develops.

Population Growth

We already know that an increase in population, which leads to an increase in total labour input, L, causes the steady-state values, K^* and Y^*, to rise in the same proportion as L. Continuing growth of the population and the labour force lead to continuing expansion of L and hence, of K^* and Y^*. For example, if L grows at 1% per year – a realistic number for the recent experience of most developed countries – then K^* and Y^* also grow at 1% per year.[4] Since K and Y grow along with K^* and Y^* in the long run, population growth can sustain long-term growth in K and Y. Hence, the economy no longer tends to constant levels of capital and output if the population is continually expanding.

Suppose that the population grows at a constant rate, say 1% per year, and that aggregate labour input, L, also grows at 1% per year. The quantities K and Y then also grow in the long run at 1% per year. Since K grows at the same rate as L, the ratio, K/L, does not change in the long run. Similarly, Y/L is constant in the long run. Therefore, although population growth can sustain long-term growth in the levels of capital and output, it cannot sustain long-term expansion in capital per worker, K/L, or output per worker, Y/L.

If the growth rate of population is positive, then the main results from the previous discussion remain valid if we reinterpret everything in terms of amounts per worker (or per person). We must, for example, replace K and Y by K/L and Y/L, respectively. Instead of steady-state levels of variables, K^* and Y^*, we have to think about steady-state values of quantities per worker, $(K/L)^*$ and $(Y/L)^*$. Also, the statements about growth during the transition from $K(0)$ to K^* – now re-expressed as $K(0)/L(0)$ to $(K/L)^*$ – translate into statements about growth of capital and output *per worker* or *per person*.[5] The previous results about convergence are correct if we say that countries with lower per capita levels of capital and output tend to have higher per capita growth rates. Similarly, the per capita growth rate for a country would tend to decline over time as the per capita quantities of capital and output increased.

Finally, we should note that the discussion in this section allows the population growth rate to be positive, but does not consider how this growth rate is determined. We should be able to apply economic reasoning to determine population growth by thinking about the factors that influence fertility, mortality, and migration. Some classical economists, such as Malthus, Ricardo, and Marx, regarded population growth as a central element of economic analysis, although their theories did not stand up empirically. The discussion at the end of this chapter considers some recent work along these lines.

Technological Progress

We already considered the effect of a one-time improvement in the technology. If the production function, $F(K, L)$, shifts upward in a proportional manner, then the $sF(K, L)$ curve shifts upward as shown in Figure 14.3. The result is that K^* increases. Steady-state output, $Y^* = F(K^*, L)$, then rises for two reasons: first, because the production function shifted upward, and second, because K^* rose. Note also that L is constant in this example. An improvement in the technology leads therefore to increases in the per worker magnitudes, K^*/L and Y^*/L.

The results for a one-time improvement in technology suggest that the economy could sustain long-term per capita growth if the production function shifted upward continually. The technology would improve in this way if producers tended over time to discover new products and methods of production or if they learned to operate their existing methods more efficiently. Economists refer to this process of learning and discovery as **technological progress**. This kind of progress is, in fact, crucial to the long-term per capita growth that the major industrialized nations have been able to sustain for almost two centuries. If the production function had remained fixed, then diminishing returns would have made it impossible to maintain per capita growth for so long just by accumulating more capital per worker. Technological progress, by allowing an escape from diminishing returns, enables the economy to grow in per capita terms, even in the long run.

The main results that we worked out before remain valid when the technology improves regularly over time. The major difference is that the per worker quantities, K/L and Y/L, no longer tend toward fixed steady-state targets, $(K/L)^*$ and $(Y/L)^*$. We have to think instead about moving targets: for example, $(Y/L)^*$ might rise over time as shown by the solid curve in Figure 14.5, due to ongoing technological change. The actual output per worker, Y/L, then gradually approaches the moving target, $(Y/L)^*$, as shown in the figure. The approach of Y/L to $(Y/L)^*$ involves the accumulation of capital – that is, K/L adjusting toward $(K/L)^*$ – just as in our previous settings.

In the long run, Y/L grows along the $(Y/L)^*$ path shown in Figure 14.5. The ratio of capital to labour, K/L, grows analogously along with $(K/L)^*$. Diminishing returns do not apply here, because the negative effect of a higher K/L on capital's marginal product is offset by technological progress. Capital's marginal product and the

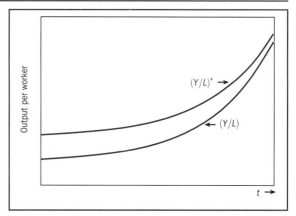

Figure 14.5 The approach of output per worker to its steady-state path

real interest rate therefore do not tend to fall along the steady-state path. (The marginal product and the real interest fall, as in the previous analysis, during the transition from Y/L to $(Y/L)^*$.)

The inclusion of technological progress affects some of the conclusions about convergence. The main new idea is that per capita growth rates are high not when Y/L is low in an absolute sense but rather when Y/L is far from $(Y/L)^*$, which is no longer constant over time. For a group of economies that have the same production function (and the same δ and s), the model still predicts that those with lower per capita product tend to grow faster in per capita terms. The learning and adaptation of advanced techniques also provides another mechanism whereby the poorer places catch up to the richer ones.

For the development of a single country over time, it is no longer necessarily true that the per capita growth rate would slow down as per capita product increased. If Y/L grows along with $(Y/L)^*$ in Figure 14.5, then the gap between $(Y/L)^*$ and Y/L does not change, and the per capita growth rate would not tend to decrease as Y/L rose. The theory says only that the per capita growth rate would fall if the spread between $(Y/L)^*$ and Y/L narrowed. For example, this framework suggests that the per capita growth rate in the US and the UK should have been relatively high at early stages of development, perhaps for much of the nineteenth century. In

Box 14.2   The Behaviour of the Saving Rate

We have assumed that the saving rate, s, does not vary as the economy grows. We now use our analysis of household behaviour from earlier chapters to consider whether this assumption is plausible. For simplicity, we think about the effects in the framework that neglects technological progress. The same ideas would still apply, however, if we extended the analysis to incorporate this progress.

As the economy grows, K/L and Y/L rise toward their steady-state values, $(K/L)^*$ and $(Y/L)^*$. The increases in K/L and Y/L affect the saving rate through two channels: a substitution effect and a wealth effect. The substitution effect involves the real interest rate – recall that a higher rate gives households a greater incentive to defer consumption from the present to the future. As K/L rises, the decline in capital's marginal product and, hence, in the real interest rate reduces the incentive to defer consumption. This effect tends to lower the saving rate as the economy develops.

The wealth effect involves the behaviour of Y/L and, hence, per capita real income. At early stages of development, real income is low in relation to the levels that will be attained later. The expectation of high future income – that is, the high ratio of long-run to current income – motivates households to consume more in relation to current income and therefore lowers the saving rate. As the economy grows and approaches the steady state, the ratio of current to future income rises. Hence, households are motivated to consume a smaller fraction of current income, and the saving rate tends to increase.

On net, the saving rate falls (or rises) as the economy develops if the effect from the declining real interest rate more (or less) than offsets the impact of growing real income. It turns out if one goes more deeply into models of saving behaviour that the net effect can reasonably go in either direction. That is, there is no presumption that the saving rate will either fall or rise as an economy develops and, moreover, the saving rate can plausibly remain roughly constant. Thus, our simplified framework that assumed a constant saving rate may be a reasonable approximation.

---

the twentieth century, however, Y/L might have been close to $(Y/L)^*$ – the steady-state path – and the per capita growth rate would not tend to fall as Y/L rose.

As with population growth, the discussion does not use economic analysis to explain the changes in technology. We would like, for example, to understand why producers carry out the research and development that leads to new products and better methods of production. We discuss at the end of this chapter some recent theories that attempt to explain technological progress.

Evidence from the US History

Table 14.1 contains data for the United States from the nineteenth and twentieth centuries on the growth rate of real gross national product (GNP), a measure of the real interest rate, and the ratios of real gross and net investment to real GNP. (The figures on GNP and investment for the nineteenth century are rough estimates.) The data are averages over 20-year intervals, except for the recent period, 1980–90, and with the exclusion of the years around the three major wars (1861–66, 1917–19, 1941–46).

A striking observation from the table is the absence of a long-term trend in the growth rate of real per capita GNP after around 1880. The six observations from 1880 to 1990 scatter around the mean of 1.6% per year. In contrast, the growth rates from 1840 to 1880 were higher than those that prevailed later.[6] For the full sample, the highest per capita growth rate, 3.3% per year, occurred in 1867–80 during the recovery from the

	Growth rates (% per year)			Interest and inflation rates (% per year)[a]			Investment ratios	
	Real GNP	Population	Real GNP per capita	R	π	r = R − π	Gross private fixed investment GNP	Net private fixed investment GNP
1840–1860	4.9	3.1	1.8	8.6	−0.5	9.1	—	—
1867–1880	5.6[b]	2.3[b]	3.3[b]	6.7	−2.4	9.1	0.17[c]	0.09[c]
1880–1900	3.2	2.1	1.1	5.6	−0.7	6.3	0.19[d]	0.10[d]
1900–1916	3.7	1.8	1.9	5.5	2.4	3.1	0.17	0.07
1920–1940	2.2	1.1	1.1	3.3	−1.6	4.9	0.12	0.01
1947–1960	3.4	1.7	1.7	2.3	2.5	−0.2	0.16	0.07
1960–1980	3.2	1.2	2.0	5.9	4.7	1.2	0.16	0.06
1980–1990	2.6	1.0	1.6	9.6	4.8	4.8	0.16	0.05

Notes and Sources: The periods exclude the years around the three major wars, 1861–66, 1917–19, and 1941–46.

For the data on real GNP, see Figure 1.1 of Chapter 1.

R is the nominal interest rate on 4- to 6-month prime commercial paper. For 1857–89, the variable refers to 60 to 90-day rates, as reported in Macaulay (1938, table 10). For 1840–56 the rates are Bigelow's estimates for the 'New York and Boston money markets', as reported by Macaulay in table 25. Interest rates since 1890 are in US Department of Commerce (1975, p. 1001) and Federal Reserve Bulletin, various issues.

The inflation rate, π, is based on the GNP deflator since 1869. For the data, see Figure 1.4 of Chapter 1. Data on the price level before 1869 refer to the consumer price index, as reported in US Department of Commerce (1975, p. 211).

The investment ratios equal real fixed, private, domestic investment divided by real GNP. Data on investment for 1869–1928 are from Kendrick (1961, tables A-I, A-III).

Data on all variables for recent years are from US Department of Commerce (1986) and U.S. Survey of Current Business, various issues.

[a] Dates for the interest rate are 1840–59, 1867–79, 1880–99, 1900–15, 1920–39, 1947–59, and 1960–79, 1980–89. Thereby the periods correspond roughly to those for the inflation rate.

[b] 1869–80 (data on real GNP for 1867–68 are unavailable).

[c] 1869–78.

[d] 1879–1900.

Table 14.1   Growth rates, interest rates, and investment ratios for the United States since 1840

Civil War. The two lowest rates, each 1.1% per year, were for 1880–1900 and 1920–40, periods that included lengthy depressions in the 1890s and 1930s, respectively.

The theory predicts declining per capita growth rates if an economy's output per worker, Y/L, is initially well below the steady-state path, $(Y/L)^*$ (see Figure 14.5). Thus, we can reconcile the theory with the facts if the US economy began in 1840 with $Y/L < (Y/L)^*$, but had got close to the steady-state path by around 1880. We can then think of the US economy as evolving since 1880 along a steady-state path in which the average per capita growth rate, 1.6% per year, was driven by technological progress. There is no tendency along this path for the per capita growth rate to rise or fall.[7]

The theory also implies that any decline over time in capital's marginal product would show up as a fall in real interest rates. To get a long time series on interest rates, we use the rate on prime commercial paper, a category that comprises short-term notes issued by established companies. (US Treasury bills were first issued in 1929.) The real interest rate shown in Table 14.1 is the nominal interest rate less the inflation rate computed from the GNP deflator.[8] We use the actual real interest rate over periods of one or two decades as a rough estimate of the expected real interest rate.

Real interest rates from 1840 to 1879 (excluding the Civil War years) were very high, exceeding 9%, and remained above 6% from 1880 to 1899. For 1900–39 (excluding the years of World War I), the real rates averaged about 4%. After World War II, real interest rates were extremely low, averaging less than 1% for 1947–79. In contrast, for 1980–89, the real interest rates averaged 4.8%, a value similar to that experienced before World War II.

The excess of the real interest rates in the nineteenth century – especially those from 1840 to 1879 – over those of the twentieth century suggests a fall in capital's marginal product from one century to the next. The pattern during the twentieth century is less clear because the average real rates in the 1980s were at least as high as those from the early years of the century. If we think of the real interest rates for the twentieth century as showing no long-term trend, then the results are consistent with rough stability of capital's marginal product over this period. We can again explain this behaviour by arguing that the twentieth-century US economy was evolving along a steady-state path, driven by technological progress. Although the ratio of capital to labour, K/L, rose over time, the technological progress offset the tendency for diminishing returns. The theory is therefore consistent with the absence of a trend in capital's marginal product and, hence, in real interest rates during the twentieth century.

Table 14.1 also shows the ratios of gross and net fixed private investment to GNP – data are available here only since 1867. The gross numbers

indicate a nearly constant ratio in the long run. The net figures suggest some long-term decline, corresponding to an increase in the ratio of depreciation to GNP. Recall that the theory of economic growth in this chapter assumed that the ratio of gross investment to output equalled a constant, s. Thus, the main conclusion from the US data is that this assumption is probably a satisfactory approximation for long-run analysis.

To summarize, we can think of the US economy as starting in 1840 with a low value of output per worker, Y/L, relative to the steady-state path, $(Y/L)^*$. The economy then went through a convergence interval in which the per capita growth rate and real interest rate were high, but declining over time. By the end of the nineteenth century, the economy had come close to the steady-state path. The economy evolved subsequently along this path: accordingly, the per capita growth rate and real interest rate showed no long-term trends during the twentieth century.

Evidence on Convergence from the US States and Regions of Western Europe[9]

Figure 14.6 considers the growth of per capita income[10] for 47 US states or territories from 1880

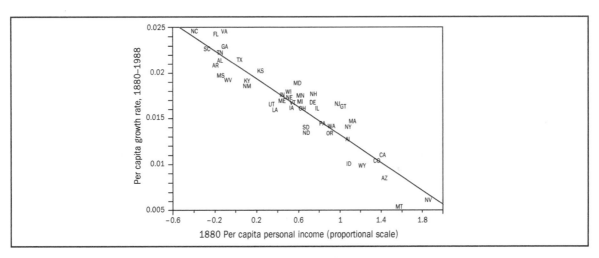

Figure 14.6   Growth of per capita income for US states, 1880–1988

to 1988. (The data for Oklahoma are unavailable because 1880 preceded the Oklahoma land rush.) The plot shows a remarkably strong inverse correlation between the average growth rate and the 1880 level of per capita income. That is, the initially poorer states grew significantly faster in per capita terms and thereby tended to catch up to the initially richer states.

Figure 14.7 depicts the convergence process in terms of the levels of average per capita income of the four regions: east, south, midwest, and west. The southern states tended to have low per capita incomes in 1880 (largely because of the Civil War) and high average growth rates thereafter.[11] The western states had high average incomes in 1880 (due principally to opportunities in mining), followed by low average growth rates. Thus, the figure shows that the average income levels for the four regions converged dramatically over the 108 years after 1880.

Although regional catch-up is part of the convergence story, the tendency for the poorer states to grow faster in per capita terms holds equally well within the regions. For example, the relatively poor eastern states, such as Maine and Vermont in 1880, tended to catch up to the relatively rich eastern states, such as Massachusetts and Rhode Island in 1880, about as fast as the typical southern state tended to catch

up to the typical western or eastern state. Thus, the data for the US states clearly reveal the convergence pattern predicted by the growth theory developed in this chapter.

We can also use the US evidence to assess the speed of convergence. The pattern displayed in Figure 14.6 turns out to imply that the spread in levels of per capita income between the typical poor and rich state vanishes at roughly 2% per year. This speed of adjustment implies that the *half life* of convergence – the time that it takes to eliminate half of the initial gap – is about 35 years. For the states to get still closer together, say to eliminate three-quarters of the initial spread, takes about 70 years. Figure 14.7 shows how these estimates of convergence times relate to the regional performance: although the level of per capita income in the south eventually got close to that in the other regions, it took about a century for this process to occur.

Figure 14.8 provides evidence on convergence for 73 regions of 7 western European countries from 1950 to 1985. (The data are for 11 regions in Germany, 11 in the United Kingdom, 20 in Italy, 21 in France, 4 in the Netherlands, 3 in Belgium, and 3 in Denmark: see Figure 14.9 and Table 14.2 for a listing of the regions.) Figure 14.8 shows that the average growth rate of per capita gross domestic product (GDP) on the vertical axis is inversely related to the 1950 level of per capita GDP, shown on the horizontal.[12] Thus, as with the US states, the poorer regions grew faster in per capita terms than the richer regions and therefore tended to catch up in levels of per capita GDP. The results for the European regions also accord quantitatively with those for the US states: the rate of convergence implied by Figure 14.8 turns out again to be about 2% per year.

Evidence on Convergence across Countries

Figure 14.10 plots the growth rate of real per capita gross domestic product (GDP) from 1960 to 1985 for 98 countries against the level of real per capita GDP in 1960.[13] This data set includes most of the countries in the world: the main

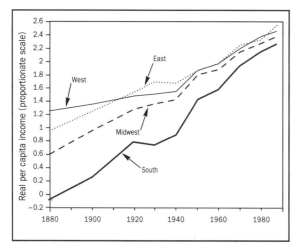

Figure 14.7 Income per capita over time for four US regions

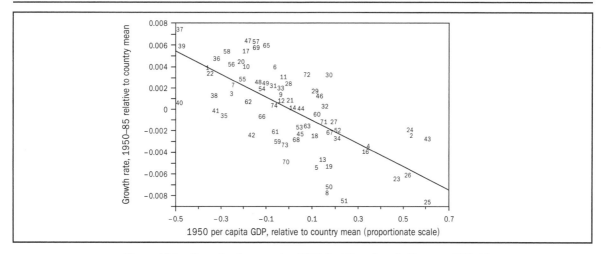

Figure 14.8 Growth of per capita GDP for 73 regions in Europe, 1950–85

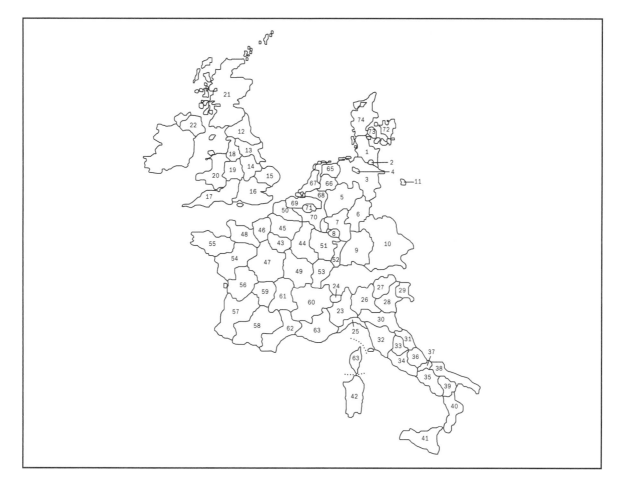

Figure 14.9 Map of regions of Europe

Germany	25. Liguria	52. Alsace	
1. Schleswig-Holstein	26. Lombardia	53. Franche-Comte	
2. Hamburg	27. Trentino-Alto Adige	54. Pays de la Loire	
3. Niedersachsen	28. Veneto	55. Bretagne	
4. Bremen	29. Friuli-Venezia, Giulia	56. Poitou-Charentes	
5. Nordrhein-Westfalen	30. Emilia-Romagna	57. Aquitaine	
6. Hessen	31. Marche	58. Midi-Pyrénées	
7. Rheinland-Pfalz	32. Toscana	59. Limousin	
8. Saarland	33. Umbria	60. Rhône-Alpes	
9. Baden-Württemberg	34. Lazio	61. Auvergne	
10. Bayern	35. Campania	62. Languedoc-Roussillon	
11. Berlin (West)	36. Abruzzi	63. Provence-Alpes-Cote d'Azur-Corse[a]	
	37. Molise		
United Kingdom	38. Puglia	*Netherlands*	
12. North	39. Basilicata	65. Noord	
13. Yorkshire-Humberside	40. Calabria	66. Oost	
14. East Midlands	41. Sicilia	67. West	
15. East Anglia	42. Sardegna	68. Zuid	
16. South-East			
17. South-West	*France*	*Belgium*	
18. North-West	43. Region Parisienne	69. Vlaanderen	
19. West Midlands	44. Champagne-Ardenne	70. Wallonie	
20. Wales	45. Picardie	71. Brabant	
21. Scotland	46. Haute Normandie		
22. Northern Ireland	47. Centre	*Denmark*	
	48. Basse Normandie	72. Sjaelland-Lolland-Falster-	
Italy	49. Bourgogne	Bornholm	
23. Piemonte	50. Nord-Pas-de-Calais	73. Fyn	
24. Valle d'Aosta	51. Lorraine	74. Jylland	

[a]GDP data from Eurostat for Corse were combined with those for Provence-Alpes-Cote d'Azur.

Table 14.2   List of European regions shown in Figures 14.8 and 14.9

exceptions are the Eastern European countries and some smaller countries with missing data. (See Table 14.3 for a listing of the countries included in Figure 14.10.) The range of real per capita GDP in 1960 is from $208 for Tanzania to $7380 for the United States (in terms of 1980 US dollars).

Unlike the regional findings depicted in Figures 14.6 and 14.7, the diagram in Figure 14.10 reveals little relation between initial per capita GDP and the subsequent per capita growth rate. If anything, the initially poorer countries grew at a somewhat below-average rate from 1960 to 1985. Thus, these data do not conform to the convergence hypothesis that came from our theory of economic growth.

Figure 14.11 limits the sample to the 20 countries that were members of the Organ-

ization of Economic Cooperation and Development (OECD) by 1960.[14] Aside from having much higher average per capita GDP than the 98 countries considered in Figure 14.10, the OECD countries are more similar in terms of basic economic and political institutions. Figure 14.11 exhibits an inverse relation between the average per capita growth rate and the initial level of per capita GDP. Thus, a pattern of convergence does show up for a relatively homogeneous collection of well-off countries. The relation does, however, differ quantitatively from that found for the regions of the United States or western Europe in Figures 14.6 and 14.8. For the 20 OECD countries, the gap between poor and rich vanishes at about 1% per year, in contrast to the 2% per year found for the regions. Thus, although convergence appears among the OECD

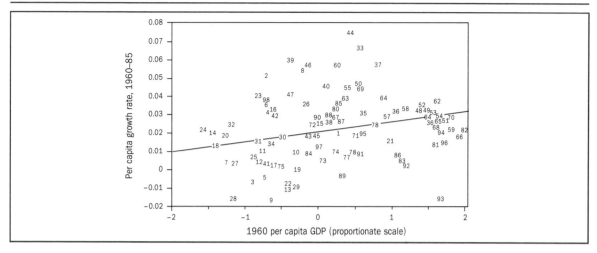

Figure 14.10   Growth of per capita GDP for 98 countries, 1960–85

1.	Algeria	26.	Tunisia	51.	Denmark	76.	Honduras
2.	Botswana	27.	Uganda	52.	Finland	77.	Jamaica
3.	Burundi	28.	Zaire	53.	France	78.	Mexico
4.	Cameroon	29.	Zambia	54.	Germany	79.	Nicaragua
5.	Central Afr. Repub.	30.	Zimbabwe	55.	Greece	80.	Panama
6.	Egypt	31.	Bangladesh	56.	Iceland	81.	Trinidad & Tobago
7.	Ethiopia	32.	Burma	57.	Ireland	82.	United States
8.	Gabon	33.	Hong Kong	58.	Italy	83.	Argentina
9.	Ghana	34.	India	59.	Luxembourg	84.	Bolivia
10.	Ivory Coast	35.	Iran	60.	Malta	85.	Brazil
11.	Kenya	36.	Israel	61.	Netherlands	86.	Chile
12.	Liberia	37.	Japan	62.	Norway	87.	Colombia
13.	Madagascar	38.	Jordan	63.	Portugal	88.	Ecuador
14.	Malawi	39.	Korea	64.	Spain	89.	Guyana
15.	Mauritius	40.	Malaysia	65.	Sweden	90.	Paraguay
16.	Morocco	41.	Nepal	66.	Switzerland	91.	Peru
17.	Nigeria	42.	Pakistan	67.	Turkey	92.	Uruguay
18.	Rwanda	43.	Phillipines	68.	United Kingdom	93.	Venezuela
19.	Senegal	44.	Singapore	69.	Barbados	94.	Australia
20.	Sierra Leone	45.	Sri Lanka	70.	Canada	95.	Fiji
21.	South Africa	46.	Taiwan	71.	Costa Rica	96.	New Zealand
22.	Sudan	47.	Thailand	72.	Dominican Republic	97.	Papua New Guinea
23.	Swaziland	48.	Austria	73.	El Salvador	98.	Indonesia
24.	Tanzania	49.	Belgium	74.	Guatemala		
25.	Togo	50.	Cyprus	75.	Haiti		

Table 14.3   Key for countries in Figures 14.10 and 14.11

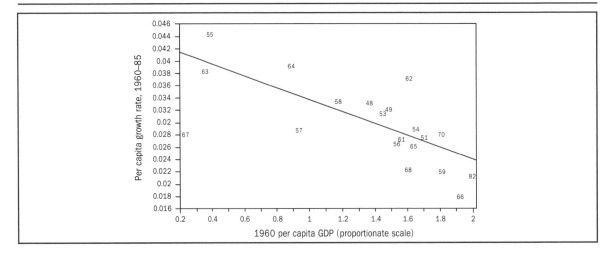

Figure 14.11   Growth of per capita GDP for 20 OECD countries, 1960–85

countries, the speed is slower than that for the regions.

In the first model that we considered, we derived the convergence hypothesis – poor economies growing faster than rich ones – by assuming that the various economies had the same steady- state values, K^* and Y^*. Figure 14.2 and equation (14.3) showed that these values

were the same if economies had the same production functions, $F(K, L)$, and also had the same depreciation and saving rates, δ and s.

In the extended models that allow for population growth and technological progress, the convergence hypothesis depends on each country having the same steady-state path, $(Y/L)^*$, shown in Figure 14.3. The poor grow faster per capita

Box 14.3 Application of the Results to Eastern Germany

An important issue is the speed with which the poor regions of the former East Germany will catch up to the prosperous West. We can apply the theory and empirical findings from the regions of western Europe and the United States to address this issue. The good news is that the convergence will occur, but the bad news is that it will not happen quickly.

There were substantial variations in estimates of East German productivity at the time of the reunification with the West in 1990. A reasonable range is from one-third to one-half the West German figure. The evidence from the US states and the regions of western Europe – which indicated that the gaps between poor and rich parts of a country vanish at about 2% per year – implies that the per capita growth

rate in the eastern parts of Germany would be initially $1\frac{1}{2}$ to 2 percentage points per year higher than in the West. This growth advantage (which declines over time as the East catches up to the West) means that it will take about 15 years to eliminate one-quarter of the gap and about 70 years to eliminate three-quarters of it. Thus, the per capita product in the East would eventually catch up to that in the West, but in a couple of generations, rather than in the couple of years or couple of decades that had been suggested by some optimistic analyses. Although the forces of convergence are powerful in the long run, anything approaching parity between eastern and western Germany is unimaginable in the short run.

than the rich if poor and rich are approaching the same (moving) target. The target is the same, however, only if the economies are basically similar: in addition to a common production function and equal values of δ and s, the countries must have the same rates of population growth and technological progress. The notion that all these characteristics are roughly the same may be satisfactory for a long-run analysis of the US states and the regions of countries in western Europe, but is inaccurate for the OECD countries and is particularly unreasonable for the heterogeneous collection of 98 countries. Thus, we should return to the theory to see how differences across economies in the steady-state path, $(Y/L)^*$, modify the convergence hypothesis.

The key idea is that per capita growth is higher the larger the gap between $(Y/L)^*$ and Y/L: Consider two countries, A and B, such that $(Y/L)_A$ is twice as large as $(Y/L)_B$. The poor country, B, grows faster than A if it has the same steady-state path as A. But if $(Y/L)^*_A$ were twice as large as $(Y/L)^*_B$, then the two countries would grow at the same rate. The point is that the theory implies a form of *relative convergence*. The growth rate does not depend on the *absolute* value of Y/L, but rather on the value measured *relative* to the economy's own steady-state position. If a country has low per-worker output, but also has low per-worker product along the steady-state path, then the theory does not predict that this country will grow rapidly.

One reason for a country to have a low value of $(Y/L)^*$ is that it has a low saving rate, s. It turns out that another reason for a low value of $(Y/L)^*$ is a high rate of population growth. A country also has a low value of $(Y/L)^*$ if it has access only to poor technologies – that is, if the level of the production function, $F(K,L)$, is low or if the technology does not improve rapidly over time. In extended versions of the growth theory that allow for a role of government, differences in government policies can work like differences in the levels of production functions. For example, if governments restrict trade, fail to protect property rights, impose high tax rates on economic activity, or provide poor infrastructure services such as highways, then the country operates as if

it had a low level of technology. Thus, bad government policies are another reason for a low steady-state path, $(Y/L)^*$.

The idea of relative convergence can explain why convergence does not show up for the broad group of countries in Figure 14.10, but does arise for the more homogeneous sub-group of countries in Figure 14.11, and appears even more strongly for the regions of the United States and western Europe in Figures 14.6 and 14.8. The countries considered in Figure 14.10 differ substantially in terms of basic political and economic institutions and are therefore likely to vary considerably in their steady-state path, $(Y/L)^*$. The poor countries are, in particular, likely to be poor for good reason in the sense that the poverty reflects inadequacies of government policies or other factors that affect the willingness to save, invest, and work. Unfortunately, these kinds of adverse conditions tend to persist over time. Thus, although per-worker product, Y/L, is low in these countries, it does not tend to be systematically low or high in relation to the steady-state value, $(Y/L)^*$. This observation explains why the poor countries in Figure 14.11 do not grow on average at high rates.

If we shift the focus to a more homogeneous collection of economies, such as the OECD countries or, even more so, to the regions of the United States and western Europe, then the similarities of policies and institutions suggest that the steady-state values, $(Y/L)^*$, would be similar. A low level of Y/L therefore signals a greater departure from $(Y/L)^*$. It follows that a simple pattern of convergence – the poor growing in per capita terms faster than the rich – shows up within these homogeneous groups. Moreover, the slower rate of convergence among the OECD countries than for the regions of the United States or western Europe can be explained by noting that the regions within a single country are likely to be more similar in terms of government policies and institutions than are the 20 OECD countries.

A further empirical challenge is to extend the analysis of growth across the broad group of countries considered in Figure 14.10 to isolate some of the factors that determine the steady-state path, $(Y/L)^*$. If we can hold constant $(Y/L)^*$, then the inverse relation between the per capita growth rate and the starting level of per capita product should appear – that is, we should see relative convergence in the data.

A recent study of economic growth across countries (Robert Barro, 1991) explored the role of a number of explanatory variables, including measures of government policies. Once these variables are held constant, the relation between the growth rate of real per capita GDP from 1960 to 1985 and the level of real per capita GDP in 1960 looks similar to the results described before for the US states and the regions of western Europe. The gap between a country's initial real per capita GDP and its own steady-state path vanishes at roughly 1–2% per year. This result from the cross-country data confirms the relative convergence that is predicted by the theory.

It is important to recognize that these cross-country findings demonstrate convergence only in a limited sense. A country tends to grow faster per capita if it starts farther below its own long-run target. This result does not mean that the typical less-developed country (LDC) in Africa, South Asia, or Latin America will tend to catch up to the currently prosperous countries. The long-run targets of these LDCs seem, on average, to be as low as their current actual positions; therefore, the LDCs on average are not growing at higher per capita rates than the prosperous countries.

The empirical results[15] also provide indications about which kinds of government policies and other variables matter for a country's steady-state path, $(Y/L)^*$. This path appears to be lower the less the country is open to international trade, the greater the distortion of capital-goods prices, the poorer the workings of credit markets, and the higher the share of government consumption expenditures in GDP. There is also an indication that the target is higher for countries that began (say in 1960) with higher stocks of human capital in the form of educational attainment. Although these results are suggestive, the precise mechanism by which this initial human capital and the various government policies matter for growth are unknown, but are the subject of intensive current research.

Recent Theories of Economic Growth (optional)

A serious deficiency of the theory is that the long-term growth rate depends entirely on factors – the rates of population growth and technological progress – that are not determined within the model. For long-term per capita growth, only the unexplained technological progress matters. In terms of the jargon used in the literature, the long-run growth rate is *exogenous*, that is, determined from outside. The framework does not provide a theory of long-run **endogenous growth** in which the long-term growth rate is determined by interactions within the model.

Research on theories of endogenous growth has been extremely active in the last few years.[16] One area involves models of technological progress that are embedded into theories of economic growth. Another area considers theories of population growth that are integrated with models of growth. Still another strand of theory has dispensed with the idea of the diminishing productivity of capital. It is possible here only to sketch some of the basic ideas in the various approaches to endogenous long-term growth.

Theories of Technological Progress

For countries on the leading edge of technology, such as the US, Japan and the EC countries, it is important to model the process of research and development, a process that leads over time to new and improved products.[17] The businesses that invest in research to come up with new ideas or better designs have to be compensated for their efforts. Typically, this compensation takes the form of exclusive or at least preferred access to the new products or methods of production for some interval of time. In some cases, the property rights in the new products or methods are enforced by patents, but more often the preferred access derives from secrecy or advantages from having moved first into a new area.

In any event, the economy's growth rate involves a tradeoff in which inventions are encouraged by a greater private reward to discoveries, whereas efficiency – after inventions have already been made – dictates free access by many competitors to the available technologies. The results in these kinds of models have implications for desirable patent policy as well as for government subsidies of research efforts. If the private benefit from research falls short of the social benefits, then the amount of research and the consequent rates of technological progress and economic growth tend to be too low from a social perspective. For this reason, some of the models in this area rationalize a public subsidy to basic research (especially to research conducted by economists!).

For most countries, the important consideration is not discoveries of basic knowledge, but rather the rate of absorption of the new methods that have been introduced by the leading countries. The advantages of being a follower – not having to invest resources in basic research – provides another force toward convergence across countries. That is, the poorer countries can grow faster because it is cheaper to adapt advanced techniques rather than to make one's own discoveries. Another point is that human capital is central to the ability to adopt new technologies. The tendency for growth rates across countries to be positively correlated with initial human capital may therefore reflect the enhanced capacity for using the technological advances that have been developed in other countries.

Population Growth

Some theories of economic growth incorporate models in which parents choose their number of children and, hence, the growth rate of population.[18] The number of children per adult amounts to a form of investment. More investment of this type, that is, a larger quantity of children per adult, substitutes for other forms of investment, especially for resources spent improving the quality of each child. Hence, the theory predicts an inverse relation between fertility and the growth rate of per capita product: this relation reflects especially the negative linkage between

fertility and the rate of investment in human capital. It is also possible, as in the classic analysis of Thomas Malthus (1809), to bring in a linkage between income and population growth that involves the response of health and mortality.

The empirical evidence across countries bears out some of the predictions about the role of population growth. For 117 countries from 1960 to 1985, there is a strong inverse association between fertility rates and school-enrolment rates. This linkage probably underlies the negative correlation between fertility and the growth rate of per capita GDP, another relation that appears in the cross-country data.

Constant-Returns Models

Diminishing productivity of capital seems natural if we define capital narrowly to include only machines and buildings. As this kind of capital rises in relation to the quantity of labour (and natural resources), we anticipate that capital's marginal product will fall. If we take a broader view of capital to include investments in persons, then the tendency for diminishing productivity is less obvious. The quantity of labour is no longer fixed, because the investments in humans effectively raise the quantity of labour available. We expect diminishing returns only if the number of bodies (or the quantity of natural resources) represents an important constraint on the production process.

We found before that an economy's long-term growth rate cannot be driven entirely by capital accumulation if capital's productivity is subject to diminishing returns. But the conclusions are different if diminishing productivity does not apply to capital, broadly construed. In this case, even without technological progress, capital accumulation can be sufficient to sustain long-term per capita growth.

One shortcoming of models without diminishing returns is that they do not predict the kinds of convergence results that we discussed before. In the constant-returns models, the growth rate does not depend on the starting level of per capita product. Thus, these theories do not accord with the empirical evidence, summarized earlier, that reveals absolute convergence for homogeneous groups of economies and at least relative convergence for more heterogeneous groups. A promising research strategy is therefore to stick with the models that featured diminishing returns, but extend them to include the theories of technological change and population growth that we sketched above.

Summary

We began with a simple model in which economic growth depended on the accumulation of capital. The workings of diminishing returns imply that the capital stock and output approach fixed steady-state values; that is, growth vanishes in the long run. The steady-state levels of the capital stock and output are higher if the economy saves a larger fraction of its output or if producers have access to better technologies. If the production function satisfies constant returns to scale in capital and labour, then the steady-state values of capital and output are proportional to the labour force.

The transition to the steady state features a declining growth rate of output and a falling real interest rate. These effects correspond to reductions in the marginal product of capital, due to diminishing returns. The model therefore predicts that an economy's growth rate of output will decline as it develops and approaches its steady state. If we consider a group of economies that have the same steady-state positions, then the initially poorer economies will grow faster and thereby converge toward the initially richer economies.

Continuing population growth leads to long-term growth of the levels of capital and output, but not to long-term growth of the per capita quantities. The theory with population growth therefore predicts that the growth rate of per capita product will be inversely related to the initial level of per capita product. Some recent theories apply economic reasoning to the determinants of population growth.

Technological progress can offset the tendency for diminishing returns and lead thereby to long-term growth of per capita output. The per capita growth rate and the real interest rate still decline in the transition to the steady state. Once an economy reaches its steady state, per capita output rises steadily, but the growth rate and the real interest rate no longer tend to decline. Recent theories try to explain the process of research and experience that leads to technological progress. Some of these theories also consider the diffusion of technologies from leading countries to followers.

The US time-series data show that growth rates of per capita GNP and real interest rates tended to decline during the nineteenth century, but have shown no systematic pattern in the twentieth century. The theoretical interpretation is that the United States was converging toward its steady-state path during the nineteenth century and has been growing during the twentieth century along a steady-state path driven by technological progress.

The experiences of the US states since 1880 and the regions of seven western European countries since 1950 show clear evidence of convergence in the sense of poorer regions growing faster than richer ones. This evidence indicates that the gap between the typical rich and poor region vanishes at roughly 2% per year. It therefore takes about 35 years to eliminate one-half of the initial gap.

The behaviour across about 100 countries in the post-World War II period shows no tendency for the poor to grow faster per capita than the rich. We can explain this failure of convergence if we assume that countries differ in their steady-state positions because of differences in government policies, saving rates, or other factors. The data are consistent with relative convergence in the sense that a country grows faster if it starts further away from its own steady-state position. In this interpretation, the typical less-developed country in Africa, South Asia, or Latin America did not grow rapidly from 1960 to 1985 because its low initial value of real per capita GDP was roughly matched by its low steady-state value.

Important Terms and Concepts

gross saving
saving rate
steady state
constant returns to scale
increasing returns to scale
decreasing returns to scale
convergence
technological progress
endogenous growth

Questions and Problems

Mainly for Review

14.1 Does a positive saving rate, s, mean that the capital stock grows over time? Explain by referring to equation (14.2).

14.2 Consider the steady-state capital stock, K^*, determined from equation (14.3). How is K^* affected by the following:
   a. An increase in the saving rate, s.
   b. An upward shift in the production function, $F(K, L)$.
   c. An increase in the depreciation rate, δ.

14.3 If labour input, L, doubles, why does equation (14.3) imply that the steady-state capital stock and output double? How does the result depend on constant returns to scale in the production function?

14.4 Explain why an increase in the capital stock, K, tends to reduce the growth rate of the capital stock, $\Delta K/K$, and the real interest rate. How do these results depend on diminishing returns to capital?

14.5 What is the meaning of the term 'convergence'? How does absolute convergence differ from relative convergence?

14.6 For the United States, Table 14.1 shows that the real interest rate had no clear trend in the twentieth century. Does this result conflict with the theoretical prediction that the real interest rate would decline as the capital stock rose? What about the observation that the real interest rate declined substantially from 1840 to 1900?

14.7 For 98 countries from 1960 to 1985, the growth rate of real per capita GDP shows little relation to the level of real per capita GDP in 1960. Does this finding conflict with our theory of economic growth? How does this question relate to the concept of relative convergence?

Problems for Discussion

14.8 Constant Returns to Scale
Suppose that the production function, $F(K, L)$, satisfies constant returns to scale. This condition means that if we multiply the inputs, K and L, by any positive number, then we multiply output, Y, by the same number. Show that this condition implies that we can write the production function as $Y/L = f(K/L)$. (*Hint*: Use $1/L$ as the number that multiplies the inputs, K and L.) What is the meaning of this result?

14.9 Growth with a Cobb-Douglas Production Function
Suppose that the production function takes the form, $Y = F(K, L) = AK^{\alpha}L^{1-\alpha}$, where $A > 0$, L is the constant labour force, and $0 < \alpha < 1$. (This form is called a *Cobb-Douglas production function*, named after the former US Senator and economist, Paul Douglas, and a mathematician associate, apparently named Cobb.)
   a. Use equation (14.3) to work out formulas for the steady- state values, K^* and Y^*, when the production function is Cobb-Douglas.
   b. What are the steady-state values of investment, I^*, and consumption, C^*?
   c. Use equation (14.2) to work out a formula for the growth rate of the capital stock, $\Delta K/K$. Can you show that this growth rate declines as the capital stock rises?
   d. With a Cobb-Douglas production function, we can write the growth rate of output as $\Delta Y/Y = \alpha \cdot (\Delta K/K) + (1 - \alpha) \cdot \Delta L/L$. (We can derive this result from calculus.) In the present case, $\Delta L = 0$. Use the answer from part c. to work out a formula for the growth rate of output, $\Delta Y/Y$. Does this growth rate decline as K rises? Does it also decline as Y rises?

14.10 Effects of Saving Behaviour on Convergence
Suppose that the gross saving rate, s, can change as an economy develops.
   a. Is equation (14.2) still valid if s is the saving rate that applies at a particular point in time?
   b. Suppose that s declines as an economy develops (because the saving rate is low when the marginal product of capital is low). How does this property affect the tendency for the growth rate of capital, $\Delta K/K$, to decline as the levels of K and Y increase? What does this behaviour mean for the convergence property?
   c. Suppose instead that s rises as an economy develops (because the saving rate is high when the level of income is closer to its steady-state value). What does this behaviour mean for the convergence property?

14.11 Absolute and Relative Convergence
Equation (14.2) implies that the growth rate of the capital stock is given by $\Delta K/K = sY/K - \delta$. Equation (14.3) implies that the (constant) gross saving rate satisfies the condition, $s = \delta K^*/Y^*$. If we substitute out for s in the expression for the growth rate, then we get

$$\Delta K/K = \delta \cdot [(Y/K)/(Y^*/K^*) - 1]$$

Note that Y/K is the average product of capital. For given L, this average product declines as K rises (because of diminishing productivity of capital).

a. Consider a group of economies that have the same steady-state values, K^* and Y^*. Does absolute convergence – poor economies growing faster than rich ones – hold for $\Delta K/K$?
b. Suppose that economies differ in their steady-state values, Y^*/K^*. Do we get relative convergence for $\Delta K/K$ but not necessarily absolute convergence?
c. Do the results in parts a. and b. depend on the assumption that the gross saving rate, s, is constant?

14.12 Growth without Diminishing Returns
Suppose that the production function is $Y = AK$ (the so-called *AK model*), where A is a positive constant.

a. What is the condition for the change in the capital stock, ΔK, in equation (14.2)? What does the $sF(K, L)$ curve look like in Figure 14.2?
b. What is the growth rate of the capital stock, $\Delta K/K$, and output, $\Delta Y/Y$? Are these growth rates positive? Does the convergence property hold in this model?
c. Discuss how the results relate to diminishing returns to capital. Is it plausible that diminishing returns would not apply?

14.13 Effects of Population Growth (optional)
Suppose that population and the labour force grow at the constant rate n and that the gross saving rate is still the constant s.

a. Is equation (14.2) valid? Does the economy still tend toward constant steady-state values, K^* and Y^*?
b. Use equation (14.2) to derive the change over time in capital per worker, K/L. (Use the condition, $\Delta(K/L) = \Delta K/L - (K/L) \cdot (\Delta L/L)$, where $\Delta L/L = n$. We can show from calculus that this condition holds exactly for infinitesimal changes.) Does K/L tend toward a constant, steady-state value, $(K/L)^*$? What determines this value? (Hint: problem 14.8 shows that if the production function, $F(K, L)$, exhibits constant returns to scale, then it is

possible to write output per worker as a function only of capital per worker: $Y/L = f(K/L)$. That is, Y/L depends only on the ratio of K to L and is independent of the scale of the economy.)
c. Does population growth lead to growth of output in the long run? Does it lead in the long run to growth of per capita output?

14.14 Effects of Technological Progress (optional)
Suppose that technological change leads to steady improvements in the production function. We can represent these changes by including time, t, in the production function: $Y = F(K, L, t)$, where t has a positive effect on Y for given values of K and L. A simple form of technological progress operates by making each worker more productive. If L is constant, then the effective number of workers, denoted by $\hat{L}$, grows at the rate $x > 0$. We can write the production function in this case as $Y = F(K, \hat{L})$, where $\Delta\hat{L}/\hat{L} = x$. (This form of technical progress is called *labour augmenting*.) The effects are then formally similar to those from population growth, as discussed in problem 14.13.

a. Is equation (14.2) valid? Does the economy still tend toward constant steady-state values, K^* and Y^*?
b. Use equation (14.2) to derive the change over time in capital per effective worker, $K/\hat{L}$. (Use the condition,

$$\Delta(K/\hat{L}) = \Delta K/\hat{L} - (K/\hat{L}) \cdot (\Delta\hat{L}/\hat{L}),$$

where $\Delta\hat{L}/\hat{L} = x$. We can show from calculus that this condition holds exactly for infinitesimal changes.) Does $K/\hat{L}$ tend toward a constant steady-state value, $(K/\hat{L})^*$? What determines this value? (*Hint*: Problem 14.8 shows that if the production function, $F(K,)$, exhibits constant returns to scale, then it is possible to write output per effective worker as a function only of capital per effective worker: $Y/\hat{L} = f(K/\hat{L})$.)
c. Does technological progress lead to growth of per capita output in the long run?

14.15 Economic Development and the Real Wage Rate
Assume that the real wage rate is determined on the labour market to equal the marginal product of labour.

a. Consider an economy with zero population growth and no technological progress. In the transition to the steady state, the capital stock rises. What happens during the transition to the real wage rate? How does the real wage rate behave in the steady state?
b. (optional) Consider an economy in which population grows at the constant rate n (see problem 14.13). Suppose that the capital–labour ratio, K/L, rises during the transition,

but stays constant in the steady state. How does the real wage rate behave in this situation?

c. (optional) Consider an economy that experiences steady technological progress (see problem 14.14). Suppose, for this economy, that the capital–labour ratio rises during the transition *and* in the steady state. What is the behaviour of the real wage rate in this economy?

14.16 Convergence and the Dispersion of Income (optional)

Consider a group of economies that satisfies our notion of absolute convergence: poor economies tend to grow faster than rich ones.

a. Does this convergence property imply that a measure of the dispersion of income, or income inequality, across the economies will necessarily narrow over time?

(This question is related to Galton's Fallacy, an idea applied by Galton to the distribution of heights in a population. If a parent is taller than average, then the child tends to be taller than average but shorter than the parent. That is, there is some tendency for reversion to the mean, an effect that parallels the convergence tendency in our growth model. Does this reversion to the mean imply that the distribution of heights across the entire population becomes narrower over time? The answer is supposed to be no, but you have to explain why.)

b. For the US states considered in Figure 14.6, a measure of the dispersion of per capita income across the states tended to decline for most of the period after 1880. The dispersion measure increased in the 1920s (a period that featured a collapse in agricultural prices) and has also risen since the late 1970s. Can you relate these observations to your answer from part a? (The behaviour since the late 1970s is not well understood.)

c. We noted that absolute convergence does not hold for the 98 countries that we considered in Figure 14.10. For these countries, a measure of dispersion shows a mild increase from 1960 to 1985. How would you account for this outcome?

Notes

1. The model of economic growth that corresponds to equation (10.2) is called the Solow model and derives from the paper of Robert Solow (1956).

2. This assumption leads to the chicken-and-egg problem of how any capital ever got produced. We could assume that people were born with a certain amount of human capital that enables them to produce something.

3. We reach the same conclusion if the economy starts with $K(0) > K^*$. Depreciation, δK, initially exceeds gross investment, $sF(K, L)$, in that case, and net investment, ΔK, is negative. Hence, K declines over time toward K^*. The steady-state capital stock, K^*, is *stable* in the sense that K approaches it for any starting value, $K(0) > 0$.

4. The labour force grows at a rate different from population if labour-force participation changes. For example, in recent years, the labour force in most developed countries rose relative to population because a larger fraction of women chose to work in the market. Two opposing forces were that people spent more time in school and tended to retire at earlier ages. In the long run, the growth of the labour force and hence, aggregate labour input, L, depends on growth in population.

5. The main complication arises in equation (14.2) if we want to interpret everything in per worker terms, including the replacement of ΔK by the change in capital per worker, $\Delta(K/L)$. The new element is that an increase in L tends to reduce K/L for a given value of K. If L grows at the constant rate n, then a higher n means that gross investment per worker has to be higher to keep K/L from falling. In this sense, n is analogous to the depreciation rate, δ, which already appeared in equation (14.2). If fact, equation (14.2) remains valid when re-expressed in per worker terms if we replace δ by $\delta + n$.

6. Note that the growth rates of population were very high in the 1800s, especially from 1840 to 1860. The pattern of high growth rates of output before 1880 is therefore more striking for the level of real GNP than for per capita real GNP.

7. Note from Table 14.1 that there was a pronounced long-term decline in the growth rate of population, from 3.1% per year in 1840–60 to 1.0% per year for 1980–90.

8. Because the GNP deflator is unavailable for 1840–60, the inflation rate for this period is computed from the consumer price index.

9. This evidence comes from studies by Robert Barro and Xavier Sala-i-Martin (1991, 1992).

10. The data refer to personal income exclusive of all transfer payments.

11. The average per capita income for 13 southern states was 43% of that for 23 eastern and midwestern states in 1880 and 82% in 1988. In contrast, before the Civil War in 1840, the available data (for a narrower concept of income) indicate that 11 southern states had an average per capita income that was 80% of that for 18 eastern and midwestern states. Thus, the southern states became markedly poorer than the northern states only because of the war.

12. The regional growth rates and levels of per capita GDP are expressed relative to the respective means for each country. The pattern shown in Figure 14.8 still appears, however, if the country means are not subtracted out.

13. The data on real GDP are from Robert Summers and Alan Heston (1988). These data use internationally comparable price indexes to measure real GDP across countries.

14. The 20 members of the OECD in 1960 were Austria, Belgium, Canada, Denmark, France, Germany, Greece, Iceland, Ireland, Italy, Luxembourg, Netherlands, Norway, Portugal, Spain, Sweden, Switzerland, Turkey, United Kingdom, and United States. Australia, Finland, Japan, and New Zealand became members later.

15. See Robert Barro (1991), J. Bradford De Long and Lawrence Summers (1991), and William Easterly (1991) for discussions of this evidence.

16. For a technical survey of this research, see Xavier Sala-i-Martin (1990).

17. Some important, but technically demanding, contributions in this area are by Paul Romer (1990) and Gene Grossman and Elhanan Helpman (1991, chapters 3 and 4).

18. See, for example, Richard Easterlin (1968), Gary Becker (1981), and Gary Becker and Robert Barro (1988).

15

Government Purchases and Public Services

This chapter introduces government purchases of goods and services and a simple form of tax revenues. Before considering these extensions to the model, it is useful to get some background by looking at data on government spending in Europe and the United States.

Data on Government Expenditures

Tables 15.1 and 15.2 summarize the evolution of government spending in several European countries between 1880 and 1989. Table 15.1, which excludes the wartime experiences, shows that

expenditures increased substantially both at the level of central government and general government – that is, central and local government combined. Expressed as a percentage of GNP, they increased, on average, more than fivefold between 1880 and 1989. For example, the average general government expenditure in the nine European countries considered increased from 8.7% of GDP in 1880 to 20.1% in 1920, 24.4% in 1938, 30.1% in 1960, and 50.1% in 1989.

The pattern of steady rise in the importance of total government expenditures conceals the divergent movements in the major underlying components. Table 15.2 shows how purchases of goods and services, at the central government

	Denmark		France		Germany		Italy		Netherlands	
	General	Central	General	Central	General	Central	General	Central	General	Central
1880	8.9	5.5			9.9	2.9		11.6		
1920	15.3	8.8	34.2	28.9				36.1		14.9
1938	16.7	8.1	29.2	22.2	36.9	29.1		25.5		19.4
1960	24.3	16.2	39.2	25.5	32.5	19		21.6		21.5
1989	58.6	39.5	46.5	20.0	46.1	29.3	58.6	47.5	50.1	27.7

	Norway		Sweden		Switzerland		United Kingdom		Average 9 countries	
	General	Central	General	Central	General	Central	General	Central	General	Central
1880	6.8	3.6		5.9			9.1		8.7	5.9
1920	12.8	7.8	10.9	5.6			27.4	21.9	20.1	17.7
1938	18.1	10.1	17.7	9.5	23.9	7	28.6	19	24.4	16.7
1960	32.3	21.5	30	20.6	17.3	7	35.3	26.5	30.1	19.9
1989	54.9	34.1	64.1	34.8	34.1	9.5	38.5	34.5	50.1	30.8

Note: France: central government does not include social security institutions. If we included them: 1989 = 42.4
Source: 1879–1970: Flora (1983); 1980–1989: IMF, Government Finance Statistics Yearbook; OECD, National Accounts.

Table 15.1 General and central government expenditure, % of GDP

	Defence	Admin. & justice	Econ. & transp.	Social security	Educ. & science	Other incl. int. on debt
Denmark						
1880	39.8	24.5	4.2	0.4	3.1	28.0
1938	9.6	6.4	10.3	37.5	13.8	22.4
1987	5.4	9.5	6.9	40.6	9.2	28.4
France						
1880	26.3	19.3	14.2	2.2	3.8	34.2
1938	40.7	10.1	8.2	13.3	9.5	18.2
1987	6.1	7.0	6.5	62.2	6.9	11.3
Germany						
1880	25.6	26.5	14.8	8.0	17.6	7.5
1925	4.0	17.2	10.6	43.3	13.6	11.3
1987	5.4	6.9	9.9	60.3	7.7	9.8
Italy						
1880	18.6	17.6	16.0	0.4	2.2	45.2
1938	32.5	8.9	15.8	7.6	5.6	29.6
1987	3.2	6.9	12.1	46.7	7.4	23.7
Netherlands						
1880	28.4	27.5	17.6			26.5
1938	15.5	35.3	6.7	10.2	15.0	17.3
1989	5.0	8.7	8.2	53.0	11.0	14.1
Norway						
1880	27.1	28.6	8.2	5.2	11.6	19.3
1938	15.7	11.6	27.8	21.5	17.3	6.1
1989	7.8	6.4	17.5	51.5	9.1	7.7
Sweden						
1880	39.4	23.3	6.7	3.5	14.9	12.2
1938	23.3	8.5	23.6	22.3	9.2	13.1
1989	6.5	7.1	8.0	57.7	8.7	12.1
United Kingdom						
1890	43.4	15.5	1.2	9.8		30.1
1938	44.4	4.1	3.4	27.6		20.5
1988	12.5	7.1	6.7	49.6	2.9	21.2
Average 8 countries						
1880	31.1	22.9	10.4	3.7	7.6	24.4
1938	23.2	12.8	13.3	22.9	12.0	15.8
1989	6.5	7.4	9.5	52.7	7.9	16.0

Table 15.2   Composition of central government expenditure (% of total expenditure)

Notes:
1. France 1880 and 1938: central government does not include social insurance institutions.
2 Germany: data refer to general government.
3. UK 1890 and 1938: social security includes education and science.
4. In computing 1880 averages, we used 1890 data for the UK.
5. In computing 1938 averages, we used 1925 data for Germany.
6. In computing 1989 averages, we used 1987 data for France, Germany, Italy and 1988 data for the UK.

Source: 1879–1970: Flora (1983); 1980–1989: IMF, Government Finance Statistics Yearbook; OECD, National Accounts.

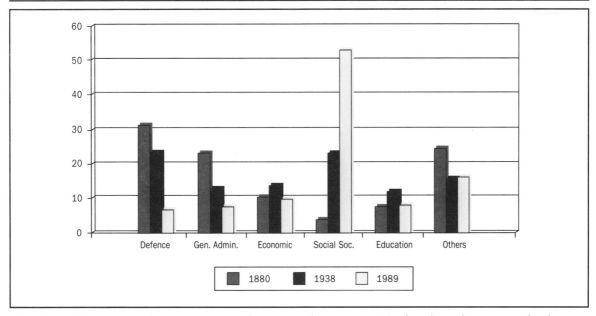

Figure 15.1 Composition of government expenditure, central government, % of total spending (average for the 8 countries of Table 15.2)

| | Occupational injuries insurance | | Health insurance | | Pension insurance | | Unemployment insurance | |
	Compulsory	Voluntary	Compulsory	Voluntary	Compulsory	Voluntary	Compulsory	Voluntary
Austria	1887		1888		1927		1920	
Belgium	1971	1903	1944	1894	1924	1900	1944	1920
Denmark	1916	1898	1933	1892	1921	1891		1907
Finland	1895		1963		1937			1917
France	1946	1898	1930	1898	1910	1895	1967	1905
Germany	1884	1871	1883		1889		1927	
Ireland	1966	1897	1911		1960	1908	1911	
Italy	1898		1928	1886	1919	1898	1919	
Netherlands	1901		1929		1913		1949	1916
Norway	1894		1909		1936		1938	1906
Sweden	1916	1901	1953	1891	1913			1934
Switzerland	1911	1881		1911	1946		1976	1924
United Kingdom	1946	1897	1911		1925	1908	1911	

Source: Flora (1983).

Table 15.3 The introduction of social insurance systems

level, have varied over time in these European countries. Until the end of World War II, the dominant component of central government purchases was defence spending. In 1880, this spending constituted between 18.6% (in Italy) and 43.4% (in the UK) of GDP. In 1938, it still accounted for almost a quarter of total spending

on average. After peaking during World War II, the share of defence steadily declined during the last forty years and accounted, on average, for 6.5% of GDP.

As emphasized by Figure 15.1, the most remarkable change in the composition of government spending is the increase in social security transfers. In 1880 these transfers accounted on average for less than 4% of central government spending. By 1938 they increased to almost 23% and in 1989 the accounted for more than half of total spending.

Under the generic name of **social security** are included several types of public services. It includes four types of social insurance schemes: (i) occupational injuries insurance, (ii) health insurance, (iii) pensions, and (iv) unemployment insurance. It also includes public health services, family allowances, social assistance, and transfer benefits to war victims and civil servants. The exact nature of these public services, the precise institutional arrangements, eligibility, and generosity of the schemes vary substantially from country to country. Nonetheless, these cross-country differences are secondary to the extent of the global expansion of transfer payments. The change in the role of the state, from being mainly involved in national security, internal safety, and justice, to that of providing assistance in the areas of health, retirement, and unemployment is an important development in modern democracies. These transformations took place mainly between the two world wars, but the involvement of the state in social services was considerably increased again in the 1960s and 1970s.

Country	Spending Ratio (%)	Country	Spending Ratio (%)	Country	Spending Ratio (%)
Austria	46	Guatemala	12	Pakistan	24
Argentina	27	Guyana	53	Panama	34
Australia	34	Iceland	36	Papua New Guinea	34
Barbados	31	India	20	Paraguay	11
Belgium	50	Indonesia	21	Peru	18
Bolivia	13	Iran	35	Phillipines	13
Botswana	37	Ireland	48	Senegal	22
Brazil	26	Israel	77	Sierra Leone	23
Burkino Faso	14	Italy	44	Singapore	20
Burma	15	Japan	27	South Africa	28
Cameroon	19	Jordan	51	Spain	26
Canada	39	Kenya	27	Sri Lanka	31
Chile	32	Korea (South)	18	Swaziland	25
Colombia	15	Liberia	32	Sweden	54
Costa Rica	22	Luxembourg	41	Switzerland	34
Cyprus	27	Malawi	27	Syria	41
Denmark	52	Malaysia	33	Thailand	17
Dominican Rep.	16	Malta	40	Tunisia	31
Ecuador	26	Mauritius	29	Turkey	23
Egypt	41	Mexico	22	Uganda	15
El Salvador	15	Morocco	32	United Kingdom	44
Fiji	26	Nepal	14	United States	35
Finland	39	Netherlands	54	Uruguay	23
France	43	New Zealand	34	Venezuela	24
Germany (West)	46	Nicaragua	21	Yemen	35
Ghana	17	Norway	51	Zaire	35
Greece	36	Oman	50	Zambia	34

Note and Source: The table reports the ratio of government expenditure to gross domestic product. Government expenditure is total spending of consolidated general government. Data are averages from 1970 to 1985 from International Monetary Fund, *Government Finance Statistics International Financial Statistics*, various issues.

Table 15.4 Government expenditures in various countries

Table 15.3 shows the year of introduction of the four main social insurance schemes in 13 European countries. In several countries these schemes were introduced on a voluntary base before the turn of the century, but in most countries they became compulsory later on, after World War I. A health insurance scheme was introduced in Germany in 1883, but in Finland only in 1963. Similarly, pension insurance was introduced in 1889 in Germany and only in 1960 in Ireland. Finally, unemployment insurance was introduced in 1911 in Ireland and the UK, but only in 1976 in Switzerland.

We can summarize the movements in government expenditures relative to GNP in Europe between 1880 and 1989 in terms of two major developments: a sharp drop in spending for the military and a more than compensating increase in social security benefits following the introduction of social security schemes, mainly during the 1920s and 1930s.

Table 15.4 shows the ratio of total government expenditures to gross domestic product (GDP) for a larger set of countries. The figures are averages from 1970 to 1985. The 81 countries listed are those for which data are available on a broad concept of government expenditures. This concept is consolidated general government, which includes purchases of goods and services, transfer payments, and net interest payments by all levels of government. The ratios of government spending to GDP range from 11% for Paraguay and 12% for Guatemala to 77% for Israel and 54% for Sweden and the Netherlands. Aside from countries that have large defence expenditures, the ratios tend to be higher for the industrialized countries than for the less-developed countries. It appears to be economic development that leads to big government – especially in the form of large transfer payments – rather than vice versa.

The Government's Budget Constraint

Let G_t denote the government's demand for commodities during period t. In terms of the national accounts, G_t corresponds to real purchases of goods and services by the total of national, regional, and local governments. Total real government expenditure equals these purchases plus the real value of aggregate transfer payments, V_t/P_t. (We do not yet consider governmental interest payments.)

Thus far, we have assumed that the government's only revenue came from printing money. The real value of this revenue is the amount $(M_t - M_{t-1})/P_t$. Now we assume that the government also levies taxes on households. (The taxes could also apply to firms, but remember that the households own the firms.) Let T_t be the aggregate dollar amount of taxes for period t. Then the real amount of tax revenues is T_t/P_t.

As before, the government's budget constraint equates total real expenditures to total real revenues. We therefore have

$$G_t + V_t/P_t = T_t/P_t + (M_t - M_{t-1})/P_t \quad (15.1)$$

Our earlier formulation fits into equation (15.1) if we set real purchases, G_t, and taxes, T_t/P_t, to zero.

We assumed before that transfer payments were lump sum. This specification means that a household's real transfer, v_t/P_t, does not depend on that household's level of income, effort at soliciting transfers, and so on. Now we assume also that the taxes are lump sum. Hence, a household's real tax liability, t_t/P_t, is independent of that household's level or type of income, effort at avoiding taxes, and so on.

In the real world, an elaborate tax law specifies the relation of someone's taxes to his or her income, business profits, sales, holdings of property, deductions from taxable income, and so on. There are lots of things people can do – including hiring accountants, working less, under-reporting income, and exploiting tax loopholes – to lower their obligations. These possibilities imply important substitution effects from the tax system on work effort, investment, relative demands for different goods (even including numbers of children), and so on. In general, people substitute in favour of the activities that lower their taxes.

In order to isolate the effects of government expenditures, we shall find it convenient initially to neglect these substitution effects from taxes. That is why we assume **lump-sum taxes**, which do not exert any substitution effects. (We bring in more realistic types of taxes and transfers in the next chapter.)

Public Production

The government uses its purchases, G_t, to provide services to households and firms. We assume that the government provides these services free of charge to the users. In most countries public services include national defence, enforcement of laws and private contracts, police and fire protection, elementary education and some parts of higher education, highways, parks, and so on. The range of governmental activities has typically expanded over time, although this range varies significantly from one country to another.

We could model public services as the output from the government's production function. The inputs to this function would be the government-owned stock of capital, labour services from public employees, and materials that the government buys from the private sector. To simplify matters we take a different approach that neglects production in the public sector. We can neglect this production if we pretend that the government buys only final goods and services on the commodity market. In effect, the government subcontracts all of its production to the private sector. In this setup, public investment, publicly owned capital, and government employment are always zero. Ultimately, the introduction of governmental production would affect the main results only if the public sector's technology or management capability differed from that of the private sector. Otherwise it would not matter whether the government buys final goods, as we assume, or instead buys capital and labour to produce things itself.

We assumed earlier that output could be labelled as consumables or capital goods. Now we introduce a third function for output: the government can purchase goods to provide public services to households and firms. As before, the suppliers of goods and services do not care whether the buyers use the goods for consumption or investment or to provide public services. The demanders of commodities – which now include the government – determine its use.

Public Services

In our model we allow for two types of public services. The first type provides utility to households. Examples are parks, libraries, school lunch programmes, subsidized health care and transportation services. An important feature of these services is that they may substitute closely for private consumer spending. If the government buys someone's lunch at school, then he or she does not buy his or her own lunch.

The second type of service is an input to private production. Examples include the provision and enforcement of laws, aspects of national defence, government-sponsored research and development programmes, fire and police services, and various regulatory activities. In some cases these services are close substitutes for private inputs of labour and capital. In other cases – such as 'infrastructure' activities like the provision of a legal system, national defence, and perhaps highways and other transportation systems – the public services are likely to raise the marginal products of private factors.

In many situations a governmental programme exhibits features of both types of services that we consider, but the mix varies across the range of programmes. In our theory, however, we proceed as if there were only one type of governmental activity. This activity yields utility directly and also provides services to producers.

Households' Budget Constraints

We have included real transfers, v_t/P_t, as a source of income for a household. Now we also have to subtract real taxes, t_t/P_t, to calculate real income after taxes. The budget constraint in real terms is now

$$y_t + b_{t-1}(1+R)/P_t + m_{t-1}/P_t + (v_t - t_t)/P_t$$
$$= c_t + i_t + (b_t + m_t)/P_t \qquad (15.2)$$

In making decisions, each household cares about the present value of real transfers net of real taxes, as given by

$$(v_1 - t_1)/P_1 + [(v_2 - t_2)/P_2]/(1+r) + \ldots$$

Consider the aggregate value of this expression. Each term involves the aggregate of real transfers net of real taxes, $(V_t - T_t)/P_t$. But we know from the government's budget constraint in equation (15.1) that this term equals the real revenue from money creation less real government purchases – that is

$$(V_t - T_t)/P_t = (M_t - M_{t-1})/P_t - G_t \qquad (15.3)$$

If the money stock were constant, so that $M_t - M_{t-1} = 0$ holds in each period, then equation (15.3) would imply that the aggregate real value of transfers net of taxes, $(V_t - T_t)/P_t$, equals the negative of real government purchases, $-G_t$. In the aggregate, households would therefore include the present value of real government purchases, $[G_1 + G_2/(1+r) + \ldots]$, as a negative item when computing the overall present value of their resources. This result makes sense because the goods, G_t, that the government buys represents a part of the output stream that is not available for households. (As in the cases discussed in Chapter 3 and the appendix to Chapter 9, the results do not change if we include the various monetary terms.)

Temporary Changes in Government Purchases

We want to explore the effects of government purchases on consumption, investment, and work effort. Consider an increase in the current level of purchases, G_1. We shall find that the effects differ depending on whether the change is temporary or permanent. To begin with, think about a temporary change: G_1 rises, but households do not anticipate any changes in future values of G_t.

Empirically, the most important example of this case is military spending during wars (if we think of the length of a period as corresponding to the expected duration of a war).

Recall that the government's budget constraint for period 1 is

$$G_1 + V_1/P_1 = T_1/P_1 + (M_1 - M_0)/P_1 \qquad (15.4)$$

An increase in purchases, G_1, must involve some combination of an increase in real taxes, T_1/P_1, a decrease in real transfers, V_1/P_1, or an increase in the real revenue from money creation, $(M_1 - M_0)/P_1$. Because we assume lump-sum taxes and transfers, our analysis of the real variables in the commodity market will be the same regardless of which combination we specify. For convenience, think of the extra government purchases as financed by more real taxes, T_1/P_1.

The higher current level of purchases, G_1, means more public services of the two types mentioned before. First, there is a positive effect on utility during the current period (because we assume that people like the services that the government provides). Suppose that the public services substitute for some private consumption but not for leisure.[1] For example, if the government provides free libraries, parks, school lunches, or transportation, then households reduce their private spending in these areas. Let's use the parameter α (the Greek letter *alpha*) to measure the size of this effect. An increase in current purchases, G_1, by one unit reduces aggregate private consumption demand, C_1^d, by α units.

It is plausible that the parameter α would decline as the quantity of government purchases rises: as the amount of public services increases, the marginal unit would substitute less well for private spending. Notice, however, that the value of the parameter α does not necessarily indicate how valuable an extra unit of public services is. People might like these services a lot even if they do not substitute much for private spending, that is, even if α is small.

Some empirical work for the US economy in the post-World War II period suggests that the parameter α is between 0.2 and 0.4.[2] That is, an extra unit of government purchases substitutes for between 0.2 and 0.4 unit of aggregate private consumption. We are therefore safe in assuming that α is positive but well below unity.

The second type of public service is an input to private production. Let's use the parameter β (the Greek letter *beta*) to measure the marginal product of public services. If the inputs of labour and capital do not change, then an increase in current purchases, G_1, by one unit raises the aggregate supply of goods, Y_1^s, by β units.[3] We assume that β is positive but less than one. Diminishing marginal productivity of public services suggests that β would decline as G_t rose, for given inputs of capital and labour.

Net investment demand depends on the schedule for capital's marginal product, on the previous stock of capital, and on the real interest rate. We assume that public services do not affect the schedule for capital's marginal product; hence, there is no direct impact of government purchases on investment demand. Any effects that arise must work through changes in the real interest rate.

Recall that the present value of households' resources includes the negative of the present value of government purchases. (This term corresponds to the present value of taxes net of transfers.) Since the increase in government purchases is temporary, the present value of these purchases rises by only a small amount. The resulting fall in wealth reduces consumer demand and increases labour supply. These changes would reinforce the effects on consumer demand and goods supply that we have already mentioned. To focus on the temporary nature of the change in government purchases, we shall find it convenient to neglect these small wealth effects. The wealth effects will, however, become important when we consider permanent changes in government purchases.

Clearing of the Commodity Market

Now we incorporate government purchases into the market-clearing conditions. Since the main new effects involve the demand and supply of commodities, we shall focus on the condition for clearing the commodity market. The new condition for period 1 is

$$
\begin{aligned}
& C^d(r_1, G_1, \ldots) + I^d(r_1, \ldots) + G_1 \\
& \quad (-)\,(-) \qquad\quad (-) \\
& = Y^s(r_1, G_1, \ldots) \\
& \quad\quad (+)\,(+)
\end{aligned}
\tag{15.5}
$$

The aggregate demand for commodities, Y_1^d, consists of consumption demand, C_1^d, gross investment demand, I_1^d, and government purchases, G_1. If consumption and investment demand did not change, then aggregate demand would increase one-to-one with an increase in government purchases. But an increase by one unit in purchases, G_1, reduces consumer demand, C_1^d, by α units. Since there is no effect on investment demand, an increase by one unit in government purchases raises aggregate demand by $1 - \alpha$ units. (Recall that we assume $\alpha < 1$.)

An increase in purchases, G_1, by one unit raises the supply of goods, Y_1^s, by β units. (*Warning:* Our analysis assumes that taxes are lump sum. When we drop this unrealistic assumption in the next chapter, we introduce some important negative effects from governmental activity on the supply of goods.) If $\alpha + \beta < 1$, then the increase in aggregate demand, $1 - \alpha$, exceeds that in supply, β. This condition turns out to be important for figuring out the effects of a temporary increase in government purchases on the real interest rate.

Consider the inequality, $\alpha + \beta < 1$. This condition says that if government purchases expand by one unit, then households and firms get back less than one unit in the combined response from the substitution for consumer spending, α, and the increase in private output, β. One easy way to satisfy this condition is to assume that public services are useless: the government essentially buys up goods and throws them into the ocean. Although this assumption, where $\alpha = \beta = 0$, is popular (and appears implicitly in many macromodels), it may not be the most interesting way to model the functions of government!

But why does $\alpha + \beta < 1$ make sense? If $\alpha + \beta > 1$, then the typical household would benefit from an increase in public services, paid for by an increase in taxes. That is because the amount that the typical household gets back – the value of the services that substitute for consumer spending, α, plus the value of the extra production, β – exceeds the additional taxes. Hence, if $\alpha + \beta > 1$, then it is plausible that the government would grow larger, and this expansion tends to reduce the values of α and β. It would, in particular, be popular for the government to expand until the condition, $\alpha + \beta < 1$, was satisfied.

Figure 15.2 shows the effects of a temporary increase in government purchases on the commodity market. Without this increase, the market clears at the real interest rate, r_1^*. Then the rise in purchases increases the aggregate quantities of goods demanded and supplied. But since $1 - \alpha > \beta$, the rightward shift of the aggregate demand curve exceeds that of the supply curve. Therefore, at the real interest rate, r_1^*, there is

now excess demand for commodities. We conclude that the real interest rate increases to the value $(r_1^*)'$.

Figure 15.2 shows that output increases. There are two elements behind this increase. First, we assume that public services are productive. Second, the increase in the real interest rate motivates people to work more.

Consider now the composition of output. We know that government purchases rise. But private uses of output – for consumption and investment – decline. Consumption demand falls for two reasons. First, there is the substitution of public services for private spending. If we are talking about more military spending, however, then this effect is likely to be weak because the parameter α would be small. Second, the higher real interest rate induces households to postpone their expenditures. This second effect accounts also for the drop in investment demand. Notice that the increase in government purchases **crowds out** private spending. Because of the higher real interest rate and the direct substitution of public services for consumer spending, the addition to government purchases induces consumers and investors to spend less.

We suggested before that investment demand is especially sensitive to variations in the real interest rate. Therefore, unless the direct substitution of public services for consumer spending is strong, we predict that the temporary increase in government purchases will mostly crowd out investment (including purchases of consumer durables) rather than consumption.

Since consumption and investment decrease, the rise in total output is smaller than the increase in government purchases. Hence, the ratio of the change in output to the change in purchases is positive but less than one. If the ratio were greater than one, then we would say that a change in government purchases has a multiplicative effect on output. But we do not get this sort of **multiplier** in the model. That is because the economy typically operates to buffer shocks rather than to magnify them. In particular, the rise in government purchases leads to decreases in private demands for consumption and investment and to an increase in work effort. Each of these

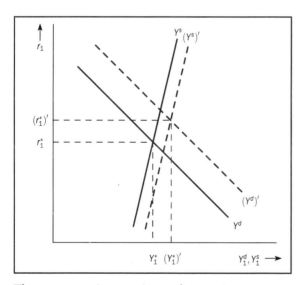

The temporary increase in purchases raises aggregate demand by more than supply. Therefore, the real interest rate and output rise.

Figure 15.2 Effect on the commodity market of a temporary rise in government purchases

responses serves to alleviate the initial excess demand for goods. (When we study the Keynesian model in Chapter 21, we shall reexamine the potential for a multiplier.)

Consider why the temporary increase in government purchases raises the real interest rate. The increase in spending, financed by a temporary increase in taxes, implies a temporary decline in households' disposable income. Since the shortfall in income is temporary, the marginal propensity to consume is small. Households therefore react mainly by reducing desired saving. When desired saving falls and investment demand does not shift, the real interest rate must increase.

The higher real interest rate is the signal for households to work harder, to produce more goods, and to reduce demands for private consumption and investment. In other words, the market uses the real interest rate to achieve the appropriate allocations over time for work effort, production, consumption, and investment.[4]

Our discussion refers to wars as cases in which government purchases are temporarily high. But we have ignored other aspects of major wars that can substantially affect the analysis. For one thing, we have neglected any negative effects of military reversals on productive capacity. These effects, an example of adverse supply shocks, would tend to reduce output. Another feature of wartime is the widespread use of rationing to hold down private demands for goods. Others are the military draft, confiscation of property, and appeals to patriotism to stimulate work and production. These instruments are examples of direct controls, which can substitute for a higher real interest rate as a mechanism for crowding out private spending and for stimulating work and production. These departures from free markets may not affect the general conclusions about the effects of wartime on the quantities of output, consumption, investment, and employment. But these controls may eliminate the increase in the real interest rate.

Evidence from Wartime Experiences

The Behaviour of Output and Other Quantities

We can assess some effects of temporarily high government purchases by looking at the most recent wars for the United Kingdom and the United States: World War I, World War II, for both the UK and the US; Korea and Vietnam for the US. (We abstract from the Falkland War and the Persian Gulf War because they were too brief to have much effect on government purchases.)

Table 15.5 describes the behaviour of military spending, real gross national product (GNP), and the major components of GNP during these episodes. We contrast the behaviour during the war years with that for a benchmark year; for example, we compare the peak year of World War II in the UK, 1943, with the benchmark year, 1938. UK real military spending in 1943 was above the benchmark value by £67.5 billion, an amount that equals 57% of trend real GNP for 1943. UK real GNP in 1918 was £20.6 billion, or 17.3% above its own trend.

Next, we calculate the ratio of excess real GNP and its various components to the excess of real military spending. For GNP the ratio in 1943 was 0.49. Hence – assuming that the boost in military spending was the major disturbance to the economy – this result supports the theory's predictions: a temporary increase in government purchases has a positive but less than one-to-one effect on output.

Since GNP rises by less than the increase in military spending, the non-military components of GNP must decline overall. The figures shown for 1943 in Table 15.5 indicate that UK gross investment declined by the fraction, 0.16, of the increase in military spending.

The final rows of the table show the effects on employment. UK total employment (numbers of persons working, including military personnel) in 1943 was above trend by 3.6 million, or 15.5% of the trend value. This total divided up between 4.3 million extra military personnel and 0.7 million

	United Kingdom			United States		
Peak year of war	1918	1943	1918	1944	1952	1968
Benchmark year for comparison	1914	1938	1915	1947	1950	1965
Excess real military spending						
UK: billions of 1985 pounds; US: billions of 1982 dollars	41.80	67.50	81.40	645.30	146.30	46.10
Excess as % of trend real GNP	53.10	56.60	16.80	66.20	11.40	2.00
Excess of real GNP						
UK: billions of 1985 pounds; US: billions of 1982 dollars	6.90	20.60	13.70	405.70	101.90	81.40
Excess as % of trend real GNP	8.80	17.30	2.80	41.60	8.00	3.60
Ratio to excess real military spending for the excess of						
Real GNP	0.16	0.49	0.17	0.63	0.70	1.77
Real personal consumption expenditures	−0.13	−0.21	−0.45	−0.08	−0.05	1.15
Durables	–	–	–	−0.04	−0.09	0.31
Nondurables and services	–	–	–	−0.04	0.04	0.84
Real gross investment	−0.06	−0.16	−0.19	−0.16	−0.26	−0.21
Excess of employment (millions)						
Total employment	1.20	3.60	2.10	8.40	1.50	2.50
Military personnel	3.60	4.30	2.70	9.90	1.90	0.70
Civilian employment	−2.40	−0.70	−0.60	−1.50	−0.40	1.80
Excess of total employment as % of trend value	6.30	15.50	5.30	14.80	2.40	3.20

Note: The method for calculating the excess or shortfall in each component is discussed in the text.
Sources:
United States: For World War II, the Korean War, and the Vietnam War, the data are from US Department of Commerce (1986). For 1915 and 1918, the data on real GNP are those shown in Figure 1.1.
Estimates for the components of real GNP use the data from Kendrick (1961, tables A-1, A-lla). The shares of real GNP in each year from Kendrick's data are applied to figures on total real GNP to estimate values for real military spending, real personal consumption expenditures, and real gross investment.
United Kingdom: Feinstein (1972), table 2, table 57.

Table 15.5   The behaviour of output and its components during wartime in the UK and the US

fewer civilian workers. (We do not consider here the likely positive effects on hours and effort per worker.)

The results for the US during World War II are similar. Because the US economy had not yet fully recovered in 1940 from the Great Depression, we use 1947 as the benchmark year. For example, the excess of US real military spending in 1944 was $645 billion, or 66% of trend real GNP. US real GNP was $406 billion, or 42% above its own trend. The excess military spending crowded out gross investment by a fraction 0.16, the same as in the UK, and total investment (gross investment plus purchases of consumer durables) by a fraction of 0.20, since consumer purchases of nondurables and services were crowded out by a fraction of 0.04. Total employment for 1944

exceeded its trend value by 8.4 million, or 15%, basically the same as in the UK. This total broke down into 9.9 million extra military personnel and 1.5 million less civilian workers.

For World War I, the impact was much larger in the UK than in the US. The excess of real military spending in 1918 was 53.1% of trend real GNP in the UK but only 16.8% in the US. Consequently, real GNP in 1918 was 8.8% above its own trend in the UK and only 2.8% in the US. Despite the difference in the magnitude of the increase in military spending between the UK and the US, the ratio of the excess of real GNP to the excess of real military spending was almost identical in the two countries: 0.16 in the UK and 0.17 in the US. This value is well below those estimated for the other wars. The computations for World War I are, however, not so reliable because the underlying data on real GNP are subject to substantial uncertainty.

Table 15.5 indicates that the excess military spending in 1918 crowded out gross investment by the fraction 0.06 in the UK and 0.19 in the US and personal consumer expenditure (which includes purchases of durables) by the fraction 0.13 in the UK and 0.45 in the US. The latter figure for the US is much greater than that found for World War II. Finally, total employment in 1918 was above its trend by 6.3% in the UK and 5.3% in the US. In this case there were 3.6 million extra military personnel and 2.4 million fewer civilian workers in the UK, whereas in the US there were 2.7 million extra military personnel and 0.6 million fewer civilian workers.

The findings from the Korean War are similar, except that the magnitudes are much smaller. US real military spending in 1952 was above the benchmark value by $146 billion, an amount that equals 11% of trend real GNP for 1952. US real GNP in 1952 was $102 billion, or 8% above its own trend. The ratio to excess real military spending for excess real GNP in 1952 was 0.70.

In 1952 US total investment (gross investment plus purchases of consumer durables) declined by the fraction, 0.35, of the increase in military spending. In contrast, US consumer expenditures for nondurables and services were actually higher by the fraction 0.04. Thus, the temporary excess of military purchases crowded out only the investment part of private spending. Recall that the theory is consistent with this outcome, because military spending would have little direct substitution for consumer spending. US total employment in 1952 was above trend by 1.5 million, or 2.4% of the trend value. This total divided up between 1.9 million extra military personnel and 0.4 million fewer civilian workers.

The results for Vietnam differ sharply from those for the other wars. To begin, using 1965 as the benchmark year, the estimate for the excess of real military spending in 1968 in the US was only $46 billion, or 2% of trend real GNP. Thus, unlike the other cases, it is doubtful that the increase in military spending was the overriding influence on the economy in the middle and late 1960s.

The estimated excess of US real GNP for 1968 was $81 billion or 4% of trend real GNP. Thus, the excess real GNP was 1.8 times the excess real military spending. Correspondingly, the total of the non-military components of GNP were above trend in 1968. For example, the ratio to excess military spending was 0.10 for total investment (gross investment plus purchases of consumer durables) and 0.84 for the consumption of nondurables and services. Hence, the United States really was enjoying 'guns and butter' at this time.

The most likely explanation for these results is that the economy was experiencing a boom in the 1960s that had little to do with the Vietnam War. This viewpoint is supported by the high growth rate of output in the period preceding the main increase in military spending. The average annual growth rate of real GNP was 5.1% from 1961 to 1965, compared with 4.3% from 1965 to 1968.

Suppose that we focus on the results for the Korean War, World War II, and World War I. Then there is an interesting comparison between the behaviour of the economy during wartime booms and during recessions. The contrast concerns the relation between changes in total output and changes in private spending. Total output rises in wars but falls during recessions, whereas private spending declines in both cases. The wartime experiences are similar to recessions in that the major adjustments to private spending show up in the investment components. (World War I may be an exception, although the data are too unreliable to be sure.) As with the postwar recessions that we studied in Chapter 12 (Table 12.2), there are relatively small reductions in consumer purchases of nondurables and services during the Korean War and World War II.

Finally, let's stress the finding that temporarily high government purchases raise total output and employment. But, as predicted, the ratio of the excess real GNP to the excess in purchases is less than one.

The Behaviour of Real Interest Rates

The theory predicts that temporarily high government purchases, as in wartime, raise the real interest rate. We have to be careful, however, when matching up this prediction with the wartime behaviour of interest rates. Recall that the previous theoretical analysis assumes that government purchases are temporarily high only for the current period. But during wars, military expenditures tend to build up for a while and then recede at the end of the war. Also, the length of the buildup and the timing of the war's conclusion (or who wins) are unknown at the outset.

One implication from the theory is that the average real interest rate should be high over the period from the peak of a war until some time after the war finishes. In line with this viewpoint, we analyze the behaviour of interest rates in the US and the UK during and after wars.

Table 15.6 refers to the US and reports averages of interest rates over six-year intervals, beginning with the peak year of each war. The figures therefore include between one and five years of peacetime after each war. Notice that the table considers the four wars that we just studied, plus the US Civil War. In each case we calculate the average for the nominal interest rate on prime commercial paper over six-year periods. Then we compute real interest rates by subtracting the average rate of change of the GNP deflator. (For the Civil War, we lack data on the GNP deflator and therefore use the consumer price index.)

For the Civil War, the average real interest rate over the period 1863–68 was 2.2%. This rate was

Period	π_t	R_t	r_t
1863–68	4.8	7.0	2.2
1918–23	2.7	5.8	3.1
1944–49	6.2	1.0	−5.2
1952–57	2.2	2.6	0.4
1968–73	5.2	6.6	1.4

Note: All values are averages, expressed at annual percentage rates, for the periods indicated. π_t is the inflation rate, based on the consumer price index for the period 1863–68 and on the GNP deflator for the other periods. R_t is the interest rate on 4-to-6 month prime commercial paper. $r_t = R_t - \pi_t$.

Table 15.6 Interest rates in the United States during wartime

substantially less than the averages for 1840–60 and 1867-80, which were each 9.1%. For World War I, the average real interest rate over the interval 1918–23 was 3.1%. This value equalled the average for 1900–16 but was below that of 4.9% for 1920–40. For World War II, the average over the period 1944–49 was −5.2%, which was well below the averages of 4.9% for 1920–40 and −0.2% for 1947-60.

For the two most recent wars, Korea and Vietnam, the average real interest rates were 0.4% (for 1952–57) and 1.4% (for 1968–73), respectively. These values do not differ greatly from the average for 1947–80, which was 0.6%.

Overall, the US data do not confirm a positive effect of wartime spending on real interest rates. US real interest rates were, if anything, below average during the wars.

For 1944–49 the substantially negative real interest rates reflect an overstatement of inflation because of the lifting of price controls. (General price controls did not apply to the earlier wars but were introduced to some extent during the Korean War.) During World War II price controls in the US kept the reported price levels below the 'true' values from 1943 to 1945, so that inflation was understated for these years. As the controls were gradually eliminated from 1946 to 1948, the reported figures caught up with the true ones and inflation was overstated. Our estimate is that, without controls, the inflation rate from 1944 to 1949 would have averaged 1.1% per year rather than the official value of 6.2%.[5] If the controls merely obscured the behaviour of the actual price level, then the lower figure would be a reasonable estimate of the true inflation rate. Using this value, the average real interest rate for 1944–49 was −0.1% rather than −5.2%. This adjusted value of −0.1% is close to the average of real interest rates for 1947–60 (−0.2%).

Even with the adjustment for price controls, we would not conclude that real interest rates were especially high during wars in the United States. A possible explanation is the resort to aspects of a command economy, in which governmental decrees on production, work, and expenditures substitute for free markets. Aside from the military draft, which applied to all the wars considered in Table 15.6, in the two world wars the government exerted direct pressures to work and produce and also rationed private consumption and investment. With few goods to buy and little option to take leisure, people would hold financial assets even if they paid low real interest rates. In other words, the command economy is in some respects a substitute for free markets with high real interest rates. Although this argument may have some validity, it also implies that the data from US wars may not be helpful for testing the theoretical link between temporary government purchases and real interest rates.

We can get around some of these difficulties by looking at the long-term relation between wartime spending and interest rates in the United Kingdom. From the standpoint of scientific inquiry, Britain was very cooperative by fighting numerous wars, especially before 1815. Prior to World War I, these wars were not accompanied by the introduction of aspects of a command economy. Thus, unlike the US case, we can be confident of predicting a positive effect of temporary wartime expenditures on real interest rates.

The solid line in Figure 15.3 shows a measure of temporary real military spending expressed as a ratio to trend real GNP.[6] The peaks in this line correspond to the seven major wars for the United Kingdom over the period from 1730 to 1918. Notice that the high points for temporary spending were 50% of GNP in World War I (1916), 16% in the Seven Years' War (1761), 9% during the War of American Independence (1782), and 7% during the Napoleonic Wars (1814).

The dashed line in the figure is the long-term nominal interest rate. The positive relation of this rate to temporary spending is clear visually and is also confirmed by statistical analysis: interest rates rose on average by 1.0 percentage point during the seven wars.[7] This change is large relative to the average level of rates, which was 3.5% from 1730 to 1918.

For some additional evidence, David Denslow and Mark Rush (1989) looked at the relation between long-term interest rates and temporary government expenditures in France from 1828 to 1869. They observed a positive relationship, which resembles the one found for the long-term British history. Thus, as with the long-term

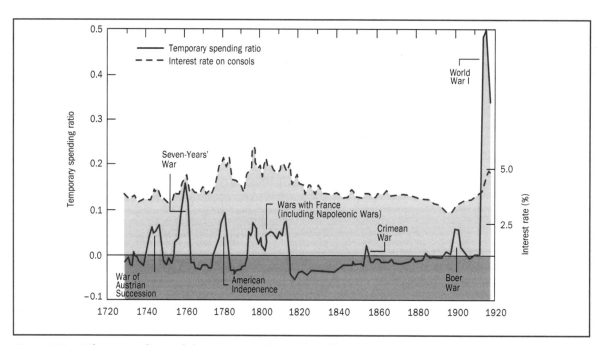

Figure 15.3   Military spending and the interest rate in the United Kingdom, 1730–1918

evidence for Britain, these findings for France are more in line with the theory than are the recent results for the United States.

Permanent Changes in Government Purchases

The previous analysis applies to temporary changes in government purchases, such as in wartime. In other cases there are long-lasting shifts in the size of government. The data that we looked at before for several European countries showed permanent increases in the ratio of total government purchases to GNP, mainly due to the increase in social transfers.

We found before that a temporary increase in government purchases raised commodities demanded and supplied. But, as shown in

Figure 15.2, the increase in demand exceeded that in supply. If the change in purchases is perceived to be permanent, then the new element is that households anticipate a sizable increase in the present value of government purchases and, hence, in the present value of taxes net of transfers. The resulting fall in wealth reduces consumer demand and raises labour supply. These responses reduce the excess demand for goods. We shall find, in fact, that an increase in government purchases now raises commodities demanded and supplied by roughly equal amounts; that is, a permanent change in government purchases does not disturb the equality between demand and supply. Let's see why this is the case.

Consider first a simplified setting in which public services are useless ($\alpha = \beta = 0$) and labour supply is fixed. In this case, a permanent increase

Box 15.1 Results when Public Services are Useful and when Labour Supply Varies

Suppose, first, that public services substitute for private consumer spending, that is, $\alpha > 0$. We know from before that the direct substitution between public and private spending implies that consumer demand declines by α units when government purchases increase permanently by one unit. If $\alpha > 0$, then households effectively lose only $1 - \alpha$ units of disposable income in each period. The other α units provide services that households no longer have to buy on the market. The wealth effect therefore implies that consumer demand falls by about $1 - \alpha$ units. (The marginal propensity to consume is still close to one here.) If we add this response to the decline of consumer demand by α units, then we find that a one unit increase in government purchases still leads to a decline by one unit overall in consumer demand. Thus, as in the case where $\alpha = 0$, the demand for goods remains equal to the supply.

Assume now that public services are productive, that is, $\beta > 0$. If government purchases

rise permanently by one unit, then the supply of goods increases by β units in each period. Consequently, households' income from production rises by β units in each period. Since the marginal propensity to consume is close to unity here, consumer demand also increases by about β units. In other words, the aggregates of goods supplied and demanded are each higher by β units. Hence, excess demand is still zero.

If $\alpha + \beta < 1$, then a permanent increase in government purchases reduces wealth and therefore motivates an increase in work effort. The higher work effort means an increase in the supply of goods and a corresponding rise in households' income from production. Since the marginal propensity to consume is close to unity, consumer demand rises by roughly the same amount. Therefore, although the rise in work effort means that goods supplied and demanded are each higher, it still follows that excess demand is nil.

by one unit in government purchases effectively subtracts one unit from households' disposable income in each period. As with a permanent shift in the production function, the marginal propensity to consume is close to one in this situation. Consumer demand therefore declines by about one unit; that is, one additional unit of public expenditure directly crowds out one unit of private consumer spending. Since government purchases are higher by one unit, the aggregate demand for goods does not change. With fixed labour supply and non-productive public services ($\beta = 0$), the supply of goods also does not change. Therefore, *a permanent increase in government purchases leaves the demand for goods equal to the supply*. This result turns out to hold even if government services are productive ($\alpha \neq 0$ or $\beta \neq 0$) or if labour supply varies. A proof appears in Box 15.1.

Figure 15.4 depicts the effects of a permanent increase in government purchases on the commodity market. Note that the demand and supply curves shift rightward by equal amounts. Therefore, aggregate demand still equals aggregate supply at the initial real interest rate, r_1^*. We conclude that a permanent expansion of government purchases has no effect on the real interest rate.

Figure 15.4 shows that output increases. This response reflects the productivity (β) of public services and a possible increase in labour supply. (Labour supply tends to rise because of the decline in wealth, as discussed in the boxed section. The increase in work effort may not occur, however, if government expenditures are financed by an income tax rather than a lump-sum tax. We consider more realistic types of taxes in the next chapter.)

Consider next the composition of output. To begin with, government purchases increase. Two forces lower consumer demand: first, public services substitute for private spending, and second, the reduction in wealth induces households to consume less. Investment is constant because the real interest rate does not change.[8] Notice the difference from the case of a temporary change in government purchases. In that case the rise in the real interest rate crowded out both forms of private spending. Now, when the change in purchases is permanent, the extra government purchases crowd out only consumer spending.

The decline in consumption and constancy of investment imply that total output increases by less than the rise in government purchases. That is, the ratio of the change in output to the change in purchases is again positive but less than one. Thus, the model still does not have a multiplier.

Consider why the real interest rate increases when the rise in government purchases is temporary but does not change when the rise in purchases is permanent. A temporary increase in government purchases implies a temporary fall in households' disposable income, an effect that decreases desired saving. In contrast, if the increase in government purchases and taxes is permanent, then the decline in households' disposable income is also permanent. The marginal propensity to consume is therefore close to one, and the effect on desired saving is small. For this reason, the real interest rate does not change.

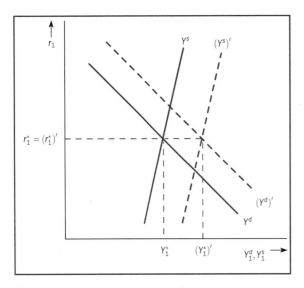

The permanent increase in purchases raises aggregate demand and supply by roughly equal amounts. Therefore, output increases, but the real interest rate does not change.

Figure 15.4   Effects on the commodity market of a permanent rise in government purchases

Change by one unit in	Estimated number of units by which real GNP increases
Temporary defence purchases	0.5 to 1.2
Permanent defence purchases	0.3 to 0.7
Permanent non-defence purchases	−0.2 to 1.3

Note and Source: The results (from Barro, 1978b) apply to US data over the period from 1946 to 1978. The results are similar from 1942 to 1978.

Table 15.7 Empirical estimates of effects of government purchases on real GNP

Table 15.7 provides empirical estimates for the US for the effects on real GNP from temporary and permanent changes in government purchases. Output tends to rise by between 50 and 120% of a temporary increase in defence purchases. These findings are broadly consistent with the less formal results that we discussed before for wartime experiences: the excesses of real GNP during World War II and the Korean War were 50–70% of the excesses of real military spending.

The table indicates that real GNP rises by between 30 and 70% of a permanent increase in defence purchases. Since the response is again less than 100%, we find that a permanent rise in purchases must crowd out some private spending.

For non-defence purchases, the data did not provide much information about temporary changes, and the results apply only to permanent shifts. The estimates are unfortunately imprecise, covering the range of responses for output from −20% to +130% of the change in purchases. Hence, although a positive effect is likely, we cannot pinpoint the magnitude.

One final point is that the empirical results suggested little role for government purchases in peacetime business fluctuations. The amount of peacetime variation in government purchases, combined with the estimated effects of these purchases on real GNP, does not account for much of the observed booms and recessions. In particular, as we saw in Table 12.2, shifts in government purchases do not have a regular association with recessions.

Summary

We introduced government purchases of goods and services as another use of output. To finance these expenditures and its transfer payments, the government levies lump-sum taxes or prints money. The government uses its purchases to provide a flow of public services. An additional unit of these services substitutes for α units of aggregate consumer spending and also raises production by β units. We assume the condition $\alpha + \beta < 1$, which means that households and firms get back directly less than the cost of an additional unit of public services.

A temporary increase in government purchases, as in wartime, raises aggregate demand by more than supply. Hence, the real interest rate and output increase. The crowding out of investment and consumption means, however, that total output rises by less than the increase in government purchases: there is no multiplier.

Variations in government purchases play a major role during wartime but not in peacetime business fluctuations. The results for World War II in the UK and the US and for Korea in the US support the theory's predictions with respect to quantities. In particular, real GNP rises but by only 50–70% of the increase in real military spending. Thus, there is crowding out of private spending, especially investment. The US data do not show a tendency for the real interest rate to rise during wartime. In contrast, the long-term data for Britain and France reveal a positive effect of wartime spending on interest rates.

A permanent increase in government purchases increases goods supplied and demanded by roughly equal amounts. Output therefore increases, but there is no change in the real interest rate. In this case, the crowding out of private spending falls entirely on consumption.

Important Terms and Concepts

lump-sum taxes
multiplier
crowding out (from government purchases)

Questions and Problems

Mainly for Review

15.1   What are the channels by which government spending affects excess demand in the commodity market? How does it affect utility? Can you think of examples of public services that are not close substitutes for consumption ($\alpha = 0$) but nevertheless provide utility?

15.2   Could government services be a substitute for leisure? If so, what additional channel of effect arises in the commodity market?

15.3   Why does the real interest rate rise as a result of a temporary increase in government purchases?

15.4   What is crowding out? Does it involve an intertemporal substitution effect alone? Could there be direct substitution of government purchases for private investment purchases?

Problems for Discussion

15.5   Government Purchases in the National Accounts
The national accounts treat all of government purchases as part of real GNP. But suppose that these purchases, G_t, are an input to private production – that is, $Y_t = F(K_{t-1}, L_t, G_t)$. Then public services are an intermediate product – that is, a good that enters as an input into a later stage of production. Hence, we ought not to include these services twice in real GNP – once when the government purchases them and again when the public services contribute to private production.
a. Suppose that businesses initially hire private guards. But the government then provides free police protection, which substitutes for the guards. Assume that the private guards and police are equally efficient and receive the same incomes. How does the switch from private to public services affect measured real GNP?
b. How should we change the treatment of public services in the national accounts? Is the proposal practical?
(These issues are discussed in Simon Kuznets, 1948, pp. 156–7, and Richard Musgrave, 1959, pp. 186–8.)

15.6   Public Ownership of Capital and the National Accounts

When the government produces goods and services, the national accounts measure the contribution to GNP by the government's purchases from the private sector of labour, materials, and new capital goods. But the accounts neglect any contribution to output from the flow of services on government-owned capital. The accounts also do not subtract depreciation of this capital to calculate net product.
a. What happens to measured GNP if the government gives its capital to a private business and then buys the final goods from that business?
b. How should we change the treatment of government-owned capital in the national accounts? Is the proposal practical?

15.7   The Role of Public Services
We assume that an additional unit of public services has two direct effects: first, it substitutes for α units of private consumption, and second, it raises production by β units.
a. Consider various categories of government purchases, such as military spending, police, highways, public transit, research and development expenditures, and regulatory agencies. How do the parameters α and β vary across the categories? Are the parameters always positive?
b. Consider a permanent increase in government purchases. How do the sizes of the responses in output and consumption depend on the values of the parameters, α and β? Explain the results.
c. Repeat part b for the case of a temporary increase in government purchases.

15.8   Prospective Changes in Government Purchases
During the current period, date 1, people find out that government purchases will increase permanently in some future period. There is no change in current purchases or in the paths of the money stock and real transfers.
a. What happens currently to the real interest rate and the quantities of output, consumption, investment, and employment?
b. What happens to the current price level and nominal interest rate?
c. Can you think of some real-world cases for which this question applies?

15.9   Effects of Government Purchases on the Real Wage Rate
Suppose that we include a labour market in the model.
a. What is the effect on the real wage rate from a temporary increase in government purchases?
b. What is the effect from a permanent increase in government purchases?

15.10 Government Employment during Wartime (optional)

In the model we assume that the government buys only final product from the commodity market. In particular, the government neither produces goods nor employs people. This assumption is basically satisfactory if the government's production function is similar to that of private producers. But the assumption is troublesome for wartime. Suppose, for example, that during World War II the government effectively removes 10 million people temporarily from the civilian labour force. But the government takes away no privately owned capital. Then, as before, assume that the government also temporarily raises its purchases of goods by a large amount.

a. Analyze the effects on the real interest rate and on the quantities of output, investment, and consumption. (How should we count the 10 million conscripts in the measure of output?) What happens to total and private employment?

b. If we include a labour market in the model, then what happens to the real wage rate?

15.11 The Price Level in the US during the Korean War

With the start of the Korean War, the US price level (GNP deflator) rose at an annual rate of 10% from the second quarter of 1950 to the first quarter of 1951. In contrast, the inflation rate was negative for 1949, 1.4% from the first quarter of 1951 to the first quarter of 1952, and 2.0% from the first quarter of 1952 to the first quarter of 1953.

The table shows for various periods the inflation rate, π_t, the monetary growth rates, μ_t, for currency and M1, the growth rate of real government purchases, ΔG_t, and the nominal interest rate on 3-month US Treasury bills, R_t. Can we use these data to account for the surge in the price level at the start of the Korean War? (This question does not have a definite answer!)

(*Hint*: Price controls were stringent during World War II. People may have expected a return to these controls under the Korean War in 1950.)

		(M1)	(Currency)		
Year and quarter	π_t	μ_t	μ_t	ΔG_t	R_t
1949.1 to 1950.2	−0.3	1.8	−1.6	2.7	1.1
Start of war					
1950.2 to 1951.1	10.0	4.0	−0.5	24.6	1.3
1951.1 to 1952.1	1.4	5.3	4.7	27.9	1.6
1952.1 to 1953.1	2.0	3.2	4.5	9.2	1.8

(Figures in % per year)

15.12 The Optimal Level of Public Services (optional)

In the model a permanent increase in government purchases raises output but lowers consumption and leisure. Recall that we used the condition, $\alpha + \beta < 1$, where α measures the substitution of public services for consumer spending and β is the marginal product of public services. We assumed also that the parameters α and β declined as the quantity of government purchases rose.

a. What happens to the typical person's utility when the quantity of government purchases rises permanently by one unit?

b. If the government wants to maximize the typical person's utility, then where should it set its level of purchases? What condition holds here for the parameters α and β?

c. Why is it not the right answer in part **b** to choose the level of government purchases that maximizes aggregate output (as measured by real GNP)?

d. Without working through the details, how does the analysis change if public services provide utility in other ways–that is, not only as a direct substitute for private consumer spending?

Notes

1. We follow here the approach pioneered by Martin Bailey (1971, ch. 9).
2. See Roger Kormendi (1983) and David Aschauer (1985).
3. David Aschauer's (1988) empirical results suggest important effects of this type from the government's contributions to 'infrastructure' but not from other types of government expenditure. The infrastructure components include highways, airports, electrical and gas facilities, mass transit, water systems, and sewers.
4. For some additional discussion of these effects, see Robert Hall (1980a).
5. These estimates, based on the behaviour of money and other variables, are reported in Barro (1978b, p. 572).
6. The details of this variable and further results are in Barro (1987). For an earlier discussion of these data, see Daniel Benjamin and Levis Kochin (1984).
7. The data are for British consols, which are government bonds that pay a perpetual stream of coupons but have no maturity date. The results refer to nominal interest rates, whereas the theory applies to real interest rates. Over the period of study, however, the long-term inflation rate in the United Kingdom was close to zero. It is therefore likely that the positive relation between temporary spending and nominal interest rates also reflects a positive relation with real interest rates.
8. We are neglecting any effects on capital's marginal product, MPK, from the changes in government purchases, G, or the quantity of labour input, L.

16

Taxes and Transfers

Thus far, we have taken an unrealistic view of governmental operations by assuming lump-sum taxes and transfers. In our model, the amount that a household or firm pays as taxes or receives as transfers has nothing to do with the household's or firm's income or other characteristics. In the real world governments levy a variety of taxes and pay out a lot of transfers, but none of them looks like the lump sums in our theory. Generally a household's or firm's taxes and transfers depend on its actions. But this dependence motivates changes in behaviour. For example, income taxes deter people from working and discourage businesses from investing. Similarly, transfers to the unemployed or the poor may motivate people not to work. Overall, the system of taxes and transfers creates a variety of substitution effects on work effort, production, consumption, and investment. In this chapter we extend the theoretical analysis to incorporate some of these effects. But before considering the theory, it is useful to start with an overview of the various tax instruments most commonly used in industrialized countries.

Sources of Government Revenues

Table 16.1 gives a broad picture of the evolution of taxation in nine European countries between 1880 and 1989. The first observation, which shows up clearly in Figure 16.1, is that tax pressure, measured as the ratio of total general government revenues (excluding social security) to GDP has increased substantially in the last hundred years. The average for these countries was 6.2% of GDP in 1880 and 29.6% in 1989.

The second observation, highlighted by Figure 16.2, is that there exist substantial cross-country differences. In 1989, the overall tax rate, i.e. total general government revenues (including social security taxes) over GDP, was as low as 33.8% in the UK and as high as 49.9% in Denmark.

These revenues are raised using a variety of tax instruments, and the particular mix of these instruments is different in each country. A detailed description of each tax structure is beyond the scope of this textbook. However, even if the cross-country differences are substantial, there are general principles that hold throughout Europe, and these are the aspects that we will focus on. In order to proceed with our analysis, it is useful to classify tax revenues on the basis of two criteria. First, we distinguish among different taxes according to the governmental authorities that are in charge of them. Second, we distinguish among different taxes according to who or what is the subject of taxation.

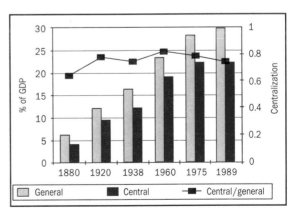

Figure 16.1 Taxes and level of government (excluding social security). Average of the nine countries in Table 16.1.

	Denmark			France			Germany			Italy			Netherlands		
	General	Central	Central/ general	General	Central	Central/ general	General	Central	Central/ general	General	Central	Central/ general	General	Central	Central/ general
1880	7.7	5.0	0.6				4.0	2.0	0.5	16.4	9.0	0.5	8.0	6.6	0.8
1920	10.8	6.5	0.6	13.7	12.5	0.9	14.8	9.8	0.7	13.5	11.5	0.9	14.8	11.0	0.7
1938	13.3	9.0	0.7	17.7	17.1	1.0	22.7	17.6	0.8	17.7	14.8	0.8	13.5	10.7	0.8
1960	24.5	18.7	0.8	21.9	20.8	0.9	22.6	19.5	0.9	19.1	16.9	0.9	23.6	23.2	1.0
1975	39.4	26.7	0.7	22.5	21.9	1.0	23.5	20.9	0.9	16.8	16.5	1.0	27.2	26.8	1.0
.... change in data source															
1989	48.6	33.2	0.7	23.7	20.2	0.9	24.0	12.1	0.5	27.0	25.7	1.0	26.4	25.3	1.0

	Norway			Sweden			Switzerland			United Kingdom			Average 9 countries		
	General	Central	Central/ general	General	Central	Central/ general	General	Central	Central/ general	General	Central	Central/ general	General	Central	Central/ general
1880	5.4	3.2	0.6	7.0	4.5	0.6				7.5	5.6	0.7	6.2	4.0	0.6
1920	7.5	3.8	0.5	12.2	7.0	0.6		3.6		20.1	18.1	0.9	11.9	9.3	0.8
1938	16.4	9.8	0.6	13.9	9.6	0.7	12.0	5.3	0.4	18.7	15.0	0.8	16.2	12.1	0.7
1960	26.8	18.2	0.7	28.5	21.8	0.8	15.4	7.6	0.5	26.0	23.2	0.9	23.2	18.9	0.8
1975	30.4	20.6	0.7	41.0	29.2	0.7	21.0	7.9	0.4	30.7	27.4	0.9	28.1	22.0	0.8
.... change in data source															
1989	33.2	23.6	0.7	35.9	24.4	0.7	20.5	9.1	0.4	27.3	23.5	0.9	29.6	21.9	0.7

Denmark: 1880 = 1882; 1920 = 1924
France: 1938 = 1935
Germany: 1880 = 1881; 1920 = 1925; 1938 = 1937
Italy: 1920 = 1921
Netherlands: 1880 = 1902; 1920 = 1922; 1938 = 1935; 1960 = 1961
Norway: 1938 = 1935; 1960 = 1961
Sweden: 1920 = 1923
Switzerland: 1920 = 1924
United Kingdom: 1880 = 1881; 1938 = 1935

Source: 1879–1975: Flora (1983); 1980–1989: IMF, *Government Finance Statistics Yearbook*; OECD, National Accounts.

Table 16.1   General and central government taxes, % of GDP (excluding social security)

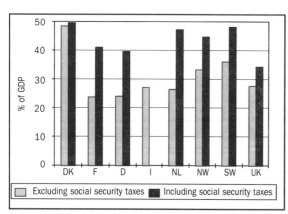

Figure 16.2   Overall tax rates, 1989

Different levels of government have the power to raise revenues. Here we distinguish between *central* government and *local* government. This distinction is unavoidably simplistic, since the precise definition of these two levels of government as well as their relative importance varies greatly across countries. Ultimately, this distinction depends on the type of political system in place, for example whether a country is an unitary state or a federation, and on the organization of its bureaucracy, whether centralized or decentralized.

Although the concept of central government is clear and relatively homogeneous across country, the international differences in the definition of local government can be enormous. In the definition of local government we include entities as large as whole states, like California in the US or Bairn in Germany, and as small as towns or boroughs within a city. Table 16.1 and Figure 16.1 describe the relative importance of central government with respect to all other levels of government. The degree of centralization, defined as the ratio of central government revenues to *general* government (i.e. all levels of government) revenues, does not display a strong trend. From Figure 16.1, we see that for the average of the nine countries considered, the degree of centralization increased from 64% in 1880 to 74% in 1989, after a peak of 82% in 1960. As expected, however, the degree of centralization is different across countries. In 1989, it ranged from 44% in Switzerland to 96% in the Netherlands.

In the following we concentrate on the tax revenues of central governments.

Types of Taxes of Central Governments

Some taxes fall on income (individual income taxes and corporate profits taxes), others on expenditures (excise, sales taxes), and some on holdings of property. But one way or another, the amount that someone pays depends on his or her economic activity: none of these levies looks like the lump-sum taxes in our theory.

One useful distinction is between *direct* and *indirect* taxes. Direct taxes, like income, property and corporate taxes, specifically target individuals and institutions and are levied on the basis of their earnings or wealth. Therefore, they require information about individuals' or institutions' income and assets. Indirect taxes, like sales taxes or excise taxes, are not levied on a particular individual or institution but on an economic transaction.

	Denmark		France		Germany		Italy		Netherlands	
	direct	indirect	direct	indirect	direct	indirect	direct	indirect	direct	indirect
1880	24.8	75.2	23.3	76.7			38.3	61.7	37.5	62.5
1920	60.0	40.0	18.9	81.1	42.5	57.5	41.0	59.0	65.5	34.5
1938	34.9	65.1	45.5	54.5	57.1	42.9	27.5	72.5	35.0	65.0
1960	43.2	56.8	39.8	60.2	47.1	52.9	24.3	75.7	58.1	41.9
					change in data source					
1975	51.2	48.7	36.8	63.0	45.0	55.0	45.8	54.2	62.1	36.9
1989	51.3	48.7	41.5	58.2	44.3	55.7	55.5	43.2	57.0	42.0

	Norway		Sweden		Switzerland		United Kingdom		Average 9 countries	
	direct	indirect	direct	indirect	direct	indirect	direct	indirect	direct	indirect
1880	0.7	99.3	22.3	77.7	6.6	93.4	27.0	73.0	20.1	68.8
1920	57.8	42.2	54.8	45.2	55.0	45.0	66.0	34.0	51.3	48.7
1938	34.2	65.8	31.3	68.7	13.0	87.0	53.0	47.0	36.8	63.2
1960	24.9	75.1	52.3	47.7	22.5	77.5	49.3	50.7	40.2	59.8
					change in data source					
1975	36.2	63.8	46.7	53.3	34.3	65.7	65.2	34.8	47.1	52.8
1989	29.7	69.7	50.2	49.7	43.1	56.9	57.6	42.3	47.8	51.8

Note: The two sources are not directly comparable for several countries.
Denmark: 1880 = 1881
Germany: 1920 = 1924
Norway: 1960 = 1961

Source: 1879–1960: Flora (1983); 1975–1989: IMF, *Government Finance Statistics Yearbook*; OECD, *National Accounts.*

Table 16.2 Central government direct and indirect taxes, % of total taxes (excluding social security)

Table 16.2 shows the historical pattern of direct and indirect taxes in the nine countries that we analyzed before. Figure 16.3 shows that indirect taxes still contribute more than direct taxes to total central government revenues. However, their relative importance has diminished, falling from 68.8% of total revenues in 1880 to 51.8% in 1989. Whereas indirect taxes (custom duties and excise in particular) were the major source of revenues for all the countries in 1880, direct taxes were more important in 1989 in five of the nine countries – Denmark, Italy, the Netherlands, Sweden and the UK.

In the following we shall briefly discuss the various tax instruments, both direct – individual income tax, property tax, and corporate tax – and indirect – custom duties, excise tax, sale tax and value-added tax (VAT). Last, we discuss social security taxes, that is taxes levied to finance the type of social security programmes described in Chapter 15.

Individual Income Tax

Income taxes are a relatively recent instrument in the history of public finance. Table 16.3 reports the dates of introduction of this type of tax. It was introduced in the UK in 1843 and in Germany only in 1924. Again, the exact structure of personal income taxes varies from country to country, but some basic principles apply almost everywhere. Usually, the computation of personal income tax begins by subtracting from a family's reported income the expenses for business purposes, deferred compensation through pension plans, and some other items to get **adjusted gross income**. Then take out various deductions for items like medical care (in countries without socialized health service), some types of interest payments, and certain other taxes. Then subtract the value of personal exemptions for dependent members of the family to get **taxable income**. Aside from any tax credits that apply, the law provides a schedule that relates the amount of tax to taxable income. (Marital status may also matter here.) But it is important to note that the tax is not a constant fraction of taxable income, that is, it is not a **flat-rate tax**. Over most ranges of income, an increase in income (that is large enough to move someone into the next tax bracket) raises the **marginal tax rate**, which is the tax rate on an additional ECU of income. This setup is called a **graduated-rate tax**. (Sometimes it is called a 'progressive tax', which seems to express someone's opinion about its merits. In contrast, a 'regressive tax' system imposes a lower rate as income rises.)

	Income tax	Corporation tax
Austria	1898	1898
Belgium	1922	1963
Denmark	1917	1922
Finland	1917	1920
France	1916	1873
Germany	1924	1924
Italy	1877	1953
Netherlands	1894	1946
Norway	1892	1922
Sweden	1903	1903
United Kingdom	1843	1947 (1966)
United States	1913	1909

Note: The separate taxation of corporate profit was introduced in the UK in 1947, but a standard form of corporate taxation was introduced in 1966.

Similarly, profit taxes were present in several countries in periods before the dates stated above. However, they were introduced only on an extraordinary basis, during times of fiscal emergency, particularly wars.

Sources: Flora (1983); King (1977).

Table 16.3   The introduction of direct taxes

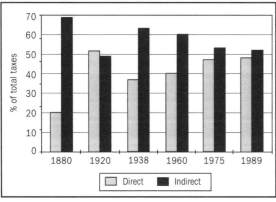

Figure 16.3   Direct and indirect taxes, central government

	Income tax	Property tax	Corporate & trade taxes	Other direct taxes	Custom taxes	Excise taxes	Turnover & VAT	Other indirect taxes
Denmark								
1881				24.8	52.7	7.4		15.1
1920	45.8	6.5		7.7	10.6	21.3		8.1
1938	10.5	6.5	4.1	13.7	18.1	37.3		9.8
1960	32.7	2.6	5.7	2.3	5.7	46.6		4.5
1975	40.6	0.7	3.9	0.5	0.5	21.6	27.8	4.3
1989	42.6	3.0	4.8	0.9	0.1	12.5	29.2	6.9
France								
1880		5.1	18.2	9.4	39.2		28.1	
1920	11.0		4.5	3.4	14.9	27.1	13.7	25.4
1938	15.2		17.7	12.6	15.4	9.9	17.2	11.9
1960	20.2		15.0	4.6	3.0	19.1	33.2	5.2
1975	18.7		17.6	6.7	0.1	10.8	41.3	5.0
1989	23.4	4.4	12.3	0.1	0.0	12.7	42.6	4.2
Germany								
1880					55.6	41.8		2.6
1924	30.4	6.9	4.6	0.6	4.9	16.5	28.0	8.2
1938	25.4	1.9	26.8	3.0	8.7	13.6	16.2	4.4
1960	28.9	4.6	12.4	1.1	4.7	15.3	27.4	5.5
1975	47.4	2.1	5.7	0.6	0.1	15.0	25.2	3.9
1989	34.3	0.4	9.6	0.0	0.0	21.0	31.5	3.2
Italy								
1880	17.3		6.0	15.1	12.2	36.8		12.7
1920	10.4		1.6	29.0	5.2	37.2	0.6	15.9
1938	19.5	3.0	1.4	3.5	4.3	36.6	10.0	21.6
1960	15.6	0.6	4.0	4.1	6.6	32.1	22.6	14.5
1975	32.9		4.7	2.9	12.3	25.4	13.2	8.4
1989	42.7	1.8	10.4	0.4	0.0	10.0	21.6	11.6
Netherlands								
1880			4.4	33.1	5.1	41.8		15.6
1920	23.6	2.2		39.5	7.0	16.7		10.8
1938	18.2	3.6		13.1	19.6	21.2	12.8	11.5
1960	40.1	1.7	14.6	2.9	10.2	8.2	18.5	3.8
1975	46.0	0.9	13.2	0.8	4.0	6.3	24.6	4.0
1989	38.5	4.5	14.1	0.0	0.0	9.6	29.6	3.8
Norway								
1880				0.7	68.9	25.0		5.4
1920	54.8			3.0	26.6	7.6		8.0
1938	26.7		2.6	5.0	26.9	20.5	7.3	11.1
1961	24.3			0.6	7.8	27.2	36.7	3.4
1975	19.1			0.5	1.2	21.8	51.4	6.0
1989	21.2	2.2	6.2	0.0	0.8	24.1	37.1	8.2
Sweden								
1880			0.6	21.8	46.5	25.7		5.4
1920	20.5		17.3	17.0	18.0	18.0		9.2
1938	31.2			0.1	17.7	28.2		22.9
1960	51.4			0.9	5.2	24.8	12.9	4.8
1975	48.9			8.4	1.3	14.6	21.1	5.7
1989	27.7	7.1	9.6	0.8	1.1	18.7	31.9	3.2
Switzerland								
1880				6.6	92.7	0.7		
1920				54.9	31.7	5.4		7.9
1938				12.9	66.1	5.1		15.9

Table 16.4 continued over

Table 16.4 continued

1960	15.8			6.7	37.3	6.6	23.3	10.4
1975	20.0			12.0	27.0	5.0	29.0	7.0
1989	28.2	8.2	6.8	0.0	15.1	6.2	32.4	3.2
United Kingdom								
1880	13.8			13.3	28.9	37.8		6.3
1920	34.2			31.7	12.8	19.1		2.2
1938	42.2			10.8	26.4	13.6		7.0
1960	41.1			8.2	23.3	15.4	8.5	3.5
1975	56.3		9.8	1.1	0.8	16.6	11.7	3.7
1989	37.4	2.8	17.4	0.0	0.0	16.3	23.8	2.3
Average 9 countries								
1880	3.5	0.0	1.8	14.8	41.3	28.5	0.0	10.1
1920	25.6	1.7	3.1	20.8	14.6	18.8	4.7	10.6
1938	21.0	1.7	5.8	8.3	22.6	20.7	7.1	12.9
1960	30.0	1.1	5.7	3.5	11.5	21.7	20.3	6.2
1975	36.7	0.4	6.1	3.7	5.3	15.2	27.3	5.3
1989	32.9	3.8	10.1	0.2	1.9	14.5	31.1	5.2

Note: Other direct taxes include: inheritance tax, land tax and extraordinary taxes.
Other indirect taxes include: turnover taxes and stamp duties on legal documents

Source: 1879–1975: Flora (1983); 1989: IMF, *Government Finance Statistics Yearbook*.

Table 16.4   Composition of central government taxes (excluding social security) (% of total taxes)

The distinction between average and marginal tax rates is important for our analysis. *Average tax rates* indicate how much revenue the government collects as a fraction of income: total revenue equals the average tax rate multiplied by the total amount of income. The effects of the tax system on people's choices depend, however, on *marginal* tax rates. These rates prescribe the fraction that the government takes from an additional ECU of income. In deciding how much to work, produce, and invest, households and firms take account of these marginal tax rates.

Table 16.4 distinguishes among the various sources of revenues of the central government of the nine European countries.[1] Figure 16.4 shows the time pattern for the cross-country averages. The importance of the income tax has increased considerably. In 1880, on average only 3.5% of total central government revenues derived from income taxation, whereas in 1989 this figure was 33.9%. Looking across countries, we notice that, in 1989, in Italy the proportion of income taxes was the highest at 42.7%, and in Norway the lowest at 21.2%.

Corporate Profits Taxes

Aside from taxing household income, governments also tax the net revenues of corporations. As for the personal income tax, corporation taxes are, for several countries, a relatively recent phenomenon. As reported in Table 16.3, a corporation tax had existed in France since 1873, but in Italy a similar taxation instrument

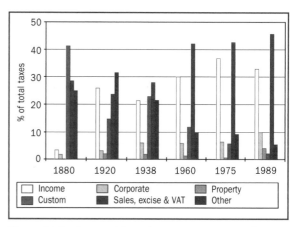

Figure 16.4   Composition of tax revenues, central government (excluding social security)

was introduced only in 1953.[2] The importance of corporate taxes has increased during the last hundred years, as shown in Table 16.4 and Figure 16.4. For the average of the nine countries, revenues from corporate taxation amounted only to 1.8% of total central government revenues in 1880 but, by 1989, they increased to 10.1%. In 1989, corporate tax revenues were as high as 17.4% of total revenues in the UK and as low as 4.8% in Denmark.

The relation of corporate taxes to corporate profits depends on various tax credits and on the rules for computing depreciation allowances and valuing inventories. These rules are specific to each country. We can think of the corporate profits tax as a levy on the capital owned by corporations. But since households own the corporations, the tax amounts ultimately to another levy on households' income from

capital. In fact, the government taxes the earnings of corporations directly and then taxes them a second time when people receive dividends or capital gains. (Economists call this *double taxation*.) For the purposes of our analysis, we can think of adding the tax on corporate profits to individual income taxes to calculate an overall tax on the income from capital.

Property Taxes

Different countries use a wide array of procedures to determine the taxes on houses, factories, and other property. We can think of the property tax as another form of tax on capital. For most purposes, we can therefore combine this tax with the individual income taxes and the corporate profits tax to find the overall tax on the income

---

Box 16.1 An Example of Income Tax: The US Federal Income Tax

Although the US income tax in 1991 was graduated, the degree of graduation had been substantially reduced by the tax reform of 1986 and by earlier tax legislation. (For a discussion of the 1986 reform, see Henry Aaron, 1987.) Figure 16.5 shows the relation of the marginal tax rate and the **average tax rate** (the ratio of taxes to adjusted gross income) to a family's adjusted gross income. The graph applies in 1991 to a married couple who have two children and do not itemize deductions. (This assumption is unrealistic for high incomes, at which most people itemize deductions.) The graph therefore incorporates a standard deduction of $5700 and personal exemptions of $8600. Note that the marginal tax rate is 0 for adjusted gross incomes between 0 and $14 300, 15% for incomes between $14 300 and $48 300, 31% for incomes between $48 300 and $96 450, 33.1% for incomes between $96 450 and $275 000, and 31% above $275 000.[3]

Figure 16.5 also shows the average tax rate as a function of adjusted gross income. The average tax rate rises steadily with income

but approaches 31% as income becomes very high. Recall that we have ignored itemized deductions and various devices that make income nontaxable. These elements weaken the tendency for the average tax rate to rise as income increases.

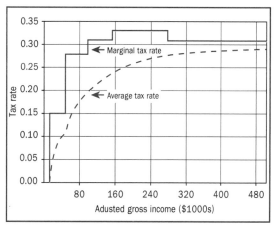

Figure 16.5 Marginal and average tax rates for the US federal individual income tax in 1991

from capital. Table 16.4 and Figure 16.4 show that property taxes are not a major source of revenues for central governments. In 1989, the average for the nine countries was 3.8% of total central government revenues, ranging from 0.4% in Germany to 8.2% in Switzerland.

Sales and Excise Taxes

Almost all countries have some form of sales taxes and special levies on particular items like gasoline, alcohol, tobacco, and other goods. As mentioned in our discussion of indirect taxes, an important feature of these taxes is that they apply to expenditures rather than to income or wealth. Many countries, including the EC member states, use a *value-added tax* (**VAT**), which amounts to a broad-based sales tax. Instead of applying to final sales, this levy depends on the value added to goods at various stages of production. Table 16.4 and Figure 16.4 show that the sum of excise, sales and value added taxes are an increasingly important sources of revenues for central governments. In fact, in 1989, this set of taxes was the largest source of central government income in all the countries considered, except for Denmark and Italy.

In the subsequent theoretical analysis, we shall focus on income taxes. Thus, in a broad sense, the analysis encompasses the types of taxes discussed in previous categories. But we should remember that sales and excise taxes operate in a different manner.

Custom Duties

Historically, one of the most important instruments has been custom duties on import and export. Table 16.4 and Figure 16.4 show that they were, in 1880, the single largest source of revenues for many countries, and the largest on average (41.3% of total revenues). Their importance, however, has been gradually decreasing and in 1989 they were reduced to 1.9% on average. This revenue contraction is due to the worldwide process of trade liberalization, as discussed in Chapter 7. It is interesting to notice from Table 16.4 that, in 1989, custom duties were practically

zero for the countries that are EC members, reflecting the absence of tariffs within the EC. The only country in which revenues from custom duties were still sizable in 1989 was Switzerland.

Social Security Tax

As discussed in Chapter 15, social security is composed of several different services, like health insurance and unemployment insurance (see Table 15.3). To finance these services, governments levy taxes (sometimes referred to as 'contributions') on both employers and employees. Unlike most other taxes, social security revenues are specifically earmarked to finance social security programmes.

Table 16.5 and Figure 16.6, show that social security 'contributions' have increased in almost all countries during the post-World War II period. On average, they rose from 5.1% of GDP in 1950 to 10.6% in 1988. Notice that total social security spending is generally greater than the revenue from social security taxes. The difference is made up by public grants, financed by using revenues from other form of taxation. The allocation of the burden of financing social security programmes varies substantially from country to country. For example, in 1988, the main source of financing came from government grants in Denmark, from taxation of employers in Italy, and from taxation of employees in the Netherlands.

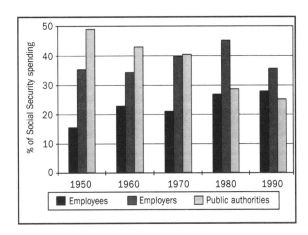

Figure 16.6 Financing of social security (sources of revenue)

	Soc.sec. taxes % of GDP	Employees Taxes	Employers taxes	Public & others
		% of social security expenditure		
Denmark				
1950	1.9	13.0	11.8	75.2
1960	2.6	14.9	10.6	74.5
1970	3.6	14.1	8.9	77.0
1980	0.8	2.9	2.0	95.1
1988	1.3	7.8	0.6	91.6
France				
1950	9.0	15.5	65.1	19.4
1960	10.6	15.6	62.9	21.5
1970	13.2	18.9	68.4	12.7
1980	16.0	32.4	59.9	7.7
1988	17.5	36.5	53.4	10.1
Germany				
1950	9.6	21.5	39.7	38.8
1960	11.0	26.2	43.4	30.4
1970	12.7	28.9	42.3	28.8
1980	15.5	55.4	48.9	-4.2
1988	15.7	57.1	51.7	-8.8
Italy				
1951	5.8	4.4	69.2	26.5
1960	8.6	12.1	60.0	27.9
1970	13.3	14.2	67.5	24.4
1980	10.8	24.7	67.5	7.7
1988				
Netherlands				
1950	5.7	13.7	54.4	31.9
1960	10.3	40.8	39.7	19.5
1970	19.3	38.5	42.9	18.6
1980	18.2	51.0	41.5	7.5
1988	20.7	63.0	41.8	-4.8
Norway				
1950	3.1	29.3	16.1	54.6
1961	5.4	32.1	28.0	39.9
1970	9.2	22.9	33.2	43.9
1980	9.1	22.3	51.5	26.2
1988	11.3	24.7	46.4	28.9
Sweden				
1950	1.8	9.8	11.0	79.2
1960	3.5	20.5	11.0	68.5
1970	9.1	11.4	27.7	61.0
1980	11.3	0.2	58.3	41.5
1988	12.0	0.3	59.9	39.8
United Kingdom				
1950	3.7	17.8	15.6	66.6
1960	3.9	20.0	17.9	62.1
1970	5.6	19.7	25.1	55.2
1980	5.5	23.5	30.2	46.3
1988	6.5	30.3	28.4	41.4
Average 8 countries				
1950	5.1	15.6	35.4	49.0
1960	7.0	22.8	34.2	43.0
1970	10.7	21.1	39.5	40.2
1980	10.9	26.5	45.0	28.5
1988	10.6	27.5	35.3	24.8

Sources: 1879–1975: Flora (1983); 1989: IMF, *Government Finance Statistics Yearbook.*

Table 16.5 Central government: social security taxes (financing of social security)

An Income Tax in the Theoretical Model

We can evaluate the main effects of taxation by examining a simple form of income tax. Assume that a household's real taxes, t_t/P_t, are a fraction, τ, of its real taxable income. (τ is the Greek letter *tau*.) Hence, for simplicity, we do not introduce a graduated-rate tax structure into the model but use instead a flat-rate tax. Also, we assume at this stage that the tax rate, τ, does not vary over time.

In the model – in which the households are the producers as well as the workers – we assume that a household's real taxable income equals its real net product, $y_t - \delta k_{t-1}$, plus real interest income, less an amount of **tax-exempt real income**, e_t.[4] Notice that we treat governmental transfers as nontaxable, which is accurate in most cases. Finally, we assume initially that there is no inflation, so that the real and nominal interest rates on bonds are equal: $r_t = R_t$. A household's real taxes are therefore given by

$$t_t/P_t = \tau(y_t - \delta k_{t-1} + r_{t-1}b_{t-1}/P_t - e_t) \quad (16.1)$$

If real taxable income is negative, then we assume that taxes are negative rather than zero.[5] We also assume that the tax parameters, τ and e_t, are the same for all households. In particular, we neglect any actions that individuals can take to affect either their marginal tax rate, τ, or their quantity of tax-exempt income, e_t. Since each household's marginal tax rate is τ, the average of these rates across households – the average marginal tax rate–is also τ.

Aggregate real tax revenues follow from equation (16.1) as

$$T_t/P_t = \tau(Y_t - \delta K_{t-1} - E_t) \quad (16.2)$$

where E_t is the aggregate amount of tax-exempt income. (Remember that aggregate real interest payments, $r_{t-1}B_{t-1}/P_t$, equal zero.) The government's budget constraint in real terms is therefore

$$G_t + V_t/P_t = \tau(Y_t - \delta K_{t-1} - E_t)$$
$$+ (M_t - M_{t-1})/P_t \qquad (16.3)$$

Here we measure aggregate real income taxes on the right side by the expression from equation (16.2).

Suppose that we take as given the amounts of real government purchases, G_t, aggregate real transfers, V_t/P_t, and the real revenue from money creation, $(M_t - M_{t-1})/P_t$. Then, for a given amount of aggregate net product, $Y_t - \delta K_{t-1}$, the two tax parameters, τ and E_t, must be set so as to satisfy the government's budget constraint: the government has to generate enough tax receipts in each period to meet the expenditures that are not covered by printing money. We shall often think about changing the marginal tax rate, τ, and then allowing the exempt amount, E_t, to vary in order for equation (16.3) to hold. In that way we can isolate the substitution effect from a change in the tax rate. Note that we do not allow the government to borrow and lend on the credit market. That is, we wait until the next chapter to allow for budget deficits or surpluses.

Households' Budget Constraints

From our analysis in previous chapters, each household's budget constraint in real terms is

$$y_t - \delta k_{t-1} + b_{t-1}(1 + r_{t-1})/P_t$$
$$+ m_{t-1}/P_t + v_t/P_t - t_t/P_t$$
$$= c_t + i_t - \delta k_{t-1} + (b_t + m_t)/P_t \qquad (16.4)$$

Recall that we treat the households as carrying out the investment expenditures. We have also subtracted depreciation from both sides of equation (16.4), so that net product, $y_t - \delta k_{t-1}$, appears on the left, and net investment, $i_t - \delta k_{t-1}$, appears on the right. Notice that real taxes, t_t/P_t, subtract from the household's disposable funds on the left side.

Now substitute for real taxes from equation (16.1) into equation (16.4) and rearrange terms to get

$$(1 - \tau)(y_t - \delta k_{t-1}) + (1 - \tau)r_{t-1}b_{t-1}/P_t$$
$$+ (b_{t-1} + m_{t-1})/P_t + v_t/P_t + \tau e_t$$
$$= c_t + i_t - \delta k_{t-1} + (b_t + m_t)/P_t \qquad (16.5)$$

The first term on the left side equals net product or income, $y_t - \delta k_{t-1}$, less the tax on this income, $\tau(y_t - \delta k_{t-1})$. In other words, the after-tax income, $(1 - \tau)(y_t - \delta k_{t-1})$, enters into the household's budget constraint. Similarly, the after-tax real interest income, $(1 - \tau)r_{t-1}b_{t-1}/P_t$, appears on the left side of equation (16.5).

The uses of funds on the right side of equation (16.5) do not involve the tax rate. This result follows because we assume no tax on the expenditures for consumption or net investment. More generally, any sales or excise taxes would enter here.

Tax Rates and Substitution Effects

We want to see how the presence of an income tax alters the various substitution effects on households. For this purpose we have to reconsider our concepts of the real interest rate, the marginal product of labour (or real wage rate), and the return to investment.

After-Tax Real Interest Rate

Households receive real interest at the rate r_t, but they pay the fraction τ of their receipts to the government. Hence, when measured net of tax, households earn interest at the rate, $\tilde{r}_t \equiv (1 - \tau)r_t$. We refer to the variable $\tilde{r}_t$ as the **after-tax real interest rate**. Notice that this interest rate appears (for period $t - 1$) on the left side of equation (16.5).

In previous chapters we discussed the intertemporal substitution effects that arise when the real interest rate changes. These effects still apply, but they refer now to the after-tax real interest rate. An increase in $\tilde{r}_t$ stimulates saving. The increase in saving reflects partly a reduction in current consumption demand and partly an increase in current work effort and the supply of goods.

After-Tax Marginal Product of Labour

When someone works an additional hour, he or she raises output, y_t, and hence income by the marginal product of labour, MPL_t. But households keep only the fraction, $1 - \tau$, of their extra income. Hence, the **after-tax marginal product of labour**, $(1 - \tau)\text{MPL}_t$, matters for the choices of work and consumption. (With a separate labour market, the after-tax real wage rate, $(1 - \tau)w_t/P_t$, would matter.)

Suppose that there is a given schedule for labour marginal product, MPL_t, when graphed versus the amount of work, ℓ_t. An increase in the tax rate, τ, lowers the schedule when measured net of tax – that is, as $(1 - \tau)\text{MPL}_t$. Households respond just as they would to a decrease in the schedule for labour marginal product: they reduce work effort, the supply of goods, and consumption demand.

After-Tax Rate of Return to Investment

An increase in the stock of capital, k_t, by one unit raises next period's net product by the marginal product of capital less the rate of depreciation, $\text{MPK}_t - \delta$. Recall that this term is the real rate of return from an extra unit of investment. But owners of capital (households) now keep only the fraction, $1 - \tau$, of this return. Therefore, the **after-tax rate of return to investment** becomes $(1 - \tau)(\text{MPK}_t - \delta)$. Producers determine their desired stock of capital, $\hat{k}_t$, by equating this after-tax rate of return to the after-tax real interest rate on bonds, $\tilde{r}_t$. That is, the condition for the desired stock of capital is

$$(1 - \tau)(\text{MPK}_t - \delta) = \tilde{r}_t \qquad (16.6)$$

Equation (16.6) implies that we can now write the function for the desired stock of capital, $\hat{k}_t$, as

$$\hat{k}_t = \hat{k}(\tilde{r}_t, \quad \tau \ldots] \qquad (16.7)$$
$$\phantom{\hat{k}_t = \hat{k}(}(-)\ (-)$$

As before, the term ... represents characteristics of the production function that affect the schedule for capital's marginal product.

For a given tax rate τ, an increase in the *after-tax* real interest rate, $\tilde{r}_t$, on the right side of equation (16.6) raises the required after-tax return from investment. Hence, the desired capital stock falls. For a given value of $\tilde{r}_t$, a higher τ lowers the after-tax return from investment on the left side of equation (16.6). The desired capital stock therefore declines again. Finally, as in earlier cases, the desired capital stock rises if there is an upward shift in the schedule for capital's marginal product, MPK_t.

As before, the desired stock of capital, $\hat{k}_t$, determines a producer's gross investment demand:

$$i_t^d = \hat{k}(\tilde{r}_t, \quad \tau \ldots) - (1 - \delta)k_{t-1}$$
$$\phantom{i_t^d = \hat{k}(}(-)\ (-)$$
$$= i^d(\tilde{r}_t, \quad \tau, \quad k_{t-1}, \ldots)$$
$$(-)\ (-)\ (-) \qquad (16.8)$$

The new features concern the tax rate. First, the after-tax real interest rate, $\tilde{r}_t$, has a negative effect on gross investment demand. Second, for a given value of $\tilde{r}_t$, the tax rate τ has a separate negative effect on investment demand.

A Change in the Tax Rate

Suppose that the income-tax rate, τ, increases. Aggregate real tax revenues are given from the tax law in equation (16.2) by $T_t/P_t = \tau(Y_t - \delta K_{t-1} - E_t)$. If the exempt amount, E_t, did not change, then real tax revenues would increase unless aggregate net product, $Y_t - \delta K_{t-1}$, fell by a great deal. Assume for the moment that this is not the case, that is, real tax receipts would rise if the exempt amount did not change.

Suppose that we hold constant the levels of government purchases, G_t, and aggregate real transfers, V_t/P_t, as well as the real revenue from money creation, $(M_t - M_{t-1})/P_t$. Then the government's budget constraint from equation (16.3) says that the amount of real taxes collected cannot change. If we raise the tax rate, then we have to increase the exempt amount, E_t, to keep real tax revenues the same. In effect, we raise the *average marginal tax rate*, represented by the parameter τ in the model, without changing the *average tax rate*. In the real world, for example, the government might increase various exemptions in the income-tax law but then raise all of the tax rates on taxable income to maintain the level of real revenues. Alternatively, the government could switch from one type of tax, such as the social security tax on wage earnings, to another, such as the individual income tax. Because the social security tax has a low average marginal tax rate, compared to the revenue that it collects, this change raises the average marginal tax rate while leaving unchanged the aggregate of real tax revenues.

The important point is that, conceptually, we want to keep separate the effects of changes in the average marginal tax rate, τ, from those of changes in government purchases, transfers, or money creation. That is why we consider first the case in which the exempt amount varies along with the tax rate to keep fixed the volume of real tax revenues. Then we can also look at cases in which tax revenues do change, along with some combination of shifts in government purchases, transfers, or money creation.

Consider whether households' wealth changes when the tax rate, τ, increases or decreases. Remember that the aggregate of households' budget constraints involves the present value of aggregate real taxes net of transfers. This present value depends on the present value of government purchases. As long as we hold this last present value fixed, a change in the tax rate does not affect the aggregate present value of taxes less transfers and therefore would not seem to affect wealth. This result turns out to be a satisfactory approximation in most cases. We shall, however, see later that it is not exact. But for now, we neglect any effects on wealth from changes in the tax rate.

Clearing of the Commodity Market

Now we incorporate the various effects from the tax rate into the condition for clearing the commodity market. The condition for period 1 is

$$C^d(\tilde{r}_1, \ \tau \dots) + I^d(\tilde{r}_1, \ \tau \dots) + G_1$$
$$(-)\,(-) \qquad\quad (-)\,(-)$$
$$= Y^s(\tilde{r}_1, \ \tau \dots) \qquad\qquad (16.9)$$
$$(+)\,(-)$$

To avoid a clutter of terms, we do not write out explicitly some of the variables that influence consumer demand, investment demand, and the supply of goods. These include the initial capital stock, K_0 and the amount of government purchases, G_1.

One new feature is that the after-tax real interest rate, $\tilde{r}_1$, appears where the real interest rate, r_1, used to appear. Given the value of $\tilde{r}_1$, the tax rate, τ, has some separate effects. First, a higher tax rate lowers the schedule for the after-tax marginal product of labour, $(1 - \tau)MPL_1$, and thereby reduces the incentive to work. This response decreases goods supply, Y_1^s, and consumer demand, C_1^d. Second, a higher tax rate lowers the after-tax rate of return to investment, $(1 - \tau)(MPK_1 - \delta)$, and thereby reduces investment demand, I_1^d. Thus, in general, *a higher tax rate tends to depress market activity*: it reduces the demands for consumption and investment, as well as the supply of goods. These results follow because a household's tax liability rises when it engages in more market activity. A higher tax rate motivates people to substitute away from market activities and toward untaxed areas, such as leisure or the **underground economy**, in which income is not reported.

Figure 16.7 shows the clearing of the commodity market. The after-tax real interest rate, $\tilde{r}_1$, appears on the vertical axis. The horizontal axis shows the levels of commodity demand and supply.

Effects of a Higher Tax Rate

Assume that the income-tax rate rises permanently from τ to τ' at date 1. Figure 16.8 shows the effects on the commodity market. First, there is a leftward shift of the demand curve, reflecting the decreases in consumption and investment demand. Second, there is a leftward shift of the supply curve. Because the increase in the tax rate

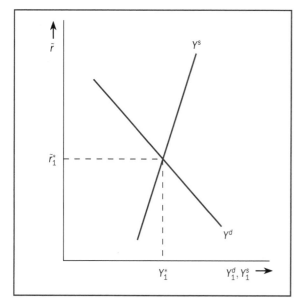

We graph the demand and supply of commodities versus the after-tax real interest rate, $(1 - \tau)r_1 = \tilde{r}_1$.

Figure 16.7   Clearing of the commodity market

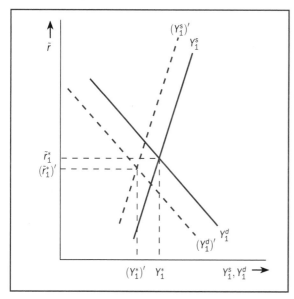

The increase in the income-tax rate from τ to τ' reduces the demand for commodities by more than the supply. Hence, output and the after-tax real interest rate fall.

Figure 16.8   Effects on the commodity market of a higher income-tax rate

is permanent, we predict little response of desired real saving. That is, at the initial value of the after-tax real interest rate, the cutback in goods supply is roughly equal to the fall in consumption demand.[6] Since investment demand also declines, the overall fall in demand is greater than that in supply. Hence, Figure 16.8 shows that the increase in the tax rate creates an excess supply of commodities at the after-tax real interest rate that initially cleared the market. The after-tax real interest rate and the level of output therefore decline.

We are, at this point, taking a short-run perspective in which the capital stock, K_0, is given. The fall in output therefore reflects a decrease in labour input, L. People work less in response to a higher tax rate because the government extracts a larger fraction of a marginal ECU of income.

Because government purchases do not change, the total of real private spending for consumption and investment must decline (to match the fall in output). Recall that the disturbance had no initial impact on desired real saving. The decline in the after-tax real interest rate reduces desired saving: therefore, real saving and hence, net investment must decline overall. We can understand this result if we think of the drop in the after-tax real interest rate as a signal that the priority for using resources to accumulate capital has diminished. From the viewpoint of the private sector, the diminished priority for accumulating capital reflects the adverse effect of a higher tax rate on the after-tax rate of return to investment.

The effect on consumption is uncertain: the decrease in the after-tax real interest rate motivates more consumption, whereas the higher income-tax rate motivates less consumption. Thus, although total output falls, the higher tax rate may crowd out enough investment to avoid a decline in consumption in the short run.

Long-Run Effects of a Higher Tax Rate

We have shown that a permanent increase in the income-tax rate, τ, leads to less investment. This effect on investment in the short run suggests that

Box 16.2 The Wealth Effect from a Change in the Tax Rate

We carried out the analysis under the assumption that the change in the tax rate left wealth unchanged. This assumption seems reasonable because we varied the amount of tax-exempt income, E_1, to hold constant the quantity of real taxes collected, T_1/P_1. But let's consider more carefully whether wealth changes.

As we discussed in Chapter 2, the effect of a disturbance on a household's wealth is positive or negative depending on whether the household can achieve a higher or lower level of utility. The increase in the tax rate that we have just considered ends up reducing the utility of the typical household. The effect on wealth is therefore negative rather than zero.

To see why, note first that someone who produces the quantity of output y_1 gets to keep only the portion, $(1 - \tau)y_1$; the remainder goes as taxes to the government. Each household's contribution to the economy's output, y_1, therefore exceeds the contribution to that

household's after-tax income, which is $(1 - \tau)y_1$.

In deciding how much to work and invest, households consider only the fraction, $1 - \tau$, of the marginal products of their labour and capital. Hence, from a social perspective, people have insufficient incentives to work and invest.[7] An increase in the income-tax rate worsens this incentive problem and thereby causes work effort and output to fall further below their socially-optimal levels. A higher tax rate therefore means that each household ends up with a smaller level of utility: each household is less wealthy.

We could modify the previous analysis to include a negative effect on wealth from an increase in the tax rate, but the general nature of the results would not change. For most purposes, we can therefore use the results that neglected the wealth effects.

---

the stock of capital would decline in the long run. To study this long-run effect, we have to use the dynamic analysis of capital accumulation and economic growth that we worked out in Chapter 14. We consider here only a sketch of these long-run effects.

We showed in Chapter 14 that the change in the capital stock is given by

$$\Delta K = sF(K, L) - \delta K$$

where s is the gross saving rate or, equivalently, the ratio of gross investment to gross output. We have just demonstrated that a permanent increase in the income-tax rate, τ, lowers investment. This change enters into the long-run analysis as a decrease in the investment ratio, s.[8] We showed in Chapter 14 that a lower s leads in the long run to a smaller stock of capital, K.

Effects of a Permanent Rise in Government Purchases under Income Taxation

In Chapter 15, we studied the effects of changes in government purchases when financed by lump-sum taxes. We shall see in Chapter 17 that temporary changes in purchases, such as in wartime, tend to be financed by government borrowing, whereas permanent changes tend to be paid from taxes. The taxes are, however, unlikely to be lump sum and are more likely to resemble the income taxes that we have considered in this chapter. We should therefore reassess the consequences of a permanent shift in government purchases when financed by a change in income taxes.

We found in Chapter 15 that a permanent increase in government purchases reduced wealth and thereby raised work effort and output. If the public services were productive, then output also increased for given inputs of labour and capital. Consumption decreased, but there were no effects on the real interest rate and investment.

Suppose now that the permanent expansion of government purchases is paid by increased income taxes and is accompanied by an increase in the marginal income-tax rate, which we represent by the parameter τ. We found before that a higher income-tax rate tends to reduce work effort. This effect offsets the tendency of more government purchases to increase work effort: hence, the overall response of labour input is now ambiguous. This uncertainty about the change in labour input means that output could also rise or fall.

Recall that a permanent increase in government purchases had no effect on investment, whereas a higher income-tax rate reduced investment. A tax-financed increase in government purchases therefore leads to less investment. This reduction of investment in the short run corresponds to a fall in the capital stock in the long run.[9]

The Relation between the Tax Rate and Tax Revenues

We combined a permanent increase in government purchases with a rise in the income-tax rate, τ, to generate more real tax revenues for each period, T_t/P_t. These revenues are given from the tax law as

$$T_t/P_t = \tau(Y_t - \delta K_{t-1} - E_t)$$

If we hold the exempt amount E_t constant, then real tax receipts increase with the tax rate only if output, Y_t, does not fall enough to reduce real taxable income, $Y_t - \delta K_{t-1} - E_t$, by proportionately more than the increase in the tax rate.

We can view the long-run movement in output, Y, in terms of the changes in the two productive inputs, K and L. We already found that a tax-financed increase in government purchases tends to reduce K, but has an ambiguous effect on L. K falls because producers get to keep only the fraction $1 - \tau$ of their output, and τ has increased. Similarly, L may fall because workers get to keep

only the fraction $1 - \tau$ of their income. The tendency of Y to decline is therefore pronounced if investment and labour input are highly sensitive to changes in the fraction of income, $1 - \tau$, that producers and workers keep for themselves.

The depressing effects of income taxation on capital and labour have to be very strong for tax revenues to fall when the tax rate rises. This outcome does, however, become more likely as the rate of tax, τ, increases. For example, when the tax rate is 10%, a 10% increase means that the new tax rate is 11%. The fraction of extra income that a producer or worker keeps, $1 - \tau$, falls accordingly from 90 to 89%, or by a percentage of 1.1%. In other words, a 10% increase in the tax rate translates into a decline by only 1.1% in the term, $1 - \tau$, that influences capital and labour. We therefore anticipate that a 10% increase in the tax rate would reduce real taxable income in the long run by much less than 10%.

Suppose that we consider higher starting values for the tax rate but continue to raise the rate each time by 10%. At a tax rate of 25%, a 10% increase (to a new rate of 27.5%) means that $1 - \tau$ falls from 75 to 72.5%, or by 3.3%. At a starting rate of 50%, a 10% increase lowers $1 - \tau$ from 50 to 45%, that is, by 10%. At the still higher rate of 75%, a 10% increase reduces $1 - \tau$ by 30%. Thus, the higher is the starting value of the tax rate, the greater is the proportional reduction of the term, $1 - \tau$, from a 10% increase in the tax rate. We predict therefore that the negative response of real taxable income to the tax rate becomes stronger as the rate of tax increases. At some point – but, surely, for a tax rate below 100% – we shall find that an increase in the tax rate reduces real taxable income by so much that real tax revenues fall.

Figure 16.9 shows the relationship between real tax receipts, T/P, and the tax rate, τ. (Think of this relation as applying in the long run, when capital and labour adjust fully to a change in the tax rate.) This relationship is called a **Laffer curve**, in honour of the economist Arthur Laffer. (For a discussion, see Don Fullerton, 1982.) When the tax rate, τ, is zero, the government collects nothing. As the tax rate rises above zero, tax

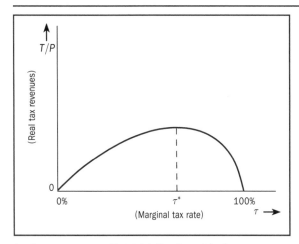

Real tax revenues. *T/P* initially rise with the tax rate τ. However revenues reach their peak when the rate is τ^*. If the tax rate rises above τ^* revenues fall and approach zero as the tax rate approaches 100%.

Figure 16.9   The relation of tax receipts to the tax rate (a Laffer curve)

revenues become positive – hence, the curve has a positive slope. As the tax rate continues to increase, however, the negative response of real taxable income becomes stronger. The slope of the curve therefore gets smaller as the tax rate rises, and the curve eventually becomes flat at the tax rate labelled τ^* in the figure. If the government raises the tax rate above τ^*, then revenues start to decline. In fact, as the tax rate approaches 100%, tax receipts approach zero. If the government wishes to maximize its real revenues, it should not choose a tax rate of 100%. Rather, the value τ^* is the tax rate that maximizes receipts.

Transfer Payments

Suppose that the government raises the aggregate of real transfers, *V/P*, and finances these expenditures with more tax revenues, *T/P*. As in the case in which government purchases increase, the rise in real taxes typically requires an increase in the average marginal tax rate, τ. We have already discussed the adverse effects on work, production, and investment from an increase in

the tax rate. Note especially that an increase in transfers, when financed by an income tax, is no longer neutral in the model.

If transfer payments are lump sum, as we have been assuming, then the analysis is finished. But lump-sum transfers make little sense. Generally the point of transfer programmes is to provide payments to persons in specified categories, for example, poor people, persons who have lost their jobs, old or sick people, farmers, college students, and others. But none of these transfers is lump sum: the amount depends in some way on a person's status.

Think about a welfare programme, in which the payments depend on a family's current or long-run income. Individuals typically face a declining schedule of transfers, possibly subject to some discrete cutoff points, as a function of market income. The important point is that the negative effect of income on benefit payments works like a positive marginal tax rate. Because transfers are sometimes cut drastically when a family's income rises, these programmes can imply high effective marginal tax rates on the earnings of low-income persons. Unfortunately, we do not have estimates for the average marginal tax rate that is implied by the full array of transfer programmes.[10]

Suppose again that the government increases taxes to finance more welfare payments. We already noted the adverse effects on work, production, and investment that derive from the increase in the average marginal tax rate, τ. But the expansion of the welfare programme means that low-income people stand to lose more benefits if they earn more market income. That is, there is also an increase in the effective marginal tax rate for potential welfare recipients. Hence, the negative influences of this change on work and production reinforce the effects from the higher tax rate on market income.

The most important and rapidly growing transfer programme in most countries is the payments to retirees and survivors under social security.[11] We have already discussed the financing of these programmes. From this standpoint, an expansion of social security leads to a higher marginal tax rate on income, τ, which has the usual adverse effects on work and production.[12] If people received social security benefits without restrictions, except for age, then the distorting influences that arise from welfare programmes would not apply. However, in some systems persons who earn income above a specified amount experience a partial or total cutoff of social security benefits. This effectively imposes a high effective marginal tax rate on these individuals. Not surprisingly, researchers find that this policy motivates people to retire earlier than they would otherwise.

Box 16.3 Marginal Tax Rate and Supply Side Economics

In 1980–81 some advocates of **supply-side economics** used a picture like that shown in Figure 16.9 to argue for an across-the-board cut in US income-tax rates. These economists contended that the average marginal tax rate on income exceeded the value τ^*, so that a general cut in rates would yield a larger volume of real tax revenues. There is, however, no evidence that the United States has reached high enough tax rates for this result to apply.

A study for Sweden by Charles Stuart (1981) provides some perspective on the US situation. Stuart estimated that the maximum of tax revenues occurs in Sweden when the average marginal tax rate is about 70%. That is, he estimated τ^* to be about 70%. The actual value of the average marginal tax rate in Sweden reached 70% in the early 1970s and rose subsequently to about 80%. (Stuart took a broad view of taxes to go beyond the income-tax law.) Sweden was therefore operating on the falling portion of the Laffer curve during the 1970s.[13] Stuart attributed part of Sweden's relatively low growth rate of per capita real gross domestic product during the 1970s (1.7% per year) to this factor.

For the United States in 1987, the average marginal tax rate from the federal income tax and social security was 32%. The rate would be higher, however, if we were able to include other taxes. Since we do not have these data, we can draw a rough comparison between the United States and Sweden by considering average tax rates.

For Sweden, the estimated value for τ^* of 70% corresponds to an average tax rate of about 50%. For the United States in 1987, a comparable figure for the tax rate, when calculated as the ratio of total government receipts to GNP, is 32%. So suppose that Sweden and the United States are roughly the same with respect to first, the value of τ^*, and second, the relation between marginal and average tax rates. Then we conclude that in 1987, the United States had a long way to go before reaching the average marginal tax rate, $\tau^* = 70\%$, at which tax revenues are maximized. We should, however, be cautious about this result for two reasons. First, the estimates for Sweden are rough. Second, we cannot be sure that the United States and Sweden have similar Laffer curves.

Lawrence Lindsey (1987) estimated the effect of the Reagan tax cuts from 1982 to 1984 on the tax payments by taxpayers in various income groups. He found that the reductions in tax rates lowered tax collections overall and for taxpayers with middle and low incomes. However, among taxpayers with the highest incomes (adjusted gross incomes in excess of $200 000), the increase of reported taxable incomes was sufficient to more than offset the decrease in tax rates. Lindsey estimated that the tax-rate cuts raised collections in this group by 3% in 1982, 9% in 1983, and 23% in 1984. Therefore, although US taxpayers as a whole were not on the falling portion of the Laffer curve, the taxpayers with the highest incomes appeared to be operating in this range.

Summary

In this chapter we expanded the model to include a simple form of income-tax law. The key parameters of this law are the marginal tax rate and the quantity of tax-exempt income. The marginal tax rate measures the extra tax that the government takes from an additional ECU of income. Households and firms take this marginal tax rate into account when deciding how much to work, produce, and invest. In contrast, the government's tax receipts equal the product of the average tax rate (total taxes divided by total income) and the amount of income.

Saving depends on the after-tax real interest rate, whereas work effort and investment depend on the after-tax marginal products of labour and capital, respectively. For a given total of real taxes collected, an increase in the marginal tax rate motivates people to substitute away from market activities, which are taxed, and toward leisure (or the underground economy). A higher tax rate therefore leads in the short run to less work, output, and investment and in the long run to a smaller stock of capital and lower levels of production and consumption.

When we combine a permanent increase in government purchases with a rise in the marginal tax rate, we change some of the results from the previous chapter. Because of the adverse effects of higher taxation, the short-run effects on labour input and output become ambiguous. Further, the higher tax rate leads in the long run to a lower stock of capital.

As the marginal tax rate rises, the quantity of real taxable income tends to fall. The sensitivity of this response becomes larger the higher is the tax rate. We can therefore draw a Laffer curve, which shows a diminishing effect of the tax rate on the quantity of real tax revenues. Eventually the economy reaches a tax rate at which revenues are at a maximum. At that point further increases in tax rates generate less real tax receipts. For Sweden, there is an estimate that this marginal tax rate is about 70%, which was reached and then surpassed in the early 1970s.

Transfer payments have allocative effects that resemble those from taxation. First, tax rates rise to finance the programme, and second, larger transfer payments mean that the potential recipients stand to lose more benefits by earning income. On both counts, an increase in transfers tends to contract real economic activity.

Important Terms and Concepts

adjusted gross income
taxable income
flat-rate tax
graduated-rate tax
marginal tax rate
average tax rate
tax-exempt income

after-tax real interest rate
after-tax marginal product of labour
after-tax rate of return to investment
underground economy
Laffer curve
supply-side economics

Questions and Problems

Mainly for Review

16.1 Distinguish between the average tax rate and the marginal tax rate. Must the two be equal for a flat-rate tax?

16.2 Why must we hold tax revenue constant when studying the effect of a change in the tax rate? What wealth effects would operate if we did not?

16.3 Explain briefly why a rise in the tax rate reduces the after-tax real interest rate in the short run but raises the before-tax real interest rate in the long run. How does the latter affect the capital stock?

16.4 Ignoring wealth effects from an increase in the tax rate, does the quantity of work decline in the long run? Explain why.

16.5 Could an increase in the tax rate reduce real tax revenues? How does the answer depend on the response of labour supply to changes in the (after-tax) marginal product of labour?

16.6 Define supply-side economics. How could the economy benefit from lowering the tax rate? Include in the answer a discussion of the wealth effects of taxes.

Problems for Discussion

16.7 The Flat-Rate Tax
Some economists advocate shifting from the graduated individual income tax to a flat-rate tax. Under the new system, there would be few deductions from taxable income, and the marginal tax rate would be constant. Because of the elimination of the deductions (sometimes referred to as loopholes), the average marginal tax rate would be lower than that under the current law.
a. What would this change do to the aggregate levels of output, employment, and investment?
b. How does the proposed flat-rate tax compare with the present social security tax?

16.8 Subsidies
Suppose that the average marginal tax rate, τ, is zero. We mentioned that an increase in the tax rate, τ, above zero – with total revenues, T/P, held fixed – reduces the utility of the typical household.
a. Explain this result.
b. Does the result mean that a reduction in the tax rate below zero would be desirable? (A negative value means that the government subsidizes production.)

16.9 Consumption Taxes (optional)
Instead of an income tax, suppose that taxes are levied on the quantity of consumption during each period. A household's real tax payments for period t are then given by the formula

$$t_t/P_t = \tau(c_t - e_t).$$

(A comprehensive sales tax on consumables might operate in this manner.)
a. Write down the budget constraints for the government and the representative household.
b. What is the after-tax real interest rate?
c. How does the tax rate, τ, now enter into the functions for consumption demand, C^d, gross investment demand, I^d, and goods supply, Y^s?
d. What is the short-run effect (while the capital stock is held fixed) of an increase in the tax rate, τ? Consider, in particular, the responses of the real interest rate and the quantities of output, work effort, consumption, and investment. Compare the results with those for an income tax.

16.10 Effects of Inflation on a Graduated Income Tax
Suppose that individual income taxes are paid in accordance with the following graduated-rate table:

Range of taxable income	Tax rate on an extra ECU of taxable income (marginal tax rate) %
ε3 540 – 5 719	11
5 720 – 7 909	12
7 910 – 12 389	14
12 390 – 16 649	16
16 650 – 21 019	18
21 020 – 25 599	22
25 600 – 31 119	25
31 120 – 36 629	28
36 630 – 47 669	33
47 670 – 62 449	38
62 450 – 89 089	42
89 090 – 113 859	45
113 860 – 169 019	49
169 020 –	50

a. Suppose that each person's real income stays constant over time, so that inflation steadily raises everyone's nominal income. If the tax law shown had remained unchanged, what would have happened over time to the average marginal tax rate and to total real tax collections?
b. Assume now that the ECU bracket limits that appear in the left column of the table are adjusted proportionally (or 'indexed') over time for changes in the price level. What then is

the effect of inflation on the average marginal tax rate and on total real tax collections?

16.11 Taxes, Inflation, and Interest Rates (optional)

Suppose that taxes are levied on nominal interest income and that the income-tax rate, τ, does not change over time.

a. What is the after-tax real interest rate on bonds? Consider a permanent increase in the monetary growth rate from μ to μ'. The acceleration of money is a surprise, but people anticipate that the higher rate of monetary expansion, μ', will continue forever.

b. Given the presence of the income tax, what is the effect of the increase in monetary growth on the inflation rate, π, the nominal interest rate, R, and the aggregate level of real money balances, M/P? (Assume that the income-tax rate, τ, is unaffected by inflation.)

c. Discuss the implications of the answer to part b. for the relation between R and π.

16.12 Effects of Transfer Programmes on Work Effort

Discuss the effects on people's incentives to work of the following governmental programmes:

a. The food stamp programme, which provides subsidized coupons for purchases of food. The allowable subsidies vary inversely with family income.

b. A negative income tax. This programme would provide cash transfers to poor persons. The amount of transfers is reduced as some fraction of increases in family income.

c. Unemployment compensation. People who work for a specified interval and who lose their jobs receive cash payments while unemployed (and 'looking for work'). The benefits can last for six months or sometimes for longer periods. What difference does it make if businesses with histories of more layoffs have to raise their contributions to the unemployment-insurance fund? (A programme that has this feature is said to be 'experience rated'.)

d. Retirement benefits under social security. What is the consequence of the income test, which reduces benefits to persons (of age less than 70) who earn labour income in excess of a specified amount?

Notes

1. Because of lack of comprehensive data before 1950, we exclude social security taxes from this table. Social security taxes are analyzed separately later in the chapter.

2. Notice that several countries used some form of taxation of company profits in earlier periods than the one stated in Table 16.4. However, these taxes were introduced only on an extraordinary basis, during times of fiscal emergency, usually associated with wars.

3. For families with adjusted gross incomes above $150 000, the marginal tax rate is the stated 31% rate plus an effect from a phase-out of personal exemptions. The phase-out is complete at an income of $275 000; therefore, the marginal tax rate reverts to 31% at that point. For families with adjusted gross incomes above $100 000 who itemize deductions (which is most families at these income levels), a phase-out of the itemized deductions raises the marginal tax rate by 0.93 percentage points until this phase-out is complete. Apparently, the main point of the 1990 tax law – which introduced these marvellous phase-outs – was to make it as hard as possible to figure out what one's marginal tax rate is.

4. The formulation assumes that interest paid by borrowers reduces their taxable income one-to-one.

5. In the real world taxes can be negative because of the earned-income credit (a payment that the government gives to low-income families that have labour income) and because households and businesses can carry over some losses from one period to the next.

6. Recall that we hold constant aggregate real taxes. The change in the aggregate of desired saving therefore equals the change in goods supply, Y_1^s, less the change in consumer demand, C_1^d.

7. The fraction τ that goes to taxes reduces the required payments of all other taxpayers (by a very small amount per person). No individual takes these benefits to others into account when deciding how much to work and invest. Economists call this an *external effect*. This effect refers to the benefits that others get from one person's actions, when the person does not take these benefits into account.

8. The higher tax rate also reduces the level of labour input, L, and therefore the level of output, Y, for a given stock of capital, K. We can show, however, that investment tends to fall as a fraction of output, that is, the ratio s declines. The capital stock falls in the long run partly because s has decreased and partly because L has declined.

9. This result follows because we assumed in Chapter 12 that a change in government purchases did not affect the schedule for the marginal product of capital, MPK. Some public services, such as infrastructure activities like highways and the maintenance of a legal system, tend to raise the marginal product of capital. In these cases, the effect on investment in the short run is uncertain: the increase in MPK tends to raise investment, but the increase in the income-tax rate tends to lower it. The long-run effect on the capital stock is also ambiguous in this case.

10. The US Council of Economic Advisers (*Economic Report*, 1982, p. 29) estimated that 'typical welfare recipients, namely

single mothers with children, face marginal tax rates in excess of 75%'.

11. One way to measure the size of this programme is by the 'replacement ratio'. This measure equals the ratio of average benefits of retirees to their average earnings just before retirement. (See Chapter 13.)

12. Because the social security tax depends on labour income, not capital income, the effects on investment are different.

13. A conceptually similar study by A. van Ravestein and H. Vijlbrief (1988) estimated that the value of τ^* for the Netherlands in 1970 was also about 70%. The actual value of τ, as estimated by the authors, rose steadily after 1970 to reach 67% in 1985. Thus, the conclusion was that the Netherlands was close to, but not yet beyond, the peak of the Laffer curve.

17

The Public Debt

In many countries, one of the hottest economic issues has been the **government's budget deficit** (which we shall define carefully later). At least from reading the newspapers, we might think that the economy suffers greatly when the government runs a large deficit. The most important task in this chapter will be to evaluate this view. As we shall see, the conclusions depart in several respects from those expressed in the newspapers.

Budget deficits arise when governments choose to finance part of their expenditures by issuing interest-bearing government bonds rather than levying taxes. The stock of government bonds outstanding is the interest-bearing part of the **public debt**. A budget deficit means that the quantity of public debt increases over time.

This chapter considers first the historical behaviour of the public debt and government deficits. With these facts as a background, we extend the theoretical model to allow for public debt. Now the government can run budget deficits rather than levy taxes. We use the model to assess the effects of deficits on interest rates and other economic variables. Next we look more closely at the cross-country differences in public debt accumulation and their relationship with differences in political systems.

Public Debt in the Long Run: The Historical Behaviour of Public Debt in the United Kingdom and in the United States

We can gauge the empirical significance of interest-bearing public debt by looking at the long-term history for the United Kingdom and the

United States. Table 17.1 shows the behaviour over the past two centuries of the central government's nominal interest-bearing public debt, denoted by B^g.[1] The table reports also the ratio of the public debt to nominal GNP, $B^g/(PY)$. We show this ratio graphically in Figure 17.1 for the United Kingdom from 1700 to 1990, and for the United States from 1790 to 1991 in Figure 17.2.

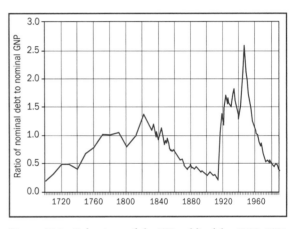

Figure 17.1 Behaviour of the UK public debt, 1700–1990

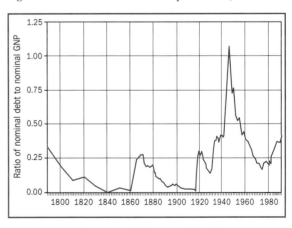

Figure 17.2 Behaviour of the US public debt, 1790–1991

	United States		United Kingdom	
	B^g ($billion)	$B^g/(PY)$	B^g (£ billion)	$B^g/(PY)$
1700	–	–	0.015	0.22
1710	–	–	0.026	0.33
1720	–	–	0.039	0.57
1730	–	–	0.038	0.56
1740	–	–	0.033	0.44
1750	–	–	0.059	0.79
1760	–	–	0.074	0.91
1770	–	–	0.11	1.22
1780	–	–	0.12	1.01
1790	0.08	0.31	0.18	1.04
1800	0.08	0.18	0.28	0.78
1810	0.05	0.08	0.43	0.93
1820	0.09	0.11	0.57	1.32
1830	0.05	0.04	0.55	1.13
1840	0.00	0.00	0.56	1.01
1850	0.06	0.03	0.56	0.94
1860	0.06	0.01	0.59	0.69
1865	2.2	0.24	–	–
1870	2.0	0.25	0.59	0.51
1880	1.7	0.13	0.59	0.43
1890	0.7	0.05	0.58	0.37
1900	1.0	0.05	0.58	0.29
1910	0.9	0.03	0.70	0.29
1919	24.2	0.31	7.5	1.30
1920	23.3	0.27	7.9	1.21
1930	14.8	0.16	7.6	1.55
1940	41.2	0.41	9.1	1.18
1945	227.4	1.07	22.5	2.27
1950	198.6	0.69	27.0	2.03
1960	207.5	0.41	29.0	1.12
1970	229.1	0.23	34.1	0.66
1980	616.4	0.23	96.3	0.42
1990	2288.3	0.41	192.5	0.38
1991	2563.2	0.45	–	–

Table 17.1　Values for public debt in the United States and the United Kingdom

Notes and Sources: For the United States: B^g is the end-of-year value (mid-year value before 1916) of privately held, interest-bearing public debt of the US federal government at nominal par value. The figures are net of holdings by the Federal Reserve and US government agencies and trust funds. (They include holdings by some government-sponsored agencies and by state and local governments.) For the sources, see Barro (1978a, table 1).

P since 1870 is the GNP deflator (1982 = 1.00). Earlier data are based on wholesale price indices, as reported in US Department of Commerce (1975, p. 201).

Y is real GNP. Estimates of real GNP for 1834–71 are unpublished data from Robert Gallman. Earlier figures are calculated from the growth rates of real output that are reported in Paul David (1967, table 1) and Alice Jones (1980, table 3.15).

For the United Kingdom: B^g since 1917 is the central government's interest-bearing public debt at nominal par value. Before 1917 the figures are the accumulation of the central government's budget deficit, starting with a benchmark stock of public debt in 1700.

P since 1830 is the GNP deflator (1980 = 1.0). Earlier data are wholesale price indexes.

PY since 1830 is nominal GNP. Earlier data are the product of *P* and an estimate of trend real GNP.

The sources for B^g are B.R. Mitchell and Phyllis Deane (1962), Mitchell and H.G. Jones (1971), and Central Statistical Office, *Annual Abstract of Statistics*, various issues. Data on *P* and *Y* are from the above and also from C.H. Feinstein (1972), Deane and W.A. Cole (1969), and *International Financial Statistics*, various issues. Recent data pertain to March of each year.

For both countries the two main positive influences on the ratio of public debt to GNP are wartime and major economic contractions. Superimposed on these infrequent positive shocks is a regular pattern in which the ratio declines over time.

In the United Kingdom the major peaks in the ratio of public debt to annual GNP are again associated with wartime: 1.3 at the end of the Seven Years' War in 1764, 1.2 after the War of American Independence in 1785, 1.4 after the Napoleonic wars in 1816, 1.3 at the end of World War I in 1919, and 2.5 after World War II in 1946. It is noteworthy that the high points for the British debt in relation to GNP were more than twice as great as those for the United States. It is also interesting that the public debt amounted to more than 100% of annual GNP as long ago as the 1760s. Large amounts of public debt are not a modern invention!

The positive effect of economic contraction on the ratio of public debt to GNP involves partly a negative effect on real GNP and partly a positive effect on public debt. This response shows up especially for the United Kingdom during the depressed periods from 1920 to 1923 and from 1929 to 1933. The ratio of debt to GNP rose from 1.2 to 1.7 during the first interval and from 1.5 to 1.8 during the second.

Periods that involve neither war nor economic contraction typically display a declining pattern in the ratio of public debt to GNP. This behaviour applies as much to the post-World War II years as to earlier periods: the ratio declined from 1.47 in

1946 to 0.38 in 1990. The ratio for 1990 was not far above the low point over the past two centuries, 0.23 at the beginning of 1914.

The experience of the United States is broadly similar to that for the United Kingdom. The major peaks in the ratio of public debt to annual GNP occur at the end of the Revolutionary War (the value for 1784 was 0.33), the end of the Civil War (0.25 in 1865), the end of World War I (0.31 in 1919), and the end of World War II (1.07 in 1945). Smaller effects – which amount to pauses in the usual downward trend in the ratio rather than to actual increases – show up for the Spanish–American and Korean wars. Little impact appears, however, for the Vietnam War. (Recall from Chapter 15 that this war exhibited only a small excess of real military spending above trend.)

Economic contractions have a positive impact on the ratio of the debt to GNP. A dramatic response to an economic downturn shows up during the Great Depression, during which the ratio of public debt to GNP rose from 0.14 in 1929 to 0.38 in 1933.

Again, during peacetime, non-recession years, the ratio of public debt to GNP tends to decline. Aside from the Great Depression, this pattern applies to much of the period before and after World War II. The ratio has, however, risen in recent years, notably from 0.23 in 1981 to 0.45 in 1991. Notice, however, that the ratio for 1991, 0.45, is not remarkable by historical standards and is still below the values for the 1950s.

Characteristics of Government Bonds

In the model the government can now borrow funds from households by selling interest-bearing bonds. We assume that these government bonds pay interest and principal in the same way as private bonds, which are already in the model. In particular, we continue to simplify matters by pretending that all bonds have a maturity of one period.[2] In the main analysis we assume also that bondholders regard public and private debts as equivalent. Specifically, we do not treat the government as more credit-worthy than private borrowers. In this case the government's bonds must pay the same nominal interest rate in each period, R_t, as that on privately issued bonds.

Our assumption about public and private bonds contrasts with our treatment of money. Because currency pays no interest, it seems that private enterprises would find it profitable to produce this stuff. In particular, the higher is nominal interest rate, R_t, the greater is the gain from entering the business of creating currency. But because of legal restrictions or technical advantages for the government in providing a medium of exchange, we assume that the private sector does not issue currency.

With respect to bonds, we assume no legal restrictions on private issues and no technical advantages for the government in providing these types of securities. Hence, we do not allow the interest rate on government bonds to differ from that on private bonds. This assumption accords reasonably well with the data if we interpret private bonds as prime corporate obligations. For example, Alesina *et al.* (1992) found that for 12 OECD countries, in the period 1979–89, the interest rate on public bonds and that on private bonds was similar, their ratio ranging between 0.89 and 0.98.

Denote by B_t^g the aggregate ECU amount of government bonds outstanding at the end of period t. We still use the symbol b for privately issued bonds. An individual's total holdings of bonds for period t are now $b_t + b_t^g$. The aggregate of privately issued bonds is still zero, that is, $B_t = 0$. Hence, the aggregate quantity of bonds held by households now equals the public debt, B_t^g. We usually think of cases in which the government is a net debtor to the private sector, so that $B_t^g > 0$. The government may, however, become a creditor and hold net claims on the private sector.[3] We can represent this case by allowing for $B_t^g < 0$.

The Government's Budget Constraint

The presence of public debt alters the government's budget constraint in two respects. First, the ECU amount of net debt issue for period t, $B_t^g - B_{t-1}^g$, is a source of funds. (Notice that the simple rolling over or reissue of bonds as they come due is not a net source of funds. What counts is the difference between the stock outstanding at date t, B_t^g, and that outstanding in the previous period, B_{t-1}^g.) In this respect the printing of money and the printing of interest-bearing debt play the same role in the financing of the government's expenditures. Second, the government's nominal interest payments, $R_{t-1} \cdot B_{t-1}^g$, appear as an expenditure. Recall that this term is zero for money.

The government's budget constraint in ECU terms for period t is now

$$P_t G_t + V_t + R_{t-1} \cdot B_{t-1}^g$$
$$= T_t + (M_t - M_{t-1}) + (B_t^g - B_{t-1}^g) \quad (17.1)$$

The two new terms are the government's interest payments on the left side, $R_{t-1} \cdot B_{t-1}^g$, and the net issue of debt on the right side, $(B_t^g - B_{t-1}^g)$. For simplicity, we return to the case in which transfers, V_t, and taxes, T_t, are lump sum.

Figure 17.3 shows how the new item of expenditure – the government's net interest payments – has behaved in the UK. The figure shows the behaviour of interest payments by the central government, expressed as a ratio to GNP. Not surprisingly, interest payments have peaks during and right after the two World Wars, when the public debt was highest. Interest payments

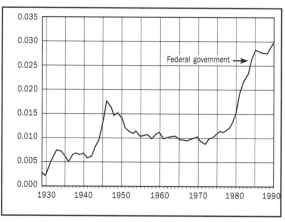

Figure 17.4   US government interest payments as a ratio to GNP

rose sharply between the mid-1970s to the early 1980s because of the increase in interest rates during that period. Figure 17.4 shows the US net federal interest payments. They were less than 1% until 1945, between 1.3% and 1.8% from 1945 to 1950, and between 0.9% and 1.2% from 1951 to 1978. For much of the latter period, the declining ratio of public debt to GNP (Figure 17.1) was offset by rising interest rates. Since 1978, the ratio of net federal interest payments to GNP has risen sharply to reach 3.0% in 1990.

The Government's Deficit

We can think of the government's saving or dissaving in the same way as for households. The national accounts define the government's nominal saving to be the change in the ECU value of the government's holdings of money and bonds. (Recall that the government holds no capital in the model or in the national accounts.) Because we think of the government as issuing money and bonds – rather than holding them – an increase in money and bonds means that the government is dissaving. Economists use the term *surplus* to refer to positive saving by the government and the term *deficit* to refer to dissaving. (When saving is zero, the government has a **balanced budget**.)

Putting this terminology together, the nominal deficit, as measured in the standard national accounts, is

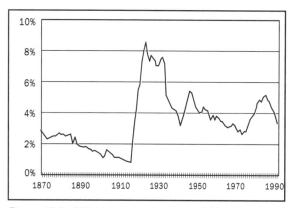

Figure 17.3   UK interest payments to GDP ratio, central government

nominal deficit (national accounts)

$$= (M_t + B_t^g) - (M_{t-1} + B_{t-1}^g) \qquad (17.2)$$

Combining the definition from equation (17.2) with the government's budget constraint from equation (17.1) leads to the usual expression for the nominal deficit:

nominal deficit (national accounts)

$$= P_t G_t + V_t + R_{t-1} B_{t-1}^g - T_t \qquad (17.3)$$

That is, the nominal deficit equals nominal expenditures – for purchases, transfers, and interest payments – less tax revenues. This is the concept of public deficit usually used in policy discussions and newspapers. This standard definition of the government's deficit, however, does not take proper account of inflation.[4] As a parallel to our treatment for households, we would define the government's real deficit – that is, its real dissaving – to be the change in the real value of its obligations in the forms of money and bonds. The appropriate definition of the real deficit is therefore

$$\begin{aligned} \text{real deficit} &= (M_t + B_t^g)/P_t \\ &\quad - (M_{t-1} + B_{t-1}^g)/P_{t-1} \end{aligned} \qquad (17.4)$$

Multiplying through by the price level, P_t, the corresponding **nominal deficit** (the ECU value of the real deficit) is

nominal deficit

$$= (M_t + B_t^g) - (1 + \pi_{t-1}) \cdot (M_{t-1} + B_{t-1}^g) \quad (17.5)$$

where $(1 + \pi_{t-1}) = (P_t/P_{t-1})$ was substituted on the right. A comparison of equation (17.5) with the national accounts' concept of the nominal deficit in equation (17.2) shows that the difference between the two measures is the subtraction of the term, $\pi_{t-1} \cdot (M_{t-1} + B_{t-1}^g)$. This term represents the reduction in the real value of the government's obligations due to inflation. If we want the real deficit (calculated by dividing the nominal deficit by the price level) to correspond to the change in the government's real obligations, then we have to deduct this term from the

standard measure of the nominal deficit.[5] The difference between the two measures of the deficit is large when the inflation rate is high. The choice of definition therefore matters a great deal for the high-inflation years, while in periods of low inflation the differences are much less significant.

Figure 17.5 report the real deficit to GDP ratio for the UK from 1900 to 1991. The solid line uses the standard definition of real deficit. The dotted line, available between 1967 to 1988, uses the inflation corrected definition of real deficit, calculated by the Bank of England.[6] As expected, the difference between the two definitions is particularly important in the mid-1970s, when the rate of inflation was especially high. Figure 17.6 graphs the inflation corrected real deficit to GDP ratio for the US, from 1930 to 1991.

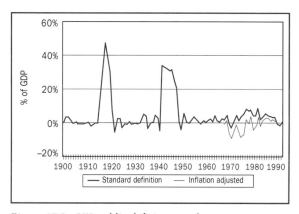

Figure 17.5 UK public deficit, central government

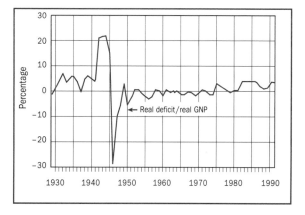

Figure 17.6 The behaviour of US real federal deficits

Note first the positive relation between the real deficit and wars in both countries. For the UK this relationship was particularly strong in the two World Wars: between 1915 and 1919 the real deficit averaged 33.4% of GDP. Similarly, between 1941 and 1945, the real deficit was, on average, 32.6% of GDP. On the other hand, the 1982 Falklands War was too short to have an impact on the deficit. We observe a similar pattern for the US. The relationship between deficits and wars stands out for World War II: the real deficit exceeded 20% of real GNP from 1942 to 1944.[7] But there is also some effect during the Korean War for 1952–53 and perhaps during the Vietnam War for 1967–68.

The second important property is the positive relation between the real deficit and economic contraction. For the US this pattern is quite clear, especially during the Great Depression: the US real deficit exceeded 7% of real GNP in 1932. The US real deficit also tended to be high during the post-World War II recessions – for example, in 1949, 1958-59, 1971, 1975–76, 1980–83, and 1990–91. The ratio of the real deficit to real GNP was 3.3% in 1975, 4.0% in 1982–83, and 3.7% in 1990–91. The pattern for the UK is less clear-cut. Nonetheless, it is true also in the UK that periods of recession tended to be associated with large public deficits. For example, if we use the standard definition of the deficit, we notice that during the early 1930s recession, the deficit increased substantially, peaking in 1934 at 5.4% of GDP. Similarly, during the 1974–75 recession, the government deficit averaged 4.5% of GDP, and during the 1980–81 recession 6.3%. However, if we use the inflation corrected measure, we see that between 1974 and 1975, the government budget was actually in surplus and not in deficit.

Summarizing, over the US and UK history, wartime spending and recession explain the bulk of real budget deficits. This relation, however, appeared to break down, in the mid-1970s in the UK and after 1983 in the US, when the Reagan tax cuts were not accompanied by comparable reductions in federal spending. For example, in the UK, from 1976 to 1978, the ratio of the inflation corrected real deficit to real GNP

averaged 2.2%, and between 1983 and 1986 3.0%, despite these being periods of strong growth (see Figure 17.6). Similarly, in the US, from 1984 to 1986, the ratio of the real deficit to real GNP averaged 4.2% (see Figure 17.5), despite the strong economic recovery and the absence of wartime expenditure. We will see later in the chapter that the relationship between recession and deficit is even more fragile in other industrialized countries in the post-World War II period.

Public Saving, Private Saving, and National Saving

Real public saving is just the negative of the real budget deficit; that is, from equation (17.4),[8]

$$\begin{aligned}\text{real public saving} \\ = -(M_t + B_t^g)/P_t \\ + (M_{t-1} + B_{t-1}^g)/P_{t-1}\end{aligned} \tag{17.6}$$

Real private saving – that is, real saving done by households – is given by

$$\begin{aligned}\text{real private saving} \\ = (M_t + B_t^g)/P_t - (M_{t-1} + B_{t-1}^g)/P_{t-1} \\ + K_t - K_{t-1}\end{aligned} \tag{17.7}$$

This result extends the measure of real saving from Chapter 12 to include the change in households' holdings of real government bonds.

The sum of public and private saving is called **national saving**. Using equations (17.6) and (17.7) this real saving by the entire nation is given by

$$\text{real national saving} = K_t - K_{t-1} \tag{17.8}$$

Thus, the key result is that real saving for the overall economy must correspond to aggregate net investment.

Public Debt and Households' Budget Constraints

As in Chapter 16, households care about the anticipated present value of real taxes. (Recall that we treat the taxes as lump sum at this stage.) We want to know how the outstanding stock of public debt and the government's current and prospective deficits affect the present value of real taxes.

To illustrate the main results it is convenient to start with a number of simplifications. First, assume that the price level and aggregate money stock do not change over time. In this case the government obtains no revenue from money creation. Second, take as given the quantity of government purchases, G_t, in each period. Third, suppose that aggregate transfers, V_t, are zero in each period. Finally, assume that the government starts with no interest-bearing debt: $B_0^g = 0$. We shall demonstrate later that the conclusions do not depend on these unrealistic assumptions.

Given our assumptions, the government's budget constraint in real terms for each period is

$$G_t + R \cdot B_{t-1}^g / P = T_t / P + (B_t^g - B_{t-1}^g)/P \quad (17.9)$$

Recall that the government starts with no interest-bearing debt at date 0. Therefore, if the government balanced its budget from date 1 onward – that is, if $B_t^g - B_{t-1}^g = 0$ in every period – then interest payments would always be nil. In this case, real purchases, G_t, would equal real taxes, T_t / P, at all times.

Suppose, instead of balancing its budget in period 1, that the government runs a deficit of ε1.00, so that $B_t^g = 1$. Because we hold fixed the quantity of government purchases, the budget constraint from equation (17.9) implies that this period's taxes, T_1, decline by ε1. That is, we are considering a *deficit-financed tax cut*. The cut in taxes by ε1 means that the aggregate of households' current disposable income rises by ε1.

Assume now that the government wants to restore the public debt to zero from date 2 onward – that is, $B_2^g = B_3^g = ... = 0$. Then in period 2, the government must raise taxes by enough to pay off the principal and interest on the ε1 of debt that it issued at date 1. The taxes for period 2, T_2, rise accordingly by $1 + R$ ECUs. Since the extra debt is paid off in period 2, taxes in subsequent periods do not change.

Overall, taxes fall by ε1 during period 1 but rise by $1 + R$ ECUs for period 2. The effect on the present value of real taxes is given by

$$(1/P).[-1 + (1 + R)/(1 + R)] = 0$$

Note that we discount the increase in next period's taxes of $1 + R$ ECUs by the discount factor, $1 + R$. Hence, the net effect on the present value of real taxes is nil. Because there is no change in the present value of real taxes, the government's deficit during period 1 has no aggregate wealth effect for households. The shift from current taxes to a deficit would therefore not affect the aggregates of consumer demand and work effort. In this sense, households view as equivalent a current aggregate tax of ε1 and a current budget deficit of 1. This finding is the simplest version of the **Ricardian Equivalence Theorem** on the public debt. (The theorem is named after the famous British economist David Ricardo, who first enunciated it.[9])

We can interpret the result as follows. Households receive ε1 extra disposable income during period 1 because of the cut in taxes. But they also face $1 + R$ ECUs of additional taxes during period 2. If households use the extra ECU of disposable income during period 1 to buy an extra ECU of bonds, then they will have just enough additional funds – $1 + R$ ECUs – to pay the extra taxes in period 2. The tax cut during period 1 provides enough resources, but no more, for households to pay the higher taxes next period. That is why there is no aggregate wealth effect and no changes in consumer demand and work effort.

We can also interpret the results in terms of saving behaviour. The budget deficit of 1 means that the government saves ε1 less than before – that is, public saving falls by ε1. Because households put all of their extra ε1 of disposable income into bonds, private saving rises by ε1. (In the case being considered, the marginal propensity to consume out of disposable income is zero and the marginal propensity to save is one.) Because the rise in private saving exactly offsets the decline in public saving, the sum of the two – national saving – does not change.

To obtain the results, we assumed that the government paid off the entire public debt during period 2; but this assumption is unnecessary for the results. To see this, assume that the government *never* pays off the principal of ε1 from the debt that it issued at date 1. Suppose instead that the government always balances its budget after the first period, so that $B_t^g - B_{t-1}^g = 0$ holds from period 2 onward. In this case, the stock of debt stays constant over time, so that $B_1^g = B_2^g = \ldots = 1$. But then the government must finance its interest payments of R ECUs in each period. (Remember that these payments would have been zero if the government had not run a deficit during period 1.) These extra expenses mean that taxes, T_t, are higher by R ECUs for *every* period after the first.

Taxes fall by ε1 during period 1 but rise by R ECUs for each subsequent period. The change in the present value of real taxes is now given by the expression

$$(1/P)\{-1 + R[1/(1+R) + 1/(1+R)^2 + \ldots]\}$$
$$= (1/P) - 1 + [R/(1+R)][(1+R)/R]$$
$$= 0^{10}$$

Hence, the net change in the present value of real taxes is still zero.

We can think of this result as follows. Households receive ε1 of extra disposable income during period 1 because of the cut in taxes. But they also face an additional R ECUs of taxes in each subsequent period. If households use the extra ECU of disposable income during period 1 to buy an extra ECU of bonds, then they receive ε1 more of principal and R ECUs more of interest in period 2. If they use the interest receipts to pay the higher taxes, then households can again buy a bond for ε1. Continuing in this manner, households can always use the interest income to meet the extra taxes in each period. The tax cut during period 1 provides enough resources, but no more, for households to pay the stream of higher future taxes. That is why the net change in the present value of real taxes is again equal to zero. Hence, we still predict no changes in the aggregates of consumer demand and work effort. Equivalently, we still predict that private

saving rises to offset the decline in public saving so as to maintain the total of national saving.

The basic conclusion is that shifts between taxes and deficits do not generate aggregate wealth effects. This result still holds if we drop many of the simplifying assumptions. If the initial level of public debt is non-zero, then the conclusion follows by considering the extra future interest payments and taxes that result from today's deficit. The results hold also if we superimpose an arbitrary pattern of transfers. Suppose, as an example, that the government reacts to higher future interest payments by reducing transfers rather than by raising taxes. Then we essentially add a new disturbance – equal decreases in future transfers and taxes – to the one that we already considered. Because this new disturbance has a zero aggregate wealth effect, the Ricardian result remains valid.

We can also allow for money creation and inflation. As one possibility, the government may react to higher future interest payments by printing more money rather than increasing taxes. In this case economists say that the government **monetizesmonetizes** part of the deficit or monetizes part of the stock of public debt. Then we essentially add another new disturbance – an increase in future money creation and a decrease in future taxes – to the one that we treated before. We know that changes in money, which finance a cut in taxes, have no aggregate wealth effect. The budget deficit therefore still has no aggregate wealth effect. Monetization of the public debt does, however, have important implications for the behaviour of prices. These effects work just like the increases in the quantity of money that we studied before: the monetization of deficits is inflationary.[11]

Finally, we can allow for non-zero deficits in future periods. As with a current deficit, these future ones do not generate any aggregate wealth effects. The aggregate wealth effect is still zero for any path of public debt. Hence, the aggregate of consumer demand does not react either to differences in the initial stock of real government bonds, B_0^g/P, or to variations in current or prospective government deficits.

Fundamentally, there is no aggregate wealth effect from budget deficits because they do not change the government's use of resources. The quantity of government purchases, G_t, is the amount of goods that the government buys during period t. Aggregate wealth effects therefore occur with changes in the present value of government purchases. But if we hold this present value constant, then there are no aggregate wealth effects from shifts between taxes and deficits.

The Effect of a Deficit-Financed Tax Cut

Recall that with lump-sum taxes and transfers, the condition for clearing the commodity market is

$$C^d(r_1, \ldots) + I^d(r_1, \ldots) + G_1 = Y^s(r_1, \ldots)$$
$$(-) \qquad (-) \qquad \qquad (+) \qquad (17.10)$$

We do not write out explicitly in these demand and supply functions the initial stock of capital, K_0, or the amount of government purchases, G_1. Also, recall that the previous analysis implies that the initial amount of real government bonds, B_0^g/P_1, does not matter for aggregate consumer demand, C^d, or goods supply, Y^s.

Suppose that the government cuts current taxes, T_1, and substitutes a corresponding increase in its interest-bearing debt, B_1^g. Assume that the government does not change either current or future purchases; thus, we are dealing with the pure effects from a budget deficit. Economists often refer to this type of action as stimulative **fiscal policy**. We found before that the replacement of current taxes by a deficit has no aggregate wealth effect. Hence, there are no effects on consumer demand or work effort. It follows that the tax cut has no impact on the condition for clearing the commodity market in equation (17.10). The real interest rate, r_1, and the quantities of output, Y_1, consumption, C_1, and investment, I_1, therefore do not change.

We can also think of the results in terms of desired saving and investment demand. Recall that the budget deficit stimulates an increase in desired private saving that exactly offsets the decrease in public saving. The budget deficit therefore has no effect on desired national saving. Because net investment demand also does not shift, the real interest rate does not have to change to maintain the equality between desired national saving and net investment demand.

The condition that money be willingly held in period 1 is

$$M_1 = P_1 \cdot \Phi(Y_1, R_1 \ldots) \qquad (17.11)$$

Suppose that the government does not change the current money stock, M_1, or the path of prospective money stocks. Then the deficit-financed cut in current taxes has no effect on equation (17.11). Hence, the price level, P_1, and the nominal interest rate, R_1, do not change. Notice also that the inflation rate, π_1, and all future price levels are unaffected by the tax cut.

We have found that a deficit-financed tax cut does not stimulate the economy or affect interest rates. Since these results are controversial and important, we shall want to see later whether modifications of the model change the conclusions.

Open-Market Operations

The inclusion of public debt in the model allows us to analyze **open-market operations**. An open-market purchase of securities occurs when the government – or a monetary authority like the Federal Reserve – buys government bonds with newly created money. In the opposite case there is an open-market sale of bonds for money. These open-market operations are the main way that national central banks actually affect the quantity of money in the United States. We shall want to see whether this realistic way of changing the quantity of money leads to results that differ from the unrealistic 'helicopter drops' of money that we studied in Chapter 9.

Consider an open-market purchase during period 1, whereby the stock of money, M_1, increases by $\varepsilon 1$, and the stock of government bonds, B_1^g, decreases by $\varepsilon 1$. Assume that no subsequent changes in money occur; that is, there is a one-time increase in the quantity of money at date 1.

Table 17.2 shows that an open-market purchase of bonds amounts to the combination of two governmental policies that we have already examined. Suppose first that the government prints an extra ECU of money, M_1, and correspondingly reduces current taxes, T_1, by $\varepsilon 1$. These changes are labelled as policy 1 in the table. Then suppose that the government raises taxes, T_1, back up by $\varepsilon 1$ and uses the proceeds to pay off $\varepsilon 1$ of the public debt, B_1^g. These changes are called policy 2 in the table. The net effect of combining these two policies is to raise money by $\varepsilon 1$, leave taxes unchanged, and reduce government bonds by $\varepsilon 1$. Thus, we end up with an open-market purchase of bonds, policy 3 in the table.

We know that policy 1 (more money and less taxes) raises the price level in the same proportion as the increase in the quantity of money. But except for a reduction in the real amount of government bonds, there are no changes in real variables. We know that policy 2 (the fiscal policy in which taxes rise and public debt declines) has no effects except for another reduction in the real quantity of government bonds. By combining the two sets of responses, we find that an open-market purchase of bonds raises the price level and other nominal variables (aside from the quantity of public debt) in the same proportion as the increase in the stock of money. Apart from the fall in the real amount of government bonds, there are no

changes in real variables. Thus, the previous results about the neutrality of money still apply to open-market purchases or sales of bonds.

Why Does the Public Debt Matter?

The results suggest that the public debt and government deficits do not matter much for the economy. But think about the parallel with private debt. The aggregate quantity of private debt is always zero, a result that also seems uninteresting. The possibilities for borrowing and lending are nevertheless important because they eliminate the need for individuals to synchronize their incomes and expenditures. The public debt plays a similar role. Because the credit market exists, the government need not match its receipts from taxes and money creation to its expenditures in each period.

The government's budget constraint from equation (17.1) implies that the real revenue from taxation and money creation for period t is

$$T_t/P_t + (M_t - M_{t-1})/P_t = G_t + V_t/P_t$$
$$+ R_{t-1} \cdot B_{t-1}^g/P_t - (B_t^g - B_{t-1}^g)/P_t \quad (17.12)$$

Suppose that the paths for the government's real purchases and transfers are given and that the initial stock of interest-bearing debt, B_0^g, is zero. If the government never issued any bonds, then its real receipts from taxes and money creation for period t would equal the given total of real expenditures for that period, $G_t + V_t/P_t$. The receipts have to be high whenever expenditures are high, and vice versa. The potential to issue

Government policy	Change in M_1	Change in B_1^g	Change in T_1
1. Print more money and reduce taxes	$+\varepsilon 1$	0	$-\varepsilon 1$
2. Raise taxes and retire public debt	0	$-\varepsilon 1$	$+\varepsilon 1$
3. Open-market purchase of bonds	$+\varepsilon 1$	$-\varepsilon 1$	0

Note: An open-market purchase of bonds – policy 3 – amounts to a combination of policies 1 and 2, which we have already studied.

Table 17.2   Open-market purchases of bonds and other government policies

debt gives the government more flexibility. The government can manage its issues of public debt to change its revenues for a period without changing the amount of expenditures for that period. By borrowing a lot when its expenditures are unusually large, for example, the government can lessen the need for abnormally high tax receipts or money creation at that time.

To bring out the main points, assume again that the stock of money is constant over time, that is, the government collects no revenue from money creation. The government's choices of public debt then dictate the timing of its real tax collections, T_t/P_t. For a given present value of taxes, the economy will respond to differences in the timing of collections only if the taxes are not lump sum. To see the nature of this response, let's reintroduce the type of income tax that we studied in Chapter 16. In this setting the aggregate real taxes for period t are given by

$$T_t/P_t = \tau_t(Y_t + R_{t-1}^g \cdot B_{t-1}^g/P_t - E_t) \qquad (17.13)$$

where τ_t is the marginal tax rate and E_t is the amount of tax-exempt real income for period t. (Note that the interest payments on the public debt – which are taxable – appear in the aggregate of households' real taxable income.)

By managing the public debt over time, the government determines the behaviour of real tax revenues, T_t/P_t, and thereby the marginal tax rates, τ_t, from equation (17.13). Consider the previous example in which current taxes, T_1, fall by $\varepsilon 1$, and the public debt rises by $\varepsilon 1$. Assume further that the government raises next period's taxes, T_2, by $\varepsilon(1+R)$ to pay off the extra debt. Unless the government has gone beyond the point of maximum tax revenues on the Laffer curve, the changes in taxes collected show up as corresponding changes in the marginal tax rates: today's marginal tax rate, τ_1, declines, and next period's tax rate, τ_2, rises. These changes motivate households to shift their income toward the current period and away from the next period. Specifically, households raise today's work but plan to reduce work in the next period. This response operates like some intertemporal-substitution effects that we considered before.[12]

Figure 17.7 shows the effect on the commodity market during period 1. The increase in today's work effort appears as a rightward shift of the supply curve. Because today's demand does not change,[13] an excess supply of goods prevails at the initial value of the after-tax real interest rate $(\tilde{r}_1)^*$. Figure 17.7 shows accordingly that the after-tax real interest rate declines, and output increases. This extra output, which reflects increased work effort, shows up partly as more consumption and partly as more investment.

The counterpart of this period's lower marginal tax rate is a higher tax rate for period 2. Figure 17.8 shows that the changes to the market-clearing diagram are opposite to those found for period 1; in particular, the Y^s curve now shifts leftward. In comparison with the values that would have arisen in period 2 with no changes in taxes, the after-tax real interest rate is higher, and output, work effort, consumption, and investment are all lower.

To summarize, when we consider income taxes, there are real effects from fiscal policy. A deficit-financed cut in today's marginal tax rate leads to increases in today's real economic activity. But the responses reverse later when

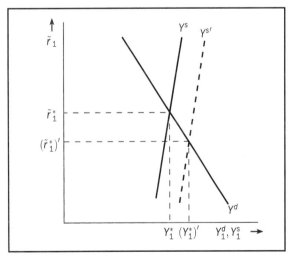

The marginal tax rate falls at date 1. The increase on today's supply of goods leads to an increase in output and a fall in the after-tax real interest rate.

Figure 17.7 Effect on the commodity market of a deficit-financed cut in today's marginal tax rate

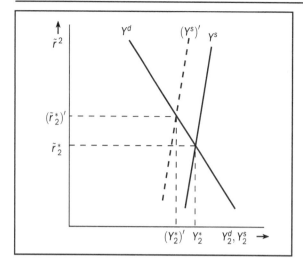

During period 2, when the government pays off public debt the marginal tax rate is higher. Therefore, output is lower and the after-tax real interest rate is higher.

Figure 17.8   Effect on the commodity market of a temporary increase in the marginal tax rate

the marginal tax rate is higher than otherwise. In our simple example, the higher future tax rate applies only to period 2. But more generally, the higher tax rate could be spread over many periods. Then the tendency for real economic activity to decline would also be spread out into the future. Overall, fiscal policy turns out to be an instrument that can influence the timing of real economic activity. But if the government uses this policy to stimulate output today, then the side effect is a reduction in output in the future.

The Timing of Taxes

The government can manipulate its budget deficits to change the relative values of marginal tax rates for different periods and thereby influence the relative levels of output at different times. But it would not be a good idea for the government randomly to make tax rates high in some periods and low in others. These types of fluctuations in tax rates cause unnecessary

Box 17.1   'Unpleasant Monetarist Arithmetic'

Thomas Sargent and Neil Wallace (1981) analyzed the effects from changes in the timing of the inflation tax. Consider a government that obtains a significant portion of its revenue from money creation. (Thus, the analysis applies especially to hyperinflations and to countries such as Argentina and Brazil that typically have high inflation.) Suppose that the government cuts current monetary growth in an attempt to reduce inflation. Assume, however, that the government does not change the current or prospective values for its real expenditures and tax receipts. In this case, the decrease in the current real revenue from printing money must correspond to an increase in interest-bearing public debt. Moreover, the financing of this higher debt later implies (with future real taxes and spending unchanged) that the future real revenue from money creation must rise. In

other words, the government is just rearranging the timing of the inflation tax; less occurs now and more occurs later.

Because future monetary growth rises, the contractionary monetary policy will be unsuccessful in generating a long-term decline in the inflation rate. In fact, if people anticipate the increase in future monetary growth, then inflation may not even decline in the short run. That is because, as discussed in Chapter 9, the expectation of higher monetary growth in the future tends to raise the current inflation rate. Sargent and Wallace conclude that a programme to curb inflation by reducing monetary growth will be unsuccessful unless it is accompanied by a plan to offset today's lost real revenue from money creation by higher real taxes or lower real government expenditures.

distortions because they give people the wrong signals in determining how to allocate work and production over time. We have seen above that the US and UK governments have not behaved in this erratic manner; rather, the public debt has typically been managed to maintain a pattern of reasonably stable tax rates over time.[14]

One example of this behaviour concerns income-tax rates during recessions. Real government expenditures typically do not decline as much as aggregate output during a recession. (In fact, items such as unemployment compensation and welfare payments rise automatically.) To maintain a balanced budget, the government would have to raise tax rates when the economy contracts. But instead of raising taxes, the government typically runs a real deficit during recessions, as we saw in Figures 17.5 and 17.6.[15]

As another example, during wartime real government expenditures are much higher than normal, and real deficits are also especially high at these times. The government thereby avoids abnormally high tax rates during wars. In this way the necessary increases in tax rates are spread roughly evenly over time. Tax rates rise somewhat during wartime but also rise afterward along with the higher interest payments on the accumulated debt.

The Conventional View of a Deficit-Financed Tax Cut

Our analysis of fiscal policy differs from that of most macroeconomic models. To see why, return to the case of lump-sum taxes, the type of taxes that most macromodels assume. For our analysis, the key point is that households regard as equivalent a current tax of ε1 or a government deficit of ε1. In particular, if the behaviour of government purchases does not change, then shifts between taxes and deficits entail no aggregate wealth effects. In contrast, most macroeconomic models assume that a deficit-financed tax cut raises households' wealth even if there are no changes in government purchases. We shall look first at the results in this case and then examine briefly the arguments that some

economists have made for a positive effect on aggregate wealth.

Suppose again that the government cuts current taxes by ε1 and runs a deficit. If the tax cut makes people feel wealthier, then aggregate consumer demand rises, but work effort and the supply of goods fall. The excess demand for goods leads to a higher real interest rate and thereby to lower investment. Thus, this analysis predicts that government deficits raise real interest rates and **crowd out** private investment.

Another way to look at the results is that the increase in households' current disposable income leads partly to more consumption and partly to more desired private saving. In particular, because the marginal propensity to consume is positive, the marginal propensity to save is less than one. It follows that the increase in desired private saving offsets only a portion of the reduction in public saving. Thus, desired national saving declines, and the resulting excess of investment demand over desired national saving leads to an increase in the real interest rate.

According to this analysis, the decrease in net investment shows up in the long run as a decrease in the stock of capital. Some economists refer to this negative effect on the capital stock as a **burden of the public debt**. Each generation 'burdens' the next one by leaving behind a smaller aggregate stock of capital.[16]

The Effect of a Tax Cut on Wealth

To reach the standard conclusions mentioned above, we have to argue that a tax cut makes people feel wealthier, even if the behaviour of government purchases does not change. We consider here two of the more interesting justifications for this assumption – one concerning the finiteness of life and the other the imperfections of private loan markets. It is worth exploring these matters in any case, because they come up in other areas, as well as in the context of public debt.

Finite Lives
Suppose again that the government cuts current taxes by ε1 and runs a deficit. We know that the

government has higher interest payments and taxes in the future and that the present value of the extra future taxes equals ε1. But assume that some of these taxes will show up after the typical person has already died. Then the present value of the extra future taxes that accrue during the typical person's lifetime falls short of ε1. Hence, there is a positive effect on wealth when the government replaces current taxes by a deficit.

Why is there an increase in wealth when people have finite lives? The reason is that the increase in wealth for the aggregate of current taxpayers coincides with a decrease for the members of future generations. Individuals will be born with a liability for a portion of taxes to pay interest on the higher stock of public debt. But these people will not share in the benefits from the earlier tax cut. If these future liabilities on descendants were counted fully by present taxpayers, then wealth would be unchanged.

Government deficits effectively enable members of current generations to die in a state of insolvency by leaving debts for their descendants. Current taxpayers experience an increase in wealth if they view this governmental shifting of incomes across generations as desirable. But, in fact, most people already have private opportunities for intergenerational transfers, which they have chosen to exercise to a desired extent. As examples, parents make contributions to children in the form of educational investments, other expenses in the home, and bequests. In the other direction – and especially before the growth of social security – children provide support for their aged parents. To the extent that private transfers of this sort are operative, the shift from taxes to deficits does not offer the typical person a new opportunity to extract funds from his or her descendants. Rather, the response to higher deficits would be a shift in private transfers by an amount sufficient to restore the balance of income across generations that was previously deemed optimal. In this case, the shift from taxes to deficits again has no aggregate wealth effect.[17]

As a concrete example, assume that a couple plans to leave a bequest with a present value of ε5000 for their children. Then suppose that the government runs a deficit, which cuts the present value of the couple's taxes by ε1000, but raises the present value of their children's taxes by ε1000. Our prediction is that the parents use the tax cut to raise the present value of their intergenerational transfers to ε6000. This extra ε1000 provides the children with just enough extra funds to pay their higher taxes. Parents and children then end up with the same amounts of consumption and leisure that they enjoyed before the government ran its deficit.

Imperfect Loan Markets

The argument that taxes and deficits are equivalent assumes also that private and governmental interest rates are the same. In practice, however, the process of lending and borrowing involves transaction costs for loan evaluations, collections, defaults, and so on. It is relatively easy to borrow if a person has a house, car, or factory to put up as collateral, but much harder if a person, such as a student, just promises to repay a loan out of future labour earnings. The interest rates for borrowing are therefore high for persons with poor collateral.

Think of the world as divided into two groups. Group A consists of individuals or companies that lend or borrow at the same real interest rate, r, as the government. Group B comprises persons or businesses that would like to borrow at this interest rate but face higher borrowing rates. Let $\hat{r}$ be the real discount rate that someone from this group uses to calculate the present value of future incomes and expenses.[18] The rate $\hat{r}$ exceeds the real interest rate, r, for those from group A.

Suppose that the government cuts taxes and runs a deficit. The cut in taxes applies partly to group A and partly to group B. As before, the aggregate of future taxes increases. Let's assume that the division of these future taxes between group A and group B coincides with the division of the tax cut. (Otherwise there is a distributional effect, which would require separate attention.) For group A, the present value of the higher future taxes equals the tax cut, and the wealth effect is nil. For group B, the present value of the extra future taxes is less than the tax cut because the discount rate $\hat{r}$ exceeds r. The members of this group are wealthier because the tax cut effectively enables them to borrow at a real interest rate, r, that is below their discount rate, $\hat{r}$. This cut in the effective borrowing rate motivates the members of group B to raise current demands for consumption and investment.

We have shown that a deficit-financed tax cut leads to an increase in the aggregate demand for consumption and investment (the demands from group A do not change, and those from group B increase). The rise in consumer demand means that the aggregate of desired private saving rises by less than the budget deficit, that is, desired national saving declines. Because investment demand (which went up) exceeds desired national saving (which went down), the real interest rate, r, must rise. This higher real interest rate crowds out current consumption and investment by the members of group A. In contrast, because of the initial stimulus to group B's demands, the consumption and investment of this group rise on net. Thus, the main effect of the budget deficit is a diversion of current expenditures from group A to group B.

In the aggregate, investment may rise or fall, and the long-term effect on the capital stock is uncertain. The major change, however, is a better channelling of resources to their ultimate uses: the persons from group B – who started with the high borrowing rates – command a greater share of current output. The deficit-financed tax cut ultimately induces the type-A people to hold more than their share of the additional public debt so as effectively to lend to the type-B people at the real interest rate, r. This process works because the government implicitly guarantees the repayment of loans through its tax collections and debt payments. Loans between A and B therefore take place even though such loans were not viable (because of 'transaction costs') on the imperfect private loan market.

This much of the argument may be valid, although it credits the government with a lot of skill in the collection of taxes from people with poor collateral. Even if the government possesses this skill, however, the conclusions do not resemble those from the standard analysis. In particular, in the analysis just presented, budget deficits are a good idea because they effectively improve the functioning of loan markets. In addition, despite the presence of imperfect credit markets, budget deficits do not necessarily reduce aggregate investment.

Social Security and Saving

Retirement benefits paid though social security have expanded dramatically in most countries, as we discussed in Chapters 15 and 16. Some economists, such as Martin Feldstein (1974), argued that this increase in social security reduced private saving. Because this effect could be quantitatively important, we want to examine it from the standpoint of our model.

The argument for an effect on saving applies when the social security system is not **fully funded**. In a funded setup workers' payments accumulate in a trust fund, which provides later for retirement benefits. The alternative is a **pay-as-you-go system**, in which benefits to old persons are financed by taxes on the currently young. In this case, the people who are at or near retirement age when the programme begins or expands receive benefits without paying a comparable present value of taxes. Correspondingly, the people from later generations pay taxes that exceed their expected benefits in present-value terms. (Most readers of this book are unfortunately in this last category.)

In most countries the social security system operates mainly on a pay-as-you-go basis. Retirees increasingly received benefits that – in present-value terms – exceeded their prior contributions.

Consider the effects of social security in a pay-as-you-go system. We neglect here the substitution effects from the taxes and transfers because we have already discussed these effects in the previous chapter. Now we look at possible wealth effects from an increase in retirement benefits, which are financed by higher taxes on workers.

The usual argument goes as follows. Old persons experience an increase in the present value of their social security benefits net of taxes. They therefore respond to the increase in wealth

Box 17.2   Empirical Evidence on the Macroeconomic Effects of Budget Deficits

Some important predictions from the standard analysis are that larger real government deficits lead to higher real interest rates, higher consumption, and lower national saving. There is little question that most government officials and news reporters, as well as many economists, believe that budget deficits raise interest rates. Nevertheless, this belief does not have much evidence to support it. For example, Charles Plosser (1982, 1987) and Paul Evans (1987a, 1987b) carried out detailed statistical analyses of government deficits and interest rates for several industrialized countries. Their major finding was that budget deficits had no significant effects on nominal or real interest rates. Thus, their evidence contradicts the standard theory in which deficit-financed tax cuts make people feel wealthier.

Despite many empirical studies for several countries, it has proved difficult to reach definitive conclusions about the effect of budget deficits on consumption and national saving. One difficulty involves the direction of causation. Budget deficits often arise as responses to business fluctuations, government expenditures, and inflation. Because these variables interact with consumption and saving, it is hard to distinguish the effects of budget deficits on the economy from the effects in the reverse direction.

One recent empirical study by Chris Carroll and Lawrence Summers (1987) avoids some of these problems by comparing the saving rates in the United States and Canada. The private saving rates were similar in the two countries until the early 1970s but have since diverged; for 1983–85 (the latest years in the study), the Canadian rate was higher by about six percentage points. After holding fixed some macroeconomic variables and aspects of the tax systems that influence saving, Carroll and Summers isolated a roughly one-to-one, positive effect of government budget deficits on private saving. This result accords with the Ricardian view.

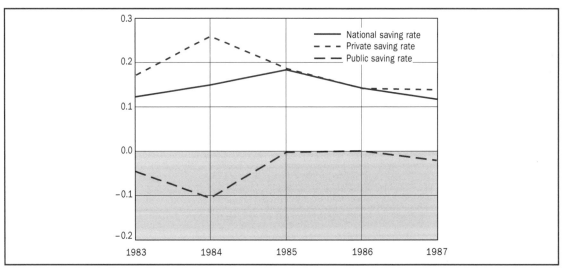

Note that the pattern for the private saving rate roughly mirrors that for the public saving rate. Therefore the national saving rate is relatively smooth.

Figure 17.9   Public and private saving rates in Israel, 1983–87

Recent fiscal policy in Israel comes close to a natural experiment for studying the interplay between budget deficits and saving rates. Figure 17.9 shows the values from 1983 to 1987 for the national saving rate, the private saving rate, and the public saving rate. (In this case, real public saving equals public investment less the real budget deficit.) In 1983 the national saving rate of 13% corresponded to a private saving rate of 17% and a public saving rate of −4%. In 1984 the dramatic rise in the budget deficit led to a public saving rate of −11%. (A principal reason for the deficit was the strong adverse effect of the increase in the inflation rate on the collection of real tax revenues.) For present purposes, the interesting observation is that the private saving rate rose from 17% to 26%, so that the national saving rate changed

little, actually rising from 13% to 15%. Then the Israeli stabilization programme in 1985 eliminated the budget deficit (along with most of the inflation), so that the public saving rate increased from −11% in 1984 to 0 in 1985–86 and −2% in 1987. The private saving rate decreased dramatically at the same time – from 26% in 1984 to 19% in 1985 and 14% in 1986-87. The national saving rates were therefore relatively stable, going from 15% in 1984 to 18% in 1985, 14% in 1986, and 12% in 1987. Although one episode cannot be decisive in verifying or refuting a theory, it is interesting that this dramatic example from Israel reveals the roughly one-to-one relationship between budget deficits and private saving that the Ricardian view predicts.

by consuming more. Young persons face higher taxes, offset partly by the expectation of higher retirement benefits. Because of this offset, the decrease in wealth for the young is smaller in magnitude than the increase for the old. Hence, the decrease in consumer demand by the young tends to be smaller in magnitude than the increase by the old. Aggregate consumer demand therefore tends to rise, or, equivalently, the aggregate of desired saving falls. The real interest rate increases accordingly, and net investment decreases. In the long run, this decrease in investment shows up as a smaller stock of capital.

This argument for social security parallels the standard view of a deficit-financed tax cut. In both cases, the increase in aggregate consumer demand arises only if people neglect the adverse effects on descendants. Specifically, an increase in the scale of the social-security programme means that the typical person's descendants will be born with a tax liability that exceeds his or her prospective retirement benefits in present-value terms. If people take full account of these effects on their descendants, then the aggregate wealth effect from more social security is nil.

As in the case of a deficit-financed tax cut, more social security enables older persons to extract funds from their descendants. But as

before, people value this change only if they give no transfers to their children and receive nothing from their children. Otherwise people respond to more social security by shifting private intergenerational transfers rather than by changing consumption. For example, the growth of social security has strongly diminished the tendency of children to support their aged parents.

On an empirical level, there has been a great debate about the connection of social security to saving and investment. First, Martin Feldstein (1974) reported a dramatic negative effect of social security on capital accumulation in the United States. But subsequent investigators showed that this conclusion was unwarranted.[19] Neither the long-term evidence for the United States nor that from a cross-section of countries in recent years provides evidence that social security depresses saving and investment.

Political Economy Theories of Public Deficit and Debt: The Relationship Between Politics and Government Budget

We argued before that budget deficits should be used by the government to absorb temporary shocks, like wars or recessions, but not to finance permanent changes in government spending. If governments systematically used government deficit to finance permanent increases in government spending, instead of raising taxes, the debt to GDP ratio would continue to increase. Eventually, the amount of real government debt would become so large compared to the level of output that it would be impossible to finance it. If a government were to follow such unsustainable budget policy, eventually it would be forced to default on its debt. The historical evidence that we presented for the US and the UK show that the public debt to GDP ratio remained, in the long run, relatively stable. For these two countries, therefore, the sustainability of debt policies is not an issue. But what about other countries?

Industrialized countries, European and non-European, while similar in most other economic dimensions, have pursued strikingly different public debt policies. Table 17.3 reports estimates of the level public debt of 17 OECD countries in 1992. For example, the gross debt (i.e. inclusive of holding of public debt by public institutions) to GNP ratio, ranges between 13.2% in Switzerland to over 130% in Belgium. In Figures 17.10 and 17.11 we show the behaviour of the national debt

	Gross debt	Net debt
Australia	18.8	
Austria	52.6	
Belgium	132.9	122.8
Canada	79.1	50.9
Denmark	61.6	28.5
France	48.5	26.7
Germany	43.5	24.2
Greece	87.1	
Ireland	108.8	
Italy	107.8	104.5
Japan	64.9	6.1
Netherlands	79.9	59.4
Portugal	46.3	
Spain	48.0	35.3
Switzerland	13.2	
UK	38.5	32.2
US	60.5	38.4

Note: These are OECD estimates, and not actual figures
Source: *OECD Economic Outlook*, Dec. 1992.

Table 17.3   Public debt in selected OECD countries, 1992 (% of GDP)

for 14 of these countries (for the others we do not have sufficiently long data series), since 1960. It is informative to divide these countries into two groups. For the first group, shown in Figure

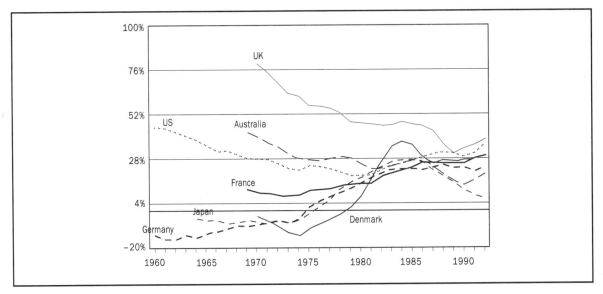

Figure 17.10   Debt to GNP ratios

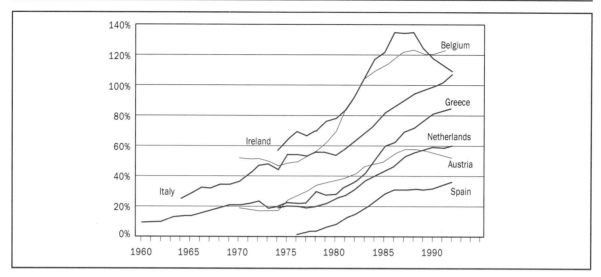

Figure 17.11   Debt to GNP ratios

17.10, the debt to GNP ratio is stable or converges toward moderate levels of about 35%. For the second group, shown in Figure 17.11, the debt to GNP ratio has an explosive pattern. In these seven countries (Austria, Belgium, Italy, Greece, Ireland, the Netherlands, Spain) public debt has been increasing almost without interruptions, for about thirty years. Only Ireland has shown, from 1988, a clear trend reversal. This pattern of debt implies that the governments of these seven countries have run large budget deficits year after year.

What are the reasons for these different debt policies? It could be argued that the observed international differences in public debt policy simply reflect differences in the shocks hitting the various national economies. However, given that our sample is limited to OECD countries whose economies are similar and highly interconnected, as we have seen in Chapter 1, this explanation is unconvincing. Recent research takes a completely different approach by focusing on the possible relationship between the political system and public debt policy.[20] It points out that governments are not simple abstract entities as we have conveniently assumed in our discussions. Economic policy decisions are a complex process deeply affected by political considerations. To set

the stage, consider Figure 17.12. Here we have divided the 17 OECD countries into three groups, depending on the nature of their electoral systems. The figure shows that the average debt and deficit to GDP ratios are markedly different across the three groups. To understand the meaning of this finding we need to describe, albeit in general terms, the essential characteristics of the political systems in these countries.

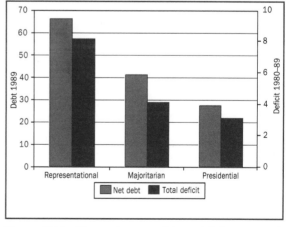

Figure 17.12   Electoral system, debt and deficit as % of GNP (group average)

The first important distinction is between *presidential* and *parliamentary* democracies. In the former, the president is voted directly into office and has significant independent authority. In the latter, the prime minister is accountable to the legislature. The first column of Table 17.4 classifies countries according to this distinction. Even though there are some mixed arrangements (Switzerland can almost be considered a multi-person presidential system, and since 1958 France combines elements of both systems), most countries are parliamentary democracies. Parliamentary systems, in turn, differ by the degree of proportionality of the electoral laws. Simplifying, column 2 of Table 17.4 distinguishes, in addition to presidential systems, between

	Type of democracy	Electoral system	Type of government			Government durability
			Majority	Coalition	Minority	
Australia	Parliament	M	26.8	73.3	0	4.44
Austria	Parliament	R	39	58.5	2.4	2.67
Belgium	Parliament	R	9.8	90.2	0	1.43
Canada	Parliament	M	80.5	0	19.5	4
Denmark	Parliament	R	0	34.1	65.9	2.11
France	President	P	41.5	39	19.5	1.29
Germany	Parliament	M	9.6	90	0	2
Greece	Parliament	R	91.2	5.9	2.9	0.97
Ireland	Parliament	M	65.9	24.4	9.8	1.9
Italy	Parliament	R	0	95.1	4.9	0.95
Japan	Parliament	M	80.5	12.2	7.3	1.67
Netherlands	Parliament	R	0	100	0	3.33
Portugal	President	P	26.7	53.3	20	1.48
Spain	Parliament	R	50	35.7	14.3	2
Switzerland	Parliament	M	0	100	0	1.6
UK	Parliament	M	92.7	0	7.3	4
US	President	P	41.5	0	58.5	5

Notes:

1. Type of democracy
Parliament = Parliamentary democracy.
President = Presidential democracy.
Greece: Dictatorship between 1967 and 1973.
Portugal: Dictatorship until 1973. New democratic constitution in 1976.
Spain: Dictatorship until 1974. First democratic election in 1977.

2. Electoral system
P = Presidential.
M = Majoritarian.
R = Representational.

3. Type of government
Majority = single party majority.
Coalition = coalition majority.
Minority = minority (coalition or single party).
The number in each column refers to the percentage of years in which the government was of each of the three types, out of the years of democratic regime. The type is defined with reference to the popular chamber.

4. Durability of the executive
Average number of years in power of the executive

Source: Grilli, Masciandaro and Tabellini (1991) and references quoted therein.

Table 17.4   Political institutions

majoritarian systems, i.e. systems with a low degree of proportionality, and *representational*, i.e. with a high degree of proportionality.[21]

Reconsider now Figures 17.10 and 17.11. Notice that all the countries with continuously increasing debt are representational systems, except for Ireland. And conversely, all representational democracies, except Denmark, have explosive debt paths. These figures, together with Figure 17.12, reveal a strong relationship between the degree of proportionality of the electoral system and debt policies. The higher is the degree of proportionality, the larger and more frequent are budget deficits.

The strong association between representational political systems and lack of fiscal discipline is also evident from the few episodes of constitutional reform that occurred in this sample period. In 1958, France reformed its electoral law and enacted a number of constitutional changes. The constitutional role of the President was strengthened relative to the Parliament and the Government. The electoral law was changed from proportional to majoritarian. The size of fiscal deficits in France changed dramatically. While in the decade 1950–59 France had an average primary deficit of 2.7 as a percentage of GNP (the largest of all countries in the sample), its average primary deficit from 1960 to 1989 was only 0.367 of GNP, one of the smallest in the sample.

Why does the degree of proportionality of the electoral system matter for public debt decisions? The main reason is that the degree of proportionality of the electoral system has a profound impact on two crucial characteristics of governments: their strength and their durability in power. Some authors, for example Alesina and Drazen (1992) and Drazen and Grilli (1993), pointed out that in many circumstances government deficits are not the outcome of optimal budget decisions, in the sense we have discussed above, for example in response to an economic recession. Public deficit is often used as a residual source of finance and may simply reflect a government's inability to cut expenditures or raise taxes. A 'weak' and divided government, without wide support in the legislature, is more likely to borrow because it lacks politically viable alternatives. Moreover, as suggested by Alesina and Tabellini (1990), public debt is a legacy deliberately left by a government to its successors. The less likely is a government to be reappointed, the stronger is the incentive to borrow rather than tax. All these observations suggest that public debt should be larger in countries with more frequent government changes from one party or leading group to another.

Following Grilli, Masciandaro and Tabellini (1991) we can use as an indicator for *government weakness* its support in the legislature. They distinguish between three kinds of government: majority, coalition and minority governments. A majority government is supported by a single party that has a majority in the legislature. A coalition government is supported by a coalition of parties, which together reach a legislative majority. A minority government is supported by a single party or by a coalition without a legislative majority. Clearly, the decision-making capacity is highest in majority governments and lowest in minority governments. They also present an index of *government durability*, the average number of years between one government change and the next. Columns 3 to 5 of Table 17.4 and Figures 17.13 and 17.14 clearly show that representational democracies tend to have shorter lived governments, and that they have majority governments less often than the other two political regimes. Average government durability is 1.9 years in representational systems, 3 years in majoritarian systems and 2.6 years in presidential systems. The percentage of governments supported by a single party majority is 27%, 57% and 47% in representational, majoritarian and presidential democracies respectively.

Summarizing, lack of fiscal discipline in industrialized countries is mostly found in representational democracies. There are two central features of representational democracies that seem responsible for excessive debt creation: the insufficient legislative support and the short durability of the governments they produce. Exactly why this is the case is still the subject of controversy and research.

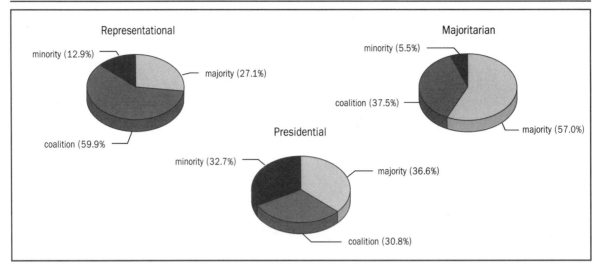

Figure 17.13   Government strength (% of democratic period)

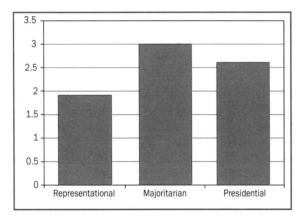

Figure 17.14   Durability of the executive (average number of years 1950–90)

Summary

The ability to issue and retire interest-bearing public debt allows government expenditures to diverge in the short run from the sum of tax receipts and the revenue from printing money. Shifts between taxes and budget deficits affect the timing of tax collections but not their overall present value. Hence, for a given path of government purchases, this type of fiscal policy has no aggregate wealth effect. In the case of lump-sum taxes, the absence of a wealth effect implies that budget deficits do not affect the real interest rate or the quantities of investment and output. This result, called the Ricardian Equivalence Theorem, says that taxes and deficits have the same effect on the economy.

Budget deficits have real effects in the presence of an income tax. These effects concern the timing of taxes; changes in the timing exert intertemporal-substitution effects on work and production. It is desirable for the government to manage the public debt to avoid large random fluctuations in tax rates from period to period. This motivation accounts for the tendency of governments to run large real deficits during wars and recessions but to run real surpluses in 'good times'.

The standard view of deficit-financed tax cuts is that they make people feel wealthier. In this case, deficits would raise the real interest rate and crowd out investment. Sometimes economists rationalize the wealth effect from a tax cut by appealing to finite lives or imperfect capital markets. But an examination of these ideas suggests that they are unlikely to support the standard conclusions.

We note that social security is analogous to public debt. If debt-financed tax cuts have little effect on real interest rates and capital accumulation, then the same conclusion holds for an increase in the scale of social-security programmes.

Finally, we review recent political economy theory of budget deficit. We discussed the possible relationship between deficit and political systems. We noticed that large public deficits are more likely in countries characterized by short lived and weak governments.

Important Terms and Concepts

government's budget deficit (surplus)
public debt
nominal deficit (national accounts)
national saving
real deficit
nominal deficit
balanced budget
Ricardian Equivalence Theorem
monetize the deficit
parliamentary democracy
representational electoral system
fiscal policy
open-market operations
full-employment deficit
crowding out (from government deficits)
burden of the public debt
fully-funded system (for social security)
pay-as-you-go system (for social security)
presidential democracy
majoritarian electoral system

Questions and Problems

Mainly for Review

17.1   What is the real deficit? Why does a rise in the inflation rate reduce the real deficit? Show how the real deficit is altered either by policy changes or by economic events such as recessions.

17.2   Suppose there is a temporary increase in lump-sum taxes. Is there any effect on households' wealth? Show how the typical household can use the credit market to offset the reduction in current disposable income.

17.3   Are government budget deficits inflationary? If so, do deficits affect the real interest rate? What about the nominal interest rate?

17.4   Why are open-market operations neutral?

17.5   Suppose that the government announces a reduction in income-tax rates to take place in some future period. What intertemporal-substitution effect will this have on current work? What effect will it have on consumption?

17.6   Compare the effect of (a) government budget deficits and (b) social security on the tax liabilities of younger people. Why do the tax liabilities exceed expected future benefits in the case of social security?

Problems for Discussion

17.7   The Aggregate Wealth Effect from a Deficit
Assume that taxes are lump sum. Suppose that the government cuts current taxes and runs a deficit. Then assume that the real public debt remains constant from period 2 onward. Also, the time paths of government purchases and real transfers do not change. Discuss the aggregate wealth effect that results from the government's current tax cut. How does this effect depend on the following considerations:
a.   Finite lifetimes?
b.   The existence of childless persons?
c.   Uncertainty about who will pay the higher future taxes?
d.   The possibility that the government will print more money in the future rather than raising taxes?
e.   The imperfection of private loan markets?

17.8   Effects of a Deficit-Financed Tax Cut
Assume that taxes are lump sum. Suppose again that the government cuts current taxes and runs a deficit. Discuss the effects for the current period on first, the real interest rate and the quantities of output and investment, and second, the price level and the nominal interest rate, assuming that
a.   The paths of government purchases, real transfers, and money creation do not change.
b.   The same as in part a, except that people expect the future growth rate of money to rise.
c.   The same as in part a, except that people expect future real transfers to fall.
d.   The same as in part a, except that people expect future government purchases to decline.

17.9 The Timing of Tax-Cut Plans

Consider two alternative plans, A and B, of cutting income-tax rates by 25%. According to plan A, the full cut is to be phased evenly in over a three-year period. The plan involves also gradual reductions over time in real government expenditures when expressed as a fraction of real GNP. Plan B yields the same present value of real tax revenues but would implement the entire cut in tax rates in the first year. Real government expenditures behave the same way as under plan A.

Compare two alternative plans with respect to the effects on work effort, production, and investment.

17.10 Social Security and Capital Accumulation

Suppose that the government introduces a new social security programme that will make payments to covered persons when they retire.

a. What long-run effects do you predict on the stock of capital?

b. How does the answer depend on whether the social security programme is fully funded or pay-as-you-go?

17.11 The Government's Stock of Gold

Most European countries' central bank (or Treasury) own large quantities of gold. Mostly because of changes in the price of gold, the market value of these holdings increased considerably between 1970 and 1992.

a. How would you modify the measure of the government's deficit to include these changes in the value of gold holdings?

b. Apply this reasoning more generally to the government's holdings of other commodities, capital goods, and land.

17.12 Temporary Consumption Taxes (optional)

Suppose that taxes are levied on consumption rather than income. An individual's real tax for period t is then $t_t/P_t = \tau_t c_t - e_t$. Assume that the government runs a deficit during period 1 and cuts the marginal tax rate on consumption, τ_1. For subsequent periods, the marginal tax rates are higher than otherwise.

a. What is the impact of the tax cut on the quantity of goods demanded and supplied in period 1?

b. What is the effect during period 1 on the real interest rate, output, work effort, consumption, and investment?

Notes

1. The data for the United States are net of holdings of public debt by various agencies and trust funds, which are parts of the US federal government, thus referred to as **net debt**. We think of the monetary authority – the Federal Reserve – as part of the central government and therefore net out the Fed's holdings of US government bonds.

2. The average maturity of marketable, interest-bearing public debt varies across countries. The maturity of public bonds ranges from few months (typically three months) to several years (thirty years bonds are not uncommon). Public bonds can even take the form of perpetuals, i.e. with no redemption rate at all.

3. Net debt was negative in Germany, Denmark and Japan in the 1960s and the early 1970s.

4. For a discussion of these effects from inflation, see Jeremy Siegel (1979).

5. Note from equation (17.3) that the subtraction of $\pi_{t-1} B^g_{t-1}$ on the right side amounts to replacing the nominal interest rate, R_{t-1}, by the real rate, r_{t-1}. Similarly, the deduction of $\pi_{t-1} M_{t-1}$ corresponds to replacing the nominal interest rate on money, which is zero, by the real rate, which is $-\pi_{t-1}$. Thus, we effectively adjust for inflation by replacing nominal interest rates by real rates. Ideally we would also adjust the measurement of the government deficit for changes in the market value of government bonds because of changes in interest rates.

6. *Bank of England Quarterly Bulletin*, June 1984, May 1988 and May 1990. For a discussion of the relationship between inflation and budget deficit in the UK, see Buiter (1985).

7. For 1946-47, the large negative real deficits reflect first, decreases in the nominal debt, and second, large increases in the reported price level. Much of these increases in the price level arose from the removal of price controls. Probably, the true price level rose more during World War II and less for 1946-47. Hence, the true real deficits for 1946-47 were not as negative as those shown in the figure.

8. If the government owned capital, then the change in this public capital would add to the measure of real public saving. But we assume in the model that the government owns no capital.

9. For discussions see Ricardo (1957), James Buchanan (1958, pp. 43-46, 114–22), and Barro (1989). Gerald O'Driscoll (1977) points out Ricardo's own doubts about the empirical validity of his famous theorem.

10. Use the condition for a geometric progression, $(1 + z + z^2 + ...) = 1/(1 - z)$, where $z = 1/(1 + R)$. The formula works if $-1 < z < 1$, a condition that holds here because $R > 0$.

11. Aris Protopapadakis and Jeremy Siegel (1987) carried out an empirical study of the relation of money growth and inflation to budget deficits and the stock of public debt. For ten industrialized countries in the post-World War II

period, there was little relation between budget deficits or public debt and the rates of growth of money or prices.

12. Because the tax law applies to income rather than spending, there is no intertemporal-substitution effect on consumer demand.

13. Investment demand may change, but this response depends on the change in the marginal tax rate for the time when the new capital stock is operational. If the changes in marginal tax rates are short-lived, then the direct effect on investment demand will be minor. For simplicity, we neglect this effect.

14. However, as we will see below, not all countries had so well-behaved governments!

15. Economists often estimate what the budget deficit would have been if the economy had been operating at a level of 'full capacity' or 'full employment'. For discussions of the **full-employment deficit**, see E. Cary Brown (1956), and Council of Economic Advisers, *Economic Report* (1962, pp. 78–82).

16. For discussions, see James Ferguson (1964). Note especially the paper in that volume by Franco Modigliani, 'Long-Run Implications of Alternative Fiscal Policies and the Burden of the National Debt'.

17. For a discussion of the interplay between public debt and private intergenerational transfers, see Barro (1974). A different view is that parents use bequests to control their children's behaviour rather than purely for altruistic reasons. For a discussion of this 'enforcement theory of giving', see Douglas Bernheim, Andrei Shleifer, and Lawrence Summers (1985).

18. For someone who is borrowing at a high real interest rate, the discount rate $\hat{r}$ equals the borrowing rate. But if the borrowing rate is high enough (perhaps infinity), then a person may end up borrowing nothing even though he or she would be willing to pay a rate that was well above r. For such a person, the discount rate $\hat{r}$ is the highest real interest rate that he or she would be willing to pay on a loan.

19. For a summary of the debate, see Louis Esposito (1978), the papers in the May 1979 issue of the *Social Security Bulletin*, and Dean Leimer and Selig Lesnoy (1982).

20. For a survey, see Persson and Tabellini (1991).

21. Here we follow Bhingam Powell (1982) who identifies the degree of proportionality with the number of representatives per district. Systems with less than five representatives per district are classified as majoritarian, with five or more as representational. Naturally, electoral laws differ on several other dimensions, which can reinforce or weaken the degree of proportionality of a political system.

18

Investment and Fiscal Policy in the World Economy

In the last six chapters we have enriched our analysis considerably. We have introduced the possibility of investing and thus to accumulate capital and to grow. We have studied the behaviour of the fiscal authorities, the impact of government spending on the economy and of the alternative forms of financing public spending. Although on several occasions we discussed the implications of our analysis for the world economy, it is still useful in this chapter to summarize the international aspects of what we have developed so far. In particular, we want to spend some time in amending the model of Chapter 7, especially to take into account private investment behaviour and public fiscal policies.

The Current Account with Investment and Government Spending

Recall from Chapter 7 that the current-account balance was given by the difference between GNP and domestic expenditure. In Chapter 7, the only source of domestic expenditure was private consumption, so that the current-account balance was given by:

Current-account balance

$$= PY_t + R_{t-1}B^f_{t-1} - PC_t \qquad (18.1)$$

We now can generalize this expression by introducing, as part of domestic expenditure, private investment and government expenditure. The current-account balance, thus, is now given

by:

Current-account balance

$$= PY_t + R_{t-1} - B^f_{t-1}P(C_t + I_t + G_t)$$
$$= \text{net foreign investment}$$
$$= B^f_t - B^f_{t-1} + H_t - H_{t-1} \qquad (18.2)$$

The equation says that the current-account balance equals net foreign investment, which is the sum of the net capital flow, $B^f_t - B^f_{t-1}$, and the change in international currency, $H_t - H_{t-1}$.

As in Chapter 7, the difference between exports and imports, or net exports, is called the **trade balance**. The trade balance now equals the total value of the goods and services produced domestically, PY_t, less the total value of domestic expenditures, $P(C_t + I_t + G_t)$.

Equation (18.2) implies

Current-account balance

$$= PY_t - P(C_t + I_t + G_t) + R_{t-1}B^f_{t-1}$$
$$= \text{trade balance} + \text{net factor income from}$$
$$\quad \text{abroad} \qquad (18.3)$$

As we discussed in Chapter 12, we can get another perspective on international borrowing and lending by thinking about the home country's saving and investment. Equation (18.3) shows that the current-account balance is $PY_t + R_{t-1}B^f_{t-1} - P(C_t + I_t + G_t)$. The expression, $PY_t + R_{t-1}B^f_{t-1} - P(C_t + G_t)$, is national saving, the part of GNP that is not spent on private consumption or government purchases. The current-account balance is therefore the difference between national saving and domestic investment – that is, if we denote national saving in dollar terms by S_t, then

$$\text{current-account balance} = PY_t + R_{t-1}B^f_{t-1}$$
$$- P(C_t + I_t + G_t) = S_t - PI_t \qquad (18.4)$$

Thus, a country runs a surplus on current account – and thereby lends funds abroad – when its national saving exceeds its domestic investment. Equation (18.4) also says that national saving, S_t, can be used either for domestic investment, PI_t, or for net foreign investment, which equals the current-account balance.

The Cyclical Behaviour of the Current Account

We argued in Chapter 12 that shocks to the production function can generate cyclical patterns for closed economies that accord in many respects with empirical regularities. The type of disturbance that fitted well was a proportional shock that affected the level of output and the marginal products of labour and capital. The effect on the production function had to persist for a while but not forever.

This kind of shock to the production function was consistent with the following facts: investment and consumption are procyclical, but investment accounts for the bulk of the fluctuations in output; employment, worker-hours, labour productivity, and the real wage rate are procyclical; and the expected real interest rate is weakly procyclical. A procyclical pattern for the real interest rate arises if the boost to investment demand (for the case of a favourable shock) exceeds the increase in desired real saving due to the temporary expansion of income. Since the relative effects on investment demand and desired real saving can depend on the particulars of the disturbance, we would not expect to find a strongly procyclical pattern for the real interest rate. A weak procyclical pattern emerges if the average shock impinges more strongly on investment demand than on desired real saving.

Consider now what this type of shock to the production function implies for the cyclical behavior of the current-account balance in an open economy. We assume that the shock applies to the home country, but not to the rest of the world. (Any disturbance that affects all countries the same way cannot affect the current-account balance for the typical country.) We assume, in particular, that the world real interest rate does not change.

The key consideration, which also determined the cyclical behaviour of the real interest rate for a closed economy, is whether the shock impacts more heavily on investment demand or desired real saving. Suppose, for the case of a favourable shock, that the increase of investment demand exceeds the rise in desired real saving due to the temporary boost in income. This condition implies that a favourable shock to the production function leads in an open economy to a current-account deficit, that is, the current account will be countercyclical. As we mentioned before, however, the relative effects on investment demand and desired real saving depend on the details of the disturbance to the production function. We would therefore not expect to find a strongly countercyclical pattern for the current-account surplus. If the average disturbance affects investment demand more strongly than desired real saving – the condition that we assumed before for a closed economy – then the current-account surplus will be weakly countercyclical.

Table 18.1 shows the correlation coefficient between the detrended current account balance and detrended real GDP for the G-6 countries. The current-account does not have a strong cyclical pattern, but it does turn out to be weakly countercyclical: the correlation with detrended real GDP is between -0.05 for Germany and -0.53 for Italy. This finding is therefore consistent with the model that incorporates the kind of shocks to the production function that we described above.

Suppose now that the disturbances to the production function for the home economy are large enough to matter for the world credit market. This situation applies if the home

	Correlation	Period
France	−0.37	1970.I–1992.II
Germany	−0.05	1968.I–1992.II
Italy	−0.53	1970.I–1992.II
Japan	−0.36	1966.I–1992.II
United Kingdom	−0.34	1955.I–1992.II
United States	−0.35	1959.I–1992.II

Table 18.1   Correlation coefficient between current account and GDP

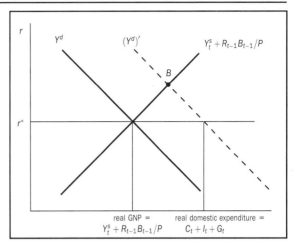

Figure 18.1   Effect of an increase in government purchases

economy is large or if the production conditions in other countries tend to be affected in the same direction (but by a smaller magnitude). We can then consider effects of disturbances to the production function on the current-account balance *and* the real interest rate. If a favourable shock impacts more on investment demand than on desired real saving, then the reaction will be partly a current-account deficit and partly a higher real interest rate. We therefore predict that the current-account surplus will be weakly countercyclical, as shown above, *and* that the expected real interest rate will be weakly procyclical, as we found in Chapter 12.

Fiscal Policy in the World Economy

Government Purchases

We learned in Chapter 15 that an important source of increased demand is a temporary expansion of government purchases, perhaps related to wartime. Because government purchases are high only temporarily, the present value of government purchases changes little. The disturbance therefore has only a small negative effect on wealth and, hence, only a minor impact on consumer demand. Given the small effect on consumer demand, the aggregate demand for goods rises on net relative to the supply. This scenario is shown in Figure 18.1, where we have assumed that the country is small and, thus, does not affect the interest rate. The home country borrows from abroad to finance its temporary increase in government purchases. By borrowing,

the country smooths out the reductions in private spending that are needed to pay for the extra government spending. A small part of the reduction in spending occurs while the government's expenditure is temporarily high. The rest of the cutback occurs in the future and corresponds to the payment of interest and principal on the accumulated foreign debt.

Suppose that the temporary government expenditures represent outlays during wartime. The international credit market then allows the combatant countries to borrow from neutrals and thereby moderate their short-run adjustments in consumption, investment, and leisure. Examples of this borrowing were the large loans from the United States to its allies during World Wars I and II, especially before the United States entered the wars. Shaghil Ahmed (1987b) studied these kinds of effects in the context of the long-term British history of wartime spending and trade balances. (Recall that we examined the data on British military spending in Chapter 15.) In line with the theory, Ahmed found a positive effect of temporary government expenditures on the trade deficit, especially from 1732 to 1830, a period that includes the major fluctuations in military expenditures (see Figure 15.3).

The wartime context suggests some serious limitations on the use of the world credit market. The possibility of a country's wartime defeat

Box 18.1   Risk of Default on Government Debt

The possibility of default on government debt is not confined to wartime situations. In fact, the most dramatic instance of sovereign debt default, the generalized debt crisis of the 1930s, was not the consequence of war defeats. In the 1930s, most Latin American countries together with several other developing countries, defaulted on their debt which, at the time, was in large part held by US and UK institutions and investors. Their default was primarily due to the worldwide recession, which triggered a widespread and substantial increase in tariffs in most of the developed countries. The recession and the increased barriers to trade made it impossible for the countries in debt to raise sufficient export revenues to meet their debt payments.[1] The point is that many different shocks may prevent a country honouring its debt obligation. How big these shocks need to be depends on the size of the debt oustanding. If a country has a small debt, only the occurrence of a very large shock can induce a default. However, if a country has a large debt, than even small shocks can create problems. Thus, the risk of default should be higher, other things equal, for countries with large debt to GDP ratios. For example, referring back to Table 17.2, the risk of default on public

debt should be higher for Italy, where the net debt is 104.5% of GDP, than for the UK, where it is only 32.2%. One way of measuring the risk of default on government debt is to look at the spread between interest rates on government bonds and interest rates on prime companies bonds. This spread will be larger in countries with higher risk of default on public debt, reflecting the higher interest rate on government bonds that investors will demand to compensate for the greater default risk. According to our argument, then, the interest rate spread should be higher for countries with a high debt to GDP ratio. Figure 18.2 shows the relationship between the interest rate spread (measured by the ratio between the two interest rates) and the size of public debt in 13 OECD countries, in the period between 1979 and 1989. Although Italy does have a higher interest ratio than the UK, Belgium has the lowest interest ratio of all countries, despite having the highest net debt to GDP ratio, 122.8% (see Table 17.2). Alesina *et al.* (1992) analyzed in detail the relationship between the interest rate risk premium on government bonds and the size of debt in these 13 countries. They found that they are positively related but that this relationship is weak.

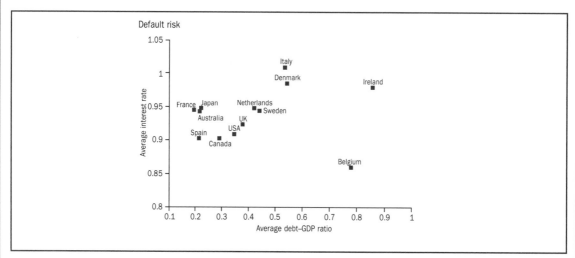

Source: Alesina *et al.* (1992).

Figure 18.2   Average interest ratio and debt–GDP ratio, 1979–89

raises the probability of default and thereby drives up the real interest rate paid on loans. Consequently, a combatant country would find it difficult to pay for government expenditures without simultaneously cutting back on private spending or raising aggregate production.

The wartime example makes clear that the loan market is helpful only if combatants have noncombatants to borrow from. As in some examples that we considered before, a worldwide disturbance differs from a localized shock. In the case of a world war, there is no one abroad to borrow from. Then the worldwide incentive to borrow drives up real interest rates (if international loan markets remain open) but leaves the typical country with a zero balance on the current account. In Figure 18.1 this outcome is represented by point B – the intersection of the supply curve with the new demand curve – which corresponds to a higher value of r_t. Similarly, as we have remarked in Chapter 7, the ability of a country to borrow on the international market to help in reducing the impact of temporary shocks depends on the country size. Unlike small countries, large countries cannot borrow heavily without driving up interest rates worldwide

Recall from Chapter 15 that a permanent expansion of government purchases differs from a temporary increase. A permanent increase in purchases leads to a roughly one-to-one cutback in consumption demand and therefore has little effect on the aggregate demand for goods. It follows that permanent changes in government purchases do not lead to significant changes in the current-account balance. Countries tend to pay for permanent increases in the size of government by lowering private spending, rather than by borrowing from foreigners.

The invariance of the current account to permanent changes in government purchases makes sense if we think of borrowing from abroad as a way for a country to smooth out its adjustment to a temporary disturbance, such as a surge in government spending. The country pays for the spending partly through small reductions in current private spending but mostly through cutbacks in private spending at later times. This process works if the increase in government spending is temporary but breaks down if the increase is permanent. If the rise in government spending is permanent, then the balanced adjustment to the disturbance is a one-to-one reduction of private spending at each date. Because current private spending then falls by as much as current government spending rises, the country does not borrow from abroad. If the country borrows instead to finance a permanent expansion of government purchases, then it finds itself in even greater stress later: since the interest and principal on the debt must be repaid, private spending in future periods would have to decline by even more than the increase in government expenditures. (The assumption here is that the home country cannot continually surprise its foreign creditors by defaulting on its debts.)

Tax Rates

Recall that the current-account balance is the difference between national saving and domestic investment, $S - I$. Changes in tax rates matter for the current-account balance if they influence desired national saving relative to domestic investment demand.

Effects on investment demand arise if the government changes the tax rate on income from capital. Therefore, a tax reform that lowers the tax rate on income from capital will result in an expansion of investment demand and – given the behaviour of national saving – a move toward deficit on the current account. This example shows therefore that a shift toward a current-account deficit is not necessarily a symptom of adverse events.

Permanent changes in marginal tax rates on labour income have little impact on desired national saving, S, and therefore have little effect on the current-account balance. A permanent cut in marginal tax rates, for example, stimulates labour supply but raises consumer demand by an amount comparable to the increase in labour income. Desired saving therefore changes little. It follows, for a given behaviour of investment demand, that the current-account balance does not change.

Desired saving responds mainly to disturbances that affect the present relative to the future. For example, a temporary cut in the marginal tax rate on labour income would increase desired saving: the current supplies of labour and goods rise, but current consumption demand increases by only a small amount. This kind of change in tax rates therefore creates a surplus on the current account.

Budget Deficits

In Chapter 17 we spent a lot of time considering whether a deficit-financed cut in taxes affects consumer demand. (For present purposes, think of lump-sum taxes, which do not affect the incentive to work today rather than tomorrow.) In the Ricardian view, as long as the present value of government purchases does not change, households do not feel wealthier if current taxes decline. Consumer demand therefore does not change, and desired private saving rises one-to-one with the budget deficit. Equivalently, the increase in private saving exactly offsets the decrease in public saving, so that desired national saving, S, does not change. With no change in national saving – and no effect on investment demand – it follows that the current-account balance, $S - I$, does not change.

To understand this result, recall that the Ricardian view implies that the households in the home country absorb all of the government's additional debt. The budget deficit therefore does not induce residents of the home country to borrow more from foreigners, and the current-account balance does not have to change.

The standard view of budget deficits – which we also discussed in Chapter 17 – starts with the assumption that a deficit-financed tax cut leads to an increase in consumer demand. That is, desired private saving rises by less than one-to-one with the budget deficit, so that desired national saving, S, declines. One rationale for the increase in consumption demand is that finite-lived individuals feel wealthier when the government uses its budget deficit to shift tax obligations toward future generations.

In a closed economy, the boost to the aggregate demand for goods leads to an increase in the real interest rate and to a fall of domestic investment. But an open economy can borrow from foreigners to pay for its increased demand for goods. We can again use Figure 18.1 to assess the effects. At the given value of the world real interest rate, r_t, real domestic expenditure rises because of the increase in consumer demand. On the production side, real GNP does not change. The gap between expenditure and GNP is the current-account deficit. Thus, when applied to an open economy, the standard analysis predicts that a budget deficit leads to a current-account deficit.

Many economists (and even more journalists) attributed the large US current-account deficits of the mid-1980s to the effects of excessive budget deficits. Despite this consensus of opinion, a careful look at the evidence does not provide much support for a linkage between budget and current-account deficits.

The first column of Table 18.2 shows the correlations between ratios of real budget deficits to real GDP and ratios of current-account deficits to GDP. The data are for ten major developed countries (Belgium, Canada, France, Germany, Italy, Japan, the Netherlands, Sweden, the United

Country	Correlation for unadjusted ratios	Correlation for ratios adjusted for cyclical variations
Belgium	0.24	−0.25
Canada	−0.15	0.02
France	0.23	0.09
Germany	−0.06	0.21
Italy	0.08	−0.43
Japan	−0.35	−0.24
Netherlands	−0.31	0.52
Sweden	0.29	0.01
United Kingdom	−0.22	−0.01
United States	0.55	0.64

Note: The data are from 1959 to 1989. The first column shows the correlation between the ratio of the real budget deficit to real GDP and the ratio of the current-account deficit to GDP. The second column shows the correlation after the two ratios are filtered for their normal relation with the movements in real gross domestic product.

Table 18.2　Correlations between the ratio of the budget deficit to GDP and the ratio of the current-account deficit to GDP

Kingdom, and the United States) over the period 1959 to 1989. For the United States, the correlation is positive: 0.55, a result that appears to corroborate the view that budget deficits caused the current-account deficits of the mid-1980s. Even for the United States, however, the correlation between the two deficit ratios is positive only because of the behaviour since 1983. From 1959 to 1982, the correlation of the two ratios for the United States is virtually nil, 0.03.

For the other nine countries, the correlations shown in column 1 of the table are all over the map, ranging between −0.35 for Japan to 0.29 for Sweden. The overall impression is that the two deficit ratios are largely independent, and there is surely no indication that higher budget deficits lead regularly to higher current-account deficits.

It is possible that the normal cyclical behavior of the two deficits makes it difficult to isolate the effect of a budget deficit – run independently of business fluctuations – on the current account. We noted in Chapter 17 that the budget deficit should rise in recessions and fall in booms – that is, the deficit should be countercyclical. In contrast, we showed earlier in this chapter that the current-account surplus was weakly counter-cyclical and, hence, that the current-account deficit would be weakly procyclical. Because the cyclical patterns – a countercyclical budget deficit and a procyclical current-account deficit – tend to create a negative correlation between the two deficits, it would be useful to purge the deficits of these cyclical influences to see whether the purged variables were related.

The second column of Table 18.2 presents the results of this exercise. The calculations first filtered out the normal reaction of the two deficit ratios for each country to the movements of real gross domestic product in that country.[2] The correlation between the filtered values was computed, and these values appear in the second column. For the United States, the correlation does go up, from 0.55 to 0.64. For the other countries, however, the correlations sometimes rise and sometimes fall: for Italy, for example, the correlation declines from 0.08 to −0.43, whereas

for the Netherlands it rises from −0.31 to 0.52. No clear patterns emerge overall and we cannot conclude from this evidence that budget deficits systematically cause current-account deficits even after we take account of cyclical fluctuations.

Paul Evans (1988) carried out a more sophisticated statistical study of the relation between budget and current-account deficits in the post-World War II period in the United States, Canada, France, Germany, and the United Kingdom. His main conclusion, consistent with the findings presented in Table 18.2, is that the data are consistent with the Ricardian view that budget deficits do not cause current-account deficits.

Fiscal Policies and Exchange Rates

We learned in Chapter 11 that one of the crucial conditions determining exchange rate behaviour is the interest parity condition:

$$\frac{(\epsilon_{t+1}^{ij})^e}{\epsilon_t^{ij}} = (1 + R^i)/(1 + R^j) \qquad (18.5)$$

or, using the logarithmic approximation:

$$R^i \simeq R^j + (d\epsilon_{t+1}^{ij})^e \qquad (18.5')$$

where $(d\epsilon_{t+1}^{ij})^e = [(\epsilon_{t+1}^{ij})^e - \epsilon_t^{ij}]/\epsilon_t^{ij}$, is the rate of depreciation of the exchange rate. Using the relationship between nominal and expected real interest rates:

$$R^i = (r^i)^e + (\pi^i)^e \qquad (18.6)$$

we can rewrite the interest rate parity condition in terms of expected real interest rates, inflation rates and the rate of depreciation of the nominal exchange rate:

$$(r^i)^e + (\pi^i)^e \simeq (r^j)^e + (\pi^j)^e + (d\epsilon_{t+1}^{ij})^e \qquad (18.7)$$

We know from Chapter 11 that if expected rate of depreciation equals the inflation differential, relative purchasing power holds. Equation (18.7) reduces then to the equality between real interest rates. An increase in the foreign interest rate, generated by a temporary increase in foreign government spending, will also raise, through international arbitrage, the domestic real interest rate, until equality between the two real interest rates is restored. But these changes in the real interest rates will not have an impact on the nominal exchange rate.

If we relax the assumption that purchasing power parity holds at all times, then a change in government spending can have an impact on the nominal exchange. There are at least two possible channels of transmission between fiscal policies and the exchange rate. First, if purchasing power parity does not hold, exchange rate depreciation and inflation rate differential do not necessarily move together. We argued in Chapter 11 that this is likely to occur in the short run. Take, for simplicity, the extreme case in which the inflation rate is the same (equal to zero) in both countries and where expectations about the future level of the exchange rate are fixed in the short run.[3] Consider again the case of a temporary increase in foreign government spending leading to an increase in the foreign interest rate. From (18.5') we see that, for the interest parity condition to hold, the increase in the foreign interest rate requires either an increase in the domestic interest rate, or an expectation of appreciation of the domestic currency or a combination of both. With the help of Figure 18.3, the analysis now follows our discussion in Chapter 11. The line stemming from the origin is the interest rate parity line. Initial equilibrium is at point A. The increase in R^j requires, for given expectation of future exchange rate, an increase in R^i and/or an increase in ϵ_t^{ij}. The new equilibrium will be somewhere between point A and point B. In a fixed exchange rate regime, where ϵ_t^{ij} is not allowed to move, the only possible equilibrium is to remain at point A. Therefore, R^i will have to raise to match the increase in R^j. Alternatively, in a pure floating exchange rate regime, it is possible for the exchange rate to move sufficiently to avoid any change in R^i. Equilibrium could occur at point B. How is this new equilibrium achieved? Remember that we are assuming that the future

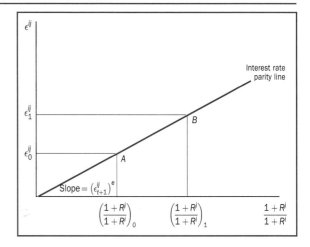

Figure 18.3   Exchange rate and interest rate parity

expected exchange rate, i.e. the slope of the interest rate parity line, remains unchanged. This will be the case, for example, if the increase in R^j is seen as short lived. Since the future expected exchange rate is unchanged, the current exchange rate depreciation, i.e. the movement from ϵ_0^{ij} to ϵ_1^{ij}, will generate expectations of a future appreciation. The size of the increase in the current exchange rate will be such to generate an expected rate of appreciation equal to the interest rate differential and thus assure that (18.5') is satisfied.

The second way in which fiscal policy can affect exchange rates is through their impact on relative prices. As we have discussed in Chapter 11, if domestic and foreign economies produce different goods, then the ratio of their prices will not remain constant, as purchasing power parity would imply, but will change depending on their relative demand and supply. If government spending is mostly directed to domestic goods, as is usually the case, then an increase in government spending would increase the demand for domestic goods relative to foreign goods and, thereby, increase their relative price.

We can illustrate this effect with the help of Figure 18.4, which describes the markets for domestic (say British) and foreign (say German) goods. On the vertical axis we measure the real exchange rate $\epsilon^{ij}P^j/P^i$, where P^j is the price of foreign goods, expressed in foreign currency, and

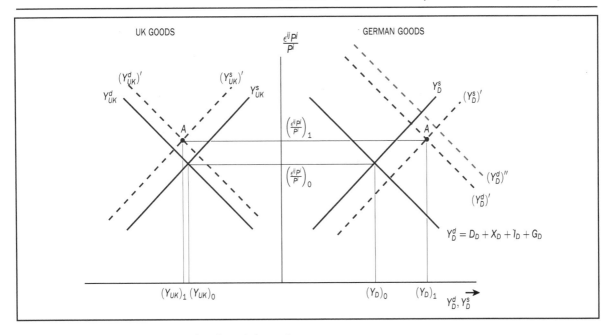

Figure 18.4 Fiscal policies, terms of trade and the exchange rate

P^i the price of domestic goods in domestic currency. The right quadrant describes the market for foreign goods. German supply of goods, Y_D^s, is a increasing function of $\epsilon^{ij} P^j / P^i$, indicating that an increase in the price of German goods, P^j, with respect to the price of British goods (expressed in Deutsche Marks), P^i / ϵ^{ij}, will motivate German firms to increase their production. The total demand for German goods, Y_D^d, is the sum of the demand for German goods by German consumer, D_D, by foreign consumer (that is, German export), X_D, by the German government, G_D, and by German firms as investment, I_D. Demand, is a decreasing function of $\epsilon^{ij} P^j / P^i$, because an increase in the relative price of German goods motivates consumers, both German and British, to switch toward British goods, i.e. both D_D and X_D decrease (while D_{UK} and X_{UK} increase).[4]

The left quadrant describes the market for UK goods. The relationship betweeen $\epsilon^{ij} P^j / P^i$ and domestic demand and supply is the opposite of that described above for the foreign economy. The supply of domestic goods decreases, while demand increases as $\epsilon^{ij} P^j / P^i$ raises. Consider now

a temporary expansion in German government spending. The demand schedule for German goods shifts rightward, by an amount equal to the increase in public spending, to $(Y_D^d)''$. This increase in the demand for German goods will tend to increase their relative price, $\epsilon^{ij} P^j / P^i$. However, in order to describe the new equilibrium we need to consider the other effects of the increase in G_D. We know that the temporary increase in G_D will increase the real interest rate worldwide. The increase in the interest rate will stimulate supply and reduce demand, both in Germany and in the UK.

In Figure 18.4, the supply schedules will move outward, from Y_D^s to $(Y_D^s)'$ and from Y_{UK}^s to $(Y_{UK}^s)'$, while the demand schedules will move inward, from $(Y_D^d)''$ to $(Y_D^d)'$ and from Y_{UK}^d to $(Y_{UK}^d)'$. The new equilibrium will be at points A. The pound real exchange rate depreciates from $(\epsilon^{ij} P^j / P^i)_0$ to $(\epsilon^{ij} P^j / P^i)_1$. Output increases, in both Germany and the UK. While the increase in output in Germany is unambiguous, the impact on UK output depends on the relative changes in UK demand and supply. A decrease in UK output is possible. What about the nominal exchange

Box 18.2   German Unification and the ERM Crisis

Several economists have suggested a link between the German unification in 1989 and the ERM crisis in September 1992. Actually, some of them, e.g. Begg (1990), predicted troubles for the ERM well before they occurred. The argument is twofold, and follows the discussion above. The unification of Germany is not without cost. The process of reconstruction and restructuring of the ex East Germany has required a large, temporary, increase in German government spending. Figure 18.5 describes the evolution of the German Federal deficit since 1987. After 1989, the federal deficit increased substantially, reflecting the desire of the government to absorb the temporary increase in spending without resorting to major tax increases, as we discussed in Chapter 17. Together with government spending, also interest rates increased in Germany from 1989, as shown in Figure 18.6. The interest rate parity condition required an exchange rate adjustment and/or an interest rate increase in the other ERM countries. Moreover, in light of the analysis above, the increase in German government spending most likely required a substantial real appreciation of the Deutsche Mark, either

through a nominal appreciation of the German currency and/or through an increase in prices in Germany and a reduction in prices in the other ERM countries. Because of the narrow limits imposed by the ERM on exchange rate movements, the interest parity condition could not be restored by nominal exchange rate changes alone. Interest rates had to increase in the rest of the EC. Similarly, the real exchange rate adjustments could not be achieved mainly through a nominal appreciation of the Deutsche Mark. Prices had to be allowed to increase in Germany, and decrease in the rest of the EC. Unfortunately for the ERM, this alternative adjustment process conflicted with policy priorities of most of the countries involved. On the one hand, Germany did not appear willing to allow for a sufficiently high inflation rate. On the other hand, neither the UK nor Italy were prepared to let their interest rates increase sufficiently. Something had to give, and this was the exchange rate system. Both Italy and the UK left, albeit temporarily, the ERM, so that the bulk of the adjustment could be achieved through the depreciation of their currency exchange rates.

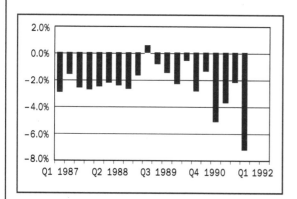

Figure 18.5   Germany federal deficit (−) (% of GNP)

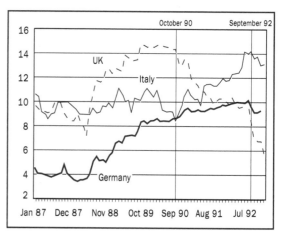

Figure 18.6   Treasury bond interest rates

rate? The pound real exchange rate depreciation can be achieved through a combination of German inflation, i.e. an increase in P^j, British deflation, i.e. a decrease in P^i, and Deutsche Mark appreciation. The relative importance of these three adjustments will depend on several factors, like monetary policies in Germany and the UK, and the exchange rate regime.

Summary

In this chapter we analyzed the open economy implication of investment and fiscal policies by extending the analysis developed in Chapters 7 and 11.

The current-account balance equals national saving less domestic investment. A temporary supply shock in one country reduces desired saving and thereby leads to a deficit on the current account. Similarly, a surge in one country's investment demand generates a current-account deficit. If the shocks apply to the entire world, then there is no one abroad to borrow from. The world real interest rate therefore adjusts to equate the world aggregates of saving and investment. If a shock to the production function affects investment demand by more than desired real saving, then the current-account surplus is countercyclical. We showed that this pattern shows up weakly in the G-6 countries.

We used the framework to analyze various fiscal policies. A temporary increase in one country's government purchases, as in wartime, leads to a cutback in national saving and therefore to a current-account deficit. In contrast, a permanent change in a country's government purchases has little effect on national saving and the current-account balance. Even if temporary, an increase in government purchases does not cause a current-account deficit if the shift applies to all countries (as in a world war). The absence of potential lenders implies that the typical country maintains a zero balance on the current account.

A cut in the tax rate on capital income stimulates investment demand and thereby leads to a current-account deficit. In contrast, permanent reductions in marginal tax rates on labour income have little influence on desired national saving and the current-account balance. If these shifts in tax rates were temporary, they would have some impact on desired saving and the current account.

Budget deficits affect the current-account balance if these deficits alter desired national saving. In the Ricardian case, budget deficits do not affect desired national saving and therefore do not influence the current account. In some other approaches, a budget deficit lowers desired national saving and thereby leads to a deficit on the current account. We showed for ten developed countries that there was no regular relationship between budget and current-account deficits.

Finally, we analyzed the possible relationship between fiscal policy and the exchange rate. We showed that temporary changes in government spending can affect the nominal exchange rate through two channels. First, because of their effect on interest rates, changes in government expenditure can bring about nominal exchange rate adjustments via the interest rate parity condition. Second, if government expenditure is biased toward domestic goods, then real exchange rate adjustments will be necessary, and these can be achieved through nominal exchange rate movements.

Questions and Problems

Mainly for Review

18.1   If a country runs a budget deficit must it also run a current-account deficit? How does the linkage between the two deficits depend on the relation between budget deficits and national saving?

Problems for Discussion

18.2   A Two-Country Model of the Current-Account Balance
Suppose that the world consists of two countries, A and B, that are roughly of the same size. Consider a temporary supply shock that affects the production function in country A but not in country B. What are the effects on the real interest rate and on the current-account balances in the two countries?

18.3   Effects of Tax Changes on the Current-Account Balance
Discuss the effects on a country's current-account balance from the following changes in tax rates.
   a. A permanent increase in the marginal tax rate on labour income.
   b. A temporary increase in the marginal tax rate on labour income.
   c. A permanent increase in the tax rate on consumption (say a general sales tax on consumables).
   d. A temporary increase in the tax rate on consumption.
   e. A permanent cut in the tax rate on income from capital.
   f. A temporary cut in the tax rate on income from capital.

Notes

1. For a discussion of the 1930s debt crisis see Eichengreen and Portes (1986).
2. The filtered part of each ratio is the part that can not be explained by the current and four annual lags of the growth rate of real GDP.
3. Recall that, under the assumption of zero inflation, nominal and real interest rates coincide.

4. For simplicity, we assume that firms and government only demand national goods for investment and public spending, so that I_t and G_t are not affected by changes in $\epsilon^{ij} P^j / P^i$. We ignore the services provided by government spending, so that supply of goods and private consumption are unaffected by changes in G_t.

19

The Interplay between Nominal and Real Variables

So far, our analysis has not stressed monetary variables as a source of fluctuations in real economic activity. Yet many economists think that movements in money and prices – that is, nominal disturbances – have a great deal to do with the short-term behaviour of real variables, such as aggregate output and employment. In this chapter we concern ourselves primarily with the empirical evidence on this important issue. But first, let's summarize what our theory says so far about the interaction between nominal and real variables.

The theory predicts that changes in the monetary base are neutral. In particular, a one-time shift in the quantity of base money leads to proportional changes in the nominal variables but to no changes in the real variables. In a closed economy, the monetary change induces proportional responses in the price level, the nominal wage rate, and the nominal values of output, investment, and so on. In an open economy with flexible exchange rates, the nominal exchange rate would change proportionately. But the important point is that there are no changes in the quantities of output and employment, the real interest rate, the real exchange rate, and so on.

We can also consider monetary disturbances in which the changes do not occur entirely at the present time. Then the anticipations of future monetary changes lead to complicated responses of the price level, as well as to shifts in the nominal interest rate. But the model still predicts no changes in the real variables. At least, the only exception in the theory concerns the transaction costs for moving between money and either goods or interest-bearing assets. Because changes in the nominal interest rate affect the real demand for money, some real effects occur through this channel. But these influences are insufficient to account for sizable fluctuations in aggregate real economic activity.

The results differ if monetary fluctuations reflect shifts in the cost of intermediation rather than changes in the quantity of base money. As examples, increases in reserve requirements or restrictions on the payment of interest on deposits raise the cost of intermediation, and a banking panic lowers households' willingness to hold deposits.[1] These cases are like reductions of the monetary base in that the price level and other nominal variables decline. But the higher cost of intermediation leads also to contractions of investment and output. Therefore, these types of disturbances move nominal and real variables in the same direction.

There are also real disturbances, such as the oil crises of 1973–74 and 1979–80, which we can represent as shifts to production functions.[2] An adverse shock reduces output and thereby lowers the quantity of real money demanded. For a given amount of base money, the price level rises. Hence, the price level moves in the opposite direction of output in this case.

In an open economy with fixed exchange rates, we found in Chapter 11 that it was not easy for the monetary authority to determine the quantity of base money once the exchange rate had been chosen. To sustain an increase in the monetary base (when this increase did not reflect a rise in the real demand for the base), governments had to restrict trade in goods or assets. Then it is not surprising that these restrictions – even if not the increase in base money itself – would have real effects.

Overall, the theory does allow for some relationships between nominal and real variables, but the sign of the interaction depends on the nature of the underlying disturbance. The key theoretical proposition, however, concerns monetary neutrality. Purely monetary disturbances – in the sense of changes in the monetary base – have no real effects. Although these monetary disturbances can create substantial variations in prices and other nominal variables, we still predict no response in the aggregates of output, employment, and so on.[3]

Most economists regard the proposition of monetary neutrality as incorrect, at least in some short-run contexts. In fact, many researchers attribute a large portion of aggregate business fluctuations to monetary disturbances, which the theory says have no important real effects. The common view is that monetary expansion tends to stimulate real economic activity, and monetary contraction tends to cause recessions.

The Phillips Curve

Economists often express their ideas about the relation between real and nominal variables in terms of the **Phillips curve** (named after the British economist A.W. Phillips). This curve is intended to summarize the relation between a measure of real economic activity – such as the unemployment rate or the departure of real GNP from its trend – and a nominal variable – such as the departure from trend or growth rate of a nominal variable, such as the price level, nominal wage rate, or the stock of money. The basic notion behind the Phillips curve is that a burst of inflation (and more monetary growth underlying this inflation) brings about an economic boom that shows up as lower unemployment and higher real GNP. This idea was presented initially as an empirical, inverse relation between the unemployment rate and the rate of growth of nominal wages. But subsequently, researchers have often

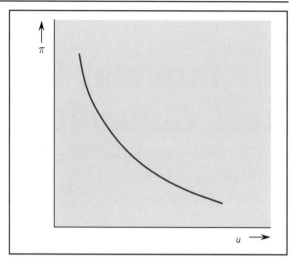

The Phillips curve associates a lower value of the inflation rate, π, with a higher unemployment rate, u.

Figure 19.1   A simple Phillips curve

replaced the rate of wage change by other measures of nominal disturbances, such as the growth rate of prices or money. Figure 19.1 shows a simple version of the Phillips curve. In this figure, a lower inflation rate, π, is associated with a higher unemployment rate, u.

Economists sometimes argue that more inflation or more monetary growth results in lower unemployment and a higher growth of output only in the short run. The economy adjusts eventually to any established rate of inflation, so that the real variables no longer depend on the behaviour of the nominal variables. Suppose that we think of the expected rate of inflation, π^e, as the rate of inflation to which the economy has adjusted itself. Then, as shown in Figure 19.2, it is only the surprise part of inflation, $\pi - \pi^e$, that would relate systematically (and presumably negatively) to the unemployment rate. This type of relation is called an **expectational Phillips curve** because the inflation rate enters relative to the amount of expected inflation. One important property of this curve is that a given unemployment rate can coexist with any rate of inflation. An unemployment rate of 6% is consistent with an inflation rate of 0%, 10%, 20%, and so on. If the inflation rate rises from 0% to 10% but the expected inflation rate rises by the same amount,

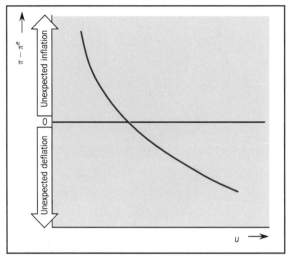

The expectational Phillips curve associates a lower value of unexpected inflation, $\pi - \pi^e$, with a higher unemployment rate, u. Thus a given unemployment rate (say 6%) can coexist with any rate of inflation.

Figure 19.2 An expectational Phillips curve

then unexpected inflation, $\pi - \pi^e$, does not change. Therefore, if the expectational Phillips curve is correct, then this kind of increase in inflation has no significance for the unemployment rate.

If the expectational Phillips curve in Figure 19.2 applies, then we can view the simple Phillips curve in Figure 19.1 as holding for a fixed value of the expected inflation rate, π^e. When π^e changes, the curve in this figure shifts. Specifically, a higher value of π^e means that a higher inflation rate is associated with any given value of the unemployment rate.

We can view much of the macrotheorizing since the 1930s as attempts to explain versions of the Phillips curve and, as a related matter, the absence of monetary neutrality. This perspective applies as much to the Keynesian theory as to the more recent monetary theories of business fluctuations. But before we explore these theories, we should understand the nature of the facts that they are trying to explain. In particular, we want to know to what extent the Phillips curve – either the simple one or the expectational variety – and monetary non-neutrality are 'facts'. In this chapter we bring out the major pieces of

empirical evidence that concern the interplay between nominal and real variables. Throughout this discussion, we look especially for findings that demonstrate the existence of the Phillips curve and the non-neutrality of money.

The Relationship between Unemployment and the Rates of Change of Wages, Prices, and Money: Long-Term Evidence for the United Kingdom and the United States

The term 'Phillips curve' derives from studies of the relationship between unemployment and the growth rate of nominal wages carried out by A.W. Phillips (1958) and Richard Lipsey (1960). Lipsey's statistical analysis documented a significant inverse relationship between the unemployment rate and the growth rate of nominal wages in the United Kingdom in the late nineteenth and early twentieth centuries. The nature of his findings shows up in Figure 19.3, which plots the British data from 1863 to 1913. The growth

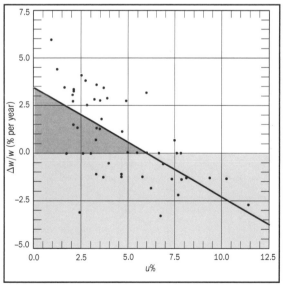

Figure 19.3 The unemployment rate and the rate of change of wages in the United Kingdom, 1863–1913

rate of the nominal wage rate, $\Delta w/w$, appears on the vertical axis, and the unemployment rate, u, is on the horizontal. The curve shows a clear negative relationship, a finding that excited Lipsey and many subsequent researchers.

The inverse relation between unemployment and the growth rate of nominal wages does not hold up after World War I. The interwar period, 1923–39, exhibited exceptionally high unemployment rates: the average value of 14.3% contrasts with that of 4.7% from 1862 to 1913. But Figure 19.4 shows that there is no significant relation between the unemployment rate and the rate of change of wages over the period 1923–39.

A different pattern of association between wage-rate changes and unemployment arises in the post-World War II period. For the years 1947–90, the relation between the unemployment rate and the rate of change of wages is significantly positive, as shown in Figure 19.5. In other words, the Phillips curve for the United Kingdom slopes in the 'wrong' direction since World War II! The most notable change, however, from the pre-World War I period is the higher average growth rate of nominal wages: 8.0% per year for 1947–90 versus 0.8% for 1862–1913 (and -0.1% for 1923–39). In comparison with the period before

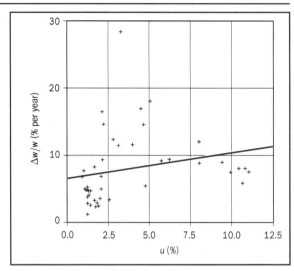

Figure 19.5 The unemployment rate and the rate of change of wages in the United Kingdom, 1947–90

World War I, the recent years involve mainly an increase in the average rate of wage change, with no significant difference in the average unemployment rate.

The results for the United Kingdom look basically similar if we replace the growth rate of nominal wages by the growth rate of either prices or the M1 definition of money. The only indication of an inverse relation between unemployment and the growth rate of a nominal variable – wages, prices, or M1 – appears in the years before World War I. Also, for any of the nominal variables, the slope of the Phillips curve has the wrong sign in the recent period.

The pattern of results for the United States resembles that for the United Kingdom.[4] Figure 19.6 shows a significantly negative association between the unemployment rate and the growth rate of wages from 1890 to 1913. Figure 19.7 shows the relationship over the interwar period, 1923–39. Although the slope is negative, this relation is not statistically significant. Unlike the United Kingdom, the unemployment rates in the United States were low during most of the 1920s. But for the 1930s, the unemployment rates were similar in the two countries.

Figure 19.8 shows the absence of a significant correlation between the unemployment rate and

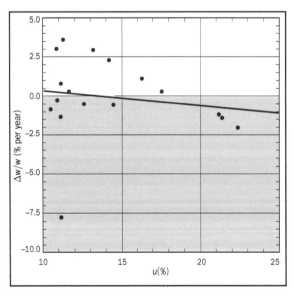

Figure 19.4 The unemployment rate and the rate of change of wages in the United Kingdom, 1923–39

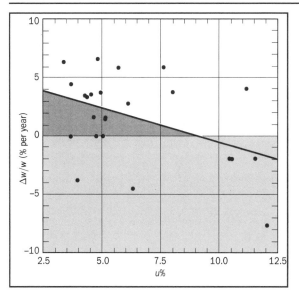

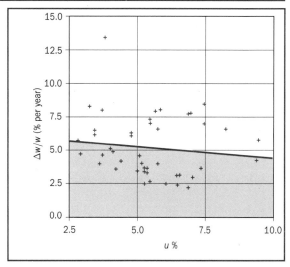

Figure 19.6 The unemployment rate and the rate of change of wages in the United States, 1890–1913

Figure 19.8 The unemployment rate and the rate of change of wages in the United States, 1947–91

the growth rate of nominal wages for the United States in the post-World War II period, 1947–91. Some weak indication of a positive relationship – that is, of a wrongly sloped Phillips curve – shows up for this period for the United States if we replace the growth rate of wages by that of either prices or a monetary aggregate, such as M1.

A clear conclusion from the data is the absence of a stable relation between the unemployment rate – or, it turns out, real economic activity more generally – and the growth rates of nominal wages, prices, or money.[5] Thus, the sharply higher growth rates of the nominal variables since World War II, compared with those before World War I, correspond to little change in the average rate of unemployment (or in average growth rates of real GNP). Hence, we can firmly reject the notion of a Phillips curve, such as that shown in Figure 19.1, that is stable over the long term. At least in the long run, it is not true that more inflation leads to a lower unemployment rate or that to have low inflation a country must accept a high unemployment rate. We consider later more detailed evidence about the short-run relation between real and nominal variables.

Cross-Country Relations between Nominal and Real Variables

Empirical studies of the Phillips curve have been conducted for other countries besides the United Kingdom and the United States. Franco Modigliani and Ezio Tarantelli (1973), for

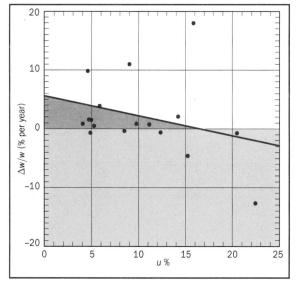

Figure 19.7 The unemployment rate and the rate of change of wages in the United States, 1923–39

example, study Italy between 1952 and 1968. They argue that a possible reason for the absence of a long-run Phillips curve is that the relationship between inflation and unemployment is not stable across different stages of economic development, because of changes in the composition of the labour force. Other studies for European economies are those of Rajindar Koshal and Lowell Gallaway (1971) on Germany, Walter Wasserfallen (1985) on Switzerland, and Martin Paldman (1980) for 17 OECD countries. In general, the evidence on the Phillips curve is mixed.

Suppose now that we look at average growth rates of real GNP for various countries and compare these with the average growth rates of prices, money, and so on. If we look at averages over several decades, then the main variations across countries would reflect differences in the long-term average growth rates of real GNP, prices, money, and so forth. Hence, the relations among these variables should indicate how differences in the growth rates of the nominal variables associate in the long run with differences in the real growth rates.

Figure 19.9 uses data from 79 countries to relate the average growth rate of output, usually over two-to-three decades since World War II, to the average rate of inflation. (Recall that we looked at these data before in Chapter 8.) There is no apparent relation between the two variables in the figure, an impression that can be verified from a formal statistical analysis. Similar conclusions apply if we relate the average growth rate of output to either the average growth rate of currency or the average growth rate of M1. Again, there is no significant long-term relation between real growth and the rate of change of the nominal variables.

Roger Kormendi and Phillip Meguire (1984, p. 147) carried out a detailed statistical analysis of the growth experience of 46 countries in the post-World War II period. One of their findings was that *increases* in inflation rates were associated with lower average growth rates of real output. This result suggests that a higher rate of inflation leads to a lower *level* of output. Thus, there is some indication of a form of Phillips curve with the 'wrong' sign. One possibility is that the

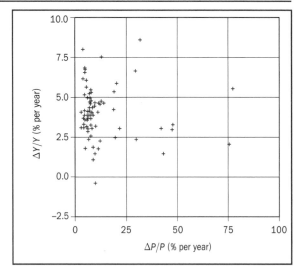

Figure 19.9   The cross-country relation between the growth rate of output and the inflation rate

transaction costs associated with higher inflation reduce the incentive for people to engage in market activity.

The Cyclical Behaviour of Money and the Price Level

The evidence already presented suggests that nominal and real variables are not related in the long run. We now want to look further at the short-run relation, specifically at the cyclical behaviour of monetary aggregates and the price level. We begin with quarterly data for 1960–92 for the G-6 countries. We use the same approach that we used before for the analysis of the cyclical behaviour of real GNP and its components (in Chapters 1 and 12), of the real wage rate (in Chapter 6), and of labour input and unemployment (in Chapter 13). In a boxed section, we use annual data for the UK and the US to examine the cyclical behaviour of monetary aggregates and the price level before World War II.

Table 19.1 shows the volatility of various monetary aggregates and the price level (GNP deflator) in this period. The monetary aggregates are M1, real M1 (nominal M1 divided by the GNP deflator), M2 and real M2.[6] We measure

	France	Germany	Italy	Japan	UK	US	Average G-6
Real GDP	0.012	0.015	0.016	0.014	0.016	0.016	0.015
M1	0.018	0.029	0.028	0.027	0.019	0.019	0.023
Real M1	0.018	0.030	0.038	0.037	0.029	0.025	0.029
M2	0.011	0.029	0.017	0.021	0.026	0.014	0.020
Real M2	0.013	0.029	0.030	0.032	0.038	0.020	0.027
GDP deflator	0.011	0.009	0.018	0.018	0.022	0.0009	0.015

Note: Samples differ across countries and series, depending on data availability.

France: GDP & GDP deflator 1967.1–1992.4.
  M1 and M2 1978.1 1992.4.

Italy: GDP 1970.1–1992.4.
  M1 1974.1–1992.4.
  M2 1962.1 1990.1.

Japan: GDP and GDP deflator 1965.1 1992.4.

UK: M0 is used in place of M1 1969.3 1993.1
  M4 is used in place of M2 1963.1 1992.4

Table 19.1 Standard deviations
  Quarterly data, 1960.1 1993.1 (unless otherwise indicated in the note)

volatility by the proportional standard deviation of the cyclical component, the same concept that we have used before. For real GNP, for example, the standard deviation of the cyclical component was, on average across the G-6 countries, 1.5%. Table 19.1 shows that the various monetary aggregates have usually a greater volatility than real GNP; in each case, the standard deviation of the cyclical component of the real monetary aggregate is as large or greater than that of its nominal counterpart. For the GNP deflator, the standard deviation of the cyclical part is on average the same as that of real GDP, but in some countries it is substantially smaller – in the US and Germany – and in others substantially larger – Japan and the UK.

Figure 19.10 shows the correlation of each cyclical component with the cyclical part of real GNP for the G-6 countries. For the nominal monetary aggregates, the average correlations across the G-6 countries were .28 for M1 and .34 for M2. Except for Italy M1, in all cases the correlations are stronger for the real counterparts of monetary aggregates: the average correlation was .43 for real M1 and .47 for real M2. Thus, the monetary aggregates are all moderately procycli-

cal, and the real monetary aggregates are more procyclical than the nominal ones.

Although money is procyclical, the price level (GNP deflator) is in all cases countercyclical: the average correlation of the cyclical component with detrended real GNP was −.39. This result is consistent with the finding that the real monetary aggregates are more procyclical than the nominal aggregates.

Table 19.2 brings out the behaviour of the monetary aggregates and the price level during the recession of 1975, the same as we analyzed in Chapter 12. The results are consistent with those shown in Table 19.1 in that the various monetary aggregates are below trend during the recessions (indicated by negative numbers in Table 19.2), whereas the price level is above trend (indicated by positive numbers).[7] On average, the nominal aggregates were below trend during the recession by 1.9% for M1 and 1.7% for M2. The corresponding figures for the real aggregates were 4.2% and 4.1%. In contrast, the GNP deflator was 2.1% above its trend on average during this recession.

The results on the nominal monetary aggregates for 1960–92 are consistent with the

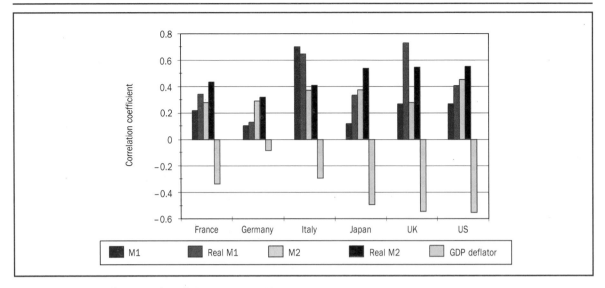

Figure 19.10   Correlation with real GDP, 1960.1–1993.1

	France	Germany	Italy	Japan	UK	US	G-6
Trough quarter of recession	1975.3	1975.2	1975.3	1975.1	1975.3	1975.1	(average)
% Shortfall of real GDP%	−2.3%	−4.3%	−3.7%	−3.1%	−3.4%	−4.5%	−3.6
M1%	%	−1.24%	−4.92%	−1.55%	−1.16%	−0.58%	−1.9
Real M1%	%	−2.54%	−5.37%	−5.18%	−5.08%	−2.90%	−4.2
M2%	%	−3.73%	−2.18%	−1.57%	2.63%	−3.70%	−1.7
Real M2%	%	−5.66%	−0.75%	−5.19%	−3.49%	−5.64%	−4.1
GDP deflator%	1.49%	1.68%	−0.01%	3.75%	3.90%	2.10%	2.1

Table 19.2   Monetary aggregates and price level during the recession of 1975
Note: Due to data availability, for the UK M0 was used in place of M1 and M4 in place of M2.

proposition that purely monetary changes have short-run effects in the same direction on real economic activity. The countercyclical behaviour of the price level indicates, however, that monetary shocks cannot be the principal disturbance that impinges on the economy. Changes that look like shifts to the production function – which move output and the price level in opposite direction – must be the dominant element. The evidence on the positive relation between money and output also does not address the question of whether shifts in money are causing changes in real economic activity or the reverse. We consider this problem of reverse causation below.

Studies of Unanticipated Money

Robert Barro (see Barro, 1981) analyzed the real effects of monetary shocks for the US in a number of papers. Other authors have applied his approach to several other countries, including most European countries.[8] The starting point in all these studies is the division of monetary growth into anticipated and unanticipated com-

Box 19.1 A Study of Price Surprises

An econometric study by Ray Fair (1979) analyzes the relation between surprise movements in the price level and the amount of real economic activity using US data for the post-World War period. He focuses on the unemployment rate, u_t, as the measure of real economic performance. The statistical procedure estimates the relation between the unemployment rate and the surprise part of the price level, $P_t - P_t^e$, where P_t is the actual price level, and P_t^e is the price that the typical person expected for period t. In other words, the study estimates a form of an expectational Phillips curve.

Fair interprets the expected price, P_t^e, as the best forecast for the actual price, P_t, that people could have made with the data available through the previous period, $t - 1$, where the periods are treated as quarters of years. Fair uses statistical techniques to obtain a best fit between the actual price level, P_t, and the lagged values of

a group of explanatory variables. Then he uses the fitted value from this relationship to proxy for the expected price, P_t^e – that is, for the best prediction of prices that could have been made from the assumed list of explanatory variables, when observed through date $t - 1$. Operationally, the constructed price surprise is similar to the cyclical component of the price level, the variable that we considered in Tables 19.1 and 19.2.

Fair finds no significant relationship between the unemployment rate and the price surprise over the period 1954–73. When he adds data from 1974 to 1977 – and thereby includes the effect of the 1973–74 oil shock on the 1974–75 recession – the estimated relation between price shocks and unemployment becomes positive. That is, the expectational Phillips curve has the wrong sign. This result accords with the finding in Table 19.1 that the GNP deflator was countercyclical during this period.

---

ponents. Conceptually, the anticipated part is usually identified with the prediction that could have been made by exploiting the historical relation between money and a specified set of explanatory variables. Unanticipated money is then the difference between the actual and anticipated amounts. Operationally, unanticipated money is similar to the cyclical component of a monetary aggregate, the concept that we used in Table 19.1 and Figure 19.10.

Next, equations for real GNP and the unemployment rate are estimated to ascertain the real effects of anticipated and unanticipated changes in money. Robert Barro found that, in the US, unanticipated M1 growth had expansionary real effects that lasted over a one- to two-year period. Conversely, the anticipated parts of M1 growth did not have important real effects. Quantitatively, he estimated that a 1% rise in money above expectations raises next year's output by about 1% and lowers next year's unemployment rate by about six-tenths of a

percentage point. Other studies for European countries reach similar conclusions as far as the impact of unanticipated monetary changes is concerned. The effect of anticipated money shocks is more controversial. Some authors have reported that, contrary to Barro's results, anticipated monetary shocks also have an impact on real variables.[9]

All these findings are consistent with the procyclical behaviour of the monetary aggregates shown in Figure 19.10.

Does Money Affect the Economy or is it the Economy that Affects Money?

The evidence that money – the monetary base or aggregates like M1 – affects output comes, first, from the observation that money and output are positively correlated, and second, from the

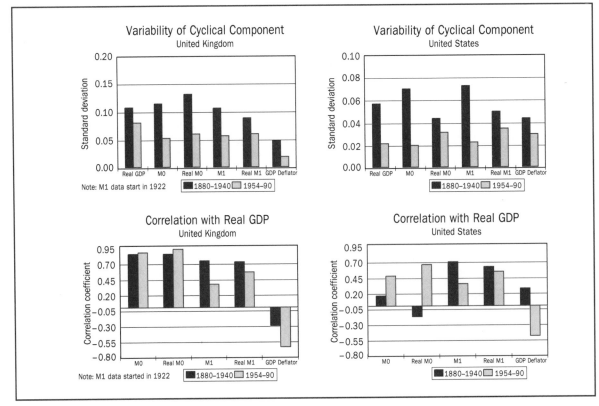

Figure 19.11

observation (which is harder to document) that movements in money precede those in output. An important question is whether these observations imply that money affects output, or instead that money responds to changes in economic conditions. Economists often refer to the latter situation as one of **endogenous money**, that is, a situation in which the quantity of money is determined by economic forces rather than being set (*exogenously*) from outside.

A banking panic is one example of a situation in which the positive association between M1 and real economic activity seems to reflect mainly the response of money to the economy. For a given quantity of base money, a banking panic tends to contract the economy and also to lower the amount of M1. Moreover, since the response of M1 may be quicker than that of real GNP, the movement in M1 could precede the change in output. In any event, the change in the quantity of

money is not the underlying causal element in this example.

In some previous cases, we considered changes in the real demand for base money while holding fixed the nominal quantity of base money. For example, a temporary supply shock reduces output and the real quantity of base money demanded. If the nominal quantity of base money does not change, then the price level would rise. But under some monetary systems, the monetary base would change automatically in these circumstances. Suppose, for example, that the monetary authority followed a rule in which it tried to offset disturbances by reducing the monetary base whenever the price level tended to increase, and vice versa. Then a supply shock would result in lower output and also smaller quantities of the monetary base and M1. In the data we would find positive associations between output and the monetary base and between

Box 19.2 Cyclical Behaviour before World War II in the UK and the US

The top part of Figure 19.11 shows the volatility of real GNP, monetary aggregates, and the GNP deflator for annual data from 1880 to 1940 (quarterly data are unavailable here) and, for comparative purposes, from 1954 to 1990. The data for M1 in the UK begin in 1922, while for the US, before 1914 we use instead of M1 (not available until then) the M2 concept of money. The main difference between the two periods is the generalized reduction in volatility of real and nominal variables after World War II, both in the UK and in the US. This decrease in variability in both output and monetary aggregates does not, however, solve the issue of whether GDP has become less volatile because money has become more stable, or vice versa.

The bottom part of Figure 19.11 shows the correlation of monetary aggregates and the GNP deflator with real GNP over the same periods. The differences in cyclicality between the two periods are much sharper for the US than for the UK. First, nominal M1 is more procyclical in the earlier period (.75 in the UK and .70 in the US) than in the later one (.37 in the UK and .35 in the US). One reason that nominal monetary aggregates like M1 were more procyclical before World War II is that business contractions in this period were often accompanied by banking panics, especially in the US. These panics led to reductions in deposits relative to currency and bank reserves and thereby led to declines in M1 for a given quantity of high-powered money.

Second, the price level is more counter-cyclical in the later period than in the earlier one. In fact, in the US, in the earlier period, the price level was procyclical (correlation with real GNP = .27) and countercyclical in the later one (correlation = −.49). In the UK, instead, it was countercyclical in both periods, but the correlation coefficient in the earlier one, −.29, was less than half the size of that of the later period, −.64.

Third, the behaviour of the monetary base was different in the two countries. The cyclicality of the monetary base has not changed significantly in the UK, being strongly procyclical in both periods. On the other hand, the monetary base has become much more procyclical in the US after World War II. In fact, the real monetary base was countercyclical before the war in the US. The differing behaviour of the price level in the US partially explains this change in cyclicality of the real monetary base.

The observations from before World War II complement those from 1954 to 1992 in the sense of confirming the procyclical behaviour of monetary aggregates like M1 or M2. The fact that shifts in the monetary base in the US were not systematically related to real economic activity in the earlier period raise some doubts about the idea that purely monetary changes – that is, shifts in the monetary base – affect real variables.

output and M1. But these associations would reflect endogenous responses of money rather than the impact of money on the economy.

The last example is important historically because monetary authorities tended to behave in the assumed manner under the gold standard, or more generally, in regimes in which the authorities attempt to fix the exchange rates between domestic and foreign currencies. (See the discussion in Chapter 11.) For present purposes, the important point is that these systems make money endogenous; in particular, they create a pattern in which the nominal quantity of money moves automatically in the same direction as the real demand for money. Because output has a positive effect on the real demand for money, the movements in output and nominal money would be positively correlated.[10] The gold standard and strictly fixed exchange rates have become less important in recent years, but monetary authorities still follow rules of behaviour that make money (the monetary base, M1, and other aggregates) endogenous. For example, as we discussed in Chapter 11, the European Exchange Rate Mechanism, by imposing limits on exchange rate fluctuations, makes money endogenous to a large extent. In this system, the nominal quantity of money tends to move in the same direction as the real demand for money; or, to put it another way, the variations in money tend to *accommodate* the movements in the demand for money. The point of this **monetary accommodation** is that it avoids changes that would otherwise have to occur in variables, such as the price level and the nominal interest rate, that influence the real demand for money, but that would not be compatible with the exchange rate within the given target zone.

But the endogeneity of money is not limited to the case of managed exchange rates. Suppose that the monetary authority has some objectives or targets for the path of the price level or the nominal interest rate. (**Interest-rate targeting** is, in fact, an important part of most European central banks' operating policy, even when they are not part of the Exchange Rate Mechanism.) If the quantity of base money did not vary, then shifts in the real demand for money would tend to affect prices and nominal interest rates. To avoid or dampen these effects, the monetary authority could adjust the amount of base money to accommodate the shifts in the demand. But, as with managed exchange rates, this pattern of endogenous money generates a positive association between money and real economic activity. Again, the existence of this association does not demonstrate that money affects the real economy.

Seasonal Fluctuations in Money

One straightforward example of endogenous money is the regular seasonal movements in the monetary base and M1. One of the functions of a central bank is to eliminate this pattern by allowing the amount of currency outstanding to vary seasonally to accommodate the regular

variations over the year of the real demand for money and thus avoid the seasonal pattern of money demand spilling over to nominal interest rates.[11]

The counterpart of the elimination of the seasonal pattern in nominal interest rates was the introduction of substantial seasonal variation into the monetary base and M1. Robert Barsky and Jeffrey Miron (1988) document these seasonal patterns for the post-World War II period in the US, and Miquel Faig (1989) analyses these patterns for the same period in Germany, the UK and Canada. These studies show that the seasonal movements in the monetary base and M1 are positively correlated with the seasonal variations of real GNP.

For example, one of the most dramatic instances of seasonality are the increases in all variables around Christmas and the reductions in all variables after Christmas. Probably all macroeconomists would accept the proposition that this seasonal behaviour is an example of endogenous money. Money is high around Christmas because real activity is high and because the central banks allow the monetary base to expand at such times. Real activity is not high in December because central banks capriciously expand the quantity of money at this time every year.

The seasonal evidence makes it clear that a positive association between money and output is not concrete evidence that money affects output. Some macroeconomists (such as Robert King and Charles Plosser, 1984) go further. They argue that the pattern of endogenous money that is so clear for seasonals applies also to the patterns that show up in business cycles. The reasoning is that, as with the Christmas season, the increase in the real demand for money during a boom induces the accommodating monetary authority to raise the nominal quantity of money at such times.

It is hard to evaluate this argument empirically. Without some additional information (such as knowledge about the effects of Christmas) it is hard to tell statistically whether the positive association between money and output that we found in Figure 19.10 reflects the influence of money on output, or vice versa. In fact, this problem of sorting out the direction of causation among variables is the most difficult problem empirical economists face.

Implications of the Evidence

If shocks to the monetary base matter for business fluctuations, then this observation would conflict with our theory. Remember that the theory predicts that changes in the monetary base would be neutral, at least if we neglect transaction costs and distributional effects. In the next chapter we explore some extensions of the theory that allow for non-neutral effects from changes in the monetary base. In evaluating these extensions, we should keep in mind the empirical evidence. There is some suggestion that monetary non-neutrality is significant, but the evidence is not very strong.

Summary

Much of the macrotheorizing since the 1930s can be viewed as attempts to rationalize a strong interplay between nominal and real variables, an interaction that shows up in various versions of the Phillips curve. We can view the Keynesian theory and more recent monetary theories of business fluctuations in this context. But before considering these theories, we should think about how much evidence there is to explain.

Neither the long-period evidence nor that from across countries suggests important effects on real variables from differences in the average growth rates of money, prices, or wages. In the long run, there is no systematic relation between real variables and nominal variables.

The data since World War II show that nominal money – the monetary base and monetary aggregates like M1 – are procyclical. The price level is countercyclical, and hence, real money is more procyclical than nominal money.

A positive association between money and output may indicate that money responds to the economy (endogenous money), rather than the reverse. The effects of banking panics on monetary aggregates like M1 are one example of this kind of effect. More generally, a positive association between money and output arises whenever the monetary authority accommodates variations in the real demand for money with movements in the nominal quantity of money. This monetary behaviour arises under fixed or managed exchange rate regimes and also in systems in which the monetary authority targets the price level or the nominal interest rate. It is unclear at this point how much of the empirical association between nominal money – the monetary base or aggregates like M1 – and real economic activity can be explained by endogenous money rather than as effects of money on the economy.

If changes in the monetary base were non-neutral and quantitatively important, then our theory would be seriously incomplete. Some of the empirical evidence is consistent with the idea that money is non-neutral, but this evidence is not very strong. Therefore, although the non-neutrality of money deserves some attention, it is likely that economists have given it too much weight. The interplay between nominal and real variables is neither as large nor as pervasive as most people believe.

Important Terms and Concepts

Phillips curve
expectational Phillips curve
anticipated money growth
unanticipated money growth
endogenous money
monetary accommodation
interest-rate targeting

Questions and Problems

Mainly for Review

19.1 What is the theoretical link between the price level and real variables? the inflation rate and real variables? Why do you think it might be important to distinguish between expected and unexpected inflation?

19.2   Consider the statement, 'Makers of economic policy face a cruel choice between unemployment and inflation.' Explain why this statement is not supported by either (a) theoretical results or (b) empirical findings on the Phillips curve.

19.3   How does the expectational Phillips curve explain the negative association between inflation and unemployment rates in the United Kingdom and United States prior to World War I? Could the absence of this negative association in subsequent years be 'explained' by shifts in the Phillips curve?

19.4   To what extent was the Great Depression (1929–33) accompanied by a change in the nominal quantity of money? in the real quantity of money?

19.5   Explain why it is important to distinguish between shifts in the nominal quantity of money and shifts in money demand. What association would we expect between the price level and real output in periods in which both types of shifts occur?

19.6   What is the meaning of the term *endogenous money*? Under what circumstances would endogenous money generate a pattern in which money and output were positively correlated?

Problems for Discussion

19.7   The Timing of Money and Output
Suppose that the data show that movements in money (say the monetary base) are positively correlated with subsequent movements in output. Does this finding imply that money affects the economy, rather than the reverse? If not, give some examples of endogenous money in which the movements of money precede those of output.

19.8   Seasonal Variations in Money
Suppose that the quantity of real money demanded is relatively high in the fourth quarter of the year and relatively low in the first quarter. Assume that there is no seasonal pattern in the expected real interest rate.
a. Suppose that there were no seasonal variations in the monetary base. What would be the seasonal pattern for the price level and the nominal interest rate?
b. What seasonal behaviour for the monetary base would eliminate the seasonal pattern in the nominal interest rate? Is there still a seasonal pattern in the price level?
c. Suppose that there is a seasonal pattern for the expected real interest rate. Can the monetary authority affect this pattern? If not, can the monetary authority eliminate the seasonal behaviour of the nominal interest rate? Is there still a seasonal pattern in the price level in this case?

19.9   Interest-Rate Targeting (optional)
Suppose that the central bank wants to keep the nominal interest rate constant. Assume that the expected real interest rate is constant, but the real demand for money shifts around (perhaps because of changes in output).
a. What should the central bank do to the quantity of money if the real demand for money increases temporarily? What if the real demand increases permanently?
b. How does the price level behave in the answers to part a? What should the central bank do if it wants to dampen the fluctuations of the price level?
c. In the real world the nominal interest rate moves around a lot. How can we incorporate this fact into the analysis?

Notes

1.   Banking panics are typically not independent of prior changes in business conditions. The potential for panics does depend, however, on some features of the financial structure. In particular, as discussed in Chapter 10, deposit insurance can prevent panics.

2.   For most purposes, we can also include here changes in government purchases and shifts in taxes and transfers. For example, an increase in marginal tax rates is analogous to an adverse shift of the production function.

3.   The variations in prices lead to changes in the distribution of real assets. Specifically, nominal debtors gain from surprise inflation, and nominal creditors lose. But the theory does not allow for effects of these types of distributional shifts on the aggregates of output and employment. One possibility would be to extend the theory so that these distributional changes did have aggregate consequences.

4.   Irving Fisher (1926) carried out an early statistical study of this type of relationship for the United States, although he used price changes instead of wage changes. This study is reprinted (under the cute title, 'I Discovered the Phillips Curve') in the *Journal of Political Economy*, April 1973.

5.   Formal statistical support for this proposition appears in Robert Lucas (1980) and John Geweke (1986).

6.   Due to data availability problems, for the UK we used M0 (monetary base) instead of M1 and M4 instead of M2.

7.   The limited availability of quarterly data for France monetary aggregate did not permit the analysis of the 1975 recession.

8.   Studies of anticipated versus unanticipated money include C. L. F. Attfield *et al.* (1981), D. Hoffman and D. Schlagenhauf (1982), Roger Kormendi and Phillip Meguire (1984), Frederic Mishkin (1982), and Mark Rush (1986).

9. For example, see Hoffman and Schlagnhauf (1982).

10. It is possible, but not inevitable, that the movements in nominal money would precede those in output. This timing depends on the precise specifications of the demand for money and the determination of output.

11. For recent discussions, see Jeffrey Miron (1986), Truman Clark (1986), and Greg Mankiw, Jeffrey Miron and David Weil (1987).

20

Money and Business Fluctuations in the Market-Clearing Model

In recent years, some macroeconomists have developed a new line of theory to explain the role of money in business fluctuations. The new approach is sometimes called *rational expectations macroeconomics*, but we shall refer to it – somewhat more descriptively – as the *market-clearing model with incomplete information about prices*.[1]

It is important to stress that the theory developed in this chapter applies mainly to the interaction between monetary and real phenomena. Thus, the evidence surveyed in Chapter 19 indicates the potential scope for the theory. That evidence suggests that there is something interesting to explain but does not imply that monetary shocks are the most important source of business fluctuations.

As with the previous analysis, this chapter relies on the conditions for general market clearing as its central analytical device. The approach also retains the assumption that households and firms behave rationally, even including the manner in which they form expectations of inflation and other variables. We introduce, however, a source of 'friction' by allowing for incomplete information about prices. An important way in which people receive information – and thereby make their allocative decisions – is by observing prices of various goods. But it would be prohibitively expensive for individuals to observe all prices instantly. Households and firms therefore typically make do with partial knowledge about the prices of different goods, about wage rates in alternative jobs, and so on. In this situation, decisions often differ from those that they would make with full information.

Variations in money and the general price level make it difficult for households and businesses to interpret the limited set of prices that they observe. Hence, when there is an increase in the general price level, a household or firm may mistakenly think that the price of its output has increased *relative* to other prices. Consequently, the household or firm tends to produce more goods than it would under full information. Because of these responses, we shall find that surprise increases in money and the general price level can lead to expansions in the aggregate level of real economic activity.

In this chapter we work out the details of a representative model from this line of macroeconomic theory. To bring out the role of incomplete information, we have to move away from the simplified model with an economy-wide market for commodities. Now we make things more realistic by including a variety of local markets on which households and firms buy and sell goods and services.

The Structure of a Model with Local Markets

Consider again the model of a closed economy in which households produce goods and sell them on a commodity market. Assume now that, instead of being identical, products differ by physical characteristics, location, and so on. We now index commodities by the symbol z, which takes on the possible values $1, 2, \ldots, q$, where q is a large number. To be concrete and to simplify matters, we usually think of z as a location – that is, a 'local market'. But more generally, we could identify this index with various characteristics of goods, occupations, methods of production, and so on. Then the value $z = 1$ might signify the automobile industry, $z = 2$ the computer industry, and so on.

Because changes in job location or type of product entail substantial costs, people do not move too often from one place or line of work to another. To capture this idea in a workable model, we assume that each household produces and sells goods in only one location during each period. But there is mobility in the sense that people may change locations at some cost from one period to the next.

We now distinguish prices by location of product and by date, so that $P_t(z)$ is the price of goods of type z during period t. Thus, $P_t(1)$ might be the price of a market basket of goods in London and $P_t(2)$ the price of the same market basket in Manchester. Correspondingly, the ratio, $P_t(1)/P_t(2)$, is the price of goods in location 1 relative to that in location 2. It is important to distinguish this *relative price* from the general price level, which we have stressed in previous chapters. By the general price level P_t we mean an average of the individual prices at date t.

To keep things manageable, we neglect any long-lasting differences across locations. That is, we ignore a variety of things that make goods permanently more or less expensive in different places. (For example, a market basket of goods costs more in Greenland than in Copenhagen.) Consequently, if the 'local price', $P_t(z)$, exceeds the average price, P_t, then market z looks relatively favourable for sellers during period t. This situation attracts producers from elsewhere, and the expansion of goods supplied to market z tends to drive down the local price toward the general level of prices. Similarly, if the local price is lower than the average price, then producers move to other territory, and this process tends to bring the local price up to the general price level. Thus, there is a process of entry to and exit from local markets that keeps each local price reasonably close to the average price. Because of this tendency for prices to converge, the long-run forecast of the price in any local market equals that for the average of the markets.

Supply of Goods in a Local Market

At the beginning of period t, a producer in market z has the stock of capital $k_{t-1}(z)$. Correspondingly, the amount of goods produced at location z during period t is given from the production function as

$$y_t(z) = f[k_{t-1}(z), \ell_t(z)] \tag{20.1}$$

where $\ell_t(z)$ is the producer's work effort. Note that we again think of each household as working on its own production process, although we could extend things to include firms and hired workers.

The nominal revenue from sales equals output, $y_t(z)$, multiplied by the local price, $P_t(z)$. But households buy goods from many locations. As an approximation, the typical household pays the average price, P_t, for its purchases. In this case, a producer calculates the real value of the revenue from local sales – that is, the value in terms of the goods that can be bought – by dividing the nominal amount by the general price level, P_t. Hence the real revenue from production is

$$[P_t(z)/P_t] \cdot y_t(z)$$
$$= [P_t(z)/P_t] \cdot f[k_{t-1}(z), \ell_t(z)] \tag{20.2}$$

The term $P_t(z)/P_t$ *is the price of goods sold in market z* relative to the average price of goods. Notice that for a given amount of physical product, $y_t(z)$, an increase in the relative price, $P_t(z)/P_t$, means a greater real value of sales. (An increase in $P_t(z)/P_t$ looks like an improvement in the terms of trade, $P/\bar{P}$, from the model of international trade in Chapter 7.)

When deciding how much to work during period t, producers and workers looked before at the physical marginal product of labour, $\mathrm{MPL}_t(z)$. (The index z means in this context that the marginal product applies to additional work and output in market z). To compute the effect on real sales revenue, producers must now multiply the change in physical product by the relative price, $P_t(z)/P_t$. Hence, the real value of labour marginal product is $[P(z)/P_t] \cdot \text{MPL}_t(z).^2$ An increase in the relative price looks to the producer just like a proportional upward shift in the schedule for labour physical marginal product. Producers therefore react to changes in the relative price, $P_t(z)/P_t$, just as they did before to changes in the schedule for labour marginal product.

Consider the response to a temporary increase in the relative price, $P_t(z)/P_t$. This change has the same effect as a temporary upward shift in the schedule for labour marginal product. Producers therefore increase work effort, $\ell_t(z)$, and the supply of goods, $y_t^s(z)$. Recall that these responses involve two types of substitution effects: first, a shift away from leisure and toward consumption, and second, a shift away from today's leisure and toward tomorrow's leisure. The second channel, which is an intertemporal-substitution effect, suggests that the current responses of work and production will be large.[3] As an example, we can think of the strong response of labour supply to the unusually high wages that firms offer during overtime periods.

Consider now the determination of investment demand. We can use the approach developed in Chapter 12 but amended for a model with local markets. Suppose that producers in market z buy capital goods from other markets at the *general* price level, P_t.[4] If capital, $k_t(z)$, rises by one unit, then next period's output, $y_{t+1}(z)$, increases by the marginal product of capital, $\text{MPK}_t(z)$. Since this output will sell at the *local* price, $P_{t+1}(z)$, revenues next period will rise by the amount, $P_{t+1}(z) \cdot \text{MPK}_t(z)$. As before, we can pretend that producers sell their used capital at the *general* price, P_{t+1}.

If we neglect depreciation for simplicity, then the nominal rate of return to investment is $[P_{t+1}(z) \cdot \text{MPK}_t(z) + P_{t+1}]/P_t - 1$. If π_t is the inflation rate (for the general price level), then this expression becomes

$$(1 + \pi_t)[(P_{t+1}(z)/P_{t+1})\text{MPK}_t(z) + 1] - 1.$$

As in Chapter 12, producers invest enough to equate this rate of return to the nominal interest rate, R_t. (We still treat R_t as determined on an economy-wide market for credit.) Writing out

this equation and simplifying leads to the condition for investment demand:

$$[P_{t+1}(z)/P_{t+1}] \cdot \text{MPK}_t(z) = r_t \qquad (20.3)$$

where r_t is the economy-wide real interest rate (defined by $1 + r_t = (1 + R_t)/(1 + \pi_t)$).

The condition for investment demand in equation (20.3) is the same as the one in Chapter 12, except that capital's marginal product, $\text{MPK}_t(z)$, is multiplied by the prospective relative price, $P_{t+1}(z)/P_{t+1}$. Thus, investment demand for period t rises with either an upward shift in the schedule for capital's marginal product or an increase in $P_{t+1}(z)/P_{t+1}$. Also, as before, investment demand falls with an increase in r_t. If actual and expected real interest rates can diverge (because of differences between actual and expected inflation), then it is the expected real rate, r_t^e, that has a negative effect on investment demand.

Consumer Demand

So far, we have examined the behaviour of producers. Now we consider the incentives of consumers, who may come from elsewhere to purchase goods. The important point is that a higher relative price, $P_t(z)/P_t$, reduces consumption demand, $c_t^d(z)$. (Note that the index z refers to goods bought in market z, although the buyers may use the goods in other locations.)

Clearing of the Local Market

If we put the pieces of the analysis together, then the condition for clearing the local market is

$$Y_t^s(z)[P_t(z)/P_t, r_t^e, \ldots] = C_t^d(z)[P_t(z)/P_t, r_t^e, \ldots]$$
$$(+) \quad (+) \qquad\qquad (-) \quad (-)$$
$$+ I_t^d(z)[P_{t+1}(z)/P_{t+1}, r_t^e, \ldots]$$
$$(+) \qquad (-) \qquad\qquad (20.4)$$

Here, we use capital letters to denote the total quantity of goods supplied or demanded in market z. Notice that a higher current relative price, $P_t(z)/P_t$, raises the supply of goods but lowers consumption demand. A higher prospective relative price, $P_{t+1}(z)/P_{t+1}$, increases investment demand.

We also include in the supply and demand functions the expected real interest rate, r_t^e. As before, an increase in r_t^e raises the supply of goods, $Y_t^s(z)$, but lowers the demands, $C_t^d(z)$ and $I_t^d(z)$.

Figure 20.1 depicts the clearing of a local commodity market. We put the current relative price, $P_t(z)/P_t$, on the vertical axis. The supply and demand curves in the figure assume a given value for the expected real interest rate, r_t^e, but assume that the prospective relative price, $P_{t+1}(z)/P_{t+1}$, moves along with the current relative price. The relative price will tend to persist in this manner if the underlying disturbances to the local supply and demand curves tend to persist.

For the supply curve, the positive slope shows the response of the quantity supplied to a higher current relative price, $P_t(z)/P_t$. For the demand curve, the negative slope shows the reaction of the quantity demanded by consumers to the higher current relative price. This higher relative price tends, however, to be accompanied by an increase in $P_{t+1}(z)/P_{t+1}$, a change that stimulates investment demand. We assume that the net effect on the demand for goods is negative and therefore draw the demand curve with the conventional negative slope.

The intersection of the supply and demand curves determines the market-clearing values of the relative price, $[P_t(z)/P_t]^*$, and local output,

$Y_t^*(z)$. For the average market – which, by definition, has not experienced unusual changes in its supply and demand curves – the market-clearing relative price must equal one, that is, $P_t^*(z)$ must equal the average price, P_t^*. The expected real interest rate, r_t^e, adjusts so that, in the average market, the quantity supplied equals the quantity demanded when $P_t(z)/P_t = 1$.

Disturbances to Local Markets

We can imagine a variety of changes in tastes and technology that affect the clearing of a local market for goods: shifts in the numbers of producers, in production functions, in the numbers of demanders, and so on. Consider, as an example, an increase in local consumption demand, $C_t^d(z)$, due to an increase in the number of shoppers in market z or due to the popularity of some new or improved product, such as CD players or personal computers.

Figure 20.2 shows the effect on a local commodity market from the increase in consumer demand. The solid lines reproduce the supply and demand curves from Figure 20.1. The new demand curve is the dashed line, labelled $Y^d(z)'$, which lies to the right of the original curve. Note that we hold constant the expected real interest rate, r_t^e, a variable that would be determined in the whole economy, rather than in a single market.

Figure 20.2 shows that the current relative price and local output increase. The rise in the relative price motivates producers to work more and

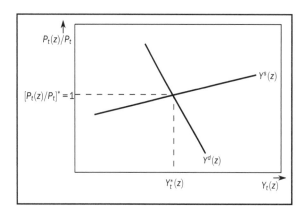

Figure 20.1   Clearing of a local commodity market

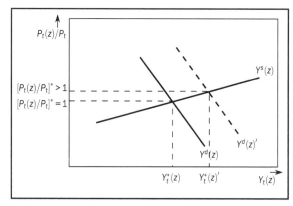

Figure 20.2   Responses to an increase in local demand

supply more goods. Thus, we can think of the high relative price as the signal that generates the unusually large volume of work and production. The high relative price persists over time and therefore stimulates current investment, $I_t(z)$. Consumption, $C_t(z)$, tends also to rise, despite the higher relative price, because of the initial boost to consumer demand. Finally, if the market-clearing relative price were initially equal to one – as is true for the average market – then the new relative price must exceed one.

Thus far, we have considered only the response of a local market to a local disturbance. Hence, we have not yet explained movements in the economy-wide totals of output and labour input. In the next section we show how a monetary disturbance may look, in each market, like a shift to local demand. Then output and labour input change just as they did in response to the shift in local demand that we just analyzed. When all markets respond this way, we end up with movements in the aggregate variables.

Changes in the Stock of Money

Consider a once-and-for-all increase in the quantity of base money, M_t. As in some cases that we explored before, this change might involve an open-market purchase of bonds by the central bank.

We found before for a closed economy that an increase in the quantity of money raised the general price level proportionately but left unchanged real variables like aggregate output and employment. This conclusion still holds when there are a variety of locations in which households produce and trade goods. As in previous analyses, we can think of households as attempting to spend their excess real money balances on the goods in various markets. Then the price in each market, $P_t(z)$, ends up rising by the same proportion as the increase in money. The general or average price level, P_t, therefore moves one-to-one with the quantity of money, and the relative price in each market, $P_t(z)/P_t$, does not change. The level of output in each market, $Y_t(z)$, also remains the same. Thus, at this point, we still lack any connection between money and real variables.

Imperfect Information about Money and the General Price Level

Now we make a crucial change in the setup to remove some information that individuals have about money and prices. The idea is that people know the prices of things that they recently bought or sold: they know the wage rate for their labour services (at least on the present job), the price of groceries at the local market, the rent on their apartment, and so on. Similarly, producers know a good deal about the costs of labour and other inputs, as well as the price of their own product. Producers and consumers have, however, much poorer knowledge about the prices of objects that they shopped for last year or perhaps have not yet examined.

We can model these ideas by assuming that sellers and buyers know the local price of goods, $P_t(z)$, but are less sure about the general or average price, P_t. The local goods represent the items that people have dealt with recently and for which they know the current price. The general price applies to other goods, which are potential alternatives to local product but for which people have a blurrier notion of the price.

As before, sellers and buyers in market z respond to their perception of the relative price, $P_t(z)/P_t$. But although they know the local price, $P_t(z)$, they are no longer certain about the general price level, P_t. We therefore have to analyze how people compute expectations of this average price under conditions of incomplete information. We rely on the concept of rational expectations, an idea that we mentioned in Chapter 8. This approach says that if people do not observe something directly – such as the current price level – then they form the best possible estimate of this variable given the information that they possess. In other words, people make efficient use of their limited data, so as not to commit avoidable errors.[5]

Consider the expectations that people have about prices for period t. Assume, for simplicity, that all markets look the same beforehand. That is, before period t, people cannot predict whether the price in market z, $P_t(z)$, will be higher or lower than the average price P_t. Then, regardless of which market a person chooses to enter, we can focus on expectations of the general price level, P_t. To keep things manageable, pretend that everyone has the same information beforehand and therefore calculates the same expectation, which we denote by P_t^e.

The expectation of the general price level depends on past information and on knowledge about the workings of the economy. We can think of this expectation as incorporating information about the quantity of money and about variables that influence the aggregate real demand for money. People can get useful information about these variables from lagged values of prices and money, from interest rates, and possibly from the government's announcements about monetary and fiscal policy. The expectation, P_t^e, therefore incorporates all of these elements.

Clearing of a Local Commodity Market When Information Is Incomplete

For a given expectation of the general price level, P_t^e, people compute the **perceived relative price** for market z as $P_t(z)/P_t^e$. We assume that sellers and buyers react to this price ratio just as they did to the actual ratio, $P_t(z)/P_t$, in the model with complete information. That is, an increase in the perceived relative price, $P_t(z)/P_t^e$, raises the supply of local goods, $Y_t^s(z)$, but lowers the consumer demand, $C_t^d(z)$.

We also continue to assume that a high relative price tends to persist and, hence, that an increase in the currently perceived relative price, $P_t(z)/P_t^e$, raises the expectation of the relative price for the next period, $[P_{t+1}(z)/P_{t+1}]^e$. The increase in the prospective relative price raises investment demand, $I_t^d(z)$. We assume, as before, that the net effect of an increase in $P_t(z)/P_t^e$ on total demand, $Y_t^d(z)$, is negative.

Figure 20.3 shows the supply and demand in a local market when people do not observe the general price level. We assume a given expected real interest rate, r_t^e, and plot the perceived

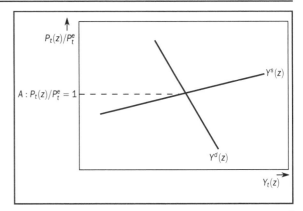

Figure 20.3   Response of a local market to the perceived relative price

relative price, $P_t(z)/P_t^e$, on the vertical axis. As before, r_t^e is determined so that the average market clears when the price ratio, $P_t(z)/P_t^e$, equals one. That is, in the typical market, supply equals demand when the local price, $P_t(z)$, equals the expected price elsewhere, P_t^e.

Changes in Money When There Is Incomplete Information

Consider again the effects of a once-and-for-all increase in the stock of money, M_t. We assume a surprise increase in money, one that people did not anticipate when they formed their expectation of prices, P_t^e. Although this expectation was rational, it could not incorporate the effects from unanticipated changes in money.

Suppose, as before, that the local price, $P_t(z)$, rises in the typical market. (We can think, as usual, of people attempting to spend their excess money balances, a reaction that bids up prices.) Since the expectation, P_t^e, is given, the rise in $P_t(z)$ implies an increase in $P_t(z)/P_t^e$. In other words, the typical person now thinks that he or she is located in a market in which the relative price is high. This belief must be incorrect, because the average across markets of the local prices, $P_t(z)$, always equals the general price level, P_t. But the surprise increase in money and prices – together with the lack of direct information about either the average price, P_t, or the quantity of money, M_t – means that the typical person underestimates the rise in the general price level. Thus, the typical person overestimates the relative price that he or she faces and reacts by raising goods supplied, $Y_t^s(z)$, and lowering goods demanded for consumption, $C_t^d(z)$. The rise in $P_t(z)/P_t^e$ implies an increase in $P_{t+1}(z)/P_{t+1}^e$ and therefore an expansion of goods demanded for investment, $I_t^d(z)$.

Point A in Figure 20.4 shows the price ratio, $P_t(z)/P_t^e = 1$, that would clear the typical local market. The surprise increase in money means, however, that the price in a typical market, $P_t(z)$, exceeds the expectation, P_t^e, as shown at point B in the figure. At point B, the supply of goods exceeds the demand; moreover, this condition applies to the typical market. Something else therefore has to happen to clear the typical market.

Effects on the Real Interest Rate

Recall that the expected real interest rate, r_t^e, equals the nominal rate R_t – which everyone observes on the economy-wide credit market – less the expected rate of inflation for the general

price level, π_t^e. Thus far, we have not allowed for any effects of the monetary disturbance on r_t^e. But for a given value of r_t^e, Figure 20.4 shows that the supply of goods would exceed the demand in the typical market, that is, excess supply of goods would apply in the aggregate. This aggregate excess supply will lead to a change in r_t^e.

Consider the results from the perspective of the typical commodity market. In Figure 20.5, the solid lines reproduce the supply and demand curves from Figure 20.4. Note that excess supply of goods prevails along the line labelled B, where $P_t(z)/P_t^e > 1$. This situation applies in the typical market after a positive monetary shock if the expected real interest rate, r_t^e, does not change.[6] We now show that r_t^e has to decline – the usual reaction to an economy-wide excess supply of goods – in order to clear the typical market.

If r_t^e falls, then the demand curve shifts rightward, and the supply curve shifts leftward, as shown by the dashed lines in Figure 20.5. That is, the fall in r_t^e motivates people in each market to consume and invest more and to work and produce less. If we shifted the curves by the right

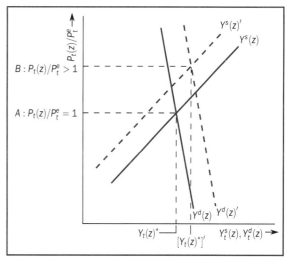

For given values of prospective relative prices and the real interest rate, the typical market would clear at point A, where $P_t(z)/P_t^e = 1$. But the surprise increase in money and prices means that the ratio $P_t(z)/P_t^e$, exceeds one, as shown at point B. Here, the supply of goods $Y_t^s(z)$ exceeds the demand $Y_t^d(z)$.

Figure 20.4 Effect of a surprise increase in money on the typical commodity market

The solid lines for supply and demand come from Figure 20.4. The decline in the expected real interest rate shifts the demand curve rightward and the supply curve leftward. Hence, the typical commodity market clears where $P_t(z)/P_t^e$ exceeds one.

Figure 20.5 Clearing of the typical commodity market after a surprise increase in money

amounts – that is, if we assumed the right amount of decline in r_t^e – then the dashed lines intersect along the line labelled B. Although people still perceive a high relative price in the typical market, this reduction in r_t^e allows the market to clear.[7]

Monetary Effects on Output, Work, and Investment

Figure 20.5 shows that output, $Y_t(z)$, rises in the typical market. The sign of this change, which is ambiguous, involves several forces. First, the high price ratio, $P_t(z)/P_t^e$, increases supply but reduces consumption demand. Second, the increase in the prospective relative price, $[P_{t+1}(z)/P_{t+1}]^e$, stimulates investment. Finally, the decrease in the expected real interest rate, r_t^e, boosts investment and consumption demand but discourages supply.

The presumption that output increases in the typical market depends on a strong positive effect from the prospective relative price, $[P_{t+1}(z)/P_{t+1}]^e$, on investment demand. If this response is strong, then a positive monetary shock will raise investment, output, and work effort. Further, since this result applies to the *typical* market, it shows up also in the *aggregates* of investment, output, and work.

Let's review the process by which a surprise increase in money and prices leads to higher work, output, and investment. First, the general rise in prices looks to local suppliers like an increase in their relative price. They therefore work more and increase production, just as they would in response to a true expansion of local demand. In other words, the suppliers confuse the change in the general price level with the type of local disturbance that warrants an expansion of their real activity. (Recall that we considered this type of local disturbance in Figure 20.2.)

Second, since the increase in $P_t(z)/P_t^e$ makes people think that the local market will remain favourable to sellers for a while, people raise their expectations of the future relative price, $[P_{t+1}(z)/P_{t+1}]^e$. The higher value of this prospective relative price stimulates investment.

Finally, since the disturbance causes an excess supply of goods in the typical commodity market, the expected real interest rate, r_t^e, must decline. This response clears the typical market by raising the demand for goods and lowering the supply.

Overall, the expansion of work, output, and investment occurs because the typical household confuses a high general price level with a high relative price in its location. Although households strive to avoid these kinds of mistakes, the available information does not allow them to distinguish all changes in general prices from those in relative prices. Also, households have to weigh their mistaken reactions to changes in general prices against the potential errors from not responding to true shifts in relative prices. In most instances the local price, $P_t(z)$, accurately signals the reward for local production and investment. An overly cautious producer who fails to react to these signals – in order to avoid the mistaken responses to changes in the general price level – will also fail to exploit a variety of true opportunities for profit.

Persisting Effects of Money on Real Variables

During recessions, variables like output, employment, and investment tend to be depressed for periods of a year or more. We want to know therefore whether the theory can account for persisting effects of monetary disturbances on real variables. One possibility is that misperceptions about the general price level persist for a long time, such as a year or more. Then any real effects from these misperceptions would also persist. But this outcome is implausible. We argued before that households would have incomplete information about prices in other markets, the general price level, and the aggregate quantity of money. But households presumably receive enough information about prices so that they would not make the same mistake in estimating the general price level for very long. Thus, it is implausible that the persistence in these errors would be as long as the persistence of booms and recessions.

The theory does not require the confusions about prices to persist in order to explain the persistence in aggregate quantities. We showed, for example, that a positive monetary shock can lead to more investment. Then, perhaps a few months later, investors recognize that they confused an increase in the general price level for an increase in their relative price. But once producers have incurred the initial costs to initiate a project, it often does not pay to terminate the project (even if the producers regret the start-up decision). Hence, investment demand may remain high even after the confusion about prices disappears. Moreover, the higher level of investment shows up later as more productive capacity, a change that tends to raise output and employment even after people learn the truth about past money and prices. Through this type of mechanism, a monetary disturbance can have a long-lasting influence on output and employment.

The Neutrality of Perceived Changes in Money

The analysis in the previous sections applies to surprise changes in money and the general price level. It is important to recognize that the confusion between general and relative prices does not occur if households and firms understand fully the movements in money and prices. To see this, suppose that everyone accurately anticipates a once-and-for-all increase in the quantity of money between dates $t - 1$ and t. Then the higher value of the money stock, M_t, shows up one-to-one as a higher rational expectation of the general price level, P_t^e. Hence, the increase of the price level in a typical market, $P_t(z)$, no longer represents a shift relative to expectations. Actual and expected prices then increase in the same proportion, and the perceived relative price in the typical market, $P_t(z)/P_t^e$, does not change. The quantities supplied and demanded in the typical market then also remain the same: hence, the quantities of output and work and the real interest rate do not change. Fully understood movements in money and prices are therefore neutral, just as in our earlier models.

Changes in the long-run averages of monetary growth and inflation would be accompanied by corresponding changes in expectations of monetary growth and inflation. The theory predicts that real variables, such as the growth rate of output and the unemployment rate, are invariant with these long-term monetary changes. The theory is therefore consistent with the long-term evidence for the United States and the United Kingdom and with the data across countries for the post-World War II period. Remember that this evidence indicates that the average rate of monetary growth or inflation bears no relation to the unemployment rate or the growth rate of output.

Implications for Monetary Policy

If changes in money can have real effects, then it is natural to think about a systematic policy of varying the money supply to stabilize the economy. Specifically, economists often advise central banks to accelerate money to bring the economy out of a recession. The theory developed in this chapter does not support this view of monetary policy.

We can think of monetary policy as a regular procedure for adjusting the quantity of money, M_t, in relation to the state of the economy. The monetary authority may, for example, expand money more rapidly than usual in response to a recession and hold down the growth rate of money in response to a boom. There is evidence that European central banks pursue this sort of countercyclical monetary policy.

What does the theory predict for the real effects of this type of policy? Given that the policy is in place, our best guess is that people take it into account when they formulate expectations of prices. If everyone knows that the central bank tends to inflate the economy in response to a recession, then households and firms raise their forecasts of money and prices accordingly. The expectation of prices, P_t^e, therefore incorporates the typical response of the central bank to the observed state of the economy. But this adjustment of expectations means that a central bank can affect money and prices in relation to people's expectations only when it departs from its usual practice. For example, if the monetary authority can observe shocks to the economy before the public does, then initially monetary policies can have an effect. However, once the shock becomes common knowledge, the central bank cannot use the element of surprise to stimulate output over the entire duration of the recession. In other words, the systematic part of monetary policy – which is the acceleration of money in response to a commonly perceived recession and the contraction in response to a commonly perceived boom – does not create any confusion between general and relative prices. These kinds of monetary changes are therefore neutral in the model. Economists call this finding the **irrelevance result for systematic monetary policy**.[8]

A great deal of actual fluctuations in money is unpredictable, and the irrelevance result does not apply to these types of monetary movements. But we also cannot think of this erratic behaviour as representing useful policy. Sometimes the changes are expansionary and sometimes contractionary but not in a way that systematically improves the workings of the economy.

Stagflation

Economists use the term **stagflation** to describe a situation in which inflation is either high or rising during a recession. During the recession of 1974–75, for example, the total unemployment in the EC increased 1.5 percentage points to 4.5%, while the annual rate of change of the GNP deflator increased from an average of about 4% over the previous ten years, to 13% in 1975. Similarly, during 1979–81, the unemployment rate increased by 2.2 percentage points, and the inflation rate rose from about 9% in 1978 to 11% in 1980.

Although stagflation is a big problem for analyses based on the Phillips curve, this phenomenon poses no difficulty for the model developed in this chapter. First, there is no relation in the theory between the perceived parts of monetary growth or inflation and the real variables. Therefore, the increase in the average growth rates of money and prices from the late 1960s to the early 1980s – an increase that was presumably perceived by everyone – gives us no reason to predict low unemployment rates.

Second, the oil crises of 1973–74 and 1979–81 constituted supply shocks, disturbances that tend to raise the general price level for a given behaviour of the money stock. Thus, we predict in these cases that a burst of inflation would accompany the shortfalls in output.

Real Effects from the Volatility of Money

Thus far, expectations of prices, P_t^e, depend only on information available before period t. Now we develop some interesting new results by allowing people to adjust their beliefs based on current information.

Recall that, during period t, producers find that goods sell locally at the price $P_t(z)$. If this price differs from P_t^e, then there are two possibilities. First, some local condition – such as a shift to demand in market z – caused the relative price of goods in this market to be either high or low. Second, the forecast of general prices may be inaccurate. That is, the general price level, P_t, may turn out to be either higher or lower than P_t^e. But by assumption, people cannot check things out directly by immediately sampling lots of prices in other markets or by observing a useful published index of current prices. Because the process of obtaining information is costly, sellers and buyers make do with incomplete knowledge about the prices of alternative goods. The observation of the local price, $P_t(z)$, does, however, convey some information about the current general price level, P_t, and we want to consider the nature of this information.

Suppose first that people can predict the general price level, P_t, with a high degree of accuracy. This situation applies if the monetary authority pursues a policy that usually provides for overall price stability. To carry out such a policy, the authority would have to avoid large random changes in the quantity of money, M_t. In this stable environment, people would not make significant adjustments to their expectations, P_t^e, when they observe the local price, $P_t(z)$. They would be confident that movements of $P_t(z)$ signalled changes in relative prices, $P_t(z)/P_t$, rather than movements in P_t. This high level of confidence in the monetary authority means, however, that people get fooled substantially on the rare occasions when monetary surprises are substantial. Even so, knowing they are right in the great majority of cases, suppliers and demanders will view changes in $P_t(z)$ as an indication that $P_t(z)/P_t$ has changed and will therefore make substantial adjustments in their quantities supplied and demand. A surprise increase in money will therefore induce a large increase in output.

In contrast, consider an economy in which money is volatile and the general price level, P_t, often departs substantially from the forecast, P_t^e. In this setting people would be much less confident that a movement in $P_t(z)$ reflected a change in the relative price, $P_t(z)/P_t$. To a significant extent they would believe that a high value of $P_t(z)$ signalled a higher than expected value of P_t. It follows that the perceived relative price, $P_t(z)/P_t^e$, and hence the quantities supplied and demanded, are not very responsive to observed changes in $P_t(z)$. A monetary shock therefore has only a small effect on real variables.

The general conclusion is that *the greater the historical volatility of money, the smaller the real effect of a monetary shock*. This conclusion follows because a greater volatility of money makes people more inclined to associate observed increases in local prices with unexpectedly high general price levels. It is therefore harder for monetary shocks to fool people into thinking that relative prices have changed.

These propositions receive empirical support from some studies of various countries during the post-World War II period.[9] First, it turns out that monetary disturbances (measured by surprise movements in M1) have a positive relation to real GNP for most countries. As the theory predicts, however, the strength of this relation diminishes as a country's rate of monetary growth becomes less predictable. Countries that display relative stability of money turn out to be the ones in which monetary shocks have a strong positive relation to real GNP. In places like Argentina and Brazil where monetary growth fluctuates unpredictably, there is essentially no connection between monetary disturbances and real GNP.

We can also use the theory to explore the relation between monetary volatility and the signalling value of the price system. We already noted that greater fluctuations in money mean that perceived relative prices become less responsive to changes in local prices. This effect means that people make fewer mistakes when the changes in prices reflect surprises in money and the general price level. But it implies that people make *more* mistakes when shifts in relative prices occur. More uncertainty about money and the overall price level means that observed prices become less useful as signals of changes in relative prices. Thus, in a general sense, the price system becomes less useful as a mechanism for channelling resources. The economy becomes less responsive to shifts in the composition of tastes and technology, shifts that require resources to move from one place to another.[10] Note especially that – in contrast to variations in the average growth rate of money – changes in the predictability of money are non-neutral. From this standpoint the best monetary policy is the one that is the most predictable.

Implications of the Model for Cyclical Fluctuations

In previous chapters, such as Chapter 12, we worked out the model's predictions about cyclical behaviour under the assumption that business fluctuations were driven by shocks to the production function. Consider now the alternative that the production function is stable and that business fluctuations are driven by monetary shocks. We can then use the analysis from this chapter to work out the implied cyclical characteristics of the principal macroeconomic variables.

Suppose that a value of money above trend corresponds to unexpectedly high levels of money (in the recent past) and vice versa. The model then predicts that an excess of money from its trend would lead to high levels of output, work effort, and investment (all relative to their trends). In other words, the theory predicts that money, labour input, and investment would be procyclical. These predictions accord with

Box 20.1   Incomplete Information about Prices and Money: Is it Significant?

A central element in the theory is that people do not observe immediately the general price level or the quantity of money. If people always knew the general level of prices – perhaps because they look regularly at a useful index, such as the CPI or the deflator for the GNP – then they would not confuse shifts in the general price level with changes in relative prices. Suppose instead that people observe quickly the quantity of money but not the general price level. Then – at least if they understand the economics taught in this book! – they can figure out the implications of the monetary movements for the general price level. They would therefore not confuse the monetary-induced parts of changes in the general price level with shifts in relative prices. But then the model predicts that the monetary changes would be neutral.

People can, in fact, observe quickly an index of prices or measures of monetary aggregates (in most industrialized countries information about the CPI, M1 and the monetary base are made public within a month lag). Most people do not, of course, bother to collect and interpret these types of data. But presumably, that is because the information is of minor value to them.

Consider the usefulness of the available indexes of prices. One reason that they may not be very helpful is that each individual cares about a market basket of goods that differs substantially from the one used in the index. Then, in order to keep well informed about prices, people would have to take detailed samples from a variety of markets. Since this process is costly, people may sometimes make significant errors in their interpretations of observed prices.

A similar argument is that the data on monetary aggregates provide little useful information. Possibly because of seasonal adjustments and the arbitrariness in defining money, the reported measures bear little relation to the concept of money that matters in the theory. This argument leads, however, to a puzzle: the reported figures – on M1 and perhaps on the monetary base – seem to have a positive relation to real economic activity in the post-World War II period. If the data are meaningless, then it is hard to explain this relation. Alternatively, if the reported measures are important, then why would people not bother to observe them?

To put the various points together, it seems reasonable that ignorance about the general price level and the quantity of money can account for small and short-lived confusions about relative prices. That is because people would find it too costly to monitor continuously and interpret the behaviour of general prices and the quantity of money. But it is unlikely that large or long-lasting confusions would arise. The costs of being misinformed about relative prices – and therefore making incorrect decisions about production, work, and investment – seem excessive relative to the costs of gathering the necessary information. Hence, this view suggests that monetary-induced confusions of general for relative prices can account for only small fluctuations in the aggregate economy. We cannot use this line of theory to explain the bulk of business fluctuations.

This conclusion is consistent with our findings about the cyclical characteristics of the principal macroeconomic variables. If monetary shocks were the main driving force behind business fluctuations, then the cyclical properties of some of the variables, such as the general price level, the real interest rate, and labour productivity, would differ substantially from the observed characteristics. We therefore conclude that business fluctuations must result primarily from other kinds of disturbances, such as the shifts to production functions that were stressed in previous chapters.

observed behaviour in the G-6 that we analyzed in Chapter 19.

The theory has, however, other predictions that are less satisfactory. A monetary shock leads, in the theory, to an increase in the general price level (relative to its trend) and to a fall in the expected real interest rate. The model therefore predicts that the price level would be procyclical and that the expected real interest rate would be counter-cyclical. These predictions conflict with the data (see Chapter 1, Chapter 12 and Chapter 19).

Since the production function was assumed to be stable and the capital stock cannot change greatly in the short run, the increase in labour input implies that the marginal and average products of labour would decline. The theory therefore predicts that labour productivity (output per worker-hour) and the real wage rate (which equals the marginal product of labour) would be low when the quantities of output and labour input were high. That is, labour productivity and the real wage rate would be countercyclical. These predictions conflict with the data (see Chapter 1 and Chapter 6).

These departures between theory and facts indicate that we cannot use the model, driven mainly by monetary shocks, to explain many of the features of business fluctuations. We can, however, fit the facts better if we reintroduce the shifts to the production function that we considered before. If business fluctuations are driven mainly by disturbances that can be modelled as shifts to the production function, then it is possible that monetary disturbances would also play a secondary role. The real effects of these monetary shocks could explain why money was procyclical. The observed cyclical behaviour of the price level, real interest rate, labour productivity, and the real wage rate would also fit the theory if shocks to the production function were typically more important than monetary disturbances.[11]

Summary

A new line of macroeconomic theory attempts to explain the role of money in business fluctua-tions. This approach retains the framework of market clearing and rational behaviour but introduces incomplete information about prices to explain some real effects from monetary disturbances. Although people form expectations rationally, the incomplete information means that surprise increases in money and the general price level make producers in local markets think that the relative price of their output has risen. Monetary injections can thereby induce expan-sions in the quantities of production, work, and investment.

Perceived changes in money and the general price level do not lead to confusions about relative prices. The perceived parts of monetary changes are therefore still neutral. This result is consistent with the absence of a long-term relation of real variables to either monetary growth or inflation.

The systematic part of monetary policy causes no confusions about relative prices. The theory predicts accordingly that this part of policy has no significance for real variables. An increase in monetary uncertainty is non-neutral, however, because it alters the information that people receive by observing local prices. Since people recognize that monetary shocks are often large, the real variables become less sensitive to monetary disturbances. But because the observed prices become less useful as allocative signals, the allocation of resources becomes less efficient. Specifically, the economy becomes less responsive to variations in the composition of tastes and technology. Thus, the model's main lesson is that monetary policy should be predictable rather than erratic.

The theory is consistent with the procyclical behaviour of money, labour input, and invest-ment, but is inconsistent with the cyclical properties of the price level, the expected real interest rate, labour productivity, and the real wage rate. Also, because the costs of obtaining information about money and prices are not very large, the theory cannot plausibly explain major business contractions. The theory may, however, serve as a useful complement to real business-cycle models in which fluctuations are driven mainly by shocks to the production function.

Important Terms and Concepts

perceived relative price
stagflation
irrelevance result for systematic monetary policy
constant-growth-rate rule
perfect foresight
discretionary policy
policy rule

Questions and Problems

Mainly for Review

20.1 Explain why it is reasonable to assume that individuals have imperfect information about the general price level. What are the costs of collecting information about prices?

20.2 Explain what a relative price is. Is the real wage rate an example of a relative price? Show how a proportional increase in $P_t(z)$ and P_t^e leaves buyers and sellers unaffected.

20.3 What are the factors that might cause the relative price in a market to remain high for many periods of time? What are the factors that cause changes in the relative price to be offset in later periods? (Consider in your answer the changes in the capital stock and in the numbers of buyers and sellers.)

20.4 Can there be unexpected changes in the quantity of money when expectations are rational? If so, does a policymaker have the option of counteracting business cycles through surprise increases in money?

20.5 When expectations are rational, any errors made in estimating the price level will not persist. How then can we explain persistent deviations of aggregate output from trend?

Problems for Discussion

20.6 Investment Demand in a Local Market
   a. Suppose that producers in market z buy capital at the price P_t. What is the condition that determines investment demand if old capital sells next period at the price P_{t+1}?
   b. What is the condition for investment demand if producers in market z buy capital locally at the price $P_t(z)$? How does the result depend on whether old capital sells the next period at price $P_{t+1}(z)$ or P_{t+1}?

20.7 Changes in the Predictability of Money
   Suppose that the fluctuations of money become less predictable from year to year. What happens to the following:

   a. The responsiveness of the perceived relative price, $P_t(z)/P_t$, to the observed local price, $P_t(z)$?
   b. The effect of a given size monetary disturbance on output?
   c. The allocation of resources?

20.8 Money and the Dispersion of Relative Prices (optional)
   The local price, $P_t(z)$, differs across locations because each market experiences local shocks to supply and demand. (Think here of changes in the composition of tastes and technology.) Thus, the model generates a dispersion of relative prices across markets at each point in time. Now suppose, as in problem 20.7, that the fluctuations in money become less predictable from year to year. Then what happens to the dispersion of relative prices across markets at a point in time?

   (There is evidence that this effect is important during extreme inflations, such as the German hyperinflation. See Zvi Hercowitz, 1982. For a survey of the related literature on price dispersion, see Alex Cukierman, 1983.)

20.9 Monetary Effects on Consumption (optional)
   In the text we noted some shortcomings of the market-clearing model with incomplete information on prices. Here, we explore another problem, which concerns the behaviour of consumption.

   We argued that a positive monetary shock could increase output, labour input, and investment. Suppose, in fact, that work effort increases, so that leisure declines.

   a. What must be the effect on consumption? (*Hint*: Does the monetary shock alter the terms on which people can substitute today's leisure for today's consumption?)
   b. Would the results change if the monetary disturbance raised perceived wealth?
   c. How do the theoretical results about consumption conform with the data on recessions in the G-6?

20.10 Monetary Effects on Real Wage Rates (optional)
   Another problem with the theory concerns the behaviour of real wage rates. We explore this problem here.

   Suppose that we allow each locality to have a labour market, on which the wage rate is $w_t(z)$. How would a surprise increase in money affect the real wage rate, $w_t(z)/P_t(z)$, in the typical market? (See note 2 for a suggestion on how to proceed.) How does the result compare with empirical evidence on the cyclical behaviour of the real wage rate?

20.11 Revisions of the Monetary Data
   a. Suppose that people observe the monetary base as it is reported from week to week. Then what does the theory predict about the effects of changes in base money on real variables?

b. Central Banks often revise their data on money – especially M1 – several months after the initial reports. (Mostly, these revisions arise because a central bank has to estimate the monthly figures on checkable deposits for some banks and other financial institutions.) What does the theory say about the economic effects of these revisions in the monetary figures? (Empirically, the revisions bear no relation to real economic activity.)

20.12 The Effects of Anticipated Policy
a. What is the irrelevance result for systematic monetary policy?
b. Does the result mean that the unpredictable parts of money do not matter?
c. Does the result mean that the systematic parts of all government policies are irrelevant? Consider, as examples, the following:
i. The unemployment-insurance programme.
ii. A policy of raising government purchases during a recession.
iii. A policy of cutting income-tax rates during a recession.

20.13 The Central Bank's Information and Monetary Policy
Suppose that the central bank has a regular policy of accelerating money during a recession.
a. Why does the theory say that this policy does not matter?
b. If the central bank observes the recession before others do, then does the policy still not matter?

c. Suppose that the central bank knows no more about recessions than anyone else does. But the central bank also knows that real activity expands when monetary growth is surprisingly high. Thus, when the economy is in a recession, the central bank attempts to expand money by more than the amount people expect. What problems arise here? (*Hint*: Suppose that people understand that the central bank is pursuing this type of policy. What then is the rational expectation of monetary growth and inflation?)

20.14 Rules versus Discretion (optional)
Assume that the monetary authority's preferred inflation rate is zero, but the authority also wants to reduce unemployment by making inflation surprisingly high.
a. Show how the equilibrium inflation rate can be high. Is the rate surprisingly high? Does the result depend on the authority's having the 'wrong' objective or on being incompetent?
b. Can the results improve if the policymaker has the power to bind himself or herself in advance to a specified inflation rate? If so, explain why this constraint (or rule) can improve matters.
c. Do you think that the policymaker's reputation may be a satisfactory substitute for a formal rule that prescribes future policies?
d. Can you think of some reasons, aside from possibly reducing unemployment, why a policy-maker might like surprisingly high inflation?

Notes

1. For a survey of the research, see Ben McCallum (1979). See also the papers collected in Robert Lucas (1981). Two early papers that stimulated much of the subsequent work are Milton Friedman (1968c) and Edmund Phelps (1970).
2. With separate labour markets, a worker would look at the local nominal wage rate, $w_t(z)$, divided by the average price of commodities, P_t. The real wage rate, $w_t(z)/P_t$, is the value of the local wage in terms of the goods that it buys on the average commodity market. Firms would hire labour until the local marginal product, $MPL_t(z)$, equalled the local cost of labour, $w_t(z)$, expressed relative to the price of the firm's product, $P_t(z)$. That is, firms would satisfy the condition, $MPL_t(z) = w_t(z)/P_t(z)$. The value of a worker's marginal product is therefore $[P_t(z)/P_t] \cdot MPL_t(z) = w_t(z)/P_t$. Thus, by responding to $w_t(z)/P_t$, labour suppliers ultimately react to the term, $[P_t(z)/P_t] \cdot MPL_t(z)$, the term that we used in the text. Because the answer is the same, we again simplify by not introducing firms or separate labour markets.
3. The higher relative price, $P_t(z)/P_t$, increases wealth for sellers in market z but reduces wealth for buyers. Because the changes in relative prices are temporary, the wealth effects will be small. We neglect these wealth effects in order to focus on the main points.

4. The main results still go through if we assume, more realistically, that producers must pay the local price, $P_t(z)$, for some of their purchases.
5. The basic idea of rational expectations comes from John Muth (1961). For a discussion of applications to macroeconomics, see Robert Lucas (1976).
6. We assume that people in all commodity markets form the same expectation, r_t^e. These expectations would actually tend to diverge because people in different markets (who observe different local prices) would have different inflationary expectation, π_t^e. The basic results would not change, however, if we added this complication.
7. Figure 20.5 depicts the situation for an average market, that is, a market that did not experience unusual changes to local demand or supply. In a market that experienced a positive shock to local excess demand (as in Figure 20.2), the perceived relative price would be even higher than that shown at point B in Figure 20.5. Conversely, the perceived relative price would be lower in a market that experienced a negative shock to local excess demand.
8. For discussions of this result, see Thomas Sargent and Neil Wallace (1975) and Ben McCallum (1979).

9. See Roger Kormendi and Phillip Meguire (1984) and C.L.F. Attfield and N.W. Duck (1983).

10. For discussions of these types of adverse consequences of monetary uncertainty, see Friedrich Hayek (1945) and Henry Simons (1948).

11. We can also explain in this way the procyclical behaviour of consumption. If only monetary shocks occur, then it is hard to explain why consumption and work effort move cyclically in the same direction.

The Keynesian Theory of Business Fluctuations

The Keynesian theory was developed to understand the tendency of private enterprise economies to experience fluctuations in aggregate business activity. More specifically, Keynes's (1935) analysis sought to explain and suggest policy remedies for the prolonged depressions that occurred in the United States during the 1930s and in the United Kingdom during the 1920s and 1930s.

The Keynesian theory focuses on the process by which private markets match up suppliers and demanders. Notably, the theory assumes that prices on some markets do not adjust perfectly to ensure continual balance between the quantities supplied and demanded. Hence, unlike our previous models, some markets do not always clear. (The imbalance between supply and demand is often referred to as 'disequilibrium', but we shall avoid that ambiguous term.) Because of the absence of general market clearing, output and employment typically end up below the efficient amounts. Although everyone could be made better off by an expansion of economic activity, the private market sometimes fails to generate this higher level of activity.

Keynesian models assume that there are constraints on the flexibility of some prices: the nominal wage rate or the nominal price of commodities responds only sluggishly to changes in market conditions. In extreme cases, the wage rate or price level is rigid – or at least fully determined from the past. Then current market forces have no influence on these prices. But economists' willingness to accept this type of assumption as reasonable has diminished with the advent of high and variable inflation in developed countries. We shall therefore also consider the possibilities for introducing some flexibility of prices into the Keynesian model.

A Simple Keynesian Model

Keynes's analysis and some subsequent treatments[1] focused on 'sticky' nominal wage rates and the resultant lack of balance between labour supply and demand. Prices for commodities were sometimes assumed to be perfectly flexible (leading to the so-called **complete Keynesian model**) but were more often treated also as sticky. In our framework, we can generate the basic Keynesian results without explicitly considering a separate labour market. Here, we treat as sticky the nominal price, P_t, for goods and services exchanged on the commodity market. (We return now to the case of an economy-wide market for goods and also assume a closed economy.) We should stress that the neglect of the labour market is purely a simplification. The same sorts of conclusions emerge if we choose instead to examine this market and postulate a sticky nominal wage rate.

Some early analyses assumed that prices were rigid. This assumption turns out to be unnecessary because the Keynesian framework can accommodate non-zero inflation rates. The crucial feature is not completely fixed prices but rather the failure of prices to clear all markets instantly. It is convenient, however, to begin with a model in which the price level is fixed. After we develop this model, we can introduce a non-zero inflation rate.

Start by writing down the standard conditions for general market clearing. For the commodity market, the condition for period t is

$$Y^s(r_t, G_t, \ldots) = C_d(r_t, G_t, \ldots) + I^d(r_t, \ldots) + G_t$$
$$(+)(+) \qquad (-)(-) \qquad (-) \qquad (21.1)$$

Recall that a higher quantity of government purchases, G_t, means a larger amount of goods supplied (because public services are productive) but a smaller amount of consumer goods demanded. We assume lump-sum taxes, although an income tax could also be considered. Equation (21.1) takes as given the stock of capital, K_{t-1}, and the characteristics of the production function.

Next we have the condition that money be willingly held:

$$M_t = P_t \cdot \Phi(Y_t, r_t, \ldots) \qquad (21.2)$$
$$(+)(-)$$

where M_t is the nominal quantity of money for period t. As usual, the aggregate real demand for money depends positively on output, Y_t, and negatively on the interest rate, r_t. We enter the real interest rate, r_t, because with a fixed price level – and hence, zero inflation – the nominal interest rate equals the real rate.

Equations (21.1) and (21.2) determine the general-market-clearing values of the interest rate, r_t^*, and the price level, P_t^*. We denote the associated general-market-clearing level of output by Y_t^*.

The departure for Keynesian analysis is that the fixed price level, P_t, differs from the general-market-clearing value, P_t^*. The standard Keynesian results emerge when the price level is excessive; that is, $P_t > P_t^*$. In this situation it will generally be impossible for the economy to attain full market clearing, as specified in equations (21.1) and (21.2). Consequently, we have to search for some concept other than supply equals demand to determine the interest rate and the level of output.

Think of starting from a position of general market clearing and then arbitrarily raising the price level above its market-clearing value. In this case, equation (21.2) can no longer hold at the general-market-clearing values of output, Y_t^*, and the interest rate, r_t^*. The excessive price level means that the quantity of money, M_t, would fall short of the aggregate quantity demanded. We can think of individuals as attempting to replenish their money balances, partly by selling bonds and partly by reducing consumer demand and leisure. The first channel suggests upward pressure on the interest rate. Since a higher interest rate raises Y_t^s and lowers $C_t^d + I_t^d$, an excess supply of commodities results. The second channel – whereby consumer demand and leisure decline – reinforces this outcome. Thus, the excessive price level leads to an excess supply of goods.

The Rationing of Sales

How does the commodity market operate under conditions of excess supply? That is, what happens when – at the going price P_t – the total of offers to sell goods exceeds the overall willingness to buy? Normally, we expect a decline in the price level, but that mechanism is ruled out by assumption. We therefore have to study the commodity market when excess supply prevails but the price level cannot fall.

Some type of rationing rule must allocate sales when there is an imbalance between the quantities supplied and demanded. The usual mechanism assumes two properties. First, no supplier or demander can be forced to sell or buy more than he or she desires, a condition that follows from the principle of *voluntary exchange*. Second, trade proceeds as long as some seller and some buyer are both made better off, that is, the market ensures the execution of all mutually advantageous exchanges, given that the fixed price P_t applies to all trades. The first condition means that the total quantity of goods sold, Y_t, cannot exceed the smaller of aggregate supply and demand; otherwise, some involuntary sales or purchases would occur. The second condition guarantees that the amount sold is at least as great as the minimum of aggregate supply and demand; if not, some mutually advantageous trades at price P_t would be missed. Thus, the combination of the two properties ensures that output is determined by the **short side** of the market – that is, by the condition

$$Y_t = \text{MIN.}(Y_t^s, Y_t^d) \tag{21.3}$$

where MIN. denotes the minimum of the variables in the parentheses.

Note that we deal here with the rationing of sales on the commodity market. In a more general Keynesian framework, we would include also the rationing of jobs – that is, sales of labour services – on a separate labour market. The people who seek jobs but cannot find them are considered to be **involuntarily unemployed**.

Under conditions of excess supply – $Y_t^s > Y_t^d$ – output is determined by aggregate demand, Y_t^d, which defines the short side of the commodity market. The typical demander therefore experiences no difficulty in finding goods to purchase from the eager suppliers. However, the representative supplier faces an insufficiency of buyers for the products that he or she offers for sale at the price P_t.[2] Thus, we have to reconsider households' decisions in the presence of this constraint. These modifications play an essential role in Keynesian analysis.

In the standard model of a competitive market, individual sellers and buyers are able to transact any amount desired at the going price. But this condition cannot hold for all suppliers when an excess supply of goods prevails. Here, we want to specify the constraint that confronts an individual supplier of goods. We assume that the total quantity of real sales available, Y_t, is somehow apportioned by a nonprice mechanism among the sellers, who offer the larger quantity, Y_t^s. In other words, some kind of rationing process assigns each producer the quantity of real sales, y_t. Notice that we consider a ration on sales rather than on purchases. A ration on purchases would arise if goods were in excess demand.

We assume that each producer regards his or her real sales limit, y_t, as a given, in the same way that they take as given the price level, P_t, and the

interest rate, r_t. We do not allow an individual to take any actions that would influence the size of the ration. That is, we exclude such possibilities as greater search for buyers, black-market activities that could involve price cutting, overstatement of the true sales offers to secure a larger individual ration,[3] and so on. Basically, the allowance for these features would amount to relaxing the constraint of the fixed price, P_t.

The Choice of Work Effort

The production function implies

$$y_t = f(k_{t-1}, \ell_t, G_t) \tag{21.4}$$
$$(+) \quad (+)(+)$$

We assume that the ration is an effective constraint on sales, that is, $y_t < y_t^s$ applies for the typical producer.[4] The level of output, y_t, is then a given to the producer rather than something that he or she can choose.

Given the quantity of capital, k_{t-1}, and the level of government purchases, G_t, the amount of work, ℓ_t, is the minimum amount necessary to produce the assigned level of output, y_t. The production function from equation (21.4) therefore determines ℓ_t for given values of y_t, k_{t-1}, and G_t. We can write the quantity of work as the function

$$\ell_t = \ell(y_t, k_{t-1}, G_t) \tag{21.5}$$
$$(+)(-) \quad (-)$$

For given values of the other inputs, ℓ_t varies directly with y_t, as shown by the graph of the production function in Figure 21.1. For any value of y_t on the vertical axis, we can read off ℓ_t on the horizontal. Note that more output means more labour input. With the labour market included, more work also means less involuntary unemployment. Increases in either of the other inputs, k_{t-1} and G_t, mean that less work is needed to produce a given amount of output; hence, ℓ_t declines in equation (21.5). (In Figure 21.1 we can verify these results by shifting the production function upward.)

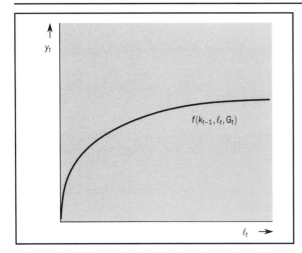

The graph of the production function shows the effect on output of more labour input, given the quantities of capital and government purchases. For a given level of output on the vertical axis the graph determines the quantity of work on the horizontal. Notice that more output means more labour input.

Figure 21.1   The determination of labour input

In the model without sales constraints, households set the level of work to equate the marginal product of labour to the value placed on an extra unit of leisure time. But an effective restraint on sales means that work effort is smaller than otherwise. Because of diminishing marginal productivity, labour marginal product now exceeds the value placed on an extra unit of leisure. Households would like to work and produce more, if only the goods could be sold at the going price. But the constraint on sales prevents the expansion of work and production. We can also say that the constraint on sales means that the economy operates inefficiently. Everyone could be made better off if work and production were higher – as they would be if all markets cleared. But in the Keynesian model, where the commodity market (and the labour market) do not clear, these efficient adjustments are assumed not to occur.

The Keynesian Consumption Function

The restraint on sales means that households receive less real income than otherwise. In our model, where the households are also the producers, each household's current real receipts from the commodity market equal the real sales ration, y_t. If prospective real sales equal the current value, then variations in y_t have a one-to-one effect on future real incomes. The effect of y_t on consumption demand would then be roughly one-to-one. If the constraint on sales is temporary, then the effect of y_t on consumption demand would be smaller.

In the more realistic case in which workers are employed by firms, an imposed limit on sales implies that firms have lower employment than otherwise. Thus, movements in households' income reflect partly changes in wage income and partly changes in profit income (since some households own the businesses). The shifts in income lead to adjustments in consumption demand, as in the simpler model in which firms and households are not distinguished.

The main point is that an increase in current output, y_t, has a positive effect on consumer demand. Hence, the consumption function, now denoted by $\hat{c}^d$, takes the form

$$\hat{c}_t^d = \hat{c}^d(y_t, \ r_t, \ldots) \tag{21.6}$$
$$(+)(-)$$

Notice that the interest rate, r_t, still has a negative intertemporal-substitution effect on current consumer demand.

The expression in equation (21.6) is called the **Keynesian consumption function**. The distinctive feature of this function is the presence of the quantity of real sales or real income, y_t. In our previous analysis, households chose consumption by considering wealth effects, the real interest rate, the possibilities for substituting between consumption and leisure, and the nature of their preferences. But now there is a separate effect from the given level of real sales in the commodity market. Anything that raises the quantity of real sales, and hence real income, y_t, spills over to increase consumption demand.

Another argument that economists sometimes use to derive the Keynesian consumption function concerns the credit market. Up to now we have assumed that this market allows households to borrow or lend any amount that they desire at the going interest rate, r_t. An alternative view is that households cannot borrow readily unless they have good collateral, such as a house, car, or business, to secure the loan. In particular, because of the costs of collection and customer evaluation, households cannot usually borrow based solely on a promise to repay out of future labour income. Economists describe as **liquidity constrained** a person who would like to borrow at the going interest rate to raise current consumption but cannot obtain a loan (at a 'reasonable' interest rate). People in this situation would alter their consumption demand, c_t^d, virtually one-to-one in response to changes in their current income, y_t. Therefore, this viewpoint can also explain why the variable y_t appears on the right side of equation (21.6) for some consumers. We shall try to evaluate the importance of liquidity constraints later on.

Determination of Output in the Keynesian Model

Putting together the results thus far, we can write the level of aggregate demand in the form

$$Y_t^d = \hat{C}^d(Y_t, r_t, \ldots) + I^d(r_t, \ldots) + G_t$$
$$(+)(-) \qquad (-)$$

where $\hat{C}^d$ is an aggregate version of the Keynesian consumption function and I^d is the investment demand function, which we have studied previously. Recall that the price level exceeds its general-market-clearing value – $P_t > P_t^*$ – and, hence, goods are in excess supply. Output is therefore demand determined, as follows:

$$Y_t = Y_t^d = \hat{C}^d(Y_t, r_t, \ldots) + I^d(r_t, \ldots) + G_t$$
$$(+)(-) \qquad (-) \qquad (21.7)$$

Equation (21.7) is the key relation in the Keynesian model. It says that output, Y_t, equals aggregate demand, Y_t^d. But the tricky aspect is that the consumption part of aggregate demand is itself a function of output. Thus, equation (21.7) says that the level of output (and hence, income),

Y_t, determines a level of demand, Y_t^d, which is, in turn, equal to output.

An important element in the determination of output is the responsiveness of aggregate consumer demand to variations in output, that is, the aggregate marginal propensity to consume out of changes in current real income, Y_t. Typically, this marginal propensity is between zero and one, with the value approximating one when people view a change in output as permanent. We denote the marginal propensity to consume by v (the Greek letter *nu*).

Consider an extreme version of the Keynesian model in which the interest rate, r_t, as well as the price level, P_t, is fixed. Later on, we shall allow r_t to be flexible. Figure 21.2, which is called the **Keynesian-cross diagram**, shows how equation (21.7) determines the level of output for a given r_t. First, the line labelled Y_t^d indicates the dependence of aggregate demand on the level of output, Y_t. Note that I_t^d and G_t in equation (21.7) do not depend on Y_t. The slope of the Y_t^d line therefore reflects only the positive effect of Y_t on C_t^d. The

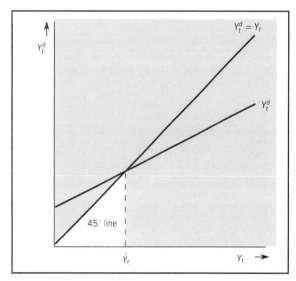

The line denoted Y_t^d shows the response of aggregate demand to changes in output Y_t. But output equals demand only along the 45-degree line. Therefore, we determine the level of output at the intersection of the curves as the value $\hat{Y}_t$.

Figure 21.2 Determination of output via the Keynesian cross diagram

slope of the line equals the marginal propensity to consume, v, which is positive but less than one. (We show Y_t^d as a straight line only for convenience.)

The 45-degree line in Figure 21.2 indicates positions for which output, Y_t, equals the level of demand, Y_t^d. Equation (21.7) therefore holds when the aggregate demand curve intersects the 45-degree line. We denote the level of output at this intersection by $\hat{Y}_t$. The Keynesian model with a given interest rate predicts that the economy's output will be this quantity $\hat{Y}_t$.

The Multiplier

To illustrate the determination of output, consider an increase in aggregate demand, Y_t^d. This increase could apply to either consumption demand or investment demand. The Keynesian model usually focuses, however, on shifts to investment demand that reflect changing beliefs about the marginal product of capital.[5]

The increase in aggregate demand leads to an increase in output, Y_t. (Recall that with excess supply of goods, output is demand determined.) The increase in output means more real income and hence a *further* increase in aggregate demand. This change leads to another rise in output, and thereby to more demand, and so on. Because each successive increase in output is smaller than the one before, the process does not lead to an infinite expansion of output. Rather, the ultimate rise in output is a finite multiple of the initial expansion of demand. To calculate the exact change, we can use the Keynesian-cross diagram.

In Figure 21.3, the aggregate demand curve is initially the one labelled Y_t^d. The intersection with the 45-degree line determines the level of output, $\hat{Y}_t$. Then an **autonomous increase in demand** of size A shifts the aggregate demand curve upward to the one labelled $Y_t^{d\prime}$ (By autonomous, we mean that the change comes from outside of the model rather than being explained by the theory.) The level of output, $\hat{Y}_t'$, corresponds accordingly to the new intersection with the 45-degree line.

The geometry of the Keynesian-cross diagram in Figure 21.3 reveals the relation between the initial and final levels of output, $\hat{Y}_t$ and $\hat{Y}_t'$. Let $\Delta\hat{Y}$ be the change in output, $\hat{Y}_t' - \hat{Y}_t$, and observe

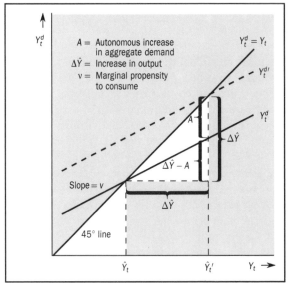

Aggregate demand increases by the amount A. The figure shows that the response of output, $\Delta\hat{Y}$, exceeds the initial expansion of demand. The geometry implies that $(\Delta\hat{Y} - A)/\Delta\hat{Y} = v$, so that $\Delta\hat{Y} = A/(1 - v)$. The term $1/(1 - v)$ is the multiplier.

Figure 21.3   The multiplier

the smaller right-angle triangle with base $\Delta\hat{Y}$. The slope of the line marked with an arrow equals the marginal propensity to consume, v. Since the vertical side of the triangle is of length $\Delta\hat{Y} - A$, the slope satisfies the relation

$$v = (\Delta\hat{Y} - A)/\Delta\hat{Y}$$

It follows that the change in output is given by

$$\Delta\hat{Y} = A/(1 - v) \qquad (21.8)$$

Thus, output changes by a multiple of the autonomous shift in demand, A. The **multiplier** is the term $1/(1 - v)$, which is positive and greater than one. Note that the higher is the marginal propensity to consume, v, the larger is the multiplier. Also, for the analysis to make sense – that is, for the ultimate expansion of output to remain finite – the marginal propensity to consume must be less than one, as we have assumed.

We can better understand the source of the multiplier by deriving equation (21.8) in an alternative manner. The autonomous increase in demand leads initially to an increase in output by the amount A. Then the rise in real income by the amount A leads to an increase in aggregate demand by the quantity vA. The additional increase in output of size vA causes demand to rise further by the amount vvA. In other words, there is a continuing sequence in which each round's increase in output is the amount v multiplied by the previous round's increase. It follows that the full increase in output comes from summing up all the rounds:[6]

$$\Delta \hat{Y} = A + vA + v^2 A + \ldots$$
$$= A(1 + v + v^2 + \ldots)$$
$$= A/(1 - v) \qquad (21.9)$$

This result coincides with the one shown in equation (21.8). We should stress two points about the derivation of the change in output, $\Delta \hat{Y}$. First, we assume that excess supply of goods prevails throughout and, hence, that producers never hesitate to meet extra demand with more output. Second, the discussion mentions a sequence of rounds only for the purpose of exposition.

In the basic model, we do not allow any time to elapse while households adjust demand or production. An autonomous increase in demand therefore leads immediately to the full multiplicative response of output, as shown in equation (21.9). More generally, we could include some dynamics, whereby output adjusts gradually toward the value dictated by the Keynesian-cross diagram in Figure 21.3.

Before going on, let's work out a third way to look at the multiplier. We can rewrite the condition for determining output from equation (21.7) as

$$Y_t - \hat{C}^d(Y_t, r_t, \ldots) = I^d(r_t, \ldots) + G_t \qquad (21.10)$$
$$(+)(-) \qquad\qquad (-)$$

The left side is the sum of desired private saving plus taxes. Equation (21.10) says that the level of output is determined so that desired private saving plus taxes equals investment demand plus

government purchases. (Equivalently, if we moved G_t to the left side of equation (21.10), then the equality would be between desired national saving and investment demand.)

Suppose that an autonomous increase in demand means that the right side of equation (21.10) rises by the amount A. (Equivalently, part of this change could show up as an increase in consumer demand and, hence, as a decrease in the left side of the equation.) If taxes do not change, then output must rise enough to generate a matching expansion of desired saving on the left side of the equation. Since the marginal propensity to consume is v, the marginal propensity to save is $1 - v$. The change in saving is therefore $(1 - v)\Delta \hat{Y}$. Since this extra saving, $(1 - v)\Delta \hat{Y}$, must balance the autonomous increase in demand, A, it follows that $\Delta \hat{Y} = A/(1 - v)$. This answer for the change in output coincides with those found in equations (21.8) and (21.9).

The multiplier is a distinctive feature of the Keynesian model and would not arise under conditions of general market clearing. To see this, assume an autonomous increase in aggregate demand, Y_t^d, with no shift in aggregate supply, Y_t^s. In a market-clearing setting, as in Chapter 5, we know that the real interest rate, r_t, rises to clear the commodity market. Since the increase in r_t reduces Y_t^d, output must rise by less than the autonomous increase in demand. (Remember that consumer demand does not depend directly on output in the market-clearing model.) Thus, the market-clearing model features a *dampener* rather than a multiplier.

The Determination of Employment

For a given level of output, Y_t, the amount of work, L_t, is the minimum amount necessary to produce this quantity of goods. That is, using an aggregate version of equation (21.5):

$$L_t = L(Y_t, K_{t-1}, G_t) \qquad (21.11)$$

For given values of the capital stock and government purchases and for a given form of the production function, anything that leads to a change in output leads to a change of the same sign for employment. The previous discussion showed that an autonomous increase in aggregate demand led to a multiplicative expansion of output. Now we find that an increase in employment accompanies the rise in output. Employment is therefore procyclical in this example.

Recall that the analysis applies in the range in which goods are in excess supply. Since the marginal product of labour exceeds the value attached to leisure time, people eagerly work more whenever it becomes feasible to sell more goods. If we introduced a separate labour market with a sticky nominal wage, then we would find that suppliers of labour – who face rationing of jobs – readily accept more work whenever the employers raise their demands. In this setting, the amount of involuntary unemployment corresponds to the gap between the aggregate supply of labour, L_t^s, and the quantity of work. Thus, increases in employment show up as decreases in involuntary unemployment. Unemployment is therefore countercyclical.

The Keynesian Investment Function

Because of the multiplier, small disturbances to the aggregate demand for goods can be magnified into sizable fluctuations in aggregate output. For example, a small cutback in investment demand could generate a recession in which real GNP and consumption fell significantly below trend. In the data, however, typical recessions feature large shortfalls in investment with relatively small contractions in consumer expenditures on non-durables and services. Recessions do not usually involve small reductions of investment that are accompanied by major declines in consumption. To explain these aspects of the data, we have to modify the Keynesian model to include a direct effect of economic conditions on investment demand.

Recall that, with excess supply of goods, producers reduce their inputs of labour services. Thereby the marginal product of labour exceeds the value of leisure time. Similar reasoning suggests that producers would cut back on their inputs of capital services. That is, when sales are rationed, producers reduce their desired stocks of capital. Thereby the marginal product of capital (less the depreciation rate) exceeds the real interest rate. The main point is that a reduction in the available real sales leads to a smaller desired stock of capital and hence to less investment demand.

We can write the **Keynesian investment function** as

$$i_t^d = \hat{i}^d(y_t, \ r_t, \ldots) \tag{21.12}$$
$$(+)(-)$$

The Keynesian investment function includes the level of output, y_t, and thereby looks similar to the Keynesian consumption function in equation

---

Box 21.1 The Investment Accelerator

The Keynesian investment function is related to the **investment accelerator**, a concept that was discussed frequently in the early literature on business cycles. The main difference is that the accelerator relates investment demand to the change in output, whereas the investment demand function in equation (21.12) involves the level of output or, more precisely, the prospective amount of output, y_{t+1}. Recall that the level of the capital stock, k_{t-1}, appears with a negative sign among the omitted terms of the investment demand function in equation (21.12). If we allowed for changes over time in the quantity of capital, then we could generate a dynamic relation for investment. This relation turns out to resemble the accelerator. For an analysis of a model with an accelerator and a multiplier, see Paul Samuelson (1939).

(21.6). Actually, what matters for desired capital and therefore for investment demand is the prospective quantity of real sales and output, y_{t+1}. A cutback in current output, y_t, reduces investment demand, i_t^d, to the extent that prospective output, y_{t+1}, also declines.

The formal analysis of the determination of output and employment does not change when we introduce the Keynesian investment function. The only difference is that we have to redefine the parameter v to be the **marginal propensity to spend**, that is, the total effect of a change in current output, y_t, on the demand for goods, y. This total effect is the sum of the marginal propensity to consume and the **marginal propensity to invest**. The latter term is the impact of a change in output, y_t, on investment demand in equation (21.12). For the analysis to go through, the marginal propensity to spend, v, must be less than one.

Recall that the multiplier in equation (21.8) is the expression $1/(1 - v)$. The term $1 - v$ is now one minus the marginal propensity to spend, rather than the marginal propensity to save. If the marginal propensity to spend, v, is less than one, then the term $1 - v$ is positive.

The new results concern the composition of output during business fluctuations. The Keynesian investment function implies that an autonomous contraction of demand can lead to a major decline of investment. At least this response follows if the contraction lasts long enough for prospective output, y_{t+1}, to decline.

If a recession does not persist long enough to have a major effect on the present value of income, then the cutback in current output, y_t, has only a minor impact on consumer demand, c_t^d. Most of the shortfall in output could then show up as less investment rather than less consumption. In other words, the Keynesian model can now be consistent with this important feature of recessions in the real world.

We mentioned before that liquidity constraints, whereby some people cannot borrow readily at the going interest rate, could be a basis for the Keynesian consumption function. But if such constraints were important, then we would expect recessions to exhibit major shortfalls in consumer expenditures on nondurables and services. In fact, the data show relatively little fluctuation in these categories of spending. The components that decline proportionately more during recessions are – aside from business investment – the purchases of consumer durables, including residential housing, automobiles, and appliances. These goods are relatively easy to buy on credit because durables serve as good collateral for loans. This observation therefore suggests that liquidity constraints do not play a key role in business fluctuations.

IS/LM Analysis and the Role of the Interest Rate

Our previous analysis, which includes the multiplier, shows how to determine the level of output for a given interest rate. As long as there is excess supply of goods, the condition for determining output is, repeating equation (21.7),

$$Y_t = Y_t^d = \hat{C}^d(Y_t, r_t, \dots) + I^d(r_t, \dots) + G_t$$
$$\quad (+)(-) \qquad (-) \qquad (21.13)$$

Our assumption to this point that the interest rate, r_t, is a given means that the analysis is seriously incomplete. We now want to go further to consider the determination of r_t in the Keynesian model. To carry out this analysis, we have to reintroduce the condition that all money be willingly held. This condition is, repeating equation (21.2),

$$M_t = P_t \cdot \Phi(Y_t, r_t, \dots) \qquad (21.14)$$
$$\quad (+)(-)$$

Given that the price level, P_t, is fixed by assumption, equations (21.13) and (21.14) determine the interest rate and the level of output. (Recall that, with no inflation, the real and nominal interest rates coincide.) Notice that equation (21.13) determines Y_t for a given value of r_t. A change in r_t would affect aggregate demand, Y_t^d, and thereby the level of output. What we want to do now is figure out the value of Y_t that corresponds to each value of r_t. That is, we want to trace out the combinations of r_t and Y_t that are consistent with the equality between output and aggregate demand, as specified in equation (21.13).

An increase in the interest rate lowers aggregate demand on the right side of equation (21.13). As with any decline in demand, the level of output falls. Accordingly, if we map out the combinations of r_t and Y_t that satisfy equation (21.13), then we determine a downward-sloping relationship. Following standard notation, we label as **IS** the curve in Figure 21.4 that shows this relation.[7] Along the IS curve, the interest rate and the level of output are consistent with the equality between output and aggregate demand.

Consider now the condition that money be willingly held, as specified in equation (21.14). Given the quantity of money, M_t, and the price level, P_t, this condition defines another array of combinations for the interest rate and output. We want to trace out the pairs of r_t and Y_t that are consistent with this condition. Since a higher value of Y_t raises the demand for money on the

right side of equation (21.14), r_t must rise to lower the demand for money back to the given level, M_t. Hence, when we map out the combinations of r_t and Y_t that satisfy equation (21.14), we determine an upward-sloping relationship. The curve designated **LM** in Figure 21.4 shows this relation.[8] Along the LM curve, the interest rate and the level of output are consistent with the condition that all money be willingly held.

The intersection of the IS and LM curves in Figure 21.4 picks out the combination of output and the interest rate – labelled $\hat{Y}_t$ and $\hat{r}_t$ – that satisfies the two necessary conditions: output equals aggregate demand, and all money is willingly held. As long as the price level is fixed, the Keynesian model predicts that the level of output will be the amount $\hat{Y}_t$ and the interest rate will be the value $\hat{r}_t$. Hence, we can use the IS/LM apparatus to analyze the determination of output and the interest rate in the Keynesian model. Because of the popularity of the Keynesian model, the IS/LM diagram has been the principal analytical tool for many economists in the last four decades.

Variations in Output and the Interest Rate

To bring out the role of the interest rate, consider again an autonomous increase in aggregate demand. If the interest rate did not change, then output would rise multiplicatively. However, the expansion of output increases the demand for money above the given quantity M_t. Households' attempts to move out of bonds and into money imply that the interest rate must increase to restore balance on the credit market. This increase in the interest rate reduces the demand for money, but it also decreases the aggregate demand for goods. Hence, the overall effect on output is less than the full multiplicative amount. In fact, the increase in output may fall short of the autonomous expansion of demand. In other words, the increase in the interest rate may make the multiplier be less than one in the Keynesian model (as it is for sure in the market-clearing model).

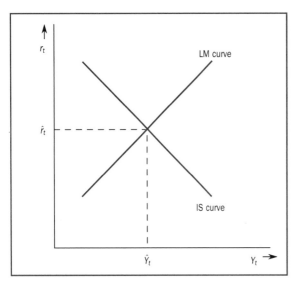

The IS curve shows the combinations of Y_t and r_t that satisfy the condition, $Y_t = Y_t^d$. The LM curve shows the combinations that induce people to hold all the existing money, M_t. Thus, the levels of output and the interest rate correspond to the intersection of the two curves.

Figure 21.4   Use of IS/LM curves to determine output and the interest rate

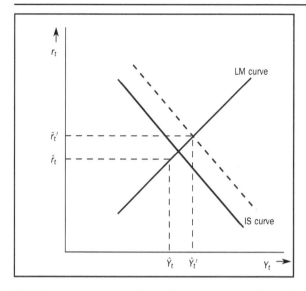

The boost to aggregate demand appears as a rightward shift in the IS curve. Since the LM curve does not shift, in this example, the figure shows that output and the interest rate rise.

Figure 21.5 Use of IS/LM curves to determine output and the interest rate

Figure 21.5 uses the IS/LM apparatus to show the results. We reproduce the solid lines from Figure 21.4. The boost to aggregate demand appears as a rightward shift in the IS curve, that is, output increases for a given value of the interest rate. The size of this shift is the change in aggregate demand, A, times the multiplier, $1/(1 - v)$. Since the LM curve does not shift in this example, the figure shows that output and the interest rate rise. The increase in output is, however, less than the full multiplier amount, which equals the rightward shift of the IS curve.

For a given amount of government purchases, it is clear that total private spending for consumption and investment increases. But because of the rise in the interest rate, it is possible that one of these components would decline. Suppose, for example, that the autonomous disturbance is an increase in investment demand. The rise in output stimulates consumer demand, but the increase in the interest rate depresses this demand. Thus, consumption may fall along with the expansion of output and investment. Similarly, if the autonomous change applies to consumer demand, then investment may decline.

Fiscal Policy in the Keynesian Model

The government can influence aggregate demand directly by changing the level of its purchases, G_t. Suppose that the government raises purchases by one unit and finances this extra spending with lump-sum taxes. Consider the case in which the rise in purchases is temporary, so that wealth effects are small. As in the analysis from Chapter 15, consumer demand falls by a fraction of the increase in purchases.[9] Thus, aggregate demand expands, but by less than one unit. In terms of the IS/LM diagram, the disturbance can again be represented by Figure 21.5.[10] Now the rightward shift of the IS curve equals some fraction of the increase in government purchases, times the multiplier, $1/(1 - v)$. Notice that output and the interest rate increase. But the increase in output is again less than the full multiplier amount.

The effects of more government purchases on private spending are uncertain. The expansion of output stimulates private demands, but the higher interest rate reduces these demands. In addition, there is the direct negative effect of government purchases on consumer spending.

Another type of fiscal policy is a reduction in taxes, financed by more issue of government bonds. Economists often argue that this policy is expansionary in the Keynesian model. But to get this answer, we have to assume that deficit-financed tax cuts make people feel wealthier. Then the stimulus to consumer demand shifts the IS curve rightward, as shown in Figure 21.5. Given this shift, there would again be increases in output and the interest rate.

Because of the higher future taxes, it can still be true (as in Chapter 17) that a deficit-financed tax cut has no aggregate wealth effect on consumer demand. Since the IS curve does not shift, output and the interest rate would not change. In other words, the Ricardian theorem – which states that taxes and deficits are equivalent – can remain valid within the Keynesian model.

If households treat a tax cut as a signal of more wealth, then the Keynesian model predicts an expansion of output. Because production and employment are constrained initially by lack of demand, the typical household ends up better off in this situation. Thus, households actually do end up being wealthier. But this result has nothing to do with tax cuts as such. In the Keynesian model, *anything* that makes people feel wealthier generates the increases in output and employment that actually make them wealthier. (Think about what would happen in this model if we assumed that households felt poorer when they saw a tax cut.)

Changes in the Price Level

Recall that the starting point for the Keynesian model was the excessive price level, $P_t > P_t^*$. If the price level declines toward its general-market-clearing value, P_t^*, then the basic constraint on the economy relaxes. We anticipate therefore that the level of output, $\hat{Y}_t$, would rise toward its general-market-clearing value, Y_t^*. To see how this works, we can use the IS/LM diagram.

Recall from equation (21.14) that the LM curve shows the combinations of r_t and Y_t that equate the amount of money demanded to the given quantity of money, M_t. A decline in the price level lowers the nominal demand for money, $M_t^d = P_t \cdot \Phi(r_t, Y_t, \ldots)$. To restore equality with the given supply of money, we need changes in r_t or Y_t that raise the real demand for money, $\Phi(r_t, Y_t, \ldots)$. Hence, the LM curve shifts rightward, as shown in Figure 21.6.

Notice that the new LM curve intersects the unchanged IS curve at a lower interest rate, $(\hat{r}_t)' < \hat{r}_t$, and a higher level of output, $(\hat{Y}_t)' > \hat{Y}_t$. We can understand these changes by recalling that a lower price level reduces the nominal demand for money, $M_t^d = P_t \cdot \Phi(r_t, Y_t, \ldots)$. Households' attempts to exchange their excess money for bonds tends to depress the interest rate, a change that leads to greater aggregate demand for goods and, hence, higher output.

Consider a sequence of reductions in the price level from its initial value toward the general-market-clearing value, P_t^*. Each reduction in the

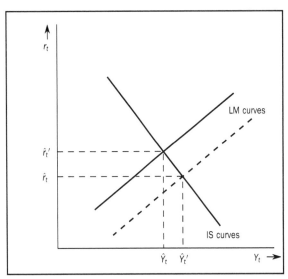

A decrease in the price level shifts the LM curve rightward. Therefore, the interest rate falls and the level of output rises.

Figure 21.6   Keynesian analysis of the effect of a decrease in the price level on output and the interest rate

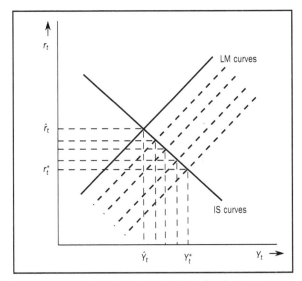

Each decrease in the price level shifts the LM curve rightward. Therefore, the interest rate falls, and the level of output rises. When the price level reaches its general market-clearing value, P_t^*, the interest rate and output attain their general market-clearing values, r_t^* and Y_t^*.

Figure 21.7   Effects of declines in the price level to the general-market-clearing value, P_t^*

price level shifts the LM curve rightward as shown in Figure 21.7. Correspondingly, the interest rate falls and the level of output rises. When the price level falls to the value P_t^*, the interest rate will have fallen to its general-market-clearing value, r_t^*, and output will have risen to its general-market-clearing value, Y_t^*.

Once the price level reaches P_t^*, further reductions in the price level would not generate more increases in output. That is because the commodity market shifts at this point to excess demand, $Y_t^d > Y_t^s$, rather than excess supply. Then the suppliers no longer produce the quantity demanded but rather produce the lesser amount, Y_t^s. Recall that the IS curve assumes that producers accommodate demand fully: $Y_t = Y_t^d$. The curve is therefore inappropriate when there is excess demand for goods.[11]

Changes in the Quantity of Money

Assume again that the price level is fixed above its general-market-clearing value, that is, $P_t > P_t^*$. Consider an increase in the quantity of money, M_t, perhaps resulting from an open-market purchase of bonds. Since P_t is fixed, equation (21.14) implies that the real amount of money demanded, $\Phi(r_t, Y_t, \ldots)$, must go up for the additional money to be willingly held. The increase in M_t therefore works just like a reduction in P_t. We can again use Figure 21.6 to analyze the effects. The rightward shift of the LM curve leads to a lower interest rate and a higher level of output.

We can interpret these results by noting that the quantity of money, M_t, rises above the amount demanded at the initial values of the interest rate, $\hat{r}_t$, and output, $\hat{Y}_t$. As before, households' efforts to exchange excess money for bonds lead to a lower interest rate and hence to higher output.

The important finding is that an increase in the quantity of money is a substitute for a reduction in the price level toward the general-market-clearing value. One way to correct for an excessive price level, $P_t > P_t^*$, is for prices to fall. But an alternative is to raise the stock of money and thereby increase the general-market-

clearing level of prices, P_t^*. Monetary expansion closes the gap between P_t and P_t^* by raising P_t^* rather than by lowering P_t.

Shifts in the Demand for Money

Notice from equation (21.14) that a reduction in the real demand for money, $\Phi(r, Y, \ldots)$, works exactly like a decrease in the price level. Both changes lead to an excess of money, M_t, over the amount demanded, M_t^d. If the demand for money falls – for example, because of a financial innovation – then the LM curve shifts rightward as shown in Figure 21.6. This change leads again to a decrease in the interest rate and an expansion of output.

These results follow because the decline in the demand for money raises the general-market-clearing value of the price level, P_t^*. From this perspective, a decrease in the real demand for money works in the same way as an increase in M_t. Both changes reduce the spread between P_t and P_t^* by raising the value of P_t^*.

IS/LM Analysis and General Market Clearing

The IS/LM framework is designed to bring out the interaction between monetary phenomena (the LM curve) and real phenomena (the IS curve). In the Keynesian model, the main source of this interaction is the stickiness of the general price level (or the nominal wage rate). That is why the IS/LM apparatus was helpful when we studied various disturbances in the context of a fixed price level.

Suppose that we return to a setting of general market clearing, where the price level is flexible. Then Figure 21.7 shows how we could use the IS/LM diagram to find the general-market-clearing values of the interest rate, r_t^*, and output, Y_t^*. The apparatus is cumbersome, however, because disturbances typically imply shifts of the IS and LM curves, as well as changes in the position of the market-clearing price level, P_t^*. The model that we developed in Chapter 5 is much simpler in the context of flexible prices.

The Supply Side in the Keynesian Model

The Keynesian model – whether the simple version we have been studying or more sophisticated versions – views aggregate demand as the central determinant of output and employment. The analysis pays little attention to aggregate supply. In formal terms, the neglect of the supply side arises because the postulated excessive price level, $P_t > P_t^*$, means that excess supply of goods and services prevails. The model assumes, in other words, that productive capacity and the willingness to work do not represent effective constraints on output. Only the willingness to spend limits the extent of economic activity in this model. This perspective explains why Keynesian analyses typically pay little attention to some matters that are important in a market-clearing framework: shifts to the production function, variations in the stock of capital, effects of the tax system on the willingness to work, and so on.[12] The neglect of these elements became embarrassing with the supply shocks of the 1970s. In fact, the failure to handle supply shocks was one of the major elements that led many economists to look for alternatives to the Keynesian model.

Inflation in the Keynesian Model

Thus far, we have assumed in this chapter that the price level was fixed. This assumption is unsatisfactory, especially for present-day economies, where inflation rates are typically positive and often highly variable over time. Since the Keynesian model does not rely on market-clearing conditions to determine the price level, we need some other mechanism to replace the assumption that prices are rigid. The usual device is an *ad hoc* adjustment relationship, whereby the price level moves gradually toward its general-market-clearing value, P_t^*. Recall that the condition, $P_t > P_t^*$, corresponds to an excess supply of commodities. An adjustment of the price level toward its market-clearing value, P_t^*, means accordingly that prices decline when goods are in excess supply and rise when goods are in excess demand.

One simple form of a price-adjustment rule is

$$\pi_t = \lambda(Y_t^d - Y_t^s) \tag{21.15}$$

where λ (the Greek letter *lambda*) is positive. The higher the parameter λ, the more rapidly prices adjust to an imbalance between supply and demand. Sometimes economists regard the reaction of prices to excess demand as different from that to excess supply. Prices are thought to rise quickly in the face of excess demand but to fall sluggishly when there is excess supply. This asymmetry would support the Keynesian focus on cases in which the price level exceeds its market-clearing value. But the reason for this asymmetry in the price-adjustment relation has not been explained.

As it stands, the price-adjustment formula in equation (21.15) has some problems. First, inflation is non-zero only if the commodity market does not clear, that is, if $Y_t^d \neq Y_t^s$. But the theory should allow inflation and cleared markets to coexist. Second, as a related matter, inflation is negative in the Keynesian case in which goods are in excess supply. Thus, we cannot use equation (21.15) to incorporate positive inflation into the Keynesian analysis.

Recall that equation (21.15) implies that the price level, P_t, moves toward the general-market-clearing price, P_t^*. But monetary growth or some other factors can lead to continuing changes in P_t^*. Intuitively, P_t would respond to the gap between P_t and P_t^*, a gap that reflects the excess supply of goods, and to the change over time in P_t^*. Call this last element π_t^* – that is, π_t^* is the expected rate of change of P_t^*. Using this concept, we might modify equation (21.15) to the form

$$\pi_t = \lambda(Y_t^d - Y_t^s) + \pi_t^* \tag{21.16}$$

Equation (21.16) says that actual inflation, π_t, exceeds the anticipated rate of change of the market-clearing price, π_t^*, when there is excess demand, and vice versa for excess supply. Thus, the actual price level, P_t, tends to approach the target, P_t^*, even when the target moves over time.

Note that equation (21.16) is consistent with non-zero inflation when the commodity market clears. A high rate of anticipated monetary growth implies, for example, high values for π_t^* and π_t. If π_t^* is positive, then π_t can be positive even when goods are in excess supply. Hence, positive inflation can appear in the Keynesian model.

We now have the following general description of a recession. First, there is some adverse shock to aggregate demand, perhaps stemming from an autonomous decline in firms' desires to invest. Then output, employment, and investment (and probably consumption) fall below their general-market-clearing values, and the unemployment rate increases. The shortfalls in quantities persist because prices (and wages) do not adjust downward immediately to reestablish general market clearing. That is, although prices are no longer

rigid, they are still sticky. But equation (21.16) says that the inflation rate, π_t, falls below the rate of change of the market-clearing price, π_t^*, and P_t falls relative to P_t^*. The resulting increases in real money balances[13] lead to decreases in interest rates, and hence to expansions of aggregate demand and output. In this way, the economy tends to return gradually to a position of general market clearing.

The role for active policy in the Keynesian model appears as a substitute for the economy's automatic, but sluggish, reaction through price adjustment. Expansions in the growth rate of money (monetary policy) or increases in government purchases (fiscal policy) can spur aggregate demand. Thereby, the model says that the recovery from a recession can be quickened.

Box 21.2 The Aggregate Supply–Aggregate Demand Model

Two problems with the usual Keynesian model are, first, it does not allow for effects on output from shifts in aggregate supply, and second, it determines the price level only by means of an *ad hoc* price-adjustment relation, such as equation (21.16). The **aggregate supply–aggregate demand (AS–AD)** model was developed in recent years as an attempt to resolve these difficulties. Although the AS–AD model has substantial shortcomings, we discuss it here because it has become popular in many textbooks.

We have already learned from Figure 21.6 that a reduction in the general price level, P_t, leads in the Keynesian model to an increase in output, Y_t. This quantity equals the amount demanded, Y_t^d. We can use this result to determine the possible combinations of P_t and $Y_t = Y_t^d$ that can prevail. The curve labelled AD (for aggregate demand[14]) in Figure 21.8 shows these combinations. As P_t declines toward its market-clearing value, P^*, the level of output rises toward its market-clearing value, Y^*.[15]

The upward-sloping curve labelled AS (for aggregate supply) in Figure 21.8 reflects the supply behaviour that we discussed in Chapter 20. Suppose that people have a given expectation, P_t^e, of the price level for period t. If P_t rises for

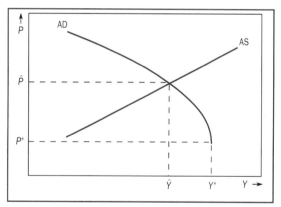

Figure 21.8 The aggregate supply–aggregate demand model

given P_t^e, then producers are motivated to raise the quantity of goods supplied, Y_t^s. Similarly, if we introduced a separate labour market and interpreted P_t as the nominal wage rate, then workers would supply more labour when the wage rate rose relative to the expected wage rate. We showed in Chapter 20 that we can get these responses of supply in a model with localized markets if people have incomplete information about the general price level. The AS curve reflects these ideas: an increase in P_t, for given P_t^e, leads to an increase in Y_t^s.

If $P_t^e = P^*$, the market-clearing value, then the quantity supplied, Y_t^s, would equal the market-clearing value, Y^*, when P_t equalled P^*. In this case, the AS curve would pass through the point, (Y^*, P^*), in Figure 21.8 and would therefore intersect the AD curve at this point. The construction in Figure 21.8 assumes instead that $P_t^e > P^*$. The quantity supplied, Y_t^s, is therefore below Y^* if $P_t > P^*$.

In the AS–AD framework, the price level is assumed to be determined at the value denoted $\hat{P}$ where the AS and AD curves intersect. The corresponding level of output is the amount $\hat{Y}$. This quantity equals the amount demanded, Y_t^d, determined along the AD curve, and also equals the quantity supplied, Y_t^s, determined along the AS curve.

Since $\hat{Y}_t < Y^*$ in Figure 21.8, we know from supply behaviour that $\hat{P}_t < P_t^e$. (Recall that $Y_t^s = Y^*$ if $P_t = P_t^e$.) As time passes, P_t^e presumably adjusts downward toward the actual price, $\hat{P}_t$. The fall in P_t^e causes the AS curve to shift rightward: the quantity supplied is higher for a given P_t if P_t^e declines. Thus, $\hat{Y}_t$ rises and $\hat{P}_t$ falls over time. The economy tends thereby toward the market-clearing position, (Y^*, P^*).

The attractive feature of the AS–AD model is that output responds to shifts to supply or demand. An expansion of aggregate demand, represented by a rightward shift of the AD curve, leads to increases in Y_t and P_t. An increase in aggregate supply, corresponding to a rightward shift of the AS curve, causes an increase in Y_t and a decrease in P_t. These changes refer to short-run situations in which the expectation, P_t^e, can be held fixed. In the long run, the adjustment of P_t^e moves the economy back to the market-clearing position, (Y^*, P^*).

The main problem with the AS–AD framework is that the various pieces of the analysis are contradictory. The AD curve reflects the underlying IS/LM model, and the key to this model is the presence of excess supply of goods (and labour). The excess supply reflects, in turn, the assumed stickiness of prices (and wages) at excessive levels. In the AS–AD model, described in Figure 21.8, the adjustment of the price level to the value $\hat{P}$ eliminates the excess supply of goods. The key features of the IS/LM model – such as the Keynesian consumption and investment functions and the workings of the multiplier – do not apply in this situation.

The AS curve assumes that producers (and workers) can sell their desired quantities at the going price, P_t. That is why the quantity supplied rises when P_t increases relative to P_t^e. This setup is inconsistent with the Keynesian idea – present in the IS/LM model and therefore in the AD curve – that producers and workers are constrained by aggregate demand in their ability to sell goods and services.

It is possible to interpret the AD curve as applying to the IS/LM model when the price level has adjusted to ensure general market clearing, as in Figure 21.7. The market-clearing value of output, Y_t^*, in this figure depends, however, on monetary disturbances because the quantity supplied is a function of the price surprise, $P_t - P_t^*$. In this case, the AS–AD model has no Keynesian features and is equivalent to the market-clearing framework with incomplete information about the general price level; that is, the model worked out in Chapter 20. In the AS–AD framework, however, the effects of unanticipated changes in the price level, $P_t - P_t^*$, are allowed to operate only on the supply side. The model ignores the effects of perceived relative prices on consumption and investment demand.

We have available, at this time, two internally consistent models that allow for significant interactions between monetary and real variables. The IS/LM model achieves this interaction by assuming that the price level is typically too high and adjusts only gradually toward its market-clearing value. The market-clearing model from Chapter 20 gets this interaction by assuming that people have incomplete information about the general price level. The AS–AD model is at worst internally consistent and at best a special case of the incomplete-information model.

Cyclical Properties of the Keynesian Model

In the Keynesian model, the cyclical properties of the major macroeconomic variables depend on whether disturbances impinge mostly on the IS curve or the LM curve. Consider first shocks to the IS curve due to changes in investment demand. An expansion of this demand leads (from Figure 21.5) to increases in output, investment, and the expected real interest rate. The change in consumption is ambiguous (the rise in income suggests more consumption, but the higher real interest rate suggests less consumption). The quantity of labour input rises along with output, and the unemployment rate falls. Since the production function has not shifted and the capital stock changes little in the short run, the rise in labour input means that labour productivity declines. To determine the effect on the real wage rate we would have to introduce a labour market. The usual assumption in the Keynesian analysis is that the real wage rate is not closely tied to the marginal product of labour and, hence, that the cyclical pattern of the real wage rate is ambiguous. Finally, the price-adjustment relation (equation [21.16]) implies that the inflation rate rises.

If we considered a shock to the IS curve that reflected a boost to consumption demand, then the only difference concerns the composition of output between consumption and investment. Consumption would rise, unambiguously, in this case, whereas the change in investment would be uncertain.

Thus, for shocks to the IS curve, the predictions of the Keynesian model for cyclical behaviour are as follows:

- **procyclical variables**: investment (probably), consumption (probably), labour input, expected real interest rate, price level.
- **countercyclical variables**: unemployment rate, labour productivity.
- **acyclical or uncertain variables**: real wage rate, quantity of money.

A comparison with the observed cyclical characteristics that we have discussed before for the G-6 countries suggests the following evaluation. To fit the dominant role of investment in observed fluctuations we would have to assume that shocks to investment demand were more important than those to consumption demand. (It also helps if investment demand is more sensitive than consumption demand to changes in output.) In the data, the cyclicity of the expected real interest rate is uncertain; hence, shocks to the IS curve – which predict a strong procyclical pattern – cannot be the whole story. The price level appears to be countercyclical, a conflict with the predictions. Labour productivity is procyclical, another conflict. The real wage rate is procyclical, whereas the model makes no prediction about this variable. Finally, we have assumed thus far that the quantity of money remained constant while the IS curve shifted.

Turn now to shifts in the LM curve due to changes in the quantity of money. An increase in money leads (from Figure 21.6) to increases in output, investment, and consumption, and to a decrease in the expected real interest rate. Labour input rises and the unemployment rate falls. Labour productivity declines, the change in the real wage rate is uncertain, and the inflation rate rises. In comparison with the results for IS shifts, the differences are that investment and consumption are both clearly procyclical, the expected real interest rate is countercyclical, and the quantity of money is procyclical. We can therefore explain the uncertain behaviour of the expected real interest rate in the data by arguing that shocks to the IS and LM curves both occur. The effects from shocks to the LM curve can also make the model consistent with the observed procyclical pattern for monetary aggregates.

Overall, the main conflict between theory and facts concerns the predictions that the price level will be procyclical and that labour productivity will be countercyclical. The failure to generate a prediction about the real wage rate is another shortcoming.

The price level is procyclical in the model because output always follows aggregate demand and an increase in demand leads to a higher inflation rate. The price level can be counter-cyclical only if a shock to aggregate supply leads to higher output and a lower inflation rate. But in the Keynesian model that we have examined, output is demand determined and is therefore invariant with shifts to supply. This shortcoming motivated some economists to develop a Keynesian model in which shifts to aggregate supply affected output. The boxed section above describes this aggregate supply–aggregate demand (AS–AD) model, but argues that it leads to logical inconsistencies.

Some economists have tried to explain the incorrect predictions about labour productivity by arguing that employment and worker-hours are inaccurate measures of labour input. In a recession, firms maintain most of their workers and paid worker-hours although the workers expend less effort than they do during a boom. (This effect is sometimes called **labour hoarding**.) Moreover, during recessions, a larger fraction of workers' effort is devoted to maintenance and other activities that do not show up in measured output. These considerations suggest that labour productivity is underestimated in recessions (when labour input is exaggerated and output is undervalued) and overestimated in booms. Hence, true productivity may be countercyclical, as predicted by the theory.

An alternative, perhaps more plausible, view is that measured labour productivity *and* real wage rates are procyclical because workers really are more productive in booms than in recessions. This perspective accords with real business-cycle models in which the booms and recessions are themselves caused by shifts to the production function and, hence, to productivity.

Sticky Prices in the Keynesian Model

All of the novel features in the Keynesian analysis, as summarized by the IS/LM model, derive from the assumption that prices (or wages) are sticky. The key postulate is that prices do not fall quickly when there is excess supply of goods. Among other things, this assumption delivers the following results:

- Output is determined by aggregate demand; supply-side elements play no important role.
- There may be a multiplier connecting autonomous shifts in aggregate demand to the responses of output.
- Whenever people feel wealthier and raise consumer demand, the expansions of output and employment actually make them wealthier.
- There are real effects from changes in the quantity of money.
- There is a desirable role for active monetary and fiscal policies.

Given all the results that follow from sticky prices, we should look further into the meaning of this assumption. Presumably the stickiness of prices does not to a significant degree reflect the costs of changing prices as such.[16] (The costs of changing production and employment – which Keynesian models usually ignore – are clearly much more important.) Instead, most macroeconomists use sluggish price adjustment as a proxy for other problems that make it difficult for the private sector to operate efficiently: costs of obtaining various kinds of information, costs of moving from one job to another, costs of changing methods of production, and so on. These types of coordination problems mean that the economy does not always react appropriately to changes in the composition of tastes and technology or to shifts in the levels of aggregate demand and supply.

There is no question that the elements just mentioned are important for explaining variations in the aggregates of output and employment and for understanding unemployment. But it is unclear that we can represent these matters by the Keynesian device of imposing an excessive price level on the trades that the private sector can carry out. Incomplete information does not mean, for example, that aggregate demand is more important than aggregate supply. Also, the gaps in people's knowledge do not necessarily imply a desirable role for activist monetary and fiscal policies.

When we allow for incomplete information and adjustment costs, we find that the allocation of resources is a hard problem for the private sector to solve. There are often mistakes, which sometimes show up as unemployment and underproduction. But the challenge to Keynesian analysis is to explain why these problems are eased if the government occasionally throws in a lot of money or steps up its purchases of goods. In the type of model that we have explored in this chapter, these policy actions look good because the assumption of an excessive price level forces the private economy to commit easily correctable mistakes. Namely, output and employment fall short of the levels at which labour marginal product equals the value of workers' time, and the marginal product of capital (less the rate of depreciation) exceeds the real interest rate. But these types of problems are transparent and easy for the private sector to solve without governmental assistance. What has not been shown is that activist governmental policies can assist when the economy has to deal with incomplete information or other serious problems.

Long-Term Contracts

It has long been recognized that the weak link in Keynesian analysis is the absence of a theory of sticky prices. One interesting attempt to explain this behaviour involves **long-term contracts**. This approach recognizes that buyers and sellers often form long-term relationships rather than dealing exclusively on auction markets, such as wholesale markets for agricultural commodities, organized securities markets, and so on. For example, the associations between employers and workers or between firms and their suppliers often extend over many years. These types of continuing interchanges frequently involve formal – though more often implicit – contractual obligations between the parties. Some presetting of prices – or, more likely, of wages – may be one feature of these contracts.[17]

Prior agreement on prices or wages may allow one party, which might be a group of workers, to shift some risk from themselves to the other party, say a large corporation. An automobile company may, for example, shield its workers from some of the fluctuations in the demand for

cars. This setup is desirable if the company is in a better position than the workers to assume risks, perhaps because the company has better access to insurance and other financial markets.

The presetting of some prices may also prevent one person from demanding 'unreasonable' terms, *ex post*. A firm might, for example, lower the wage rate after an employee had incurred significant costs in moving to a job. Similarly, a builder might raise the price for a construction project at a time when delays became prohibitively expensive. In these cases the market – for builders, workers, and employers – may be competitive beforehand but more like a monopoly later. Some of these problems can be avoided by entering into prior contractual arrangements about prices and other considerations.

Some economists have used the contracting approach to rationalize the stickiness of prices or wages in Keynesian models.[18] Suppose, as an illustration, that two parties agree on a price, P, over the life of a contract.[19] In some cases the chosen price will be the best estimate of the average market-clearing price during the contract, P^*, given the information available at the outset. Unanticipated events – such as monetary disturbances – lead, however, to departures of the price from its market-clearing value. When the contract expires, the parties will agree to a new price, which equals the anticipated market-clearing price over the next period.

At any point in time, there is an array of existing contracts, which specify prices that likely depart somewhat from market-clearing values. If there has been a recent monetary contraction, for example, then the typical price will be above its market-clearing value (and vice versa for monetary expansion). As more people renegotiate contracts, the average price adjusts gradually toward the average market-clearing value. We can, in other words, use this model to rationalize a price-adjustment relation like that in equation (21.16):

$$\pi_t = \lambda(Y_t^d - Y_t^s) + \pi_t^*$$

The gradual response of the average price to excess demand corresponds to the process of

Box 21.3 Some Empirical Evidence on the Contracting Approach

As we discussed above, the presence of long-term labour contracts has been used to justify the Keynesian assumption of downward rigidity of wages which, in turn, is considered to be responsible for large variations in unemployment. Several authors have studied the relationship between unemployment and wage rigidities in Europe. Dennis Grubb, Richard Jackman and Richard Layard (1983) analyze nineteen OECD countries,[20] and find that the unemployment rate is significantly higher in countries with greater real wage rigidities. As is common in this literature, they define wage rigidities as the degree of responsiveness of the real wage rate to unemployment: the lower this responsiveness, the greater the degree of wage rigidity. Similar results are reported by George Alogoskoufis and Alan Manning (1988) for a similar set of countries.[21] However, although these are important findings, they cannot be used as evidence in favour of a contract based theory of unemployment. The point is that we cannot directly impute the existence of this type of real wage rigidities to the existence of nominal wage contracts and nominal wage rigidities. There is no clear link, in fact, between the empirical measure of rigidities used in these studies and the existence of long-term contracts.

More direct evidence on the importance of labour contracts is provided by two studies on Canada and the US, respectively. According to theories in which contracts are the basis for the Keynesian model, countries in which long-term labour contracts are pervasive (and have little indexation) should show substantial responses of real wages and, hence, of employment and output, to nominal disturbances. Industries with lots of indexation would be affected little by nominal disturbances. Shaghil Ahmed (1987a) used a data set for 19 industries in Canada over the period 1961–74. He used these data because an earlier study by David Card (1980) calculated the amount of indexation – that is, automatic adjustment of wages for general inflation – in each industry's labour contracts. (Indexation ranged across the industries from zero to roughly 100%.) According to theories in which contracts are the basis for the Keynesian model, industries with little indexation should show substantial responses of real wages and hence, of employment and output, to nominal disturbances. Industries with lots of indexation would be affected little by nominal disturbances.

Ahmed found that nominal shocks – based on unanticipated changes in money or some other nominal variables – had positive effects on hours worked in most of the 19 industries. These results are consistent with some other findings that we discussed in Chapter 19. The important point for present purposes, however, is that the extent of an industry's response to nominal disturbances bore no relation to the amount of indexation in that industry. Those with lots of indexation were as likely as those with little indexation to respond to nominal disturbances. This finding is damaging to theories that use long-term contracts as the basis for the Keynesian model.

Mark Bils (1989) studied labour contracts for 12 manufacturing industries in the United States. He reasoned that if the signing of new contracts was important, then he should find unusual behaviour of employment and real wages just after these signings. His results were mixed. On the one hand, some industries – especially motor vehicles – turned out to exhibit significant changes in employment subsequent to new labour agreements. Prior changes in employment tended to be reversed just after a new contract. These results, although applying only to a few industries, provide some support for the contracting approach. On the other hand, Bils did not find any corresponding changes in real wage rates after new labour contracts were signed. Since these changes in wage rates are central to the contracting approach, it is difficult to reconcile this part of Bils's findings with that approach.

recontracting, and the anticipated rate of change of the market-clearing price, π_t^*, reflects the known factors that negotiators take into account when setting prices or wages at the start of contracts. Note that an excessive price – that is, excess supply of goods and services – is no more likely than too low a price. The price-adjustment relation would be symmetric and would therefore not support the Keynesian focus on excessive price levels.

Although the contracting viewpoint may rationalize a process of gradual price adjustment, there are difficulties in using this analysis to explain Keynesian unemployment and underproduction. The Keynesian results emerge when prices or wages are above market-clearing values *and* when the quantities of output and employment equal the smaller of supply and demand. Recall that this short-side rule for determining quantities accords with voluntary exchange on an impersonal market. But the rule is not generally sensible in a long-term contract, which is now the theoretical basis for sluggish price adjustment.

In an enduring relationship, in which long-term contracts arise, firms and households do not have to change prices or wages every instant to get the 'right' behaviour of quantities. Workers can, for example, agree in advance that they will work harder when there is more work to do – that is, when the demand for a firm's product is high – and vice versa when there is little work. Unlike in an auction market, these efficient adjustments in work and production can occur even if wages do not change from day to day. (For large short-term increases in work, contracts may prescribe overtime premiums or other types of bonuses.) The important point is that stickiness of wages does not necessarily cause errors in the determination of the levels of employment and production.

Similarly, suppose that inflation is sometimes higher than expected and sometimes lower. Firms and workers know that inflation – if not accompanied by some real changes – does not alter the efficient levels of work and production. It is therefore reasonable to agree on a contract that insulates the choices of quantities from the rate of inflation. Over many periods – where the effects of unanticipated inflation on real wage rates tend to average out – both parties to a labour contract would benefit from this type of provision. (When inflation gets very high and unpredictable, however, firms and workers prefer either to index wages to the price level or to renegotiate contracts more frequently.)

One important lesson from the contracting viewpoint is that stickiness of prices or wages need not lead to underproduction and unemployment. Within a long-term agreement, it is unnecessary for prices and wages to move all the time to attain the general-market-clearing values of output and employment. Thus, stickiness in prices and wages no longer tends to generate Keynesian results. Rather than supporting the Keynesian model, the perspective of long-term contracting demonstrates that output and employment can be determined efficiently – as if prices and wages always adjusted to clear markets – even if prices and wages are sticky.

Summary

In the Keynesian model the price level (or the nominal wage rate) exceeds the market-clearing value. The resulting excess supply of goods and services means that output is determined by aggregate demand. Correspondingly, there is underproduction and unemployment.

In the simplest Keynesian model, in which the interest rate is given, an increase in aggregate demand leads to a multiplicative expansion of output. The increase in demand could reflect an autonomous shift to investment or consumption demand or could come from an increase in government purchases. The expansion of output is accompanied by increases in employment, investment, and consumption. If we include the Keynesian investment function and the dependence of consumption on long-run income, then the model can match the empirical observation that investment is more volatile than consumption.

The IS/LM analysis shows how to determine the interest rate along with the level of output. In this model, an increase in aggregate demand may no longer have a multiplicative effect on output:

the increase in the interest rate crowds out the demands for consumption and investment.

In the Keynesian model, a decrease in the price level implies more real money balances and a lower interest rate. The fall in the interest rate stimulates consumption and investment demand, and this increase in demand leads to an expansion of output and employment. Similarly, an increase in the quantity of money or a cutback in the demand for money leads to a lower interest rate and thereby to higher levels of output and employment.

We can incorporate inflation into the Keynesian model by using a price-adjustment formula that relates inflation positively to the excess demand for goods. When the commodity market clears, the inflation rate equals the anticipated rate of change of the market-clearing price. This mechanism allows the price level to fall, relative to the market-clearing value, during a recession. The resulting increases in real money balances lead to decreases in the interest rate and to increases in aggregate demand. Thus, the economy adjusts automatically toward the market-clearing levels of output and employment. In the Keynesian model, active monetary and fiscal policies can speed up this gradual process of automatic adjustment.

The Keynesian model can account for many observed features of business fluctuations. The Keynesian model predicts, incorrectly, that the price level would be procyclical and that labour productivity would be countercyclical. The model also makes no clear prediction about the cyclical behaviour of the real wage rate.

Some novel features of the Keynesian analysis are the following:

- Output is determined by aggregate demand; supply-side elements play no important role.

- There may be a multiplier connecting autonomous shifts in aggregate demand to the responses of output
- Whenever households feel wealthier and raise consumer demand, the expansions of output and employment actually make them wealthier.
- There are real effects from changes in the quantity of money.
- There is a desirable role for active monetary and fiscal policies.

These features follow from the assumption that prices are sticky downward. Most macroeconomists use sticky prices as a proxy for the coordination problems that characterize the private sector's reaction to fluctuations in aggregate supply and demand and to shifts in the composition of tastes and technology. But when economists model these problems in terms of incomplete information, costs of moving, and so on, the Keynesian features noted above do not tend to emerge.

An interesting rationale for sticky prices concerns long-term contracts. Each (explicit or implicit) contract specifies a wage or price over an interval of time. Then the gradual process of recontracting means that the average wage or price adjusts gradually toward the average market-clearing value. Although this perspective may account for sticky prices, it is less successful in explaining the Keynesian predictions about quantities. That is because sensible agreements would allow for efficient adjustments of work and production even if wages or prices do not change from day to day. Thus, the existence of long-term contracts does not explain the type of unemployment and underproduction that arises in Keynesian models.

Important Terms and Concepts

complete Keynesian model
short-side rule (for determining quantities)
involuntary unemployment
Keynesian consumption function
liquidity constraint
aggregate supply-aggregate demand (AS-AD)
  model
autonomous change in demand
multiplier
Keynesian investment function
investment accelerator
marginal propensity to spend
marginal propensity to invest
IS curve
LM curve
Keynesian-cross diagram
labour hoarding
long-term contracts
menu costs

Questions and Problems

Mainly for Review

21.1   a. Contrast the form of consumption demand in the Keynesian model with that in Chapter 5. Why does a change in current income not affect consumption demand in the market-clearing model?
  b. Make the same comparisons for investment demand.

21.2   What is involuntary unemployment? Are the temporary layoffs of workers on long-term contracts an example of involuntary unemployment?

21.3   How does output adjust to ensure the aggregate-consistency condition for the commodity market [equation (21.7)]? Would this result apply if goods were not in excess supply?

21.4   Explain how an increase in the quantity of money reduces the real interest rate in the Keynesian model. Why does this effect not arise in the market-clearing model?

21.5   What is the output multiplier for an increase in government purchases? Discuss how the size of the multiplier is affected by:
  a. Whether government purchases are tax financed or deficit financed.
  b. Any increases in the interest rate.

  c. Whether government purchases are temporary or permanent.

21.6   Assume that the price level is fixed at a level that is 'too high'. Show in this case that the interest rate and output must adjust to ensure the condition that all money be willingly held. Can the interest rate be too high as a result? How does a downward adjustment of the price level bring down the interest rate and eliminate excess supply of commodities?

Problems for Discussion

21.7   The Paradox of Thrift
  Suppose that people become 'thriftier' and thereby decide to save more and consume less.
  a. For a given interest rate, what happens to the quantities of output and employment? What happens to the amount of private saving? (*Hint*: What happens to the quantity of investment?) If the amount of private saving falls when people become thriftier, then there is said to be a *paradox of thrift*.
  b. Re-do the analysis when the interest rate is allowed to adjust. What happens now to the amount of saving? Is there a paradox of thrift?
  c. Can there be a paradox of thrift in the market-clearing model, in which the price level is also allowed to adjust? What accounts for the differences in results?

21.8   The Multiplier
  Consider an autonomous increase in investment demand.
  a. Why is there a multiplicative effect on output if we hold fixed the interest rate?
  b. Is there still a multiplier when the interest rate adjusts? How does this answer depend on the magnitudes of the following:
  i. The sensitivity of aggregate demand to the interest rate?
  ii. The sensitivity of money demand to output?
  iii. The sensitivity of money demand to the interest rate?

21.9   Perceived Wealth in the Keynesian Model
  Suppose that the Prime Minister makes a speech and announces that we are all wealthier than we previously thought. If we all believe the Prime Minister, then what does the Keynesian model predict for the changes in output, employment, and 'wealth'? Explain these results and contrast them with the predictions from the market-clearing model.

21.10 A Change in Inflationary Expectations
  Consider an (unexplained) increase in inflationary expectations, π^e.
  a. How does this change affect the IS curve?

b. How does it affect the LM curve? (Recall that money demand depends on the nominal interest rate, $R = r + \pi^e$.)

c. What happens to the level of output, the real interest rate, and the nominal interest rate? Explain these results and contrast them with those from the market-clearing model. (*Hint*: How does the change in inflationary expectations compare to an autonomous shift in the demand for money?)

21.11   **Extreme Cases in the IS/LM Analysis**
Consider the following extreme cases (which have sometimes been suggested, but have not been supported empirically).

a. Suppose that money demand is insensitive to the interest rate. What does the LM curve look like? In this case what is the effect on output and the interest rate from a disturbance that shifts the IS curve?

b. Suppose that money demand is extremely sensitive to the interest rate (sometimes called a *liquidity trap*). How does the LM curve look in this case? What is the effect now from a shift in the IS curve?

c. Suppose that the interest rate has a negligible effect on aggregate demand. How does the IS curve look in this situation? What are the effects from a shift in the LM curve?

d. Finally, suppose that aggregate demand is extremely sensitive to the interest rate. Draw the IS curve and describe the effects from a shift in the LM curve.

21.12   **Stagflation in the Keynesian Model**
Suppose that we define stagflation as an increase in inflation during a recession.

a. Assume that a recession stems from an autonomous decline in aggregate demand. Can we get stagflation from this disturbance in the Keynesian model?

b. Is there some other way to generate stagflation in the Keynesian model?

21.13   **The Cyclical Behaviour of the Real Wage Rate** (optional)
Consider a positive shock to the IS curve. We showed that output and the inflation rate would rise in the Keynesian model. What happens over time to the nominal wage rate and therefore to the real wage rate? What are the implications for the cyclical behaviour of the real wage rate?

Notes

1. See Don Patinkin (1956, ch. 13) and Robert Barro and Herschel Grossman (1976).
2. In a disaggregated setup, excess supply could appear in some markets and excess demand in others. The standard Keynesian model applies when the great majority of markets experience excess supply.
3. It is common practice for the Treasury of several countries to ration sales of bonds to potential bidders in accordance with the quantity requested if the sale is oversubscribed at the acceptable price. Hence, an aggressive bidder at Solomon Brothers decided that it would be desirable to submit enormous bid quantities for US Treasury bills. The US Treasury reacted by limiting the quantity bid by a single purchaser to a specified fraction of the total issue. The bidder at Solomon Brothers got into trouble when he used various devices to get around the US Treasury's restrictions.
4. We do not allow producers to store up excess output as inventories. This option becomes important if people perceive the state of excess supply to be temporary. For extensions of the Keynesian model to include inventories, see Ajit Chaudhury (1979) and Alan Blinder (1980).
5. Keynes attributed a large part of these disturbances to *animal spirits*, by which he meant spontaneous shifts in optimism or pessimism. These shifts caused businesses to alter their expectations for the profitability of investment. See Keynes (1935, ch. 12).

6. The formula for a geometric series implies that $1 + \nu + \nu^2 + \ldots = 1/(1 - \nu)$ if $-1 < \nu < 1$.
7. The terminology IS refers to the equation of investment demand to desired saving. Recall from equation (20.10) that the condition, $Y_t = Y_t^d$, is equivalent to an equality between investment demand (plus government purchases) and desired private saving (plus taxes). The apparatus in Figure 21.4 comes from John Hicks (1937).
8. The letter L is often used to denote the demand-for-money function; hence, the terminology LM refers to the equation between the demand for money, L, and the quantity of money, M.
9. Public services substitute for α units of private consumer spending, where α is a positive fraction.
10. This diagram applies if the change in government purchases has no direct effect on the demand for money. Otherwise, there is also a shift of the LM curve.
11. Under excess demand it is purchases of goods and services, rather than sales, that have to be rationed. For a theoretical discussion, see Robert Barro and Herschel Grossman (1976). For empirical applications to the (previously) centrally planned economies of eastern Europe, see David Howard (1976) and Richard Portes and David Winter (1980).
12. The Keynesian model considers these factors to the extent that they influence investment or consumption demand. Also, the supply of labour services matters when computing the amount of involuntary unemployment.

13. The discussion assumes that the growth rate of the market-clearing price, π_t^*, reflects an equal growth rate for the quantity of money. The growth rate of money therefore exceeds that of prices.

14. The term 'aggregate-demand curve' is unfortunate because the AD curve is not a demand curve in the usual sense. The curve shows the combinations of P_t and Y_t that are consistent with the condition, $Y_t = Y_t^d$. The level of Y_t shown along the curve therefore equals the quantity demanded, but only because the actual quantity produced has already been equated to this demand.

15. If P_t fell below P^*, then excess demand for goods would result. We have not studied the determination of output under conditions of excess demand, but an analysis of this situation indicates that output would fall below Y^* (see Robert Barro and Herschel Grossman, 1976). Output is maximized not by making P_t as low as possible, but by setting it equal to its market-clearing value, P^*.

16. Until recently most macroeconomists seemed to agree that the direct costs of adjusting prices were unimportant for understanding macroeconomic phenomena. Yet a recent literature relies on **menu costs** for changing prices. For a discussion, see Laurence Ball, Greg Mankiw and David Romer (1988).

17. Some major papers in this area are Donald Gordon (1974), Costas Azariadis (1975), Martin Baily (1974), and Herschel Grossman (1979).

18. See, for example, Jo Anna Gray (1976), Stanley Fischer (1977), and John Taylor (1980).

19. The contracting theory actually motivates the presetting of a relative price or a real wage rate rather than nominal prices or wages. Yet many labour contracts are not explicitly 'indexed', that is, do not contain automatic adjustments of nominal prices or wages for changes in the general cost of living. Firms and workers apparently find it convenient to frame their contracts in nominal terms even when inflation is moderately high and variable. But inflation does tend to produce contracts with shorter durations.

20. The countries are Australia, Austria, Belgium, Canada, Denmark, Finland, France, Germany, Ireland, Italy, Japan, Netherlands, Norway, New Zealand, Spain, Sweden, Switzerland, the United Kingdom and the United States.

21. They analyze the same countries as Grubb, Jackman and Layard with the exception of Australia, Canada and New Zealand.

Monetary Policies, Credibility and International Coordination

An exciting recent development in macroeconomics is the application of models of strategic behaviour to the study of government economic policies. The initial inspiration for these ideas came from the distinction between anticipated and unanticipated monetary and price changes in the kinds of models that we have considered in Chapter 20. For example, if only unanticipated money and unexpected changes in the price level matter for real variables, then policymakers who wish to affect real variables have an incentive to surprise people. But if individuals form expectations rationally, then it is difficult to fool people systematically.[1] The resolution of these conflicting objectives involves the strategic interplay between the policymakers and individuals in the economy.

The applications of this strategic approach are wide-ranging. There are many situations in which strategic interaction among economic agents is critical, and the literature on the subject, although recent, is vast. We first consider monetary policies in a closed economy and then extend the analysis to an international framework.

Rules versus Discretion in Monetary Policies

Suppose that the monetary authority can use its instruments to achieve any desired rate of inflation, π. It would be more realistic to assume some error between the desired and actual inflation rate, but that change would not affect the basic results. The policymaker wants to reduce unemployment or raise the level of output but can do so only by creating a positive amount of unexpected inflation, $\pi - \pi^e$. This surprise inflation would correspond to a positive amount of unanticipated money growth. For a given expected rate of inflation, π^e, the unemployment rate decreases with π. This result holds in the expectational Phillips curve shown in Figure 19.2 and in the model worked out in Chapter 20. We can summarize this relationship with:

$$x = x(\pi - \pi^e) \tag{22.1}$$

where x is the variable of concern of the policymaker, such as employment or output. The variable x can also represent government revenue, which is typically enhanced by unexpected inflation.

Define x_0 to be the value that x would attain in the absence of any inflation surprises, that is when $\pi = \pi^e$. The authority is assumed to have a target value for x, $\bar{x}$, that exceeds $x_0 : \bar{x} > x_0$. The excess of $\bar{x}$ over x_0 tempts the government to create surprise inflation. The monetary authority is assumed, however, not to like inflation for its own sake; for given unemployment, the policymaker prefers an inflation rate of zero. Hence, for given π^e, an increase in π above zero entails a tradeoff between the benefits of lower unemployment (or higher output or revenue) and the costs of higher inflation. The resolution of this tradeoff determines the inflation rate, denoted by $\hat{\pi}$, that the policymaker selects.

The policymaker's selected inflation rate, $\hat{\pi}$, would generally depend on people's expected inflation rate, π^e. Write this dependence as the function, ψ (the Greek letter psi) – that is,

$$\hat{\pi} = \psi(\pi^e) \qquad (22.2)$$
$$(+)$$

To illustrate this relationship, consider Figure 22.1. This graph assumes that expected inflation is zero. The horizontal axis measures inflation, and the vertical axis shows the corresponding level of welfare.

The first component of welfare measures the gains in employment due to inflation surprises. Since expected inflation is zero, unexpected inflation equals realized inflation. At zero inflation, there is no inflation surprise and thus no gain in employment. If inflation is positive, instead, then employment increases. The higher inflation, the higher employment and thus welfare. (We assume here that more employment is always better.) This relationship is represented by the solid line in the upper part of the figure.

The second component of welfare is the direct disruptive effect of inflation on economic activity. We assume that living with inflation is costly, and that these costs are higher as inflation rises. For example, when inflation is high, optimal money

balances are low and, thus, individuals have to engage in frequent transfers from savings to checking accounts. Firms and shops also have to revise their prices more frequently when inflation is high. This relationship is represented by the dotted line in the lower part of the graph.

Total welfare, the dashed line in Figure 22.1, is the sum of the two components. The monetary authority would choose the inflation rate at which welfare is maximized, that is, $\hat{\pi} = \pi_1 > 0$.

Notice that we started with the assumption that expected inflation was zero, then we found that the inflation rate chosen by the monetary authority would be positive. Our initial assumption about π^e was therefore not a good one. It would not be rational for individuals to set their expectations of inflation to zero in this situation because they could easily figure out that the monetary authority would have an incentive to choose a positive level of inflation.

Suppose, then, that expected inflation is positive, say equal to π_1. This case is described in Figure 22.2. The costs of inflation are the same as before, because they do not depend on expected inflation. The benefits, however, are smaller. For example, if inflation is set to zero, then the inflation surprise is negative. Employment will decrease and thus the benefits of inflation would be negative. More generally, as shown in Figure 22.2, the whole schedule representing the benefits from inflation is lower than before. The level of inflation that maximizes welfare is now $\hat{\pi} = \pi_2 > \pi_1$. Notice, therefore, that the monetary authority's choice of inflation is a positive function of inflation expectations. If π^e is higher, then the monetary authority would have to set a correspondingly higher value of π to maintain the surprise, $\pi - \pi^e$. For this reason, the policymaker's choice, $\hat{\pi}$, tends to increase with π^e, as shown in equation (22.2). We represent this relationship in Figure 22.3.

Consider the top graph in Figure 22.3. It highlights two characteristics of the policy function, $\hat{\pi} = \psi(\pi^e)$. First, as we have seen, $\pi > 0$ holds if $\pi^e = 0$; that is, the policymaker finds it worthwhile to inflate if people expect zero inflation. Second, the slope of the function, $\psi(\pi^e)$, is flatter than that of a 45-degree line, that is, an

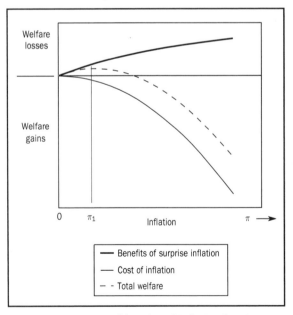

Figure 22.1   Costs and benefits of inflation for given expected inflation, $\pi^\varepsilon = 0$

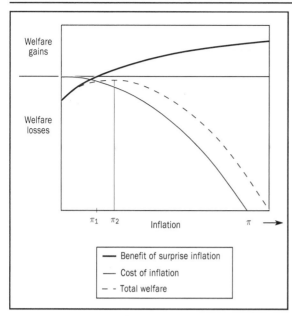

Figure 22.2   Costs and benefits of inflation when $\pi^e = \pi_1$

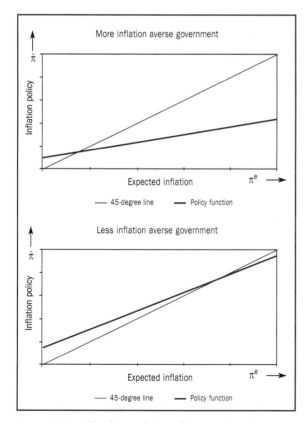

Figure 22.3   The shape of the inflation policy function

increase in π^e raises $\hat{\pi}$ by less than one-to-one.[2] The intercept and the slope of the government policy line depends on the monetary authority's evaluation of the tradeoff between inflation and output. In particular, the more the authorities value low inflation compared to high output, the lower the intercept and the flatter the line. Conversely, the more the authorities value output, the higher the intercept and the steeper the line, as shown in the bottom graph of Figure 22.3.

Next we have to model expectations. Consider how an individual would form a rational expectation of inflation in this model. Suppose that each person knows everyone else's expectation, π^e, and also knows what the government is trying to do: set $\pi = \hat{\pi}$ to achieve a desired tradeoff between unemployment and inflation. Then each individual can figure out the policy-maker's choice, $\hat{\pi}$, and compute the rational expectation, $\pi^e = \hat{\pi}$. Thus, rational formation of expectations corresponds to the 45-degree line shown in Figures 22.3 and 22.4.

The intersection of the two lines determines the equilibrium inflation rate, $\pi^* = (\pi^e)^*$ in Figure 22.4. This value satisfies two conditions: first, at $\pi^e = \pi^*$, the policymaker – who is trading off the benefits of lower unemployment against the costs of higher inflation for a given value of π^e – selects the value $\hat{\pi} = \pi^*$, because this point lies on the line, $\hat{\pi} = \psi(\pi^e)$. Second, the expectation, $\pi^e = \pi^*$, is rational because it is the best possible forecast

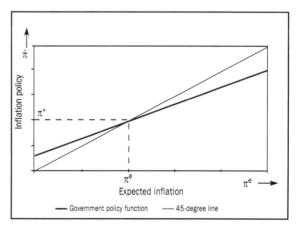

Figure 22.4   Determination of inflation

of inflation. (In this model – but not in the extended versions we consider later – the forecast error is zero; that is, people have **perfect foresight**.)

We can clarify the nature of the results by thinking about some (made-up) numbers. Conjecture that $\pi^e = 0$. Facing this belief, the policymaker finds that the optimal choice for $\hat{\pi}$ is, say, 5%. But any individual can figure out, by knowing what the government is up to, that the policymaker would pick 5% inflation if everyone expected zero inflation. More generally, everyone knows that the government will engineer high inflation if people expect low inflation. Hence, $\pi^e = 0$ is an irrational expectation, and each individual would switch to $\pi^e = 5\%$.

If everyone expects 5% inflation, then the government would set $\hat{\pi}$ to be, say, 7%. Everyone would therefore switch to $\pi^e = 7\%$, an expectation that motivates the government to pick $\hat{\pi} = 8\%$, and so on. In the equilibrium, perhaps at 10% inflation, the government is motivated to pick $\hat{\pi} = \psi(10\%) = 10\%$, and people also expect inflation to be 10%. This result applies when the two lines intersect in Figure 22.4. At this point the government attaches such a high cost to additional inflation that it is not motivated to surprise people by choosing a still higher inflation rate. Hence, people regard 10% inflation as credible.

The nasty aspect of the equilibrium is that it entails a high inflation rate, $\pi = \pi^*$ in Figure 22.4, without any benefits from *surprisingly* high inflation. Since π^e is correspondingly high, the inflation surprise, $\pi - \pi^e$, is zero. Employment and output therefore receive no stimulus (and the government gets no extra revenue from surprise inflation). From Figure 22.3 we see that the equilibrium inflation rate would be higher if the government is known not to be very inflation averse.

The economy would perform better with zero actual and expected inflation because the costs associated with inflation would be lower. In that case the inflation surprise, $\pi - \pi^e$, is still zero, but at least the inflation rate is low. It is clear, however, from Figure 22.4 that $\pi = \pi^e = 0$ is not an equilibrium in this model. If $\pi^e = 0$, then the

policymaker would pick $\hat{\pi} > 0$, and – since people know that the policymaker would behave this way – $\pi^e = 0$ is inconsistent with rational expectations.

The high inflation result, $\pi = \pi^e = \pi^* > 0$, is often referred to as the **inflationary bias** of **discretionary policy**. This outcome results if the policymaker can make no commitments or binding promises about future actions. In contrast, a policymaker who can make such commitments is thought of as operating subject to a **policy rule**. One simple form of rule specifies a constant rate of monetary growth or a constant rate of inflation (so-called **constant-growth-rate rules**). In the present setting, in which inflation is costly and there is no uncertainty, the best thing that the monetary authority could do is to commit to zero inflation. (Later on we will see that in other models the optimal rule would be more complicated.) With this commitment, $\pi = \pi^e = 0$ would be attainable and also superior to the discretionary result, $\pi = \pi^e > 0$.

Figure 22.4 illustrates the tension in a rule with zero inflation. At $\pi^e = 0$, the policymaker really wants to renege on commitments and set $\pi = \hat{\pi} > 0$.[3] If this repudiation is feasible, then individuals presumably would have known it in advance and would not have maintained expectations of zero inflation. Then the equilibrium tends toward the discretionary one worked out before in Figure 22.4. To avoid this outcome, it is crucial that commitments be well enforced. They have to be strong enough so that policymakers cannot overturn them later even if they want to. To the extent that 'sovereign power' makes such commitments infeasible, the outcomes tend to look more like the high inflation under discretion and less like the low inflation under rules.

An important point is that the high inflation result under discretion can arise even if the policymaker is well meaning and competent. The force that drives the result is the benefit from the inflation surprise. In the example just considered, this benefit arises if, first, an increase in surprise inflation reduces unemployment and, second, if the decrease in unemployment is desirable. The last property holds if the private economy tends to generate unemployment rates that are too high on average. Two possible reasons for this market failure are the existence of income taxes and the availability of unemployment-insurance benefits. The Keynesian model, discussed in the previous chapter, suggests that price or wage stickiness may be another reason why unemployment might be too high on average.

Even if unemployment and output do not respond to unexpected inflation, the results go through in terms of fiscal considerations. Surprise inflation tends to improve the government's budget situation – for example, by lowering the real value of the nominal debt outstanding. A benevolent government would value this change because it could then reduce its reliance on distortionary taxes.

Similar results about policy come up in many areas in which the policymaker (and perhaps the nation as a whole) would benefit if people were surprised after the fact. Debtor countries may, for example, surprise creditors by defaulting on foreign debts, governments may surprise owners of capital by assessing high tax rates on existing capital (so-called *capital levies*), tax collectors may surprise people by announcing tax amnesties, governments may fail to honour patents after inventions have been made, and so on. In all of these areas, the surprise is tempting after the fact. But if people understand the government's incentives, then expectations before the fact will take account of the likelihood of subsequent policy actions. The equilibria then have undesirable properties: excessive inflation, too little foreign borrowing, low investment, poor tax compliance, and a low volume of inventions. To avoid these outcomes governments would like to promise that they will resist the temptation to surprise people later. But the credibility of these commitments is a major problem.

Making Monetary Policies Credible

Central Bank Independence

The discussion has stressed the importance of the credibility of monetary policies. Many economists soon recognized that the credibility of monetary policies is linked to the anti-inflationary reputation of the monetary authorities. Following this observation, Rogoff (1985), building on work by Barro and Gordon (1983), suggested that a way to improve the credibility of monetary policies was to delegate them to an inflation averse central bank. As we have seen in Figure 22.3, the size of the inflationary bias is negatively correlated with the degree of inflation aversion of the monetary authorities. Accordingly, it would be optimal to delegate monetary policies to a central banker who has no output or employment target, but cares only about setting inflation to zero. In this case, the central banker would not be tempted to create inflation surprises, because he or she is not trying to achieve a level of employment greater than x_0. In terms of Figure 22.4, this central banker has a policy function that coincides with the horizontal axis, and the equilibrium inflation rate is zero.[4]

Several authors, such as Bade and Parkin (1982), Grilli, Masciandaro and Tabellini (1991) and Alesina and Summers (1991), investigated how this mechanism could be implemented in practice. How can the public be convinced that monetary policy is under the control of an inflation-averse monetary authority? These authors suggested that the anti-inflationary reputation of a central bank is closely related to its degree of independence from the government.

It is likely that the inspiration for these theories was provided by the observation that Germany, the country with the best post-war record on price stability, has a central bank that is famous for its tough anti-inflationary stance and its independence from the German government. The evidence regarding the relationship between central bank independence and inflation performance goes, however, beyond the German case. Figure 22.5 presents the relationship between inflation and a measure of central bank independence (discussed below) for 18 industrialized countries in the period 1950–89. There is a clear negative relationship between central bank independence and the inflationary record. Portugal and Greece have very dependent central banks and have experienced the highest inflation

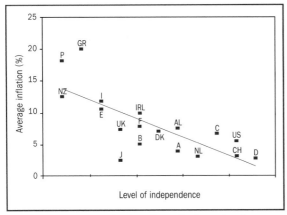

Figure 22.5 Central bank independence and inflation, 1950–90

levels. In contrast, Germany, Switzerland, and the United States have the most independent central banks and the lowest average inflation.

How can we define and measure the degree of independence of a central bank? This task is difficult and, to some extent, arbitrary. Nonetheless, there exists general agreement about the institutional characteristics of a central bank that enhance or diminish her autonomy. In a recent study, Grilli, Masciandaro and Tabellini (1991) propose to measure central bank independence according to two criteria: the political autonomy and the economic autonomy of a monetary institution.[5]

Countries	Appointments			Relationship with government		Constitution		Index of political independence	
	(1)	(2)	(3)	(4)	(5)	(6)	(7)	(8)	(9)
Australia		*					*	*	3
Austria						*	*	*	3
Belgium				*					1
Canada	*	*					*	*	4
Denmark		*				*	*		3
France		*		*					2
Germany		*		*	*	*	*	*	6
Greece			*					*	2
Ireland		*				*	*		3
Italy	*	*	*		*				4
Japan							*		1
Netherlands		*		*	*	*	*	*	6
New Zealand									0
Portugal					*				1
Spain				*	*				2
Switzerland		*			*	*	*	*	5
UK					*				1
US				*	*	*	*	*	5

Notes: (1) Governor *not* appointed by government; (2) Governor appointed for >5 years; (3) All the Board not appointed by government; (4) Board appointed for >5 years; (5) No mandatory participation of government representative in the Board; (6) No government approval on monetary policy formulation is required; (7) Statutory requirements that central bank pursues monetary stability amongst its goals; (8) Legal provisions that strengthen the central bank's position in conflicts with the government are present; (9) Overall index of political independence, constructed as the sum of the asterisks in each row.

Source: Grilli, Masciandaro and Tabellini (1991).

Table 22.1 Political independence of central banks, 1989

Political Autonomy of a Central Bank

Political autonomy is defined as the ability of a central bank to pursue monetary stability without political constraints or governmental influence. Table 22.1 summarizes the most important elements that affect political autonomy in 18 industrialized countries. First, autonomy is enhanced if the price-stabilization role of the central bank is explicitly stated in the statutes. In this way, the bank's role cannot be easily and arbitrarily changed by the particular government in power. Among the EC countries, only the central banks of Denmark, the Netherlands, and Germany have the objective of price stability explicitly stated in their statutes.

A second important element that protects the autonomy of a central bank is the guarantee for the governor and the board of directors of sufficiently long terms of office. Short terms of office could make the directorate of the bank more vulnerable to politically opportunistic pressures because of the almost constant uncertainty regarding their reappointment. In the EC, of the central banks with a specific duration for the governor's office, the longest is that of Germany, eight years. In Italy, France and Denmark, the governor's mandate does not have an explicit duration. This setup does not, however, imply a lifetime appointment. To the contrary, the experience shows that this arrangement facilitates sudden dismissals of the governor. Similar arguments hold for the board of directors of a central bank. The eight-year term in Germany is longer than that of any other European country. For example, the term is six years in France, four in the United Kingdom, and three in Italy.

A third important factor that influences the independence of a central bank from political pressures is whether the statute of the bank excludes the participation of the government in monetary policy decisions. This participation could be in the form of the requirement of formal government approval of monetary policy or in the form of the presence of government officials on the central bank board. The statute of the Bundesbank, for example, explicitly forbids any government participation of this sort. Other EC central banks are, however, much less strict.

For example, in France and the United Kingdom, governmental representatives are part of the central bank boards, and monetary policy must be explicitly approved by the government.

Economic Autonomy of a Central Bank

The second dimension of independence of a central bank is its economic autonomy, that is, the ability to use, without restrictions, monetary policy instruments to pursue the objective of price stability. Table 22.2 summarizes the most important elements that affect economic autonomy. The most important and common constraint on the daily management of monetary policy derives from the central bank's obligation

Countries	Monetary financing of budget deficit					Monetary instruments		Index of economic independence
	(1)	(2)	(3)	(4)	(5)	(6)	(7)	(8)
Australia	*	*	*	*	*	*		6
Austria			*	*	*	*	**	6
Belgium		*		*	*	*	**	6
Canada	*	*	*	*		*	**	7
Denmark		*			*	*	**	5
France				*	*	*	**	5
Germany	*	*	*	*	*	*	*	7
Greece				*		*		2
Ireland		*	*	*		*		4
Italy				*				1
Japan	*			*		*	*	5
Netherlands		*	*	*		*		4
New Zealand		*	*			*		3
Portugal				*		*		2
Spain		*	*				*	3
Switzerland		*	*	*	*	*	**	7
UK	*	*	*	*		*		5
US	*	*	*	*	*	*	*	7

Notes: (1) Direct credit facility: not automatic; (2) Direct credit facility: market interest rate; (3) Direct credit facility: temporary; (4) Direct credit facility: limited amount; (5) Central bank does not participate in primary market for public debt; (6) Discount rate set by central bank; (7) Banking supervision *not* entrusted to the central bank (**) or not entrusted to the central bank alone (*); (8) Overall index of economic independence (being the sum of the asterisks in columns 1–7).

Source: Grilli, Masciendaro and Tabellini (1991).

Table 22.2 Economic independence of central banks, 1989

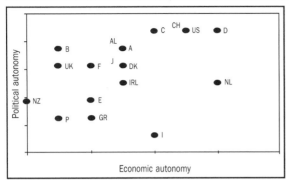

Figure 22.6   Central bank independence, 1989

to finance public-sector deficits. This constraint is particularly important for countries with high levels of public debt, such as Belgium, Ireland, and Italy. Here again, the Bundesbank has strict regulations that severely limit advances to the German government. The arrangements are different in France and Italy; for example, the central banks are allowed to grant credit to their finance ministries.

Figure 22.6 plots the results of this classification.[6] The figure shows that, in 1989, there were differences in the level of independence of national central banks. The central banks of Germany, Canada, Switzerland and the United States enjoyed a high level of autonomy, whereas those of Portugal, Greece, and Spain had a very low one. Once again, these indexes must be interpreted with caution. For example, although the tables suggest that the Bundesbank and the Federal Reserve are highly independent, they are still subject to political interference. More important, the relationship between monetary credibility, central bank independence, and low inflation has received much attention in recent years by policymakers, and several countries are in the process of introducing (for example France and Spain) or have already introduced (New Zealand) wide-ranging reform of their central banks to increase their independence.

Monetary Policy in the Presence of Shocks

We now extend the analysis to the realistic case in which the economy is subject to real shocks.

Suppose that the monetary authority's target variable, say output, depends on a productivity shock, ϵ, so that equation (22.1) becomes:

$$x = x(\pi - \pi^e) + \epsilon \qquad (22.3)$$

The productivity shock is zero on average, but it is sometimes positive and sometimes negative. As before, we assume that $\bar{x} > x_0$, where x_0 is now the level of output that corresponds to $\pi = \pi^e$ and $\epsilon = 0$. Thus, the government still wants to engineer inflation surprises to try to reach $\bar{x}$, an objective that we call **output targeting**.

We assume, in addition, that the government values stability, that is, it dislikes output fluctuations. This objective motivates the government to try to use monetary policy to avoid variations in output when productivity shocks are non-zero. Consider, for example, a negative shock, $\epsilon < 0$. The monetary authorities would like to create a positive inflation surprise to stimulate output and thereby offset the negative impact of the real shock. Let's call this second government objective **output stabilization**. It is important to keep the two government objectives separated because they have different implications for the conduct of monetary policy.

We describe the new equilibrium in Figure 22.7. Consider first a zero productivity shock, so that there is no need for output stabilization. The only objective of the government is output targeting, and the problem is analogous to the case considered before. In particular, the policy function of the government is the one described in Figure 22.4 and is now reproduced as the darker line in Figure 22.7.

Consider now a negative output shock. In addition to output targeting, the monetary authority would like to create a positive inflation surprise to stimulate output and compensate for the negative real shock. Thus, for every level of expected inflation, they would like to generate a larger level of inflation than in the previous case of zero shock. The relevant policy function becomes the top dotted line in Figure 22.7.

A positive output shock has just the opposite implication. Now the authorities would like to generate a negative inflation surprise to compensate for the positive real shock. For each level of

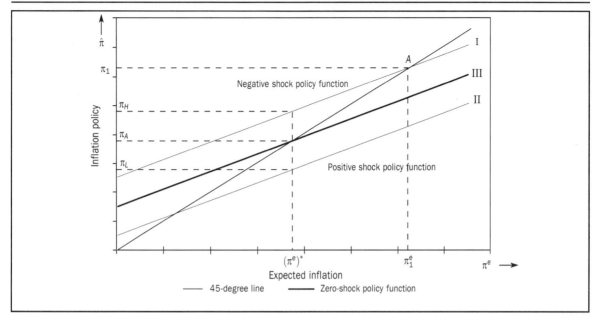

Figure 22.7   Determination of inflation in the presence of shocks

expected inflation, the authority would like to set a lower level of inflation; hence, the policy function is given by the lower dotted line in Figure 22.7. Note that, for a negative shock, both the output targeting and the output stabilization objectives create an incentive for positive inflation surprises. In contrast, for a positive shock, the two effects offset.

Consider now how expectations are formed in this environment. If the public has the same information as the government about output shocks and revises its expectations before the government can take any policy action, then the presence of shocks has no consequence. In essence, the analysis is the same as that without shocks. Because it observes output shocks, the public knows the position of the government's policy function and thus can correctly predict the rate of inflation. For example, in the case of a negative output shock, the public is aware that the government's policy function is line I in Figure 22.7, and will set expectations at π^e. Equilibrium is at point A, the inflation surprise is zero, and output equals $x_0 + \epsilon$. Again, monetary policy has no real effects.

To depart from this neutrality result, we have to assume either that the government has an informational advantage, that is, that it observes real shocks before the public (and does not broadcast the information to the public), or that the public cannot respond quickly to the information, for example, because of nominal labour contracts.[7] In both cases, the important consideration is that expectations do not take into account the particular realization of the shock.

To be concrete, assume that the government observes the real shock, ϵ, as soon as it occurs, but the public sees this shock only with a lag. As before, when they compute expectations, individuals take account of the government's incentive to create inflation, but they do not know the value of ϵ. Individuals realize that, because of output targeting, the monetary authorities will create positive inflation even when $\epsilon = 0$. As before, individuals expect a level of inflation, $(\pi^e)^*$, given by the intercept of the 45-degree line and the zero-shock policy function. The output-stabilization objective does not alter this expectation. Since the real shock is zero on average, the public's best guess about the position of the government's policy function is line III in Figure 22.7, that is, the policy function that corresponds to $\epsilon = 0$. Expected inflation is set at $(\pi^e)^* = \pi_A$, that is, the level of inflation that would prevail when $\epsilon = 0$.

On average – that is, when $\epsilon = 0$ – inflation and expected inflation coincide at π_A, and output equals x_0. Therefore, the economy still experiences high inflation without an increase in the average level of output.

In periods of negative real shocks, the monetary authority's policy function is line I in Figure 22.7. Since expected inflation is $(\pi^e)^*$, the government's optimal choice of inflation is π_H, and inflation is higher than expected, $\pi_H > (\pi^e)^*$. This positive inflation surprise tends to stabilize output around x_0. Conversely, when the shock is positive, inflation will be lower than expected, $\pi_L < \pi^e$. The negative inflation surprise will, once again, stabilize output around x_0.

Output targeting is still ineffective in this framework. Because of their informational advantage, however, monetary authorities can generate inflation surprises when the real shock is non-zero and, hence, they are able to reduce the impact of the real shock on output. Nonetheless, monetary policy still suffers from excessive inflation. A preferable equilibrium would feature a mean inflation rate that was zero, rather than positive. Notice that the inflationary bias derives only from the output-targeting objective, not from the output-stabilization objective. In order to remove the inflationary bias, therefore, the monetary authorities must credibly renounce the output-targeting objective.

Several authors have argued that the solution proposed in the previous section – the delegation of monetary policy to an independent central bank that cares only about minimizing the inflation rate – may not be the best solution in the presence of real shocks. By committing to a zero inflation policy, the monetary authority forsakes not only output targeting, but also the possibility of offsetting the impact of real shocks on output. The desirability of appointing a completely inflation averse central banker depends on how effective monetary policy is in offsetting real shocks, compared to the size of the inflationary bias that is introduced by retaining monetary discretion.[8]

Monetary Policy in a Monetary Union: Conflict Among Stabilization Objectives

Up to now we have considered the issue of monetary policy from a purely domestic perspective. The main problem facing the monetary authority, or the national central bank, was the credibility constraint imposed by the presence of rational domestic agents. No mention was made of potential constraints imposed by international factors. In this and the next section, we widen the scope of the analysis to consider how monetary policies are affected by international elements. As discussed in Chapter 11, a form of international constraint on domestic monetary policy is imposed by membership in a fixed exchange rate system or a monetary union. The problems raised by the two systems are similar, but the second is of particular interest because of the recent movement in the European Community toward the creation of a **European Monetary Union (EMU)**.

The foundations of EMU are contained in the 1991 Maastricht Treaty. Although this treaty deals with several institutional features of the EC, the most relevant aspect is the creation of a monetary union among the EC member states. A European monetary union involves the creation of a common currency and a single monetary authority (the **European System of Central Banks, ESCB**, and the **European Central Bank, ECB**). In BOX 22.1 we discuss in more detail the timing and likelihood of EMU. Here we are concerned with the economics behind this project. Why this desire for a monetary union? What are its advantages and disadvantages?

Advocates of EMU usually refer to three types of benefits from such a monetary arrangement. First, the system eliminates the transaction costs from exchanging currency on the foreign exchange market whenever transactions involve individuals from different countries. Second, the union reduces the uncertainty associated with unpredictable fluctuations of exchange rates. Third, the arrangement enhances the credibility of monetary policy in the EC. This last argument parallels the analysis in the previous sections.

Monetary policy in the EC will be conducted by the ECB instead of the various national central banks. As we have seen in Figure 22.6, the central banks of several EC countries are not very independent from their governments and, thus, lack credibility. The Maastricht Treaty purports to establish the ECB as an independent institution. In fact, the ECB has been modelled after the German Bundesbank and, according to the indicator of political and economic independence discussed in the previous section, the ECB and the Bundesbank are virtually identical. Therefore, countries with low levels of independence of their central banks, such as Greece, Portugal, and Spain, will enjoy more credible monetary policies by joining EMU. It remains to be seen, however, whether the political pressures that will be exerted by various countries will lower the degree of credibility relative to that achieved by some other countries, notably Germany.

A monetary union, in any case, is not without its costs. The usual view is that the main shortcoming of a monetary union is the loss of monetary independence, that is, the inability to pursue income targeting and stabilization at the national level. As we discussed before, the inability to follow income targeting is an advantage because it increases the credibility of monetary policies. The loss of national income stabilization, on the other hand, would be costly if monetary policy were effective in offsetting real shocks. Since the EMU's monetary policy will have to be set at the European level, the ability to offset country-specific real shocks will be reduced. This consideration is more important the greater the difference between the real shocks that affect the various countries. If the differences are large – and if monetary policies actually help to stabilize output – then the cost of joining a monetary union could be substantial.

This line of argument suggests that we can evaluate the cost of joining a monetary union by constructing an index of 'cyclical distance' between the EC and each of the twelve member countries. This measure uses the standard deviations of the cyclical component of a country's GDP and its correlation coefficients with the cyclical component of the global EC GDP. These distances are reported in Figure 22.8.

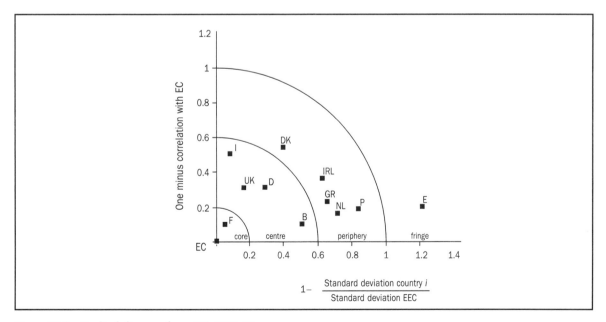

Figure 22.8   Cyclical distance from EC, 1960–90

The figure is constructed so that the origin coincides with the EC average. The vertical axis measures (one minus) the correlation coefficient of a country's output with the EC's output. The horizontal axis measures (one minus) the ratio of a country's standard deviation of output to the EC's standard deviation of output. Some caution is necessary when inspecting this figure, because the output series that we observe already reflect the effects of national monetary policies, which we would like to exclude from the analysis. In any event, the figure suggests that, from the standpoint of stabilization, the countries that have the most to lose from a monetary union are those at the periphery of Europe: Portugal, Ireland and Greece. The country least affected on these grounds is France.

It is interesting to note that the countries that have more to lose from the stabilization point of view are also the ones that could gain more in terms of enhanced credibility of their monetary policies. For example, Portugal, Greece, Ireland and Spain are among the countries with the largest distance from the EC and, at the same time, the countries with the least independent central banks and highest rates of inflation.

International Aspects of Economic Policies: The Benefits of International Coordination

From our previous discussion it may seem that common monetary policies are not a good idea, because they prevent governments from following their own stabilization objectives. The analysis assumed that the effects of policy actions remained limited to the country in which the policy was implemented. In some cases, this assumption can be misleading.

The problem is that in an economically integrated world the impacts of policies are rarely confined within national boundaries. This observation implies that policies that would be chosen when a country is considered in isolation may be undesirable when the international implications are considered. Several economists have suggested that when the effects of national

policies spill over to other countries it is appropriate to discuss and coordinate these policies at an international level. The argument in favour of policy coordination is not confined to monetary policies, but applies to any policy that has international ramifications.

To develop the argument in general terms, consider a policy objective χ (the Greek letter *chi*), and a policy instrument σ (*sigma*), which can be used to affect the objective. Note that we are not implying that it is correct or beneficial to try to pursue a particular policy objective, or that the policy instrument, σ, is the best way to reach the policy goal. The point that we want to make here is more limited. Even if we were to agree on the desirability of certain policy objectives and on the particular policy tool best suited to achieve them, we have to pay attention to the policies of other nations.

To study the issue of policy coordination, we have to consider the behaviour of at least two policymakers, one domestic and one foreign. Each policymaker tries to control his or her target with a particular instrument. In terms of previous examples, they may be trying to stabilize output by mean of monetary policy, or they may be trying to control their currency exchange rates by varying the money supply or the discount rate. The difference with the previous setup is that we now allow foreign policy actions to affect domestic objectives, and vice versa. As examples, the exchange rate can be affected by the other authority's decisions about interest rates, and the level of domestic output can be affected by foreign government spending. We assume that the target variables, χ in the domestic country and χ^* in the foreign country, are determined by:[9]

$$\chi = \chi(\sigma, \alpha\sigma^*) + \epsilon \qquad (22.4)$$

and

$$\chi^* = \chi^*(\sigma^*, \alpha\sigma) + \epsilon \qquad (22.5)$$

where, σ is the setting for the domestic policy instrument and σ^* the setting for the foreign policy instrument. We assume that χ depends positively on σ and that χ^* depends positively on σ^*. Notice that each country's policy instrument enters the other country's function multiplied by the parameter α. This parameter measures the direction and intensity of the policy spillover. If α is positive, then the foreign policy – in the sense of a higher value of σ^* – has a positive effect on the domestic target, χ. This effect is larger the higher the value of α.

We assume that the policy instruments, σ and σ^*, also impose a direct cost in each country. As an example, we assumed before that policy-makers disliked inflation (the policy instrument in our earlier analysis).

Note that we assume in equations (22.4) and (22.5) that the targets, χ and χ^*, are hit by the same real shock, ϵ. In terms of the previous section, we are assuming that national real shocks have the same variance and are perfectly positively correlated. Thus, we are neglecting any potential policy conflict that reflects differences in the shocks that each country faces. The thrust of the argument would not change if we were to complicate the model to allow for differences in national shocks.

We assume that each country's authority is aware of the impact of its policy, σ, on the foreign outcome, χ^*, and of the effect of foreign policy, σ^*, on domestic outcome, χ. In other words, they know the forms of equations (22.4) and (22.5). We assume, however, that each authority is concerned only with the stabilization of its own policy target, and not with the stabilization of the other country's target. The setting of policies in this framework depends on the degree of cooperation between the two policymakers. We consider two possible alternatives: one in which they do not cooperate at all and another in which they cooperate fully.

Non-Cooperative Policies

In the first scenario, the two authorities set policies independently of each other. This independence does not mean that each authority ignores the actions of the other when determining policy. On the contrary, policy decisions depend crucially on beliefs about the other policymaker's behaviour.

To be concrete, suppose that the government's objective is to stabilize employment in the manufacturing sector. To achieve this goal, it can decide how much of its budget to allocate to purchases of manufactured goods, thus sustaining the demand for those products. (Recall that we are not arguing that the policy objective and the policy instrument are sensible.) We assume that the direct cost of the policy is that public spending on other programmes, say on the preservation of the environment, has to be cut. In terms of equations (22.4) and (22.5), χ and χ^* are domestic and foreign manufacturing employment, and σ and σ^* are government spending on manufactured products. The cost of using σ and σ^* is that spending on parks and the environment has to be cut. We also assume that α is positive because a part of the increase in government purchases of manufactured goods falls on foreign products.

Consider the decision of the authority at home when ϵ is negative, that is, when there is a negative shock to employment in manufacturing. This case is analyzed in Figure 22.9. The horizontal axis measures foreign government spending on manufacturing, and the vertical axis does the same for the domestic authorities. If the foreign authorities were to set their policy to zero, then there would be no spillover on employment at home. Hence, the domestic authorities will have to set σ sufficiently high to offset the shock completely on their own. This outcome is given by point A. The other extreme is one in which the foreign authorities set σ^* at such a high level that domestic employment has been sufficiently stabilized with no need for further domestic policy action. This result is given by point B.

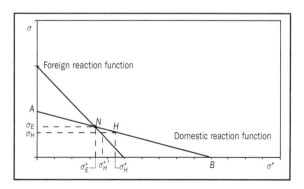

Figure 22.9 Non-cooperative policies

The line connecting point A to point B is the domestic authority's policy function or **reaction function**. It indicates the best domestic response to the foreign policy action. The higher is foreign spending on manufactured goods, the lower domestic spending needs to be to stabilize domestic employment. Note that, from the point of view of the domestic authorities, point B is much more attractive than point A because, at B, stabilization is achieved without the need for high government spending on manufactured goods. A similar argument holds for the foreign country: the higher is public spending on manufactured goods in the domestic economy, the lower is the need for foreign spending. The second line in the figure represents the foreign policymaker's reaction function.

The equilibrium in this model is at point N, where the two lines cross. Only at this point is each country's policy decision the best response to the other country's action. In other words, N is the only point that belongs to both reaction functions. To clarify this result, consider why point H in the figure cannot be an equilibrium. At point H, if the foreign authority sets spending at σ_H^*, then the domestic authority would set spending at σ_H. But if the domestic authority sets spending at σ_H, then the choice of the foreign authorities would be $(\sigma_H^*)'$, not σ_H^*. Only at point N are the two policy responses consistent with each other.

The equilibrium level of spending depends crucially on the size of the spillover parameter, α. Figure 22.10 shows that an increase in α leads to a decrease in the equilibrium level of spending.

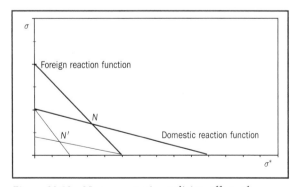

Figure 22.10   Non-cooperative policies: effect of an increase in α

Since a higher α means that foreign spending has a greater effect on domestic employment, the domestic authorities will set a lower level of σ, for each value of σ^*. Hence, the domestic reaction function shifts downward. A similar argument holds for the foreign reaction function, which shifts leftward. Thus, the equilibrium moves from point N to point N'.

Cooperative Policies

The important aspect of the non-cooperative equilibrium is that it is not optimal, in the limited sense that a different set of policies could achieve a better tradeoff between stabilization objectives and the cost of policy action. The problem with the non-cooperative equilibrium at point N in Figure 22.9 is that, in setting policy, each policymaker ignores the positive effect that its actions have on the foreign economy. Since they care only about stabilization of their own economy, they underestimate the value of spending and, consequently, spending is set too low in equilibrium. (In contrast, if the spillover parameter α were negative, then spending would end up too high.) Global welfare could be increased if each authority took account of the effects of its policies on the rest of the world. This consideration suggests that the outcome might improve if policy were coordinated.

Figure 22.11 compares the non-cooperative equilibrium (point N) with the equilibrium that arises when the policymakers cooperate (point C). A simple way to derive a cooperative equilibrium is to construct the (hypothetical) policy function that each authority would have if it were to value the stabilization of foreign employment as much as the stabilization of domestic employment.[10] The cooperative functions are shown by the two solid lines in the figure. Since the foreign impact of domestic spending is considered, policymakers are more prone to adopt high spending, that is, these policy functions lie above the ones for the non-cooperative case. Consequently, in the equilibrium, the share of public spending on manufacturing is higher in both countries. (If we had assumed a negative coefficient α, then we would have obtained the opposite answer.)

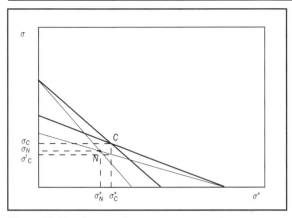

Figure 22.11 Cooperative vs non-cooperative equilibrium

The cooperative equilibrium, although more desirable than the non-cooperative one, may not be feasible without a credible commitment by the two authorities. Otherwise, each authority may 'cheat' and set its spending below the amount shown at point C in the figure.

Consider, for example, the incentive of the domestic authority after it agrees to set spending at σ_c. Although the solid lines in Figure 22.11 show the best policies when domestic and foreign welfare are considered, the dotted lines still show the best responses from a selfish perspective. If the domestic authority believes that the foreign authority will set spending at σ_C^*, then it prefers to set spending at σ_C', rather than σ_C. In other

---

Box 22.1 Will EMU Ever Happen? The Problem of Economic Convergence within the EC

The Maastricht Treaty not only introduced the goal of a European Monetary Union, but also established the timing and conditions for its occurrence. According to the Treaty, the earliest date for the beginning of EMU is 1997. The start of EMU in 1997 is conditional on a majority (seven at the moment) of the EC member states qualifying to be part of the monetary union. In order to qualify, a country must satisfy several economic preconditions laid out in the Treaty in terms of exchange-rate convergence, fiscal convergence, and monetary convergence. The exchange-rate criterion is simple: a country's exchange rate must have remained in the Exchange Rate Mechanism without any devaluation during the previous two years. The fiscal criteria refer to government deficits and public debt accumulation. The general total gross debt outstanding should not exceed 60% of GDP and the general government net borrowing should not exceed 3% of GDP. The monetary criteria set limits for the inflation rate and long-term interest rates. The annual growth rate of the consumer price index should not exceed by more than 1.5 percentage points that of the third lowest in the EC. The interest rate on long-term government securities should not exceed by more than 2 percentage points the highest interest rate among the three EC countries with the lowest rate of inflation. Only the countries that satisfy all the preconditions can join the monetary union. Thus, if EMU were to start in 1997, it must include at least seven EC countries.

Figure 22.12 shows which countries satisfied the fiscal and monetary preconditions in 1991. Of the 12 countries, only 5 satisfied all 4 preconditions: Denmark, France, Germany, Luxembourg and the United Kingdom. The situation worsened in 1992–93. First, during and following the exchange-rate crisis of September 1992, several ERM members devalued their currencies (Portugal, Spain, Ireland) or left the ERM altogether (Italy and the United Kingdom). The fiscal deficits soared in Germany after the unification and rose in France and the United Kingdom, mainly because of recessions.

Consequently, the number of countries that satisfied the preconditions was only three in mid-1993. The likelihood that EMU will start in 1997 is, therefore, quite low. The next possible date for the beginning of EMU is 1999. According to the Treaty, by that time EMU will be allowed to start regardless of the number of countries that actually qualify for it. Thus, if EMU were to start in 1999, then it could include only one country! Nonetheless, the future EMU is still far from certain.

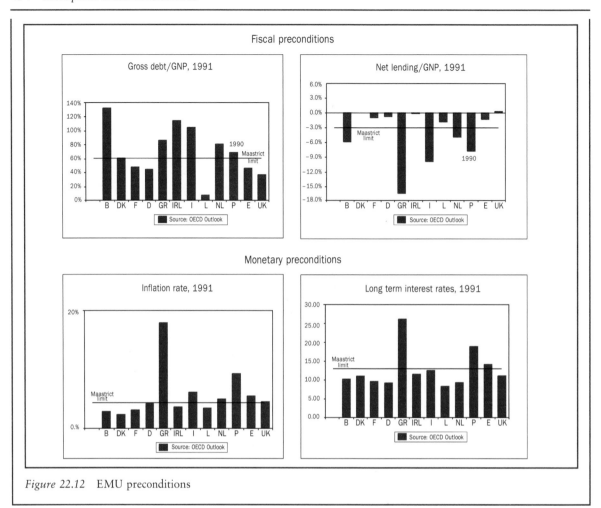

Figure 22.12   EMU preconditions

words, the domestic authority would like the foreign authority to behave altruistically, but prefers to act selfishly in return. Clearly, the foreign authority has the same incentive. If there does not exist a clear commitment not to act selfishly, then cooperation would not be credible and, thus, the only equilibrium is the non-cooperative one. In the attempt to outsmart each other, the two policymakers end up hurting themselves.

Cooperation, however, is not always beneficial. For example, Rogoff (1985) and Canzoneri and Henderson (1991) showed that when there are many spillovers and the authorities are able to coordinate their actions only to deal with a few of them, coordination may actually be harmful.

Taking care of just some of the spillovers, in fact, can intensify the impact of the other spillovers so much that the situation as a whole may actually worsen. Cooperation in this case would be counterproductive.

Many economists have argued against international cooperation of policy and in favour of competition among governments on more general grounds. If policy spillovers are absent or difficult to quantify, policy coordination may evolve into a policy cartel and have all the harmful implications that usually apply to cartels among private firms. Competition can impose discipline on governments and reduce their monopoly power to extract rents.

Summary

A new line of macroeconomic theory attempts to explain the formation of monetary policies. This approach builds on Keynesian models and on models of incomplete information about prices to justify the existence of real effects from monetary disturbances. Although people form expectations rationally, surprise increases in money and the general price level may raise production and employment.

We started by analysing the effects of monetary policies in a closed economy in which the policymaker systematically tries to create surprise inflation to increase the level of output. In equilibrium, this attempt is unsuccessful and results in a high level of inflation with no gains in output. Although it would be better for the policymaker to abandon these attempts and follow a low-inflation policy, a commitment to low inflation may lack credibility. We discussed ways to make anti-inflation monetary policy credible: for example, the delegation of monetary policy to an independent central bank can help.

We introduced shocks to output and showed that the monetary authority might be able to offset these shocks and thereby help to stabilize output. These possibilities are limited, however, because they depend on the policymakers having superior information about shocks or the private economy's presetting of prices or wages.

We then pursued two open-economy extensions. First, we analyzed monetary policies in a monetary union. We saw that the costs and benefits of a monetary union depend on the difference in the cyclical behaviour of the economies that belong to the union. Second, we introduced spillover effects from the policy of one country to the economies of other countries. In this circumstance, the coordination of monetary policies may be beneficial. Without coordination, policy responses tend to be too high or too low, depending on whether the spillovers are positive or negative.

Important Terms and Concepts

perfect foresight
discretionary policy
constant-growth-rate rule
central bank independence
cooperative equilibrium
policy spillover
output targeting
output stabilization
inflationary bias
policy rule
reaction function
non-cooperative equilibrium
European Monetary Union (EMU)
European Central Bank (ECB)
European System of
   Central Banks (ESCB)

Questions and Problems

Problems for Discussion

22.1   Rules versus Discretion
       Assume that the monetary authority's preferred inflation rate is zero, but the authority also wants to reduce unemployment by making inflation surprisingly high.
       a. Show how the equilibrium inflation rate can be high. Is the rate surprisingly high? Does the result depend on the authority's having the 'wrong' objective or on being incompetent?
       b. Can the results improve if the policymaker has the power to bind himself or herself in advance to a specified inflation rate? If so, explain why this constraint (or rule) can improve matters.
       c. Do you think that the policymaker's reputation may be a satisfactory substitute for a formal rule that prescribes future policies?
       d. Can you think of some reasons aside from possibly reducing unemployment why a policymaker might like surprisingly high inflation?

22.2   Monetary Policy in a Monetary Union.

Assume that the EC has a single currency and a single central bank (ECB). Assume that the EC as a whole is hit by a negative real shock. Analyze the cost and benefit of belonging to the monetary union for France, Spain and the United Kingdom under the following assumptions:

a. France's shock is identical to the EC-wide shock.

b. Spain's shock has the same sign (that is also negative), but is much larger than the EC-wide shock.

c. The United Kingdom's shock has the same size but the opposite sign (i.e. it is positive) shock than the EC-wide shock.

d. What policy would France, Spain and the United Kingdom implement in this circumstance if they were not part of the monetary union?

22.3   Negative Policy Spillover

Discuss, with the help of a figure like Figure 22.11, the difference between non-cooperative and cooperative equilibrium when foreign policies have a negative impact on the domestic economy, that is, when $\alpha < 0$.

Notes

1. Abraham Lincoln had a somewhat different view: 'you may fool all of the people some of the time; you can even fool some of the people all of the time' (quoted in Alexander McClure, 1901, p. 124).

2. It is possible to show that this property holds if the cost attached at the margin to more inflation rises as the inflation rate increases.

3. The outcome, $\pi > \pi^e = 0$, is preferred to the rules solution, $\pi = \pi^e = 0$, as well as to the discretionary result, $\pi = \pi^e > 0$. However, $\pi > \pi^e$ is inconsistent with rational expectations in this model. The policymaker cannot systematically set inflation above expectations because it is infeasible to fool people consistently.

4. We shall see in the next section that appointing a central banker who cares only about zero inflation may not be optimal in general.

5. The classification proposed by Grilli *et al.* (1991) extends earlier work by Bade and Parkin (1982).

6. The vertical axis plots the index of political independence, column (9) in Table 22.1, and the horizontal axis the index of economic independence, column (8) in Table 22.2.

7. In Chapters 20 and 21 we expressed doubts that these types of market imperfections could be the source of large and persistent effects of monetary policy on output. We argued that if such effects existed then they are likely to be short-lived. It is important to stress, therefore, that the analysis developed in this and the following sections is only short-term. Although monetary policy might be used to briefly offset unexpected temporary shocks, it cannot be used systematically to change the level of output.

8. The characteristics of the optimal central bank depend on several factors, which are discussed in Rogoff (1985), and Persson and Tabellini (1991).

9. A detailed study of international policy coordination is by Matthew Canzoneri and Dale Henderson (1991).

10. While in the discussion above we assume, for simplicity, the existence of just one cooperative equilibrium, in reality there are many and the difficulty is to reach an agreement on which one to implement. For example, one equilibrium may be one in which both authorities increase spending by the same amount, a second equilibrium one in which the domestic country increases spending much more than the foreign country and so on. It is clear that these different equilibria are not equivalent in terms of welfare for the two countries. Each country would prefer equilibria in which they increase spending the least while the other country increases the most. Which equilibrium is chosen depends on the relative bargaining strength of the two countries. For simplicity, we consider only the symmetric equilibrium that is obtained assuming that the two countries increase spending by the same amount and, thus, split the gains from cooperation equally.

Bibliography

Aaron, Henry J., "Symposium on Tax Reform," *Journal of Economic Perspectives* 1, Summer 1987, 7–119.

Abraham, Katharine G., and Lawrence F. Katz, "Cyclical Unemployment: Sectoral Shifts or Aggregate Disturbances," *Journal of Political Economy* 94, June 1986, 507–22.

Ahmed, Shaghil, "Wage Stickiness and the Non-Neutrality of Money: A Cross-Industry Analysis," *Journal of Monetary Economics* 20, July 1987a, 25–50.

———, "Government Spending, the Balance of Trade and the Terms of Trade in British History," *Journal of Monetary Economics* 20, September 1987b, 195–220.

Alchian, Armen A., and Harold Demsetz, "Production, Information Costs, and Economic Organization," *American Economic Review* 62, December 1972, 777–95.

Alesina, Alberto, and Allan Drazen, "Why are Stabilisations Delayed?," *American Economic Review* 81(5), December 1991, 1170–88.

Alesina, Alberto, and L.H. Summers, "Central Bank Independence and Macroeconomic Performance – Some Comparative Evidence," *Journal of Money Credit and Banking*, 1991.

Alesina, Alberto, and Guido Tabellini, "Voting on the Budget Deficit," *American Economic Review* 80(1), March 1990, 37–49.

Alesina, Alberto, Mark de Broeck, Prati Alessandro and Guido Tabellini, "Default Risk on Government Debt in OECD Countries," *Economic Policy* 15, 1992, 427–63.

Alogoskoufis, George S., "Aggregate Employment and Intertemporal Substitution in the U.K.," *Economic Journal* 97, June 1987a, 403–15.

———, "On Intertemporal Substitution and Aggregate Labor Supply," *Journal of Political Economy* 95, October 1987b, 938–60.

Alogoskoufis, G. S., and A. Manning, "On the Persistence of Unemployment," *Economic Policy* 7, 1988, 427–69.

Ando, Albert, and Franco Modigliani, "The 'Life-Cycle' Hypothesis of Saving: Aggregate Implications and Tests," *American Economic Review* 53, March 1963, 55–84.

Aschauer, David A., "Fiscal Policy and Aggregate Demand," *American Economic Review* 75, March 1985, 117–27.

———, "Is Public Expenditure Productive?" Presented at conference of National Bureau of Economic Research, Cambridge, Mass., July 1988.

Attfield, C.L.F., D. Demery, and N.W. Duck, "A Quarterly Model of Unanticipated Monetary Growth, Output and the Price level in the U.K.," *Journal of Monetary Economics* 8, November 1981, 331–50.

Attfield, C.L.F., and N.W. Duck, "The Influence of Unanticipated Money Growth on Real Output: Some Cross-Country Estimates," *Journal of Money, Credit and Banking* 15, November 1983, 442–54.

Auerbach, Robert D., *Money, Banking and Financial Markets*, 2nd ed., Macmillan, New York, 1985.

Azariadis, Costas, "Implicit Contracts and Under-employment Equilibria," *Journal of Political Economy* 83, December 1975, 1183–202.

Bade, R., and M. Parkin, "Central Bank Laws and Inflation – A Comparative Analysis," mimeo, University of Western Ontario, 1982.

Bagehot, Walter, *Lombard Street*, Scribner Armstrong & Company, New York, 1873.

Bailey, Martin J., *National Income and the Price Level*, 2nd ed., McGraw-Hill, New York, 1971.

Baily, Martin N., "Wages and Employment under Uncertain Demand," *Review of Economic Studies* 33, January 1974, 37–50.

Ball, Laurence, N. Gregory Mankiw, and David Romer, "The New Keynesian Economics and the Output-Inflation Tradeoff," *Brookings Papers on Economic Activity*, 1988.

Baldwin, Richard, "The Economic Effects of 1992," *Economic Policy* 9, 1989.

Banca Commerciale Italiana, *Tendeze Monetarie*, November 1991.

Bank of England, *Quarterly Bulletin*, various issues.

Barnett, William A., Edward K. Offenbacher, and Paul A. Spindt, "The New Divisia Monetary Aggregates," *Journal of Political Economy* 92, December 1984, 1049–85.

Barro, Robert J., "Are Government Bonds Net Wealth?" *Journal of Political Economy* 82, November/December 1974, 1095–118.

———, "Comment from an Unreconstructed Ricardian," *Journal of Monetary Economics* 4, August 1978a, 569–81.

————, "Unanticipated Money, Output and the Price level in the United States," *Journal of Political Economy* 86, August 1978b, 548–80.

————, "On the Determination of the Public Debt," *Journal of Political Economy* 87, October 1979, 940–71.

————, "Output Effects of Government Purchases," *Journal of Political Economy* 89, December 1981, 1086–121.

————, "Government Spending, Interest Rates, Prices and Budget Deficits in the United Kingdom, 1730–1918," *Journal of Monetary Economics* 20, September 1987, 221–47.

————, "The Ricardian Approach to Budget Deficits," *Journal of Economic Perspectives* 3, Spring 1989, 37–54.

————, "Economic Growth in a Cross Section of Countries," *Quarterly Journal of Economics* 106, May 1991, 407–43.

Barro, Robert J., and R. J. Gordon, "A Positive Theory of Monetary Policy in a Natural Rate Model," *Journal of Political Economy* 91, August 1983, 589–610.

Barro, Robert J., and Herschel I. Grossman, *Money, Employment and Inflation*, Cambridge University Press, Cambridge, 1976.

Barro, Robert J., and Chaipat Sahasakul, "Average Marginal Tax Rates from Social Security and the Individual Income Tax," *Journal of Business* 59, October 1986, 555–66.

Barro, Robert J., and Xavier Sala-i-Martin, "World Real Interest Rates," *NBER Macroeconomics Annual 1990*, MIT Press, Cambridge, Mass., 1990.

————, "Convergence across States and Regions," *Brookings Papers on Economic Activity* no. 1, 1991, 107–82.

————, "Convergence," *Journal of Political Economy* 100, April 1992, 223–51.

Barsky, Robert B., and Jeffrey A. Miron, "The Seasonal Cycle and the Business Cycle," unpublished, University of Michigan, Ann Arbor, Mich., July 1988.

Batten, Dallas S. *et al.*, *The Conduct of Monetary Policy in the Major Industrial Countries: Instruments and Operating Procedures*, Occasional Paper, IMF, no. 70, 1990, Washington.

Baumol, William J., "The Transactions Demand for Cash: An Inventory Theoretic Approach," *Quarterly Journal of Economics* 66, November 1952, 545–56.

Becker, Gary S., "The Demand for Children," in *A Treatise on the Family*, Harvard University Press, Cambridge, Mass., 1981.

Becker, Gary S., and Robert J. Barro, "A Reformulation of the Economic Theory of Fertility," *Quarterly Journal of Economics* 103, February 1988, 1–25.

Begg, David, *et al.*, "Monitoring European Integration," *CEPR annual report: the impact of Eastern Europe*, London, Centre for Economic Policy Research, 1990.

Benjamin, Daniel K., and Levis A. Kochin, "War, Prices and Interest Rates: Gibson's Paradox Revisited," in Michael D. Bordo and Anna J. Schwartz, eds., *A Retrospective on the Classical Gold Standard, 1821–1931*, University of Chicago Press, Chicago, 1984.

Bernanke, Ben S., "Irreversibility, Uncertainty, and Cyclical Investment," *Quarterly Journal of Economics* 98, February 1983a, 85–106.

————, "Non-Monetary Effects of the Financial Collapse in the Propagation of the Great Depression," *American Economic Review* 73, June 1983b, 257–76.

Berndt, Ernst R., and David O. Wood, "Engineering and Econometric Interpretations of Energy-Capital Complementarity," *American Economic Review* 69, June 1979, 342–54.

Bernheim, B. Douglas, Andrei Shleifer, and Lawrence H. Summers, "The Strategic Bequest Motive," *Journal of Political Economy* 93, December 1985, 1045–76.

Bienefeld, M. A., *Working, Hours in British Industry*, Weidenfeld and Nicolson, London, 1972.

Bils, Mark, "Testing for Contracting Effects on Employment," Rochester Center for Economic Research, working paper no. 174, January 1989.

Bird, Roger C., and Ronald G. Bodkin, "The National Service Life Insurance Dividend of 1950 and Consumption: A Further Test of the 'Strict' Permanent Income Hypothesis," *Journal of Political Economy* 73, October 1965, 499–515.

Black, Fischer, "Banking and Interest Rates in a World without Money," *Journal of Bank Research*, Autumn 1970, 9–20.

Black, Stanley W., "International Money and International Monetary Arrangements," in Ronald W. Jones and Peter B. Kenen, eds., *Handbook of International Economics*, vol. 2, North-Holland, Amsterdam, 1985.

Blanchard, O. J., and L. H. Summers, "Hysteresis in Unemployment," *European Economic Review* 31, 1986, 288–95.

Blinder, Alan S., "Inventories in the Keynesian Macro Model," *Kyklos* 33, no. 4, 1980, 585–614.

Bloom, Murray T., *The Man who Stole Portugal*, Charles Scribner's Sons, New York, 1966.

Board of Governors of the Federal Reserve System, *Banking and Monetary Statistics, 1941–1970*, Washington, D.C., 1976.

————, *Annual Statistical Digest 1970–1979*, Washington, D.C., 1981.

————, *Annual Report*, 1984.

————, *Federal Reserve Bulletin*, various issues.

Bohn, Henning, "Budget Deficits and Government Accounting," unpublished, the Wharton School, University of Pennsylvania, Philadelphia, 1991.

Bomberger, William A., and Gail E. Makinen, "The Hungarian Hyperinflation and Stabilization of

1945–1946," *Journal of Political Economy* 91, October 1983, 801–24.

Bordo, Michael D., and Lars Jonung, "The Long-Run Behavior of the Income Velocity of Money in Five Advanced Countries, 1870–1975: An Institutional Approach," *Economic Inquiry* 19, January 1981, 96–116.

Boskin, Michael J., "Social Security and Retirement Decisions," *Economic Inquiry* 15, January 1977, 1–25.

Boskin, Michael J., ed., *The Crisis in Social Security*, Institute for Contemporary Studies, San Francisco, 1977.

Boskin, Michael J., Laurence J. Kotlikoff, Douglas J. Poffert, and John B. Shoven, "Social Security: A Financial Appraisal across and within Generations," *National Tax Journal* 40, March 1987, 19–34.

Bresciani-Turroni, Costantino, *The Economics of Inflation*, Allen & Unwin, London, 1937.

Brown, Charles, Curtis Gilroy, and Andrew Koehn, "The Effect of the Minimum Wage on Employment and Unemployment: A Survey," *Journal of Economic Literature* 20, June 1982, 487–528.

Brown, E. Cary, "Fiscal Policy in the Thirties: A Reappraisal," *American Economic Review* 46, December 1956, 857–79.

Brunner, Karl, "The Role of Money and Monetary Policy," Federal Reserve Bank of St. Louis, *Review*, July 1968, 9–24.

Buchanan, James M., *Public Principles of Public Debt* Irwin, Homewood, Ill., 1958.

Buckmaster and Moore, *Index-Linked Gilt Book*, London, May 1985.

Buiter, Willem, "A Guide to Public Sector Debt and Deficits," *Economic Policy*, A European Forum 1, November 1985, 13–60.

Bulow, Jeremy, and Kenneth S. Rogoff, "Sovereign Debt: Is to Forgive to Forget?" Unpublished, Stanford University, Stanford, Calif., February 1988.

Burda, Michael, "Reflections on 'Wait Unemployment' in Europe," Economic Policy Panel, London, April 1988.

Burtless, Gary, "Jobless Pay and High European Unemployment," in Robert Lawrence and Charles Schultze, eds., *Barriers to European Economic Growth*, Brookings Institution, Washington, D.C., 1987.

Butter, F. A. G. den and Fase, M. M. G., "The Demand for Money in EEC Countries," *Journal of Monetary Economics* 8(2), September 1981, 201–30.

Cagan, Phillip D., "The Monetary Dynamics of Hyperinflation," in Milton Friedman, ed., *Studies in the Quantity Theory of Money*, University of Chicago Press, Chicago, 1956.

———, "The Demand for Currency Relative to the Total Money Supply," *Journal of Political Economy* 66, August 1958, 303–28.

———, *Determinants and Effects of Changes in the Stock of Money, 1875–1960*, Columbia University Press, New York, 1965.

Calmfors, Lars, and John Driffill, "Bargaining Structure Corporatism and Macroeconomic Performance," *Economic Policy* 6, 1988, 13–62.

Campbell, Colin D, "Introduction," in *Controlling the Cost of Social Security*, Lexington Books, Lexington, Mass., 1984.

Canzoneri, Matthew B., and Dale W. Henderson, *Monetary Policy in Interdependent Economies: A Game Theoretic Approach*, Cambridge, Mass. and London, MIT Press, 1991.

Card, David, "Determinants of the Form of Long-Term Contracts," Princeton University working paper no. 135, June 1980.

Carlson, John A., "A Study of Price Forecasts," *Annals of Economic and Social Measurement* 6, Winter 1977, 27–56.

Carroll, Chris, and Lawrence H. Summers, "Why Have Private Savings Rates in the United States and Canada Diverged?" *Journal of Monetary Economics* 20, September 1987, 249–79.

Caskey, John, "Modeling the Formation of Price Expectations: A Bayesian Approach," *American Economic Review* 75, September 1985, 768–76.

Cecchini, Paolo, *The European Challenge, 1992 – The Benefits of a Single Market*, Aldershot, 1988.

Central Statistical Office, *Annual Abstract of Statistics*, London, various issues.

———, *Monthly Digest of Statistics*, London, various issues.

Chaudhury, Ajit K., "Output, Employment and Inventories under General Excess Supply," *Journal of Monetary Economics* 5, October 1979, 505–14.

Clark, Kim B., and Lawrence H. Summers, "Labor Market Dynamics and Unemployment: A Reconsideration," *Brookings Papers on Economic Activity* no. 1, 1979, 13–60.

———, "Unemployment Insurance and Labor Market Transitions," in Martin N. Bally, ed., *Workers, Jobs and Inflation*, Brookings Institution, Washington, D.C., 1982.

Clark, Truman A., "Interest Rate Seasonals and the Federal Reserve," *Journal of Political Economy* 94, February 1986, 76–125.

Coase, Ronald H., "The Nature of the Firm," *Economica* 4, November 1937, 386–405.

Cukierman, Alex, "Relative Price Variability and Inflation, a Survey and Further Results," *Carnegie-Rochester Conference Series on Public Policy* 19, Autumn 1983, 103–58.

Cumby, Robert, and Maurice Obstfeld, "International Interest Rate and Price level Linkages under Flexible Exchange Rates: A Review of Recent Evidence," in John F. O. Bilson and Richard C. Marston, eds., *Exchange Rate Theory and Practice*, University of Chicago Press, Chicago, 1984.

Darby, Michael R., "Three-and-a-half Million U.S. Employees Have Been Mislaid: Or an Explanation of Unemployment, 1934–1941," *Journal of Political Economy* 84, February 1976, 1–16.

Darby, Michael R., John C. Haltiwanger, Jr., and Mark W. Plant, "Unemployment Rate Dynamics and Persistent Unemployment under Rational Expectations," *American Economic Review* 75, September 1985, 614–37.

David, Paul A., "The Growth of Real Product in the United States since 1840," *Journal of Economic History* 27, June 1967, 151–97.

Davis, Steve J., and John Haltiwanger, "Gross Job Creation, Gross Job Destruction, and Employment Reallocation," unpublished, University of Chicago, 1992, forthcoming in the *Quarterly Journal of Economics*.

Deane, P., and W. A. Cole, *British Economic Growth 1688–1959*, 2nd ed., Cambridge University Press, Cambridge, 1969.

De Long, J. Bradford, and Lawrence H. Summers, "Equipment Investment and Economic Growth," *Quarterly Journal of Economics* 106, May 1991, 445–502.

Denslow, David A., and Mark Rush, "Supply Shocks and the Interest Rate," *Economic Inquiry* 27(3), July 1989, 501–10.

Department of Employment and Productivity, *British Labour Statistics, Historical Abstract 1886–1968*, London, 1971.

Dewey, Davis R., *Financial History of the United States*, 11th ed., Longmans, Green, New York, 1931.

Dotsey, Michael, "The Use of Electronic Funds Transfers to Capture the Effect of Cash Management Practices on the Demand for Demand Deposits," *Journal of Finance* 40, December 1985, 1493–503.

Drazen, Allan, "Monetary Policy, Capital Controls and Seigniorage in an Open Economy," in Marcello De-Cecco and Alberto Giovannini, eds., *A European Central Bank? Perspectives on Monetary Unification after Ten Years in the EMS*, Cambridge University Press, Cambridge, New York and Melbourne, 1989.

Drazen, Allan, and Vittorio Grilli, "The Benefits of Crises for Economic Reforms," *American Economic Review* 83(3), 1993, 598–607.

Easterlin, Richard A., *Population, Labor Force, and Long Swings in Economic Growth*, Columbia University Press, New York, 1968.

Easterly, William R., "Government Induced Policy Distortions and Economic Growth," unpublished, The World Bank, Washington, D.C., 1991.

Eaton, Jonathan, Mark Gersovitz, and Joseph E. Stiglitz, "The Pure Theory of Country Risk," *European Economic Review* 30, June 1986, 481–513.

Economic Report of the President, United States Government Printing Office, Washington, D.C., various issues.

Economist Intelligence Unit, Ltd. (U.K.), *Quarterly Economic Review of Saudi Arabia*, Annual Supplement, 1985.

———, *Country Profile, Saudi Arabia, 1987–88*, London, 1987.

Edwards, Sebastian, "On the Interest Rate Elasticity of the Demand for International Reserves: Some Evidence from Developing Countries," *Journal of International Money and Finance* 4, August 1985, 287–95.

Eichengreen, Barry, and Richard Portes, "Debt and Default in the 1930s: Causes and Consequences," *European Economic Review* 30(3), June 1986, 599–640.

Eisner, Robert, *How Real is the Federal Deficit?*, The Free Press, New York, 1986.

Eisner, Robert, and Paul Pieper, "A New View of the Federal Debt and Budget Deficits," *American Economic Review*, 74, March 1984, 11–29.

Eisner, Robert, and Robert H. Strotz, "Determinants of Business Investment," in Commission on Money and Credit, *Impacts of Monetary Policy*, Prentice-Hall, Englewood Cliffs, N.J., 1963.

El-Agraa, Ali M. (ed.), *The Economics of the European Community*, Philip Allen, Oxford, 1990.

Emerson, Michael, *What Model for Europe?*, MIT Press, Cambridge, Mass., 1988.

Emerson, Michael, *et al.*, *The Economics of 1992. The EC Commission's Assessment of the Economic Effects of Completing the Internal Market*, 1992.

Esposito, Louis, "Effect of Social Security on Saving: Review of Studies Using U.S. Time Series Data," *Social Security Bulletin* 41, May 1978, 9–17.

Evans, Paul, "Interest Rates and Expected Future Budget Deficits in the United States," *Journal of Political Economy* 95, February 1987a, 34–58.

———, "Do Budget Deficits Raise Nominal Interest Rates? Evidence from Six Industrial Countries," *Journal of Monetary Economics* 20, September 1987b, 281–300.

———, "Do Budget Deficits Affect the Current Account?" unpublished, Ohio State University, August 1988.

Faig, Miquel, "Seasonal Fluctuations and the Demand for Money," *Quarterly Journal of Economics* 104(4), November 1989, 847–61.

Fair, Ray C., "An Analysis of the Accuracy of Four Macroeconometric Models," *Journal of Political Economy* 87, August 1979, 701–18.

Fama, Eugene F., "Short-Term Interest Rates as Predictors of Inflation," *American Economic Review* 65, June 1975, 269–82.

———, "Financial Intermediation and Price level Control," *Journal of Monetary Economics* 12, July 1983, 7–28.

Fay, Jon A., and James L. Medoff, "Labor and Output over the Business Cycle: Some Direct Evidence,"

American Economic Review 75, September 1985, 638–55.

Feinstein, C.H., *National Income, Expenditures and Output of the United Kingdom 1855–1965*, Cambridge University Press, Cambridge, 1972.

Feldstein, Martin S., "Social Security, Induced Retirement, and Aggregate Capital Accumulation," *Journal of Political Economy* 82, September/October 1974, 905–28.

Feldstein, Martin, and Charles Horioka, "Domestic Saving and International Capital Flows," *Economic Journal* 90, 1980, 314–29.

Feldstein, Martin S., and Andrew Samwick, "Social Security Rules and Marginal Tax Rates," National Bureau of Economic Research, working paper no. 3962, January 1992.

Ferguson, James M., ed., *Public Debt and Future Generations*, University of North Carolina Press, Chapel Hill, 1964.

Fischer, Stanley, "Long-Term Contracts, Rational Expectations and the Optimal Money Supply Rule," *Journal of Political Economy* 85, February 1977, 191–206.

———, "Seigniorage and The Case for a National Money," *Journal of Political Economy* 90, April 1982, 295–313.

Fisher, Irving, "A Statistical Relation between Unemployment and Price Changes," *International Labor Review* 13, June 1926, 785–92, reprinted as "I Discovered the Phillips Curve," *Journal of Political Economy* 81, March–April 1973, 496–502.

———, *The Theory of Interest*, Macmillan, New York, 1930.

———, *The Purchasing Power of Money*, 2nd ed. (1922), Augustus Kelley New York, 1971.

Fisher, Irving, assisted by Harry G. Brown, *The Purchasing Power of Money: Its Determination and Relation to Credit Interest and Crises*, A.M. Kelly, New York, 1963.

Fleisher, Belton M., and Thomas J. Kniesner, *Labor Economics: Theory, Evidence and Policy* 3rd ed., Prentice-Hall, Englewood Cliffs, N.J., 1984.

Flood, Robert P., and Peter M. Garber, "An Economic Theory of Monetary Reform," *Journal of Political Economy* 88, February 1980, 24–58.

Flora, Peter, *State, Economy and Society in Western Europe 1815–1975: A Data Handbook in Two Volumes*, London, Macmillan, 1983.

Foley, Duncan K., and Miguel Sidrauski, *Monetary and Fiscal Policy in a Growing Economy*, Macmillan, New York, 1971.

Friedman, Milton, "The Quantity of Money – A Restatement," in *Studies in the Quantity Theory of Money*, University of Chicago Press, Chicago, 1956.

———, *A Theory of the Consumption Function*, Princeton University Press, Princeton, N.J., 1957.

———, *A Program for Monetary Stability*, Fordham University Press, New York, 1960.

———, "Free Exchange Rates," in *Dollars and Deficits*, Prentice-Hall, Englewood Cliffs, N.J., 1968a.

———, "Inflation: Causes and Consequences," in *Dollars and Deficits*, Prentice-Hall, Englewood Cliffs, N.J., 1968b.

———, "The Role of Monetary Policy," *American Economic Review* 58, March 1968c, 1–17.

———, *The Optimum Quantity of Money and Other Essays*, Aldine, Chicago, 1969.

Friedman, Milton, and Anna J. Schwartz, *A Monetary History of the United States, 1867–1960*, Princeton University Press, Princeton, N.J., 1963.

———, *Monetary Statistics of the United States*, Columbia University Press, New York, 1970.

Frowen, Stephen, and Philip Arestis, "Some Investigations of Demand and Supply Functions for Money in the Federal Republic of Germany," *Weltwirtschaftliches-Archiv* 112, 1976, 136–64.

Fullerton, Don, "On the Possibility of an Inverse Relationship between Tax Rates and Government Revenues," *Journal of Public Economics* 19, October 1982, 3–22.

Garber, Peter M., "Transition from Inflation to Price Stability," *Carnegie-Rochester Conference Series on Public Policy* 16, Spring 1982, 11–42.

Geweke, John, "The Superneutrality of Money in the United States: An Interpretation of the Evidence," *Econometrica* 54, January 1986, 1–22.

Giavazzi, Francesco, "Incentives to Fix the Exchange Rate," *European Economic Review* 32(2–3), March 1988, 382–7.

Giavazzi, Francesco, and Alberto Giovannini, *Limiting Exchange Rate Flexibility: The European Monetary System*, MIT Press, Cambridge, Mass., 1989.

Glass, Carter, *An Adventure in Constructive Finance*, Doubleday, Page & Co., New York, 1927.

Goldfeld, Steven M. "The Demand for Money Revisited," *Brookings Papers on Economic Activity* no. 3, 1973, 577–638.

———, "The Case of the Missing Money," *Brookings Papers on Economic Activity* no. 3, 1976, 683–730.

Goodfriend, Marvin, "Monetary Mystique: Secrecy and Central Banking," *Journal of Monetary Economics* 17, January 1986, 63–92.

———, "Interest Rate Smoothing and Price Level Trend Stationarity," *Journal of Monetary Economics* 19, May 1987, 335–48.

Goodhart, Charles A.E., *Money, Information and Uncertainty*, Macmillan, Basingstoke, 1989.

Gordon, Donald F., "A Neo-Classical Theory of Keynesian Unemployment," *Economic Inquiry* 12, December 1974, 431–59.

Gorton, Gary, "Banking Panics and Business Cycles," unpublished, Federal Reserve Bank of Philadelphia, February 1986.

Gottfries, Nils, and Horn, Hendrik, "Wage Formation and the Persistence of Unemployment," *Economic Journal* 97(388), December 1987, 877–84.

Gray, Jo Anna, "Wage Indexation: A Macroeconomic Approach," *Journal of Monetary Economics* 2, April 1976, 221–36.

Greenwood, Jeremy, "Expectations, the Exchange Rate and the Current Account," *Journal of Monetary Economics* 12, November 1983, 543–70.

Grilli, Vittorio, *Financial Markets and 1992*, Brookings Papers on Economic Activity, vol. 2, 1989, 301–24.

Grilli, Vittorio, Donato Masciandaro and Guido Tabellini, "Political and Monetary Institutions and Public Financial Policies in the Industrial Countries," *Economic Policy* 13, 1991, 341–92.

Grossman, Gene M., and Elhanan Helpman, *Innovation and Growth in the Global Economy*, MIT Press, Cambridge, Mass., 1991.

Grossman, Herschel I., "Risk Shifting, Layoffs and Seniority," *Journal of Monetary Economics* 4, November 1979, 661–86.

Grubb, Dennis, Richard Jackman and Richard Layard, "Wage Rigidity and Unemployment in OECD Countries," *European Economic Review* 21(1/2), March/April 1983, 11–39.

Haberler, Gottfried, *Prosperity and Depression*, 2nd ed., League of Nations, Geneva, 1939.

Hall, Robert E., "Investment, Interest Rates, and the Effects of Stabilization Policies," *Brookings Papers on Economic Activity*, no. 1, 1977, 61–103.

——, "A Theory of the Natural Unemployment Rate and the Duration of Unemployment," *Journal of Monetary Economics* 5, April 1979, 153–70.

——, "Employment Fluctuations and Wage Rigidity," *Brookings Papers on Economic Activity*, no. 1, 1980a, 91–123.

——, "Labor Supply and Aggregate Fluctuations," *Carnegie-Rochester Conference on Public Policy* 12, Spring 1980b, 7–33.

——, "The Importance of Lifetime Jobs in the U.S. Economy," *American Economic Review* 72, September 1982, 716–24.

——, "Consumption," in Robert J. Barro, ed., *Modern Business Cycle Theory*, Harvard University Press, Cambridge, Mass., 1989.

Hamermesh, Daniel, *Jobless Pay and the Economy*, Johns Hopkins University Press, Baltimore, Md., 1977.

Hamilton, James D., "Oil and the Macroeconomy since World War II," *Journal of Political Economy* 91, April 1983, 228–48.

——, "Uncovering Financial Market Expectations of Inflation," *Journal of Political Economy* 93, December 1985, 1224–41.

Hawtrey, Ralph G., "The Portuguese Bank Notes Case," *Economic Journal* 42, September 1932, 391–98.

Hayashi, Fumio, "Why is Japan's Saving Rate So Apparently High?" *NBER Macroeconomics Annual 1986*, MIT Press, Cambridge, Mass., 1986.

Hayek, Friedrich A., "The Use of Knowledge in Society," *American Economic Review* 35, September 1945, 519–30.

Hercowitz, Zvi, "Money and the Dispersion of Relative Prices," *Journal of Political Economy* 89, April 1981, 328–56.

——, "Money and Price Dispersion in the United States," *Journal of Monetary Economics* 10, July 1982, 25–38.

Hicks, John, "Mr. Keynes and the 'Classics'," *Econometrica* 5, April 1937, 147–59.

——, *Value and Capital* 2nd ed., Oxford University Press, Oxford, 1946.

Hoffman, Dennis L., and Schlagenhauf, Don E., "An Econometric Investigation of the Monetary Neutrality and Rationality Propositions from an International Perspective," *Review of Economics and Statistics* 64(4), November 1982, 562–71.

Howard, David H., "The Disequilibrium Model in a Controlled Economy: An Empirical Test of the Barro–Grossman Model," *American Economic Review* 66, December 1976, 871–79.

Ingram, James C., *International Economics*, Wiley, New York, 1983.

International Monetary Fund, *International Financial Statistics*, various issues.

Jackman, Richard, Christopher Pissarides and Savvas Savowi, "Labour Market Policies and Unemployment in the OECD," *Economic Policy: A European Forum* 5(2), October 1990, 449–90.

Jevons, W. Stanley, *Money and the Mechanism of Exchange*, Appleton, New York, 1896.

Jones, Alice H., *Wealth of a Nation to Be*, Columbia University Press, New York, 1980.

Jones, Robert A., "The Origin and Development of Media of Exchange," *Journal of Political Economy* 84, August 1976, 757–76.

Judd, John P., and John L. Scadding, "The Search for a Stable Money Demand Function," *Journal of Economic Literature* 20, September 1982, 993–1023.

Katz, Lawrence F., and Bruce D. Meyer, "The Impact of the Potential Duration of Unemployment Benefits on the Duration of Unemployment," unpublished, Harvard University, Cambridge, Mass., May 1988.

Kendrick, John W., *Productivity Trends in the United States*, Princeton University Press, Princeton, N.J., 1961.

Kenny, Lawrence W., "Cross-Country Estimates of the Demand for Money and Its Components," unpublished, University of Florida, Gainesville, Fla., 1988.

Keynes, John Maynard, *The General Theory of Employment, Interest and Money*, Harcourt Brace, New York, 1936.

Keynes, J. M., *Activities 1940–1946: Shaping the Post War World – Employment*, London, Macmillan, 1980.

Kindleberger, Charles P., *Manias, Panics and Crashes: A History of Financial Crises*, London, Macmillan, 1978.

King, Mervin with J. A. Kay, *The British Tax System*, Oxford University Press, 1977.

King, Robert G., and Charles I. Plosser, "Money, Credit and Prices in a Real Business Cycle," *American Economic Review* 74, June 1984, 363–80.

Klein, Ben, "Competitive Interest Payments on Bank Deposits and the long-Run Demand for Money," *American Economic Review* 64, December 1974, 931–49.

Kormendi, Roger C., "Government Debt, Government Spending, and Private Sector Behavior," *American Economic Review* 73, December 1983, 994–1010.

Kormendi, Roger C., and Phillip G. Meguire, "Cross-Regime Evidence of Macroeconomic Rationality," *Journal of Political Economy* 92, October 1984, 875–908.

Koshal, Rajinder K., and Lowell E. Gallaway, "The Phillips Curve for West Germany," *Kyklos* 24(2), 1971, 346–9.

Kreinin, Mordechai E., "Windfall Income and Consumption – Additional Evidence," *American Economic Review* 51, June 1961, 388–90.

Kuznets, Simon, "Discussion of the New Department of Commerce Income Series," *Review of Economics and Statistics* 30, August 1948, 151–79.

Kydland, Finn E., and Edward C. Prescott, "Rules Rather than Discretion: The Inconsistency of Optimal Plans," *Journal of Political Economy* 85, June 1977, 473–91.

——, "Business Cycles: Real Facts and a Monetary Myth," Federal Reserve Bank of Minneapolis, *Quarterly Review*, Spring 1990, 3–18.

Lahaye, Laura, "Inflation and Currency Reform," *Journal of Political Economy* 93, June 1985, 537–60.

Laidler, David E., *The Demand for Money Theories and Evidence*, 3rd ed., Harper & Row, New York, 1985.

Landsberger, Michael, "Restitution Receipts, Household Savings and Consumption Behavior in Israel," unpublished, Research Department, Bank of Israel, 1970.

Law, John, *Money and Trade Considered (1705)*, Augustus Kelley, New York, 1966.

Layard, Richard, Stephen Nickell and Richard Jackman, *Unemployment*, Oxford University Press, 1991.

Leimer, Dean, and Selig Lesnoy, "Social Security and Private Saving: New Time Series Evidence," *Journal of Political Economy* 90, June 1982, 606–29.

Lilien, David M., "Sectoral Shifts and Cyclical Unemployment," *Journal of Political Economy* 90, August 1982, 777–93.

Lindbeck, A., and D. Snower, "Union Activity, Unemployment Persistence, and Wage–Employment Ratchets," *European Economic Review* (Proceedings) 31, 1987, 157–67.

Lindbeck, A., and D. Snower, *The Insider–Outsider Theory of Unemployment and Employment*, Cambridge, Mass., MIT Press, 1988.

Lindsey, Lawrence B., "Individual Taxpayer Response to Tax Cuts: 1982–1984," *Journal of Public Economics* 33, July 1987, 173–206.

Lipsey, Richard E., "The Relation between Unemployment and the Rate of Change of Money Wage Rates in the United Kingdom, 1862–1957: A Further Analysis," *Economica* 27, February 1960, 1–31.

Long, John B., Jr., and Charles I. Plosser, "Real Business Cycles," *Journal of Political Economy*, 91, February 1983, 39–69.

Loungani, Prakash, "Oil Price Shocks and the Dispersion Hypothesis," Rochester Center for Economic Research, working paper no. 33, January 1986.

Loungani, Prakash, and Mark Rush, "The Effects of Changes in Reserve Requirements on Investment and GNP," unpublished, Federal Reserve Bank of Chicago, December 1991.

Loungani, Prakash, Mark Rush, and William Tave, "Stock Market Dispersion and Unemployment," *Journal of Monetary Economics* 25, June 1990, 367–88.

Lucas, Robert E., Jr., "Adjustment Costs and the Theory of Supply," *Journal of Political Economy* 75, August 1967, 321–34.

——, "Understanding Business Cycles," *Carnegie-Rochester Conference on Public Policy* 5, 1976, 77–29.

——, "Two Illustrations of the Quantity Theory of Money," *American Economic Review* 70, December 1980, 1005–14.

——, *Studies in Business-Cycle Theory*, MIT Press, Cambridge, Mass., 1981.

Macaulay, Frederick R., *The Movement of Interest Rates, Bond Yields and Stock Prices in the United States since 1856*, National Bureau of Economic Research, New York, 1938.

McCallum, Ben T., "The Current State of the Policy-Ineffectiveness Debate," *American Economic Review* 69, proceedings, May 1979, 240–45.

McClure, Alexander K., *Abe Lincoln's Yarns and Stories*, W. W. Wilson, New York, 1901.

McCulloch, J. Huston, "The Ban on Indexed Bonds, 1933–77," *American Economic Review* 70, December 1980, 1018–21.

MaCurdy, Thomas E., "An Empirical Model of Labor Supply in a Life-Cycle Setting," *Journal of Political Economy* 89, December 1981, 1059–85.

Maddison, Angus, *Dynamic Forces in Capital Development*, Oxford University Press, 1991.

Malthus, Thomas R., *An Essay on the Principle of Population*, R. C. Weightman, Washington, D.C., 1809.

Mankiw, N. Gregory, and Jeffrey A. Miron, "The Changing Behavior of the Term Structure of Interest Rates," *Quarterly Journal of Economics* 101, May 1986, 211–28.

Mankiw, N. Gregory, Jeffrey A. Miron, and David N. Weil, "The Adjustment of Expectations to a Change in Regime: A Study of the Founding of the Federal Reserve," *American Economic Review* 77, June 1987, 358–74.

Mansfield, Edwin, *Microeconomics* 5th ed., Norton, New York, 1985.

Marston, Stephen T., "Employment Stability and High Unemployment," *Brookings Papers on Economic Activity*, no. 1, 1976, 169–203.

Miron, Jeffrey A., "Financial Panics, the Seasonality of the Nominal Interest Rate, and the Founding of the Fed," *American Economic Review* 76, March 1986, 125–40.

———, "A Cross-Country Comparison of Seasonal Cycles and Business Cycles," unpublished, University of Michigan, Ann Arbor, Mich., October 1988.

Mishkin, Frederic S., "Does Anticipated Monetary Policy Matter?" *Journal of Political Economy* 90, February 1982, 22–51.

———, "Are Real Interest Rates Equal across Countries? An Empirical Investigation of International Parity Conditions," *Journal of Finance* 39, December 1984, 1345–57.

Mitchell, B. R., *European Historical Statistics, 1750–1975*, 2nd ed., Macmillan, London, 1980.

Mitchell, B. R., and P. Deane, *Abstract of British Historical Statistics*, Cambridge University Press, Cambridge, 1962.

Mitchell, B. R., and H. G. Jones, *Second Abstract of British Historical Statistics*, Cambridge University Press, Cambridge, 1971.

Modigliani, Franco, "Long-Run Implications of Alternative Fiscal Policies and the Burden of the National Debt," in James M. Ferguson, ed., *Public Debt and Future Generations*, University of North Carolina Press, Chapel Hill, 1904.

Modigliani, Franco, and Richard Brumberg, "Utility Analysis and the Consumption Function: An Interpretation of Cross-Section Data," in Kenneth Kurihara, ed., *Post-Keynesian Economics*, Rutgers University Press, New Brunswick, N.J., 1954.

Modigliani, Franco and Ezio Tarantelli, "A Generalisation of the Phillips Curve for a Developing Country," *Review of Economic Studies* 40(2), April 1973, 203–23.

Molle, Willem, *Regional Disparity and Economic Development in the European Community*, Saxon House, Farnborough, England, 1980.

Morgan Guaranty Trust, *World Financial Markets*, New York, February 1983.

Mundell, Robert A., *International Economics*, Macmillan, New York, 1968.

———, *Monetary Theory*, Goodyear, Pacific Palisades, Calif., 1971.

Musgrave, Richard, *Theory of Public Finance*, McGraw-Hill, New York, 1959.

Mussa, Michael, "Empirical Regularities in the Behavior of Exchange Rates and Theories of the Foreign Exchange Market," *Carnegie-Rochester Conference Series on Public Policy* II, 1979, 9–58.

Muth, John F., "Rational Expectations and the Theory of Price Movements," *Econometrica* 29, July 1961, 315–35.

Nelson, Charles R., and G. William Schwert, "Short-Term Interest Rates as Predictors of Inflation: On Testing the Hypothesis that the Real Rate of Interest Is Constant," *American Economic Review* 67, June 1977, 478–86.

Nickell, Stephen, *The Investment Decisions of Firms*, Cambridge Economic Handbooks, Cambridge University Press, 1978.

Nickell, Stephen and Paul Kong, "An Investigation into the Power of Outsiders in Wage Determination," *European Economic Review* 36(8), December 1992, 1573–99.

Ochs, Jack, and Mark Rush, "The Persistence of Interest Rate Effects on the Demand for Currency," *Journal of Money Credit and Banking* 15, November 1983, 499–505.

O'Driscoll, Gerald P., Jr., "The Ricardian Nonequivalence Theorem," *Journal of Political Economy* 85, February 1977, 207–10.

Organisation for Economic Cooperation and Development, *Main Economic Indicators*, Paris, various issues.

———, *National Accounts, Main Aggregates* vol. 1, 1952–1981, Paris, 1983.

———, *National Accounts of OECD Countries*, Paris, various issues.

———, *OECD Economic Outlook*, Paris, September 1987.

Organization of American States, *Statistical Bulletin of the OAS*, various issues.

Padoa-Schioppa, Tommaso and Saccomanni, Fabrizio, *Agenda for Stage Two: Preparing the Monetary Platform*, London, Centre for Economic Policy Research, 1992.

Patinkin, Don, "Price Flexibility and Full Employment," *American Economic Review* 38, September 1948, 543–64.

———, *Money, Interest and Prices*, Harper & Row, New York, 1956.

Persson, Torsten, and Guido Tabellini, *Macroeconomic Policy, Credibility and Politics*, Fundamentals of Pure and Applied Economics; Harwood Academic Publishers, 1991.

Phelps, Edmund S., "The New Microeconomics in Employment and Inflation Theory," in *Macroeconomic Foundations of Employment and Inflation Theory*, Norton, New York, 1970.

Phillips, A. W., "The Relation between Unemployment and the Rate of Change of Money Wage Rates in the United Kingdom, 1861–1959," *Economica* 25, November 1958, 283–99.

Pigou, Arthur C., "Economic Progress in a Stable Environment," *Economica* 14, August 1947, 180–88.

Pissarides, C. A., "Job Matchings with State Employment Agencies and Random Search," *Economic Journal* 89(356), December 1979, 818–33.

———, *Equilibrium Unemployment Theory*, Cambridge Mass. and Oxford, Blackwell, 1990.

Plosser, Charles I., "The Effects of Government Financing Decisions on Asset Returns," *Journal of Monetary Economics* 9, May 1982, 325–52.

———, "Fiscal Policy and the Term Structure," *Journal of Monetary Economics* 20, September 1987, 343–67.

Portes, Richard, and David Winter, "Disequilibrium Estimates for Consumption Goods Markets in Centrally Planned Economies," *Review of Economic Studies* 47, January 1980, 137–59.

Protopapadakis, Aris A., and Jeremy J. Siegel, "Are Money Growth and Inflation Related to Government Deficits? Evidence from Ten Industrialized Economies," *Journal of International Money and Finance* 6, 1987, 31–48.

Powell, Bhingam A., *Contemporary Democracy: Participation Stability and Violence*, Harvard University Press, 1982.

Ramaswami, Chitra, "Equilibrium Unemployment and the Efficient Job-Finding Rate," *Journal of Labor Economics* 1, April 1983, 171–96.

Ramsey, Frank P., "A Mathematical Theory of Saving," *Economic Journal* 38, December 1928, 543–49.

Rees, Albert E., "Patterns of Wages, Prices and Productivity," in Charles Myers, ed., *Wages, Prices, Profits and Productivity*, Columbia University Press, New York, 1959.

Ricardo, David, "Funding System," in P. Sraffa, ed., *The Works and Correspondence of David Ricardo*, Cambridge University Press, Cambridge, 1957.

Rogoff, Kenneth S., "Can International Monetary Co-operation be Counter Productive?" *Journal of Money, Credit and Banking*, 18, 1985, 447–57.

———, "Reputation, Coordination, and Monetary Policy," in Robert J. Barro, ed., *Modern Business Cycle Theory*, Harvard University Press, Cambridge, Mass., 1989.

Romer, Christina D., "Spurious Volatility in Historical Unemployment Data," *Journal of Political Economy* 94, February 1986, 1–37.

———, "Gross National Product, 1909–1928: Existing Estimates, New Estimates, and New Interpretations of World War I and Its Aftermath," National Bureau of Economic Research, working paper no. 2187, March 1987.

———, "The Prewar Business Cycle Reconsidered: New Estimates of Gross National Product, 1869–1908," unpublished, University of California, Berkeley, June 1988.

Romer, Paul M., "Capital Accumulation in the Theory of Long Run Growth," in Robert J. Barro, ed., *Modern Business Cycle Theory*, Harvard University Press, Cambridge, Mass., 1989.

———, "Endogenous Technological Change," *Journal of Political Economy* 98, October 1990, 571-S102.

Rotwein, Eugene, ed., *David Hume — Writings on Economics*, University of Wisconsin Press, Madison, 1970.

Runkle, David E., "Liquidity Constraints and the Permanent Income Hypothesis: Evidence from Panel Data," unpublished, Federal Reserve Bank of Minneapolis, November 1988.

Rush, Mark, "Unexpected Monetary Disturbances during the Gold Standard Era," *Journal of Monetary Economics* 15, May 1985, 309–22.

———, "Unexpected Money and Unemployment," unpublished, University of Florida, Gainesville, Fla., September 1986.

Sachs, Jeffrey D., "The Current Account and Macroeconomic Adjustment in the 1970s," *Brookings Papers on Economic Activity* no. 1, 1981, 201–68.

Saidi, Nasser, "The Square-Root Law, Uncertainty and International Reserves under Alternative Regimes: Canadian Experience, 1950–1976," *Journal of Monetary Economics* 7, May 1981, 271–90.

Sala-i-Martin, Xavier, "On Growth and States," Harvard University PhD, 1990.

Samuelson, Paul A., "A Synthesis of the Principle of Acceleration and the Multiplier," *Journal of Political Economy* 47, December 1939, 786–97.

Sargent, Thomas J., "The Ends of Four Big Inflations," in Robert E. Hall, ed., *Inflation: Causes and Effects*, University of Chicago Press, Chicago, 1982.

———, *Macroeconomic Theory*, New York, Academic Press, 1979.

Sargent, Thomas J., and Neil Wallace, "Rational Expectations, the Optimal Monetary Instrument, and the Optimal Money Supply Rule," *Journal of Political Economy* 83, April 1975, 241–54.

———," Some Unpleasant Monetarist Arithmetic," Federal Reserve Bank of Minneapolis, *Quarterly Review*, Fall 1981, 1–17.

Scoggins, John F., "Supply Shocks and Net Exports," unpublished, University of Alabama at Birmingham, 1990.

Siegel, Jeremy J., "Inflation-Induced Distortions in Government and Private Saving Statistics," *Review of Economics and Statistics* 61, April 1979, 83–90.

Simons, Henry C, "Rules versus Authorities in Monetary Policy," in *Economic Policy for a Free Society*, University of Chicago Press, Chicago, 1948.

Solon, Gary, "Work Incentive Effects of Taxing Unemployment Benefits," *Econometrica* 53, March 1985, 295–306.

Solow, Robert M., "A Contribution to the Theory of Economic Growth," *Quarterly Journal of Economics* 70(1), February 1956, 65–94.

Spindt, Paul A., "Money Is What Money Does: Monetary Aggregation and the Equation of Exchange," *Journal of Political Economy* 93, February 1985, 175–204.

Spinelli, Franco, "The Demand for Money in the Italian Economy 1867–1965," *Journal of Monetary Economics* 6(1), January 1980, 83–104.

Stuart, Charles E., "Swedish Tax Rates, Labor Supply and Tax: Revenues," *Journal of Political Economy* 89, October 1981, 1020–38.

Summers, Robert, and Alan Heston, "A New Set of International Comparisons of Real Income and Price levels, Estimates for 130 Countries, 1950–1985," *The Review of Income and Wealth* 34, March 1988, 1–25.

Taylor, John B., "Aggregate Dynamics and Staggered Contracts," *Journal of Political Economy*, 88, February 1980, 1–23.

Tesar, Linda L., "Savings, Investment and International Capital Flows," *Journal of International Economics* 31(1–2), August 1991, 55–78.

Thornton, Henry, *An Enquiry into the Nature and Effects of the Paper Credit of Great Britain (1802)*, Augustus Kelly, Fairfield, N.J., 1978.

Timberlake, Richard H., Jr., *The Origins of Central Banking in the United States*, Harvard University Press, Cambridge, Mass., 1978.

Tobin, James, "The Interest-Elasticity of Transactions Demand for Cash," *Review of Economics and Statistics* 38, August 1956, 241–47.

———, "A General Equilibrium Approach to Monetary Theory," in *Essays In Economics*, vol. 1, *Macroeconomics, Markham*, Chicago, 1971a.

———, "Deposit Interest Ceilings as a Monetary Control," in *Essays in Economics*, vol. 1, *Macroeconomics*, Markham, Chicago, 1971b.

Topel, Robert, and Finis Welch, "Unemployment Insurance: Survey and Extensions," *Economica* 47, August 1980, 351–79.

United Nations, *Statistical Yearbook*, various issues.

U.S. Bureau of Labor Statistics, *Employment and Earnings*, various issues.

U.S. Department of Commerce, *Fixed Reproducible Tangible Wealth In the United States, 1925–85*, Washington, D.C., 1987.

Historical Statistics of the U.S., Colonial Times to 1970, Washington, D.C., 1975. National Income and Product Accounts of the U.S., 1929–1982, Washington, D.C., 1986.

———, Statistical Abstract of the United States, various issues.

———, *Survey of Current Business*, various issues.

Van Ravestein, A., and H. Vijlbrief, "Welfare Cost of Higher Tax: Rates: An Empirical Laffer Curve for the Netherlands," *De Economist* 136, 1988, 205–19.

Varian, Hal R., *Intermediate Microeconomics*, Norton, New York, 1987.

Walre de Bordes, J. van, *The Austrian Crown*, King, London, 1927.

Wasserfallen, Walter, "Forecasting, Rational Expectations and the Phillips Curve: An Emprirical Investigation," *Journal of Monetary Economics* 15(1), January 1985, 7–27.

Winston, Gordon C., "An International Comparison of Income and Hours of Work," *Review of Economics and Statistics* 48, February 1966, 28–39.

World Bank, *World Development Report 1987*, Oxford University Press, New York, 1987.

Index